Man in the Primitive World

An Introduction to Anthropology

E. ADAMSON HOEBEL

Professor of Anthropology, University of Utah

McGRAW-HILL BOOK COMPANY, INC.

New York : Toronto : London

1949

572
H67m
3 2173
Feb' 55

MAN IN THE PRIMITIVE WORLD

VII

To
FRAN AND BART

PREFACE

Anthropology is one of the most recently developed fields of scientific study. It is empirically rigorous, and it is still vigorous in its growth. This book has been created in response to the need for reappraisal and reformulation of the data of a growing science. As an introduction to general anthropology it endeavors to introduce the student of man to the fundamentals of most aspects of the subject matter of anthropology. It also undertakes to state the more important problems of the science as they have been formulated in the present stage of anthropological knowledge.

As an introduction to anthropology this book has been written primarily for the student, fellow worker in other sciences, and the lay reader who desires an orientation in the science of anthropology. The data have been selected with this goal in mind.

An attempt has thus been made to provide enough descriptive and factual materials to give substance to the work and reality to the patterns of conduct described herein. Yet it is easily possible to gag the novice in anthropology with a surfeit of strange tribal names and miniscule customs to such a degree that digestion of the essential principles to be derived from the study of anthropology is made impossible. We have felt constantly for the best balance between overfeeding and underfeeding of facts.

Facts, however, are not enough. All phenomena have their meanings, but they never speak for themselves. Science is as much interpretation as it is observation, and a good introduction to anthropology must balance valid fact with sound interpretation.

Anthropology has traditionally concentrated its attention on prehistoric and primitive man. As the science of man it may, however, properly include man on any level of culture, primitive and civilized, within its scope; it may properly include man on any time plane, prehistoric, historic, and contemporary, within its purview. Anthropology must bring its conclusions to bear upon the problems of modern society; it must place its methods at the disposal of all other sciences.

Nevertheless, its great contribution to knowledge has been derived from its special quality as a comparative science. By means of anthropological study of societies unlike our own, we have been able to break through the mental crust formed of our own cake of custom. It is still best to keep anthropology firmly rooted in the data of primitive society. Anthropologists should not presume to displace sociologists, economists, political scientists, and psychologists in the study of contemporary society. In keeping with this conviction, this book is primarily a study of man in the primitive world.

It is nevertheless desirable and necessary to relate new facts to the preexisting knowledge of the student. In addition, in times like these the ultimate justification for anthropology is the contribution it can make to the solution of the problems of man. Anthropology should be studied with reference to the modern world. Consequently, in addition to providing lucid descriptive fact we have striven continuously to create a fresh and comprehensive integration of fact and interpretation through the formulation of significant principles relative to the interests of the intelligent person in the modern world of science.

Science, like culture, of which it is but a part, is a continuous growth process nourished by the contributions of many minds. The author of any general introduction to a science draws naturally on the thought and labors of a multitude of predecessors and coworkers. The footnotes throughout this book indicate the specific sources of a good deal of the factual data and thought worked into this book. Yet the greatest and most influential sources of the thinking and knowledge that have entered into the development of a book cannot always be footnoted. Such are the contributions of my teachers, whose impress in classroom, seminar, field work, and discussion was not by means of the printed page alone. Franz Boas, Ruth Benedict, and Karl Llewellyn at Columbia; Ralph M. Linton (in field work among the Comanches and later at Columbia); Robert H. Lowie, Alfred L. Kroeber, and Max Radin at California; Edward A. Ross, Kimball Young, Norman Cameron, and William H. Sheldon at Wisconsin; Leopold von Wiese and Ferdinand Kühn at Cologne; and C. G. Dittmer and H. P. Fairchild at New York University were those whose marks rest most heavily and to whom my personal debt of gratitude can never be repaid in full measure. Anyone who reads this book will also find that the mark of the late Bronislaw Malinowski is heavy upon its pages. Although it was never my privilege to work directly under him, his influence was not to be escaped.

The names of numerous anthropologists appear in the footnotes and bibliography in direct evidence of my indebtedness to their work. Many others, especially among my contemporaries, have made felt their unlabeled and imponderable influences. Scientists form a close fellowship of persons and ideas, and one of the special delights of being an anthropologist derives from the fact that anthropologists enjoy an even closer fellowship than most other scientists.

Since in certain aspects it inevitably and properly follows that the viewpoints and methods of some of these upon whom I have leaned and from whom I have learned are more or less incompatible, it naturally follows that the creative privilege and scholarly duty of selection and synthesis has been freely exercised in the writing of this book.

Not all those from whom anthropology springs are teachers in universities or professional anthropologists. Among the Comanche, Seed Eater Shoshone, Cheyenne, Keresan Pueblo Indians, and Japanese-American evacuées in the Granada War Relocation Center who have patiently aided my field investigations are many good friends, who have contributed much of what they know to my fund of anthropological fact. Except for my Pueblo and Japanese-American friends, they have been named in my previous works. Yet I would salute them again!

A teacher learns from his students while they struggle to learn from him. The results of nineteen years of teaching at New York University, with brief sessions at the University of Washington, Claremont Colleges, and the University of Chicago, have helped to shape the growth of this introduction to anthropology.

I am indebted to the following publishers for permission to reprint quotations:

Columbia University Press: A. Kardiner, *The Psychological Frontiers of Society*, p. 120; W. Whitman, *The Pueblo Indians of San Ildefonso*, pp. 99–100; Appleton-Century-Crofts, Inc.: P. Radin, *Crashing Thunder: The Autobiography of an American Indian*, pp. 27–28; Doubleday & Company, Inc.: E. A. Hooton, *Man's Poor Relations*, pp. 124–125 and 331–332; Houghton Mifflin Company: R. F. Benedict, *Patterns of Culture*, pp. 75–76; Rinehart & Company, Inc.: R. H. Lowie, *The Crow Indians*, pp. 177–178 and 190–191; University of Chicago Press and the Chicago Natural History Museum: *Indians before Columbus*, Figs. 29, 62, and 85; Yale University Press: G. B. Grinnell, *The Cheyenne Indians*, Vol. I, pp. 50 and 51; William Morrow & Company, Inc.: M. Mead, *Coming of Age in Samoa*, pp. 202–203; *The Atlantic Monthly:* F. C. Hibben, "Corn," Vol. 175, 1945, p. 121.

Illustrations have been obtained from the following museums, whose officers have generously granted permission for reproduction in each instance as indicated in the captions accompanying the illustrations: The American Museum of Natural History, Brooklyn Museum, Chicago Natural History Museum, Museum of Art (Rhode Island School of Design), The Museum of Modern Art, National Museum of Canada,

Peabody Museum of Archaeology and Ethnology, Harvard University, Peabody Museum of Salem, United States National Museum, Smithsonian Institution, The University of Pennsylvania Museum.

A partner on my earliest field trips was my wife, Frances Gore Hoebel. Later we were joined in our investigations by our son, Bart. At the age of five he eyed a group of Indian girls picnicking in Yosemite Park. "Dad, aren't those girls Indians?" he demanded. "Well, why don't you go talk to them? You might learn something." I offer this as evidence that he, like his mother, has nourished an active interest in anthropology that has been a sustaining stimulus through the years. At large and in many specific ways they have more than earned the right to have this book dedicated to them.

E. Adamson Hoebel

Salt Lake City, Utah
April, 1949

CONTENTS

C. Status and Social Role

D. Property

E. Social Control

F. Religion

PART FIVE: SOCIETY AND CULTURE

Part One: Introduction

CHAPTER 1

ANTHROPOLOGY: THE STUDY OF MAN

Augustine observed that "Man wonders over the restless sea, the flowing water, the sight of the sky, and forgets that of all wonders man himself is the most wonderful." It is the truth in that statement that justifies the study of anthropology, for anthropology is the study of man (Gr. *anthropos* man + *logia* a study). Man, who is the greatest of all wonders, deserves study for his own sake, even though it were to bring no more reward than satisfaction to the probing curiosity of mind, which is in itself one of the wonders of man. Nevertheless, out of such study grows knowledge. And out of such knowledge grows power, the power to control nature and shape man's destiny. Thus anthropology, like any disciplined study of natural phenomena, leads not only to the satisfaction of intellectual curiosity; it inevitably becomes a tool in the hands of man. It is a practical undertaking through which to learn the nature of man, to the end that we may more effectively understand man's problems and how to solve them. The study of anthropology underlies all the social sciences; it makes a contribution to almost every branch of learning one might name, excepting perhaps the sciences that deal only with inorganic matter.

Anthropology is unique in that it is both a natural science and a social science. Man is a part of what we call *nature* (the forces that create the phenomena of the material world). He is therefore a natural phenomenon. He is a part of the organic material universe—a biological specimen, a member of the animal kingdom. The history of his individual growth and of his development as a species is *natural history*. It is for this reason that our museums of natural history always include anthropological exhibits in their halls and have an important place for anthropologists on their scientific staffs. But anthropology is more than mere *human biology*. It is the study of man—and of all his works. In its fullest sense it is the study of the races and customs of mankind. In these customs we see social behavior, and because anthropology is also the *science of custom*, it is a social science as well as a natural science.

1

Physical Anthropology. All living forms of humanity today belong to a single biological species—*Homo sapiens*. This was not so in prehistoric times when there were a number of different species, and even genera, of men and ape men struggling for survival. Today, within the sole surviving species there are a great number of *breeds* and *varieties* of mankind. It is the concern of physical anthropology to study the greatest possible number of well-selected samples of human beings to determine the general characteristics of the family as a whole and the special characteristics of the different genera, species, breeds, and varieties. Physical anthropology is therefore the study of the physical characteristics of the human race as such.

When dealing with prehistoric man the physical anthropologist must work almost entirely with skeletal material. Mummies are rare and are survivors from relatively recent times when they do occur. Russian anthropologists hopefully expect to discover some day a complete prehistoric Ice Age man, frozen and preserved by the same natural, "Birds Eye" process that has yielded perfect specimens of the extinct woolly mammoth from the Siberian ice deposits. Lacking adequate numbers of mummies and having no "Birds Eye men" as yet, the physical anthropologist working on prehistoric man is in consequence confined to skeletal materials, fossilized and unfossilized. This study of the bony structure of an animal form is called *osteology* (Gr. *osteon* bone + *logia* a study), and it is the foundation of all physical anthropology, as the skeleton is the foundation of the body.

When dealing with living races, however, the physical anthropologist has the entire body at hand for comparative study. For static comparison he may treat the mere form of the body and its organs, including not only the skeleton but muscular contour, eye color, skin color, hair form and color, and in addition, the internal organs. His aim is to characterize *human morphology* (Gr. *morphe* form + *logia* a study). Here he is using the methods of *comparative anatomy* (Gr. *ana* up + *temnein* to cut). An anatomist is one who cuts up! For purposes of metric comparison the physical anthropologist has charted numerous fixed points upon the human body that can be used as bases for measurement. Such measurements may be treated statistically; range of distribution, averages, indices, may be obtained and compared for different populations. This is the phase of physical anthropology known as *anthropometry*—the measurement of man.

The modern physical anthropologist is not satisfied with static data from the human body, however. He wants to discover what is to be known about similarities and differences in the functioning (*e.g.*, basal metabolism, pulse rate, growth rates) of the human body in different populations throughout the world. His method here is that of *comparative human physiology* (Gr. *physis* nature + *logia* a study), which is the study of the dynamic working processes of living organisms. When the data of this type of investigation are treated by statistical method, we have the branch of physical anthropology known as *biometrics* (Gr. *bios* life + *metron* measure).

The beginning student in anthropology will not have to concern himself with the techniques of all these specialized branches of study, but the results of detailed research by careful investigators in all these fields lie behind what the sound anthropologist has to tell him about the realities of race.

Culture. The behavior of man is even more wondrous than his body. Though man be only a supersimian on a petty planet, the measure of his accomplishments is great and the follies of his misbehavior tragic. Whatever he does is fraught with fascination and significance for the science of custom. The human being, as the most highly and most recently developed product of a billion and a half years of organic evolution, is the most plastic and adaptable of all living creatures. Man's unique quality is his ability to invent new forms of behavior that are not biologically predetermined by any hereditary set of the organism. Though the biological imperatives of hunger, sex, and bare-bones survival are minimal requirements, which man may never totally ignore, he is free to experiment with many different ways of meeting these needs. Beyond the basal biological requirements there stretches a practically unlimited area for further development of "noninstinctive" behavior.

Infants indulge in random behavior in the early stage of their development, but adult society bends its efforts at the earliest possible moment toward reducing this random behavior to ordered patterns. These behavior patterns define the characteristic and standard behavior for the members of any society. An Andaman Islander, from the Indian Ocean, weeps copiously when he greets a good friend whom he has not seen for a long time; a Frenchman kisses his comrade on both cheeks; while we content ourselves with seizing his hand. The circumstance is the same in all instances, but the total situation is defined differently in terms of standard behavior among different people. This is the effect of *culture*.

The concept of culture is anthropology's greatest single contribution to modern thought. *Culture is the sum total of learned behavior patterns which are characteristic of the members of a society and which are, therefore, not the result of biological inheritance.*[1] This is the cultural whole. There are also sub-elements to culture known as *culture complexes* and *culture elements,* or *traits* (see page 431). Culture is wholly artificial in that it is the result of social invention. It is transmitted and maintained solely through learning. Culture is "noninstinctive."

Every separate society has its distinctive culture. The consequent effect is that the members of every single society behave differently from the members of other societies in some significant respects. Change the culture of a society, and the behavior of individuals in that society changes with it. Culture exists initially only in the behavior of individuals; but culture is superindividual in that each person, as he is born and develops, comes under the sway of preexisting culture patterns and is molded by them—or at least affected by them. The dynamics of this process are for later study, however. It is important at the outset just to know the nature of culture or the totality of custom, *i.e.,* the learned ways of man.

Cultural Anthropology. To study culture is to study the social behavior of man. The phase of anthropology that devotes its attention to the customs of mankind is called *cultural anthropology,* in contradistinction to physical anthropology. It is customary to classify culture as *material* and *nonmaterial,* and cultural anthropology deals with both. Material culture, it should be realized, is always a product of the nonmaterial. Artifacts (tools, weapons, etc.), houses, monuments, and pictures are all objects of material culture, but they are the products of ideas and techniques that were in themselves behavior patterns—nonmaterial culture. Material culture is therefore but a concrete objectification of nonmaterial behavior patterns. It might be said that material culture is what goes into museums, while nonmaterial culture is what goes into books. It is likely, however, that the museum anthropologist of today would take strenuous exception to such a pat statement. In the last century, and well into this, it is true that museums were chiefly interested in collecting objects, especially objects that would look well in display cases. But today museum anthropologists are no longer collectors and custodians of musty curios. It is humor but not fact for Will Cuppy to quip, "Anthropologists are folks who live in museums." [2] They, too, recognize the importance of the total cultural significance of material objects.

---

[1] The classic definition of culture is that of Sir Edward Tylor, who first formulated the concept. Tylor's statement reads, "Culture . . . is that complex whole which includes knowledge, belief, art, morals, law, custom and any other capabilities and habits *acquired by man as a member of society." Primitive Culture,* Vol. 1, p. 1.

[2] W. Cuppy, *How to Tell Your Friends from the Apes,* p. 22.

This leads us to our second point with respect to material culture. Not only is every object of material culture the product of nonmaterial culture patterns, but every object has its specifically defined uses or functions, as determined by the culture complex in which it is embedded. For an example, Professor Malinowski effectively pointed out that the simple digging stick, or dibble, can also be used as a punting pole, a walking staff, or a rudimentary weapon. "It is the diversity of function not the identity of form that is relevant to the student of culture." [3] The cultural anthropologist is less interested in a stick in a museum case than he is in

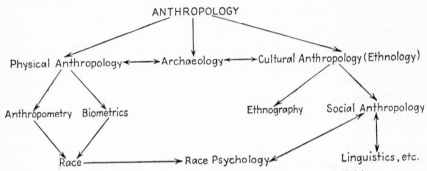

FIG. 1. Anthropology and the interrelations of its main subdivisions.

the uses to which the stick is put in the culture from which it came and the attitudes of the users toward such a stick.

Social Anthropology. Sometimes the concept of *social anthropology* is used synonymously with that of cultural anthropology. From what has been said in the previous section it should be clear that this is not strictly accurate. Social anthropology is actually a subsection of cultural anthropology, since its interest is in social behavior per se and only very incidentally in the technical aspects of material culture.

Students often express curiosity as to the relation of sociology to anthropology. It is at this point that the relationship stands out most succinctly. Sociology and social anthropology are, in their broadest senses, one and the same. Both of them are the study of social interrelationships and the behavior of men, *i.e.*, the relations of men to men. They also have a close identity with *social psychology*, which is the special study concerned with social stimuli and the social responses of the individual person. Although social anthropology, sociology, and social psychology are closely similar, if identified by their interests, nevertheless they exist

[3] B. Malinowski, "Culture" (*Encyclopedia of the Social Sciences*, Vol. 4, 1931), p. 625.

as separate academic disciplines in actuality. The reasons for this are historical, as the anthropologist is fond of saying. Each field has had a different background, uses somewhat different methods of investigation, and has differing traditional attitudes and concepts. Sociology and psychology grew primarily out of philosophy and have been struggling violently to get away from it ever since they attained their adolescence. Anthropology stems primarily from natural science and carries a greater measure of the natural-science tradition. Still, the methodological differences between these fields of study grow less with each passing year as anthropology becomes more interpretative and sociology more objective, so that today the measure of difference is one of convenience. The anthropologist concentrates chiefly on the society of primitive peoples and the sociologist concentrates on our own contemporary civilization. The social psychologist roams happily between them manipulating his tests and measurements.

Ethnology and Ethnography. Cultural anthropology has two further subdivisions that are given names of common use: *ethnology* (Gr. *ethnos* race + *logia* a study) and *ethnography* (Gr. *ethnos* race + *graphein* to write). Neither of these names means exactly what a literal transcription of its Greek roots would imply. They are not studies of races, which is the work of physical anthropology, but rather of the cultures of the world. Ethnography is strictly descriptive and is going out of fashion. It presumes merely to give a noninterpretative, photographic picture of a series of cultures. It is the collection of data only, the raw material for ethnology. Ethnology, as the science of culture, completes the process of extracting meaning from the data through classification, analysis, and the formulation of principles.

Special Areas of Study. There are, lastly, several additional fields in which the anthropologist frequently specializes, though the fields are not peculiarly anthropological. Most important of these is *archaeology* (Gr. *archaios* ancient + *logia* a study). The hallmark of the archaeologist is the spade; he is a digger whose job is to extract skeletal material and artifacts from the ancient sites of human habitation. He serves the physical anthropologist, the cultural anthropologist, and the historian with tangible remains from prehistoric and historic times. Since prehistoric men leave no written records, the products of the archaeologist's scratching in the dirt are frequently all we have to go on. Archaeology has become a highly exacting science requiring many routine hours of work in the laboratory and in the field, but it has the never-diminishing lure of the treasure hunt to infuse it with an aura of glamour.

Linguistics is another field the anthropologist makes his own. Since language is the great medium of cultural transmission and is in itself a most important cultural phenomenon, the anthropologist must deal with it. It is not enough that he surmount the barrier of language in order to obtain the facts of a culture from a strange people. Language as a cultural fact must be studied and analyzed to learn what it will reveal as to the mental habits and interests of a people. There is also an archaeology of language, the discovery of fragments of the history of a people by digging out word roots and language forms that give clues to past events or practices and beliefs long since abandoned but still existing as word fossils. The systematic analysis of language forms and functions, with comparative study of languages, makes up linguistics.

The full scope of anthropology will unfold only as one becomes acquainted in the subsequent chapters of this book with the subject matter presented there. It is obvious, since anthropology treats all phases of culture, that it is also concerned with such specialties as handicrafts, art, dance, music, folklore, economics, religion, government, and law, in addition to the areas of study presented in the discussion of this chapter.

Part Two: Ancient Man and Prehistoric Culture

CHAPTER 2

HUMAN ORIGINS

Anthropology is a historical science. It is concerned with biologic and social processes, the regular sequences of conditions in growth and change. Life exists through time, and so does all matter. The life process consists of continuous change, and it must be followed from its beginning to its end if it is to be understood in its entirety. The same is equally true of social and cultural processes, for society too is a continuum that exists through time. Neither life nor society is ever static.

The evolutionary aspect of life was realized to a certain extent by the thinkers of the classical world, but it was the great intellectual achievement of the nineteenth century to put the facts of evolution to use in the analysis of natural and social phenomena. To Charles Darwin (1809–1882) and his epoch-making book, *The Origin of the Species* (1859), goes full credit for the first comprehensive formulation and systematization of the biologic processes in terms of developmental sequences. Darwin's great contribution was to demonstrate that the life processes result in variation and the production of new forms. By the process of *natural selection* forms that are well fitted to their natural environment tend to survive and forms that are ill fitted tend to be eliminated. This is the famous doctrine of the *survival of the fittest*. In consequence of variation and natural selection, Darwin showed that through evolution new and more complex forms emerge from older and simpler forms of life. The process has been one of development from simple and homogeneous life forms to organisms of ever-increasing complexity and heterogeneity, and there has been a continuous linkage of all existing species to preexisting species. This is the *principle of evolution,* sometimes called *Darwinism* or *evolutionism.*

The principle of evolution is the foundation stone of anthropology in its biological aspect, and it is the purpose of this and the succeeding chapter to delineate the elemental facts of life's emergence and development.[1]

[1] The application of the principles of evolution in the field of social anthropology

The Origin of the Earth. The earth is itself a heavenly body, a planet, and a member of the solar system, revolving on an elliptical orbit around the sun and accompanied by its satellite, the moon. More than two billion years ago there was no earth and no solar system. There was a giant star instead. In the violent disruption of this virgin star the earth, Mercury, Venus, Mars, Saturn, Jupiter, Neptune, Uranus, and Pluto were born. The residual core of that giant star remained to constitute our sun. Mighty though it is, the sun is but a remnant of its former self.

The stupendous disruption of the great star probably occurred when the path of its orbit brought it in close proximity to a still greater star. An actual collision was not necessary to wreck the smaller of these two stars. It was sufficient that the sun came close enough to the larger mass of its passing competitor to be subjected to the tremendous power of its gravitational pull. This produced a tidal distortion that became greater and greater as the two bodies approached nearer and nearer to each other, until, as they at last sped past each other, the pull of the greater star exceeded that of ours to such a degree that it ripped great masses of sun stuff out into space. These were the *planetesimals*. Together, with the sun as a nucleus, they probably formed a stellar complex not unlike the spiral nebulae that can be observed through a good telescope today. Each of the countless thousands of planetesimals moved on its own elliptical orbit about the vestige of the sun. A few of them were much larger than the others, and, in consequence, they exerted a gravitational attraction upon the smaller bodies that came within their range. Like giant vacuum cleaners the larger bodies swept along their orbits, gathering in the lesser planetesimals, rolling up their bulk like ever-increasing snowballs. The occasional meteors that come flaming through our atmosphere today are merely belated arrivals at our planet, which is the current product of the evolutionary growth of one of the larger original planetesimal nuclei.[2]

The earth probably had a thin atmosphere at first, which grew heavier as the earth increased in mass and gravitational power through the

---

is a point of considerable confusion and disagreement among anthropologists. At first, the principle was enthusiastically and uncritically applied to produce simple and all-embracing theories of social origins and evolution. With the turn of the century a critical reaction set in. This reaction all but devastated the entire concept of social evolution. A positive attitude toward the concept was very nearly tabued among anthropologists and it has been only in the last few years that an inclination to recognize the residual values in the concept has become manifest. A detailed discussion of this problem is reserved for Chap. 34.

[2] This discussion is a simplified presentation of the famous Chamberlin-Moulton planetesimal hypothesis of the origin of the solar system. See T. C. Chamberlin, *The Origin of the Earth*.

addition of more and more planetesimals. Water vapor condensed to form rain, which in turn ran down from the higher surfaces of the unevenly piled planetesimal drifts to form lakes and oceans. Increasing pressure on the interior of the earth's mass, together with heat liberated by the decomposition of radioactive substances, raised internal temperatures sufficiently to melt those parts of the "heterogeneous mass" which had the lowest melting points. Within the solid mass of the earth "bubbles" of molten rock developed, which gradually worked their way toward the surface until many of them broke through in fiery volcanic action. When the molten masses cooled, they had formed lava fields and the tough igneous rocks. All this time, rain was washing down the high spots into the ocean basins where the water sifted out the sediments so that they came to rest in sedimentary layers. These were later compressed into strata of sedimentary rocks, some of which were metamorphosed (changed) into crystalline rocks by later and more severe pressures.

From its very inception the atmosphere has been busy tearing down the elevated masses and drowning them in the seas. For various physical and chemical reasons the earth materials that go into the sea are heavier than those that remain on land; the result is that the rocks underlying the ocean floors have a greater specific gravity than do those of land areas. The distribution of weight about the earth's surface is not even, and it is subject to a constant gradual disturbance and readjustment of position. Usually the lighter land masses are forced upward as the ocean basins settle. Thus, the areas around the continents are lifted above the waters, and the process of their demolition (erosion) begins anew. The process of uplifting occurs unevenly around the earth's surface, however, and land areas can also sink beneath the seas.

Successive elevations and subsidences result in different layers of sedimentary rocks, each distinguishable from the others. These layers are the pages of earth's history that the geologist reads. The layers formed earliest are at the bottom of the heap, and although not all the layers built up through time occur in any one place, by integrating the layers found in different parts of the world geologists have succeeded in completing the total sequence.

From the disruption of the sun star to the relative completion of the nuclear core of the earth (when it had acquired the bulk of its planetesimals) to the formation of its first oceans is known as *cosmic time*, a period that may have lasted half a billion years, but of this period there is no direct geological record. *Geologic time* began with the deposition of sedimentary rocks, the first of which were laid down some one and a half billion years ago. This span of time is divided by modern geologists into five eras, each named according to its most characteristic forms of life. Figure 2 presents in a simplified manner the sequence of eras and periods, with their outstanding life forms.

The Origin of Life. It is most probable that life made its first appearance upon this earth soon after the beginning of geologic time. This is indicated by the presence of carbon in Archeozoic sedimentary deposits of Ontario, Canada, a condition which the paleontologist Charles Schuchert declares "indicates unmistakably that life was already in existence." [3] Yet just how life began or where this momentous and mysterious event occurred is still unknown, for protoplasm, which is the basis of all living matter, is such "an inconceivably complex physiochemical organization" [4] that it has defied final scientific analysis up to the present. True, the chemical elements that go into protoplasm are known, but its molecular and atomic structure is so complex that the compounds that are built up from these elements within the protoplasm cannot be stated. The most we can say is that life first began when the several elements that make up protoplasm occurred initially in proper combination in suitable environmental conditions—whatever they may have been. Then these elements combined to form a unique matter which is colloidal in form, which can maintain itself by borrowing energy and materials from its surrounding environment (a biologic process called *metabolism*), which can grow and increase its mass, which can reproduce itself and maintain continuity, which is marked by rhythmicity in its vital processes, which is irritable (responds to stimuli) and which is marked by adaptability (the capacity to adjust to environmental changes). [5]

Since the first successful formation of unicellular protoplasm (*protozoa*), life forms have progressively evolved into differential forms of increasing complexity. The manner in which new forms of life come into being is a question of genetics, and like the nature of life is still in the early stages of scientific investigation. Nevertheless, though the *how* of evolution is not satisfactorily established, the fact of progressive evolution in forms of life from the simplest to the most complex varieties is convincingly revealed in the story of the rocks.

The long and intricate path of evolution has led upward through successive geological strata. Protozoa and metazoa prevailed during the Archeozoic and Proterozoic eras, respectively (more than two-thirds of

[3] C. Schuchert, "The Earth's Changing Surface and Climate during Geologic Time" in *The Evolution of Earth and Man*, p. 65.

[4] L. L. Woodruff, "The Origin of Life" in *The Evolution of Earth and Man*, p. 83.

[5] H. H. Newman, "The Nature and Origin of Life" in *The Nature of the World and Man*, pp. 166–176.

ERAS	PERIODS	DURATION OF PERIODS	PERIOD STARTED, B.C.	DOMINANT LIFE
CENOZOIC	PLEISTOCENE	1,000,000	1,000,000	MAN
CENOZOIC	PLIOCENE	6,000,000	7,000,000	MAN
CENOZOIC	MIOCENE	12,000,000	19,000,000	APE
CENOZOIC	OLIGOCENE	16,000,000	35,000,000	APE
CENOZOIC	EOCENE	25,000,000	60,000,000	MAMMAL
MESOZOIC	CRETACEOUS	65,000,000	125,000,000	REPTILE
MESOZOIC	JURASSIC	35,000,000	160,000,000	REPTILE
MESOZOIC	TRIASSIC	35,000,000	195,000,000	REPTILE
PALEOZOIC	PERMIAN	25,000,000	220,000,000	AMPHIBIAN
PALEOZOIC	CARBONIFEROUS	85,000,000	305,000,000	AMPHIBIAN
PALEOZOIC	DEVONION	50,000,000	355,000,000	FISH
PALEOZOIC	SILURIAN	40,000,000	395,000,000	FISH
PALEOZOIC	ORDOVICIAN	85,000,000	480,000,000	INVERTEBRATE
PALEOZOIC	CAMBRIAN	70,000,000	550,000,000	INVERTEBRATE
PROTEROZOIC	PRECAMBRIAN	650,000,000	1,200,000,000	METAZOA
ARCHEOZOIC	PRECAMBRIAN	650,000,000	1,850,000,000	PROTOZOA

Fig. 2. The geologic ages and the forms of life.

geologic time). Shell-bearing marine animals and primitive fishes left their fossil marks in the rocks of the early Paleozoic; insects, amphibians, and primitive land plants first appeared in the middle of the same era, and early reptiles showed up in the later phases. The Paleozoic era endured for approximately one-sixth of geologic time. The Mesozoic was the Age of Reptiles, the time when cumbersome dinosaurs dragged their ungainly hulks about the landscape, an era that consumed almost one-twelfth of the billion and two-thirds years of geologic time. In the last of the eras, the Cenozoic, in which we are still living today, the cereals, fruits, higher mammals, apes and monkeys first emerged, to be followed later in the era by the forerunners of man and, at last, by man himself. The Cenozoic is the shortest of all the eras, for it has thus far consumed less than one twenty-fifth of geologic time. Each successive era, though notably shorter in duration than those preceding it, nevertheless brought forth more numerous life forms in ever-increasing complexity than those which had previously run their courses.

The evolution of life continues to this day, and there is every reason to believe that it will continue so long as life exists. The history of living matter has been one of continuous change and progressive development since life first came into being in the Archeozoic. Nor has anything occurred to indicate that the process has been arrested. Indeed, man has greatly hastened the evolutionary process among many life forms by turning it to his own ends through the skillful techniques of plant and animal husbandry. Many more new varieties of plants and animals have been deliberately brought into being by the efforts of man during the past hundred years than in any other equal span of time in all history or prehistory.

New forms come into being, and old ones sometimes disappear. If man has had a hand in bringing forth new life forms, he is also responsible for the disappearance of many others. The extinction of a variety or species is the mark of its failure in the struggle for existence. Many forms of life developed to fit a particular environmental complex (which included not only the physical environment but other life forms as well) only to fall by the wayside when "critical periods" of change in earth conditions so altered life conditions that they were no longer fit to survive. Farewell to the dodo, brontosaurus, stegosaurus, pteranodon, and archelon; life marches on!

Evidences for the Evolutionary Origin of Man. An adequate presentation of the full body of evidence for the evolutionary origin of man from lower animal forms would require many volumes. Obviously, no attempt to treat all the data can be made here. Yet the types of evidence upon which the biologist and anthropologist rest their identification of man with the lower animal forms can be briefly stated.

Comparative Anatomy. By comparison and contrast of skeletons (Fig. 3), organs, and musculature of man and the living apes, we know precisely in what respects man and the anthropoids are similar and in what respects they differ. Every bone that is present in each of the apes is also present in man (except the thirteenth rib). The dissimilarities in the skeletons of man and apes exist in the shapes of the various bones. The bones are alike in number and function; they differ merely in form. In man these differences in form are associated primarily with the attainment of upright posture, greater prehensibility of the fore limbs (arms), greater stability of the hind limbs (legs), greater brain size, and reduction of the face and jaws. No zoologist, unhampered by theological or anthropocentric prejudices, would have the slightest hesitation in classing man with the apes and monkeys as a primate on the basis of *comparative anatomy* alone.

Vestigial Remains. Functional analysis of the organs of the human body reveals many structures whose presence is understandable only in the light of the principle of development of the human species from lower biological forms. These are organs which serve no discernible physiological function in the body of man, organs which are atrophied counterparts of homologous organs that function effectively in other primates or other lower animal forms. Hence they are called *vestigials* or *dysteleologies* (Gr., *dys*, bad + *telos*, end, purpose + *logy*, study; *i.e.*, without purposes), purposeless relics from former times.

The presence and distribution of body hair on man is an obvious vestige. The hair patterns on man and the apes are closely identical, and although body hair may be useful to apes, it has long since become so slight and atrophied on man as to be without value; indeed, its superfluity is such as to give rise to a flourishing depilatory business in our culture. The same may be said of the vermiform appendix, which serves a definite digestive function in apes, monkeys, and other herbivorous animals, but not in man. The third molar, or wisdom tooth, in the reducing jaw of man is another organic superfluity. It is healthy and useful in the other primates, but there is hardly a place for it in our dentition. Overcrowding causes frequent impaction; it is more subject to decay than the other teeth; and according to Keith's studies of the English population, a lucky fifth of the population of that country do not even develop the rudimentary third molar.[6]

The coccyx, formed of the last four caudal vertebrae at the bottom of the spine, is a hidden vestigial tail, which is folded under and does not

[6] A. Keith, *The Antiquity of Man*, Vol. 2, p. 401.

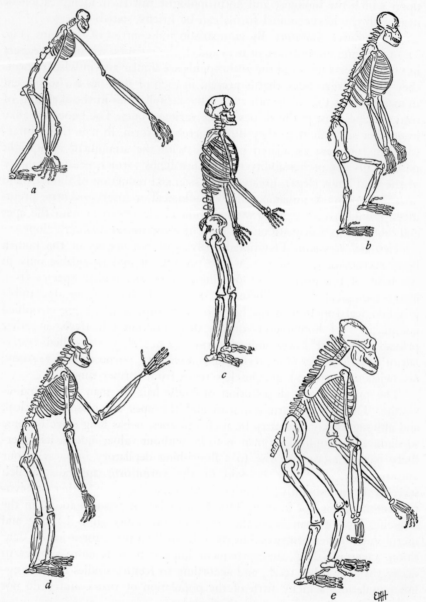

Fig. 3. The skeletons of man and the anthropoid apes: *a*, gibbon; *b*, orang-utan; *c*, man; *d*, chimpanzee; *e*, gorilla.

show on most of us at birth. It is external in the human embryo during its second month of growth and even today a few persons are born with the coccyx showing.

Numerous muscles occur in different parts of the body, which are not functional in man, although their homologues are functional in other primates.[7] Most of us have acquaintances who can wiggle their ears, but although the rest of us have vestigial ear muscles, we possess these muscles in such atrophied form that this entertaining simian capacity is beyond us.

All these vestigials are anatomical lags. Indeed, if one takes the pessimistic point of view enunciated by the physical anthropologist Hooton, it seems as if most of the human body is formed of anatomical lags, many of which, although they function (in contrast to the vestigial organs), do so with lamentable insufficiency. For alas, in standing on his hind legs man throws undue stresses and strains upon his bodily structure for which it was not originally constructed in the days when our mammalian ancestors ran on all fours. The convex arch of the spine of the quadruped is a fine supporting structure, but the S-curved columnar spine of man is apt to be too weak for its job; more than this, it throws too much weight on the wedge-shaped sacrum. The frequently lamentable result is sacroiliac displacement. To add to our woes, our visceral organs no longer rest in a neat underslung basket of ribs; instead, they drape down into a poorly supported abdomen. Result: rupture of the abdominal wall or the displacement of internal organs.

We also carry a crowded tangle of unnecessarily long (for our type of diet) intestines, a heritage from our herbivorous ancestors. Our overstrained hearts must work excessively hard to pump an adequate stream of blood to our enlarged brains, now in a position above the heart instead of on the same level, as among quadrupeds.

These are only a few of the inherited inadequacies of the human species that Hooton calls our "original biological sins."[8]

Sum up the many anatomical lags in the human body (which represent imperfect evolutionary adjustments to new demands put upon old structures), add to them the hundred or so vestigial organs (which represent old and now useless structures upon which no bodily demands are made), and you will agree with Wallis that man "is, indeed, a walking museum of antiquities."[9]

[7] See E. A. Hooton, *Up from the Ape*, pp. 232–233, for a discussion of some of these muscles.

[8] E. A. Hooton, "The Wages of Biological Sin" (*The Atlantic*, Vol. 164, 1939), pp. 435–445.

[9] W. D. Wallis, *An Introduction to Cultural Anthropology*, p. 19.

Recapitulation in Embryonic Development. Each human being is launched upon his life cycle as the result of the fertilization of a female ovum by a male sperm. Through cell division and multiplication the ovum increases in size and complexity, passing through the simple multi-cellular stages of the *blastula* (a single-layered cellular mass) and the *gastrula* (a double-layered, cuplike cellular mass), into the advanced embryonic stage, through the fetal stage, which is reached in the second month, on to birth after nine months. The process of growth is not complete even then, of course, for a long period of postnatal development is required to produce the adult human being. The entire life history of the individual, from conception to full development and inevitable death, is termed *ontogeny*.

At various stages of embryonic development characters such as the notochord, gill arches, and gill grooves are present. They represent important features of certain early evolutionary forms that are not present in the fully developed human being. In broader terms, the human embryo passes through successive stages *roughly* similar to an undifferentiated cell mass, a coelenterate, a worm, and a generalized fish; finally, it takes on mammalian qualities and is ultimately born a man-child; although even a proud parent frequently finds it difficult to agree that a newborn infant looks like a human being (Fig. 4).

Thus, it has long been held that the human embryo recapitulates the evolutionary history of the human race. This is known as the *recapitulation theory*. Provided one does not take the theory too literally or interpret it too narrowly, it is sound and useful. When we say that the human embryo is fishlike at a certain stage, we do not mean that it is identical with the comparable embryonic stage of a fish. Human ontogeny is always unique, and a human embryo can always be identified for what it is at whatever stage of growth it may be. Nevertheless, it seems to be established that in a generalized way "ontogeny repeats phylogeny," or "each individual climbs his family tree."

Blood Relationship of Man and the Primates. If the principle of recapitulation in embryological development is subject to some qualifications as evidence of man's relation to lower animal forms, the evidence to be found in experimental blood tests with man's relatives is not.

Since the epoch-making medical discoveries of Pasteur and Koch, the marvelous antitoxin capabilities of animal organisms have become familiar to the millions of persons who have been vaccinated. Vaccines are serums produced by injecting the toxin, or disease virus, into an animal whose physiological system produces antibodies to destroy the toxin. Serum derived from the extracted blood of the medium animal contains the active

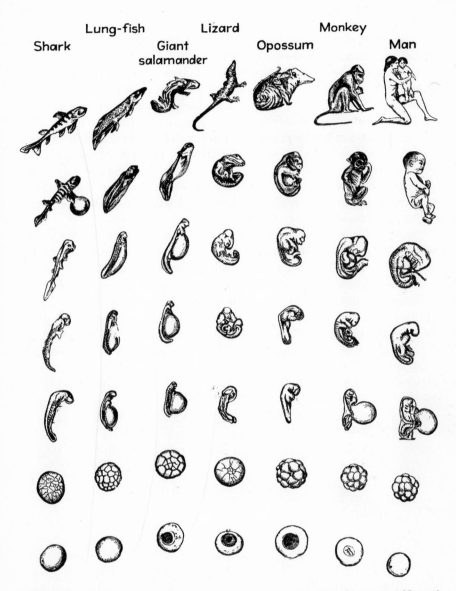

Fig. 4. Comparative stages in embryonic development. (*American Museum of Natural History*.)

antibodies, and this serum properly introduced into the human venal system will in the fortunate cases produce immunity to the disease for which the serum is a specific.

The principles underlying this process have suggested a series of highly significant blood-relationship tests in the following manner: The blood of a dog, let us say, injected into a rabbit (any tractable animal will do) causes the rabbit's system to produce antibodies to counteract the alien (dog) blood. A serum produced from this rabbit's blood may be called *antidog serum*. When mixed with the blood of a dog it causes a white precipitate to form. The same reaction occurs, though with less intensity, when the antidog serum is mixed with the blood of a wolf, fox, or any other member of the canine family. The closer the relationship to the dog, the stronger the reaction. But the antidog serum produces no reaction when mixed with the blood of a cat, a hog, a monkey, a man, or any noncanine.

Anticat serum produces a like precipitation when mixed with cat, tiger, lion, or any other feline blood; but it does not precipitate when mixed with the blood of a nonmember of the feline family.

Similar results will occur for any animal family for which an antiserum can be produced. So it goes for man and the apes and the monkeys. Antihuman serum produces a cloud of white precipitate when mixed with human blood, a lighter cloud when mixed with the blood of an ape, and a still weaker cloud when mixed with the blood of the various monkeys. A slight reaction is even produced in mixing the antihuman serum with the blood of the lemur and tarsius, living representatives of the most primitive primate forms from which man, the anthropoids, and monkeys have developed during the last sixty million years. Blood will tell, and "the blood of the common ancestor still flows in man, the higher apes, and, in more diluted form, the Old and New World monkeys." [10]

Fossil Man. Lastly, there is the fascinating evidence offered by the recovered skeletons of fossil men. Their bones have been lifted out of the past to offer mute testimony of the antiquity of man and his early nature. They form a host of "missing links" that piece together to weave a pattern of evolutionary trails out of apedom into humanity. Each year, as new discoveries of fossil men are brought to light, the pattern becomes more complex but its certainty is made clearer. The fossils and the way they form the pattern of relationship to lower forms will require for exposition the whole of the next chapter.

[10] *Ibid.,* p. 13.

CHAPTER 3

FOSSIL MAN

Primate Phylogeny. Man is not, as the common misconception has it, "descended from the monkeys." Such a popular idea is a vulgar corruption of the evolutionary concept of the descent of man; it was never advanced by Darwin or by any of his scientific followers in biology or anthropology. In the preceding chapter several types of evidence were presented to show the bases on which the close relationship of man to the apes and monkeys is predicated. From these and similar data the principle that man has evolved, or ascended, from lower animal forms is derived. Two separate ideas are involved in this statement. The first rests upon the zoological proposition that two or more animal forms that show a large number of significant similarities in form and function must be more or less closely related. The second proposition is that close relationship means common ancestry. Further, the greater the detailed similarity in form and function, the more definite and extensive is the commonness of ancestry.

Because man and the living anthropoids have so many detailed traits in common, this is scientific evidence of their common ancestry. This must not be taken to mean, however, that the numerous kinds of monkeys, apes, and men have *a* common ancestor. The primate order has enjoyed sixty million years of evolutionary development since the beginning of the Eocene period. During the protracted span of the Eocene, Oligocene, and Miocene periods there have occurred hundreds of varieties and breeds of numerous primate genera. It is therefore wrong to speak of any of these forms as *the* missing link, as though there is just one ancestral form. It must be realized at the outset that there are a number of series of missing links, which make a complex pattern back to remote antiquity. *There is no common ancestor but many ancestral predecessors.* A complete family tree of man, the apes, and monkeys will include a truly bewildering number of fossil ancestors.

Though man is not descended from the apes, we are, nevertheless, justified in referring to the traits of man's prehuman ancestors as "simian" or "apelike." This is permissible because the apes have not evolved as far from the common ancestral forms as we have. Our prehistoric ancestors carried some of the primitive traits of the common

21

ancestral forms that we have ultimately forgone and the apes continue to retain. At no time has the human line passed through an evolutionary stage in which it exhibited total forms exactly like any of the living

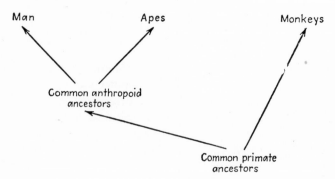

Fig. 5. Diagram of the actual relationships of man, the apes, and monkeys.

apes. Since the days of divergence from the common ancestors, the apes have all continued to evolve in the direction of their own peculiar specializations at the very time that human forms were developing their own unique traits. The difference is that the apes have evolved to a much more limited extent. To say that a trait is "simian" means indirectly that it is primitive, in the sense that ape traits are (except for specializations) not greatly different from those of the common ancestors of apes and men.

The simple way of putting it is to say that the present-day apes are our relatively undeveloped collateral relatives, "cousins," and the living monkeys are in varying degree less developed and more remotely related "cousins." Diagrammatically this relationship would be expressed as in Fig. 5. The erroneous popular idea of the descent of man from the apes and monkeys would have to be diagrammed as in Fig. 6.

Fig. 6. Diagram of the erroneous popular conception of the descent of man from the apes and monkeys.

Though the diagram given in Fig. 5 is correct so far as it goes, it does not go far enough. It is possible, on the basis of fossil primates already discovered, to elaborate such a chart in great detail. In fact, it is quite possible to include so much detail as to discourage any but the specialist. To avoid such a result and to keep the diagram comprehensible to the novice, a considerable number of known fossil genera and species of the primates have been excluded from presentation in the elaborated chart of primate phylogeny given in Fig. 7. This chart gives the dramatis personae of main characters in the drama of primate evolution; it shows their relationships to each other as delineated at

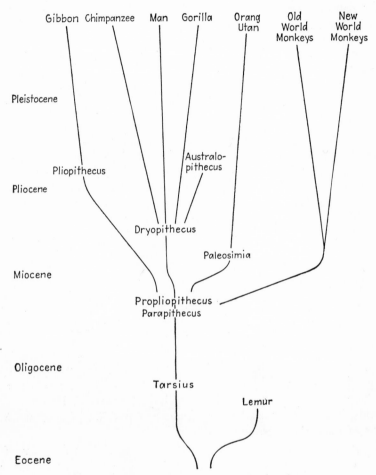

Fig. 7. Probable phylogenetic tree of the primates.

present by the weight of competent authority. The subsequent paragraphs undertake a synoptic summary and interpretation of the significance of each of the types that has a place on this family tree.

Lemuroids. The little lemurs are the earliest fossil primates that may clearly be distinguished from the tree-dwelling mammalian insectivores of the Cretaceous period of the Mesozoic era who were ancestral to all the primates. The lemur is itself a primate, but because it is the most primitive and ancient primate known, it takes the important place as common ancestor to all other primate forms. Fossil lemurs occur in Eocene deposits in both the Old World and the New, but living types occur naturally only in the tropical areas of the Old World, particularly in Madagascar.

Tarsioids. The minute tarsius, hardly bigger than a mouse, occurs as a fossil in the Lower Eocene deposits of Europe and North America. The antiquity of tarsioids therefore approximates that of the lemuroids, but they are less primitive. This means that tarsius is to be regarded as evolutionarily more progressive and biologically a higher type than the lemur. The timid and nocturnal tree-dwelling tarsius still lives in the jungle forests of the East Indies. Its eyes are set in complete sockets (previous mammals lacked this trait), which face forward in the face. It puts a premium on seeing over smelling; and it prefers to convey food to its mouth with its front paws rather than to nuzzle it. In consonance with these propensities, it took to sitting on its haunches, and it exhibits a much-reduced snout. Recession of the face and the freeing of the fore limbs for handling, by use of the rear limbs for support and locomotion, are progressive traits established by the tarsioids and improved upon by the Old World monkeys and apes. Ultimately man attained superior proficiency in all these respects. The tarsius itself did not progress very far along these lines, but its valid claim to honor is that it founded the family line and established important traits leading to the higher primates.

Parapithecus. Parapithecus is a fossil primate known only from a lower jaw and teeth found in Lower Oligocene deposits at Fayum, Egypt. The nature of its dentition shows it to be ancestral to the Old and New World monkeys and the tailless anthropoids, including man. It holds, in consequence, the very important position of *a* common ancestor of man, the apes, and monkeys.

Propliopithecus. This animal is also represented by a fossil jaw fragment from the very same deposits of the Oligocene at Fayum that yielded the remains of parapithecus. Propliopithecus is to be regarded as of approximately similar age as parapithecus, but evolutionarily more advanced. Its position is that of a descendant of a parapithecus type of ancestor. Because of its pronounced gibbonoid tendencies, it is considered to be ancestral to the Lower Pliocene pliopithecus, who is the direct and immediate ancestor of the modern gibbons of the Malay Archipelago.

Paleosimia. Paleosimia is a fossil ape found in the Middle Miocene deposits of India. Its traits mark it as a direct ancestor of the forest orang-utans of present-day Indonesia. Paleosimia is in no respect ancestral to man, an indication that the orang-utan line differentiated from the humanoid stem long before the separation of the chimpanzee and gorilla branches. The same is true of the gibbons.

Dryopithecus. Of the greatest importance is the versatile genus of dryopithecus. Possessed of notable biological lability, this genus differentiated into at least a dozen species. The common characteristics of the genus are such as to make this animal without doubt the form from which all types of man ultimately derive. But not only was dryopithecus the progenitor of all humanity; it also was the genetic source of the lines of the gorilla, chimpanzee, and a number of extinct genera of superapes, such as australopithecus (see below). These distinctive genera of man and apes probably were derived from differing species of dryopithecus. *Dryopithecus fontani* probably produced the gorilla. *Dryopithecus rhenanus* probably produced the chimpanzee. At least one other dryopithecus species, possibly *darwini*, produced the lines of humanoids. The marked dissimilarity between the basic races of man at the opening of the glacial age leads to the possibility that two or more closely similar dryopithecus species gave rise to humanoid descendants. Man, it is now clear, evolved differentially and simultaneously in many parts of the Old World.[1]

The dryopithecus apes lived six million or more years ago in a time that may be looked upon as the crucial evolutionary period in the emergence of man. This was the period when the anthropoids of large bulk gave up tree life to come down to earth. Some of the forms grew larger brains and took to the habit of standing on their hind legs when they walked. These were the ones whose descendants were destined in due time to become men.

Dawn Men. From the time of dryopithecus to the emergence of modern man, approximately 800,000 generations of anthropoids have lived, bred, and died. The changes occurring in any one generation of any one type would not be noticeable except as individual variations. But cumulative variations in a given direction throughout 800,000 generations can measure up to some mighty alterations, such as produce entirely new genera and many new species. So emerged the ape men and men from lower apes.

Australopithecus africanus. In australopithecus we have a remarkable intermediary creature that was less than man and more than ape, but

[1] F. Weidenreich, "Some Problems Dealing with Ancient Man" (*American Anthropologist*, Vol. 42, 1940), pp. 381–382.

more ape than man. It first became known from a complete natural endo-cranial cast with fossil face and jaws taken in 1924 from a quarry near Taungs, in South Africa. A number of specimens of the same or closely

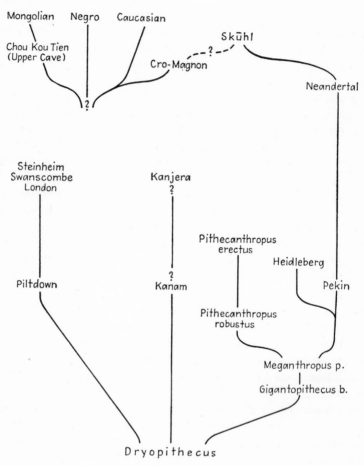

Fig. 8. Probable phylogenetic tree of fossil men.

related species have subsequently been recovered in Central Africa. The original skull was that of a five-year-old infant. Adults have a cranial capacity of approximately 600 cc. A brain of this volume is no larger than those of the larger gorillas and chimpanzees. From this, and the nature of the cortical surface, it is to be inferred that the Taungs superape was not notably superior to the gorilla or chimpanzee in mental status. Nevertheless, in a number of important features australopithecus was decidedly human. This is especially true of its dentition and of certain facial features.[2] Australopithecus may be classified as a superior ape that had humanoid tendencies. It could in no sense have been a human ancestor, however, because its age is Early Pleistocene, a time when man was already well beyond the ape level.

Pithecanthropus erectus. A half-century ago pithecanthropus stirred the interest of the world as "the missing link found." Uninformed skeptics are sometimes inclined to doubt the reliability of provisional reconstructions of whole creatures based upon fragmentary remains. In the case of pithecanthropus, this was done on the basis of the skullcap, a left femur (thighbone), and a few teeth. These were the sole parts that Eugene Du Bois originally discovered at a site near Trinil, Java. Nevertheless, when a competent scientist shapes a reconstruction to fill in the gaps left by missing parts, he is working not by blind guesswork but on the basis of close familiarity with the comparable parts of apes and humans. Given a few essential clues, he can reconstruct a model of the original with impressive probability of high accuracy. In the case of the reconstructions of Java man from the original Trinil fragments, their accuracy has been brilliantly substantiated by the recent discovery (1936 to 1939) in Java of fairly complete skulls from three more pithecanthropus individuals. These fuller skulls prove that the early reconstructions were wholly correct.

Pithecanthropus, or Java man (Fig. 9), has the external cranial appearance of a refined gorilla: heavy, jutting brow ridges; low, receding forehead; narrow temporal regions; skull broad at the base; sharp, angular occiput; immense, prognathous upper jaw; heavy, chinless lower jaw; broad, depressed nose. It lacks the great sagittal and occipital crests of the gorilla, however, and it does not have the massiveness of teeth and jaws of the gorilla.

In spite of any primitive superficial appearances, the real test of a man is his brains. On this count, pithecanthropus deserves to be recognized as a human creature, albeit of a low order. Du Bois's original pithecanthropus has a cranial capacity computed at 985 cc. The 1939 find is equally large-brained, while the specimen found in 1938 is smaller with a capacity of 830 cc. These figures may be set against the range and mean of the normal brains of adult modern man so that their significance may be understood. The probable range for pithecanthropus is from about 775 to 1,000 cc., with a mean of perhaps 900 cc. From these data it can be seen that the pithecanthropus type just reaches the minimum

---

[2] A. Keith, *New Discoveries Relating to the Antiquity of Man.* Chaps. 2–7 detail a careful descriptive balance of the simian and human traits of australopithecus.

of brain size for humanity. On this basis alone, he must be evaluated as less than true man. On the other hand, pithecanthropus appears in a very favorable light when considered against the brain ranges and means of the great apes.

A question may be raised as to the validity of comparisons based on mere brain size, since it is well established that there is no correlation

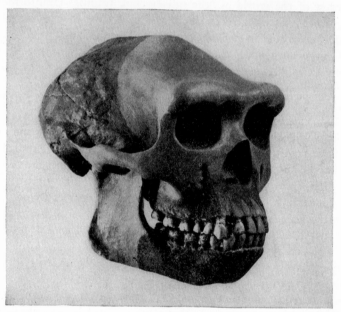

Fig. 9. Restored skull of Java man (*Pithecanthropus erectus*). (*American Museum of Natural History.*)

between brain size and mental ability within the present human species except in pathological cases of micro- and macrocephalics. Nevertheless, as between the several primate genera and in comparison to even lower animal forms, brain volume, cortical surface area, and the relative development of the different parts of the brain are determinable and significant indicators of relative mental capacity. Thus, not only does the brain volume of pithecanthropus indicate his advance far beyond the ape stage, but careful studies of the endocranial casts, which indicate general cortical conformations, have demonstrated that qualitatively, as well as quantitatively, the brain of the pithecanthropus race deserves to be put within the human category. The possessor of such a brain is a man and not an ape man.[3]

[3] F. Tilney, *The Brain from Ape to Man*, Vol. 2, p. 884.

Nothing is definitely known of Java man's body, except for the intriguing thighbone. This is quite enough to prove that he was bipedal and upright, 5 feet 2 inches in height. The fact of his upright posture is predicated by the slight curvature of the bone, which is more like the slender straight femur of man than like the curved heavy femur of an ape; the stature is derived from the femoral length-height ratios of apes and men. A well-developed posterior ridge, the *linea aspera*, along which

NORMAL RANGE IN BRAIN SIZE FOR ADULT HOMO SAPIENS, CUBIC CENTIMETERS

Minimum	Mean (approximate)		Maximum
	Female	Male	
1,000	1,300	1,350	2,000

RANGE IN BRAIN SIZE FOR ADULT GREAT APES, CUBIC CENTIMETERS

Minimum	Mean	Maximum
290	425	650

the extensor muscles of the thigh are anchored, also tells the story of upright posture for its owner. One of the recently discovered pithecanthropus skulls includes the *foramen magnum*. Its position under the skull, intermediate between that of an upright man and a quadrupedal ape, gives additional confirmation of the evidence supplied by the thigh.

Java man may be pictured as a human being of the most low-browed sort. Bull-necked, pinheaded, with beetling eyes under a pre-frontal escarpment, a broad flat nose over a large mouth, and no chin, his appearance had little to commend him. But for all that, and because of that, he is a transitional man, a branch of mankind leaving apedom behind. Therein lies his importance.

Pithecanthropus Precursors. One of the most assiduous of recent searchers after the remains of ancient man is von Koenigswald. Just prior to the outbreak of the Second World War he recovered in China four gigantic humanoid teeth three times as large as any previously known teeth of men—teeth that were 1½ times as large as the largest teeth of any known gorilla. The probable age of these monstrous grinders is Late Pliocene, and Weidenreich has identified them as the teeth of a gigantic genus of pithecanthropus progenitors to whom he has given the scientific name *Gigantopithecus blackii*, in honor of Davidson Black, pioneer student of ancient man in China.

In Java, von Koenigswald and his assistants found skull fragments of another overgrown type of early man, whose teeth indicate probable descent from gigantopithecus. This specimen is probably ancestral to pithecanthropus, and because it is large but not gigantic, his genus name, ascribed by Weidenreich, is *Meganthropus* and his species name is *paleo-javanicus*, because he lived in ancient Java.

And yet another species of pithecanthropus is indicated by Weidenreich on the basis of von Koenigswald's discoveries. This is a more rugged specimen of pithecanthropus who belongs not to the species *erectus* but, rather, *robustus*.[4]

Thus, in a few short years, the systematic and purposeful researches of von Koenigswald, analyzed and interpreted by Weidenreich, have revealed three ancestral progenitors of the famous old *Pithecanthropus erectus*. As one follows them back into antiquity, each is successively larger than the other.

Apparently, a very sharp mutational break produced an oversized Dawn man out of a dryopithecus species. The resultant giantism was subsequently progressively modified in a reversal of the usual evolutionary trend, which is from small to larger sizes.

However that may be, it is no longer possible to maintain, as did Weidenreich even as late as 1940, that *Pithecanthropus erectus* is the most primitive type of fossil man ever found.[5]

Sinanthropus pekinensis. In the quarries located at the little Chinese village of Chou Kou Tien, in the environs of Peking, are some remarkable caves anciently filled in with rich fossil-bearing travertine. In a little more than ten years of systematic excavation (1927 to 1939) these quarries have yielded fossilized remains of thousands of Ice Age mammals and portions of skeletons of more than forty prehistoric men, women, and children—members of a number of ancient races, from the primitive type

[4] F. Weidenreich, "Giant Early Man from Java and South China" (*American Museum of Natural History, Anthropological Papers*, Vol. 40, 1945), pp. 1–134.

[5] F. Weidenreich, "Man or Ape?" (*Natural History*, Vol. 46, 1940), p. 35.

now known as *Peking man* to a local Oriental variety of prehistoric *Homo sapiens*. It is with the Peking race (not *Homo sapiens*) that the present discussion is concerned.

The general similarity of Peking man and Java man is immediately striking. Prehistoric man spread far in his racial dispersions. The familiar contour of the Java skull is found again in the skull of Peking man (Fig.

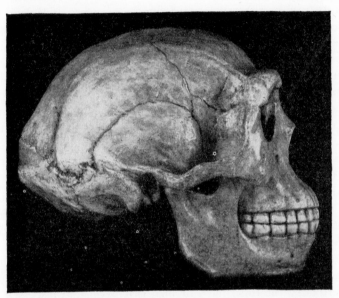

Fig. 10. Restored skull of Peking man (*Sinanthropus pekinensis*). (*American Museum of Natural History*.)

10). There is the same receding forehead, sloping back from heavy supra-orbital ridges, the same angular occiput, the same narrow constriction of the frontal regions (as viewed from above); Peking man is definitely a close relative of pithecanthropus. His brain, with its average of about 1,000 cc., is more copious, but not much. His face projects somewhat in the snouty manner of Java man and his canine teeth are moderately tusklike. His whole dentition is, in fact, very primitive but nevertheless human. His chin recedes in the simian manner, but on the whole the structure of his jaw is human enough. So few body bones have been found in conjunction with the multiplicity of skulls recovered, that suspicion is warranted that Peking man was the victim of a group of cannibals who beheaded its Pekinese victims and took its gruesome trophies to the Chou Kou Tien caves in order to crack the skulls open for a feast on brains. Yet from the materials that are available, it is apparent that Peking man was an upright biped whose fore limbs were freed from the necessity of aiding in locomotion; its prehensile hands with their opposable thumbs were wholly free for manipulatory activities and toolmaking. Peking man, although apparently contemporary to Java man, represents an improvement in evolutionary form of the same racial stock that produced the Java race. Peking man, it may be concluded, represents an early link in the evolution from the very primitive Java race to the Late Pleistocene Neandertals who lived 900,000 years after Java man (see below).

Eoanthropus dawsoni. Evidence has been accumulating in recent years to undermine the old idea that Asia is the original center for the emergence of man. The newer facts make it quite probable that there was no single center for the origin of man but that several kinds of men were evolving from several superape types in all parts of the Old World: Europe, Africa, and Asia. It is not to be forgotten that Eocene, Oligocene, and Miocene fossil primates are found over all the Old World and even in the Western Hemisphere. The earlier primates were by no means confined to Asia. Dryopitheci are found in the western, as well as in the eastern, extremes of the Eurasiatic continent; and Africa, not Asia, is the home of australopithecus. Africa produced the chimpanzee and gorilla, while Asia's best are the orang-utan and gibbon. With respect to the quality of its known prehuman anthropoids, Asia is at the present moment a poor second to Africa.

Nevertheless, the fossil races of man that have been discussed are of Asiatic occurrence. These must now be balanced by a consideration of the very famous Dawn man of Piltdown, England, discovered in 1909 to 1911 by a lawyer, Charles Dawson. First, it must be emphasized that the Piltdown fossil is fully as old as, and possibly older than, either Java or Peking men. It was found in deposits of the first glaciation—in circumstances that suggest that the fossil had actually been washed down from older deposits into a glacial stream bed. This opens the possibility that the Piltdown race lived in preglacial, or Late Pliocene, times. Archaeological evidence (see page 45) makes this possibility highly probable. This means that the Piltdown type of humanity was well established in the extreme west of Europe while the lowly Java man was yet abroad in Asia.

The first discovered remnants of Piltdown man consisted of large cranial fragments and the right half of a lower jaw. In 1915, Dawson also discovered smaller fragments of another individual of the same race in the same geological level that had yielded the first finds, but two miles distant.

The astounding feature of Piltdown man is his cranial development (see Fig. 11). For contrast, one may well compare the smooth rounded contours of the skull of Piltdown man with those of Java, Peking, and Neandertal man (Fig. 12). The vaulted capacious forehead should be

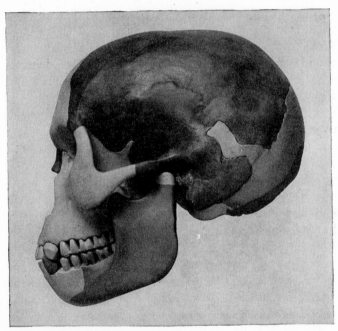

Fig. 11. Restored skull of Piltdown man (*Eoanthropus dawsoni*). (*American Museum of Natural History.*)

noted, and the deep, full occiput. The skull also has a broadness that, combined with its longitudinal fullness, gives it a cranial capacity of 1,400 cc.—a brain volume equal to that of any average modern male. Qualitatively, too, the brain of Piltdown man apparently measures up to high human standards. Keith reports on the basis of his investigations of the endocranial casts that the convolutions of the cortical surface of Piltdown differ in no essential respect from the external brain conformations of living races of men. There is no question but that Piltdown man achieved prodigious mental development at an early age.

The joker in the case of Piltdown man has been his anomalous jaw. The primitive, chinless mandible with its projecting tusklike canine tooth is so apelike in appearance that many skeptics have refused to believe that such a jaw could have been appended to such a skull. There are scientists who have been under the sway of the popular notion that a he-man chin is the essential correlate of a strong mind. Therefore, while the facts necessitate the acceptance of the validity of the skull and jaw as authentic fossils of genuine antiquity, a number of authorities have vigorously contended that the finds at Piltdown actually represented no more than the fortuitous association of a human skull with the jaw of a giant gibbon. In the quarreling over the matter of the linkage of the jaw and skull, the real significance of the Piltdown race was slighted: the fact that a creature with a modern type of brain was in existence a million years ago. The question of what kind of a jaw he had is actually of secondary importance.

Fortunately, two discoveries have routed the mandibular skeptics to establish the anomaly as a fact. First, Keith's ever-meticulous study has shown that the teeth of Piltdown man, though retarded in their evolutionary development, were actually in the process of changing from ape characteristics to human; they are intermediary in form and position. The dentition proves the jaw to be definitely not that of an ape. Secondly, the 1915 discovery of the fragments of the second Piltdown individual included a molar tooth in addition to cranial fragments. The skull fragments duplicate the characteristics revealed by the skull of Piltdown I, and the tooth is identical with the molars embedded in the jaw of the first Piltdown man. This gives basis to the conclusion that jaw and skull belong together, for the purely fortuitous association of an ape jaw with a human skull, along with the complete disappearance of the human jaw and the ape's skull, is not likely to occur twice in the same location. There is no reasonable alternative to the fact that Piltdown man was a "chinless wonder."

A more serious consequence than the reluctance of some anthropologists to accept the implications of the association of the jaw with the skull of Piltdown has been the consistently facile rejection of a number of fossils of apparent early glacial age which are modern in type. This has been done on the basis of the apt formula that Early Pleistocene man had to be apelike, in the manner of pithecanthropus. This unreasonable obtuseness has lead to the arbitrary closeting of such really important finds as those made at Galley Hill, near London (1888), at Paris (Grenelle and Clichy, 1869), and in Italy (Olma, 1863, and Castenedolo, 1860 and 1880). These last-mentioned are all fossils of modern types that were discovered embedded in mid-glacial and early glacial deposits. In some instances, it is true, the circumstances of the discoveries were equivocal, but this is not so in all of them. They were rejected because they were too modern for their antiquity, *i.e.*, they did not fit into the then-existing schemes of human origins, which did not allow for a great antiquity of the human race. Too great a mental wrench was called for to make possible the acceptance, at the time, of these fossils for what they apparently are. Nor was the significance of the Galley Hill type of man realized even with the discovery of Piltdown man. Piltdown man had been tentatively suggested by a few authorities as a possible ancestor to modern man, but the intervening links between Piltdown and modern man were thought to be still a blank record. Europe was deeded over to the Neandertalers without a keen search of the title.

New discoveries in London in 1925 fortunately caused the issue to be reopened. In that year, Lloyd's of London began the construction of a new home office on the site of the famous old East India House in the heart of the Old City, only a stone's throw from London Bridge. There, excavations 42 feet beneath the street level, on a glacial age terrace of the River Thames, brought forth a fossil skull, known as the *London skull*. The precise age of this skull is mid-glacial (500,000 years). It has some traits that approximate the Neandertaloid (see below), but, in the main, its affinities are Piltdown, and London man is a Piltdown descendant. More of this same type of man seem recently to have been discovered at Swanscombe, England (1935), and Steinheim, Germany (1938), for both are modern type mid-glacial skulls that Keith analyzes as of Piltdown affinity.[6]

The conclusion is that we are not so lacking in fossil representatives of the Piltdown line of descendants as had been thought. The discoveries of the last ten years have produced some very fine examples; Galley Hill man and his continental counterparts must be reconsidered as probable representatives of the same racial line. Piltdown man rises to a stronger and stronger position as a possible ancestor, or near ancestor, of modern man. This is a claim that cannot be made with much force for Java and Peking men.

Homo kanamensis. No synoptic survey of the fossil ancestors of man would be adequate without reference to a few of the recent and impor-

---

[6] A. Keith, "A Resurvey of the Anatomical Features of the Piltdown Skull with Some Observations on the Recently Discovered Swanscombe Skull" (*Journal of Anatomy*, Vol. 63, 1938–1939), pp. 155–185, 234–254. In *New Discoveries Relating to the Antiquity of Man*, Chaps. 29 and 30, Keith presents detailed data and evaluations on the London skull.

tant discoveries that have been coming from central Africa in the region of Lake Tanganyika. In the spring of 1934 Leakey recovered a chin fragment of highly mineralized bone from deposits of probable Early Pleistocene age. The symphysis of this chin fragment is in all respects the prognathous chin of modern man, so that its possessor was very likely a member of the genus homo. If the geological age claimed for the specimen by its discoverer is correct, then we are confronted by a third type of humanity existent at the opening of the glacial age one million years ago. It may or may not be that Kanam man is the direct ancestor of modern man; more evidence is needed before that claim may be given unqualified acceptance. Especially desirable would be the recovery of adequate skull remains of Kanam man. A possible indication of the cranial qualities of Kanam man is advanced by Leakey, however, in the form of skullcaps from nearby deposits of mid-glacial age at Kanjera. It is suggested that Kanjera man, who is semimodern in cranial form, is a descendant of Kanam man.[7]

Homo neandertalensis. The fossil men who have thus far been discussed were all Dawn men, men who lived at the very dawn of the human era and who were prototypic of the true men to come later. It has already been seen that during the long stretches of the middle phases of the glacial period descendants of the Piltdown lineage were present in Europe and England. It seems almost as though they must have been limited to sparse and scattered populations, however, because the Neandertals and Neandertaloids so definitely dominate the scene from the time of the first interglacial epoch to the peak of the fourth glaciation (750,000–40,000 B.C.). Not only did the Neandertal race dominate Europe in these times but Neandertaloid descendants of Java and Peking types of men flourished throughout Africa and Asia too. Over 40,000 generations of the Java-Peking-Neandertal line lived and succeeded each other, suddenly to vanish from the earth. The survival destiny of no biological form is guaranteed against all comers and all contingencies.

The Neandertal species of the genus homo existed in a number of races and varieties (for the specific meaning of these terms see Chap. 6). With its wide distribution and environmental separatism, many local modifications occurred; however, all Neandertal types have fundamental characteristics in common.

The first Neandertal man was discovered in 1848 at Gibraltar, too early to be recognized at the time for the special human type that it is. A subsequent discovery in 1856 of a fairly complete skeleton in a cave in the valley of the Neander, a little stream near Düsseldorf-on-the-

[7] L. S. B. Leakey, *The Stone Age Races of Kenya.*

Rhine, led to the recognition of the type as a unique human species and gave the form its species name *Neandertalensis*. The particular skeleton found at Neandertal has been superseded as the type of specimen by that of the famous old man of La Chapelle-aux-Saints, a cavern in south-western France. This is the Neandertaler whose skull is shown in Fig. 12.

All the important external superficial characteristics listed for the Java-Peking men may be seen again in the skull of the Neandertal. The

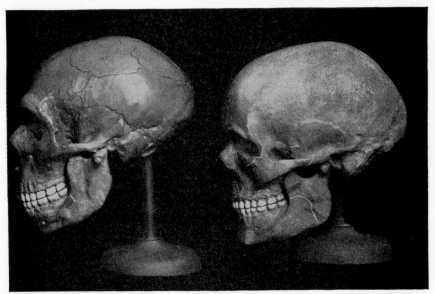

Fig. 12. Skulls of Neandertal man (left) and Cro-Magnon man (right). (*American Museum of Natural History.*)

main points of difference between Neandertal man and his Java-Peking predecessors are traits of qualitative improvement brought about by evolutionary development. Whereas the Java and Peking brains were at the lowest extreme of human brain volume, Neandertal man reached the higher limits, though some specimens also fall in the lower brackets. The range of brain volume of Neandertal man coincides with that of modern man—from 1,000 to 2,000 cc. with the mean at about 1,400 or 1,500 cc. Though quantitatively the equal of modern man in brain size, Neandertal man's mental equipment was not qualitatively up to the standard of ours. This judgment rests upon the fact that a smaller proportion of the brain volume and surface area occurs in the frontal lobes of Neandertal man than is the case with modern man. The frontal area of the brain is the associational area that is so greatly involved in the higher processes of thinking. Because of the poorer development of the frontal regions of the brain, the forehead of Neandertal man, though it is more vaulted than is the case with his Java and Peking predecessors, is still somewhat recessive and low.

The Neandertal jaw is set with human, non-ape-like teeth. The chin of the Neandertal jaw does not recede to the extent of the chins of Java and Peking men; neither does it project, as does modern man's. Neandertal man was developing a chin, but in a very tentative manner.

The face is exceptionally long and full, with eyes set deep under overhanging bony ridges. The nose is wide and low-bridged, the cheeks round and full over their bony foundation. The dental arches are prognathous.

Fortunately, more is known of the body of Neandertal man than is the case with many of his predecessors, for Neandertal man served archaeology by instituting the practice of burial—a great aid to the fossilization process and a boon to anthropologists.

The stature of Neandertals is less than 5½ feet; their bodies are robust with broad shoulders and deep chests. Posture, although classed as upright since the Neandertalers were habitually bipedal, hardly approached the military ideal. This was caused by the forward projection of the face with its heavy jaws, which made necessary a tilting up of the head to allow adequate room for jaw operation. To support such a head in this position a heavy neck musculature, anchored to massive backward-projecting spines on the neck vertebrae, was required. The whole spine was short and thick, lacking the characteristic S curvature that modern man has developed in consonance with his upright posture. The arms of these men were short and heavy, the forearm being particularly short—a most un-ape-like specialization of the species. The legs, on the other hand, show much in common with the chimpanzee and gorilla. Their component bones are short and massive, with enlarged joints that reveal in their conformation a propensity to habitual squatting. The same features develop on the articulating surfaces of the ankle joints of modern primitives who squat habitually. The thighbones are moderately curved in consonance with upright posture.

Such are the main contours of Neandertal man; his skin and hair color are of course unknown, as are the shape of his lips and the form and distribution of his hair. Of his works we shall speak in the next chapter.

It has been reiterated in these pages that Neandertal man stood at the end of a Neandertal-Peking-Java line of evolution. These three races are by no means the sole known representatives of the line, for its collateral branches are studded with intermediary types of fossils that may be called *Neandertaloids*. Some of the more famous representatives of this group are the Heidelberg man (*Homo heidelbergensis*), known from a massive fossil lower jaw found in the first interglacial sands of Mauer-on-the-Neckar, near Heidelberg; the Ehringsdorf, Weimar, and Krapina men from the second interglacial deposits of south Germany and Jugoslavia; Solo man (*Homo soloensis*) from the Solo River, near Trinil, Java, a mid-glacial deviant Neandertaloid that is closely related to the remarkable fossil man found at Broken Hill, Rhodesia, in South Africa (*Homo rho-desianensis*). This peculiar type of man has a large (1,300 cc.) but primitive brain housed in a low-vaulted skull behind dikelike supraorbital ridges, below which hangs a huge elongated face.

Palestine Man. Excavations around the Sea of Galilee since 1925 have yielded a golden harvest of Neandertaloids. The Holy Land was a favorite haunt of Neandertalers in the dim eras before Biblical times: the caves of its hills are rich in the remains of prehistoric men. It is exciting enough to discover prehistoric fossil men in Palestine, but it is not this that stirs the interest of the scientific world so much as does the nature of the Palestinian Neandertals found at Mount Carmel. The fossil Neandertalers from this site were numerous and so variable in their characteristics that they range from standard type Neandertals to modified Neandertals with distinct modern qualities. This last group, known as the Skhūl race, may be looked upon as a Neandertal variety that was evolving into *Homo sapiens* form. Or it may be held to be the result of intermixture between Neandertals and some *Homo sapiens*. The first opinion is held by McCown and Keith, the discoverers of the Palestine group. It is revolutionary in its proposal that modern man was produced as a result of quite recent mutations of the Neandertalers, an idea that has been consistently championed for some time by the Smithsonian anthropologist Ales Hrdlička, who has been looked upon as an anthropological heretic because of it.[8] That the Skhūl race is intermediary between the Neandertals and modern man cannot be doubted, but there is as yet little inclination among the majority of anthropologists to accept the possibility that modern man developed from the Neandertals. Even when taken to mean that there was miscegenation between the two types of man, however, the evidence is of revolutionary import. It dissipates the formerly held idea that racial antipathy was so strong between Neandertal man and the modern man who succeeded him that no intermixture whatever took place. Present evidence does not go far to indicate any such measure of congeniality between these two forms of humanity in prehistoric Europe,

[8] A. Hrdlička, "The Neandertal Phase of Man" (*The Smithsonian Institution, Annual Report,* 1928), pp. 593–623.

but in Palestine the two types seem to have attained a measure of biological assimilation.

Homo sapiens Cro-Magnonensis. Object of paeans of anthropological praise is Cro-Magnon man. A modern man in all physical characteristics, upright and generally magnificent of stature, large-brained, with a high smooth forehead on a finely shaped head, broad-faced with jutting chin— he was a paragon of athletic beauty. Endowed with artistic skill and aesthetic imagination, this is one race that replaced the Neandertals. The origin of the Cro-Magnon is an unsolved mystery; whether he evolved by mutation from the Neandertal type, or by gradual development from the Piltdown-London prototypes of modern man, or outside Europe from unknown ancestors, remains to be determined. Whatever his origin, Cro-Magnon man, at the height of the fourth glaciation, took over a large part of western Europe that had previously been under the control of Neandertals. Where Cro-Magnon man waxed, Neandertal man waned and disappeared. Here was struggle for survival on the grand scale, truly affecting the destiny of all mankind for all human time to come. So ended the million-year epoch of the Java-Peking-Neandertal heritage. The epitaph of the Neandertal species may be read in the recent judgment of Howells, "modern man as a whole is no descendant of the known Neandertals, and . . . he did not pass through a Neandertaloid phase in his main line of ancestry." [9]

Cro-Magnon man is not an early ancestor of *Homo sapiens*. He *is* a *Homo sapiens*, who lived from 40,000 until 15,000 B.C. He was probably related to the present Caucasian or white race. This last fact is not based on any knowledge of his skin color or hair form; it rests upon the identity of his well-known skeletal characteristics.

Cro-Magnon man, it should be realized, was not the only form of *Homo sapiens* inhabiting Europe in the last phase of the glacial age. There is, for example, the provisional Aurignacian race, *Homo sapiens aurignacianensis*, as represented by the fossil men from Paviland Cave in Wales, from Combe-Capelle, France, and Predmost in Czechoslovakia. This race is similar in many counts to the men of Galley Hill and London. From this fact, the Aurignacian race is to be looked upon as a European correlate of the Piltdown-London racial line. It is an oversimplification to attribute the glories of Upper Paleolithic culture (see next chapter) to Cro-Magnon man alone. Aurignacian man most certainly had a hand in it, too.

[9] W. W. Howells, "Fossil Man and the Origin of Races" (*American Anthropologist*, Vol. 44, 1942), p. 189.

Africa also offers its share of Upper Paleolithic varieties of *Homo sapiens*, numerous specimens of which have been unearthed from the Sahara to Cape Town. Some of these forms prove to be ancestral to the few surviving Bushmen of the Kalahari desert. Others are prototypic ancestors of the Negro race. One famous pair of this type made its way north of the Mediterranean to be buried in the grotto of Grimaldi on the Italian-French border of the Riviera.

Postglacial Men. The last glaciation was well along with its melting dissipation when the Cro-Magnon phase came to a close about 15,000 B.C. By this time the cultures of the Near East were so advanced that great expansions of populations were possible in that part of the world. Multitudes of men began the penetration of western Europe, ranging up the river valleys that lead into the Mediterranean and Black Seas. They opened the gates to the dawn of civilization.

Up to this stage of man's history all the known fossil races of man had been longheaded. Now for the first time the roundheaded races made their appearance. They are best known in their earliest occurrence from the multiple burials of skulls in nests in southeastern Germany. These burials appear to be interments attendant upon the sacrificial beheading of the victims, mostly women and children. Round heads, long heads, and medium heads occur together in the nests—evidence that the new races were intermixing as the invasions went on. These were the harbingers of the Mediterranean and Alpine white races that were later to establish themselves in numerous locales of Europe, and, ultimately, over the world. The Nordics, for whom such extravagant claims have recently been made, arrived later upon the scene from unknown sites of origin to contest with the Mediterraneans and Alpines for position in Europe and North Africa, and also to intermix with these peoples to form the present populations of Europe, America, and many other parts of the world.

New World Man. Since the mention of lemuroids and the branching of the New World monkeys from the primate trunk in the Oligocene period, not a word has been said in this chapter about primate ancestors of man in the Western Hemisphere. The good reason for this lies in the fact that New World primate evolution never went beyond the lowly long-snouted, tailed monkeys of South America. The western continents were incapable of producing any of the higher ape forms. There was no dryopithecus here to provide the seed from which to evolve man. Hence, no human foot trod these soils until man in the Old World had reached the stage where he was ready and able to leave the Siberian wilds to cross the old land bridge at Bering Straits and work his way down and across the vast reaches of North America, then to press on through the narrows of Central America into South America, so on down to the southern tip at Tierra del Fuego. Current evidence indicates that the first of the migrations that accomplished the aboriginal peopling of the Americas began at about the time of the Cro-Magnon displacement of the Neandertals, or possibly a little later. From that day to this, the New World has been the promised land of immigrants, but it has proven barren soil for the antiquarian anthropologist who seeks the ancestors of man. Rich it is, though, in rewards for the anthropologist who is content to work with more recent men and cultures. The archaeology and ethnology of the American Indians are a complex and rewarding field of study, though their prehistory is brief from the anthropological point of view.

CHAPTER 4

THE OLD STONE AGE

The seeds of cultural capacity are in the great apes, whose potentialities for learning, discovery, and invention have been investigated and carefully described in the works of Köhler, Yerkes, and others. It has been shown that the higher apes possess the capacity to perceive the applicability of observed phenomena to the attainment of desires: invention. They apply sticks as levers and stones as hammers; they fit sticks together to extend their reach; they use them as vaulting poles to extend their jumping capacities—and as jabbing rods to annoy unwary hens about the ape farm. Such activities are only the simplest of their many capacities in the production of new tools and new ideas. Such patterns of behavior are not inborn. They are not instinctive; they are protocultural, the stuff out of which culture develops. The apes fall short of culture because their discoveries and inventions do not persist. The apes lack the ability to produce language (though they do, of course, communicate on an elemental emotional level), and their memory span is so short that their communicable noninstinctive accomplishments flourish only as short-lived fads without the permanence of true culture traits.[1]

It is impossible to say at precisely what time in prehistory protoculture shaded into genuine culture, for the element of permanence is a relative thing, and the transition from the one to the other must have been very gradual. But when the brains of our subhuman ancestors had developed sufficiently to make possible permanent habits of toolmaking and lasting social inventions, the long process of cultural development was truly under way. The era of the great event was the Late Pliocene.

The Dawn Stone Age. The earliest known remains of man's handiworks are found in the Late Pliocene deposits of East Anglia (England); the geological estimate of their age is 1,300,000 years. Near a town known as Bramford, the great amateur archaeologist J. Reid Moir discovered numerous peculiarly shaped stones that he subsequently named *rostrocarinates*, meaning beak-keeled (Fig. 13). The very peculiarity of these stones with their chipped surfaces, which at one end resemble the curved beak of a bird, is what proves them to be the works of men. The dis-

---

[1] This subject is treated more fully in Chap. 33.

tinctive form into which these pieces of flint were shaped could be the product of no other force than the controlled handiwork of intelligent man.

The rostrocarinate is a fairly advanced type of implement that must have been preceded by less definite types of tools. And indeed, such cruder tools, or *eoliths* (Gr. *eos* dawn + *lithos* stone), are found in many parts of the world. An eolith may be said to be a stone crudely chipped

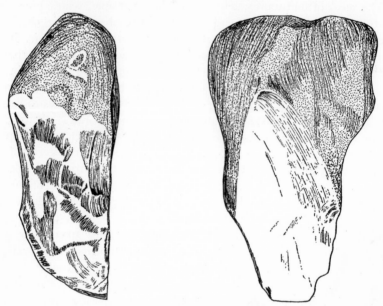

FIG. 13. Rostrocarinate from the Sub-Red Crag of Bramford.

with the intent of making it fit a useful purpose. There is no doubt that early man put stones to use without chipping them, just as the chimpanzee does, or anyone may do to pound a stake, crack a nut, or drive off an inquisitive cow at a picnic. Such stones, although temporarily used as tools, are, nevertheless, not eoliths. The hallmark of the eolith is that it is purposefully worked to improve its effectiveness. An eolith might with equal appropriateness be called a *teleolith* (Gr. *telos* end, purpose + *lithos* stone).

The need for cutting and scraping instruments led to the invention of eoliths. Natural hammerstones can be found ready to hand in great profusion in most places. It is otherwise, however, with stones that must have a sharp, lasting working edge. Flaked flint has just this quality. Because of its nature, flint sometimes flakes under natural conditions such as earth movements, glacial action, and grinding among the rolling rocks on the bed of a fast-flowing stream. By such means as these, so-called "natural eoliths" have been produced without being touched by the hand of man. Such stones may have given men the first thought that they could convert flint into useful tools. Or the workman, using a flint nodule as a hammerstone, might have accidentally broken off flakes with sharp edges. However it may have been, natural eoliths were not good enough, and long before the time of Java and Piltdown men their predecessors were struggling to shape flint nodules and flakes into tools and weapons.

Rhythm holds an intense satisfaction for man. In the production of eoliths this became manifest in a regular tendency to strike blows that retouched the edge of a cutting flake along one side of the flake only. The early workman's percussion strokes did not fall at random.

Many eoliths from the site at Piltdown prove that Piltdown man was a maker of stone tools. More than this, his immediate successors in the territory were responsible for a truly remarkable implement of bone fashioned from the thigh of a mammoth. The tool is nearly 1½ feet long and pointed at one end (Fig. 14). Probably bone tools were numerous in Eolithic days, but unless bone fossilizes it is less durable than stone and specimens are few.

Fig. 14. Pointed implement carved from the thighbone of a Pliocene elephant (*Elephas meridionalis*).

Early man also probably made tools of wood, but wood is even less durable than bone and specimens are fewer still. However, the wooden digging stick, or dibble, is universal among all the lowest primitive food gatherers, and it must be looked upon as one of the most indispensable items in the inventory of Eolithic culture.

Another significant feature of Eolithic culture as it is revealed in England is the evidence of the regular use of fire in the camp sites of Foxhall. Some of the very earliest cultures evidently included the techniques of control of fire. The use of fire in domestic activity is now a universal culture trait indispensable in human activities. We have long since left flint flaking behind as an industrial need, but it is improbable that we shall ever progress beyond the need to use fire.

The Lower Old Stone Age. Overlooking a pleasant valley in the Pyrenees is a remarkable prehistoric site in the cavern of Castillo. Here was a favorite haunt and home of prehistoric man. In thirteen distinct layers of debris, 45 feet in thickness, all the cultures of the *Paleolithic* (Gr. *palaios* ancient + *lithos* stone) *Age* of Europe from the Acheulean (see below) upward are represented. Excavations have laid open, to be read like the pages of a book, the whole sequence of the works of the Neandertaloids and their Upper Paleolithic successors. Many other stations in Europe and Africa have yielded rich harvests of Stone Age cultures corresponding to those found at Castillo, but none have offered so complete a record in one place.

The various Paleolithic cultures receive their queer-sounding names after the geologist's practice of naming rock formations from the place of original discovery or their most typical locality. The unfolding of Old World prehistory in the last half of the nineteenth century was largely the work of French archaeologists digging in France. They gave the newly discovered Stone Age cultures their names after localities in France in the manner listed below (read from bottom to top to obtain the chronological order):

Mesolithic............	Azilian-Tardenoisian	(from Le Mas d'Azil and Fère-en-Tardenois)
	⎧ Magdalenian	(from La Madeleine)
Upper Paleolithic.....	⎨ Solutrean	(from Solutré)
	⎩ Aurignacian	(from Aurignac)
	⎧ Mousterian	(from Le Moustier)
Lower Paleolithic.....	⎨ Acheulean	(from Saint-Acheul)
	⎩ Chellean	(from Chelles)
Eolithic..............	Pre-Chellean	

The Lower Paleolithic period forms a continuous evolution of a single culture complex, modified by cross-fertilizations. Its outstanding feature is the hand ax, also known as the *coup de poing* (Fr. blow of the fist). In most Pre-Chellean industries this implement has no definite shape other than that predicated by the natural shape of the flint nodule from which the ax was made. Chellean man, however, had learned to shape his implements by means of a better technique (Fig. 15); and Acheulean man further refined the hand ax so as to produce a thin even implement, neatly worked over its entire surface. In the Mousterian culture the *coup de poing* was reduced in size and was superseded in importance by the *Levallois flake*.

The Levallois flake was the product of a special technique developed in the Baltic region. Its infusion into the Acheulean culture set a technical tradition that outlived the Lower Paleolithic and contributed to the abandonment of the *coup de poing*. In the Levallois method a flat surface was found or prepared on the nodule of flint to serve as a striking platform. A well-delivered blow on this plane caused a large flake to break off at a 120-degree angle to the plane. The smooth, slightly rounded surface of the fraction face of the flake was left untouched, while the outer face of the flake was shaped by percussion into the desired form. Many varieties of scrapers and points were made by this method in the Mousterian epoch. A close parallel to the Levallois flake is found in the tools of the Clactonian culture from the vicinity of Clacton-by-the-Sea, England.

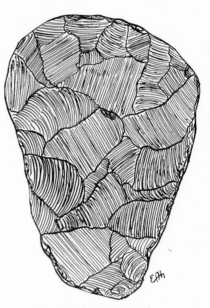

The racial nature of the men of Clacton and the Levallois cultures is as yet unknown. They may well have been of the Piltdown-London line. But the Chellean-Acheulean-Mousterian culture carriers were Neandertaloids and Neandertals who worked Levalloisian ideas into the Acheulean and Mousterian phases of their culture history.[2] And when Neandertal man finally vanished, the Chellean-Acheulean-Mousterian cycle came to an end.

Fig. 15. Chellean hand ax.

In the times of the Eolithic and Pre-Chellean cultures of the Late Pliocene, the climate of Europe and England was gentle and warm; much more so than is the case today. Warm-water corals and mollusks lived in the North Sea. The now extinct southern mammoth and *Elephas antiquus* roamed the prairies and softwood forests of Europe. There were other large mammals, such as the hippopotamus, Etruscan rhinoceros, and saber-toothed tiger; the primitive and diminutive Steno's horse made his precarious way among these larger brutes. So did wild cattle and deer.

　　[2] Recent technical discussions among European prehistorians have been much concerned with the possibility that the flake cultures were produced by *Homo sapiens* (neanthropic) types of prehistoric men, while the core cultures may have been the work of the Neandertaloid lines. For a critical evaluation of this literature, see R. J. Braidwood, "The Interrelations of Core and Flake Tool Traditions in Europe" in *Human Origins*, 2d ed., pp. 145–152.

Eolithic man lived in the open, contesting with these creatures for watering places—and existence. He was not then a cave dweller, nor was he in interglacial times, for man loves the sunshine and forsakes it for the gloomy chill of caves only when forced to do so by glacial weather or fear of attack. The camp sites of Stone Age man were by preference the sun-warmed banks of watercourses. Who among us does not prefer the bathing beach to the air-raid shelter or dugout—unless it be a Dunkirk beach?

In times of the glacial advances the whole face of Europe was changed. Although the glaciers were never extensive enough to smother the entire land surface with ice, they were the result of drastic climatic changes that brought long cold winters and short fleeting summers. In many places man adjusted to the change by making cultural modifications in his modes of living. He retired to caves, warmed himself by fire, and stripped heavy-coated animals of their furs to provide a warm covering for himself. Other animals, however, having no culture, could not wait for biological changes. They had to retire to more comfortable climates in Africa and south Asia. The southern mammoth and the straight-tusked elephant disappeared, to be replaced by the woolly mammoth, the woolly rhinoceros, the monster cave bear, and the hardy reindeer. Their charred and broken bones are found in profusion in the hearths of the Late Mousterian culture, mute testimony to the prowess and culinary tastes of Neandertal man.

The glacial period began one million years ago, and its remnants are with us still in the small glaciers of our northern mountains. The four periods of glacial advance alternated with periods of interglacial warmth, such as the present. The glaciations and their interglacial interludes were probably not of equal length, but for convenience we may roughly calculate each period as of 150,000 years' duration.

On this basis, the correlation of the Lower Paleolithic cultures with the four glaciations and three interglacial periods gives approximate antiquities for the various Old Stone Age cultures as shown in Fig. 16.

The Upper Old Stone Age. The eventful racial revolution of the fourth glaciation (when *Homo sapiens* replaced Neandertal man) was accompanied by a far-reaching cultural revolution. The Lower Paleolithic gave way to the Upper. It is a truism that all revolutions retain something of the order that preceded the revolution. The cultural revolution of the Upper Paleolithic is no exception. Although the spirit of Upper Paleolithic culture was wholly different from that of the Lower Paleolithic, there was nevertheless a carry-over of basic toolmaking techniques from the one to the other. The method of making the Levallois-

Mousterian points was continued, but the form of the products was modified to meet the new needs of Upper Paleolithic man. There is evidence in this of culture contact between Neandertal man and *Homo sapiens,* even if there was little miscegenation.

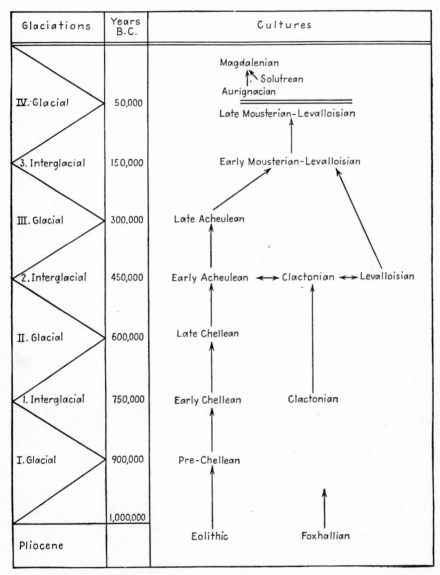

FIG. 16. Main Paleolithic culture sequences of western Europe.

The essential difference in form between the Aurignacian points of the first period of the Upper Paleolithic and the Mousterian is in the prevalence of elongated surface flaking. This was a method for making a usable flake tool with a minimum of effort. The typical *Audi* blade (Fig. 17A) of the opening phases of the Aurignacian culture had not yet attained this quality, but as the Aurignacian period went its way the Audi

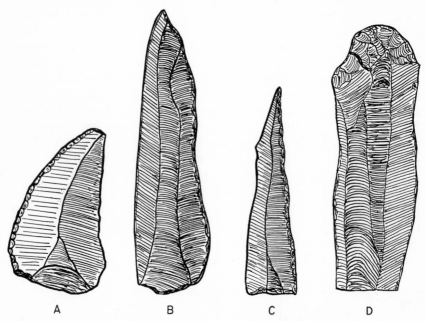

A   B   C   D

Fig. 17. Upper Paleolithic blades from France: A, Audi blade; B, Châtelperron blade; C, gravette; D, carinate blade.

blade was gradually replaced by the long narrow sparsely flaked *Châtelperron* point (Fig. 17B). This in turn gave rise to the very sharp cutting and engraving tool known as the *gravette* (Fig. 17C). Peculiar blades shaped like dumbbells were also produced, which were probably used as shaft shavers. Neat little planing tools, known as *gravers*, or *carinate blades* (Fig. 17D) were quite numerous. In addition, points with tangs for handles were finally produced in Late Aurignacian times.

The specialization in form seen in Aurignacian flint implements is much greater than that found in any culture of Neandertal man. But the artisans of the Aurignacian and Magdalenian periods were indifferent flint workers at best. They were bent on exercising their talents in other fields. The situation offers a good example of the *principle of skewed elaboration in culture.* It is a characteristic of culture growth that the development of most cultures tends to be lopsided. The full potentialities of cultural activity are so great for man that no people has succeeded in giving equal attention to all the possible features of cultural development that lie within its grasp. Attention becomes focused upon some few fields of activity. Here the imagination takes hold to develop the particular phase of culture with exuberance and often with exaggerated lack of restraint. With respect to the possibilities of a well-rounded whole, a skewed culture results.

In the case of the Aurignacian and Magdalenian cultures, this skew was in the direction of the elaboration of thaumaturgy (magic) and art. Beyond the demands of minimum necessity Aurignacian and Magdalenian men had little interest in practical toolmaking. They preferred bending the world of fantasy to their practical needs. There is no doubt but that they were skillful and successful hunters, who relied on effigies and abracadabra to produce results and give them confidence to attack wild beasts. Smoothly finished weapons were not so important.

What has just been said of the Aurignacian and Magdalenian cultures does not hold for the intrusive Solutrean. After some 10,000 years of Aurignacian supremacy the carriers of an alien culture pressed into western Europe from the regions of the Danube. They were the Solutreans, who succeeded for a time in displacing some of the Aurignacian Cro-Magnons. But the latter were too numerous and too strong for the Solutreans; in time they sponged up the Solutreans and their culture. Nevertheless, Solutrean culture, although it disappeared, did not fail to leave its mark. Its crossing with the Aurignacian produced a hybrid vigor that gave great impetus to Aurignacian trends. An outburst of Stone Age cultural advance followed in the Magdalenian to produce the greatest marvels of cave art. The Solutrean contact also stimulated the industrial interests of the Aurignacian. In the Magdalenian fine barbed harpoons of reindeer horn, tastefully decorated, were the outcome of an evolution from the bone javelin point of the Solutreans.

It may be said of Solutrean man that he was a true artist in flint working. At the height of his technique the Solutrean workman gave form, rhythm, and symmetry to his products beyond the needs of industrial utilitarianism. The best of his willow-leaf and laurel-leaf points (Fig. 18) are the results of precocious effort.[3]

[3] *Cf.* N. C. Nelson, "Prehistoric Archaeology" in *General Anthropology*, Chap. 5. This is a systematic treatment of the subject, which gives excellent brief interpretations of prehistoric archaeology in Asia, Africa, and Oceania; it also discusses the world-wide diffusion of basic material culture.

Stone Age Art. It is in the field of art that the accomplishments of the men of the Upper Paleolithic have led to the sobriquet, "Paleolithic Greeks." The aesthetic sensitiveness and technical proficiency of these ancient cave dwellers is truly awe-inspiring. They surpassed many later primitives in ability, while some of their sculpture compares favorably

Fig. 18. Solutrean laurel-leaf point.

with good modern works. They were versatile, too. Painting, engraving, sculpture, and modeling were familiar media of expression. Furthermore, they were skilled in all fields. Their art began in experimental crudeness and developed steadily to the sure technique of masters. It offers a golden field for the study of developmental processes in art because the sequences in improvement are clearly discernible in archaeological series.

Although they represent different techniques, engraving and painting were closely integrated by the Aurignacian-Magdalenian artists. Their development went hand in hand to produce closely similar forms of expression. It appears that when an engraving was made first, its incised lines were always painted in afterward. And sometimes a wall surface was given a paint wash, after which the engraving was incised. The effect was to set out the engraving in fresh contrast to the painted background.

Early Aurignacian engravings and paintings were no more than crude stiff outlines. Upper Aurignacian pictures were more accurate representations, and in the Lower and Middle Magdalenian real skill in composition, contour, and the use of polychrome was reached. Some comparative examples from the four phases of Aurignacian-Magdalenian art are given in Fig. 19.

Sculpture does not show such a progressive trend, since most of the known examples reveal reasonably good technique, whatever the phase. Mural sculpture was wall engraving developed to produce medallion types of low and high relief. The best work was done, however, in sculpturing in the round on bone, antler, and ivory, in shaping such articles as dagger grips and dart throwers in animal and bird forms. Exotic figurines of little female idols were fashioned in stone and ivory (Fig. 20). The most famous example of plastic modeling is a family group of a bison bull, cow, and calf from the cavern of Tuc d'Audubert.

Much light is shed on the beliefs and mentality of Upper Paleolithic man by the art that he produced. If ever an art reflected the spirit of its culture, it was this. There has been much argumentative exchange of

FIG. 19. Four phases of Upper Paleolithic art; *a*, phase I, early Aurignacian; *b*, phase II, late Aurignacian; *c*, phase III, early Magdalenian; *d*, phase IV, middle Magdalenian.

opinion between utilitarian-minded anthropologists and aesthetically minded "art-for-art's-sakers." Anthropologists have insisted on the magico-religious utilitarianism of the art. Aestheticians have insisted that it manifests the artistic genius of its makers. Both are right, but the anthropologists more so.

Upper Paleolithic art had the gross purpose of filling men's stomachs and maintaining the population by serving as a magical aid in hunting and procreation. But beyond these ends to which his art was but a means, the Upper Paleolithic artist used his art as an end in itself. He produced not merely images but beautiful images. He strove not only to produce magically efficacious representations of the goals of his desires; he also developed artistic skill for the intrinsic pleasure it gave him.

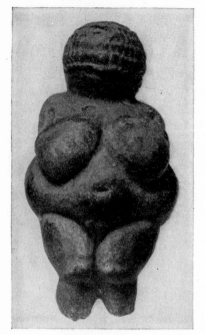

FIG. 20. The Venus of Willendorf. A prehistoric fertility statuette from the Aurignacian epoch. (*American Museum of Natural History*.)

It is likely, however, that magical purposes never left his mind. Especially is this evident in the case of his mural art, which is rarely found where it may easily be viewed. The Upper Paleolithic artist did not adorn the walls of his homesite in the entrance to a cavern. No, his art works are found deep in the earth's bowels, in the dark mysterious caverns where the artist worked by the fitful smoky flare of a stone lamp. There he drew his animals: the woolly mammoth, bison, reindeer, wild cow, bear, woolly rhinoceros, horse, and ibex—most of them animals long since extinct in Europe. And again and again he painted red gashes on their bodies, gashes dripping with blood. He often showed projectile points piercing their flesh. Sometimes he drew hunting clubs beside the beasts. He did not draw actual hunting scenes, but contemporary artists who lived in East Spain to the south of the Pyrenees did. His paintings were effigies designed to play their part in imitative magic (see Chap. 28), since he thought, as primitive man has ever since, that harm done an image is harm done the real thing.

Not all magic is aimed to do harm; some of it may be wholly beneficent. This is particularly true of fertility magic, magic that constitutes the main content of fertility cults. Aurignacian men were especially fond of statuettes of pregnant women, of whom the Venus of Willendorf (Fig. 20) is the most famous. The parts of her torso that swell with pregnancy are given lavish exaggeration. The face, arms, legs, and feet are ignored. The artist has composed her with selective interest. The detail of her coiffure shows that hairdo had its social (probably cult) significance 30,000 years ago and that the beautician existed as an artisan long before our era.[4]

Females were the more frequent objects of artistic representation, but males as masked dancers were sometimes portrayed.

Upper Paleolithic art may be summed up as vividly realistic, an art of flesh and blood, a functional art that aided in survival, eagerly used by a hunting people living in a glacial age.[5]

The Transitional Period. The flourishing Upper Paleolithic cultures reached their zenith in the Middle Magdalenian. Then the fourth glaciation rapidly receded under the warming seasons of a changing climate. The flower of the Magdalenian culture had bloomed and was quickly going to seed. The animals Magdalenian man had known retreated northward year by year as new animals came from the south to replace them. With the new fauna came new races of men from the south and east to overwhelm and absorb the Cro-Magnons. It was a period of cultural depression, known as the *Mesolithic* (Gr. *mesos* middle + *lithos* stone) *Age* because it stood midway between the Old Stone Age and the New.

The Mesolithic is an age much disparaged in most anthropological writings because the fine art had disappeared, the elegant harpoons of the Magdalenian had become poor staghorn imitations, and flints were mostly pygmy microliths. If one looks back only to the glories of the Upper Paleolithic, then the Mesolithic culture seems poor indeed. But if one looks forward from the Mesolithic to the Neolithic, then it will be realized that the Mesolithic was a period of transition and readjustment when profound changes were taking shape.

Mesolithic man painted, but he did not paint pictures. He was content to daub simple marks on pebbles. A degenerate art, some say. However, the modern abstractionist in art can without difficulty appreciate what the Mesolithic dauber was about. Mesolithic art was purely intellectual and symbolic. By a gradual process of conventionalization, pictures had become so simplified that a few strokes set a hieroglyph, which conveyed the meaning of a picture without actually being a picture. Time was saved, if one understood the conventional meaning of the hieroglyph, because it served the intellectual purposes of magic and communication as well as the finest polychrome. Aesthetics languished, it is true, but the

---

[4] See Chap. 11 for a discussion of hair treatment as adornment and status symbolism.

[5] G. G. MacCurdy, *Human Origins*, Vol. 1, Chap. 8, presents the best and most richly illustrated discussion of Paleolithic art available in English.

intellect was fertilized, and the germ of one of the greatest of all inventions, writing, was planted.

The transitional period to the New Stone Age was of short duration in Europe (15,000–8,000 B.C.). Man, it has been seen, had gone through a million years of painful learning. He had learned to master flint working and had created magic and religion to aid him in mastery over the wild beasts. Now he was embarking on the mastery of the mind. Standing on the threshold of manifold discovery, he was about to raise the curtain on the dawn of civilization.

CHAPTER 5

THE DAWN OF CIVILIZATION

The Neolithic, or New Stone Age, lasted less than one-hundredth as long as the Old Stone Age, but it witnessed many times the accomplishments of all the million years of the Paleolithic. It was an age that brought forth one astounding invention after another to revolutionize the ways of man.

Foremost of all accomplishments was the domestication of plants and animals. Plants tamed and nursed in domestic gardens yielded their harvest for the food pots and storage bins of Neolithic man: barley, wheat, millet, peas, and lentils. All can be bought from the shelves of our stores today. Flax was raised to provide fibers for the looms of the times. The dog, horse, pig, goat, sheep, and cow were tamed and bound to the domestic economy of man. Thus the hunter's camp and cave gave way to the farmer's homestead and garden. The foundation for future urban civilization was laid.

In the Neolithic Age it was discovered how to mold clay into vessels; how to fire them to make them lasting; how to decorate them to make them pleasing.

In the Neolithic Age it was discovered how to weave the fibers of plants into cloth as a substitute for the furs of animals to provide warm garments for the body of man.

It was discovered how to combine stout logs, wattles, and thatch with clay and mud to make weather-tight shelters. Houses were invented.

It was discovered how to adapt the elasticity of wood to the needs of the hunt and war. The bow was invented.

It was discovered how to hollow out logs to provide a vessel of some stability and lightness for water transport. The canoe was invented.

It was discovered that wet sandstone can wear down harder stones when used as an abrasive; that chipped flint tools can be polished down to an attractive smooth luster; that igneous rocks, which defy chipping, can be worn into a desired shape by abrasion. The era of polished stone was inaugurated. This is the prehistorian's symbol of the New Stone Age: the polished stone tool. Yet striking as the innovation of polished stone may be, it is the least important of the accomplishments of the Neolithic Age that have been listed above.

Polished stone would in due course of time be superseded by bronze, and later by iron, but other inventions of the times were destined to more lasting significance. The Neolithic domesticated plants and animals, weaving, pottery, water transport, and housing have all remained indispensable features of civilization. Even the bow played an important role in war and hunting until the recent invention of gunpowder provided a better means of projectile propulsion.

There was yet another invention of the Neolithic that has not yet been mentioned—writing. All peoples have a language, but only civilized man has written language. The power of the written word was unknown before Neolithic times, except as nascent hieroglyphs were formulated in the Mesolithic—the painted pebbles of Azil and the symbols on the cave walls of eastern Spain (see pages 184–185).

Although the descriptions of Neolithic culture in this book shall be confined to the New Stone Age in Europe, it is improbable that any of the basic inventions of the Neolithic actually originated in Europe. The cradle of the New Stone Age was in the East—probably in Asia Minor (not enough is known about the prehistory of the Far East to be able to ascertain its original contributions to the Neolithic). All Neolithic innovations appeared in the east before they made their way into European life. Thus there is a definite lag between the Neolithic dates for Asia Minor and Europe. In Asia Minor, for example, the earliest Neolithic datings are about 18,000 B.C., while in central Europe the equivalent culture dates from not before 10,000 B.C. at the earliest. But the development of civilization meant more rapid spread of communication and diffusion of culture, so that toward the end of the New Stone Age the gap had closed, and Europe was only 2,000 years behind the Near East. These are the circumstances that led the eminent English authority V. Gordon Childe to comment, "It must then be admitted that true civilizations had grown up and were well established in the Ancient East while Europe was still sunk in epipaleolithic barbarism." [1]

Thus, when we discuss certain features of the Neolithic Age as it occurred in Europe, we are not actually treating the origin of the New Stone Age. The value of confining this treatment to the Neolithic of Europe is to maintain the continuity of development from the Old Stone Age as we have seen it in Europe and to avoid unnecessary complexities. The elaboration of culture had by Neolithic times resulted in so much regional differentiation and parochialism that it has become impossible to present even the European Neolithic in general terms. The most usable

[1] V. G. Childe, *The Dawn of European Civilization*, p. 23.

example is perhaps found in the Scandinavian Neolithic culture, briefly described below.

The Scandinavian Neolithic. About 10,000 years ago the retreat of the northern ice sheet freed the west Baltic area from its cold grip and left moist rich lowlands open for occupation. Scattered throughout the glacial till of this country were many large nodules of high-grade flint brought by the moving ice from the high countries to the north and abandoned by the ice in its retreat. Migrations of men followed hard on the heels of the retreating glaciers, and many habitations were founded amid the peat bogs along the low shores of the North Sea and the fresh-water lake that has since become the salt-water Baltic Sea.

In the transition from the Old Stone Age to the New, the local populations of this area lived mostly as fishermen and shellfish eaters. Great quantities of oyster and clam shells were accumulated under and around their pine-raft dwellings anchored along the shallow shores of the sea and lakes. The heaps of shell are tokens of the many meals of mollusks that nourished these prehistoric men. Numerous broken utensils went the way of the shells, and sometimes good artifacts inadvertently slipped from careless hands to pile up with the refuse that formed the great shell heaps, or kitchen middens, of the era. The kitchen midden phase, known also as the *Ertebolle*, marked the opening of the Neolithic in the north. Its inventory included chipped-stone implements, a crude pottery of coarse paste, and numerous articles of bone and staghorn. There was probably little agriculture at this early stage of the New Stone Age.

The full Neolithic that followed in Scandinavia may be divided into two phases: (1) the epoch of the axes, and (2) the epoch of the stone graves.

In the epoch of the axes the Scandinavian flint work attained unparalleled excellence. The ripple-chipped daggers and spearheads of this culture represent perfection in the flint-chipping arts. Axes were also usually of flint. They were first roughed into shape by the chipping method and then polished down completely, or partially, to a lustrous finish. Toward the middle of the epoch of the axes the discovery was made that it is possible to drill through solid igneous rock by pouring wet sand under a rotating drill of reed, bone, or wood. The application of this discovery made possible the hafting of axes through a center hole. The ax thus produced is superior to the flint ax, and the latter went out of style. Improved pottery was developed during the epoch of the axes, and the introduction of agriculture was pushed ahead.

Refinements of these inventions continued during the epoch of the graves. In addition, wooden plows were introduced, and boats were developed out of canoes. But most impressive of all were the great stone monuments of the *Megalithic* (Gr. *megas* great + *lithos* stone) cultures of Scandinavia and the western continental rim.

Cro-Magnon man had been caught up in imaginative sympathetic magic. Neolithic man in his turn became engrossed in the imaginative worship of the sun and the dead. He raised vast monumental symbols of solid rock to make his intangible beliefs objectively perceptive. With what must have been incredible toil, he and his fellows moved and raised huge stones by sheer primitive force combined with elementary engineering. Some of these monuments were single standing stones; others of them were chambered sepulchers; and yet others were raised in combinations to constitute ceremonial plots. The most ancient form of the Neolithic burial chamber of Europe is the *dolmen* (Breton, *dol* table + *men* rock), so called because it was constructed of a flat rock laid horizontally like a table top over several supporting boulders set on edge. Thus a rough closed chamber was formed in which interments were made. Usually, but not always, the dolmen was covered with an earth mound, called a *tumulus;* the dolmen and tumulus together constitute a *barrow*. In the later phases of the Neolithic, simple dolmens were elaborated into multi-chambered dolmens consisting of several connecting dolmens under a single tumulus. Some types of dolmens had a long narrow passage leading into the main burial chamber, as the elongated entrance of an Eskimo iglu leads to the domed ice hut. This kind of dolmen is known as a *passage grave*. A still later development was to construct only the passage without the main dolmen. Such a structure is a *hallcist*. Ultimately, in the Late Neolithic, very small hallcists, only large enough to encase a single individual, became the favored burial receptacle. So the dolmen evolved to the *cist*.

Some enthusiastic diffusionists, notably the English anthropologists G. Elliot Smith and W. J. Perry, look upon the Neolithic burial mounds as evidence of Egyptian explorer-adventurers in the North. Certainly, the burial chamber has a wide distribution along the Atlantic and North Sea coasts and in the vicinity of the Black Sea, too, but the lack of conformity in specific detail to the Egyptian *mastaba*, from which the diffusionists suppose the Neolithic forms to be derived, argues against the validity of the theory.

A single, standing stone is a *monolith*, or if we prefer Breton usage for the many monoliths that dot their homeland, we may call it a *menhir* (Breton, *men* stone + *hir* long). Neolithic man raised thousands of menhirs, probably to serve as monuments, even as we raise large stone blocks as enduring memorials to great events and persons. But because they are more than mere memorials, menhirs have a fetish quality among many primitive peoples. Jacob, for example, when he saw the ladder to Heaven and heard the voice of God, commemorated the miracle with a sizable rock, declaring, "And this stone, which I have set for a pillar, shall be God's house. . . ." [2] In this way the stone became a memorial and the abode of a spirit.

A single monolith can kindle a sympathetic imagination. A cromlech or an alignment, however, presents a mysterious majesty that excites almost unlimited speculation and wonder. Of the great cromlech of Stonehenge, in England, more than a thousand articles and books have been published, some born of mere fancy and others of scientific labor.

A *cromlech* (Welch, *crom* concave + *llech* stone) consists of menhirs arranged in a circle to form a ceremonial ring—an outdoor temple. At Stonehenge the great stones were hewn and shaped, some of them fitted so as to form a semicircle of doorframes within the western circumference of the great circle. Outside the circle, on the mid-line of an avenue that stretches away from the cromlech to the east, stand two large stones in alignment with the central portal of the circle. By means of astronomical calculation it has been determined that at the instant of the rising sun on the day of the summer solstice on or about 1680 B.C., these stones would have cast their long shadow through the portal to fall upon the altar stone within the ring. Thus is Stonehenge dated.

Because other cromlechs and alignments also have a solstitial orientation, there can be no question but that great annual rites were held at these prehistoric sites to do worship to the sun at the moment of the year when the sun's power was greatest.

Several thousand years later the American Indians of the Plains were found in much the same activity in a very similar setting. In the sun dance of the Indians, however, the pillars of the outdoor temple are of wood rather than stone, and a new temple is erected for each annual ceremony. Even as the sun dance lodge of the Indians is a sort of circular cromlech, so the entire camp of the assembled tribe forms a great camp circle around the lodge. A wide-open mouth is always left on the east side of the circle, so that the rising sun may shed its first golden rays directly into the dance lodge to fall upon the expectant worshippers. Though much of the old religion of our Plains Indians is gone, most of

[2] Genesis 28:22. Other Biblical references to the raising of menhirs occur in Genesis 35:20; Joshua 4:1–9; I Samuel 7:12.

the tribes still practice the sun dance, because they still sincerely revere the Sun Father.[3]

Similar in function to the cromlechs, but different in form, are the alignments. An *alignment* is a form of ceremonial plot in which menhirs are set in a series of rows. At Carnac, in Brittany, stands the most famous of all alignments—three groupings of monoliths that stretch across the level fields for nearly two miles in widely spaced ranks ten to thirteen rows deep. No fewer than 2,210 monoliths stand to this day in the grand arrangement where they were set by mystic worshippers in Late Neolithic times.

The great stone monuments of the Megalithic cultures of the Neolithic are solid evidence that in those days religion had come to play a role of great importance in the affairs of men. It had passed the phase of individual power and magic. Religious order must surely have been mainly in the hands of permanent priests, who had the power and authority needed to organize extensive concerted effort on the part of the tribesmen. In this there was also something of the germ of government.

The Bronze Age. Bronze is an alloy of copper and tin. Its discovery or invention marked the third great revolutionary innovation in the technological culture of prehistory. The introduction of bronze ushered in the ages of metallurgy, and all that they would bring in their train.

Before the use of bronze had made its way into the cultures of Europe, there was a brief and fleeting era of copper, which was used raw without smelting. It was merely beaten into shape, as the Indians of the Great Lakes region of North America were working copper in the seventeenth century. Most of the raw copper used in antiquity came from the isle of Cyprus, which has given the name *cyprolithic* to the Copper Age. Some authorities, however, prefer the term *chalcolithic* (Gr. *chalkos* copper + *lithos* stone) as being more directly descriptive.

The copper phase was by no means universal in prehistory; its distribution is largely determined by the accidental fact of the natural distribution of raw copper nuggets. In Old World prehistory, once the use of copper was established, the discovery of bronze followed in rapid order. The Copper Age lasted no more than a few centuries.

It is probable that bronze was discovered by accident rather than invented by design. The likely situation would be one in which rocks with a high copper content, also containing some tin, were used in the build-

[3] See pp. 420–421 for a consideration of sun cults in primitive religion. Volume 16 (1921) of the *Anthropological Papers of the American Museum of Natural History* is devoted to a number of papers describing and analyzing the sun dances of most of the Plains Indian tribes.

ing of primitive hearths. The accidental result might have been that particularly hot fires reduced the copper and tin to a molten state. It then ran down to the ground and flowed in little rivulets into depressions that formed natural molds. To the wonderment of men, it hardened upon cooling into a tough, durable, rustless, attractive metal. Then some ingenious mind hit upon the idea of pressing a stone ax head into the ground to form the depression into which the molten alloy would flow. Result: a perfect reproduction of the stone celt in bronze!

The first step in the transition from the New Stone Age to the Age

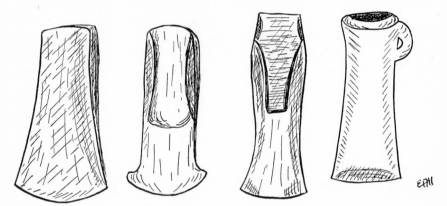

Fig. 21. Evolution of the Bronze Age celt.

of Bronze literally exemplifies the principle that new inventions are molded in the case of old forms. Usually it is enough at first for men to be able to seize upon the new medium. Only later as they become familiar with it do they begin to play with it sufficiently to break free of the old molds to create new forms. Thus the bronze celt gradually began to outgrow its old form; wings and flanges were added to give stability to the hafted ax head. In the final stage, the wings had grown so large that at last they met to form a complete socket. This then gave birth to the idea of molding the ax in the form of a cup to receive the L-shaped handle. The transformation of the celt was complete in the last phase of the Bronze Age (Fig. 21).

Bronze gave rise to the development of many other types of weapons. Long swords grew out of the chipped-stone dagger. In the Early Bronze Age these swords were of the poniard type—suitable for punching an adversary full of holes. In the Late Bronze Age broad-bladed swords with double edges for two-way hacking were perfected—suitable for butchering an opponent. A modified bronze dagger fastened at right angles to a long shaft produced the halberd popular in the wars of the Middle Ages. Slim handsome battle-axes with tasteful decoration were developed out of the Neolithic polished stone ax with the haft hole. Bronze spear-heads replaced the more fragile ones of flint. Bows also persisted, though apparently without great popularity, since Bronze Age arrowheads are relatively scarce. The men of this period seemed to prefer the rough-and-tumble of hand-to-hand combat.

The great variety of weapons and their numerous occurrence indicate that Bronze Age life was not particularly peaceful. Villages were some-what like fortified camps, and men went forth well armed. But man is a peculiar creature who exerts his ingenuity in the creation of better and more effective ways of killing his fellow men, at the same time racking his brains to find means of nullifying his lethal capacities. For every kill-ing tool he invents, he is soon busy thinking up a defensive specific. Then he feels impelled to produce some new offensive weapon for which there is no defense. This results in progress: e.g., it cannot be denied that the development of the modern airplane has been greatly fostered by its use for war. Thus, just as in the present century the submarine has led to the depth bomb, the tank to the land mine, and the airplane to the antiaircraft gun, so the sword, spear, and halberd of the Bronze Age led to the bronze shield, helmet, and cuirass. But shields and helmets ante-date the Bronze Age, for shields of wood, wicker, and leather are used as defenses against stone axes, wooden clubs, spears, and arrows by primitives who are ignorant of metallurgy. Neolithic man, too, must have protected himself with such devices. It is not to be supposed, how-ever, that the rank and file of men in the Bronze Age carried the hand-some bronze shields that are to be seen in the British Museum, or wore the becoming bronze helmets. The ordinary man had no better defensive equipment than had the fighter of the New Stone Age. Precious bronze armor was for chiefs.

But though war engenders production and stimulates progress, it is not productive. The life-giving heart of Bronze Age civilization was not in warmaking but in the husbandry that made a nursery of the soil and barnyard. Farming was pushed farther than it had been in the New Stone Age. Improvements in crops came about because of selective breeding and better methods of cultivation. Wood plows were extensively used, and bronze sickles are common finds. The men of the times still fished, and they made harpoons and fishhooks of their new metal. Seagoing boats capable of carrying a number of passengers were developed from the dugout canoe.

Life was rich and full. The needs of food and shelter were well met, nor was the vanity of man and woman neglected. Numerous bronze razors prove that the rite of shaving held a fashionable sway. Simple and ornate bronze safety pins (fibulae) were worn as brooches by both sexes. Elegant bracelets and necklaces of bronze and gold were abundant.

Commerce flourished in steady streams of traffic up and down the valleys of the stately rivers of Europe and Russia. Where the overburdened merchant cached his wares along the valleys are now found hundreds of archaeological treasure-troves.

Habitations were gathered in larger settlements. Houses were mostly two-room structures of palisaded logs covered with thatched roofs. In Switzerland pile dwellings, such as had been made in Neolithic times, continued to persist. But in the advanced centers of civilization great palaces of stone and plaster were built.

Megalithic monuments continued to be built in the north and west, as in the New Stone Age, but the practice was gradually falling into disregard as burial in cists became more popular; still later, toward the end of the Age of Bronze, cremation became fashionable.

Pottery became more and more a craft of skill, with localities vying with one another until such a bewildering variety of local styles was developed that the study of Bronge Age pottery has become a field of modern scholarship in itself.

Although decorative art flourished on jewelry and pottery, there was little pure art in the Bronze Age. Nevertheless, crude but expressive pictographs were carved into the rocks of the North to leave a documentary record of many phases of the life of the times (Fig. 22). In decorative art, stylized geometric figures and spirals played the dominating role.

The Bronze Age, which began in Europe about 2500 B.C., had run its course at the opening of the first millennium before Christ. During its span it gave rise to such rich and vigorous protoclassical civilizations as Minos in Crete, Mycene in Greece, and the early dynasties of Egypt and Babylonia. It was the heroic age of Homer.

Then came a new metallurgic discovery—iron. In the year 1400 B.C. iron was well known in Egypt. It had established itself 500 years later (900 B.C.) as a widely used metal in Europe. The Iron Age was at hand.

The Iron Age. The cultures of the Iron Age are for the most part no longer a subject of prehistory. Any student of classical civilization is fully familiar with the life and cultures of ancient Greece, Rome, and the Near East. Writing, which had had its tentative beginning in the Mesolithic era, had reached a high stage of development by the time of the Iron Age, except for the barbarians of the hinterlands. In the many civilized cultures of the Iron Age written records were inscribed not only on tablets of rock and clay or on walls and monuments but were carried on parchment scrolls and papyri, too. They speak to the modern scholar in the very words of the people who wrote them. They are in-

Fig. 22. Bronze Age pictographs from Sweden. Plowman, charioteer, and proto-Viking crew.

finitely better raw materials for culture history than the meager archaeological treasures of the anthropologist.

The Bronze Age forms the bridge by which we leave prehistory and enter the historic era of man's existence. It is the solid link by which our present is tied to our once-forgotten past. There is a perfect continuity from the Old Stone Age to the present historic era through the New Stone Age and the Ages of Bronze and Iron.

The student who is familiar with the Gauls, the Belgians, the Helvetians, and the Britons of Caesar's time knows the tribes of the Late Iron Age in central and western Europe. But they represented only the most backward and conservative peoples of the Iron Age. One would refer with greater justice to the accomplishments of this era by under-taking a study of the great civilizations of Greece, Egypt, Rome, and Mesopotamia. In these centers the arts flourished; mathematics, astron-omy, and philosophy flowered; and empires were in existence. However, this is beyond the immediate sphere of the anthropologist. The scholar in ancient history and classical civilization is more competent to deal with the details of such cultures than is the anthropologist, unless the classicist has confined his attention solely to literature without realization of the broader features of his great subject.

Part Three: Race and Culture

CHAPTER 6

RACES OF MANKIND

The subject of race is implicitly difficult to analyze in scientific terms. The perplexity of the problem is still further complicated by the emotional atmosphere that today surrounds the subject. Such hideous mischief has been wrought in the name of prostituted concepts of race by political schemers and bigots that among some anthropologists there has been (and is) a strong attempt to banish the evil by conjuring away the concept of race by word magic.

However, races have been with us for a long time and will continue to be around for some time to come. Therefore, it behooves the anthropologist, the student of man, scientifically to consider the races of mankind.

Race Defined. To the physical anthropologist *a race is a biologically inbred group possessing a distinctive combination of physical traits that tend to breed true from generation to generation.* Three factors are embraced within this definition: inbreeding, distinctive combination of physical traits, and breeding true. Each of these factors may be considered in turn.

Inbreeding. Inbreeding is the result of isolation and limited mobility. Isolation among men is the consequence of geographic circumstance *and* social inhibitions.

Space and physiographic features are the primary geographic stimulators of inbreeding. North American Indians did not mate with Australians, because 12,000 miles of ocean separated them. The Polar Eskimos in northwest Greenland were so isolated that until their illusion was shattered by the arrival of the first Europeans, they thought they were the sole inhabitants of the earth. When we consider that the Polar Eskimos numbered no more than a few hundred individuals, we can realize how close their inbreeding had to be. In fact, in almost any of the smaller primitive tribes (and this includes the majority of all tribal groups) every person is apt to be a genetic relative of every other.

Social isolation, in contrast to geographic isolation, is man-made. Whether we like to admit it or not, human beings in general prefer to associate with their own kind. They incline to be suspicious of differences and to give warm approval to likenesses of themselves. The *consciousness of kind*, which the sociologist Giddings saw as the basis of social groupings, has its counterpart in a *consciousness of difference*. *Endogamy*, or marriage within the group, is a consequence of these two sets of attitudes The function of endogamy is to regulate marriage in a way that preserves the cultural identity of the group. Its biological effect is to produce intensification of distinctive physical traits through inbreeding. Social distance has the same physical consequences as geographical distance.

The effect of inbreeding is to intensify or narrow the distribution of genetic traits within a population. The physical characteristics of the individuals within the population then reveal a greater degree of standardization than is the case where there is little or no inbreeding. Any unique qualities of genetic composition become more marked, and racial differentiation is thereby enhanced.

This fact has been demonstrated over and over again in animal husbandry.

Among biologists a fundamental principle is that "general anatomical resemblances imply relationship and that detailed similarities of face and form mean that the individuals possessing them have in common all or nearly all of their ancestors." [1] It is assumed in physical anthropology, therefore, that groups of persons who bear distinctive anatomical resemblances are more closely related to each other (inbred) than to others.

If one attempted to prove this with absolute conclusiveness, it would be necessary to work out complete genealogical records for a large sample in every racial population. This would be a hair-shirt task, which no anthropologist has tried for a large group. The simple reason is that it is impossible to accomplish.

Distinctive Physical Traits. The question as to what constitutes a realistic combination of distinctive physical traits is the one that poses the greatest difficulties. What traits legitimately go into the combination and what must be left out?

There is obviously considerable overlapping of single traits among the different races. Only the Negro has a distinctive lip, for instance. This means that a generalized lip form occurs in all other races. Black hair dis-

---

[1] E. A. Hooton, *Up from the Ape*, p. 1.

tinguishes the Negro from the blond Nordic but not at all from the multitudinous Mongolians. Thus the fact that any one of the physical traits found to be characteristic of a race may be found in other races has in itself neither positive nor negative significance. Any suggestion that the presence of a single trait in two different races indicates genetic affinity between the races would be absurd. The fact that certain Melanesians possess "Semitic" noses cannot be used as evidence of Semitic ancestry for those Oceanic Negroes. On the other hand, neither can it be said that the fact of this nose is not an important element in the cluster of distinctive traits that characterizes each of these groups.

The whole concatenation of traits marks the race. Yet an individual person rarely possesses all the traits that characterize his race. If, for purposes of illustration, we say a particular race has twenty-five traits in a distinctive combination, it does not mean that every person who properly is a member of that race possesses all twenty-five traits.

The Swedes, for example, are a notably homogeneous population with unusually distinctive physical traits: flaxen hair, blue eyes, light skin, long heads, etc. Retzius and Furst, in 1898, in measurements of 45,000 Swedish army recruits, found that only 11 per cent possessed *all* the traits that go to make up the distinctive Nordic combination; 29 per cent had all traits except that they were roundheaded.

Should we not conclude from this fact that the racial combination is an imaginative idealization of types that rarely occur in fact? Those who would wish away races answer "Yes."

It is a fact that race-conscious persons hold an image of racial types in their heads. The type consists of all the distinctive traits of a race in combination. When these persons associate an individual with a given race, because that individual has one or more of the type traits, they either overlook the presence of nontypical traits or they impute the type traits to the person being considered. Correction of such false perception is a matter of social psychology.

The scientifically oriented observer will make no such error, because he knows that a race is statistically determined on the basis of biologically derived data.

Statistically, any student of elementary biology knows that all biological traits are variable. He also knows that each trait is limited in its range of variability, that the variables tend to cluster around a norm or mean, and that the occurrence of extreme forms of the variable become less frequent the farther they vary from the norm. Statistically, when plotted for frequency distributions, variables usually form a hump-backed curve with the same number of units falling on each side of the mean. This is the old familiar frequency curve. In a normal distribution curve the mean (average) coincides with the mode (variable of greatest frequency) and the median (mid-point between the two extremes of the range). In a skewed or lopsided curve these three types of norms will not coincide (Fig. 23). In such a case physical anthropologists usually use the mean as expressive of the physical trait characteristic of the group. Thus, according to Hooton, the mean stature for Ainus is 157.9 cm. (5 feet 3 inches), for Negritos 150 cm. (4 feet 9 inches), for Nilotic Negroes 175 to 180 cm. (5 feet 10 inches to 6 feet), and for Nordics 172

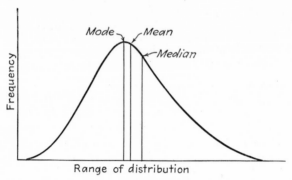

Fig. 23. Three kinds of norms in a skewed frequency distribution curve.

cm. (5 feet 8.8 inches).[2] We can properly say that the Ainu and Negrito races are short and the Nilotic Negroes and Nordics are tall.

In detailed specialized studies, physical anthropologists usually give the total range of distribution with coefficients of deviation.

Figure 24 illustrates comparative distributions with respect to the relative statures of Navajo Indian and white American girls of college age (16 to 24 years, average age 20 years). These comparative data show some overlapping in the ranges of distribution for the two groups. Some Navajo girls are taller than some white girls. However, although 5 per cent of the Navajo girls are less than 4 feet 9 inches (1,500 mm.) in stature, not a single white girl is shorter than this. On the other hand, although 28 per cent of the white girls are more than 5 feet 4 inches (1,640 mm.) tall, not a single Navajo girl exceeds this height.

The average (mean) stature of the Navajo girls is an even 5 feet (1,556 mm.; Probable Error [P.E.] ± 2.81; Standard Deviation [S.D.] 41.70 ± 1.99). The average (mean) stature of the white girls is 5 feet 3 inches (1,628.05 mm.; P.E. ± 3.75; S.D. 55.59 ± 2.65).

[2] *Ibid.,* pp. 503*ff.*

The shortest Navajo girl is 4 feet 7 inches (1,420 mm.) tall and the tallest Navajo girl stands 5 feet 4 inches (1,640 mm.). Among the white girls the shortest of the group is 4 feet 11 inches (1,520 mm.) and the tallest is 5 feet 8 inches (1,760 mm.). The range of variability between the shortest and the tallest Navajo girl is 8.6 inches; between the shortest and the tallest white girl, 9.4 inches.[3]

It will be seen that the difference between the average heights of the two groups is approximately 3 inches. Thus the differences between the

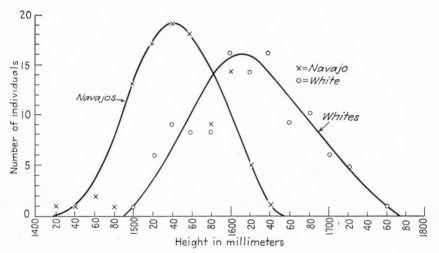

FIG. 24. Frequency distribution of stature among 100 Navajo and 100 white American girls of college age.

tallest and the shortest within each of the groups is greater than the difference between the means of the two groups.

A recent tendency among some anthropologists has been to emphasize that in such single traits the groups are more akin to each other than are the extreme members within one of the groups. This is perfectly true, and it should serve to warn us against overemphasis of racial differences, but it does not wholly negate the significance of the differences that are to be discerned in the averages.

Breeding True. There is no such thing as a pure race on the face of the globe today. Race mixture has obviated that possibility. Whether there were pure races in the prehistoric past, we do not know. That there never will be a pure race in the future is a certainty.

[3] M. G. Steggerda, "Physical Measurements on Negro, Navajo and White Girls of College Age" (*American Journal of Physical Anthropology*, Vol. 26, 1940), p. 420.

There is much talk about pure races, but just what a pure race is supposed to be is hardly ever made clear. Theoretically, it would consist of a limited population that has been inbred for an indefinite number of generations without any outside admixture, so that the mean and range of variation for each family of brothers and sisters would be the same throughout the population. Every family would have the same genetic background. Except for very small, long-isolated populations, this condition is never even approximated. There are no pure races.

Nevertheless, there still remain races. In a racial group children tend to have the same physical characteristics as their parents, in spite of the fact that some individuals may depart so far from the norm in a number of traits as to appear to belong to another race altogether. Some dark Swedes may look more like Mediterranean Spaniards than like Scandinavian Nordics. Nevertheless, in a mating of dark Nordics the majority of their children revert toward the blond Nordic norm.

Most dark Nordics are biologically phenotypes. It so happens that dark pigmentation of eyes and hair are incomplete Mendelian dominants. Therefore, it is necessary for a Nordic to receive only one dark-eyed determinant gene in his double combination of genes to produce a dark-eyed phenotype. A dark-eyed Scandinavian mating with a blue-eyed Scandinavian will still produce some dark-eyed offspring, and dark or mixed (hazel)-eyed descendants will be perpetuated in the Scandinavian population. Nevertheless, the whole population in each succeeding generation will tend to have the same distribution of traits and means for these traits as the preceding parental generation. But note that we say *will tend to have*. Once a dominant trait not characteristic of the group as a whole is introduced into the population, the dominant phenotype will tend to spread, even though no new additions are made from the outside.

If absolute breeding true were the case, there never could be any modification of racial traits—and it must be kept in mind that even supposedly nonadaptive physical traits do change through the years. The germ plasm is not immutable, nor are races irrevocably fixed for all time.

The Origin of Races. The problems involved in the genetics of racial origins are so vast and so difficult that we have as yet nothing but the most meager knowledge as a start on their solution. The handful of geneticists in the world has not managed to progress very far beyond fruit flies and peas. And the equally small handful of physical anthropologists has not gone very far beyond determination of the main characteristics of man's somatology. In this age of advanced learning, if we were as interested in the development of man as we are in his destruction, we would find the problems of human biology no more difficult to solve than those of atomic fission. But who can interest a government in a two-billion-dollar research program in the scientific analysis of man?

For the present, the most we can say is that science does not know how new traits become established in the human genetic stream. This is a bald confession that we know nothing about how any race develops the traits that differentiate it from another.

We feel rather confident that most racial traits are nonadaptive, which is to say that they are not specialized responses to differential features of environment. There is no known functional advantage in round-headedness over longheadedness; neither correlates one way or the other with intelligence or any known environmental factor. Tallness of stature cannot be demonstrated to have any superior survival value in and of itself. The physical environments of the Caucasians and Mongolians have not been appreciably unlike. Both, as a matter of fact, show extreme ranges in climate and altitude, so environment can hardly account for their differences in pigmentation. Perhaps Negroes may have developed heavy pigmentation in response to tropic life, but it is not proved. Such minor racial traits as musculature of the face are unlikely to be adaptive traits. Yet the facial muscles of the Caucasian, Negro, and Mongolian are so different that Washburn says students working on Mongolian cadavers in Asiatic medical schools run into difficulties and confusion because the English-language textbooks they use are written in terms of Caucasian musculature. The differences are great enough to cause trouble.[4]

Yet it is unlikely that these racial differences represent special adaptations to environmental conditions.

Modern Races. Before the modern age of exploration and mass migration the great races of the world were highly localized. The Negroes were centered in Africa and the islands of the Southwest Pacific. The Mongoloids held sway in Asia and North and South America. The Caucasians were limited to Europe, western Asia, Asia Minor, and North Africa.

Since 1500 A.D. the Caucasians have swarmed from their European hive to establish themselves over the face of the globe. In North America, New Zealand, and Australia they have almost wholly displaced the aboriginal populations.

[4] S. L. Washburn, "Thinking about Race" (*Science Education.* Vol. 28, 1944), p. 68.

Ever since Neolithic times mankind, like Gaul, has been divisible in three parts: Mongoloid, Negroid, and Caucasoid. These are the three primary racial categories. Each in turn may properly be subdivided into secondary races, as follows:

Caucasoid	Mongoloid	Negroid
Nordic	Asiatic	African
Mediterranean	Oceanic	Oceanic
Alpine	Amerind	Negrito

Perhaps we should be content with these main subvarieties and not venture into the maze of further subdivision of the three great races. Most anthropologists agree on the units just listed, but they begin to fall out with one another when it comes to determination of more specialized categories. This is because the smaller divisions, although localized, have often been subject to crossings between the subvarieties, so that it is difficult to decide whether they possess any distinctive group of characteristics or not. Examples of these more doubtful subraces among the Caucasians would be the Dinaric, which is probably due to a Nordic-Armenoid cross, and the Baltic, probably due to Alpine-Nordic-Mongoloid crossing.

In addition to the three primary races, there are several important intermediary races that cannot be put under any of the main racial categories. These are the Australian, Ainu, Polynesian, and Bushmen races.

The relations of all these races to each other is diagrammatically shown in Fig. 25. The relative distance from the nearest point on the periphery of one circle to that of another indicates the approximate relation of those two races. The small circles falling outside the three larger ones are intermediary races, and the arrows indicate the stocks with which they have the greatest affinity.

Caucasians. The white race is not actually white, but relative to other races it is light-colored. Eye color among Caucasians varies from light blue to dark brown. Hair is ash blond to black, of fine to medium texture; it may be straight, wavy, or curly, but rarely kinky and never woolly. The males grow hair on their chests, arms, legs, and faces as well as on the tops of their heads. The nose is narrow and high, rarely broad or flat. Although the forehead is usually sloping, the face is not prognathous. Chins tend to jut and lips are thin. Stature is medium to tall.

Within the Caucasian race the Alpines are concentrated in East Central Europe and Asia Minor. Recent migrations have sporadically distributed them in western Europe, North Africa, and North America in particular. They are brachycephalic (cephalic index 83 to 88) and have broad faces with sharp square jaws. They are brunettes through and through; eyes and hair are brown to black; the skin is olive-hued. The nose is well padded with adipose tissue at the tip, and it tends to be broad.

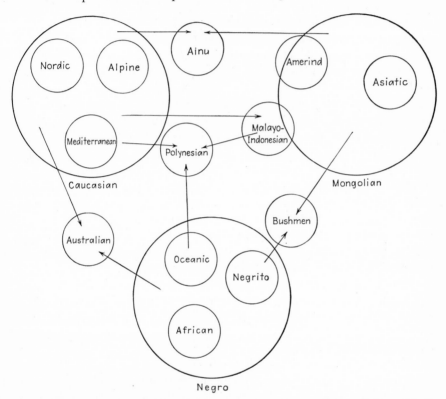

Fig. 25. The races of mankind. Positions of circles indicate relative affinities. (*Modified from Kroeber.*)

The body is usually solid and heavy, rarely exceeding medium stature. Alpine men can grow fine dark beards; and if hair on the chest indicates masculinity, they have more of what it takes than any other Caucasians.

The Mediterranean is also brunette, but, unlike the stocky Alpine, he is on the average slight of stature. His tendency is to be slight in youth and fat in maturity (this applies to the female also). The race is dolichocephalic (C.I. 72 to 76) with narrow high foreheads unmarked by any protrusion of a supraorbital ridge. Hair is black or dark, usually handsomely wavy and rarely straight. Although luxuriant on the head, it is sparse on the face, limbs, and body. Eyes are brown; the skin is light brown or pale olive. Noses are narrow and high-bridged. Spaniards represent the most commonly seen Mediterraneans in America. Some Britishers are Mediterraneans (especially Welchmen), but the bulk of the Mediterraneans are found in the Iberian Peninsula, Egypt, and Italy, and among the Berbers and Arabs of North Africa.

The mean Nordic (statistically speaking) is low in pigmentation; his hair is blond (from towheaded to light brown); eyes are blue, gray, or hazel. Head form is dolichocephalic; the face is also narrow and angular. Jaws and chin are usually prominent; the nose is narrow and usually high. Hair is sparse on the body, thin on the head, and usually falls out in adult males—a price a man must pay for being a Nordic. In form Nordic hair is straight or wavy but seldom curly. The characteristic Nordic is tall and slender. His body is relatively small, but his legs are long. His chest is usually shallow and flat. Nordics do not have to worry too much about their waists, but there is much evidence in this country that they are not satisfied with themselves as paragons of physical perfection. Numerous males hopefully respond to physical-culture advertisements urging them to develop manly chests with bulging pectoral muscles. The females spend millions of dollars and uncalculated time in attempts to make their hair curly, while both sexes go to great lengths through natural and artificial means to attain the skin color of Mediterraneans.

Nordics predominate in the populations of Scandinavia and the Baltic shores of Germany. Many representatives of this race are found in Britain and its dominions, and among the Old American population of the United States. Nordic enclaves are also found scattered throughout Europe and North Africa.

Mongolians. The most populous of the present-day races is the Mongoloid. The most outstanding Mongolian physical trait is the "slant eye," more elegantly known to anthropologists as the *internal epicanthic fold*. The infants also have a unique feature in the Mongolian patch: a purplish, triangular area of skin at the base of the spine. Mongoloids are midway between Caucasians and Negroes in pigmentation. Skin color is brown or yellowish tan. Eyes are brown or dark brown, and the hair is as black as the Negro's. It is very coarse and straight, growing long on the head and shunning the face and body. Most Mongoloid populations are brachycephalic, but there are exceptions among the American Indians and Eskimos. The malars are broad and high while the nose is squat and low-bridged, thus giving most Mongoloids a flat-faced appearance. In stature they are usually short and squat, due mostly to their short bandy legs, since actually their body trunks are fairly long.

The Mongolians proper are found in north, central, and southeastern Asia. The American Indians are predominantly Mongoloid and are usually classified as such by most anthropologists. However, they most certainly picked up some Negroid and Caucasian ancestry long, long ago, before they left the Orient, since non-Mongoloid traits are evident in ancient skeletons and in the features of a number of Central and South American groups, as well as in North America. Therefore, in Fig. 25 the circle representing the Amerinds overlaps the Mongoloid circle.

The same has been done for the Malayo-Indonesian race of Southeast Asia and the Indonesian archipelago. The Mongoloid strain is so strong in the majority of the Malayo-Indonesians that the variety deserves to be linked with the Mongoloid race. Yet it is not submerged in it, since a considerable degree of Mediterranean Caucasian heredity is obvious. Indonesians, the older population found predominantly in the interiors of the islands of the East Indies, are clearly a Mediterranean offshoot derived in all probability from south India. The Malays, who came into Indonesia within the last several thousand years, picked up a strong Mongolian strain from immigrants who came into Southeast Asia from South China in recent times. They have given the Mongolian cast to the present Malayo-Indonesian race.

The result, as it is to be seen in these people, is a short, well-formed population averaging hardly more than 5 feet in stature. Skin color is brownish and eyes are brown. They have black hair with a definite reddish strain in it; where Indonesian elements predominate the hair is wavy and the head long; where Malay traits predominate the hair is usually straight and the cephalic index brachy- to mesocephalic.

Negroes. There is no justification for speaking of Negroes as the "colored race," since all races are more or less colored. In fact, if black is an absence of color, Negroes may better be called *colorless.* Admittedly Negroes are the possessors of the darkest pigmentation of all mankind; nevertheless, few Negroes are actually black. Most are dark brown or brownish-black in skin color. Negro hair is prevailingly black, coarse, and wiry, and tightly curled, kinky, or woolly. Negro heads are with few exceptions long and narrow. The occipital region juts out, as does the lower portion of the face, which in appearance is accentuated by the thick, everted mucous membrane that forms the lips. The Negro nose is broad, with flaring alae and a broad, deeply depressed bridge. The hair on the head, though thick, is short in length, while the male beard is sparse and the body is not given to much hair growth. Stature is medium tall; the forearm is long; the legs thin (*i.e.,* the calves do not develop thick musculature); feet are flat-arched with a prominently protruding "larkspur" heel. No shoes made in America today are properly designed for Negro feet.

The African Negro is the variety most familiar in Europe and the Americas. Originally, he inhabited most of Africa south of the Sahara and Egypt, but the seventeenth to nineteenth centuries saw the forced migration of several million Negroes from the West African Sudan to the New World.

East Africa produces a remarkable subvariety of Negro known as the Nilotic, who outdoes the Nordic in growing long legs on a slender short body. He averages 6 feet 9 inches in height.

The Oceanic Negro is a denizen of the South Seas, who first came to the attention of more than a handful of Americans when our troops made landings in the Solomons, New Hebrides, New Caledonia, and New Guinea. Physically, Oceanic Negroes are generally similar to African Negroes with these notable exceptions: the hair is more often frizzly and bushy;[5] the supraorbital ridge is pronounced; the nose is prominent, "hooked," and depressed at the tip; and the lips are thinner and less everted than the African's.

The pygmy races of the world are all Negroid. This special variety is hence called *Negrito,* or "little Negro." The scattered distribution of these little men indicates great antiquity for the race, which is found in small groups in the depths of the Congo jungle, in the Malay jungles of Southeast Asia, in the interiors of New Guinea and the Philippines, and on the Andaman Islands of the Indian Ocean.

The Negritos are very small, averaging less than 4 feet 9 inches. Their skulls are mesocephalic with bulging foreheads, above which sprouts a tightly spiraled crop of close-growing hair. They vary from blackish- to reddish-brown in skin color, but the hair is consistently black. Their noses are exaggeratedly flat and broad, and their facial prognathism is marked. Their little bodies are lightly muscled, and their stomachs are prone to be potbellied. All in all, the physical endowment of the Negrito is so meager that it almost certainly has handicapped him in his precarious struggle for survival against the more powerfully built races of predatory men.

Composite Races. The South African Bushman is a Negrito with Mongoloid eye form and Mongoloid skin color. His triangular-shaped face with its protruding cheekbones also reflects Mongoloid characteristics. In spite of the absence of any historical data to support the con-

---

[5] This trait led G.I.s to call the Melanesians "fuzzy-wuzzies." Although Kipling's Fuzzy-wuzzy was a Sudanese African, the G.I. had good precedent. The Papuan got his name from the Malay word meaning "frizzly hair."

clusion, these marked Mongoloid traits indicate an ancient Negrito-Mongolian cross as the origin of the Bushman race. Archaeological evidence proves that Bushmen have been in South Africa for at least 15,000 years.

The fact that the dark brown Australians are called *blackfellows* leads to the easy error of thinking of them as Negroes. They decidedly are not. Nevertheless, they must possess some Negroid ancestry (probably Tasmanian). Their hairiness of head and body and the waviness of their hair indicate a strong probability of archaic Caucasian ancestry, such as is predominant in the Ainus (see below).

The Australian aborigine is physically a "low brow." His forehead slopes back from the heaviest supraorbital ridges of any surviving race. His skull is narrow and houses a brain that is notably smaller in volume than that of any other living race. His face juts forward, and his dental arches even more so. His dark brown eyes are set beside a deeply depressed nasal root, below which the broad thick tip of the nose flares up in a great bulb. The whole face is compressed from symphysis to nasion. The Australian is neither very short nor very tall. Like the Nordic and Nilotic, he grows a slender short body on a pair of pipestem legs. Australia is the land of retarded zoological oddities, and Australian man is a slightly retarded representative of *Homo sapiens*.

When the first Mongoloid invaders of Japan landed several thousand years ago, they found an unusual people in possession of the islands. These were the primitive Ainus—a people of swarthy "white" skin, abundantly covered with wavy black hair on head, face, and body. Their eyes were light brown under heavy brow ridges similar to the Australian's. Noses, too, were Australoid, only less so. In stature they were short and thickset. The prehistoric Japanese disputed the possession of the islands with these people, gradually crowding them into the northern recesses and at the same time interbreeding to some extent, so that today some Mongoloid traits crop up in what is otherwise a unique race among all the races of mankind.

If it comes to pass at some future date that miscegenation blends all the races of man into one standardized variety, then that variety may reasonably be expected to look somewhat like the polyglot Polynesians. Such a prospect is genuinely gratifying, for rare is the person who dissents from the judgment that they are a handsome and comely people of great ability. Yet the Polynesians are thoroughly mongrelized; predominantly they are Mediterranean Caucasian (from south India and akin to the Hindus) mixed with Oceanic Negroes and south Asiatic Mongoloids. The race is very similar to the Malayo-Indonesians except that the stronger Mediterranean heredity gives a wavy form to the hair, elongates the face and body, lightens the skin, and produces a high nose. Negroid traits show up in a tendency to fullness of lips. The dominant round-headedness of the Mongoloid characterizes most Polynesians. Hair grows luxuriantly on the head, but as is to be expected in a Mediterranean-Mongoloid-Negro mixture it shuns the face and body.

Blood Relationship. In this introduction to racial anthropology the diagnostic traits of race have been limited exclusively to morphological traits. Classifications by blood types are inconclusive.[6] Other physiological and psychological factors are reserved for discussion in the next chapter.

There has been some recent insistence upon a "genetic theory of race" in which analysis of races is to be in terms of genes, not morphology.[7] The time may come when it will be possible to describe races in terms of gene components, but that time is not yet here. For the present, we shall continue to use physical traits for diagnostic purposes, taking care to isolate culturally conditioned traits from genetically determined ones. Only the latter are to be treated as racial.

During the recent war the American Red Cross felt that it was necessary to segregate Negro blood from white in "blood bank" collections. Even though the Red Cross was itself aware of the fact that racial traits are carried in the germ plasm and not in the blood, it felt compelled to such segregation because of the popular belief that hereditary traits are "in the blood." This action of the Red Cross involved it in a tempest of controversy, aligned it with a false and undemocratic position, and created additional work in the extra handling and classification of Negro blood and plasma. Fortunately, when it came to saving lives through the use of plasma and fresh blood, the Army medical corpsmen generally ignored the racial classifications that the Red Cross had so painstakingly maintained.

Anthropologists are in no position to criticize the action of the Red Cross, however, since we have consistently contributed to popular misconception and are continuing to do so at this very moment.

Like any thoughtless person, we speak of "blood relationship." In all our discussions of kinship (a subject of consuming interest to anthropologists) we regularly use the term "blood relationship group." The terms "consanguine family," "consanguinity," "consanguine relatives," are all in constant use along with the synonym "blood relatives." It is not necessary to cite cases. One can pick up any current book or monograph in ethnology, or any issue of the *American Anthropologist*, and he is likely to find sufficient instances without painstaking research.

---

[6] See Hooton, *op. cit.*, pp. 554–563, for a contemporary summary of the facts.
[7] Cf. M. F. Ashley-Montague, *Man's Most Dangerous Myth*.

But a moment's reflection shows us how false this terminology is. The clan, for instance, is not founded on any blood tie, nor is any other relationship of family or kin. The relationship may be genuine or fictive, but it rests on a genetic principle and nothing else.

The error is even more egregious in physical anthropology when we commonly speak of racial ancestry in terms of blood. It is not unusual, for example, to hear a contemporary anthropologist say that the composite Polynesian race is predominantly Caucasian with a definite Mongolian admixture and a minority element of Negro blood. We still speak of halfblood, fullblood, and pureblood Indians.

The error of the anthropologist is shared by his fellow scientists. We unthinkingly perpetuate the timeworn popular fallacy of hereditary continuity through blood. In the interests of scientific accuracy it is incumbent upon us to cease. The imprint of accurate word usage based upon scientific fact must be stamped upon the lexicon of all men by scientists. It is our responsibility not to permit ourselves to be bound by popular word usage based on age-old error, especially when the error serves to generate and perpetuate untold mischief in the affairs of men.

A simple correction can easily be made. For "blood relationship" and "consanguine" substitute "genetic relationship" and "genetic group." For Negro, Caucasian, and Mongolian "blood" substitute "ancestry" or "hereditary or genetic component" unless it is blood you are talking about and not racial heredity. For "halfblood," "fullblood," and "pureblood" substitute "hybrid" and "unmixed."

This is not the only contribution anthropologists can make to the improvement of race relations, but it is an important one.

CHAPTER 7

RACIAL SUPERIORITY

The question of whether some races are superior or inferior to others raises the deeper question, "Superior in what?" Nilotic Negroes are obviously superior in stature to Negritos; Nordics are obvious superior in average stature to Malayo-Indonesians. This, however, is not the kind of superiority on which the "racial issue" turns. The alleged superiority or inferiority is a functional one. Do some races have superior capacity for cultural attainment? Are they inherently more intelligent? Do they have an inherently greater capacity for leadership and domination, which justifies their control and exploitation of less fortunately endowed races?

Racism is the doctrine that assumes as self-evident the proposition that "one group has the stigmata of superiority and the other has those of inferiority." [1] Science presupposes that superiority and inferiority must be determined by careful sifting of all the evidence that can be marshaled on the subject. Prejudiced opinion and demagoguery do not provide acceptable bases for determining the facts. The sociologist Edward A. Ross put it tersely when he penned the judgment, " 'Race' is the cheap explanation tyros offer for any collective trait that they are too stupid or too lazy [and we would add, too dishonest] to trace to its origin in the physical environment, the social environment, or historical conditions." [2] This declaration was long anticipated by the economist John Stuart Mill when he wrote, "Of all vulgar modes of escaping from the consideration of the effect of social and moral influences on the human mind, the most vulgar is that of attributing the diversities of conduct and character to inherent natural differences." [3]

To what conclusions does the nonvulgar anthropological consideration of the facts of physical anthropology, race psychology, anthropogeography, sociology, and culture history lead?

Anatomical Superiority. First, are some races more advanced in biological evolution than others? A positive answer would indicate general functional superiority. *Homo sapiens* is unquestionably more advanced

[1] R. F. Benedict, *Race: Science and Politics*, p. 5.
[2] E. A. Ross, *Social Psychology*, p. 3.
[3] J. S. Mill, *Principles of Political Economy*, Vol. 1, p. 390.

than Java man, and there can be no gainsaying his functional superiority. Further, *Homo sapiens* is undoubtedly more advanced than was *Homo neandertalensis*, a fact that probably contributed to the extinction of Neandertal man. However, all living races are members of the *Homo sapiens* group, and functional differences between the varieties of *Homo sapiens* are not so obvious.

Physical anthropologists are in general agreement that the Australian race is retarded in biological evolution and physically more primitive than other races. Yet the question of its intellectual inferiority is undetermined. True, the Australian possesses one of the world's rudest cultures, but, because of his isolated location, this point does not prove inherent incapacity to do better. The psychologist Porteus attempted a serious evaluation of native Australian endowment by means of a large variety of tests and observations.[4] His psychological results are utterly inconclusive, except to demonstrate the power of cultural influences in causing differential behavior. For instance, the solution of problems by the individual acting alone is the basis of most psychological tests. Porteus found to his dismay that it is difficult to get Australians even to attempt to solve a problem alone, since they are used to acting and thinking in concert. All problems in tribal life are debated and worked out by the council of elders until a unanimous decision is reached. The natives even felt that Porteus should have helped them solve the tests, especially when in one group they had made him a tribal member! Speed has no meaning to the Australian, whose skill in the hunt demands "sustained muscular control, and undivided attention, an extreme sensory wariness, inexhaustible *patience and concentration* of purpose."[5] Yet speed is an important factor in many intelligence tests. Hence, the results of such tests, which naturally show the Australian up poorly, have no validity. There can be no doubt that tests designed to take full account of skills that are important in the native Australian environment would measure differences between individual natives with reasonable significance. Equally likely is the probability that Australians would obtain a higher rating than whites if both were subjected to those tests. And such results would be just as unfair to the whites as the present tests are to the Australians.

When we return to matters of physical anthropology, we find prejudiced laymen likening Japanese to monkeys and Negroes to apes. Both comparisons lead to the inference of evolutionary backwardness and inherent inferiority. Southern gentlemen argued in the ante-bellum debates

[4] S. D. Porteus, *The Psychology of a Primitive People.*
[5] *Ibid.,* p. 64. Italics are the author's.

on slavery that Negroes were physically and spiritually subhuman, devoid of souls, and therefore not subject to the moral injunction against enslavement of human beings. Some people still argue that the body proportions, facial projection, and flat broad noses of the Negroes put them nearer to the apes in physical development; that these features are prima-facie evidence of their inferiority.

Greater or lesser similarity to simian physical characteristics for particular traits is actually a valid measure of evolutionary development constantly relied upon by physical anthropologists in their attempts to determine whether a fossil find is human, ape, or intermediary.[6] Yet when applied to the modern races of man this technique proves nothing at all. A comparison of the primary races will quickly show why.

	Most simianlike	Less simianlike	Least simianlike
Cephalic index.........	Mongolian	Caucasian	Negro
Cranial capacity.......	Negro	....	Mongolian, Caucasian
Eye color..............	Negro, Mongolian	....	Caucasian
Nasal index...........	Negro	Mongolian	Caucasian
Hair form.............	Mongolian	Caucasian	Negro
Hair length...........	Caucasian, Mongolian	....	Negro
Body hair.............	Caucasian	....	Negro, Mongolian
Lip form.............	Mongolian	Caucasian	Negro
Lip color.............	Mongolian	Caucasian	Negro
Facial prognathism.....	Negro	Caucasian	Mongolian
Eye form.............	Caucasian, Negro	....	Mongolian

This is by no means an adequate balance sheet; there are innumerable detailed features of anatomy that could be listed. All we have undertaken to demonstrate is that with respect to the superficial traits on which popular judgment rests, no race comes out ahead of the others. Negroes are most "apelike" in five of the selected traits, whereas Caucasians come closest in three. But Negroes are least "apelike" in six of the traits and Caucasians are least in only three. The whole argument turns out to be as puerile as the reasoning of one Herman Gauch, who became an official anthropologist of the Nazi regime after genuine anthropologists had become exiles, when he said, "If non-Nordics are more closely allied to monkeys and apes than to Nordics, why is it possible for them to mate

---

[6] *Cf.* A. Keith, *New Discoveries Relating to the Antiquity of Man*, Chaps. 5 and 6, for a skillful application of such criteria in the evaluation of *Australopithecus africanus*.

with Nordics and not with apes? The answer is this: it has not been proved that non-Nordics cannot mate with apes." [7]

Attempts have been made to correlate racial intelligence with average brain size. It is a fundamental fact of evolution that brain size and complexity increase relatively with each successive emergent animal form. Functional adaptability increases with larger and more complex brains, as we compare one genus with another. Within the Caucasian race, several methodologically sound studies correlating brain size with school and university grades and I.Q. have been made. Klineberg, on consideration of these studies concludes, "In general there appears to be an exceedingly small, though positive correlation between head size and intelligence." [8] However, judicious interpretation explains this difference as due to good conditions of nurture, which produce brighter people as well as larger stature, which in turn is consistently correlated with larger brains. If this be true, the correlation between brain size and intelligence is due to external factors, not inheritance.

When the problem of brain size as related to racial intelligence is tested, the results are wholly inconclusive. Australians, Pygmies, and Negroes have smaller average brains than do Mongolians and Caucasians. In the case of the Pygmies it is a function of small body size. Racists have seized on the smaller brain size of Negroes as evidence of inferiority. But on the basis of such reasoning we should have to acknowledge the large-brained Eskimos as our intellectual superiors and include the Negro Kaffirs and Amakosa along with them. The extinct and primitive Neandertal would also rate as our equal if not our superior.

In the case of the Neandertal man, anatomical evidence indicates qualitative inferiority of the brain, because of the relative smallness of the frontal lobe and the simplicity of convolutions. It has not yet been possible to establish similar deficiencies for any of the living races.

Another popular basis for assumption of racial superiority is body odor. How often has one heard the exclamation in defense of discrimination against Negroes, "They smell so!" There is little doubt that Negro perspiration has a different odor than that of Caucasian. There is equally strong evidence that the body odor of whites is sharply distinguishable by Chinese and their water buffaloes and dogs. These animals are violently upset by the scent of whites, and the Chinese find our "smell" quite distasteful. However, they are too mannerly to admit it except in closest confidence. We know little or nothing about the biochemistry of human perspiration. We do not know what produces diversity of body odor.

[7] H. Gauch, *New Foundations for Research into Social Race Problems.*
[8] O. H. Klineberg, *Race Differences*, p. 80.

Diet is definitely a factor, but there is a good possibility that inherently different organic functions are also important.

A tentative conclusion to the effect that distinctive body odors may be inherent racial traits does not carry a correlative one that a particular odor is superior or inferior to another. We are merely prone to accept our body odor, because we are used to it. But even we react obsessively to the unpleasantness of our own aroma, if we are to judge by popular response to soap advertising and the flourishing sale of perfumes.

Psychological Superiority. The really crucial issue is whether the mental processes and psychological aptitudes of different races are inherently different. Then follows the problem, if they are different, is it possible to determine whether the psychological traits of some races are inferior to those of others? Animal breeders and fanciers are thoroughly familiar with inherent differences in temperament, physiological function, and learning capacities in different breeds or varieties within the same species of animal. It must be recognized that a similar possibility exists in the case of the human animal. Inasmuch as the nervous system of man is a part of his biological system, it is quite possible that inherent differences in the structure and functioning of the nervous systems of different races do exist.

There are three possible approaches to the scientific solution of this problem: (1) Neurological analysis of the anatomy and physicochemical functioning of the nervous systems of different races, which, unfortunately, calls for a refinement of laboratory technique far beyond that yet developed by neurologists. (2) Controlled psychological experimentation, in which the cultural and environmental factors are held constant or eliminated, so that the inherent functional capacities of different races may be measured. (3) Anthropological analysis of the cultural accomplishments of different races.

Race Psychology. The last three decades have witnessed a flurry of activity among experimental psychologists attempting to measure inherent race differences. Hundreds of experiments of varying worth have been undertaken. Many of the earlier ones have been analyzed and summarized in the books of Garth [9] and Klineberg. [10]

Tremendous interest was first raised by the published results obtained from the Army alpha and beta tests of the First World War, and subsequently hundreds of tests of various races and nationalities were undertaken during the 1920's. The results of these tests gave Negroes and Mongoloids definitely lower ratings than Caucasians. By the Binet tests, the Negro I.Q. averages around 99, American Indian 75.3, Chinese and

---

[9] T. E. Garth, *Race Psychology.*   [10] Klineberg, *op. cit.*

Japanese 99, and Caucasians 100. Since Terman, who had the prestige of authority behind him, had expressed the opinion that the Binet scale is a true test of native intelligence, the inferiority of Negroes and other non-Caucasian races then seemed to be scientifically proved. At last, social discrimination justified by racial superiority, in the eyes of its protagonists, seemed to have an irrefutable *raison d'être*.

More experience with the tests has sobered the psychologists, however. By their own work they have demonstrated that emotional maladjustment, amount of schooling, language facility, and kinds of attitudes (motivation) toward the testing process can drastically alter the results of the tests. Criticism from anthropologists has evoked a realization that tests designed on the basis of one type of cultural experience are not valid when applied to persons trained under markedly different cultures. Our comments on Porteus's experience with Australians illustrated this. Intelligence and aptitude tests measure innate ability plus experience, modified by emotional and cultural factors.

The first caution signs against uncritical use of the Army results in racial interpretation of differential intelligence were raised in Yerkes's original presentation of the data.[11] It was shown that Negroes from the North rated much higher than Negroes from the South. The Army testers observed that this fact could be due to better economic, social, and educational opportunities for Negroes in the North. They thus gave implicit recognition to the effect of environment on intelligence performance. They also noted that the difference could be taken to mean that naturally intelligent Negroes leave the South (selective migration). It was further noted that Negroes from some Northern states rated higher median scores than did the white draftees from some Southern states. Since Northern whites obtained higher intelligence grades than Southern whites, the inference was rather clear that the better general educational and economic environment of the North was the crucial element.

These figures created no public furor until Benedict and Weltfish wrote a little popular pamphlet on race a quarter of a century later.[12] When this pamphlet was selected for reading by the soldiers of the Second World War, the Kentucky chairman of the House Military Affairs Committee rose in wrath against its "insult" to white supremacy and won for it thereby a wide popular circulation. Such are the consequences of censorship.

The Army testers had left open the question as to whether the high

[11] R. M. Yerkes (ed.), *Psychological Examining in the U. S. Army* (Memoirs of the National Academy of Sciences, Vol. 15, 1921).

[12] R. F. Benedict and G. Weltfish, *The Races of Mankind*.

performance of Northern Negroes was due to their innate capacity or to the more favorable environment of the North. The problem was tackled by Klineberg in the 1930's. The first step was to obtain the school records of Negro children in Charleston, Nashville, and Birmingham. The percentile rankings of children who were known to have left for the North were compared with those who stayed in the South. Klineberg found that "The migrants as a whole were almost exactly at the average of the whole Negro school population in these three Southern cities." [13]

Next Klineberg and his assistants measured 3,000 Southern-born Negro children in the schools of New York City. Five different standard intelligence and performance tests were used. It was found that the I.Q. and N.I.T. ratings of new arrivals (less than one year in New York) were lowest, and that these ratings improved in regular progression for each additional year of residence in New York, until the same level was reached as is shown by the Negro children born in the North. The factor of mixed ancestry was properly taken into account, and a check was made to determine that the more recent arrivals were not of inferior rating in the South.

The Klineberg studies demonstrate conclusively that the lower I.Q. ratings of Southern Negroes are in large measure an I.Q. *retardation* caused by inadequate schooling and a cultural environment different from that presupposed by the standard intelligence tests. Modification of education and cultural environment in the direction of that enjoyed by whites, in the case of New York City Negroes, narrows the gap between the I.Q. averages of white and Negro children. The gap is not wholly closed, for Klineberg found that twelve-year-old New York Negro school children are still six to eighteen months lower in mental age than are white children of the same chronological age.

It remains perfectly true that the bulk of intelligence tests give American whites higher median I.Q. ratings than American Negroes.[14] But it is just as true that

The widely accepted belief in the hereditary group differences in intelligence which the test results seem to demonstrate must for the present be regarded as unproved. If intellectual differences between racial and social groups do exist (and this point is still debatable) the testing technique is nevertheless incapable of proving their existence.[15]

[13] Klineberg, *op. cit.*, p. 184.

[14] H. E. Garrett, "Negro-White Differences in Mental Ability in the United States" (*The Scientific Monthly*, Vol. 65, 1947), pp. 329–333.

[15] O. H. Klineberg, "Mental Tests" (*Encyclopedia of the Social Sciences*, Vol. 10, 1933), p. 326.

The reason lies in the pervasive influence of very subtle cultural differences that the tests cannot control.

In summary, the evidence from psychology is largely negative. It demonstrates that (1) so-called "intelligence tests" measure innate skill plus cultural experience. No test has yet been evolved that can eliminate the cultural factor, and differential ratings of the various races in intelligence tests must be critically evaluated; (2) aptitude tests do reveal racial differentials in visual, motor, and vocal skills, but these too are subject to cultural influences that have not been eliminated in tests and measurements; and (3) many skills of intelligence and aptitude definitely change when the cultural environment changes.

The whole result of scientific race psychology is to throw the explanation of significant behavior as between people of different races over into the field of cultural experience. The findings of psychology harmonize with those of anthropology and history, which we shall now treat simultaneously.

Race and Culture History. It is the opinion of anthropologists that all races except, perhaps, the Australian aborigines are equally capable of cultural development and that culture operates independently of racial heredity. How then, it is often asked, can it be that some races are culturally more advanced than others? How does one account for the fact that the Negroes never attained civilization until it was brought to them by Caucasians? Is it not true that the highest modern civilizations have been developed by the European whites?

There are three principles to be grasped in formulating the answers to these questions: (1) Although all cultures are fundamentally similar in their nuclear cores, the range of cultural variability as manifest by human societies is truly remarkable. Limits to the range of culture are imposed by the physical nature of man. These limits are so basic and so generalized, however, that they are common to all races of man. The forms of variation are the result of the processes of culture growth, not of racial predisposition. (2) The behavior and cultural ingenuity of different peoples within any given race are so variable that obviously the racial factor can be of little importance. (3) The same people may exhibit astounding cultural energy at one period of their history and be almost wholly devoid of it at another. Peoples who have been culturally quiescent for centuries suddenly burst into a veritable fury of cultural development without any determinable change in racial composition.

The Japanese are the most spectacular example in modern times. The Chinese illustrate the principle in reverse; they have been in the forefront of civilizational development for many centuries in the past, only to have lapsed in more recent times into creative quiescence and social disorganization.

In European history the facts confound the racists again and again. Cicero said of the Britons, "Do not obtain your slaves from the Britons, for the Britons are so stupid and so dull that they are not fit to be slaves." Yet what was to be the relative position of Cicero's descendants and the Britons 2,000 years later? The Romans looked upon the Germans as inherently incapable of high civilization, as many Americans now look upon Africans and Asiatics. The American error is compounded, since the non-Caucasian peoples of Asia and Africa have in the past produced high cultures of considerable richness. It is easy for North Europeans and their American descendants to forget how late they came to the forefront of civilization and cultural development. The centers of cultural invention did not shift to North Europe until after the Renaissance, only 500 years ago. During the Dark Ages, the Maya Indians of Central America showed greater cultural accomplishments than the European whites.

The history of the Uto-Aztecans is also pertinent. The Aztecs, Comanches, and Shoshones are all Indians who speak similar languages indicative of a common historical background. They are racially quite similar, and 600 years ago they stood as lowly hunters and gatherers at the bottom of the cultural scale, living in the western deserts of the United States and possessing a meager cultural equipment. Historical events radically altered their basic characters and cultural development.

The Aztecs wandered southward until they settled in Central Mexico in the midst of several high cultures that had been greatly influenced by the Mayan tradition. In A.D. 1325 they founded Tenochtitlan (the present Mexico City), and 200 years later they were overlords of the land: maize growers, road builders, astronomers, artists, and possessors of a city with public buildings of cut stone so magnificent that stout Cortez cried out that in all Andalusia there was nothing to compare with its glory.

The Comanches wandered into the southwestern plains of the United States at a somewhat later date. There they acquired Spanish horses and guns and came into contact with the warlike tradition of the Plains tribes. They became truculent, nomadic robbers and fighters, so violent that to this day the plainsman's simile, "as wild as a Comanche," is still heard in the West.

The Shoshones, who retain the attitudes and culture once shared with the Comanches, obtained neither guns nor horses. They were regularly mauled by the Blackfeet, who had guns and horses, so they timidly hid out in the desert—peaceable, because they dared not make war. They developed a strong inferiority complex, and they are the only Indians the author has ever worked with who welcomed the coming of the whites. "If the white man had not come, there would be no Indians left," they say. By Indians, they mean themselves.

As circumstances found them, the Aztecs and Comanches had become definitely superior people, the Shoshones miserable by any man's count. But race was a constant element. The accidents of culture history had frowned upon the hapless Shoshones.

The problem of what causes cultural spurts is a complex and difficult one that must be analyzed in terms of cultural process, to which the last section of this book is devoted. Outstanding among the multitude of factors is cross-fertilization of cultures; the stimulation of new ideas and new ways of doing. Isolated peoples always stagnate, be they Mongolian, Negro, or Caucasian. But the bent of the culture is important, too—a backward-looking, ancestor-worshipping culture is not readily amenable to change and further development. The physical environment is also influential. Each of these can be shown to be active factors. But since it cannot be shown that races differ in the possession of hereditary mentality and capacities, because the performance of different groups within a single race ranges from high to low and because the performance of a single racial group varies so markedly through time, it becomes evident that race per se is of small moment in cultural achievement.

Therefore, the present view of anthropology in regard to race may be summed up in these terms: (1) It must be acknowledged that there is the possibility of innate physiological and psychological differences between racial groups; (2) however, no such differences have been scientifically isolated and unequivocally established; (3) and such differences as are indicated are so slight in their apparent effect on human behavior that, when compared to the proved influence of culture in determining the action of men, race differences are of such relative insignificance as to be of no functional importance. Culture, not race, is the great molder of human society.

Part Four: Primitive Society

A. Subsistence and Crafts

CHAPTER 8

FOOD GETTING

Man eats to live. The cravings of a hungry stomach are but sensory stimuli that set the organism into food-getting activities. Ingestion of food is an absolute necessity to the maintenance and functioning of the organism. Food as fuel to be released as energy is necessary to bodily action. Food as repair material to replace the continuous loss of substance from the body is necessary to bodily maintenance. True foods are either energy yielders or nonenergy yielders, and man must get an adequate intake of both. The latter supply inorganic materials for body replacement. In addition, man must take in indigestible materials, expressively called *roughage*, to assist the passage of true food and its residues through the alimentary canal.

Food getting is a physical imperative, subsistence a fundamental interest, hunger a diffuse primary drive.

The society that fails to solve the problems of development of minimal subsistence techniques is doomed. The ghost of Malthus haunts all mankind.

The subsistence resources available to a people depend upon three factors: the natural environment, culture, and population. People who subsist by collecting and gathering roots, berries, seeds, and insects are for the most part directly dependent upon what the natural environment offers for the taking. People who have acquired the techniques of planting, cultivating, and harvesting crops, or the husbandry of animals and who have mastered methods of cooking or otherwise changing the chemicophysical substance of natural products, so as to make them useful or more desirable as foods, are less directly dependent upon the natural offerings of their physical environment. As man learns to expand his food-producing resources through cultural techniques and devices, he pushes back the specter of starvation and lays the base for the expansion of society.

The natural environment does not absolutely determine the nature of the foodstuffs a society can enjoy. Deserts can be made to bloom and bear fruit. Hothouses can be built in the Arctic, and ice cream can be frozen on a Pacific isle. Yet only quite advanced cultures make such things possible. Nor do food-getting techniques dictate the details of all aspects of culture. Great variations occur in the cultures of hunting peoples and, more especially, of gardeners.

Modern anthropology rejects the cruder aspects of environmental determinism espoused by the anthropogeographers of an earlier day. Nonetheless, the nature of the physical environment does influence the materials and modes of subsistence of any people, especially primitive. Therefore, we shall briefly delineate the chief types of physiographic environments and note their societal possibilities.

Classification of Environment. Chapple and Coon [1] have advanced for use in anthropology a classificatory scheme of terrestrial environments taken from the work of the geographer Preston James.[2] The classification is fairly generalized, since the divisions represent combinations of elements (vegetation, climate, soil, orientation of land) as they exist over wide areas. Finer distinctions would lead to a multiplication of categories beyond the eight that are here given.

1. Dry Lands (Deserts). Annual rainfall ranges from zero to 15 inches and there is a great diurnal range of temperature. Vegetation is sparse and animal life naturally limited. Water sources are irregularly distributed and directly influence the distribution of human and animal life. Oases make possible sedentary gardening and pastoral existence. Rivers that have their sources in mountain areas bring water to some deserts and support gardening cultures along their courses, as is the case with the Pueblos of the Southwest. Otherwise, desert environments tend to support only the most primitive hunters and collectors, as was the case with the Shoshoneans in the Great Basin, the natives of the "Dead Heart of Australia," and the African Bushmen who, although they enjoyed a more favorable locale in recent prehistoric times, have been forced to take refuge in the inhospitable Kalahari Desert, first because of Bantu pressure and lately by the aggressions of South African whites.

2. The Tropical Rain Forests. These occur along the equator. Heavy rains and high temperatures produce luxuriant growths of vegetation, which are so heavy as almost to choke out animal and human life. In

[1] *Principles of Anthropology*, pp. 73–95.
[2] *An Outline of Geography.*

the *true rain forest* it rains every day, as many a veteran of the Solomon and New Guinea campaigns knows but too well. There are no seasons, and plant life blooms the year round. Sunlight rarely penetrates to the ground, where in the dank, dim gloom of the forest there is little game. Gardening is difficult. The jungle quickly swallows such clearings as are laboriously hacked out for garden patches. Only when peoples of high cultures and large populations undertake thoroughly to strip the jungle and to grow rice do rain-forest lands lend themselves well to habitation. This has been done in Southeast Asia. In the *semideciduous rain forest*, seasonal rains alter the situation somewhat. Trees shed or fade annually, thus giving surface undergrowth a chance for thicker development. Typical inhabitants of the rain forests are the Amazonian Indians, Congo Negroes, Melanesians, and Indonesians.

3. *Mediterranean Scrub Forests*. Adjacent to a desert and the sea, shut off from the desert by mountains, and lying in the temperate zone, the scrub-forest lands enjoy mild rainy winters and dry hot summers (*viz.*, California). Scrub broadleaf trees provide bountiful nuts, and small game is abundant. Although limited in extent, these areas readily support various types of human societies. Typical peoples are the coastal and mountain Indians of California.

4. *Temperate Forests*. The temperate forests are well watered, but not excessively so. Winter and summer seasons are well defined, and trees are both deciduous and evergreen. Game is usually fairly abundant, but natural food plants are limited. Gardening is possible, but it requires much work in the clearing of land. Great areas of woodland must be stripped before extensive populations can be supported. The temperate forests are suitable for a fairly rugged sort of primitive existence. Early civilization was nourished best in scrub-forest environments, but modern times have witnessed the inexorable conquest of the temperate forests primeval, which now are the home of over half the earth's peoples. The temperate-forest areas advance in importance as culture is developed to the levels of machine technology. Types of peoples are the Woodland Indians of eastern North America and the Northwest Coast of the same continent, and the prehistoric peoples of Europe.

5. *Boreal (Northern) Forests*. Because of their subarctic location, the northern forest belts have long cold winters and short summers. Broadleaf trees are rare; the conifers are fairly alone. Fur-bearing animals abound, and gardening is all but impossible. Only hunters can make out in this rugged environment where no advanced cultures have as yet been located. Type of peoples are the Nascapi and other eastern Algonquians, and the Athabascan-speaking tribes of the interior Canadian Northwest

6. Polar Deserts and Tundras. The Arctic and Antarctic land areas are either ice-capped, barren, or covered with bush and sedge grass. The explorer Stefansson may call it "The Friendly Arctic," but fewer than fifty thousand of the earth's two billion people find it a fit place to live. The one-sixth of the earth's land area within the polar zone supports 0.025 per cent of humanity. Typical peoples are the Eskimos, the Chukchi and Yukaghir in Siberia, and the Ona and Yahgan in Tierra del Fuego.

7. The Grasslands. Prairies and steppes are the two great types of quasi-arid grasslands within the temperate zones. In lower latitudes are found the tropical grasslands known as *savannas*. These areas are the most favorable in the world for the proliferation of game, large and small—bison in America—and numerous varieties in the African Sudan. Primitive people without domesticated transport animals can exist in the grasslands only in small groups of nomadic hunters or as gardeners in river bottoms. Pastoralists, of course, flourish in such areas, and hunters equipped with horses can do very well indeed. Types of peoples are the Plains Indians in North America, Kirghiz in Turkestan, Mongols in Asia, and Masai in East Africa.

8. Mountain Areas. Except in the boreal and polar regions, mountain areas can present most of the geographic zones in a vertical succession. Consequently, they provide a number of variant possibilities for different types of societies and cultures, although difficulties of transportation and communication tend to hold them back. Outstanding among mountain cultures is that of the Incas of Peru.

Before we undertake to describe various food-getting techniques of primitive men, let us clarify what is meant by such terms as "hunters and gatherers," "lower hunters," "higher hunters," "gardeners," "hoe culture," "agriculture," and "pastoralism." These are all categories for the classification of peoples or cultures in terms of their *predominant* subsistence techniques, for the activities of men are multifarious, and even industrialized men garden, hunt, fish, and occasionally collect wild berries and nuts as well as maintain pastoral flocks and herds.

Food Gatherers. Collecting and gathering is the rudest and the most primitive technique for the acquisition of food. In its lowest forms it requires no tools whatsoever. Hands with which to pluck and arms with which to convey the edible plunder to the mouth suffice. This is the technique of our anthropoidal relatives. Few contemporary primates have been carefully observed under natural conditions, but we have an admirable account of a day's jaunting of a group of chimpanzees in French

Guinea (West Africa) as reported by Dr. Henry Nissen.[3] Nissen's observations lead to the following data on chimpanzee food habits: Thirty-four foods eaten during the dry season were identified, of which there were twenty-eight fruits, three stalks or stems, two blossoms, and one leaf. It is possible that eggs and small birds and rodents are consumed, but this is not confirmed. When eating (which takes 3 to 6 hours per day), a chimp ensconces himself in a crotch or upon the branch of a tree. Steadying himself with one arm, he uses his free arm to pluck the fruit and bring it to his mouth. Or, he may reach out and bend in a branch to eat directly from it. Or, caring nothing for the fate of the tree, he may break off a branch to strip it of fruit. He never eats with his feet, which is to his credit, and he always tries to eat everything within reach before moving to another spot. If the band moves before he has finished off one spot, he may snatch a branch of fruit and munch upon it as he shuffles along. Chimpanzees are not inhibited by any sense of delicacy that prohibits spitting out food they do not like. They feel perfectly free to eat what they prefer of some object and to throw the rest away without tasting. When hungry, the chimpanzee bolts almost everything. When full, he becomes quite finicky and leaves a careless litter of unwanted scraps beneath his tree.

Although Köhler demonstrated that chimpanzees are smart enough to invent simple tools with which to reach food when they are locked in a cage and not allowed to eat naturally, there is no indication that wild chimpanzees ever bother to make even the simplest tools for use in food getting. Their relation to nature is one of direct dependency. Hypothetically, this was true of the earliest ape men of Pliocene times. It would not be true of the Dawn men of Early Pleistocene times, since we have incontrovertible evidence that these men made tools. If they made tools, we may feel certain they used them. And so, a million years ago man had already left "pure collecting" and was *working* upon his physical environment.

To illustrate the subsistence techniques of a group of lower hunters and collectors, we might describe the activities of one or another Australian tribe, or the Tasmanians, Semangs, Andaman Islanders, African Pygmies, or African Bushmen. Any of numerous California tribes would do equally well, as would one of the three main tribes of Tierra del Fuego. However, we shall make the Great Basin Shoshoneans our exemplar.

[3] H. W. Nissen, *A Field Study of the Chimpanzee* (Comparative Psychology Monographs, Vol. 8, No. 1, Serial No. 36, 1931).

In 1860, Abbé Domenech noted of the Great Basin Shoshone, "According to the season, they emigrate from one place to another to seek miserable roots, which form their only nourishment; even animals are seldom to be found there." [4] It is because of their root-grubbing activities that the Shoshonean food gatherers are known throughout the Western states as *Diggers*. Steward lists over 100 species of seeds, roots, and nuts known to have been eaten by the Shoshones. [5] Roots were extracted with a simple pointed digging stick, or dibble. Seeds were collected with the aid of a woven basket and a fanlike beater wherewith to knock the grass seeds into the basket. Of all the delectable seeds offered by the desert, those of the sunflower were the most prized. Roasted lightly and ground on a stone metate, they were reduced to an oily paste, which tasted "just like peanut butter." In field work among the members of the *H3kandika* (Seed Eater) Shoshones, who live on Bannock Creek in Idaho, gallon jars of peanut butter make most acceptable presents. They stimulate memories of olden days. Pine nuts also played a great part in the social economy of the various Shoshones—with results that we shall look into under the heading of land ownership (see Chap. 23).

Not only was the environment exploited for roots, berries, and nuts, but vermin were looked upon as an epicurean godsend. Regular communal grasshopper drives were organized. A sizable pit, 3 or 4 feet deep and 30 or 40 feet across, was laboriously prepared. Then men, women, and children formed a large circle, which converged slowly on the pit as they drove the grasshoppers before them with brush beaters. A good drive netted countless grasshoppers, which could then be roasted to provide a feast of plenty.

Ants were a more favored delicacy, because of the pungency of their taste when properly prepared. In March, when the ants had left the larva stage but were not yet up and around, a woman would scoop up an entire ant nest in her large scallop-shaped winnowing basket. With dextrous and wonderful manipulation she shook the basket so that the ants gathered in its heel, while the sand and dirt bounced off the outer edge. When only ants remained, she scooped up hot coals with the basket. Rapidly jouncing them in the air, she kept the coals and ants turning together and the basket from burning up. When at last the legs were burned from the ants and their bodies properly toasted, her motions were deftly altered; the ashes marched off the edge of the basket, while the

[4] E. Domenech, *Seven Years' Residence in the Great Deserts of North America*, Vol. 1, p. 242.

[5] J. H. Steward, *Basin-Plateau Aboriginal Sociopolitical Groups* (Bureau of American Ethnology, Bulletin 120, 1938), pp. 21–32.

ants once again foregathered in its heel. They were then dumped upon a grinding stone, rolled out, and reduced to a delectable paste (from the Shoshone point of view). This recipe is known as Shoshone *ante-pasto*.

Small rodents were trapped by means of simple deadfalls. Rabbit hunting took the form of a great communal hunt under the direction of a hunt chief.[6] Nets were set up and beaters drove the quarry into the waiting meshes. Soft robes were plaited from thin strips of rabbit fur for winter use. Antelopes were occasionally hunted in much the same way, but with the addition of magical lures and antelope disguises worn by the hunters. A fence of brush supplanted the nets of the rabbit hunt.[7]

Deer, mountain sheep, and mountain goats were sometimes pursued alone by the most energetic hunters. A hunter with much endurance would chase a deer or sheep for two whole days until exhaustion of the quarry made it possible for him to get close enough for a shot. Should this seem like incredible exertion, perhaps the motivation can better be appreciated if we quote Lewis and Clark on the meat hunger of the Shoshones. One of the expedition's hunters had killed a deer on Friday morning, Aug. 16, 1805. The Shoshones accompanying Captain Lewis, after a pell-mell race to the spot where Lewis's man had dressed the deer,

. . . all dismounted and ran tumbling over each other like famished dogs; each tore away at whatever part he could, and instantly began to eat it; some had the liver, some the kidneys, in short no part on which we look with disgust escaped them; one of them who had seized about nine feet of the entrails was chewing at one end, while with his hands he was diligently clearing his way by discharging the contents at the other.[8]

This method of eating "sausage" was still remembered by Shoshone informants in 1934.

Shoshone deer hunting was much like that of the Tarahumara Indians of Mexico, of whom Bennett and Zingg report

Hunting deer consists of chasing the deer for two days—never less than one day. The Tarahumara keeps the deer constantly on the move. Only occasionally does he get a glimpse of his quarry, but he follows it unerringly through

[6] Communal rabbit hunts extend down through the Southwest into the Pueblos, where participation is not only a lark but a religious duty, and into the various groups of the Gila River area.

[7] Antelope and buffalo drives were performed by the Plains tribes in a somewhat similar manner.

[8] M. Lewis and W. Clark, *History of the Expedition of Captains Lewis and Clark, 1804–5–6*, Vol. 2, p. 401.

his own uncanny ability to read the tracks. The Indian chases the deer until it falls of exhaustion, often with its hoofs completely worn away.[9]

Fear of starvation constantly haunted the Shoshones. Like the Eskimos, they sometimes took a desperate last resort in cannibalism. But cannibals were feared and hated, and occasionally lynched.[10]

It would be an error to conclude from the above remarks that the Shoshones were devoid of all fastidiousness. They would and will eat neither dogs nor coyotes, for Coyote is a supernatural culture hero—a lovable rapscallion, who figures in many a myth as an Indian equivalent of Tyll Eulenspiegel. He is the younger brother of Wolf, whom some Shoshones look upon as the Supreme Deity.[11] To kill a coyote or his cousin the dog is unthinkable; to eat them, impossible. Modern Shoshones, in 1934, were even loath to eat the surplus Navajo sheep sent them by the government. Skinned sheep look too much like dogs.

Bands of food gatherers are necessarily seminomadic. They must cover wide areas to skim off sufficient provender to keep them alive. But a given band tends to stay within its own familiar territory, because (1) any animal may secure food and water more efficiently if it knows the land; (2) all human groups practice some storage of food; (3) they may also practice conservation of food resources; (4) their movements are hindered to a certain extent by their possession of material goods; and (5) property concepts are universal among mankind; tacit agreement allocates to each group its landed property unless the equilibrium is upset by war and migration.[12]

Such bands are usually bilateral or patrilineal in social organization, so far as present evidence goes.

Hunters. Hunters always rely to some extent upon berries, nuts, and roots to round out their diet. But they are distinguished from collectors and gatherers in that they are predominantly predatory carnivores in their subsistence habits. Man is omnivorous by nature. This more than any other single trait distinguishes him from his vegetarian anthropoidal relatives. When or how the revolutionary meat-eating habit first took hold in the evolutionary development of man we do not know.

[9] W. C. Bennett and R. M. Zingg, *The Tarahumara*, p. 113.

[10] E. A. Hoebel, *The Political Organization and Law-ways of the Comanche Indians* (American Anthropological Association, Memoir 54, Contributions from the Laboratory of Anthropology, 4, 1940), p. 141.

[11] R. H. Lowie, "The Northern Shoshone" (*American Museum of Natural History, Anthropological Papers*, Vol. 11, Part 2, 1909), pp. 233 ff.

[12] J. H. Steward, "The Economic and Social Basis of Primitive Bands" in *Essays in Anthropology in Honor of Alfred Louis Kroeber*, p. 332.

It is difficult for man to down his animal victims without the aid of tools. In almost all hunting situations he relies upon some inventive device to assist him in bringing down his quarry. Thus he uses clubs, spears, darts, arrows, deadfalls, pitfalls, snares, nets, weirs, hooks, axes, knives, and poisons to accomplish his ends. He may enlist the aid of a dog or mount a horse or camel. Perhaps he may fashion a boat to bring him to his quarry. Whatever the device he may use, hunting techniques are those of assault (shooting, spearing, clubbing, axing, stabbing), trapping and snaring, the pitfall and poisoning. Shooting, while the most commonly preferred technique among recent primitives, was probably the last of these methods to appear in human prehistory. The bow was not invented until Late Paleolithic or Early Neolithic times. Neandertal man had clubs, spears, and hand axes. While there is no direct evidence that he utilized traps and snares or pitfalls, it is likely that he had invented simple devices of this order. There is no way of knowing whether he wittingly used poisons or not.

Because it is so efficient a weapon, the bow had attained almost world-wide distribution by the seventeenth century. The skill of most primitive hunters in tracking game to bring them within bowshot is so well known as not to bear repeating here. Devices of disguise are cleverly used in some tribes. Bushmen artists have depicted disguised bowmen stalking the unwary ostrich. Western Indians were wont to wear antelope skins to approach that fleet and shy beast. Cheyennes shot eagles on the wing by hiding under grass in a pit from which they slowly rotated a stick with a bit of cloth on the end. This aroused the curiosity of the king of birds, who warily soared lower and lower until the patient hunter could spring from his blind for a shot.

In the jungles of Malaysia and South America and the woodlands of Southeastern United States, the blowgun with dart is often preferred for the hunting of small game and birds. The heavy jungle growth inhibits any long-distance shooting, and in such a setting darts are often more effective than arrows, especially in South America and Indonesia, where darts are poison-tipped.

The hunting of larger animals is not usually a matter of technique pure and simple. Ritual and magic are evoked to reinforce the hunter, whose anxiety for personal safety and fear of failure are overriding. Much of the cave art left by Cro-Magnon man is eloquent, if mute, evidence of this. His painted figures of animals are frequently wounded and pierced with figures of darts. We do not know what ritual formulas gave efficacy to Cro-Magnon animal effigies. But a Winnebago Indian yet living tells of a very holy hill in Wisconsin in which was a cave wherein lived twenty spirits, called *Those-who-cry-like-babies.*

My father had control of them [says Crashing Thunder in his autobiography], and when he wished to bless a man he would take his bow and arrows and, holding them in his hands, lead the man around the hill and into the lodge [*i.e.,* into the hill]. There he would look for a stone pillar, and upon it, at about arm's length, he drew the pictures of a number of different animals. My father possessed only one arrow, but that one was a holy one. Then dancing around the stone pillar and singing some songs, he finished by breathing upon the pillar. Finally he walked around it and shot at it and when he looked at the stone, it had turned into a deer with large horns which fell dead at his feet. . . . My father was a very famous hunter and my brother wished to be like him.[13]

Whaling among the Eskimos and certain Northwest Coast Indians is assuredly one of the bravest and most technically skillful hunting-by-assault accomplishments of any primitive people. To reinforce his hunting skills, to give social recognition to the outstanding hunter, and merely in consequence of his belief in the spirit nature of whales and all the denizens of the animal world, the Alaskan made of whale hunting not only a hunt activity but a fulsome cult of magical and religious observances.

Lantis's analysis of the Alaskan Whale Cult [14] has revealed it as a complex of technological, economic, sociopolitical, magico-religious elaborations. Anthropologists and institutional economists well know, if the followers of Adam Smith did not, that "economic man," who rationally seeks the greatest return for the smallest investment of capital and the least expenditure of effort, is a theoretical figment of scholastic imagination. The Whale Cult is only one example among the many that come to our attention when we observe actual subsistence activities by means of field work. Whale hunting, then, in addition to the actual chase, which involves skilled use of boats, paddles, harpoons, lines, and floats to locate, trail, attack, destroy, and land the great sea monster, is worked into a web of behavior and beliefs that includes the following chief elements:

1. The headman of a whaling crew is a headman of the local group. Whaling leadership is integrated with social leadership.

2. Distribution of the parts of the whale is regulated by customary usage in accordance with which the boat owner, harpooner, and others hold particular rights.

[13] P. Radin (ed.), *Crashing Thunder,* pp. 27–28.
[14] M. Lantis, "The Alaskan Whale Cult and Its Affinities" (*American Anthropologist,* Vol. 40, 1938), pp. 438–464.

3. Initiation into the Whale Cult is through a long arduous period of instruction in which the young whaler learns the rituals and songs and seeks a vision.

4. Special amulets to ensure good luck are used in the whale hunt and hidden away in a secret cave between seasons. Knowledge of such caves and the use of the amulets is passed from father to son.

5. Whaling songs are sung. They are private incorporeal property (see pages 344–345).

6. The season of whaling is a special ceremonial and tabu season. The whalers are isolated from the main village. They are unclean, must sleep in the open, and (in northern Alaska) must not eat raw meat.

7. Whalers must be sexually continent before and during the whaling activities.

8. All those left in the village during the actual hunt must neither sleep nor work.

9. The wife of the chief whaler must remain quietly at home without eating, "in order to draw the whale to her."

10. Corpses or parts of the bodies of deceased whalers are used in ceremonial preparation for the hunt or are carried in the whaleboat.

11. All gear must be repaired and cleansed before the onset of the whaling season, otherwise the whale will be offended.

12. When the whale is hauled ashore it is given a symbolic drink of water by the whaler's wife.

13. As the whale is cut up, certain parts of his body are ceremonially handled, and very special rituals are performed to return the whale's spirit to the sea unangered. It is given food, and no disturbing noises are permitted.

14. The length of the ritual period following a whale killing is the same as for a human death (3 to 5 days).

This is only a brief sketch of the Whale Cult complex, but it should serve to indicate how much more there is to hunting than tracking and killing.

Gardeners. Of the million or so years that man has sojourned on this planet, for over 900,000 of them he made his way as a gatherer and lower hunter. His subsistence has been that of a savage for all but a small fraction of his existence.

The Neolithic Age saw the emancipation of man from the meager and relatively unreliable resources offered by wildlife. Through the domestication of plants and animals the hunter became the farmer and the herdsman.

There is no reason to suppose that one or the other form of domestication came first. The domestication of both plants and animals was a gradual process, which took place in a number of different parts of the world along independent lines. Domestication consists merely in controlled cultivation and husbandry. A domesticated plant is one that is useful to man and is cultivated by him. Dandelions are noxious weeds in the lawn to most persons, but cultivated dandelions may be purchased from vegetable stands in city areas settled by Italian-Americans.

The first steps in plant cultivation were probably taken in the area of weed elimination and control (a weed being any plant that is held to be undesirable). A patch of wild plants was tended, and weeds cut or uprooted. The Kwakiutl Indians' care for their wild clover patches would be an example of this. Clover beds were the properties of specific families, who dug them for their roots. The main roots were never dug and such pieces as were not considered good for food were, if they had been dug up, replaced in the ground for future growth.[15]

Real domestication begins, however, when seeds, roots, or shoots are deliberately planted or stored from one season to the next, for later planting to bring forth a crop. This calls not only for foresightedness and self-restraint (you can't eat your seed and plant it, too) but it also requires clearing of the forest and preparation of the soil—both arduous tasks. The idea of plant domestication is hard to come by, but even before the Age of Exploration had spread European traits over the world, the bulk of mankind's societies consisted of preagricultural gardeners. Most of North America was inhabited by hunters and collectors. However, all of the Prairie and Eastern Woodland tribes south of the Great Lakes and the St. Lawrence River raised maize, beans, and squashes. The Southwest Indians were intensive gardeners and growers of maize, as were all the Mexican and Central American tribes, the Andean peoples, and to a lesser extent those of northern and eastern areas of South America. Manioc was and is cultivated throughout the tropical rain forest of that continent.

Agriculture, which involves use of the plow, was never attained by the American Indians before the European invasion.

In the Old World only the peoples on the extreme fringes of the continental masses remained collectors or hunters in late pre-Columbian times. Across the north of Siberia, the Samoyed and Yukaghir hunters held a thin fringe, with the Gilyak on the northeast coast. Africa was

---

[15] E. S. Curtis, *The Kwakiutl*, p. 43.

given over wholly to pastoralists and food-growing peoples, except for the Bushmen, Congo Pygmies, and a few other scattered groups. All Indonesians, except for a few small groups, are gardeners.

Agriculture in the Old World attained a continuous distribution from Europe and the Mediterranean scrub forests of North Africa into India by way of Turkestan through a narrow corridor, with a slender appendage down the valley of the Nile. Isolated agricultural areas appear in China and Indo-China.

The domesticated plants of the Old World are numerous, but a half-dozen grains are the old Neolithic staples. Such grains as oats, wheat, rye, barley, and millet are only modified grasses whose seed heads have been enlarged by selective breeding. Indeed, according to the Russian botanist Vavilov, in Iranian Asia Minor wild rye is looked upon as a noxious weed inimical to the growth of cultivated wheat and barley.[16]

Old World domestication of most plants took place in the Near East. The environment is mountainous (Type 8) with dry lowlands and humid highlands. Winters are rainy and cool, summers dry and hot. Sauer writes

> In this habitat the crops are fall-sown, make a large part of their growth of stalk and leaf in cool weather, and complete their maturity during the long summer days of warmest weather. These climatic adaptations made easy diffusion of such plants into northwestern Europe. . . . In the European lands there was still the same condition of a cool, moist starting period, though the start was shifted to spring, and maturity still took place during the long days of mid-summer.[17]

Old World farinaceous plants are sown broadcast.

In this process of development it would be wrong to think of any one tribe as being responsible for the domestication of all, or even one, plant. The process was long and slow, with many people and many tribes working upon the problem. However, there is little doubt that in the Old World, where plant domestication was first accomplished 15,000 to 20,000 years ago, the triumphant attainment was encompassed in the Iranian highlands.

Lightly forested highlands may strike the reader as strange places for the origins of gardening. Clearing forests is hard work, and it would seem

---

[16] N. Vavilov, *Studies on the Origin of Cultivated Plants* (Bulletin of Applied Botany and Plant Breeding, Leningrad, 1926), pp. 109*ff*.

[17] C. Sauer, "American Agricultural Origins" in *Essays in Anthropology in Honor of Alfred Louis Kroeber*, p. 285.

at first careless thought that open country would be more suitable. However, two factors militate against horticultural origins in open lands. Deserts are deficient in water, even if the soil is friable. Archaeological evidence does not support the thesis that gardening first began in "irrigation oases" of the arid river valleys in the Old and New World. Grasslands are impenetrable to planting by peoples who do not have heavy plows. Even our own pioneers avoided the heavily sodded prairies, until special sod-breaking plows were developed (which was not so long ago). Although the best grain-producing lands in the world are the American and Russian prairies (Type 7), they have become so only under modern conditions. Tropical rain forests (Type 2) can be made to support gardens by primitive men, but the environment was not conducive to first efforts at plant domestication. Archaeological evidence and botanical facts do not indicate great antiquity for domesticated jungle plants.

Clearing the forest for planting requires energetic labor; it is not for lazy men. But for people who are not rushed for time it can be effectively done with primitive tools by the "slash and burn method." Each tree is "girdled" by cutting a ring through the bark and cambium layer. Death follows. The dead trees may then be burned out or left standing. Their leafless branches no longer shade the ground. The weedless floor of the virginal forest is a light rich humus, and the gardeners simply plant among and around the dead stumps. Stumps are a serious nuisance only to the farmer with a plow.

Recent evidence has shown that American horticultural origins were probably diffusely centered in northern South America (not in the Mayan peninsula of Yucatan, as earlier theorists supposed). The tuberous potato was domesticated in the Andean highlands; the area where maize was first developed out of pod corn [18] is undetermined, but the probabilities point to Paraguay or eastern Bolivia; peppers and peanuts come from Brazil; [19] and manioc and sweet potatoes were the original contributions of the prehistoric people of the tropical lowlands. It is obvious that American agricultural origins were multiple. Culture growth is always the result of contributions from many sources.

Maize ultimately became the most important of all American foods, but it appears not to have been the first to be domesticated. It is quite possible that manioc and the potato were earlier forms. Americans, to whom potatoes are either Irish, Maine, Long Island, Idaho, or sweet, may

[18] Corn in which each kernel is protected by a pod covering.
[19] P. C. Mangelsdorf and R. G. Reeves, "The Origin of Maize" (*American Anthropologist*, Vol. 47, 1945), pp. 235–243.

be amazed to learn that the illiterate Aymara Indians of Bolivia are such fastidious potato connoisseurs that La Barre recently listed 209 Aymara identifications for native potatoes! [20]

The use of manioc as a basic foodstuff by Amazonian Indians reveals a genuine ingenuity. Sweet manioc, which grows wild, gives relatively small yields. The domesticated forms with large yields contain much poisonous prussic acid. This necessitates a leaching process of some complexity before the manioc tubers can be converted to edible cassava. The roots, after being dug, must be sliced and fermented to free some of the poisons. Next they are pulped on hand graters and then wrung dry of liquids. The dried pulp must then be ground to a flour and heated to free the remaining volatile poisons. Safe bread can then be baked.

Beans and squashes also underwent domestication by the Indians, ultimately to become with corn "the triumvirate that forms the basis of much of American Indian agriculture." [21]

The roles played by wheat and barley in Europe and Asia Minor and by maize and manioc in the Americas are played by rice in Asia and Indonesia. Dry-rice cultivation is the simpler and more ancient method of growing this staple. Wet rice, grown on irrigated fields or paddies, rewards the great efforts expended in irrigation engineering by producing much larger yields than the more primitive dry-rice techniques. In India and China rice irrigation has replaced dry planting, but in western Indonesia irrigated rice agriculture has not yet reached the interior of the large western islands (Sumatra, Java, Borneo). As practiced by the Siang Dyaks of Central Borneo, whose methods are typical enough, each man selects a sloping plot for clearing and planting. If it is a new one, he cuts partially through the trees on the lower side of the slope. Large key trees at the top of the plot are then felled so as to smash down the lower trees. All are trimmed, left to dry, and after several weeks, burned. In all this he is usually helped by neighbors, whom he must help in turn. Work parties often get drunk on rice wine at lunch time, when the party phase washes out the work aspect of the joint undertaking.

Planting is done by poking holes in the ground with a pointed stick, after which a couple of grains of rice are dropped in. Weeding is done occasionally, but it is so disheartening a task that most gardeners prefer to clear a new field every two or three years. In Borneo, where culture

[20] W. La Barre, "Potato Taxonomy among the Aymara Indians of Bolivia" (*Acta Americana*, Vol. 5, 1947), pp. 83–102.
[21] G. F. Carter, "Origins of American Indian Agriculture" (*American Anthropologist*, Vol. 48, 1946), p. 1.

is primitive and communities small, there is still more than enough land to support this wasteful method of land use.[22]

High cultures enjoy no such margin of safety. The *milpa* system, as it is known among the Mayas, was (and still is) [23] basically similar to the *ku, kaingin,* or *jhum* system, as it is known in Borneo. In J. E. Thompson's account in *The Civilization of the Mayas* we read that

> The Maya system of agriculture was primitive. Land suitable for agriculture was prepared by burning off trees and undergrowth. After the first rains, the sower, with a bag of seed and a sharp-pointed stick, crossed and recrossed the field, making a hole with his stick in the ground at every pace, and throwing a few grains of maize into the pit. . . . At the end of the season the field was abandoned, and next year the Maya farmer marked out a new piece of land to be cleared and sown. In the course of time and with the large increase of population that undoubtedly occurred, the Mayas must have been driven farther and farther afield in search of virgin soil. The exhausted soils nearer home must have been resown after shorter and shorter periods of recuperation. In time the yield of the district would have fallen below the level of consumption, and, faced with evacuation or starvation, the people chose the former.[24]

In this we have one of the theories to account for the decline and abandonment of the great urban centers of the Old Empire of the Mayas (320–890 A.D.). Morley has advanced the theory that intensive slash and burn gardening by the ancient Mayas resulted in the invasion of grasses that converted the tropical forest of southern Yucatan to tough sod savanna. With their primitive dibbles they were unable to pierce the sod, he thinks, and so by the natural consequences of their own efforts, they were driven from their cities.[25] Thompson's present view, however, relies on less direct factors than the effect of *milpa* farming on the soil or vegetation. Old Maya cities were not urban centers of population concentration. They were religious and court centers supported by *milpa* farms more or less evenly distributed for miles around, not clustered like European peasants beneath the walls of citadels. Such a pattern requires a pacifistic state of society. It is quite possible that the upset of the delicate social balance by the introduction of war forced the abandonment

---

[22] J. H. Provinse, "Cooperative Ricefield Cultivation among the Siang Dyaks of Central Borneo" (*American Anthropologist*, Vol. 37, 1939), pp. 77–102.

[23] See R. Redfield, *The Folk Culture of Yucatan*, pp. 115ff.

[24] (Field Museum of Natural History, Anthropology Leaflet 25, 4th ed., 1942), p. 15.

[25] S. G. Morley, *The Ancient Maya*, pp. 71–72.

of Mayan centers in southern Yucatan around 900 A.D.[26] Whatever the true explanation, high cultures rest precariously, if the base is *milpa.*

Wet-rice irrigation was probably developed in India some 3,000 or more years ago, whence it spread into China, Southeast Asia, and western Indonesia. Prior to its penetration of Indonesia, yams, taro, and millet were the staple crops of this part of the world. In the central islands of Indonesia (the eastern Lesser Sundas and the southern Moluccas), American maize introduced in post-Columbian times has won out over rice as the staple crop while in the extreme east, where Indonesia merges into Melanesia, sago prevails. Rice cultivation belongs to the Asiatic, not the Oceanic province.

Wet-rice culture requires extensive water control and irrigation systems, which sustain and require heavy population density combined with societies that are confined to specific localities because of the amount of work that goes into the building and maintenance of the system. The most populous areas of the world are those of wet-rice-growing societies in the Orient.

The economic organization of irrigation cultures is too complex for us to attempt to analyze here. Barton has given us a useful study of the Philippine Ifugaos,[27] to which the reader may refer, and Linton has published some illuminating materials on the social adjustments that were forced when a primitive dry-rice culture changed over to wet-rice techniques in Madagascar.[28]

To an even greater degree than is true of hunting technology, gardening techniques become woven into elaborate tapestries of magic and religion.[29] Gardening gives greater food leeway to man than hunting, but the very fact that it leads to greater populations brings about two direct consequences: (1) There is a greater stake in the success of the food crop; and (2) supernaturalism is embellished as a projective aid to crop security. Where the magician once reigned, the secular experts in the Department of Agriculture now wrestle with the eternal problems of the "ever-normal granary."

[26] J. E. S. Thompson, "A Survey of the Northern Maya Area" (*American Antiquity*, Vol. 2, 1945), pp. 2–24.

[27] R. F. Barton, "Ifugao Economics" (*University of California Publications in American Archaelogy and Ethnology*, Vol. 15, No. 5, 1922).

[28] R. M. Linton, "The Tanala," in A. Kardiner, *The Individual and His Society;* also, *The Tanala, A Hill Tribe of Madagascar* (Field Museum of Natural History, Anthropological Series, Vol. 22, 1933).

[29] Cf. B. Malinowski, *Coral Gardens and Their Magic* for an exhaustive analysis of this aspect of Trobriand culture.

Pastoralism. All gardeners have some domesticated animals. They may or may not be eaten. Indeed, so frequent is the abjuration of the flesh of domesticated animals among their primitive masters that Lowie recently concluded that "the original reasons for keeping animals were not practical ones." [30] Domesticated animals are kept for emotional reasons as pets or as objects of religious sacrifice. However, pigs, goats, and dogs, although not eaten, are not as economically useless as is often imagined. Hambly notes that goats, for instance, are ubiquitous and neglected in Africa; they are neither milked nor used extensively as a meat supply. But "goats pick their own food supply, and since they are almost omnivorous in their selection of vegetable food, there is no cost of maintenance." [31] What Hambly failed to note is that in their omnivorousness goats are good garbage disposers. So are pigs and dogs, a fact which has led Asheley-Montague to suggest this as the original reason for the domestication of dogs in Neolithic times. [32]

The fact that most primitive peoples ignore or are ignorant of the half-dozen practical uses for domestic animals seems to be what led Lowie to his conclusion.

The known utilitarian uses to which domestic animals can be put are (1) consumption of their meat and blood; (2) use of their hides; (3) use of hair or wool for weaving or felting; (4) milking and dairying; (5) load carrying or pulling; (6) riding. [33]

That the Chinese do not milk cattle and will eat no cheese or dairy products (although they are not averse to beef as food), while East Africans make a cult of sour milk religiously and economically along with adoration of sacred cows and just plain cows, is one of anthropology's prize curiosa. Africans, for all their preoccupation with sour milk, never acquired the art of cheese making, and butter is less often eaten than smeared in the hair or used for oiling the body. Beef is eaten only occasionally. Women may toil under heavy loads, but cattle must not be burdened nor set to pulling loads. In East Africa south of Abyssinia, the art of riding is totally unknown to the native peoples. So, although the cult of the cow is the dominant theme of most East African cultures, the use of the cow falls far short of full realization of all potentialities.

[30] R. H. Lowie, *An Introduction to Cultural Anthropology*, pp. 51–53.

[31] W. D. Hambly, "Source Book for African Anthropology" (*Field Museum of Natural History, Anthropological Series*, Vol. 26, Part 2, 1937), p. 596.

[32] M. F. Asheley-Montague, "On the Origin of the Domestication of the Dog" (*Science*, Vol. 96, 1942), pp. 111–112.

[33] C. D. Forde, *Habitat, Economy, and Society*, p. 401.

Of course, we in our use of horses reverse the situation. We ride them, make them haul burdens, and pet them. But we neither milk nor eat them. The Mayor of New York City in 1943 insisted that the eating of horseflesh is "immoral and uncivilized," and upon these lofty if narrow-minded principles he forbade the selling of horse meat as a wartime measure to relieve an acute meat shortage.

Pastoralism is an adjustment to ecological factors on the part of advanced primitives. Forest dwellers cannot become pastoralists, while dwellers in the grasslands and deserts cannot readily become gardeners. Men strive to penetrate all habitable areas of the globe. In dry grass and steppe areas men on the lower levels of economic development may be collectors or hunters. If they move on to higher levels, they must become herders. Only when civilizational techniques produce the plow may agriculturalists successfully move into the more favorable semiarid regions.

Pastoralism is preeminently an Asiatic-African economic complex. In Africa it covers the whole Sahara, where it centers on the camel and horse, as in eastern Arabia. In the northern Sudan and most of East Africa it combines with hoe culture, and in the extreme south the Hottentots and Hereros live on their cattle. The great Asiatic steppes, from the east shores of the Caspian to the boundaries of China, from the Himalayas to the Arctic wastes, support such eminently pastoral peoples as the Finn, Kazak, Tatar, Altai, Kalmuck, and Mongols, and the reindeer-breeding Ostyak, Tungus, Yakut, Yukaghir, Chukchi, Koryak, and others.[34]

In the New World only the Navajos became real pastoralists—and that only in modern times with sheep acquired from the Spanish. In the southern Plains such tribes as the Comanche became quasi herders but not pastoralists in the mid-nineteenth century. Their horse herds numbered in the thousands, but horses were eaten only occasionally, milked never, and used mostly for riding and trade.

Domestication of animals came late in human history. The dim brain of prehistoric man was slow to realize that some animals might better be made slaves to man's will than victims of his weapons. Yet once this realization dawned, in Neolithic times, it became the fashion to experiment with a variety of beasts. But of the hundreds of animal species, although many have been tamed from time to time, less than two dozen have attained any domesticated significance. Of these, the dog alone has world-wide distribution. Otherwise, the llama and alpaca in the Andean highlands, the guinea pig in the Guianas and Andes, and turkeys raised

[34] Cf. N. T. Mirov, "Notes on the Domestication of the Reindeer" (*American Anthropologist*, Vol. 47, 1945), p. 396.

for feathers in the Southwest pueblos complete the list in prehistoric America.

In the Old World, primitive man had the dog, pig, cow, buffalo, yak, camel, horse, reindeer, sheep, goat, ass, chicken, duck, goose, pigeon, and peacock.

No new animals have been brought under human domination since the Bronze Age.

CHAPTER 9

HOUSING

One might think that after a million years of experience man would have mastered the housing problem. The need for shelter is, after all, one of the most elementary of the basic needs of mankind. That the majority of humanity lacks enjoyment of decent, healthy housing is a sad reflection on the seamy side of man's technical and social incapacities. Rural hovels and crowded, dirty city tenements do put a roof overhead, but so does a doghouse. Rationalized, functional dwellings are within human vision but still out of reach for all but a precious few.

In the realm of housing man has remained throughout the ages strangely conservative. Again and again, he has modified his dwellings not at all or only with the most perverse obstinacy when improvements were known or at hand.

Certainly, he has not concentrated his interest or attention on the problem of providing functionally sound housing to anything like the degree of assiduity with which he has attacked problems of myth making, religion, art, song, and dance. If this sounds like gross exaggeration, consider the Navajo in his wood and dirt hogan making intricate sand paintings and performing his nine-day chants. Consider the Australian with his bush windbreak putting on elaborate initiatory rites. Or, consider the earth-lodge Pawnee with his elaborate *hako* ceremony.

It must be concluded that so physically elemental is the need for shelter that it is easily and simply satisfied. The feelings of insecurity and inadequacy that myth, magic, and religion strive to overcome are so deep and diffused that elaborate cultural inventions are devised to satisfy them. Further, man's earliest childhood experiences are closely associated with the particular type of dwelling possessed by his family. Basic habits are linked to a definite form of dwelling. Changes in house patterns mean changes in individual personality and, indeed, in family and kinship structures and function. More than that, changes in house form may very well necessitate changes in the entire societal structure. Navajos, for instance, if they were to give up their widely scattered and separated *hogans* for the consolidated, communal dwellings of the pueblo type, would have to reorganize their lives and stop being Navajos as we now know them. They could not continue under their present amorphous system of social organization nor nurture their individualistic separateness. Contemporary Pueblo Indians, as they become "Americanized," tend to build small individual houses away from the old communal structure. This takes place because in the rural West the original American pattern of separatistic dwellings is still closely tied to personal individualism and family exclusiveness, both important features of American private-property-based society. But at the very time that Pueblo Indians are gradually abandoning their communal apartment houses as a step in Americanization, industrial urbanism is forcing a greater and greater percentage of the American population out of separate dwellings into mass-housing structures.

The intimate and subtle relations between house forms and the functional manifestations of individual, familial, and kinship behavior and the more general aspects of social and economic institutions have been grossly neglected in anthropological and sociological literature. More than half a century ago, Lewis Henry Morgan attempted a pioneer study in the relation between house form and social living.[1] His keen mind perceived the possibility of close interrelations, but his study was vitiated by his preconceptions. His study of house forms and house life was tailored to fit his assumptions. The pertinent presuppositions were: (1) The gens (clan) was universally "the unit of social organization and government, the fundamental basis of ancient society."[2] (2) Since food and house hospitality are universal among American Indians, it follows that the law of hospitality implies common stores and communistic living in large households.[3] (3) "These and other facts of their social condition embodied themselves in their architecture."[4] From these premises Morgan attempted to demonstrate that the housing of the Iroquois, Pueblo Indians, and the Northwest Coast tribes were manifestations of primitive communism. The individualistic Ojibways in their one-family huts gave him a momentary pause. They certainly were not practicing communal living in the nineteenth century, but he thought they must have done so in ancient times.

In all this Morgan grappled with some truth and a large amount of error. Social organization and type of dwelling are interrelated. Emphasis upon kinship tends to gather relatives under a common roof. This, however, is not necessarily a communistic unit. It may be merely a joint-family household. And the clan, as we shall see later (Chap. 18), is not characteristic of the more primitive levels of human society.

[1] L. H. Morgan, "Houses and House Life of the American Aborigines" (*Contributions to American Ethnology*, Vol. 4, 1881).

[2] *Ibid.*, p. 2.

[3] *Ibid.*, p. 61.

[4] *Ibid.*, p. 105.

Somewhat later Wilhelm Wundt [5] expressed a different theory of the influence of dwelling types upon social forms. He observed that occupation of a small cave by a single family must have produced separatistic social attitudes and behaviors. On the other hand, occupation of a large cave by several families would tend to produce the joint family as a communal type of social organization. All subsequent dwelling forms and arrangements, he thought, continue to reflect this basic contrast between the single family unit and the multiple family dwelling. For Wundt the impress of early cave life was indelibly stamped upon subsequent social history.

Caves. Caves have served as homes for man since the earliest Pleistocene times. If not too damp, they serve as comfortable shelters from beast, weather, and prowling enemies. Archaeologists always probe cave sites when looking for remains of ancient man, because the chances of finding some human refuse in a cave are always good. Not that there is the least evidence that primitive men suffered from agoraphobia. Nor is there much empirical evidence to support the psychoanalytical notion that our earliest ancestral dwellings were preferably caves, because in the snug, enveloping darkness of the comfy cavern our unsophisticated ancestors subconsciously recaptured the ineffable sense of security once enjoyed in the prenatal state. For it is, in fact, in the womb alone that the perfect environment is enjoyed. But if a cave was the best adjustment to psychic need that primitive man could work out, his was a sad state indeed.

We need not waste tears over this consideration, however. Although caves have served man well as homes (and the times may yet again come when any number of us will be grateful for a good deep cave), caves are few and men are many. There never were enough to go around. More than that, caves have a number of serious disadvantages as homesteads. They may not be well situated with respect to water and game. They cannot be moved around, and in consequence they inhibit the nomadic tendencies that are so characteristic of collectors and hunters. They are always unhealthy spots. Garbage accumulations are bothersome. If dampness is present, arthritis threatens, as well as rheumatic fever.

No, even Old Stone Age man chose an open camp site, climate permitting. And, by and large, mankind has preferred building shelters and houses to curling up in nature's holes in the ground. After all, our primate relatives do not patronize dens. Every one of them sleeps above ground. Chimpanzees, gorillas, and orang-utans fashion nests on the ground or in trees. Of these the orang does the best job.

---

[5] *Völkerpsychologie*, Vol. 7.

Just before dark the animal stands upright on a forked branch, using one arm as a support and with the other drawing in distant branches, breaking them, and piling them up all around him until he is in the center of a circle of twigs 45 cm. or more in height. He then breaks off smaller twigs and puts them across to form the floor of the nest, next comes a process of stripping leaves from the branches to line the nest. These are pressed into the crevices. Finally, the orang lies down and draws over himself and interlaces the remaining twigs, which are piled up, so that a domelike roof covers him completely.[6]

F<small>IG</small>. 26. Tehuelche Indian family with wind screen. (*American Museum of Natural History*.)

Windscreens. There are no universal house forms among men, but the simplest homes of wandering food gatherers are not much more than nests. Murdock describes the usual Tasmanian shelter as "a simple windbreak, constructed of interlaced boughs or strips of bark in the form of a crescent and open on the leeward side." [7] This is the exact counterpart of the Shoshone windbreak used in summer wanderings. The natives of Patagonia huddled before similar shelters made of skins (Fig. 26). For more permanent settlements beehive-shaped grass houses, called *wickiup*, were the Shoshones' highest attainment in housing.

The Arunta *wurley* is no more than a lean-to constructed of leafy branches laid against a horizontal pole supported in the crotches of two

[6] E. A. Hooton, *Man's Poor Relations*, pp. 124–125.
[7] G. P. Murdock, *Our Primitive Contemporaries*, p. 5.

upright sticks set into the ground 6 to 8 feet apart. In the jungles of the Malay Peninsula Negrito Pygmies build lean-tos of palm leaves on a frame very much akin to the *wurley*. The hut of the African Pygmy is only a dome of light sticks not more than 5 feet high and thatched with broad leaves (Fig. 27).

Huts. Thus the homes of the most primitive peoples of modern times are hardly more ingeniously devised than are the nests of the great apes.

Fig. 27. Congo Pygmies with beehive huts. (*American Museum of Natural History*.)

They are little valued and readily abandoned—hardly to be considered as real property. However, they have possibilities. Elaborations of these little hovels of grass and sticks have served to house the greater part of mankind in the eras of precivilization. Throughout the vast areas of the tropical rain forests and the woodland areas, pole and thatched houses made of vegetation prevail. They may be semispheric domes, as the Ojibway bark *wigwam* or the South African hut of the Zulu and Hottentot. Or they may be cones, as the Shoshonean adaptation of the Plains Indian *tipi*. But more commonly, they will be found to be oblong, gabled structures formed by joining two lean-tos at the ridge in the form of a pup tent. The gabled structure, however, is almost always raised on walls. By such simple means the internal cubage, or volume of usable living space, is greatly increased without much additional effort. The additional effort is nevertheless sufficient that except for certain Mongolian tribes only sedentary peoples expend it. This means that such houses are generally confined to those people who have attained a gardening economy or have a dependable localized source of food such as fish. In Indonesia and Melanesia and again in South America, such houses are raised on stilts as a protection against vermin, flood water, and excessive dampness during the rainy season, and often as a defense against marauders. In the coastal

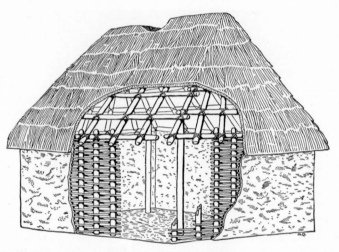

Fig. 28. Construction of the rectangular gable-roofed house with mud-on-wattle walls of the prehistoric Middle Mississippi Indians. (*Chicago Natural History Museum.*)

areas of the Melanesian Islands pile dwellings are commonly built over the waters of lagoons, just as the Neolithic lake dwellers of Switzerland built their homes on the shores of the sub-Alpine waters.

The walls and roofing of primitive houses are variously made of snow, thatch, bark, mats, hides, felt, mud, planks, or stones. Thatch and mats prevail in tropical forest regions (Fig. 28), but in the Puget Sound area mat houses were common for summer use. Bark was extensively used in the eastern (temperate) woodlands of North America. Hides were in common usage on the plains and among Eskimos for summer tents. Felt, used in the same manner as mats or hides, finds preference among Mongols and culturally related Asiatics. Mud is used either as covering for earth lodges in temperate or subarctic regions or as wall material in semi-arid regions where rain will not too quickly reduce such a house to a puddle. Plank houses were concentrated on the Northwest Coast of North America (Fig. 29) and nearby Siberia. Stone houses were built only by extremely sophisticated primitives—Mayas, Aztecs, Incas, *et al.* in Central and South America, Pueblo Indians in the Southwest, and the early predecessors of Mediterranean civilization.

The Pit House. A distinctly different line of development in house forms is to sink the floor of the house into the ground before raising the

Fig. 29. Kwakiutl Indian plank house with totem pole and heraldic paintings. (*American Museum of Natural History.*)

superstructure above it. This technique is adapted to the conditions of temperate climates with cold winters. For obvious reasons, it never occurs in the tropical areas where the ground is too soaking wet. The semi-subterranean house has two advantages: (1) It is easier to keep warm, and (2) it can be made roomy without raising high side walls. The first reason is the functionally effective one, since many primitive people have solved the problems involved in getting sufficient inside height when building above ground.

The earliest known house sites, which date from the Mesolithic period (*ca.* 12,000 B.C.) at Campigny in France and elsewhere, are shallow pits over which half-dome superstructures were apparently raised.

Among recent primitives the pit house has found greatest favor with numerous peoples of western North America.

The description of the pit houses seen by Lewis and Clark just below The Dalles of the Columbia River could very well have applied to the Campignian house types of 14,000 years ago.

They are sunk about eight feet deep [the captains wrote] and covered with strong timbers, and several feet of earth in a conical form. On descending by means of a ladder through a hole in the top, which answers the double purpose of a door and a chimney, we found that the house consisted of a single room nearly circular and about sixteen feet in diameter.[8]

Among the Wishram tribe of the Columbia Basin from one to six families occupied a single house, the size varying accordingly. All the people in the house were related patrilineally. Such houses were used as winter dwellings. In the summer, these people used houses of mats laid over frames.[9]

In northern California only the men's clubhouses (see Chap. 21) are semisubterranean.

Far to the east in the great valley of the Missouri River and its drainage the advanced, sedentary gardeners (the Village tribes of the Plains—Mandan, Hidatsa, Arikara, Omaha, Pawnee) lived in so-called "earth lodges" that were impressive enlargements of the pit-house idea. In construction, a stick was thrust into the ground at the place to be occupied by the fireplace. This served as the focus for a 10- to 30-foot rawhide rope that was used to describe a complete circle. The sod within the circle was removed and the floor was excavated about 1 foot deep. Crotched poles 10 feet high were set within the circle every 8 feet or so and joined with horizontal beams. Midway between this circle of posts and the fireplace four to eight large crotched pillars were raised in a square or circle. These, too, were joined by beams. Posts for an entrance hall were also set. Palisaded walls of split posts were laid against the frame. Long, tapering tree trunks formed the roof. Above the fireplace a 3-foot smoke opening was left. Outside the walls and roof willow withes were horizontally lashed and then covered with a heavy thatch

[8] M. Lewis and W. Clark, *History of the Expedition of Captains Lewis and Clark, 1804-5-6,* Vol. 2, pp. 253–254.

[9] L. Spier and E. Sapir, "Wishram Ethnography" (*University of Washington Publications in Anthropology,* Vol. 3, No. 3, 1930), pp. 202–221.

of coarse grass. Over this was placed a thick coating of sod laid to lap like shingles. Thus by combining logs, thatching, matting, and mud a truly impervious, if lightless, habitation was manufactured. To the Omaha Indians an earth lodge was a mansion, a tangible evidence of social importance, for "the erection of this class of dwelling required considerable labor, hence only the industrious and thrifty possessed these lodges." Others lived in tipis. Usually only one family was housed in a lodge, but if there were two, each took one side.[10]

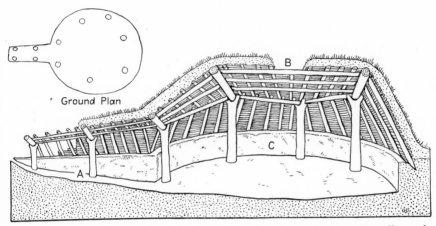

Fig. 30. Cross section and ground plan of a prehistoric pit dwelling, Mogollon culture: A, entrance; B, smoke hole; C, excavated earth wall. (*Chicago Natural History Museum.*)

Pueblos. From pit house to the great five-storied apartment buildings of the Southwest pueblos is a far cry across the span of a millennium.

Three main archaeological patterns of prehistoric culture have been found in the Southwest. The first is the Anasazi, of which the living pueblos of today are a part. Because of its geographical localization on the high plateaus of northern Arizona and New Mexico and southern Utah and Colorado around the Four Corners,[11] it is sometimes referred to as the *Plateau culture*. It must not be confused with the ethnologist's Plateau Culture Area, which is located on the Columbia River Plateau. The second is the Hohokam, also called the *Desert culture*, for its location in the central and southern Arizona deserts. The third is the

[10] A. C. Fletcher and F. LaFlesche, *The Omaha Tribe* (Bureau of American Ethnology, Annual Report 27, 1911), p. 88. See also G. R. Wilson, "The Hidatsa Earthlodge" (*American Museum of Natural History, Anthropological Papers*, Vol. 33, 1934), p. 5.

[11] The only place in the United States where four states touch each other.

Mogollon-Mimbres, also known as the *Mountain culture*, because of its association with the mountainous area of southeastern Arizona and southwestern New Mexico. In their earliest known phases (about 2,000 years ago) each of these cultures included pit houses as the dwelling type (Fig. 30).

The evolution of the Anasazi pattern begins with what is known as

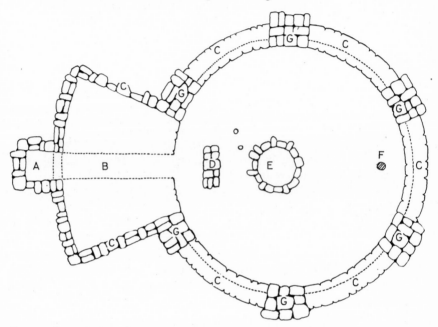

FIG. 31. Ground plan of a Mesa Verde type kiva. This so-called "keyhole" type is said by contemporary Pueblo Indians to represent a kachina mask. (*Chicago Natural History Museum.*)

the *Basket Maker period* (100–500 A.D.). Basket Maker houses were constructed of inclined posts, poles, and twigs laid horizontally to form a dome around and above a saucer-like pit 10 to 20 feet in diameter. The frame was plastered over with mud. These individual houses were built in small groups, either within shallow caves or in the open.

In the succeeding Modified Basket Maker period (500–700 A.D.) pit houses still prevailed. They now consisted of a framework of four or five uprights supporting a flat roof. Entrance was gained either through the smoke hole over the fire pit or through a projecting passageway on the south side of the house. A low ridge of mud separated the south from the north half of the house. A new type of feature that marks this period, however, was the building of long, flat-roofed structures of poles and mud that housed two rows of contiguous rooms. Some of these buildings were in the shape of crescents. Two lines of architectural development had emerged.

In the period of the Modified Basket Maker, the pit houses were used for ceremonial and dwelling purposes. The multiroomed surface houses

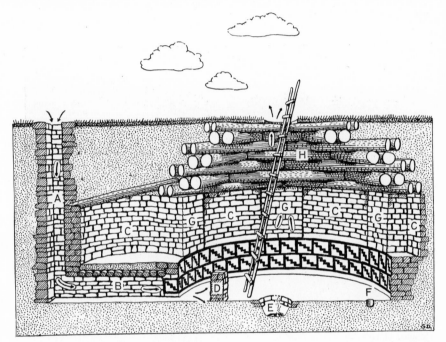

FIG. 32. Cross section of a Mesa Verde type kiva: A, vent; B, air duct; C, wall; D, deflector and back wall of altar; E, fireplace; F, sipapu, or entrance to Underworld; G, pilasters; H, roof timbers. (*Chicago Natural History Museum.*)

were apparently used mostly for storage. Later, in the Pueblo periods, the pit house evolved into the underground ceremonial chamber or *kiva* (Figs. 31 and 32). The above-ground storage rooms became the multiple apartment houses for which the Pueblo Indians are justly famous. The climax was reached between 1000 and 1300 A.D. in the Pueblo III period. To this period belong the famous cities in the caves, including Cliff Palace in Mesa Verde National Park. Of the open sites of this period, Pueblo Bonito in Chaco Canyon, New Mexico, is best known (Fig. 33). These buildings contained hundreds of rooms built of coursed masonry walls rising often to four stories. The modern pueblos are merely shrunken survivals of the great period.

Between the communal houses of the pueblos and the general configuration of Pueblo culture (see pages 445–446) there is a close
nexus. The pueblos of the Great Period were defensive citadels as well
as domiciles. The outer ground-level walls of the open-site pueblos were
blank surfaces with no doors or windows. To get in a house one had to
climb to the roof and go down the smoke hole as in the pit house. To
the hostile outer world the pueblo turned its back. It faced inward upon

Fig. 33. Pueblo Bonito. A Pueblo III ruin, Anasazi culture, Chaco Canyon, New
Mexico. (*Photo by the author.*)

the court in which the public dances of its rich ceremonialism occurred.
The great building formed a compact, architecturally integrated, inturned
whole. The members of the pueblo were forced to live in the closest intimacy with each other; not just the members of one family, but all families, all clans were piled together in a great heap. The cooperative emphasis of Pueblo life was required by the nature of their housing, if
nothing else. And, of course, their housing could not have come into
being had they not simultaneously been developing cooperative values.
But the crowded intimacy of Pueblo living seems also to have left its
impress in the form of excessive touchiness, backbiting, fear of witchcraft, and factionalism. "Chronic cabin fever" is the diagnosis of W. W.
Hill. "Cabin fever" produces centrifugal forces pushing toward breakup
of the pueblo. Well-integrated religio-ceremonial structures counteract
this tendency to a great degree in Pueblo society. In the political sphere,

however, the pueblos have failed in the development of governmental mechanisms that combine reasonably centralized authority with flexibility in the handling of divergent interests. This is, of course, the eternal problem of healthy government. In the case of the pueblos, their compact form of housing contributed to an intensification of the imperative need for political skill.

We would agree with the conclusion of Steward in speaking of the Basket Maker and Pueblo I cultures, "It is difficult to reconcile the division of the early villages into small house clusters with any other social unit than the unilateral lineage or band." [12] Steward and Titiev [13] both suggest that a movement of consolidation of independent clans or bands in Pueblo II times resulted in the building of communal houses. "The formally separated small groups are amalgamated, but do not lose their social and ceremonial integrity." [14] And because these formerly discrete groups did not lose their integrity when compressed into the larger pueblo units, plus the irritability engendered by too close living, vindictive factionalism is an inherent aspect of pueblo life. Quarreling has led again and again to the breakup of pueblos and the establishment of new settlements. The hundreds of ruined pueblos that make the Southwest an archaeologist's paradise are rich testimony to the long Pueblo struggle to adjust their house forms to their social conservatism.

Earlier in this chapter it was remarked that the Navajos could not adopt the pueblo house form and remain Navajos in spirit and action. We have seen something of the difficulty the Pueblo Indians themselves have had to reckon with in the solution of their housing problem. Those who have wondered how it is possible for the Navajos after centuries of contact with the Pueblos—centuries in which they have absorbed much of Pueblo ritual imagery and arts—to live even yet in wretched log and mud hogans, when they have for so long had the exemplar of Pueblo masonry houses before them, may find the answer in the Navajo's devotion to his form of social organization. Present-day Navajo social forms are undoubtedly much closer to the kind of society that was enjoyed by the Basket Maker and Pueblo I peoples than are those of the modern Pueblo Indians. The scattered Navajo communities of individual hogans are not greatly different from the ancient open-site pit-house villages of the Anasazi.

[12] J. H. Steward, "Ecological Aspects of Southwestern Society" (*Anthropos*, Vol. 32, 1937), p. 99.
[13] M. Titiev, "Old Oraibi" (*Papers of the Peabody Museum of American Archaeology and Ethnology, Harvard University*, Vol. 22, No. 1, 1944), pp. 96–99.
[14] *Ibid.*, p. 96.

Joint Family Houses of the Jivaro and Iroquois Indians. The buildings of the Great Pueblo period were properly communal dwellings. Communal houses of a different sort occur in parts of Southeast Asia, South America, and in interior New Guinea. The notorious head-shrinking Jivaros of eastern Ecuador exemplify the South American pattern. The unit of Jivaro social organization is the patrilineal family group living under a single roof. "Such a household is quite independent and self-sufficient, being subservient to no one." [15] The typical Jivaro house is about 75 feet long and some 40 feet wide, elliptical in shape, with parallel sides and rounded ends. The walls are made of 10-foot laths of palm or bamboo lashed vertically to the frame. The roof is thatched. At each end of the house is a door of heavy planks, which must be lifted and set aside to gain entrance. These doors are barred from the inside. An interesting sexual dichotomy reserves one door for men only and the other for women. In like wise, one half of the interior is for men, the other half for women. Each man has his private sleeping platform against the wall on his side; each woman has her platform on the woman's side. Women's platforms are enclosed with mat walls. The men seek no such privacy. Thus, within the *jivaria* separation is based upon sex. Although several conjugal families may be living in a single house, they are not spatially separated on a family basis. Most lamentably, we know nothing about interpersonal relations within the household group, or how the Jivaros manage their sex life.

In Jivaro society there are no clans, villages, or other forms of social organization beyond the isolated household, except a loose and amorphous federation of five or six households under a common war leader.

In the long house of the Iroquois Indians we find an internal organization more typical of joint family households. The structure of an Iroquois long house is something like that of a Quonset hut. A rounded roof of slabs of dried bark is laid on vertical walls. The house may be enlarged or shortened merely by adding or removing sections at either end. Doors are at the ends, with an open passage down the entire house, which in one instance was 100 yards long—the length of a football field. On either side of the passage were cubicles about 12 feet wide and deep, closed on the sides but wide open to the passageway, like the long corridor of bedrooms in the Tuileries. Murdock refers to these as apartments.[16] More seemingly, they were compartments. At the back of each

[15] M. W. Stirling, *Historical and Ethnographical Materials on the Jivaro Indians* (Bureau of American Ethnology, Bulletin 117, 1938), p. 38.
[16] Murdock, *op. cit.*, p. 298.

was a sizable shelf, 6 feet deep and the width of the cubicle. Here a whole conjugal family slept at night. On the back wall was a shelf for utensils, and between each living compartment and the next was a storage closet. A number of closets were kept at either end of the house, too.

Now who lived in this big building, and what were their arrangements? Each long house "belonged" to a lineage of related women.

At the head of the long house was an influential older woman. The household certainly included all her daughters and their husbands and children. It usually included her sisters and their families as well, and also the families of her married granddaughters. All the women of the long house, in theory at least, belonged to the same clan. The long house bore the name and clan insignia of its dominant matrilineal family (except in the case of the somewhat patrilocal Seneca tribe). Married men were supposed to move into the long house of the wife, but the son of an influential mother married to a girl from a family of less account might choose to stay in his mother's home. And, of course, since the Iroquois were given to adoption of captive enemies as replacements for dead relatives, there were always some of these in the household.

The women could throw out their husbands at any time. For the dispossessed divorcé there was nothing to do but to pick up his gear and get. He had no legal claim on children or home.

The social organization of the Iroquois long house was that of a joint matriarchate (see the discussion of the susu, pp. 221–226). Segregation within the long house was not Jivaro-wise by sexes but rather by conjugal families. Each woman with her husband and bratlings had her cubicle. Eating was partly a joint family, partly a separate family affair. Each conjugal family shared a cooking fire with the occupants of the opposite compartment. Down the center of the passageway lay a hearth for each pair of families.

Iroquois long houses could encompass quite a conglomeration of relatives. But they did not pose the onerous dilemma that bedeviled the Pueblos. Living was close, but the entire village was not housed in one building. A village consisted of several to many long houses within a protective palisade. A number of villages together made up a tribe (whereas among the Pueblos each village was usually a tribe in itself). The six original Iroquois tribes made up the Iroquois nation. Loyalties reached out far beyond the lineage group in the long house. Further, the Iroquois were militant expansionists. They could release their internal tensions in outward aggression.

In Southeast Asia, where long houses are common, a recent survey of data has revealed some interesting facts.[17] Long houses tend to be associated with clans. Where the village unit is formed on territorial rather than kinship bonds, as in Java and the Philippines, each family has its own separate house. The lineage and joint family do appear to go together. Morgan had a certain amount of truth to back him up. But lineages and clans do not by any means always live in long houses, while some clanless people do. The relationship is not absolute.

[17] E. M. Loeb and J. O. M. Broek, "Social Organization and the Long House in Southeast Asia" (*American Anthropologist*, Vol. 49, 1947), pp. 414–425.

CHAPTER 10

HANDICRAFTS

The workaday world is the humdrum world of the manipulators of tools. Man is a tool maker and a tool user. There are few operations that he performs with his bare hands or feet.

Dawn man fashioned the first eoliths, the forerunners of the vast fabricating machines of modern technology. From the first clumsy artifacts of a million years ago to the mechanical marvels of the present, man has steadily improved his mechanical devices in a continuous effort to meet his physical needs and psychic wants more satisfactorily.

Stone Implements. Almost all primitive peoples were dependent upon stone as the material from which to make cutting and scraping implements. The greater part of the prehistoric span of man's existence in Europe was the Stone Age. In North and South America, although the peoples of high culture knew metallurgy, it is proper to say that all the Indians were Neolithic men, as were all the Oceanic peoples of the Pacific, although it must be remembered that on coral islands rocks other than flint had to be used. Africa south of the Sudan was given over to tribes with lithic technologies, while many of the Sudanese Negroes were well advanced in ironworking and bronze casting.

Although the course of European Paleolithic and Neolithic cultures has already been indicated, a discussion of stone artifacts is still very much in order.

The most fundamental classification of stone implements is that which draws a distinction between chipped and abraded (polished) artifacts. Method of production is the criterion. We have already seen that chipping was the exclusive stone-working technique of the Old Stone Age. Although it seems most reasonable to suppose that Early Paleolithic men must have experimented with abrasive techniques, the economy of effort found in chipping was sufficient to win preference for that method for hundreds of thousands of years.

Flint, chert, and chalcedony are preferred materials because of their fracture qualities. By percussion delivered by means of a hammerstone, which is a round or ovaloid igneous or metamorphic rock held in the hand, a fresh nodule of flint may be forced to yield flakes from its surface. Since the outer edge of the flake (that which is farthest removed from

131

the point of percussion) is almost always thin and sharp, many flakes may be used as crude cutting or scraping tools with no further preparation. The residual core of the nodule is also suitable for use as a crude ax. Thus are formed the two basic subdivisions of chipped implements, flake and core. The addition of pressure flaking makes it possible for skilled workmen possessing high-quality flint to elaborate specialized forms of flint artifacts. The basic flake implements possessed by almost all primitives are scrapers, points, and awls. Scrapers are used mostly in the preparation of skins or in the shaping of wooden shafts for weapons and tools. Points are used as penetrating heads for various kinds of projectiles (darts, arrows, spears), or as knife blades. Cores may also be worked into scrapers and points, but generally they are shaped to form hand axes or celts.

Abrasion is used to shape rocks that fracture poorly or with great difficulty. The use of wet sand or sandstone is almost an essential for the process. The outer surface of an intended artifact may be worn into shape by rubbing on sandstone or with a piece of sandstone held in the hand. Tough stone is even sawed in two by the use of thin slabs of sandstone or by pouring wet sand under a piece of wood that is rubbed back and forth. Sawing, however, is relatively rare.

Drilling through solid stone has been within the capabilities of most primitive peoples since Neolithic times. The drills are ordinarily nothing but wooden rods or tubes rotated between the hands or by mechanical means. Again, wet sand does the actual cutting. But think how many drills must be used to go through a 2-inch piece of basalt! Although rotation between the hands was unquestionably the most primitive and earliest drill technique, it is probable that Neolithic man hit upon the bow drill, since he had the bow and arrow. Also, in later Neolithic times he produced many polished axheads with drilled transverse haft holes. However, in modern times hand drilling has had a much wider distribution than the bow drill, even among peoples who possess the bow and arrow; thus it by no means follows automatically that the one leads to the other. The trick of the bow drill, as every Boy Scout who has passed his fire-by-friction test knows, is to wind the bowstring once around the drill, hold the top of the drill in a hand socket, then saw back and forth with the bow like a cello player. The Eskimo takes a bite on the socket instead of a handgrip. The strap drill works on the principle of the bow drill except that there is no bow. The ends of the working thong are simply held in the hands and drawn back and forth. Really clever is the pump drill. By first winding up the string on the drill shaft and then pushing the crossbar down, a spin is imparted to the drill. The momentum given to it by the stone or pottery flywheel automatically rewinds the string. Another downward push keeps it spinning.

The process of drilling a hole in a stone hammer head is actually the most advanced technique for hafting purposes. The simplest form of hafting is to bind a strip of sapling around the stone. Elaborations of

FIG. 34. Polished stone ax from the Mount Hagen district, New Guinea. An example of artistic overelaboration of a utilitarian object. (*The Museum of Modern Art.*)

this technique, using cord or rawhide, occur in all parts of the world. An advantageous improvement is to groove the axhead by grinding or pecking in order to give a firmer setting to the head. Staghorn sockets were developed by Neolithic Swiss lake dwellers to form a type of compound hafting for their celts. Elaborate compound haftings are characteristic of eastern New Guinea, where, in the Mount Hagen district, hafted stone axes reach a sublime degree of monstrosity (Fig. 34).

Mauls of stone differ from axes only in that axes are intended for chopping and therefore have sharp edges. Mauls are intended for crushing or driving and therefore have round or blunt edges. What appear to be grooved mauls but yet have no abrasion scars from use as mauls are apt to be either loom or snare weights, or fish-net sinkers.

Other common primitive creations are milling stones consisting of a broad flat base rock, often with a wide shallow groove in it, and an oblong rounded stone with which to crush seeds or nuts. Following the custom of Southwestern archaeologists, the base stone is called a *metate* (Aztec, *metlatl*), while the grinding stone (muller) is called a *mano* (Spanish, hand).

Wooden Implements. In Chap. 4 it was asserted that Stone Age man relied as much upon wood for artifacts as he did upon stone. This statement rests upon inference from recent primitive cultures rather than direct archaeological evidence. Wood is perishable, but all primitives make considerable use of wood. Eskimos use relatively less of it than most peoples, for the simple reason that trees do not grow in the Arctic. Northwest Coast Indians, endowed as they are with excellent workable cedar, have turned wood to an unusually great number of uses. A Northwest Coast inventory would include plank houses, wooden totem poles, adze handles, canoes, paddles, clubs, bows, arrows, helmets and slat armor, bowls, dishes, spoons, boxes, rattles, batons, and masks in a profusion of carved and painted varieties.

Eastern Woodland Indians preferred to use the bark of the birch for canoes, boxes, and housing, while Plains Indians seized upon hides and Pueblo Indians use wood only sparingly. Skillful in pottery, they prefer utensils of clay and homes of adobe and stone. Tropical tribes in Africa, Oceania, and South America, who find themselves in rain forests with plenty of wood at hand, use it extensively. Polynesian wooden clubs are a sophisticated transformation of the caveman's bludgeon (Figs. 35 and 36).

A universal and fundamental use of wood that should not be overlooked is in firemaking. We have discussed the drill as a stone perforator. It is even more widely used as a fire starter in America, Asia, and Africa. By setting the drill in a wood socket and pouring dry tinder about it, it is possible to generate enough heat by friction to start a fire. Hand rotation, strap, bow and pump methods are all used. The fire-plow is a simpler but less efficient device. Named by Tyler the "stick and groove method," the implement consists of a grooved board lying on the ground and a blunt stick, which is pushed back and forth with vigorous pressure until friction-generated heat kindles fire—a method concentrated primarily in Polynesia. In Indonesia a variant form is preferred, the fire saw. In this method a piece of split bamboo is sawed so rapidly that the dust ignites.

Bone and Shell. The skeletons of vertebrates and the shells of crustaceans find their uses in primitive material culture. The reader will remember that one of the earliest artifacts from the Piltdown deposits is a pointed implement fashioned from the thighbone of the Southern elephant (Fig. 14). Unworked shells make serviceable if not durable scrapers and saucers. Caribbean Indians rubbed heavy seashells into polished celts like those of stone. The long bones of birds and animals splintered and polished to a smooth point have always found favor as

Fig. 35. Carved Maori war club, New Zealand. (*Peabody Museum of Salem.*)

Fig. 36. Carved Fijian war club. (*The University of Pennsylvania Museum.*)

perforators and awls, and the earliest needles were always made of slivers of bone. Fishhooks made of bone occur almost everywhere. Harpoon heads of bone, antler, or ivory were characteristic of Magdalenian man and Eskimos alike.

One of the most interesting bone implements is the garden hoe produced by Indians in the eastern Plains area from the shoulder blade of the bison. The scoop-shaped scapula was lashed at right angles to a wooden handle and used exactly as we use a hoe today. Alaska Eskimos use whale scapulas as handleless snow shovels.

Traps. Traps and deadfalls have been previously mentioned as primitive food-getting devices. The ingenuity of such machines, as in the

Arawak Indian bow-and-arrow trap shown in Fig. 37, occasionally reaches Rube Goldberg proportions. This is an unusual variation of the much more common spring trap in which the animal puts his head in a noose to get the bait, releases the trigger, and is hoisted, if not by his own petard, at least in consequence of his own action. Deadfalls are forms of traps in which the animal who tugs at the bait releases a trigger that literally brings down the roof on his head.

Fish weirs, commonly used on the west coast of North America, in South America, and the African Sudan, consist of fencelike obstructions across a river or lagoon designed to lead the fish through a funnel into

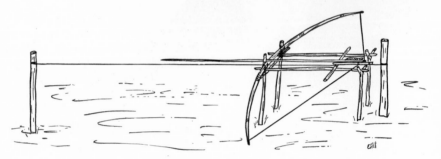

FIG. 37. Arawak Indian bow-and-arrow-set trap.

a large basket or crib. Although he can wriggle into the funnel, the poor fish cannot reenter the narrow spout.

To detail all the trap forms devised by clever primitives is an impossibility here. It is probable that all recent primitives have utilized some means of trapping or snaring animals. It is also likely that man in the Early Paleolithic was already cheating his dim-witted animal brethren with crude but carefully prepared snares.

Bags and Baskets. All human beings have need of artificial containers. Skin pouches or bags may serve to meet this need, as evidenced by the hand or shoulder bag of modern woman and the brief case of the lawyer or professor. Primitive containers may also be made of wood or of plastics, such as clay. But of all these possibilities, baskets, which are containers made of interwoven reeds, grass, or shredded bark (bast), have by far the widest distribution.

Basket making is a truly ancient craft. Direct archaeological evidence yields basketry remains from the Neolithic sites of Europe, and in the Southwest elaborate basketry skill gave the Basket Maker name to the potteryless pre-Pueblo inhabitants of the area.

The simplest basketry container (made by the marginal food collectors, the Fuegians and other southern South Americans, the Australians and Bushmen) is a loose, open-weave bag such as that used to package onions and oranges in the United States.

Bags of genuine netting are not so much woven as worked out in crochet patterns. *Knotless netting*, as this technique is called, occurs throughout a large part of the Western Hemisphere and in Oceania and Australia (Fig. 38).[1]

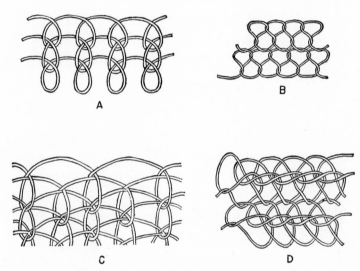

Fig. 38. Knotless netting: A, half hitch around a half hitch; B, hourglass pattern; C, half hitch through a half hitch with two alternating and intertwining strands; D, hourglass with lower loop interlocking with two adjacent loops to the right. (*After Davidson.*)

A basket differs from a bag in that it is at least semirigid if not actually stiff. It is built upon its own frame, or its foundation is formed as it is made. The body is produced by the interlocking of long strips or threads of fibrous materials in the form of dried reeds, grasses, split cane, or shredded bark. Basketry materials can be found in all environments inhabited by man.

Plaiting. The technologically simplest basket-making method is that of wickerwork or plaiting. Every reader of this book has done plaiting with paper in kindergarten. It is the alternating over-and-under technique (Fig. 39c). However, virtuosity such as that displayed by the Hopi of

[1] D. S. Davidson, "Knotless Netting in America and Oceania" (*American Anthropologist*, Vol. 37, 1935), pp. 117–134.

Third Mesa [2] in producing wicker trays of sumac and rabbit brush is not kindergarten work. In method, plaiting and wickerwork are alike, except that plaiting is work in very soft and pliable materials and wickerwork makes use of stiff materials.

Twilling. Twilling is plaiting with variations. Instead of plaiting in and out, over one under one, the basket maker goes over two or more

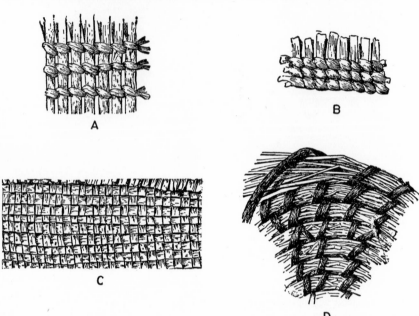

Fig. 39. Basketry techniques: A, open twining; B, close twining; C, plaiting; D, coiling. (*After Wissler.*)

strands and under two or more. Each row is offset from the one next to it, so the effect produced is that of a series of staircases or slanting lines.

Wrapping. Wrapping utilizes a slightly different technique. The foundation of the basket consists of stiff parallel rods. A pliable strand is turned or wrapped once around each rod in a continuous series. It is a basket-making method that is relatively little used.

Twining. This is a step more complicated. In its simplest form two strands of pliable material are simultaneously woven in and out between parallel foundation strands. As each strand is passed between two foundation strands (from over to under and vice versa), it is given a half twist

[2] The Hopi villages are located on three mesas in northeastern Arizona. From east to west the mesas are named First, Second, Third.

(Fig. 39*a*). The foundation strips are thus firmly bound on both sides in a way that gives much strength to the weaving. Soft grasses or strips of rabbit fur twined in this way produce a cloth-like material. In fact,

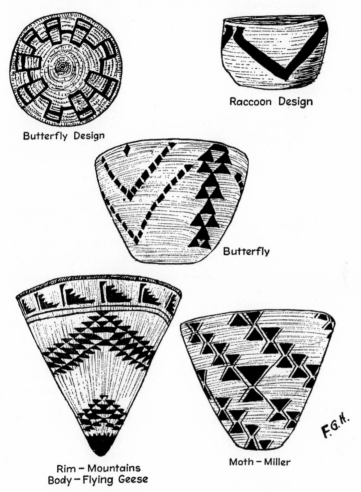

Butterfly Design

Raccoon Design

Butterfly

Rim – Mountains
Body – Flying Geese

Moth – Miller

FIG. 40. Basketry designs of the Maidu Indians of California. (*After Boas.*)

twined rabbitskin robes to be worn in the winter were the sole clothes of many peoples of the Great Basin and California.

Coiling. Coiling is the most sophisticated and painstaking of all basketry methods. As a technique it has little in common with plaiting, twilling, and twining, except the use of a foundation of one or more rods or a bundle of grass. Presumably it represents a distinct inventive idea. A spiral coil of the foundation material is built up like rope coiled un the deck of a ship by a careful sailor. It is permanently bound by a strand of pliable material wrapped around the bundle that is to be sewed into position. A hole is then punched through the outer edge of the coil already in place. The binding strand is pushed through this hole and back up around the outside coil to hold it in place. Figure 39d shows this method better than words describe it.

Coiled basketry has a sporadic distribution about the surface of the globe that suggests independent invention in several areas. A continuous distribution occurs from northeast Asia through Alaska, down through the Mackenzie-Yukon area into the Great Basin, California, and the Southwest. In extreme isolation, the Labrador Eskimos and the Tierra del Fuegians also make it. In the Old World the coiling technique occurs in Africa, Indonesia, and Australia.

Twined and coiled baskets are used to hold not only dry stuffs but also water. To carry water in a basket may seem as silly as bailing with a sieve, but if baskets are closely woven and sealed with clay or pitch, they will do. The Shoshone Indians make their drinking-water baskets slightly permeable like Western water bags. Enough liquid seeps through to keep the water cool by evaporation, and a gentle flavoring of pine gum makes a delectable desert drink.

In North America there is a close association between tightly twined and coiled basketry, and stone boiling as a method of cookery. Preheated stones are grasped with wooden tongs and held in the basketful of water. The heat of the stones brings the water to a boil. In the Plains area a pouch of skin suspended on four stakes was used in the same way.

Conversely, where pottery is well developed, basketry is not used for cooking purposes. Once the techniques are known, pottery is quicker and easier to make than baskets. More than that, it is more efficient for cooking purposes, since it may be put directly over the fire.

The Pomo Indians of California are acclaimed as the world's finest basket makers. They not only used the three basic basket techniques, but they practiced five kinds of twining (plain, diagonal, three-strand, three-strand braided, and lattice). Coiling was done on a one- or three-rod base. The variety of forms, however, is too great to describe here.[3]

There are also many modifications on the basic patterns practiced by various people in different parts of the world. The reader interested in

[3] See S. A. Barrett, "Pomo Indian Basketry" (*University of California Publications in American Archaeology and Ethnology*, Vol. 7, 1908).

the details should go to the classic work of Mason on American Indian basketry.[4]

Pottery. The making of pottery is one of the higher accomplishments of primitive life. Paleolithic man never achieved it, for not until Neolithic times, some 15,000 years ago, was the first pottery invented. The earliest migrants to North America left Asia before the technique of pottery making had spread to Siberia. There are no shards associated with early prehistoric finds on this continent. Not until the Modified Basket Maker period (500–700 A.D.) did the people of the Anasazi culture, who were later to become such skilled potters, get their start on ceramic vessels.

In Central America and the Andean region archaic pottery horizons are earlier by perhaps a thousand years. It is most likely that pottery was independently invented in one or another part of this area, whence it spread out to other parts of the New World. Patagonians and Tierra del Fuegians never received the invention, while basket-making Californians and Shoshoneans rarely found the urge to copy their neighbors in the Southwest. Northwest Coast Indians were satisfied with their baskets and wooden boxes, while other Indians of the Canadian woodlands utilized bark utensils. Thus, the extreme western and northern areas of North America were never penetrated by pottery, except for the western fringe of Alaska, where pottery forms diffused from Siberia in relatively recent times.

All peoples of Africa make some pottery, but it has received scant attention as an artistic craft on that continent where woodworking, metalworking, and weaving are of more interest to the natives.[5]

The potter's art extends across Asia through Indonesia into the Pacific. Good pottery is made in Melanesia and Guam, and Pelew and Yap in western Micronesia, but to most Micronesians and the Polynesians it became a lost art—and for good reason.

Many unthinking people [says the Maori anthropologist Te Rangi Hiroa (Peter H. Buck)] have criticized our Polynesian ancestors for their lack of pottery and loom weaving. . . . Pottery was made in Fiji; then why, ask our critics, was it not made in Tonga and Samoa? The answer is absurdly simple—

---

[4] O. T. Mason, *Aboriginal American Basketry* (United States National Museum, Report, 1904), pp. 171–548. For a discussion and analysis of ethnological problems in basketry, see G. Weltfish, "Prehistoric North American Basketry Techniques and Modern Distributions" (*American Anthropologist*, Vol. 32, 1930), pp. 454–495.

[5] Omitted from the scope of this statement are the ancient civilizations of the Lower Nile and Asia Minor.

there is no clay in Tonga and Samoa. . . . The distribution of clay in the Pacific ends with the continental islands of Fiji.[6]

Polynesians hit upon the substitute device of the stone oven for cooking purposes.

In general, except for the gap just mentioned, the distribution of primitive pottery follows the distribution of gardening and agriculture. Food gatherers and hunters are too far removed from the centers of pottery invention to have received the art by diffusion, or, because of their nomadic life, they have rejected clay pots as too burdensome.

Pottery Techniques. A primitive potter must successfully complete six steps in the making of even the simplest pot:

1. She must know where to find decent clay. Surely the reader as a child has hopefully made at least one crude clay vessel only to have it crack and crumble upon drying. Clay is a disintegrated pelitic rock consisting essentially of hydrous aluminum silicate with various impurities. The relative proportions of silica and aluminum oxide plus the nature and quantity of the impurities determine the quality of the clay for pottery purposes.

2. The clay must be prepared: (*a*) Most primitive potters first dry the clay and then pulverize it so that coarse extraneous materials may be sifted out. Clay of homogeneous texture is thus procured. (*b*) The mechanical and chemical composition of the clay is usually adjusted by the addition of tempering materials, which may be powdered shell, mica, quartz, sand, or even crushed potsherds. Tempering serves to give the clay a workable and binding consistency. It also prevents cracking and checking on drying. Archaeological specimens indicate that the earliest Neolithic potters did not add artificial temper to their clay. (*c*) The clay must be moistened to a proper working consistency.

3. The clay must next be shaped into a vessel.

4. After this is completed, the pot must be air dried.

5. Decoration, if any, is applied before or after air drying, depending upon the nature of the decorative process. Glaze may be added at this point.

6. The final and critical step is the firing of the pot.

Steps 3, 5, and 6 deserve to be discussed in some detail. In shaping a pottery vessel there are three possible techniques, all of which were known to primitive man. The least used, but possibly the oldest, is to mold the clay about a basket or gourd, which is burned out in the firing process. This method is wasteful of labor and baskets, truly a long way

---

[6] P. H. Buck, *Vikings of the Sunrise*, p. 46.

to a pot. Modeling may be either from a solid lump of clay or from built-up coils that have been rolled out like long snakes. Either process may be done with or without a paddle and dolly. And either method may be used with or without a potter's wheel.

The potter's wheel need not be a true wheel, *i.e.*, it does not have to be round in circumference; it can be a square platform—or octagonal. But it must embody the basic principle of the wheel, namely, a plane rotating on an axle. This principle no American Indians, not even the sophisticated Mayas, Incas, or Aztecs, were ever able to discover for themselves. Hence, all Indian potters were wheelless.

In the Old World the potter's wheel appears to have been invented in Egypt some 5,000 years ago. It spread throughout Bronze Age Europe and eastward through India.

In the use of the wheel, the lump of clay is centered directly over the axle, and in the hands of a skillful worker the revolving mass seems miraculously to grow up and out into a vase.

In the coiling of pottery a piece of clay is always first laid down as a base. Pueblo Indians start the bottom coils in a tray or pottery bowl to provide a support and a turning base. Other peoples invariably use a flat rock or piece of board. If the pot is a large one, when the side walls are half built it must be set aside to dry for a while in order to become stiff enough to hold its shape. When the whole pot has dried to a leathery consistency, it is pressed smooth with the worker's fingers or with a rounded dolly of stone or clay held against the inside wall, while the outer surface is patted or rubbed into shape.

Attractive corrugated ware for household use was made by prehistoric Pueblo Indians, who instead of obliterating the coils, pinched or pressed down the outer rounded edges.[7] A much more primitive decorative device was to pat the surface of the pot with a cord-wrapped paddle, imparting to it a textilelike surface.

In the European Neolithic, cord imprints were applied in horizontal series to what the Germans have called *Schnurkeramik*. The other great class of European Neolithic pottery was produced by scratching in bands of incised lines or punctate dots, the so-called *Bandkeramik*.

More sophisticated artisans obtain decoration through slip, painting, method of firing, and sculpture. A slip is a surface wash of very fine clay which when baked produces a smooth finish. Use of a clay of different composition from the body produces a different exterior color.

---

[7] See R. Bunzel, "The Pueblo Potter" (*Columbia University Contributions to Anthropology*, Vol. 8, 1929) for a comprehensive analysis of an important pottery complex.

Painted designs are put on before firing. The paint changes color in baking.

All primitive pottery is baked or fired, but a kiln is not necessary for this purpose, and few primitive potters have them. Several pots are fired at once to save labor. They are simply piled up in inverted fashion (the bottom ones resting on rocks) and covered with a heap of wood or dry dung, if that is available. The latter makes a very hot fire; even without the use of bellows, temperatures of 1200 to 1700F. are produced.

If the potter wants to turn out creamy ware or shades of buff, brown, orange or red, she does not inhibit or smother the fire. Without knowing exactly what happens in chemical terms, she does know that plenty of air produces those colors, dependent upon the chemistry of the clay. All combustible materials in the clay are oxidized. If she wants black pottery, she smothers the fire with wet grass, peat, wood, or powdered dung. The oxygen in the clay is driven out by reduction, and carbon deposited by the smoke produces black coloration.

Glazing was known to few primitives. It is attained by applying a slip or painted design of lead oxide, silica, or salts in solution. At high temperatures they fuse and impart a glassy luster.

The final technical step in pottery making (porcelain) was never attained by any primitive people. Invented by the civilized Chinese, who developed it into a high art imitated by Europeans, chinaware is nothing but very thin pottery made of pure pipe clay (kaolin) fired at such high temperatures that it fuses throughout.

In Africa a very few closed families of artisans among the Ashanti and at Bida in Nigeria make glass beads and bangles. The origin of the industry or its antiquity are unknown, but it is not likely to have been a native invention.

Weaving. Weaving is an outgrowth of netting and basketry. Its product is textile fabric. It differs from basketry in that the strands used are so pliable and fine that they must be worked on a loom,[8] which is a device for holding the warp[9] threads taut. Such strands are, of course, string or thread made of animal or vegetable fibers. They may also be narrow strips of fur, although woven fur robes are not considered to be true cloth.

The manufacture of twine is a universal trait of human culture. By the most primitive method fibers are simply rolled between the palms or between the thigh and the hand. Spindles were independently developed

---

[8] Knitting and crocheting are special forms of close netting, not weaving.

[9] The *warp* is the group of parallel-lying foundation threads over and through which the *weft*, or *woof*, is woven at right angles.

in Egypt, and much later in Central and South America. The primitive spindle is nothing more than a long narrow stick with a stone or pottery collar near one end to keep the thread from running off. A rough string of fiber wound several times about the spindle and held taut with the left hand is tightly twisted and simultaneously wound around the spindle, which is spun with the right hand. Several spinnings are needed to produce an even thread.

In spite of the fact that cord or thread making is universal, weaving is not. Although an ancient art in the Mediterranean area, India, Indonesia, and prehistoric Europe, it did not extend deeply into the tropical forests of Africa (although it is practiced in the Sudan), nor was it known to the Bushmen. We have already noted that, like pottery, it was a lost art in Polynesia, where its absence was adequately met by bark cloth (as also in the African Congo). In Melanesia a limited amount of weaving was done, but here, too, the preference was for bark cloth. There was no weaving in primitive Australia.

In the Americas, the Andean region around 1200 A.D. became the center for some of the finest and most complicated hand-woven fabrics the world has ever known. The direction of the textile industry became one of the chief interests of the Inca government, which levied taxes, fines, and tribute in cloth. Great stores of perfect cloth, well-preserved in the high dry climate, have been recovered by modern archaeologists and collectors.

Archaeological stratigraphy gives a clear sequence for the development of looms in this area. The belt loom was the earliest (Mochica culture, 600–700 A.D.). It was followed by a horizontal frame loom supported on stakes, which is to this day preferred by Aymara Indians in their loom work. Finally, it was followed by a vertical four-pole frame loom built against the wall.

From the Inca center true loom weaving is distributed north and south along the Andean cordillera, up through Central America and Mexico into the Southwest. Simple frame weaving is done in the Amazonian basin, as is also belt loom work; frame weaving occurs in the Gran Chaco and the Pampas but disappears completely in the extreme south. Native American cotton is the chief material used from the Southwest down through South America.

Weaving was absent in California and the Plains area, but very primitive "suspended warp" weaving was done on the Northwest Coast and in the woodlands of the Mississippi Valley and the Southeast.

Suspended warp weaving is done without a true loom. It calls for finger weaving without the aid of a heddle. Chilcat blankets from the

Northwest Coast are the most famous product of this kind of weaving (Fig. 41). The warp of shredded cedar bark is suspended free-hanging from a horizontal pole supported on two uprights. The weaving is done from top to bottom as the weaver works the woolen weft in and out with her fingers.

True looms must meet two needs: (1) They must keep the warp taut; and (2) they must have some arrangement whereby a whole group

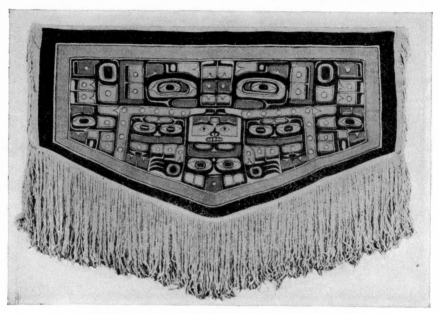

Fig. 41. Chilcat blanket. (*American Museum of Natural History.*)

of warps can be lifted at once, so that the weft may be passed through the *shed* (the open space between the lifted warps and the dormant ones) in one movement. When the lifted wraps are released, the shed closes as they fall back into place and the weft falls automatically into its over-and-under position.

The device that performs this function is known as the *heddle*. There must always be at least two heddles to any loom. The most primitive heddle is a simple stick, which need be only a little wider than the web (the breadth of the warps). One heddle is passed under every alternate warp. The remaining warps are tied to the second heddle. By alternately lifting each heddle, the warps can be shifted for simple weaving. After the weft is passed through the shed by means of a *bobbin*, it is hammered tightly against the woven material with a flat stick (the batten) or a comb. Design patterns are woven in by use of more than two heddles or by laying in differently colored wefts and warps.

The belt or waist loom solves the problem of warp tension by tying one end of the loom to a pole and the other to a belt around the weaver's waist. Larger looms may have a four-pole frame, or the warp poles may be lashed to ceiling or floor.[10]

Felting. If weaving and spinning are a way to interlock fibrous materials to form a compact cloth covering, so is felting, in which animal wools are matted together by wetting, beating, forming in sheets, compressing, and drying.

Because of the relatively greater complexity of the weaving process, it was at one time assumed that felt was the earlier invention. But the world-wide distribution of weaving as against the limitation of felting to Asia and Europe makes it clear that felting is a special and later invention. For all their skill in weaving, and in spite of the fact that they possessed an excellent supply of wool in the llama and alpaca, the Andean Indians never felted at all. Of course, felting is possible only where woolly animals provide a source of materials.

Bark Cloth. In such tropical areas as Indonesia, Oceania, Central Africa, and Central and South America, bark fibers are used as equivalents of wool. The principle underlying the manufacture of felt and bark cloth is the same: a sheet of material is produced by matting fibers so tightly that they adhere permanently. However, geographical distribution and analysis of the complexes make it quite clear that bark-cloth manufacture was independently invented and not derived from felting or vice versa.

A full comparative study of bark-cloth techniques in all parts of the world is yet to be done.[11] But in general the process is the same everywhere. The fibrous inner bark of a suitable tree such as the paper mulberry (which is cultivated for the purpose in Polynesia) is stripped, scraped, and beaten out with a grooved wooden mallet or paddle on a wood anvil. It may or may not be soaked in water as a part of the preparatory process. Where it is, there is no limit to the size of the cloth

[10] *Cf.* C. Amsden, "The Loom and Its Prototypes" (*American Anthropologist,* Vol. 34, 1932), pp. 216–235.

[11] An excellent prototype of such a study was done by Raymond Kennedy, who demonstrates that the internal congruity of technical steps and linguistic terminology associated with bark-cloth manufacture in Polynesia and Indonesia is such that it must be inferred that Polynesian bark-cloth manufacture originated in Indonesia. See his "Bark Cloth in Indonesia" (*Journal of the Polynesian Society,* No. 172, 1934).

that can be made, since one piece may readily and effectively be "felted" into another.

Indonesians and Polynesians decorate their *tapa* cloth with stamped designs carved into wooden blocks and printed over the surface of the material in brown vegetable dyes (Fig. 42). Polynesian block-print designs have come recently into fashion in California play-clothes cottons.

Fig. 42. Samoan bark cloth or tapa. (*American Museum of Natural History.*)

Metallurgy. Metallurgy is scarcely a primitive craft, for it requires the kind of technical knowledge that is more closely allied to civilization than to savagery. Yet preliterate people do acquire metalworking. This was probably true of the North Europeans of the prehistoric epochs of Bronze and Iron. It was true of the African Negroes of the nineteenth century and also of the Peruvian Indians and Indonesian peoples. All were close to the threshold of civilization.

The beating out of gold nuggets or chunks of pure copper does not constitute metallurgy. Indians in the copper-rich regions of Lake Superior made tubular arrow- and spearheads of beaten native copper. Copper pieces are found in mounds of the prehistoric Hopewell culture of

Illinois and Ohio. Eskimos fashioned a few rare tools out of the iron residue of meteorites found on the frozen surface of the ground. But not a single North American Indian knew how to smelt a metal.

The Mexicans, who knew how to melt gold nuggets with the aid of blowpipes, came close to the secret of the reduction of ores. The Peruvians found the secret in the smelting of copper and tin, which were mined from hills looked upon as sacred shrines. Inca metalworking processes included smelting, alloying (bronze), casting, hammering, repoussé, incrustation, inlay, soldering, riveting, and cloisonné.[12] Skill in goldworking by the highly honored profession of goldsmiths was the bait that brought the gold-greedy conquistadores down upon the hapless Indians.

The Negroes of Africa concentrated upon the more prosaic tools of the blacksmith's forge. From iron smelted in little furnaces with hand bellows they shaped such utilitarian tools as knives, adzes, axes, and hoes. However, bronze casting in West Africa reached a peak of artistic perfection in the work of the Bina at Benin that has made the Benin masks precious collectors' items. The Benin method of casting is the "lost wax" or cire-perdue technique in which a model is first made of wax and then covered with clay. The wax is then melted out to make room for the molten metal. When the clay molds are broken, the casting is freed.

[12] J. H. Rowe, "Inca Culture at the Time of the Spanish Conquest," in *Handbook of South American Indians*, Vol. 2, p. 246.

CHAPTER 11

CLOTHING AND ORNAMENT

Man is a rebel against nature. He is prone to accept few things as they come. In all matters it is his irrepressible belief that by his tinkering he can improve upon them. His instrument is culture.

In all times and climes, man undertakes to effect what he vainly believes are improvements upon his bodily appearance. His sartorial accomplishments, both primitive and civilized, are wonderful if not always beautiful to behold. The time and effort that has gone into painting, pricking, scarring, puncturing, and otherwise mutilating and deforming the human body for aesthetic and status reasons is beyond all calculation. We shall leave it to sociologists and economists to conjure up their guesses as to how many billion dollars are spent per year on clothes and cosmetics in this most advanced of civilizations. Suffice it that in the critical year of 1947 one of the burning American issues was whether the American woman would or would not take on a "new look." As if there could have been any doubt about it!

The Naked Savage. People who wear little or no clothing are no contradiction to what has just been said. Be man ever so unclothed, he is never unadorned. If he wears not so much as a G-string, he certainly sports a nose, ear, or lip plug, or bears his tattoos or scarifications, or paints his face, or curls his hair or cuts it off, or blackens his teeth, or knocks them out, or perhaps merely files them to a point.

The sense of modesty is merely a habit, no instinct. The discomfiture that is felt when one's sense of modesty is disturbed is a diffused neurophysiological upset of a large part of the nervous and organic system, shock-stimulated by a behavior situation that contrasts sharply with those to which a person has been intensely habituated. And of course, there is more than the element of mere habit in the total situation. There has also been a strong ideational indoctrination that penalties, social or supernatural, accompany any departure from the habituated pattern. Apprehension of dire consequences contributes much of the tone of fear and anxiety that colors the feelings of immodesty.

To this day, old-timers among Comanche males feel acutely uncomfortable and indecent if they thoughtlessly go out without a G-string, even though fully clothed in American store pants and shirt.

150

A favored tale among anthropologists is that of Baron von Nordenskiold, who in his Amazonian travels undertook to purchase the facial plugs of a Botocudo [1] woman, who stood all unabashed in customary nudity before him. Only irresistible offers of trade goods at long last tempted her to remove and hand over her labrets. When thus stripped of her proper raiment, she fled in shame and confusion into the jungle. After all, the close identification between the Botocudo as a person and the *botocudo* as a plug is such that to become unplugged is most un-Botocudo.

Such circumstances make it perfectly clear that the use of clothing does not rise out of any innate sense of modesty, but that modesty results from customary habits of clothing or ornamentation of the body and its parts.

Among primitive peoples the use or nonuse of clothing is more or less functional, although not wholly so. People who dwell in the tropical rain forests tend to get along with a minimum of clothing. This is true in Africa, the Americas, and Oceania. Generally, however, the men wear some sort of a pubic covering, a suspensory or supporter. It is hardly necessary to seek magical reasons for the widespread use of this device, as was done by the early anthropologist Waitz,[2] and after him by Sumner.[3] It is a practical device that lends physical comfort. Notions of mystic shielding of the male sex organ from evil influences, if they exist, are more likely to be secondary developments. Certainly, the conspicuous coverings of gleaming shells, gourds, bark, hide, cloth, or grass do not serve to divert attention but rather to attract it.

An alternative to the rigid sheath is a small apron of leather, grass, or cloth worn in front, or fore and aft, or between the legs and about the waist. Such a garment is frequently worn by women as well as men. It is the basic, and often the only, bit of clothing for most primitive peoples.

When warmth is needed, something more must be added. Most races of mankind are so relatively hairless as to need artificial insulation. Hence, we rob the animals of their hairy covering—skin and all. The

---

[1] "The *Botocudo* owe their name to the large cylindrical wooden plugs worn by men and women alike in the ear lobes and lower lips. These cylinders, of light wood (*Chorisia ventricosa*), were 3 to 4 inches (7.6 to 10 cm.) in diameter and 1 inch (2.5 cm.) thick. The ears were perforated at the age of 7 or 8, the lips a few years later." A. Metraux, "The Botocudo," in *Handbook of the Indians of South America*, Vol. 1, p. 534.

[2] F. T. Waitz, *Anthropologie der Naturvölker*, Vol. 6, pp. 575–576.

[3] W. G. Sumner, *Folkways*, pp. 432, 456.

trapper flays the beast and prepares the hide, the tailor shapes it, and the lady of fashion slips the skins of animals over her own when she makes her winter excursions. Wool coverings are also produced at the expense of animals, but not necessarily by lethal methods.

Shoshoneans weave rabbitskin robes, as did the early prehistoric Basket Makers. African Bushmen provide themselves with skin cloaks. The Yahgan of Tierra del Fuego wore a small sealskin, sea-otter, or fox cape as the sole protection against a nasty subantarctic climate—except for a small pubic covering worn by women. The Ona of the same area and the nearby Tehuelche (Fig. 26) sported longer and larger capes. The Tasmanians wore no proper cloak, but the men were given to draping and tying sundry strips of fur around their shoulders and limbs. For the most part, the Tasmanians smeared themselves with grease and red ochre as proof against cold, as did also the Fuegians. The Central Australians, like the Tasmanians, deviate from the norm of collectors and gatherers who live in the temperate zone in that they have no cloaks. They seem never to have hit upon the idea of wearing skin for clothing. For the men a conspicuous pubic tassel suspended from a belt of human hair plus arm bands of twisted fur suffice. A woman is dressed if she has a string of beads around her neck.

When we turn our attention once again to South America, we find that the fur mantle is worn by Patagonians and Indians of the Gran Chaco in inclement weather. The famous woven wool ponchos of the Andean Indians are undoubtedly a cultural elaboration of this more primitive covering.

In North America, the buffalo-hide robe of the Plains Indians was also a form of cape, a large one, later to be replaced by the trader's blanket, which is to this day the symbol of the conservative Indian, the "blanket Indian," who clings to the old ways. Even in rugged Northeastern Woodlands the draped robe was the chief item of winter clothing, besides leggings and moccasins. In the Southeastern states the natives went naked except for a loin cloth. When cold did sweep down from the north, they, too, cast on a loose robe or cape of fur.

The Tailored Man. Tailoring, it may be seen from our remarks, was not one of the more widely esteemed human arts. Most of mankind, including such sophisticates as the Greeks and Romans and the late Mahatma Gandhi, have done quite well without it. The feature that is unique about tailoring is that by means of sewing, clothing may be made more or less to fit the human frame. The very idea of tailoring is "fit," and "well-tailored" means more fit rather than less. In temperate and arctic climates it is functionally advantageous to have tailored clothes.

The insulating efficiency of clothing is greatly enhanced by the closed, tubular effect of the tailored garment, which gives little room for the play of chilly breezes upon the body. In the tropical rain forest or torrid desert the very advantages of tailored clothing become its disadvantages.

Two factors, therefore, have combined to limit the pre-Columbian distribution of tailored clothing to Europe, northern Asia, and the northern half of North America: (1) selective adjustment to climatic factors; and (2) the fact that tailoring is an advanced technique, which the lowly Fuegians, who certainly could have used warm garments,[4] were incapable of inventing for themselves.

That cultural improvements are not *ipso facto* beneficial is incidentally demonstrated in the debilitating effect of the introduction of European clothing among the Yahgan, of whom Cooper writes:

> The clothing of the Yahgan seems to us utterly inadequate, given the climatic conditions—temperatures commonly around and well below freezing point in winter, high winds, frequent snow, hail, sleet, and cold rain—but in view of the seeming role played in their decline by introduced European clothing and their relative good health prior thereto, perhaps their clothing was reasonably well-adapted to the environment.

In this case, we would observe that it is not so much that their clothing was reasonably well adapted (which it was not) as that they were physiologically reasonably well adapted to a *specific* environmental situation. The adjustment was more biological than cultural. The introduction of tailored European clothing was a cultural modification that so altered the total environment of the Yahgans as to disturb disastrously the biological balance between them and their physical world. Inexorable extinction apparently stalks them.

This, of course, has been a common consequence of culture contact when very primitive peoples find their environment drastically unsettled by incursive elements emanating from a suddenly presented, unlike, and higher culture.

To return to the problem of the distribution of tailored clothing, it originally was made among the arctic and subarctic peoples of Siberia and North America and the ancient Chinese. The distribution in North America, as Wissler pointed out,[5] was coterminous with the distribution of caribou; in Asia the association was coterminous with the reindeer. Although the Northwest Coast Indians could easily have adopted the tail-

---

[4] J. M. Cooper, "The Yahgan" in *Handbook of South American Indians*, Vol. 1, p. 87.

[5] C. Wissler, *The American Indian*, p. 62.

oring te·hnique (they did sew boxes together), they did not do so. The northern bison hunters of the Plains did, however, make loosely tailored shirts and dresses of the modified poncho type.

Real tailoring is done by the Eskimos and Indians of the Canadian woods. Coats are fitted with genuine sleeves and necks. Eskimo garments with the fur turned in and the outer skin dyed and decorated are not only functional but aesthetic.

The diffusion of tailoring in prehistoric times raises several unsolved problems. Did it spread from the ancient civilization of China to the Siberian barbarians, thence east and west? Or did the primitive skin workers of north Asia develop it, whence it came to the Chinese?

The westward diffusion into Europe proper did not occur until a number of centuries after the conquests of Caesar. And finally, since the bursting of the confines of Europe in modern times, when tailored clothing became the symbol of the European conqueror, human creatures in all parts of the world have now enclosed their bodies in suits and dresses. The lovely tapa sarong of the Polynesian has given way to the missionary's Mother Hubbard. But lo, our parents having "civilized" the Polynesian out of the sarong, we moderns have taken its charms for our own.

Shoes and Hats. A properly dressed American woman never goes to church or afternoon tea without shoes and hat. The upper and nether extremities must be covered. Shoes and hats, like tailored clothing, may be functional—or mere status symbols.

Among primitives footgear is more common than headgear. The status functions of headgear can be served readily enough by hairdos. The protective functions of hats are also notably less important than the protective function of shoes.

Here again, the physical environment is an important factor in influencing the adoption or nonadoption of an element of material culture.

The problem of fabricating a foot covering that will stand up under the wet rot of the tropical jungle is practically insoluble. Even our best efforts with all the resources of science were not very satisfactory in the South Pacific campaigns of the Second World War. Jungle primitives prefer to go barefoot. An unshod foot dries more quickly and comfortably than one encased in a soaking and muddy moccasin. For this reason the highly sophisticated Indians of the Northwest Coast rain forest went barefoot, even in southern Alaska.

The simplest footgear is a piece of hide folded about the foot. When tailored, it becomes a moccasin of the type made famous by North American Indians. Further development of this form produces the boot. The so-called "Arctic boot" is an adjunct of true tailoring. This is not at all surprising, since anyone skilled enough in cutting and sewing to make a boot is *ipso facto* skilled enough to tailor clothing, and vice versa. Further, the same climatic circumstances that lend to tailored clothes their functional value act likewise with respect to boots. People who have to plod around in snow and cold find high tops more comfortable. Who enjoys walking through snowdrifts in oxfords? However, we have learned in anthropology not to expect that necessity necessarily mothers invention. The Indians of the North American boreal forests (the Canadian woodlands), who make tailored clothing and are confronted with heavy snows, make moccasins instead of boots, in spite of the fact that the more northerly of these Indians have contact with boot-wearing Eskimos. The boot of the Eskimos, worn from Greenland to Alaska, was undoubtedly borrowed from the Siberian herders and hunters. It is quite definitely an Asiatic trait.

The high, thigh-length, Cavalier-style riding boot of the Tehuelche Indians of the Patagonia pampas (whence comes its name, "the Patagonian boot") is apparently a post-Columbian adoption. The early, horseless "foot Tehuelche" wore a kind of moccasin stuffed with straw.[6] Because of its association with the horse, a post-Columbian acquisition, the Patagonian boot is hardly to be considered an independent primitive invention. But it is interesting to note that similar boots were not adopted in the Amazon, where the natives still prefer to go barefoot, or in the Andean region where the prehistoric sandal holds sway.

The sandal is the other type of primitive footgear that finds great favor. In its simplest form it is a piece of leather roughly fitted to the sole and held firm by thongs passing over the foot.

Basketry-type sandals with woven fiber soles were very popular with prehistoric Southwestern Basket-Maker Indians. Wissler noted that "in eastern North America moccasins were discarded when walking in the rain, in wet grass, or upon moist ground."[7] This was also true of the Incas with their rawhide-soled sandals, which would go soft and feel squishy when wet, then become hard and out of shape when dried. Wissler cites a correlation between the sandal and textile clothing in both the Old World and the New.[8] This correlation is most probably an indirect one. It is not that weaving gives rise to the use of sandals, but rather that each is an aspect of sedentary life; ergo, of higher primitive culture as such.

[6] J. M. Cooper, "The Patagonian and Pampean Hunters" in *Handbook of South American Indians*, Vol. 1, p. 144.

[7] Wissler, *op. cit.*, p. 65.

[8] *Ibid.*, p. 64.

The Hairdo. Concern with the coiffure is one of the most intense interests of mankind. We know not when the earliest prehistoric men and women first began to play with the cranial hair. Archaeological evidence from the Upper Paleolithic in Europe decisively demonstrates that Cro-Magnon man and his contemporaries laid great emphasis upon the female hairdo. In the Aurignacian statuette of the Venus of Willendorf (Fig. 20), no facial features were carved by the artist. To him there was no interest in a pretty face. But the pattern of the hair style is meticulously incised.

This trait of the Venus of Willendorf in the Aurignacian epoch, 30,000 to 40,000 years ago, were not a mere accident but a strong feature of the culture, for a similar degree of care was lavished upon the hair pattern of the female head from the *Grotte du Pape* at Brassempouy.

All recent primitives, from those of the lowest cultures to the highest, treat the hair. Add to this the fact that all civilized people do likewise, and we see that here is another universal trait in human culture.

The trimming and arrangement of the hair is not merely a matter of decoration and ornamentation; in culture after culture, it serves to symbolize social position. The most basic status represented in the treatment of the hair is that of sex. Males and females within any given society almost without exception have different ways of fixing the hair. With us the symbolism is so strong that short-haired women are considered mannish and long-haired men effeminate.

Less universally, hair styles are used to indicate age status. Omaha Indian boys had their heads shaved close, with isolated tufts of hair left here and there. Men wore either their full head of hair lying loose, or they shaved it off, except for a continuous roach along the sagittal line. Likewise, it used to be that young girls in our society wore their hair down, until after adolescence they were privileged to put it up. Today rigid custom is weakened, but the flavor of the symbolism remains. Matrons strive for "that girlish look" by wearing their hair in a long bob, while teen-agers put on sophisticated airs with the upsweep. It is all very confusing to the bewildered male, who is the intended victim of these tactical subterfuges.

Among the Omahas the shaved head of the boys indicated more than just age status, for the patterns of the remaining tufts were different for the boys of each clan. "The cutting of the hair was done, it was said, in order to impress on the mind of a child, as in an object lesson, the gentes [patrilineal clan] to which a playmate belonged." [9] This selfsame practice

[9] A. C. Fletcher and F. LaFlesche, *The Omaha Tribe* (Bureau of American Ethnology, Annual Report 27, 1911), p. 198.

is widespread among Sudanese West Africans. There the pates of children are divided into patterns of diamonds and squares formed by parting the hair and gathering it into tightly tied tufts. In Africa, the various patterns indicate different social affiliations. In America, some of the styles can frequently be seen on small Negro children, but among American Negroes, who have long since lost all vestiges of African clan organization, the practice apparently [10] expresses no more than a style convention that is but a survival of the old practice. A definitely New World symbolism has arisen among American Negroes in the matter of hair form. The passion for hair-straightening and kink-removing compounds among American Negroes reflects an identification of nonkinky hair with the social status of Caucasians.

The varieties of hair decoration are so multifarious the world over that it is not possible to attempt a distributional summary here. Mention should be made of the localized Melanesian custom, particularly in New Ireland, of bleaching out black hair to a reddish orange with lime. This phenomenon confounded any number of American G.I.s when they were first confronted with it in the South Pacific.

A closing comment on this subject would reemphasize the vital significance of the relation between hair treatment and formal social position. What is the meaning of the colloquialism, "They really let their hair down and had a good time?" Do we actually let down our hair? Only figuratively. What is let down are the customary restraints that keep us within our more cautiously preserved social roles. Let-down hair is ordinarily hidden from the public view, as is also the "uncensored" personality.

Cosmetics and Jewelry. Americans spend an estimated 700 million dollars on cosmetics in a normal year.[11] It is not the primitive but the universal man in us that accounts for this seeming extravagance. Viewed from the apex of a lofty asceticism, cosmetic aesthetics seem basely barbaric. Lotions, pastes, powders, pigments, and synthetic essences to alter the texture, color, feel, and smell of the external surfaces of the human body are neither primitive nor civilized. They are only the universal cultural responses to the basic human need for favorable response. They are designed to heighten the stimulus intensity of the physical presence of one person upon the touch, smell, sight, and perhaps taste of others. The others are usually of the opposite sex, but not exclusively so. If person-

[10] There has been no investigation into the possible functional significances of hair arrangements in American Negro children.

[11] J. Gunther, *Inside U.S.A.*, p. xii.

ality is the social stimulus value of an individual, then cosmetics intensify personality.

Rouge is the most common cosmetic for two reasons: (1) red ochre (iron oxide) occurs in many places and is readily procurable; and (2) red is the primary color with the longest wavelength perceptible to the human eye, the color with the greatest natural stimulus value. When mixed with grease, it may be harmlessly applied to the human body. Yellow, black, blue, and white are the other favored colors.

Body painting among primitive peoples is for the most part limited to special occasions. Such occasions are, of course, usually ritual and cere-monial. They are events out of the ordinary, and painting changes the individual from an ordinary person to a man of distinction. War paint is usually linked to magical potency and serves less to frighten the enemy than to bolster the faint heart of its wearer. Thus, much of primitive cosmetic practice takes on symbolic values.

The trouble with paint and cosmetics, as every woman knows, is that its application is not lasting. The solution hit upon by many peoples is tattooing.

In North America, light tattooing runs from the Eskimos down the West Coast and into South America. The two high centers of the art, however, were Polynesia and Japan. Curiously, the status associations of tattooing in Polynesia and the civilized world are just reversed. With us soldiers and sailors in the lower ranks, longshoremen, and unskilled laborers are the persons who usually get themselves tattooed. For persons of higher status, it is definitely *déclassé*. But within the lower classes it serves as a symbol of masculinity and toughness. In Polynesia, the higher the social status, the fuller the tattooing. It extended over face, body, and limbs; in some overenthusiastic cases even to the tongue. The process was long-drawn-out and painful, but socially rewarding.

The technique of tattooing is to puncture the skin with needles carry-ing an indelible dye—usually carbon black. This posed a problem for Negroes and the Australian Blackfellows. No white dye for tattooing was ever discovered by them. The solution hit upon in Africa and Aus-tralia is to incise the skin instead of puncturing it. Then by rubbing ashes, grit, or other irritants into the wounds scar tissue can be encour-aged to form, so that a series of raised lumps remain in a permanent visible pattern.

In Central Australia cicatrization or *scarification*, as the process is called, is a part of the adolescent initiatory rites for boys. The patterns are simply parallel rows of lines on the chest and back, but they are absolutely necessary to manhood. So important are they as symbols of manhood that individuals voluntarily repeat the operations in later life to keep their scars large and fresh.

In Africa, scarification among the Congo Bantus is also part of the initiatory rite or follows after. The designs are in some instances elaborate geometric patterns (Fig. 43; also Fig. 59).

German corps (fraternity) students and university men give great kudos to dueling scars. Reputedly they have great sex appeal. A wound that does not fester and leave a glaring scar is a dead loss. So important are the duel-born scarifications that German impostors have been known to slash themselves with a razor and rub in salt to leave the impression that they, too, bear the scars of honor.

Decorative Deformations and Mutilations. Tattooing and scarification are only superficial ornamental embellishments impressed upon the body. Piercing of the nasal septum, the lips, or ears so that sundry bones, feathers, shell, wood, or metal ornaments may be shoved through them extends from the most primitive to highly civilized peoples. The invention of the screw and spring clip has only

Fig. 43. Cicatrization. Maipimbe tribe, Congo, West Africa. (*American Museum of Natural History.*)

recently obviated the need for ear puncturing among our own ladies, who find the functionally atrophied external ear a convenient appendage from which to dangle pretty baubles.

Incas, in South America, and Bagandas, among others in Africa, gradually extend the ear lobes to receive thin disks as much as 6 to 8 inches in diameter. Inca nobility wore disks of gold. Baganda women, with their huge lip labrets, are familiar to all circus sideshow visitors.

Separation of the cervical vertebrae and extension of the neck in ringed brass collars by Burmese women is another familiar distortion.

Cranial deformation was much esteemed as a mark of beauty by various Northwest American Indian tribes (*viz.*, the Flatheads of Idaho) and also by the Incas and other Andean peoples, who bound a flat board against the frontal region of the head of a baby in the cradleboard in order to produce a recessed forehead and a high, peaked occipital. Binding with cloth to produce long heads was also practiced.

Circumcision and subincision are not so much mutilations for ornamentation as they are mystical and status operations. The one is the removal of the foreskin of the penis; the other a slitting of the skin and urethra along the length of the male sex organ. Among the Central Australians they symbolize masculinity in a male-dominated and ideologically masculine society; like scarification, the operations (often fatal) are performed without anesthesia and with flint knives on adolescent boys as a part of initiation into manhood. Most African tribes also circumcise at adolescence, and for similar reasons.

Filing or knocking out of incisor teeth occurs in scattered distribution from Australia up through Melanesia and Indonesia, and over into Africa. Prehistoric Europeans and American Indians spared themselves this mark of distinction. Of all the decorative blemishes imposed by man upon himself this is perhaps the most foolish. Scarification, tattooing, and circumcision may be painful, but except as they cause death through infection, they do not inhibit the healthy functioning of the body. The deliberate destruction of the teeth does just that.

Yet, as has been shown throughout this discussion, what is lost physically is gained socially. Mind triumphs over matter. No matter if the psychic satisfactions are not rational. The need that is met is elemental. The fashion and jewelry industries, the cosmetic manufacturers and purveyors, the beauticians, all may rest secure that their services have a future—as long as all mankind's.

CHAPTER 12

ART

The urge to beautify is one of the most interesting and unique, certainly one of the most remarkable, characteristics of the human being. Unlike so many of the basic drives that may be more or less directly linked to the imperatives of biological survival, the aesthetic and artistic drives are much more obtuse in their origins and functions. Man could survive without art, but to do so he would have to return to an ape level of existence. To be artless is to be dehumanized. Not without reason are the arts and belles-lettres known as the *humanities*.

By art we mean the overt expressions of impulses in line, form, color, rhythm, and word as drawing, painting, sculpture, dance, tone, poetry, and literature. The impulses are emotive and rational, but feeling tone predominates over thought.

The basic function of art as art is to release tensions by enabling the artist to externalize some of his emotions and ideas in an objective way. The release of the tensions brings satisfaction and pleasure. The viewers of an art object are stimulated to sensuous perceptions that likewise produce emotional responses ultimately resolving into a pleasurable feeling of euphoria and balance. This is not to deny, however, that the artistic experience may be highly disturbing and may even cause the artist great discomfiture while running its course. The end product, however, is a state of euphoria; the person who is initially complacent, or chronically so, never creates or responds to art.

Thus even from the individualistic point of view, art never exists literally for art's sake alone. It exists for psychophysiological reasons. And because our scientific knowledge of the physiology of emotion is as yet so crude, we understand little of the workings of the artistic impulses. Aesthetics, the study of beauty, remains almost entirely a branch of philosophy, for beauty is subjective.

But art may not be seen in its entirety if analyzed only from the individualistic point of view. Art is also a social expression, and it inevitably becomes a part of culture. Further, since man is always a creature of society and the child of culture, art *ipso facto* serves social as well as individual interests and needs. Art is inextricably tied to religion and magic. Yes, and to politics. It cannot help expressing and reflecting social relations and systems. It can serve to sustain them, as Renaissance art served medieval Christianity; or it can strive to destroy them as does the anarchistic art of the Dadaists, who hold modern civilization to be so false and meaningless that the honest artist can only lampoon and destroy it with senseless combinations of line and color.

What Is Primitive Art? The only safe answer to this question is that primitive art is the art of primitive peoples. It is impossible to define primitive art merely as crude art, for some primitive forms of artistic expression are exceedingly complex. It is impossible to label it as "childish"; for some primitive art is precocious in technique and sophis-

Fig. 44. Bushman rock painting. The dancers.

ticated in ideology. It is impossible to identify it as naturalistic, for some primitive art is highly stylized and conventionalized. The art of primitive peoples runs a wide gamut from technical clumsiness to high skill, from childlike simplicity to confusing complexity, from naturalism and realism to conventionalized abstraction.

Even when we eliminate the more florid forms of primitive art from our consideration and concentrate our attention on the arts of the most primitive of known peoples, this is still true. Bushman art is naturalistic and full of vitality (Fig. 44). Australian art is highly stylized and in certain forms abstract and symbolic. Eskimo art is naturalistic and technically quite sophisticated (Fig. 45). Shoshone art is almost wholly nonexistent.

No qualities that characterize primitive art universally can be adduced from the art of primitive peoples, unless it be that no primitives ever solved the problem of perspective—with which most of them never dealt.

The so-called "primitivists" in recent Occidental art are not true primitives. In stripping down their art forms to what they see as essential simplicity they are not necessarily emulating primitive art, even though they have been consciously influenced by the art of certain primitive peoples, especially African sculpture.

The "primitives" in American painting cannot be considered truly primitive either. They were only the untutored early representatives of an American offshoot of the European cultural tradition. They are called *primitives* only because they were early nineteenth century with reference to a very limited art history, and because they were crude in their technique.

Since, as most art students now agree, an art can be aesthetically the art of a culturally primitive people without itself being "primitive,"

Fig. 45. Eskimo carving in ivory.

primitive art must be defined by extraartistic means, *viz.*, its association with a preliterate culture.

Decorative Art. Decorative art is the work of the artisan, not the artist. It is the embellishment of an artifact. Plains Indian moccasins were embroidered with dyed porcupine quills. Later, when traders made colored beads available, beadwork replaced quillwork. Basket makers find that variations in twilling produce interesting and pleasing designs within the structure of the basket. They discover that the use of varicolored fibers makes possible tasteful coil and twill work. Potters discover that slips and painting make infinite variety a potentiality in ceramic production. Clay vessels can be mere household articles, or, by attention to line and form, they can be transformed into objects of pure beauty. Rawhide boxes could have been left as crude and undecorated as our corrugated shipping cartons. But Plains Indians preferred to decorate them with geometric designs in color.[1] A lime spatula could be a simple stick, but the natives of eastern New Guinea prefer to carve out a handle with painstaking skill. Northern Shoshones were content with roughed-out spoons of mountain-sheep horns, but Northwest Coast Indians worked intricate totemic designs into their handles (Fig. 46).

[1] *Cf.* L. Spier, "Plains Indian Parfleche Designs" (*University of Washington Publications in Anthropology*, Vol. 4, No. 3, 1931), pp. 293–322.

These are all examples of decorative embellishment—superfluous modification in line, form, and color of useful articles—superfluous in the sense that they do not contribute to the utilitarian effectiveness of the

Fig. 46. Northwest Coast Indian carving on the handle of a spoon fashioned from a mountain-sheep horn. (*American Museum of Natural History.*)

article. But they please their owner, impress his guests, and whet the acquisitive appetites of museum collectors.

A valid principle seems to be that as soon as a people solves the fundamental technical problems in the production of an artifact or tool, the artistic impulse begins to assert itself. The more aesthetically endowed individuals begin to "play" with the surface in an effort to increase the pleasing potentials of the object.

The history of automobile design compresses the whole process within the span of a generation. Motors were first attached to carriages with only as much modification of the erstwhile horse-drawn vehicle as the mechanical needs of the device dictated. The problem was to make a four-wheeled vehicle that was automotive; inventive concern was almost wholly concentrated on mobile power and its problems. By 1935 these problems, so far as the internal-combustion engine is concerned, were for the most part mastered. Creative interest shifted more and more to body design and appearance until by 1940 the industrial artist had almost superseded the automotive engineer in importance in Detroit.

As a rule, technique must first be mastered before decorative art worthy of being called art develops. Beyond mastery of technique, the more leisure the subsistence techniques and resources of a people's culture allow, the greater the likelihood of decorative embellishment. This must not, however, be taken as a bald assertion that leisure produces art. It does not. Surplus energies and time may be directed into other channels to satisfy other interests such as war, trading, or games.

Decorative art may be purely *formal*, or it may be *representative*. Formal decoration is characterized by its concentrated emphasis upon form and design without reference to meaning or thought. Examples of this would be the perfect shaping of a pottery bowl, the turning of a beautiful rim. Designs in coiling, weaving, and twilling that come out of the arrangement of warp and weft (see Fig. 40), the introduction of decorative bands about the rims of baskets through the process of binding the edges to avoid raveling, are further examples of formal decoration that results primarily from industrial technique. However, formal decoration not imposed by technical needs is world-wide. Decorative bands incised or painted about the neck of a pot or the edges of a box are purely *superimposed* on the functional structure of the artifact. Such formal design elements are not extensions of technique, but rather expressions of the universal "feeling for form" that prompts man to emphasize the form of his object.

Thus, the ubiquitous formal decorative art that has been so assiduously studied by anthropologists and so generally spurned by art historians ("because it is not *pure* art") springs from two fundamental sources. As Boas has put it, such art "is not necessarily expressive of purposive action," *i.e.*, the artisan is not consciously producing an artistic product, but rather it is based upon "reactions to forms that develop through mastery of technique" and secondly, "the formal interest is directly due to the impression derived from the form. It is not expressive in the sense that it conveys a definite meaning or expresses an aesthetic emotion." [2]

Decorative art may also be representative, *i.e.*, the design or figure portrays some object. It presumes to represent the real thing. If the

Fig. 47. Stylized realism. Carved stone head from Oaxaca, Mexico. (*American Museum of Natural History.*)

representation is faithful to the original model, it is said to be natural, or naturalistic, as was European cave art, or as are the delightful dancing figures conceived by the Bushman artist. Naturalistic art may be stylized to a degree, as indeed are the Bushman figures with their long limbs, narrow torsos, and fluid movements. The meaning of "style" in representative art can be quickly grasped by comparing Egyptian naturalistic representation of dancers with the Bushman's. Figure 47 shows us an extraordinary Zapotec piece of naturalism in sculpture from Oaxaca.

[2] F. Boas, *Primitive Art*, pp. 62–63.

Mexico. The same people were also capable of marked stylization, as seen in the clay representation of a tiger god in Fig. 48. Style means a departure from absolute naturalism. Artists always compose their creations to some degree. Documentary photography or the snapshots of

Fig. 48. Decorative elaboration. Terra cotta funerary urn from Oaxaca, Mexico. (*American Museum of Natural History*.)

most amateurs are not art. But by selective lighting, screening, and retouching, photography can be made to approach art. A textbook line illustration of an anatomical specimen is a scientific representation, but hardly ever art. Style denotes a standardized selective modification of the real image in a way that produces an aesthetically effective and distinctive representation.

Style in Northwest Coast Art. One of the most distinctive of all primitive art styles is that of the Northwest Coast of North America in the carving and painting of masks, totem poles, boxes, rattles, dishes, spoons, canoes, houses, and other objects. Exaggerations in representative art have led not to geometric design but to a unique stylization in which a body form can still be distinguished, in spite of the fact that it is weirdly distorted in size and arrangement. Since all Northwest Coast art objects are utilitarian in intent, the form of the object on which the decorative element is placed determines the shape of the piece. The representation of the image is, therefore, more or less subordinated to the object. The art is definitely not free art.

The effects of this subordination of the art to the object are most interesting. The artist is given, so to speak, a decorative field that he must cover. He abhors blank spaces. He also wants all his decorative elements to represent some aspect of animal life. Hence, he is impelled to dissect, dismember, distort, and remold his creatures to fill the space, be it the surface of a box, bowl, wooden hat, or rattle. Distortion becomes such that the representation is in the end a caricature. But sheer design does not annihilate representation wholly, because the impulses of the Northwest Coast artist are not unalloyedly aesthetic. Totemic heraldry, with its rich mythology of clan and lineage origins from heroic animal ancestors, pervades most Northwest Coast art. The representative art portrays not just an animal but an animal that symbolizes some mythical or historic event in the social background of the artist. This interest in the art counterbalances the tendency for caricature to get out of hand. The device by means of which this purpose is made effective is the standardization of certain immutable symbols based on one or a few outstanding anatomical traits of the natural creature portrayed. Thus, no matter how weird the distortion in the interests of design or in the flight of imaginative fancy, the message to be conveyed by the representation cannot be lost in meaningless form and line.

The marks of the beaver in Northwest Coast art are the most readily recognizable—his flat, scaly, mud-slapper tail and his efficient cutting teeth. These are always present in any artistic representation of the beaver. In Fig. 49A we see a Haida Indian totem-pole beaver. He may be quickly recognized by his two great incisors and his crosshatched tail, which, since the pole is to be viewed from the front, is curled up between his legs, for otherwise it could not be seen. Since the beaver is a woodworker, he is often, but not always, shown with a chunk of a log in his paws. One other important landmark is the projecting ear. Although it will be observed that stylization of the face is in the direction of the human visage (all the mythological creatures talk, think, and act like human beings) the ears above the head are sure distinctive evidence that a nonhuman animal is represented.

The bear in Fig. 49B fills in a square design area. Again the ears prove him to be an animal. The teeth are bear teeth, but the most important mark is found in the long claws of the paws. Notice, too, how the bear

A

B

C

Fig. 49. Northwest Coast art (Haida): A, carved totem-pole beaver; B, painted bear on a flat surface; C, painted shark (dogfish). (*After Boas.*)

looks as though he had been split down the back and then opened to fill out the flat space.

This tricky device is shown at its best in the treatment of the shark, shown in Fig. 49C. The distinguishing shark features, which are all on the face, are (1) a large mouth, drawn down at the corners, (2) many sharp teeth, (3) gill slits on the cheeks, (4) large round eyes, (5) a high tapering forehead on which are drawn two circles like eyes and gill slits to form a pseudo subface. Since these features are all best seen from the front, the shark head is never shown in profile. Yet the side of the body must be shown in profile. In order that symmetry may be attained, the artist has split the fish down the back and folded the two sides out to the right and left of the head. What looks to us, at first glance, like wings are but the outspread right and left sides of the shark's body. Not to leave a large void beneath the body, the pectoral fins are much enlarged; and then to keep the whole within the confines of the rectangular decorative area, the split tail is turned down and inward at both ends of the body.

Thus we see how the Northwest Coast artist with great skill and ingenuity compromised and balanced his hunter's interest in animal anatomy, his artistic interest in design, his abhorrence of blank spaces, and his totemic mythology into a sophisticated art style. In the struggle between representation and symbolism neither won. Northwest Coast art is both representative and symbolic.

Variations in Styles. An interesting aspect of primitive art is the occurrence of different art styles within the same culture, each style associated with a specific aspect of the culture and not transferable to other phases. On the Klamath River, among the Yurok Indians, naturalistic representations are permissible on woodwork but absolutely tabu on basketry, where only geometric patterns are allowed. Why? Naturalism in basketry designs is sure to bring bad luck, especially eye trouble, as happened to a woman once, according to the old wives' tales.[3]

Sculptured representations of Cook Islands gods reveal a nice contrast of styles between two closely related objects. Private gods, belonging to individual persons, are represented by grotesque but utterly realistic figurines carved in a highly stylized manner and yet essentially naturalistic. Clan and tribal gods, on the other hand, "were usually represented by highly abstract wood carvings most of which bear no recognizable relation to the human figure."[4] The clan deities are highly stylized and abstract (Fig. 50). The knobby projections running down the body should be viewed from the left. Then they may be seen as a series of highly conventionalized human heads and figures.

[3] L. O'Neale, lecture, *Seminar in Psychological Approaches to Culture*, University of California, spring, 1941.
[4] R. M. Linton and P. S. Wingert, *Arts of the South Seas*, p. 27.

A most interesting example of symbolic abstraction is found in the worship of ceremonial tools as representing the god of a cult of craftsmen. The superbly fashioned adze from Cook Islands (Fig. 51) is the

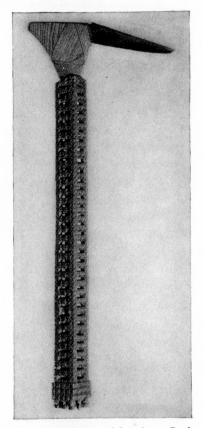

Fig. 50. Carved wood representation of a clan deity from Cook Islands, Polynesia. (*Peabody Museum of Archaeology and Ethnology, Harvard University.*)

Fig. 51. Ceremonial adze. Cook Islands, Polynesia. (*Smithsonian Institution.*)

apotheosis of their basic tool. They literally worshipped the tools with which they worked. Nevertheless, the Cook Islanders, although their craftsmanship was suffused with religious and magical power, knew that good work calls for good tools and that unnecessary decorative embellishment can impair function. Therefore, although their tools and objects

of use are created with a strong feeling for form, they are rarely decorated. All the decorative effort goes into the deified objects.

In this context, the mastery of functional form by the Micronesians
should be mentioned. Only a people who have "found their aesthetic
expression in fine craftsmanship and functional design rather than elaborate decoration" [5] could produce such an exquisitely modern piece as the
wooden dish from Matty Islands shown in Fig. 52.

Religion and Art. Religion and art are by no means inseparable, but
for deep-rooted reasons they have a strong affinity.

Fig. 52. Wooden dish from Matty Islands, Micronesia. A fine example of functional
art. (*University of Pennsylvania Museum.*)

In essence religion is subjective—a matter of belief. Yet the covert
concepts of religious belief are always translated to overt ritual and
ceremonial forms. Religion needs objectifying, and art is one medium of
outstanding effectiveness. By artistic embellishment the paraphernalia of
religion and magic may be lifted out of the realm of ordinary artifacts
or activities to become endowed with the qualities of the unusual that
should be associated with the supernatural—the sacred.

Yet even more important than the elaboration of religious paraphernalia is the representation of the spirits and gods. Gods are imaginative
conceptions who exist in belief. The belief takes on a more convincing
sense of reality if it can be translated into concrete form. Paintings and
statues objectify the subjective concepts of the divinities. The presence
of a god at a ceremony is more directly felt by the majority of men if
the god is there in solid stone or wood looking down on the believers.
It is true that the Judaeo-Christian religious tradition tabus all representations of God the supreme deity, but the myriad representations of
Christ, the Virgin Mary, and the host of saints proves that the principle
is not wholly invalid for the Occidental religions.

[5] *Ibid.*, p. 71.

The representation or symbolization of primitive gods is done usually in the medium of sculpture or painting, or a combination of both.

Primitive religious sculpture appears in the form of masks or statues —idols. Without artists there can be no idolatry.

The use of masks to portray supernatural beings is prevalent among primitives in all parts of the world. Only Polynesia and Micronesia, in the Pacific, and the Plains and Basin areas in the United States are con-

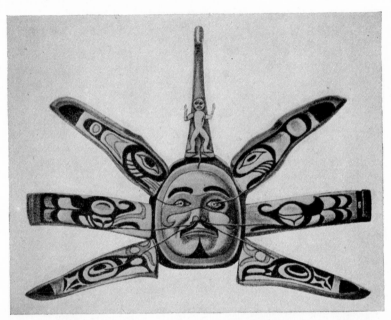

FIG. 53. Kwakiutl Indian double mask shown in the open position.

spicuous in the absence of masking. In the religion of the Plains Indians deities are of little importance and ritualism is poorly developed. There is nothing much to mask. In Polynesia, although the pantheon is elaborate and gods are portrayed as statues as we have noted for Cook Islands masking is abjured, for reasons that are obscure.

In North America the masks of the Northwest Coast reach a richness of variety and form that is rivaled only in parts of Melanesia. Many Northwest Coast masks, by means of hinges and strings, have movable parts that may be manipulated by the actor to heighten the dramatic effect. Some, like the Kwakiutl mask depicted in Fig. 53, have an inner and an outer face to portray the dual character (human and animal) of the early mythological progenitors. The combination of factors that has produced the exotic elaborateness of Northwest Coast masking is in the main (1) a social organization emphasizing hereditary status based in part on descent from mythological ancestral lineage founders, (2) elaboration of dance drama depicting the deeds of the mythical heroes, (3) technical mastery of the skills of carving, and (4) a vigorous creative drive to translate ideas and mental imagery into objective representations.

Fig. 54. Carved wooden masks of the Iroquois Indian False Face Society. (*National Museum of Canada.*)

At the eastern end of our continent, Iroquois masks as made and used by the False Face Society of curers are not so rich in variety nor so elaborate as those of the Northwest Coast, but they bear the stamp of a grotesquely humorous realism designed to frighten away evil spirits (Fig. 54). While the intent of the masks is serious, one cannot help feeling that the artist carves with his tongue in his cheek.

A mask is not necessarily art. Dime-store false faces for Halloween are genuine attempts at representation of something or other, and they surely titillate the spines and hair roots of small boys and girls, but it is unlikely that they ever raise the pulse of an art critic. Some Pueblo

Indian masks have artistic qualities. Many do not, for they are nothing more than cylinders that cover the head like an inverted bucket (Fig. 55). Although Pueblo masks have various appendages and are painted, little effort is expended to work out notable patterns of line or color. Southwest Indians do little wood carving, and none of their masks are made of wood.[6] Leather (occasionally gourd or wicker) is the material used—a medium that does not lend itself to delicate molding or modeling.

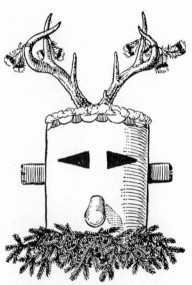

FIG. 55. Kachina mask. Santa Ana Pueblo. (*After White.*)

Although Pueblo design in pottery has reached a high art level, only the crudest of geometric design patterns are transferred to the masks. Thus in spite of the ritual importance of masks in Pueblo society, they have failed to become objects of creative artistic interest. All the ideological stimuli for artistry in masks are present, but unlike the cultural situation on the Northwest Coast, no suitable technical medium is at hand in the Pueblo cultural tradition; the Pueblo religious craftsman has turned his creative aesthetic interests elsewhere.

Masking associated with religious belief has generated rich art products in both Africa and Melanesia, but of the two areas Melanesia has been the more prolific. Hence we shall briefly discuss its products. In Africa and Melanesia the worship and veneration of ancestral spirits looms large in virtually all tribal religions (see Chap. 29). In Melanesia, particularly, the masks are ancestral representations used in elaborate memorial rites. On the island of New Ireland, this complex reached its most elaborate expression in the ritual and art of the *malagan*, a system of festivals in memory of the recently deceased.

Tradition decreed so strongly that these be performed that the survivors of the deceased would lose caste if they did not conform, while their prestige would be enhanced in proportion to the magnificence of the ceremonies held. This attitude served as a powerful incentive to provide the maximum of food for the feasts and the richest possible carvings.[7]

[6] E. C. Parsons, *Pueblo Indian Religion*, Vol. 1, p. 340.
[7] Linton and Wingert, *op. cit.*, p. 160.

Some of these carvings were intricately worked plaques, but most of them were masks. Colored in red, yellow, blue, and white, they are truly

FIG. 56. Boar's head mask, carved and painted wood. New Ireland, Melanesia. (*Chicago Natural History Museum.*)

spectacular and impressive (Figs. 56 and 57). Obviously they are the work of professional artists, who are in fact well paid for their services, which are secretly performed within a high-walled enclosure close by the cemetery of the clan that is holding the *malagan*. The sculptors work for nearly a year preparing the boards and masks before they are all finally ready for public display and use. In style, as Wingert has noted, the basic carving, although complex, is well organized, while the painted surface designs are overelaborate, even jittery.

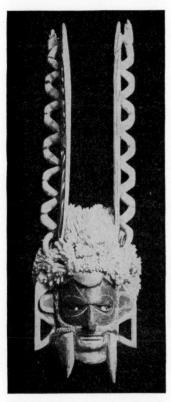

Fig. 57. Human mask, carved and painted wood. New Ireland, Melanesia. (*Museum of Art, Rhode Island School of Design.*)

Fig. 58. Ancestral figure from the Ivory Coast, West Africa. (*Brooklyn Museum.*)

Statuary as a medium of primitive religious art is common in Africa and Melanesia, and also in Polynesia and Central America. African statuary has had considerable influence upon modern European artists because of its direct naturalism and its general simplicity of mass and line, coupled with intensity of subject matter. It possesses a living quality eagerly sought after by modernists. It embodies the people's hopes and fears; it terrorizes or delights them as it portrays the nature of the gods on whom they lean or before whom they prostrate themselves.

This is true of African sculpture, as well as Polynesian and Melanesian. The artist is close to his work, and his work is close to the interests and well-being of his people. He is in his society what the modern artist would like to be in ours.

Mass, solidity, and plainness of surface are the impressive features of African Negro sculpture, even though the figures are not usually very

FIG. 59. Bakongo fetish figures. (*Brooklyn Museum.*)

large. These qualities are partly induced by the nature of the material in which the artist works, partly by his own inimitable style. The material is hardwood—mahogany, aristocrat of timbers, and ironwood—tough challenging material. No light-minded whittler can work the sculptor's transformation on such a block. The wood is close-grained and invites a high polish with dark lustrous tones. The glistening high lights of the smooth Negro skin are beautifully reflected in the finished statues. The wedding of subject matter and materials is perfect.

African Negro sculpture is characteristically disproportionate (Figs. 58 and 59). The head is always too large for the torso; the legs are squat and sturdy. All the work is subject to the limitations of the mass of the block with which the artist works. That is to say that the African woodworker is no joiner. Since he cannot attach projecting pieces to the mass, the arms must be formed close to the body. The legs must be confined within the area of the original block. Such limitations contribute to the feeling of compactness that emerges from the art. Concentration of attention on the head of the statue, lineal elongation of the body, and dwarfing of the lower limbs is a matter of stylistic choice in the African tradition.

It is true that to those of us who have been trained in the naturalistic idealism of sculpture in the Greek tradition, African distortions appear at first as shocking grotesquerie. But, with familiarity, the cubic way of cutting out of surfaces, the rhythm that moves between the parts of the statue, the basic simplicity in its generalization of the human figure, and the exquisite texture of the finish combine to caress the aesthetic sense of the sympathetic observer.

Yet our emotional response is only a dilute aesthetic reaction hardly comparable to the tremendous emotional significance of these statues for the Africans. The overtones with which the mortuary and fetishistic pieces are freighted for the native can never be sensed by outsiders. Most African statues represent dead ancestors; they are created to house their spirits. The statue, when the spirit has taken up its abode, is in the true sense a fetish.[8] It is not just a work of art to be viewed objectively in a museum. It is a personage, alive with all the pulsating powers of the personality it represents—powers that are superhumanly potent because the one it represents is no longer mere man but god.

To go into a consideration of Melanesian statuary is not possible here. The varieties of form are too great. But from one end of the area to the other, representative ancestral sculpture is found. Most of it, particularly that of the Papuan area, has none of the stylistic slickness of the African work. Color and form in Melanesia are violent and disturbing. This, however, is not true of the ancestral fetishes fashioned from tree fern and set up about the dance clearings on Ambrim Island in the New Hebrides. While it is extremely unlikely that a Melanesian would be moved to laughter at the sight of a group of bug-eyed statues peering out from the jungle, the reader may decide for himself whether or not a ludicrous gathering is portrayed (Fig. 60).

Symbolism in Art. A symbol is any phenomenon that stands for something else in the idea system of a culture. It is so closely identified with the symbolized object in meaning that it stimulates like responses.

A general characteristic of symbols is their nondiffuseness. In one

[8] See R. H. Lowie, *Primitive Religion*, pp. 268–270.

form or another, symbols are always overt; they must be seen, heard, felt, or smelled. They condense abstractions into delimited objects. Words are vocal symbols.

Art symbols are combinations of line, color, texture, form, and sound that stand for concrete objects or abstractions. They also possess definite aesthetic qualities.

Symbolic art is at the opposite pole from naturalistic representation.

Fig. 60. Ancestral figures carved in tree fern. Ambrym Islands, New Hebrides, Melanesia. (*Chicago Natural History Museum.*)

Stylization and conventionalization are intermediate forms. In conventionalized art the process of selection and elimination of detail has gone so far that while a perceptible similarity to the original object is still preserved, the representation has become more symbolic than naturalistic.

Evolution in Art. The genetic relation of symbolism to naturalism in art has long stimulated the interest of anthropologists. In the late nineteenth century it posed one of the primary problems upon which such writers as Balfour, Haddon, and Holmes worked.[9] Current anthropological interest is focused upon the sociopsychological functions of symbolism rather than upon its evolution, but the genesis of symbolism remains an important cultural problem.

Meaningless geometric decorative design is rare among primitives;

[9] H. Balfour, *The Evolution of Decorative Art*; A. C. Haddon, *Art in Evolution*; W. H. Holmes, *Ancient Art of the Province of Chiriqui* (Bureau of American Ethnology, Annual Report 6, 1888), pp. 13–186.

there is almost always some consciousness of symbolization. But the degree of consciousness may be more or less sharp, the meaning of the symbols more or less standardized, according to the person and the culture.

Thus, among the Arapaho, according to an early study by Kroeber,[10] beadwork patterns had the symbolic values shown in Fig. 61. However, certain patterns had multiple symbolic values variously interpreted in accordance with their context and the intent of the beadworker. The simple diamond, listed as a star symbol, can also stand for a navel, an

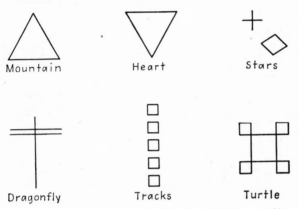

FIG. 61. Conventional symbols in Arapaho beadwork designs. (*After Kroeber.*)

eye, a lake, a person, life, a buffalo wallow, or the interior of a tipi. The personal factor loomed so large in symbolism that conscientious Indians refuse to interpret the ornamentation on another person's article, on the ground that they do not know the artist's intent. Nowadays, however, Indians engaged in commercial trading will make up glib and cryptic interpretations for the white man who insists on knowing the meaning of the designs. It is all a part of the sale.

Associative symbolism can be arrived at from two directions. Geometric forms may be created out of doodling, or the inherent limitations and possibilities of a technique, such as twilling and weaving, may suggest an idea that is associated with the form, just as people try to tell what the ink blots remind them of in Rorschach tests. Or, on the other hand, the artist may make a naturalistic representation of something. Then, through the course of time, the naturalistic form is transformed into a conventionalized symbolism by subsequent artists.

[10] A. L. Kroeber, "Decorative Symbolism of the Arapaho" (*American Anthropologist,* Vol. 3, 1901), pp. 308*ff*.

One of the best demonstrations of the second process is that advanced by Holmes in his discussion of Chiriquian pottery designs.[11] Among the several design motifs discussed by Holmes that of the alligator is

Fig. 62. Conventionalization and abstraction of alligator designs on Chiriquian pottery. (*After Holmes.*)

most arresting. In Fig. 62 some of the alligator designs are arranged to show progressive abstraction from stylized representations.

In the upper left of Fig. 62 is the painted figure of an alligator with upturned snout and tail and dots to represent his scales. Below him is a conventionalized figure of an alligator that is almost unrecognizable, while below it appears a meandering abstraction that would be hard to identify as an alligator symbol if it were not that more realistic representations are available for comparison.

[11] Holmes, *op. cit.*, pp. 171–186.

In the upper right of Fig. 62 is a simple curvilinear representation of an alligator that is progressively simplified through symbolic abstraction to become a mere curved line and a dot.

The "alligatoric" symbol encased in the circular field in the right bottom of Fig. 62 is apparently abstracted from the sort of alligator picture embraced in the trapezoidal field shown to the left of it. To fit his picture into the field or area to be covered by the picture the artist has bent the tail of the alligator down while curving the tip inward. The head is turned in to fit into the dip formed by the beast's sagging back. The legs and the double-hooked representation of scales at the back of the neck form three appended units.

Although the complex spiral shown within the circle is a far cry from an alligator, it is most assuredly derived from the idea of the alligator represented to the left of it. It occurs on pottery of a type that is commonly decorated with alligators; it has the same inturned hook of the tail; it has three semicircular protuberances (no more, no less) just as the alligator has three groups of semicircular legs and neck scales; the inner loop of the spiral corresponds to the hooked loop of the alligator's nose. What looks like geometric scribbling is a meaningful symbol abstracted from a stylized representation of a real animal form.

Holmes was quite convinced that in the case of Chiriquian forms a definite evolution from realistic through conventionalized to abstract symbols occurred. Critical objections have been raised to this thesis because it implies a temporal sequence from a typological classification, and Holmes had no proof that the realistic forms were actually earlier in time. Boas and others have pointed out that since in some known instances the evolution of an art style is found to have moved from geometric figures to realistic,[12] there is no justification for assuming priority of naturalistic forms unless there is stratigraphic or actual historical evidence for implying such a time sequence.

While it is true that there is no direct evidence of temporal sequence in the Chiriquian series, the probability that the abstract designs of Chiriquian ware are the derivatives of the realistic designs is certainly much greater than the reverse possibility.

Art and Writing. All art is a form of communication. Writing is communication by means of visual symbols substituted for spoken words. All writing is, therefore, symbolic and its origins lie in symbolic art.

[12] See F. Boas's study of Eskimo needlecases. Archaic geometric decorative elements are shown to have evolved into animal figures. *Decorative Designs of Alaskan Needlecases* (United States National Museum, Reports, Vol. 39, 1908), pp. 221–344.

Conventionalization is usually discussed as a process of degeneration of art. This is true only when conventionalization reflects a decline in technique—a simplification of line and form due to slovenliness on the part of the artist. It is not true when the interest of the artist is actually shifted from the *image* of the object portrayed to its *meaning*. To portray an object faithfully requires dextrous technique in motor control.

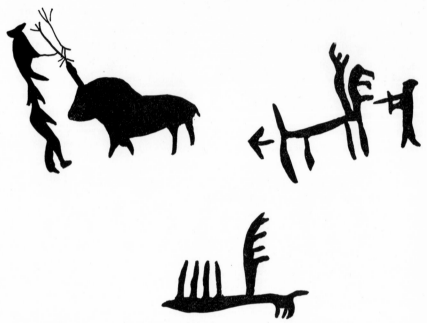

FIG. 63. Three degrees of conventionalization in the representation of the stag in the East Spanish art from Cogul.

To abstract the meaning of an object and to be able to represent it with a simple symbol requires a degree of mental sophistication that is on a higher level of performance.

When archaeologists lament the "decline" of Paleolithic art and its "degeneration" to the red ochre paintings on pebbles in the Mesolithic culture of Mas d'Azil in France,[13] they are shedding useless tears. The degenerate figures on the painted pebbles are the rudiments of an embryonic system of writing. Lament the invention of writing, one of the greatest intellectual feats of human history! Lament the attainment of the

[13] For example, H. F. Cleland, *Our Prehistoric Ancestors*, p. 63. "The art of the Late Paleolithic had completely disintegrated and now consisted merely of crude geometric designs painted on pebbles and cave walls."

one feature of culture that all anthropologists agree distinguishes civilized culture from primitive.[14]

In the cavern of Cogul, in Portugal, is a painted wall upon which prehistoric man of the Capsian culture has left many pictures of cattle, antelopes, and a ring of half-clothed females dancing about a phallic male. One of the pictures is that of a man confronting a stag (Fig. 63). On another part of the wall is a crudely conventionalized picture of a

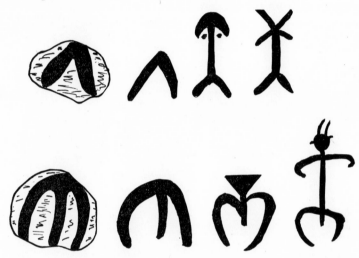

Fig. 64. Female and male symbols (?) on painted pebbles from Mas d'Azil (left) compared with female and male pictographs from late Upper Paleolithic cave art in East Spain. (*After Obermaier.*)

hunter, who has just shot a large arrow at a stag. In yet another spot is a very queer figure. By itself it would be no more intelligible to us than the Chiriquian alligator symbols. We know, however, that the Capsian hunters were very much interested in dead deer, and with the more naturalistic examples before us, we can compare the number of prongs in the forklike projections on this figure with the prongs of the antlers in the naturalistic pictures. That a deer is meant is certain. Furthermore, since the four feet of the object are sticking straight up in the air, we may feel reasonably sure that this is the symbol for a dead deer.

Presumably, this is a magical hunting symbol to help the deerslayer. A Winnebago Indian yet living has described in detail the working of such magic. A vital fragment of his story is given in Chap. 8.

[14] L. A. White excepted. White would substitute the invention of the steam engine as the critical trait. *Cf.* "Energy and the Evolution of Culture" (*American Anthropologist*, Vol. 45, 1943), pp. 354–355.

What took place at Cogul occurred elsewhere on the Iberian Peninsula. Obermaier, in arguing for a genetic relationship between the Azilian painted pebbles and the painted petroglyphs of the Spanish caves and rock shelters, prepared the comparative chart shown in Fig. 64. On the left of the double line are petroglyphs from the Spanish caves. To the right are figures taken from the Azilian pebbles. Clearly, the Azilian ⋀⋀ symbolizes a squatting female, and the ⋀ is a male. Azilian man had progressed from picture writing to ideographs. Such is the first step in the evolution and origin of all systems of writing. The scribe is the intellectual offspring of the artist.

B. Marriage and Kin

CHAPTER 13

SELECTIVE MATING AND PREFERENTIAL MARRIAGE

Mating is a biological imperative deeply rooted in the sex drive and the need to reproduce. No human society can escape from the dictates of its imperative, and mating is therefore a universal feature in the social life of all peoples of all times. By mating is meant *the pairing off of individuals of opposite sex under the influence of the sexual drive.* It is preponderantly a psychophysical phenomenon, basically instinctive in nature. But among human beings it is definitely influenced by various culture patterns that control the forms of its expression. The purpose of this chapter is to describe the nature of the cultural controls of mating.

Mating implies more than mere sexual intercourse; a degree of permanence is involved in the association of the mated pair. However, mating is not to be confused with marriage because, intimately related though the two may be, they are not inseparable. As in the case of nonhuman animals, mating can occur on a purely biological plane, without benefit of marriage—the connubial institution. Conversely, marriages can occur without mating.

In spite of the fact that marriage meets basic biological needs, it is a social institution determined *in toto* by culture. *Marriage is the complex of social norms that define and control the relations of a mated pair to each other, their kinsmen, their offspring, and society at large.* It defines all the institutional demand rights, duties, immunities, etc., of the pair as husband and wife. It is the institution that shapes the form and activities of the association known as the *family.*

Premarital Mating. In contrast to our fairly strict usages, a great number of primitive societies accept free premarital sexual experimentation without disapproval. Of the Trobriand Islanders it is written, presumably without exaggeration, that

. . . chastity is an unknown virtue among these natives. At an incredibly early age they become initiated into sexual life, and many of the innocent-looking plays of childhood are not so innocuous as they appear. As they grow up, they live in promiscuous free love, which gradually develops into more permanent attachments, one of which ends in marriage.[1]

In the absence of the severe guilt feelings that ordinarily color premarital sex activity among our youthful population, premarital activity may function among primitives to prepare young people for marriage. It can provide an intimate test of the compatibility of mating pairs before they actually enter into marriage with all its social and economic responsibilities. This is Malinowski's principle of the *social function of premarital sexual activity*.[2] There is little doubt but that the end to which Malinowski calls attention may so be served in some societies, but it seems more likely that societies are apt to permit the free play of the biological drives before marriage because of sheer indifference to the effects of such activity. At any rate, not much emphasis can be placed upon the function of premarital experience as a factor in mate selection in the vast number of primitive societies in which the boy or girl have very little to say as to whom they shall marry. It will be shown later to how small a degree marriage in primitive society is concerned with sexual gratification and personal compatibility on the basis of romantic love. Primitive societies are much more concerned with (1) the biological perpetuation of the group, (2) the perpetuation of the culture and social existence of the group through proper nurture and training of the oncoming generation, and (3) last but not least, the furthering of immediate special interests in prestige, property, and prerogatives of the *extended families* of the pair to be joined in marriage.

This last point is well illustrated in the practices of the Philippine Ifugaos, who permit free premarital sexual activity only for members of those classes in which there is not much stake in property and prestige. Each night adolescent boys of the lower and middle classes must seek the congenial comfort of the house of a widow, which also serves the regular purpose of a dormitory for unmarried adolescent girls because custom does not permit them to sleep under the family roof. In the deep of the night the boys try their luck at love-making. Much experimentation in different dormitories ultimately leads to a permanent attachment to some one girl—a form of companionate marriage that eventually blossoms into a fully accredited marriage when the numerous exchange gifts have been made and family rituals of marriage have been observed.

[1] B. Malinowski, *The Argonauts of the Western Pacific*, p. 53.
[2] B. Malinowski, "Culture" (*Encyclopedia of the Social Sciences*, Vol. 4, 1931), p. 630.

However, the upper class Ifugaos behave in quite a different manner, since their parents do not care to run the risk of permitting their children to mate in accordance with mere amatory affection and personal compatibility. Family status among the Ifugao rests heavily on property; marriage is a useful instrument for augmenting the status of the next generation by combining the resources of two families of property. To have a scion find a compatible but propertyless bride in the damsels' dormitory is for the upper class Ifugao a greater calamity than for an American blue blood to marry a chorus girl. To avert such an eventuality, rich children of the Ifugaos are betrothed in infancy, or even before birth. A contract marriage is arranged by the parents, who guarantee the amount of land and other goods that will be conveyed to the bride and groom. Throughout childhood the boy and girl take turns living in each other's parents' homes, until they establish a home of their own on marriage, shortly after adolescence.[3]

A similar picture, in which freedom is allowed some young persons but not others, is derived from Samoa and elsewhere in Oceania. Boys and girls of the commoner class are allowed virtually unrestricted sex freedom "under the palms," but woe to the royal princess who does not preserve her chastity and is exposed at the public rituals of defloration when the emissaries of another village come to claim her for their royal chief.[4]

Among the American Indians of the Plains we again find premarital unchastity the rule (except for the strict Cheyennes), but families of high standing endeavored to inculcate virtuous behavior in their daughters. The girl who retained unimpugned chastity until marriage was greatly respected in public opinion and doubly cherished by her husband.

This seeming paradox crops up in many ways in numerous societies, civilized and uncivilized. It certainly manifests a conflict of interests and values. Important elements in the situation include the desire of the individual for biological gratification between the attainment of puberty and marriage, on the one hand, and the sense of enhanced value in exclusive possession, on the other.

The illustrations cited above indicate that economic factors definitely influence the imposition of checks on free premarital sexual activity. This must have played an increasingly important role in the unfolding of human history as societies built up more and more property. The con-

[3] R. F. Barton, *Philippine Pagans.* Also, "Ifugao Law" (*The University of California Publications in American Archaeology and Ethnology*, Vol. 15, 1919), pp. 15–22.

[4] M. Mead, *Coming of Age in Samoa*, p. 98.

trol of mating in order to effect the control of property therefore looms as something of a necessity among civilized peoples in a way that is not the case with the more propertyless primitives. Mating becomes more than the crude expression of biological drives. It also binds and directs the disposition and control of property. Mating becomes subject to social limitations that override mere amatory whim.

While economic determinism has a sturdy finger in the pie, other factors must be also recognized. Religious belief is pervasive. In the area of sex control its power cannot be overestimated. The Polynesian princess must lead a carefully guarded life, because she is inherently charged with *mana* and therefore tabu to ordinary mortals. Inca maidens dedicated to serve the sun in the nunneries of Cuzco were required to remain virgins until they were married off to some worthy dignitary, who was the recipient of royal favor from the demigod, the Great Sun, the ruling Inca. Rome had her vestal virgins. And the military societies of the Cheyenne Indians each had four honorary virgins to perform ritual services in the society ceremonies. Sexual life is often incompatible with religion.

Shamans are generally devoted to this principle. Unless they are engaged in fertility rites to bring on a crop of babies or corn, they almost universally submit themselves to temporary celibacy when they are about to invoke their mystic powers. The belief is that the female physiology is itself charged with a mystic power of great potency. In this man-dominated world the unique female power is looked upon as evil and dangerous, dangerous especially to the mystic powers of men. Contamination of a male's supernatural power by the negative power of the female is believed to result from sexual association. When this attitude is exaggerated it leads to the sexual asceticism of some of the Late Classical cults and early Christianity, an asceticism that survives in the celibacy of the Catholic clergy and the Puritan distrust of sex that is embedded in much of our culture. Such intense elaboration of sex asceticism is only another example of the principle of skewed elaboration of culture. Sociology can induce few good functional reasons for its existence. Psychiatry and psychology can adduce manifold instances of malfunctioning as a result of it—the psychotic and neurotic quirks of the repressed personality.

Mating Prohibitions. The special checks upon premarital sexual activity discussed above are as nothing compared to the general mating prohibitions that exist in every human society of which we have knowledge. These prohibitions do not put a stop to all mating activities, but they operate to prevent mating or sexual association between persons of certain defined statuses. Since mating prohibitions exist in all societies known to us, this means that permissible total promiscuity has never been observed among human beings. *Hypothetical promiscuity* has been advanced as the condition of human sexual activity in early prehistoric times, and numerous fantasies of anthropological theory have been put forward with this as a base.[5] Yet the evidence on which the hypothesis rests is so slight and equivocal that the theories based on it are compounded more of imagination than objective fact.

Whatever may have been the practices among our subhuman ancestors, social order and promiscuity do not mix. This is one of the most ancient social discoveries made by man. It is so important that it has been put into universal practice.

Incest Prohibition. Mating with any person who is *socially defined* as a genetic relative is forbidden. Any such prohibited mating is incestuous. The prohibition of sex relations between genetic relatives is therefore known as the *incest tabu*. It automatically follows in the case of forbidden sex relations that marriage between persons subject to this rule is also forbidden.

Incest tabus are universal among all peoples, because incest is repugnant to the least as well as to the most civilized people. The universality of incest prohibition and the fact that it is concerned with a basic biological act have lead to the common view that it is instinctive. Universality, however, is not in itself any evidence of instinct. As well say that fire making is an instinct, because all peoples practice it! The weight of the evidence is on the other side; incest prohibition is not instinctive. Rather, it is rooted in a social, not a biological, basis.

Let us observe how this works. The tabu on the mating of brother and sister is almost universal, as is mating between parent and child. The exceptions that bar universality are few and far between, nor do they in any case apply to the entire population of any society. The exceptions to the brother-sister rule are the famous cases of the royalty of Egypt, Hawaii, and Inca Peru. In these instances marriage between brother and sister of royal lineage was required in the belief that the supreme royalty was divine, marriage with mortals a corruption and lese majesty. But alas for ideals! Cleopatra, although she married her twelve-year-old brother, saw to his murder while she mated with Julius Caesar and Mark Antony.

Another special and very peculiar exception to the brother-sister tabu exists among the Balinese, who suppose that boy and girl twins have been

---

[5] L. H. Morgan, in his *Ancient Society*, was the outstanding early progenitor of the idea; R. Briffault, in *The Mothers*, is the modern protagonist of the notion.

too intimate in their mother's womb. The penalties for incest are severe in Bali, but in the case of baby twins, temporary banishment of the parents and "erring" twins, followed by a ceremony of purification and atonement, negate the sin. This makes it permissible for the mating in the womb to be completed as a true marriage in later life.[6] Ordinary brother-sister marriages are said to have been permissible among the aboriginal Ainus of Japan, but the evidence for this is merely mythological. Myth is not good historical evidence.

Such permissible marriages within the family show that when social considerations make it desirable there is no horror of sex relations within the family.

More remarkable than the exceptions to the narrow rules of incest prohibition are the arbitrary practices of many primitives in the extension of the scope of relationship terms to include persons of diverse genealogical status in an arbitrarily established social status. Indian boys and girls who have gone to white schools talk of "my sister" and "my Indian sister." What is the distinction? To us a sister is a girl born of the same mother as oneself. However, Catholics do stretch the term to include nuns, and members of a sorority extend the term to include each other. When the Indian boy of today makes the distinction of "sister" and "Indian sister," he is trying to make clear that the Indian concept of "sister" is somewhat different from the white man's. If the speaker is a Seed Eater Shoshone from Idaho, "sister" in its native sense means not only "daughter of my own mother" but includes *all* female cousins through both father and mother. Primitives take their relationship terms quite literally; therefore, a girl called "sister" *is* a sister and must be treated as such in all respects. Sex relations and marriage with all "sisters" are therefore automatically tabued.

This broadening of relationship categories has been aptly called *lumping* by Lowie.[7] It is the usual characteristic of relationship systems that are identified as *classificatory*. Because most primitive systems are classificatory, many individuals are embraced within the incest prohibitions by the simple fiat of a social system that dubs them as "father," "mother," "brother," or "sister" when in biological fact they are no such thing.

The Shoshones and the Hawaiians lump all cousins in a single sibling (brother and sister) category. Most other primitives indulge in a curious

---

[6] J. Belo, "A Study of a Balinese Family" (*American Anthropologist,* Vol. 38, 1936), p. 30.

[7] R. H. Lowie, "Kinship" (*Encyclopedia of the Social Sciences,* Vol. 3, 1931), pp. 568–572.

discrimination that intensifies the impression of arbitrary disregard of biological reality. A certain type of cousin is classified as "brother" or "sister," but another type of cousin is regarded as not being a relative at all. The first type of cousin we call *parallel cousin,* because the parents through which they are related are of like sex. The other type of cousin we call *cross-cousin,* not because of any temperamental peculiarities but because the parents through which they are related are of opposite sex; there is a crossing over from one sex to the other in the genealogy of relationship. In any tribe in which cross-cousins are distinguished from parallel cousins, cross-cousins are never reckoned as belonging to the same kinship group. In the dogma of the social system they are *not* relatives. The logic of such a premise produces a biological absurdity, but let the biologist protest in vain! To marry a parallel cousin may be incest, to marry a parallel cousin who is a member of one's own clan *is* incest, but to marry a cross-cousin may be the thing to do. It may even be the required thing to do! Thus one is forbidden to marry a first cousin of parallel relationship, while it is good form to marry a first cousin of cross relationship. Both are equally close in genetic kinship, but the second is no relative at all in *sociologically determined* kinship.

There are many other equally arbitrary extensions and distinctions in the classification of relatives that make the social relations of primitive man different from ours. Elaboration of this subject requires such special treatment that full discussion of it is reserved for a separate chapter on Kinship Systems and Terminology (Chap. 17). The essential point at this stage is that sociological factors play a more important role in the definition of incestuous relations than do the facts of biological reality. Incest prohibitions are not biologically based and therefore are not instinctive.

It has been argued by Westermarck [8] and Morgan, [9] among earlier anthropologists, that primitive man became cognizant of racial deterioration resulting from close inbreeding. They averred that on this basis primitive man preserved his racial stamina by preventing close inbreeding through the establishment of incest prohibitions. The fact is, however, that inbreeding does not necessarily produce physical deterioration. It depends on the nature of the inbreeding stock. Inbreeding does no more than intensify the traits the stock possessed at the outset. Recessive traits have a better chance of obtaining somatic realization where inbreeding is marked. If undesirable recessives are in the stock, they may well come to

---

[8] F. Westermarck, *The History of Human Marriage,* Vol. 2, pp. 218–241.
[9] Morgan, *op. cit.,* p. 424.

the fore and deterioration may then result. Nevertheless, it is equally true that inbreeding intensifies the influence of dominant traits. A stock with desirable dominants becomes stronger. The end result may be good or bad; it all depends on the distribution of traits with respect to dominance and desirability. Among the mountaineers of Kentucky the inbred populations of some pocketed valleys have been observed to send young men and women of consistently superior mentality to Berea College. The populations of other pocketed valleys in the same area are distinguished for the occurrence of epilepsy and a plethora of morons. Cleopatra, the last of the Ptolemies, product of twelve generations of brother-sister marriages, was hardly a specimen of physical degeneration, whatever may be said of her morals.

If biological factors do not suffice to explain so important a social phenomenon as incest prohibition, it behooves the anthropologist to discover what nonbiological factors may be responsible for such rigorous and universal rules. Unfortunately, all explanations of incest prohibitions must forever remain hypotheses, for the insurmountable reason that no observations can be made on any group of people in which there is an absolute absence of rules restricting mating and inbreeding. Nor is it probable that an experimental incestuous society will ever be set up for scientific study. We can therefore do no more than accept as most probable that hypothesis which most reasonably fits the known facts. Of the many hypotheses that have been advanced to date, Malinowski's is by far the most satisfactory.

Malinowski posits the proposition that sexual affection is anteceded in the development of the individual by strongly conditioned parental and fraternal affection, based on intimate family associations, which occurs before the maturation of the sex drives. These are the affective emotions that cement the bonds of family and kin, that give solidarity to the foundation group of any society—the group of immediate kinsmen. The family is founded in part upon the sexual association of spouses, between whom the sex drive may have legitimate play. But sex is a dangerous element. From its drives arise powerful emotional disturbances of great disruptive potentiality. In preadolescence the sex drives are unmatured; they are not yet dangerous. On maturation under unrestricted conditions, however, gratification of the sex drives would frequently be sought with those nearest at hand, toward whom one already has affection, the members of one's own household. This would naturally lead to mating between siblings and parents and offspring. The violent emotions engendered by sexual affection would blast and disrupt family unity built upon the earlier established filial-fraternal affections. *A house divided against itself cannot stand; it will become all one thing, or all the other.* Promiscuity and the family cannot exist side by side; sex relations, except for those of the father and mother, must be barred. Thus the preservation of the intimate kin group, the foundation unit of society, is maintained.[10]

The punishments, or negative sanctions, for the violation of the incest tabus vary greatly from one society to another, but a definite regional distribution of characteristic reactions is discernible. In Australia, where kinship is a subject of intense interest, most tribes punish incest with death. Plains Indians, on the other hand, do not consider incest either a crime or a sin. They simply look upon it as impossible behavior, so inconceivable that only insane persons indulge in it. Yet the punishment was mild in the few rare cases that have been recorded. A Dakota father of an incestuous brother and sister proclaimed, "Now I am the father of dogs!" Comanche informants cannot remember a single actual case of incest among their people, nor can they stretch their imaginations sufficiently to give a specific statement of what the public reaction would have been had such a case occurred, except to say that the people would have shunned them and called them *keshuant*, crazy.

In ancient Bali the punishment was poetic and devastating. The hapless couple were adorned with yokes customarily worn by pigs. They were then made to crawl on all fours to drink from the swill trough of the hogs. After this humiliation, they were banished forever from the village, and their lands were confiscated. No other village would take them in for fear of ill luck and disaster. They were doomed to a fearsome existence alone in the jungle.[11]

The forensic Ashanti of the West African Sudan give vivid reasons for the imposition of the death penalty for incest. According to them, if the sinful crime were to have gone unpunished

. . . hunters would have ceased to kill, children would have ceased to have been born, crops would have refused to bear fruit, the ancestral spirits would have been infuriated, gods would have been angered, clans would have ceased to exist, and all would have been *basa basa* [chaos] in the world.[12]

Exogamy. Exogamy (Gr. *ex* outside of + *gamos* marriage) results from the application of the incest prohibition to marriage. It may be defined as *the social rule that prohibits a person from marrying within a defined social group of which he is a member.* Exogamy applies for the

---

[10] B. Malinowski, "Culture" (*Encyclopedia of the Social Sciences*, Vol. 4, 1931), p. 630.

[11] Belo, *op. cit.,* p. 29.

[12] R. S. Rattray, *Ashanti Law and Constitution*, p. 304.

most part to kinship groups, real or putative. The Chinese usage that persons of the same surname may not marry, because similar surnames imply kinship, rests on this principle. It is as though all Smiths were forbidden ever to marry any other Smith on the grounds that all Smiths are relatives!

The dogma of clan kinship is always that clan members are common relatives. Clan exogamy is therefore universal wherever there are clans.

Locality exogamy sometimes occurs where there is a presumption of common blood among all the members of a local community. The Ona of Tierra del Fuego liked to go as far from home as possible to find a wife for this reason. This type of exogamy is especially concentrated in India, but it also has a fairly wide distribution among the South Slavs. Elsewhere it is only of sporadic occurrence.

Incest prohibitions and their exogamic corollaries are negative principles, which limit mate selection with a "Thou shalt not." Every human being, civilized or savage, is confronted by such rules when it comes to choosing a mate. We are never permitted free choice in the selection of mates. Personal affinity, we find, is shackled by the binding chains of social permissibility.[13]

Preferential Mating. So integral and important an element in social structure is the family that for most societies culture not only defines whom one may marry but goes much further to prescribe certain classes of persons with whom one ought, or must, marry. These limitations constitute the rules of preferential mating. Each type of preferential mating has its own functional reasons for being and must therefore be explained separately. Furthermore, the operation and effect of any particular type of preferential mating may be different in different cultural contexts. This raises the necessity of special examination of the exact nature of the requirements in each culture if an exact analysis is hoped for. To do this is beyond our powers in an introduction to anthropology, but the main characteristics of preferred marriage forms can be adequately formulated in terms of general principles.

Endogamy. Endogamy (Gr. *endo* within + *gamos* marriage) is the converse of exogamy. It is *the social rule that requires a person to marry within a defined social group of which he is a member.* The occurrence of endogamy is much less common than is exogamy. Unlike exogamy, there is no particular universal type of social group to which the endogamous rule applies. Nevertheless, endogamy is found to some degree in

---

[13] The poignancy of personal tragedy when persons of forbidden relationship have the misfortune to fall in love is delicately exemplified in O. La Farge's story of the Navajo youth, *Laughing Boy.*

many societies, although the rule is not always explicit and verbalized. It frequently expresses itself as a tendency, without actually being a requirement. It may also apply to any kind of a social group. The discussion of incest prohibitions has shown, however, that because of the prevalence of exogamic rules, the application of endogamy to family or clan is most exceptional. Rules of exogamy and endogamy are contradictory and cannot apply simultaneously to the same social group. They do, of course, exist side by side in the same culture.

The world's most famous system of endogamy is the caste organization of India with its 2,000 or so castes and subcastes, between which marriage is formally prohibited.

The African Sudan exhibits numerous tribes in which a like caste endogamy is prevalent on a considerably more modest scale. Among the East African Masai, ironworkers form a pariah occupational caste subject to the domination of the warrior caste. Each caste marries within its own numbers. The neighboring Ruanda are divided into castes made up of the lanky, ruling, pastoral nobility—alien conquerors from the north, the horticultural Hutu, and the lowly Twa hunters. A ruling caste Tussi may on occasion marry a Hutu woman, if his fortunes have sunk so low that he cannot find a mate of his own rank. But neither a Tussi nor a Hutu will stoop to marriage with a Twa.[14]

Transplanted Africans and Orientals in North America find themselves subject to the same type of hierarchal caste endogamy in our culture.

While castes are explicitly endogamous, social classes are prone to exhibit similar tendencies without recourse to explicitly prescribed rules. We are all familiar with this manifestation in many subtle ways. Its roots are in the desire to retain the exclusive and distinctive qualities of self-regarding in-groups. Intermarriage is a leveler and universalizer of culture and race. In-groups who cling tenaciously to dogmas of self-righteousness and superior goodness, who implicitly feel that their values are too dear to leave open to competition, raise the barricade of endogamy. Mohammedans may not marry infidels; orthodox Hebrews may not marry Gentiles on pain of banishment from church and family, followed by the performance of mourning rituals for the dead. Stumbling blocks are put in the path of marriage between Catholic and non-Catholic.

Special forms of endogamy, which occur among primitives, include the locality endogamy of the Bella Coola Indians of the Northwest Coast.

---

[14] See R. H. Lowie, *The Origin of the State*, pp. 29–33, for a detailed discussion of Ruanda caste interrelations.

These people place great value on the sacred stories that are told in family rituals as a part of the family inheritance. If outsiders marry into the family they will have a right in the stories too. Marriage within the village bars outsiders and prevents too great a depreciation of the fiduciary value of the tales.

The Todas of India require clan exogamy, but marriage must be within the moiety (half of the tribe) to which a person belongs.

Tribal endogamy, while rarely an explicit rule, is frequently a strong tendency. Westermarck has suggested that there is an instinctive basis for such endogamy on the grounds that mating between creatures of different species rarely occurs among animals, and mating between animals of different genera never takes place.[15] However, the cogency of the argument is hard to see, since all living human beings belong to the same species. Rather, men live by values—the values which are familiar and the values which they believe promote their special well-being. And the values of the out-group are always a potential challenge to the values of the in-group; unless the in-group develops a cosmopolitan disregard for its own uniqueness, it will take refuge in *social distance*. Endogamy is its strongest shield.

Affinal Marriage. Much more specific than mere endogamy are the rules of preferential mating that bring about marriages between in-laws. We call these *affinal marriages, i.e.,* marriage to a relative through marriage.

Levirate. Marriage of a woman to her brother-in-law, known as the *levirate* (L. *levir,* brother-in-law), is the most popular affinal marriage form among the peoples of the world. Under the simple levirate the marriage occurs only after the death of the husband, when the widow is inherited by the dead man's brother. In the case of the *junior levirate,* only a younger brother may be the inheritor. This handy practice occurs in all parts of the world, among peoples of the most diverse levels of cultural development. The rude Australians made it a rule; the Biblical Hebrews approved of it; and the civilized Incas provided for the inheritance of all a man's secondary wives by his younger brother, or perhaps his sons. An Inca first wife never remarried. She was supported by the state, if necessary, with a widow's pension proffered by an effective social-security system.

Whether the young man who finds himself with his brother's widow on his hands likes it or not depends partly on personalities, but also on cultural determinants. The Comanche inheritor of a widow is apt to look

---

[15] Westermarck, *op. cit.,* Vol. 2, pp. 35–38.

on it as a right and a privilege, especially since the widow may not marry another man without that person's obtaining a quitclaim from the heir. And that requires a consideration—a horse or two, or perhaps some blankets. In other cases there is no element of choice for the collateral heir. The woman is his willy-nilly. Her family has a claim on him, as much as he has a claim on her. His family also has a voice, as in the case of a Shoshone Indian who in 1933 was forced to divorce the wife of his own choice in order to marry his dead brother's wife. His people wanted to keep the girl in the family, and the laws of the United States do not permit a man to have two wives.

The purpose of the levirate is not hard to discern. It effects a continuation of the link between the two kin groups that was established through the original marriage. It is a manifestation of the intergroup character of marriage in that the defunct husband's kin have the privilege and right to prevent the widow from leaving their group. Her obligation is not alone to the man she married but also to his kin. Of equally great importance, in view of the fact that in primitive society the children usually follow the mother when a home is broken, the children are not lost to the father's group. On the other hand, the claims of the widow's kin upon the group of the defunct husband are maintained in the substitution of a brother. The situation is one of balanced reciprocity.

Anticipatory Levirate. Fraternal polyandry has recently been reported as occurring among some of the Shoshone tribes of the Nevada desert.[16] The Seed Eater Shoshones of the Snake River Desert of Idaho and their close relatives, the Comanches, did not go so far as that but they did come close to it in a practice that the author has elsewhere named the *anticipatory levirate.*[17] With the thought in mind that each may some day inherit the other's wife, a married man was wont to extend the sexual favors of his wife to an unmarried younger brother. In return he expected reciprocity when his brother had a wife to share. A man always calls his brother's wife "wife," and again the implications of the kinship term are taken seriously. By this arrangement a brother simply enjoys the privileges of the levirate while his married brother is still living. A sort of attenuated fraternal polyandry results.

Sororate. As in the levirate a living brother takes the place of the dead father in a bereaved household, so in the sororate a sister is substituted for the mother. Therefore, in the sororate a bereaved husband marries his

[16] W. Z. Park, "Paviotso Polyandry" (*American Anthropologist*, Vol. 39, 1937), pp. 366–368.

[17] E. A. Hoebel, "Comanche and Hɜkandika Shoshone Relationship Systems" (*American Anthropologist*, Vol. 41, 1939), p. 447.

deceased wife's sister. From the woman's angle, a girl marries her dead sister's husband.

The sororate goes hand in hand with the levirate; each is the complement of the other. It is observed by virtually every tribe of North America outside of the Pueblo area and is found widely distributed throughout the world.

The common mistake of confusing the sororate with *sororal polygyny* should be avoided. Under the true sororate a man is married to but one sister at a time. Under sororal polygyny he does not wait for the death of his wife to marry her younger sister; he takes her when she becomes of age.

Secondary Affinal Marriages. The subjection of the individual to group identification takes a bizarre turn when the levirate and sororate principles are extended to affinal relatives of a higher or lower generation. This results in such peculiarities as marriage (1) of a man to his wife's brother's daughter; (2) of a man to his wife's father's sister; (3) of a woman to her husband's sister's son.

When a tribe uses a patrilineal system of descent reckoning (see page 203), a man's wife's brother's daughter belongs to the same kin group as his wife. Her sociological status is that of his wife. Why not make her a wife? This is also true for a man's wife's father's sister. No matter that the secondary wife may be twenty years older or younger. A wife is a wife for all that.

If a tribe uses a matrilineal system of descent, it so happens that a woman's husband's sister's son belongs to the same kin group as her husband and has the same sociological status as her husband. Why not make him a husband? Or, look at it from the man's point of view. In a matrilineal system a boy usually inherits from his maternal uncle (mother's brother). Why not inherit his wife? Marriage of a boy to his mother's brother's wife is marriage of a woman to her husband's sister's son, seen other end to.

Marriage with secondary affinal relatives is not common; only a minority of human societies find it worth bothering with. But in a strong clan system, inclined to extend the logic of clan identity, these marriages follow naturally enough.[18]

Filial Inheritance. Attention has already been called to the Inca practice of permitting a brother or a son to inherit the secondary wives of a dead man. Inheritance of the wives of his father, who were not his uterine mother, is also known to have been practiced by the Caribs of

[18] See L. A. White, "A Problem in Kinship Terminology" (*American Anthropologist*, Vol. 41, 1939), pp. 569–570.

South America and by a number of African tribes. Filial inheritance is obviously possible only where there is polygamous marriage. It also serves to keep the women in the family.

Kin Marriage. The primitive practice of marriage with cross-cousins has already been noted in the discussion of incest and its prohibition. Cross-cousin marriage is simply the most common form of a type of connubial union that we shall call *kin marriage,* marriage with a genetic relative. This type of marriage has recently been discussed in detail by Loeb and Toffelmier who call it "an incestuous marriage; because it involves the sexual union of persons related by blood ties." [19] This type of marriage is not actually incestuous, however, because marriage with relatives who are not looked upon as members of the kin group is not incestuous. A marriage is incestuous, it must be emphasized, *only* if it is forbidden on the grounds of real or putative relationship. In terms of social reality only those relatives are kin who are recognized as members of the kin group.

Marriage with a genetic relative who is not a member of the kin group is especially prized in many parts of the primitive world. The marriage may be not to any genetic relative, but only to particular relatives: notably, (1) cross-cousins; (2) mother's sister (or sister's son); (3) father's sister (or brother's son); (4) sister's daughter (or mother's brother); (5) sister's son's daughter (or father's mother's brother), an occasional Australian form. Types 2 to 4 are marriages between persons we would call uncle and niece, aunt and nephew. Type 5 would be a marriage between a granduncle and grandniece!

Marriage of cross-cousins is by no means a freak occurrence. It is the preferred union, a "must" among virtually all the tribes of North and Central Australia and a large part of Melanesia. Many people of Asia marry in accordance with its dictates, even those of ancient China. The Negroes of Africa follow the practice (except for the Sudanese). Polynesians, on the other hand, never took to the notion, except the natives of Tonga who have had close contact with the Melanesian Fijis. In America cross-cousin marriage occurs in California, the Great Basin, and sporadically among Algonquians of the Northeast.

To some peoples it is a matter of indifference whether one marries a cross-cousin related through one's father or one's mother. This is the case with the Dravidians of India, who are given to *symmetrical* cross-cousin marriage. In other societies such tolerance is lacking. It may be insisted that marriage be either on the mother's side or the father's. The Haidas

[19] "Kin Marriage and Exogamy" (*Journal of General Psychology,* Vol. 20, 1939), p. 181.

of the Northwest Coast have a predilection in common with the Melanesian Trobriand Islanders, who permit marriage only with the father's sister's daughter. The Haidas' neighbors, the Tsimshian tribe, chose the other alternative, permitting marriage only with the mother's brother's daughter. The result is *asymmetrical* cross-cousin marriage.

Marriage of a man to his sister's daughter is characteristic of the Indian tribes of the South American tropical forest. Its only other occurrence in the wide world is among the Tungus of Siberia and in India. The great gaps in its distribution indicate clearly that as between the Old World and the New the trait is an independent invention. Within the Amazonian region, however, the occurrence of the trait among so many contiguous tribes indicates diffusion. Gillin suggests on the basis of his observations among the Caribs, who are clanless and who practice sister's daughter marriage, that the marriage form is correlated to levirate and sororate practices and not to the influence of a clan system.[20] However, a definitive functional-distributional study of the complex is necessary before this point may be considered settled, since it is quite possible that the clanless Caribs have borrowed the marriage practice from tribes who may have invented the custom because of paternal clan interests.

Why cross-cousin marriage? Why should some societies practice the symmetrical, others the asymmetrical, form? The second question can sometimes be answered in terms of the specific kinship organization of particular tribes. The first question, however, is much more baffling. It is a bête noir of anthropology. Because of its great importance, it demands analysis but it refuses to yield a satisfactory general answer.

Nevertheless, one thing is clear. Cross-cousin marriage is linked to clan organization, even though it does appear among a few tribes who do not have clans.

When descent is analyzed in tribes possessing clan systems it can readily be seen that parallel-cousins *may be* members of the same clan, but cross-cousins *can never be* (Fig. 65). It thus works out that parallel-cousins may be classified as brother and sister, between whom marriage is forbidden. Cross-cousins do not belong to the recognized kin group, are never called brother and sister, and are eligible as potential mates because they do not have the status of relatives. These circumstances make cross-cousin marriage possible but they do not explain why it should become a *preferred* marriage form.

[20] J. P. Gillin, "The Barama River Caribs of British Guiana" (*Papers of the Peabody Museum of American Archaeology and Ethnology, Harvard University*, Vol. 14, 1936), p. 90.

Most of the plausible explanations of cross-cousin marriage that have been advanced by anthropologists apply to specific conditions as they exist in particular tribes or areas. Because what applies in one place does not apply in another, Professor Lowie has expressed the cautious opinion that "cross cousin marriage is in all probability not a phenomenon that has evolved from a single cause but one that has independently risen in several centers from diverse motives." [21]

Lowie's observation is undoubtedly true if the investigator is considering the diverse manifestations of cross-cousin marriage in different societies in different places. Yet the suggestion of Loeb and Toffelmier that

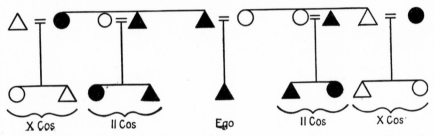

FIG. 65. The separation of parallel- and cross-cousins in a moiety system with patrilineal descent.

cross-cousin marriage and all other forms of kin marriage are generated by the same factors that give rise to incest tabus is deserving of serious consideration.[22] The very fact that incest tabus are universal means that there must be a universal desire, or likelihood of desire, for sex relations with close kin. We hold with Malinowski that the desire must be repressed for the good of social solidarity. Yet if the desire to mate with a close relative can be gratified without danger to the social order, why not permit it? In fact, why not encourage it? Primitives whose social order makes it possible do precisely that. They encourage a person, even require a person to marry a genetic relative who is not a member of the functioning kin group. First cross-cousins stand closest in this harmless relationship. They are the very ones who are most frequently prescribed by the rules of preferential mating. Other kin marriages are less direct methods of attaining the same end. Thus the desire for sexual activity with a close genetic relative is safely satisfied without breaking in upon the sociologically defined extended family.

Another possibility can be found in the widespread hostility and social restraint manifest in the relations of married persons to their own parents-

[21] R. H. Lowie, *Primitive Society*, p. 31.
[22] Loeb and Toffelmier, *op. cit.*, pp. 181–184, 224.

in-law (see Chap. 14). In cross-cousin marriage the father-in-law and the mother-in-law will necessarily be a person's mother's brother or father's sister, depending on the type of cross-cousin marriage followed, while in an inter-familial exchange marriage (see page 210) the parents-in-law will be aunt and uncle. This brings about the salubrious result of putting the favored avuncular or amitate personages, the very ones with whom pleasant and familiar relations have existed since childhood, in the position of parents-in-law. Such an arrangement should work to neutralize the inherent in-law antagonisms. If this were generally found to be the case, we would find a very strong functional reason for cross-cousin marriage without recourse to subconscious compensations such as suggested by Loeb and Toffelmier. At the present moment, however, this suggestion is no more than a hypothetical suggestion that calls for empirical testing with statistical correlation.

CHAPTER 14

MARRIAGE

The basic purpose of marriage is to stabilize mating. Infancy among human beings is long drawn out. The absolute dependency of children upon adults for sheer physical survival endures for eight to ten years at the very least. Yet even a longer period of training and development is required before the child has acquired the minimum of skills and knowledge to make him a sufficient adult in any society. For those who are going to play the more specialized roles in an advanced society, infancy is extended through a full third of modern life expectation. It has been written that "college prolongs infancy." Even without sarcasm this is true. Training in the specialized aspects of our culture is so complex that the select few who go to colleges to receive it are not ready to begin their roles as adults until twenty full years of life are past.

The continuance of a society and its culture require that some man and woman, or group of men and women, be fixed with the responsibility of providing the necessary care and training without which children perish or fail to acquire the cultural techniques and values to which their society holds. E. W. Burgess, long an expert and scientific student of the family, believes that the fact of paramount significance for our understanding of the family is that "the sexual impulse in itself is not sufficient to insure more than the casual union of the sexes." [1] Anthropological evidence concurs in this conclusion. Marriage fixes responsibility. Put another way, the function of marriage is to make the world safe for the family. As was observed in the last chapter, marriage is the institution that defines the interpersonal relationships that determine the form and pattern of the association we know as the family. Marriage is, therefore, a culture complex. It is the characteristic behavior, as family members, of the group of people who make up a family. This means, of course, that for descriptive purposes marriage and the family are really one and the same. It is for analytical reasons solely that we draw a distinction between them.

In this chapter attention shall be devoted to the ways in which primitive peoples enter into marriage, and how they may get out of it, if that

[1] E. W. Burgess, *Introduction* in *The Negro Family in the United States*, p. xi.

is permissible. In the next chapter, we shall look into the forms the family assumes and the special functions it fulfills.

Marriage by Purchase. Below the civilized level the formal payment of a price for a bride is the normal, or most usual, method of getting a wife. Marriage by consideration, or *bride price*, was found to prevail in 303 of the 434 tribes statistically sampled by the English anthropologists Hobhouse, Wheeler, and Ginsberg.[2] It is the common thing in Africa;[3] it is the regular practice among the patrilineal tribes of Indonesia; and it occurs in one form or another in all other parts of the world.

It must not be assumed that bride purchase means women are mere degraded slaves to be sold from the auction block of a marriage mart—a sordid commercial commodity. A commercial element necessarily colors the institution, for after all, a family with five daughters to "sell" and one son for whom a bride must be purchased, is economically better off than the family with one daughter to sell and five sons to be provided for. But women are not fluid goods in a free market. Husbands are never permitted to resell the wives they have acquired by purchase.

Nor does the occurrence of bride price mean that the position of woman in terms of prestige, privilege, power and labor is necessarily high or low. It does mean, however, that women have value as members of the kinship group. The value of a particular woman in terms of bride price is determined by a compound of her personal attractiveness in beauty and skills and the social and economic status of the groom's family balanced against the bride's. The personal attractiveness of the groom as a prospective son-in-law usually acts to win him a lower bride price.

The social prestige of a married woman is directly influenced by the amount of the bride price that has been paid for her. A twenty-cow wife in East Africa has a definite forensic advantage in any argument with the woman for whom but ten cows have been paid. Her husband and children enjoy a like glory in terms of her worth in bride price. Among the Yuroks of California this is so fixed that the social status and wergild of a man are determined absolutely by the bride price paid for his mother.

A number of factors underlie bride purchase, but the basic principle is the supremacy of the kin group over its individual members. In no society does the person stand alone as an individual. This is particularly

---

[2] L. T. Hobhouse, G. C. Wheeler, and M. Ginsberg, *The Material Culture and Social Institutions of the Simpler Peoples.*

[3] The Native Administration Act of 1927, Union of South Africa, in recognition of the importance of bride price to native society expressly forbids any court from setting aside *lobola* or *bogadi* as "repugnant to natural law." J. Lewin, *Studies in African Native Law*, p. 57.

true in primitive societies where status as a member of a group of kinsmen is the primary determinant of the individual's social position.

In spite of what aspirant youth may feel about it, marriage is not a concern of the marrying pair alone. Society at large has its stake in the affair and what ensues from it. The families of the principals to a marriage have their very direct interests in its many ramifications.

To understand marriage at all, and primitive marriage especially, it is necessary to grasp this basic principle: *marriage constitutes an alliance between two kin groups in which the couple concerned is merely the most conspicuous link.* Everyone learns, sooner or later, if he does not know it now, that when he marries the "one and only" he marries not only her but all her relatives as well. Brides, of course, have the same experience.

The kin-group alliance is shaped as a kind of implicit contract. Tangible evidence of the contract helps to solidify it. Symbolic gestures such as marriage feasts and rituals serve this function well. This is also the effect of gift exchange at marriage. When gift exchanges are customarily equal, no one comes out ahead. This is the case with the Cheyenne Indians. A boy who has set his heart on a particular girl talks it over with his family. If they think the choice is a good one, after taking into consideration not only the qualities of the girl but also the character of her family, they muster their nicest transferable possessions to place at the disposal of the young swain. These are carefully loaded on a fine horse. They then call upon a respected old woman to lead the horse to the tipi of the girl's elder brother. There she stakes it out for all the camp to see, while she enters the lodge to press the suit of her protégé. The elder brother calls in his cousins for a family conclave. If they decide the proposal is acceptable, they unload the horse and distribute the gifts among themselves, the brother taking the horse. All then disperse to their separate lodges to rustle up what each will offer as a return gift. Each is expected to bring back in the next day or two something equal in value to what he has received. In the meantime, the bride is made beautiful, and when all is ready she is mounted on a good horse, the presents are loaded on another, and the old woman is called upon to lead the bride and the gift horse back to the groom's tipi. There she is received by all his family, and her accompanying gifts are distributed among them in accordance with what they gave. So far as economic value goes they are exactly where they were before. What then has been gained?

Perhaps we can understand the social function of such activity better if we reflect on our own elaborate gift exchanges at Christmas time. The energy, trouble, and effort in acquiring and distributing suitable gifts is immense and often discouraging. As often as not, we end up with a collection of items we would just as soon do without. Nevertheless, in the exchange we reaffirm and bind anew the friendships and relationships we value or find desirable.

The line between gift and purchase is gossamer thin. So, on occasion, is the line between gift and bribe. In either case, the differences lie in the attitude of the giver and receiver and the tone of the situation as it is customarily felt in the community. This makes it sometimes difficult to determine whether the social practice in a given tribe is bride purchase or merely gift. When a Comanche gives arrows or a horse to a girl's elder brother in preparation for a marriage proposal, it probably is to be considered as a gift, since the elder brother is not obligated to release his sister in exchange. Yet a man knows what the other has in mind when he gives these gifts, and acceptance does impose a measure of claim upon his sister. In this sense, the gift is a purchase price.

Since gift giving as a smoother-of-the-way is apparently a universal practice, it is probable that gift giving as a step in marriage exists as a weak form of bride price in most societies in which the overtures are made by the men.

Bride price is a stepping up of gift giving and an aspect of gift exchange when women have come to acquire a highly esteemed significance as an element in the family structure. Some tribes explain it as a compensation to the parents for the trouble they went to to raise the girl. Others simply say that her family has something the groom badly wants; therefore he must pay. The extent to which bride price is correlated with patrilineal descent systems has not been statistically determined, but the adhesion of these two forms has been definitely noted for Indonesia.[4] When the woman is removed from her family to that of her husband's, and more especially, when her children belong to her husband's family rather than her own, then her family really is losing something for which they may require a payment in equalization. In Bali, the natives feel that bride price removes the woman from the protection of her domestic gods and validates the sway of her husband's family gods over her.

Bride price thus effects the transfer of the girl from one family group to another. But there is more significance to it than this. It is not so much the purchase of a bride as it is of posterity. Children are the goal, offspring who will perpetuate the husband's family line. This is what gives bride price its special association with patrilineal descent. A sterile bride is a bad bargain. It is therefore common among African Negroes for the

---

[4] B. ter Haar, *Adat Law in Indonesia*, pp. 169–173.

bride's family to substitute a younger sister without charge, if no issue is forthcoming from the first daughter for whom they have received bride price. As an alternative, the sum of the bride price may be refunded. This is often difficult, however, because the capital received in payment for the daughter may already have been invested in the purchase of a wife for a son. Thus, it has been reported (for the Thonga, for instance) that the family may be required to surrender their son's wife to their son-in-law in lieu of their barren daughter. These same requirements hold if the married daughter deserts her husband, who has paid for her.

Linton's report on the Vezo Sakalava of Madagascar shows to what extent bride price is actually the purchase of a right to children among these people. In the case of divorce, neither a refund of the cattle paid nor the substitution of another woman is socially permissible. The divorced wife may remarry, but only with her former husband's permission. This will be forthcoming upon agreement by the wife and her new husband-to-be that the first children born to them (up to the limit of three) will be deeded over to the first husband, who is the one that paid the bride price to her family. The woman nurses and keeps the children until weaning, whereupon they are turned over to her first husband and become his legal heirs without the formality of adoption.[5] All this illustrates another basic principle to be referred to in more detail later on, viz.: *among primitives sociological fatherhood is generally of more significance than biological fatherhood.*

A nice Sakalava refinement is that although legally a divorced husband may demand a refund, good form does not countenance it. That would be putting material values above human values! Such a man puts cattle above children.

Finally, among the Bavenda of South Africa, if the bride price is paid in installments, the children do not pass to the husband's family until the sum is paid in full.

A unique twist to bride price as a means of obtaining offspring is found among the Dahomeans of West Africa. A married woman may pay the bride price to obtain a second wife for her husband as a means of providing him with children. These children call their sire's first wife "father," because she, after all, is the one who paid for them.[6] This may seem to be carrying the principle of sociological fatherhood a bit far, but who can deny that it is logical?

[5] R. M. Linton, "The Tanala" (*Field Museum of Natural History, Anthropological Series,* Vol. 22, Chicago, 1933).

[6] M. J. Herskovits, "A Note on 'Woman Marriage' in Dahomey" (*Africa,* Vol. 10, 1937), pp. 335–341.

The medium of bride price varies in different parts of the world. In East and South Africa among the cattle raisers, the purchase price is primarily in cows. Among certain Indians of California it is in dentalium shells. On the Northwest Coast of North America it is in blankets and coppers. The Kazaks of Central Asia find horses, cattle, sheep, and camels acceptable according to the means of the groom. An African Hottentot pays in cattle and a girdle of ostrich shell beads to his future mother-in-law.

Suitor Service. A cheap but not easy way to obtain a wife is to work for her. Jacob put in seven years of labor to win the hand of Rachel, plus seven for Leah, who was not part of his bargain. Among the Siberian Chukchi, Koryak, and Yukaghir tribes service for the bride is the regular practice; it seems to have replaced bride price as the earlier form of acquisition of a wife.

Scattered tribes in all parts of the world have been found to require service in the bride's household as the price the groom must pay. Many of these tribes allow no alternative, but in others suitor service is simply a substitute for payment of the bride price—like the vagrant who washes dishes in the kitchen to pay for his meal.

The obligation of a son-in-law to work for his wife's parents may be an enduring responsibility. Although the Comanche Indians do not require outright suitor service, a son-in-law is expected to send a good share of the game he slays to the tipi of his mother-in-law. This is why parents want their daughter to marry a good hunter. A son-in-law does not have to do this, but if he does, he is a good son-in-law, and he is a poor son-in-law if he does not. His reward will be a younger daughter to become his second wife. But no meat, no second daughter.

Exchange Marriage. Another inexpensive way to get a bride is to swap sisters. This results in a form we know as *interfamilial exchange marriage*. In this arrangement a brother and a sister are married to a sister and her brother, and a man's wife's brother is also his sister's husband—a two-way brother-in-law. Since both the families come out even, there is no need for either bride price or suitor service, although gift exchanges are still allowed.

From the point of view of cementing family alliances, this method of acquiring a mate is best of all. It is easy to see that it doubles the connecting link between the two groups and it is the most equitable in all respects. Add to this the fact that in Australia and Melanesia, where interfamilial exchange marriage is most common, the exchange is preferably between cross-cousins, and it can be seen that the bond is even more firmly cemented.

The difficulty with this practice is, however, that it is not so easy to make a double match as it is a single one. The Shoshone Indians of the Snake River Desert in Idaho prefer this form of marriage to all others, and their whole system of kinship terminology is predicated upon it.[7] Yet in recent times, at least, such marriages have been in actuality few and far between.

Marriage by Capture. Novelists and romanticists dwell on the hoary days when the caveman was supposed to beat his beloved into insensibility with a knobby club, then to drag her by her flowing hair to his lair where she forthwith became his loving wife. This is the wishful notion of the "get 'em young, treat 'em rough, and tell 'em nothing" school. When anthropology was young, serious consideration was given to this fantasy as the earliest method of getting a wife. Suitors' trials and sham battles at marriage were thought to be symbolic survivals of the scuffles that accompanied the abduction of the feminine prize. It is still a popular notion that the harmless rice thrown at the escaping bride and groom is a gay vestige of the days when rocks and spears were hurled instead.

Mock capture is a real and not uncommon practice. When a young Bushman and his bride are to be married the folk gather from all around to join in the wedding feast. In the midst of the meal the groom seizes the bride. This is the signal for all her relatives to grab their dibbles and set to beating him. A minor battle royal takes place among the guests while the groom receives his drubbing. If he can keep his hold on the girl, the boy succeeds in his marriage. If he lets go under the hail of blows, he loses her.[8]

The African Bahima subject the bride to a tug of war between her clan and the groom's, who always wins. When the final pull is given in the groom's favor, the bride is hustled to a cowhide and raised from the ground by the groom's cohorts, who rush off with her, chased by friends and relatives.[9]

Of course, the hilarious horseplay that climaxes our own weddings and the escape of the bride and groom in a cloud of exhaust smoke (provided a spark plug has not been removed), are cut of the same cloth.

If this is not a survival of bride capture, what then is it? Modern anthropology prefers a functional to a pseudohistorical explanation. More properly, it is to be understood as a symbolic expression of latent and repressed hostilities of the two marrying families. True, they are to be

[7] *Cf.* E. A. Hoebel, "Comanche and Hȝkandika Shoshone Relationship Systems" (*American Anthropologist*, Vol. 41, 1939), pp. 440–457.

[8] G. W. Stow, *The Native Races of South Africa*, p. 96.

[9] J. Roscoe, *The Northern Bantu*, Vol. 2, p. 256.

allied in marriage. But alliance is only possible where differences exist. Alliance always involves a measure of antagonistic cooperation. Common interests dominate any alliance or it will not be forged. Yet the antagonisms are there to be felt, unconsciously or otherwise. The bride-giving family resents the successful intrusion of the suitor, and they are given the ritual opportunity of letting him know it in a harmless way. Thus are the deep emotions of resentment drawn off. Likewise, any feeling that the swain is unworthy of the precious daughter may be met by forcing him to prove his worth.

All this is not to contend that marriage by capture does not exist. It does. But we must dispel the notion that it could ever have been the prevailing technique in any supposed stage of human history. Rather, it is a supplementary way of getting a wife. Its advantage is that it is cheap and adventuresome, if risky. On the other hand, its disadvantages, aside from risk, are heavy. Since marriage is an alliance between kin groups, capturing a wife brings none of the advantages that are to be derived from such an alliance. There are no wife's relatives to back a man up or contribute their share of property. The man who captures his wives will, therefore, be at a disadvantage as against the man who has got his by reciprocal means. His children will not have the advantages and status his wife's family might bestow, and if his sole wife is from an alien tribe, his children will not be raised in the pure tradition of his own culture.

Plains Indian warriors, like the men of many another primitive tribe, do capture and mate with alien women. Many are the nations who have considered women the legitimate prize of war. However, unless a man is poorly off, he first marries a girl of his own tribe in the regular manner. His captured "wives" are secondary additions to his household: his concubines and his wife's household drudges. Here, as elsewhere, the position of the captive woman may be closer to that of a slave than of a true wife.

Again and again, we find that the abduction of women is the cause of bitter wars and annihilations. Helen of Troy may be the most famous such *bella causus belli*, but she was neither the first nor the last among her sex.

Inheritance of Wives. Inheritance of widows through the operation of the levirate and filial inheritance is of course of extreme importance as a form of marriage. However, nothing further need be added here to what we have already said in the previous chapter on this subject except to note that the Palvic and Bura tribes of Northern Nigeria allow a man to inherit his grandfather's wives.

Adoptive Marriage. In Indonesia and modern Japan a man may obtain a wife by being adopted into her family.[10] It is a device by which a patrilineally organized family may maintain its line when there are no sons. By legal fiction the son-in-law thus becomes a "son" in his wife's family, and his children belong to her family and not his. A queer quirk of this device is the fact that technically the groom's bride becomes his own "sister." It is necessary that the people close their eyes to this bit of logic, for that, of course, would be incest. Convenience masters logic and the husband is a "son" of his father-in-law for purposes of reckoning descent.

Fictive Marriage. Adoptive marriage is a form of fictive marriage in that it is assumed that the son-in-law is a son. More extreme forms of fictive marriage occasionally occur. Among them are the special practices of the Kwakiutl and the Nuer. In the case of the Kwakiutl the inheritance of chiefly prerogatives passes from a titled man to his grandson through his son-in-law, the grandson's father. It is not possible for the titles to pass to succeeding generations through the chief's sons directly. If there are no daughters, such inheritance would be blocked for lack of a son-in-law were it not for fictive marriage.

In such a case [writes Boas], a man who desires to acquire the use of a crest and the other privileges connected with the name performs a sham marriage with the son of the bearer of the name. The ceremony is performed in the same manner as a real marriage. In case the bearer of the name has no children at all, a sham marriage with a part of his body is performed, with his right or left side, a leg or an arm, and the privileges are conveyed in the same manner as in the case of a real marriage.[11]

The son-in-law begets children by a second wife.

Among the Nuers of the upper Nile, when a man has been murdered and the murderer's kinsmen have paid cattle in settlement, the blood money is used in part to "marry a wife to his name to give him heirs."[12] Who sires the children is not reported.

Elopement. Elopement is a safety valve. It is one of those saving cultural forms whose function is to provide an acceptable byroad wherewith to escape the dictates of formal custom. Marriage as we have seen is never left open to the untrammeled choice of the marrying individuals. There are incest and exogamic prohibitions; there are the limita-

[10] ter Haar, *op. cit.*, pp. 175–176; J. F. Embree, *The Japanese Nation*, p. 162.

[11] F. Boas, *Social Organization and Secret Societies of the Kwakiutl Indians* (United States National Museum, Report, 1895), p. 359.

[12] E. E. Evans-Pritchard, *The Nuer*.

tions of preferential mating; and there are the personal prejudices of family members to be met. On the other hand, there is love. Few people are so given to romantic love as are Americans. In our individualistic sentimentalism we exalt the ideal of marriage based on love—that mysterious psychophysiological reaction. Although many primitive cultures do not allow very much weight to love in marriage (indeed, many seem to ignore it entirely), the fact is that all primitives have their amorous likes and aversions too.

From the evidence it would appear that elopements take place in every known society. When familial or social disapproval blocks a fervently desired marriage, or when a planned marriage with a distasteful partner is about to be forced on the unwilling one, elopement is a way out. The tribes that require that elders and relatives seek the consent of marriageable youths to the arrangements they plan for them are surely a minority among mankind. This makes a general human necessity of the path of elopement.

Of course, the existence of a formal rule does not mean that it will always be insisted upon. Cheyenne men hold the legal right to dispose of their sisters as they wish. But as Calf Woman put it, "Kind-hearted brothers always found out how their sisters felt about it before they promised them to any man."

It is difficult to formulate a generalization concerning the status of elopement marriages. In the case of the Cheyennes the elopement would ultimately be recognized as a marriage and be validated by gift exchanges only if the pair ran off before the girl had actually been engaged by her brother to another man. It was a different matter if the promise had already been made. In several Cheyenne cases brothers committed suicide when their sisters eloped after they had been promised to someone else.[13]

In parts of the Pacific area the tendency to *cultural orthogenesis* has resulted in elopement becoming the *regular* way of getting married. This is the situation in a number of Australian tribes. According to the reports of Howitt,[14] elopement is the *reductio ad absurdum* of overdeveloped marriage rules among the Kurnai tribe. Broad rules of exogamy combine with narrow rules of localized mating (*i.e.*, the mate must be taken from a specific band) to narrow strictly the field of legitimate choice. Old men dominate the society and have the first choice of young girls. Matters are so carefully controlled that a boy can scarcely find a girl he can rightly marry. Fortunately for the Kurnai, they make "pretend rules" of these principles. Most marriages of young couples are by elopement,

[13] K. N. Llewellyn and E. A. Hoebel, *The Cheyenne Way*, Chap. 9.
[14] A. W. Howitt, *The Native Tribes of South-east Australia*, pp. 273ff.

and customarily medicine men are expected to help them escape. What then? The righteous citizenry (most of whom married in just this way) are terrible in their anger. A posse of vigilantes sets forth to do social justice. The couple flees to a traditional asylum. If they are overtaken, they are cruelly wounded and may be killed. Once at the place of asylum, however, they are safe. They stay there until a baby is born. Then they may return home to face a softer music, for they will merely be given a beating and then be accepted as legitimately married.

Divorce and the Dissolution of Marriage. In spite of the desire of kinsmen to retain the marriage link, primitive marriages are brittle things. Romance and individual desire may not play so great a role in determining the choice of a first partner as it does with us, but they are permitted more sway in the shifting of mates after marriage. Only a small proportion of marriages among primitives are for life. In principle, the primitive marital bond is relatively loose.

Hobhouse, Wheeler, and Ginsberg found in their study that of 271 tribes only 4 per cent forbid divorce; 24 per cent allow it for specific cause; 72 per cent permit it on the basis of mutual consent based on incompatibility or whim.[15] The sample may not be statistically perfect. Nevertheless, the results just quoted are probably not too far from accurate fact.

Aside from the economic arrangements that may have to be untangled where a high bride price was paid or a rich dowry given, divorce does not entail such difficulties among the primitives as it does with us. The first reason rests in the fact that although religious ritual may enter into the marriage ceremonies, marriage is hardly a religious affair. In addition, the problem of the care and disposition of the children is more easily handled. Ordinarily, they go with the mother. It has already been noted that sociological fatherhood is more significant to primitive man than is biological paternity.

There is little evidence on record to indicate that when the primitive mother remarries the emotional transition for the children is difficult. If the mother does not remarry right away, it is easy for her and her brood to settle among her relatives, for the tribal community is small and she has not been far from her kin at any time. If she is a captive from an alien tribe, she probably remarries without delay. Unmarried adult women are unthinkable to most primitives.

The prevalence of wife stealing is another important unsettling factor. In societies in which sexual competition among the men is a means

---

[15] Hobhouse, Wheeler, and Ginsberg, *op. cit.*, Chap. 3.

of attaining social status, no home is truly safe. Eskimos may cooperate economically, but they engage in violent competition for women. To steal another's wife and get away with it proves the abductor a better man than the loser. The risk is great, however, because the husband, if half a man, will attempt to murder the absconder. A would-be wife taker often anticipates this by killing the husband first and marrying the widow afterward.

In the 1920's Knut Rasmussen visited a village of Musk Ox Eskimos in Canada. He found that every adult male in the community had been involved in a murder centering about wife stealing! [16]

Special practices, such as the licenced wife stealing of the Crow Indians, may also break up the family. This is a phase of competition between two rival military associations, the Foxes and Knobby Sticks. Each spring one or another of the fraternities is privileged to capture any wife of a member of the other fraternity, provided she has had premarital sexual relations with the captor. The husband may not resist the abduction or take his wife back. The triumph of the kidnapping fraternity is supreme.

After an abduction there was a ceremonial display of the captive women. The successful club would announce: "One of the Lumpwood girls (Fox) has married one of us Foxes (Lumpwoods) of her own accord!" They took her to the club lodge, where they kept up drumming, singing, and dancing most of the night. She was the only woman present. Her kidnaper's family treated her as a real bride, bringing her an elk-tooth dress and other garments. Early the following morning an old member went through camp, shouting: "We are going to have a good time today, get your horses and prepare for today's big dance!" The stolen woman dressed up in her new clothes, her face painted with red stripes, while the members painted as though for war. She was to ride behind a member who had once saved a Crow from a pursuing enemy, taking him up on horseback behind himself and thus earning the title of akbapicere (one who takes someone behind). Any other man presuming to ride with the woman was jeered and at once thrown off by the rival club. There were, in fact, further restrictions. The feat must have been achieved on the war-path, not while defending the camp against hostile attack, in which case the danger was not reckoned so great. Further, the horse mounted by the pair must be one cut loose from its picket in the enemy camp; otherwise the riders were thrown off, the bridle was torn, and the horse turned loose. The entire club paraded in regular formation, two abreast, with the leaders and rear-men in the van and rear, respectively; only the akbapicere and the woman remained outside the line. Similarly, they kept outside the circle formed by

[16] K. Rasmussen, *Across Arctic America*, p. 250.

the society in the center of the camp, where the dancing commenced and continued until evening. The society losing the woman looked on ostentatiously during the performance with feigned indifference. At last the members of the triumphant club returned to the lodge, leaving the woman in her lover's custody.[17]

Cheyennes and other Plains tribesmen considered it a great feat ceremonially to throw away wives at a special dance. The Cheyenne warrior tossed a stick among the male spectators and whoever was struck by it had to marry the woman, if only for a day.

In general, men are allowed more leeway in the matter of divorce than are women. Many tribes allow the injured wife, as well as the husband, to sever the tie when the other spouse is unfaithful, but many other tribes give the man power to divorce his unfaithful wife without giving like power to the wife. Matrilineal descent plus uxorilocal residence, of course, strengthen the hand of the woman. Among the highly matrilineal Hopi and Zuñi, where women own the houses, a woman can divorce her husband simply by setting his gear outside the door. Any man who comes home to see his pile of belongings outside the door knows just what that means. It is his time to go home to mother.

The causes of divorce and the grounds for it may be two quite different things. Yet it may be illuminating to close this chapter with a listing of what the Ifugao of northern Luzon consider as grounds for divorcement:

1. A bad omen of the bile sac of the sacrificial animal at any one of the four feasts of the marriage ritual
2. A bad omen of the bile sac at any of the three principal rice feasts of either family during the first year after the completion of the marriage rituals
3. Barrenness
4. Continuous dying of offspring
5. Permanent sexual disability
6. Unwillingness to perform the sexual act
7. Neglect in time of sickness, "failure to cherish"
8. Insulting language by an in-law
9. Reduction of the area of fields agreed on in the marriage contract
10. Selling of a rice field for insufficient reason and without consent of the other spouse
11. Continued refusal of a father-in-law to deliver the fields called for in the marriage contract when the couple reaches a reasonable age
12. Incurring of unreasonable debts

[17] R. H. Lowie, *The Crow Indians*, pp. 190–191.

13. Chronic laziness or shiftless conduct
14. Failure to perform certain special duties involved in getting married
15. Any legal offense by a kinsman of one spouse against a kinsman of the other
16. Insanity
17. Extreme jealousy
18. Incompatibility
19. Dereliction of affection
20. Desertion
21. Adultery

Certain of these grounds are based on the willful wrongdoing of one spouse against the other. In these cases, the injured partner may obtain the divorce and claim damages. In the case of bad omens, fate is set against the marriage, but without blame to anyone, so no damages need be paid. Insanity and sexual incompetence are not matters for blame, since they are beyond control of the individual, yet they make fulfillment of the marriage functions impossible; hence, divorce is reasonable, but no damages may be claimed. Neither the Ifugao nor any other primitive people provide for alimony. It is always assumed that the divorcée will soon remarry. In the interim, her relatives will care for her and her children.

Here, then, in the case of the Ifugaos, is an almost completely rational handling of the divorce problem in which the social functions of marriage are the standards against which the continuance or discontinuance of the maintenance of connubial pairing shall be tested.[18]

[18] R. F. Barton, "Ifugao Law" (*University of California Publications in American Archaeology and Ethnology*, Vol. 15, No. 5, 1922), pp. 30–31.

CHAPTER 15

THE FAMILY

The essential function of the family is to provide a basic group in which children receive their primary care and social training in an atmosphere of emotional intimacy. Families emphasize the emotional interdependence of their members to a degree that quite consistently exceeds that of any other social group. Affection, loyalty, cooperation, and standing together are almost always enjoined upon family members even though not always successfully evoked. The emotional content of family attitudes is such that any threat to family security, such as incest or adultery, is officially, at least, met with violent reactions. So far as the evidence goes, homicide and adultery are the two acts that are legally punishable in all societies.[1]

Although we have just spoken of *the essential function of the family*, the reader has probably noticed that two functions were stated: (1) care and social training of offspring and (2) maintenance of an atmosphere of emotional intimacy. Other groups and associations can and do provide for the care and social training of children, even to the extent of displacing or acting as a total substitute for the family, *viz.*, orphanages and correctional homes for the unlucky among us, or boarding schools and summer camps for the children of the wealthy. But none of these succeed in providing the exclusive in-group feeling characteristic of the family. That feeling appears to be a concomitant of the psychological need for a sense of security.

It is on this basis that we identify the universal emotional atmosphere as a functional characteristic of primary significance in the family.

The provision of care and training calls forth a number of correlated activities of an economic nature: the procurement of food, shelter, clothing, and other material needs. The family is thus always an economic unit in production and consumption. Adults as well as children naturally benefit in this. Marriage and the formation of a family, even without children, is considered an essential for almost all adults in all primitive societies. The customary division of labor prevents either a

[1] An exception is W. H. R. Rivers's report on the Todas of India, among whom he found no social disapproval of adultery.

man or a woman from performing all the economic functions necessary to a satisfactory life. A helpmate, or economic complement (the spouse), is needed.

From the point of view of the individual, this may provide the strongest motive for getting married. Certainly, in those societies in which free premarital sex life is openly countenanced, it is not the sex interest that prompts marriage, for in such a case, rather than opening the door to sex life, marriage limits it. On the other hand, where premarital sexual experience is prohibited or inhibited, marriage may be partially motivated by the desire to satisfy the sex drive.

However, from the discussion in this and previous chapters, it should be evident that marriage and entering into the family relationship are the results of social rather than individual motivations.

Multiple Family Membership. Every person is a member of at least four families. This may sound like a startling statement but a moment's consideration will show that it is commonplace fact.

Each legitimate child is a member of the *conjugal family* into which it is born. This is the common type of family, which comes into being with the marriage of a mating pair; it consists at marriage of husband and wife (or wives and husbands) and later includes such offspring as are forthcoming. The conjugal family is the type with which each of us is intimately familiar. It is the type of family we ordinarily have in mind when we use the word "family." Anthropologically, however, with the need for a nicer precision of identification at hand, we label this kind of family "conjugal," because it is the type of family in which two or more spouses come together to conjugate in the biological (not grammatical) sense. For this reason, some sociologists call this familial form the *family of procreation.*[2] Others name it the *biological family;* while the older fashion was to call it the *small family (Kleinfamilie).*

In addition to being born into a conjugal family, when an adult marries he founds a new conjugal family in conjunction with his mate. The married adult is thus a member of *two* conjugal families. He is a member of the first as an offspring, and of the second as a (pro)creator. In the first, his relation is that of child to parent and sibling to sibling. In the second, his relationship is that of parent to child and spouse to spouse. The statuses and roles of the individual are quite different in each of the conjugal families to which he belongs. It must be realized, therefore, that from the point of view of the interacting individual the two families are

[2] J. L. and J. P. Gillin, *An Introduction to Sociology*, p. 209.

quite different as social experience. Yet, as we view them from the outside, both families are identical in form.

The conjugal family is always bilateral. Since it takes two to make a conjugal family, and since each spouse already belongs to a preexisting family, the marriage union links two units into a new one. The child has its ties to both its father's and its mother's conjugal families as well as to the one into which it is born.

The Extended Family. The family tie does not stop short with parents and children. The bond of close kinship embraces uncles and aunts, cousins, parents, grandparents, and grandchildren. Some sort of group organization of these relatives is always present. This is what we know as the *extended family*. These extended family relationships are quadrilateral. Unless the unilateral principle is operative, the individual can count on the support of his relatives in all four of his extended families.

The multilateral extended family, however, has an inherent weakness. It spreads itself in too many directions. Its boundaries become too blurred and diffused. There are so many individuals within it that their interests are apt to cut across each other. Conflicts of loyalty are engendered. What is more defective, its very diffuseness makes the maintenance of effective loyalty truly difficult to accomplish. A weak extended family weakens the individual and, indeed, the whole social structure.

Many societies have found a corrective in the unilateral principle. This is a selective device in which for purposes of social organization one side of the relationship tree is arbitrarily ignored, while the other side is given reinforced recognition. If a child belongs to the paternal extended family of its father, the relationship is *patrilineal*. If the child belongs to the mother's maternal family, the extended family is *matrilineal*. In a given tribe, one of these principles usually prevails to the exclusion of the other, although this is by no means always the case.

Further consideration and elaboration of the unilateral principle produces the lineage and clan as significant kinship groups above and beyond the family, a subject to be discussed in the next chapter.

The Susu. However much we may cherish the conjugal family as a social unit, it is functionally far from ideally suited to the ends it must fulfill. In the first place, the conjugal family is very unstable. There is the constant possibility of divorce, and where divorce is not countenanced emotional disturbances arising from the incompatibility of the father and mother can easily destroy the affective solidarity that is so important to good family functioning. If a primary purpose of marriage is to fix the biological father of children with the economic and social responsibility of providing for his children's nurture, this essential social need is seriously impaired when the father divorces the mother. True enough, the consequences of a conjugal family breakup are not so serious in a primitive society where the mother is securely embedded in the protection of her extended family and where remarriage is easier than is usually the case with us. Nevertheless, the brittleness of the conjugal family is a definite deficiency.

Also, the conjugal family is a temporary association. It begins and ends with the union of the married pair and the dispersal of the children.

Furthermore, upon marriage a person enters a new conjugal family and his loyalties are split. From our own experience we know the tensions that can result from the pull of loyalty to our husbands or wives as against our fathers and mothers.

The instability of the conjugal family and its short time span also limit its usefulness as a means of inheritance of property and perquisites.

In order to overcome these disadvantages, many primitive societies utilize the *susu* along with the conjugal family.

Before describing the susu it may be well to say a few words about nomenclature. The susu does not exist in our culture, and if it ever existed in the historical past in the cultures from which ours is traditionally derived, we have no record of it. Not possessing it, not even knowing there could be such a thing until anthropology recently discovered it among other peoples, we have no name for it in our vernacular. When science is confronted with a new material or phenomenon, a new label must be provided. Ordinarily, this is done by coining a new compound from Latin or Greek roots—often with horrendous results. Or, the new thing may be labeled with a descriptive grouping of adjectives, adverbs, and nouns already in the language. Or, we may take over a foreign word from some culture in which the thing already exists. There are precedents for all three in anthropology. Anthropology, which is itself a relatively new phenomenon, is named in accordance with the first practice. The term "secondary affinal marriage" to identify a particular kind of mating illustrates the second. The incorporation of such words as *tabu* (from the Polynesian) and *totem* (from the Algonquian) into everyday usage illustrates successful innovations by the third method. No method is necessarily better than another; all should be investigated when a new name is needed. However, in anthropology, if a primitive term fits the thing with "alluring brevity and phonetic suggestiveness," it should be utilized. Anthropologists owe more to primitive men than they do to the Greeks and Romans.

Goldenweiser and Linton have each advanced a nomenclature for the type of institution we are now considering. Goldenweiser has called it the *unilateral family*.[3] Linton has labeled it the *consanguine family*.[4] The susu, it is true, is unilateral, but it is better not to call it a family. The term "consanguine," for its part, means blood relationship, a concept that we would have interdicted. Something new is needed.

Susu is the name the Dobu tribe gives to the primary unilateral relationship group that complements and completes the conjugal family. The Dobu susu has been described and analyzed in clarity and great detail by Fortune in his well-known book *Sorcerers of Dobu*.[5] All anthropologists are familiar with the term; it has "alluring brevity and phonetic suggestiveness"; and it is devoid of all preconceptive and misleading connotations. Therefore, it shall be used for the type of organization now to be described.

The nuclear basis of the susu is the brother-sister relationship. The husband does not enter into it at all. His role, except as procreator, is replaced in part or wholly by the mother's brother. Generally, in Melanesia the father raises his garden produce not for his wife and his own children but for his sister and her children. A man's brother-in-law must in turn provide for his children. The main burden of educating the boys in men's work falls on the mother's brother. His nephews inherit most of their goods from him. He sponsors their entrance into various clubs and societies. He passes on his social prerogatives to his nephew, not to his son. Where the susu organization is highly institutionalized, the father, as we know him, is almost entirely ruled out of the picture (see avunculate, pages 242–243).

The susu tends to extend unilineally down the generations, so that it includes a brother and sister (or group of brothers and sisters), the sisters' children, their daughters' children, daughters' daughters' children, etc.

Susus are always matrilineally oriented, since the male role in the child nurture group is directed toward patronage of his sister's children, rather than his own.

Except for procreation, the susu is competent to take over every function exercised by the conjugal family. There is reportedly only one known societal organization in which this has actually occurred, however; this is the famous Nayar caste of the Cochin state on the Malabar coast of

---

[3] A. Goldenweiser, *Anthropology*, Chap. 22.

[4] R. M. Linton, *The Study of Man*, p. 161.

[5] R. F. Fortune, *Sorcerers of Dobu*; see also R. F. Benedict, *Patterns of Culture*, Chap. 5.

southeast India. The Nayars are supposed to have been the ruling caste
of the aboriginal society predating the Hindu influx. Today they form
the third-ranking caste of a complex and caste-dominated society. Above
them is the royal house of great wealth and power, which may have
emerged long ago from the Nayars themselves. Beneath the royal house
(but far above the Nayars in sublimity) is the caste of Nambudiri Brahmans, whose sacred families are patrilineally organized on a strict basis
of primogeniture. The Nayars are a closed caste of land owners and professional soldiers, who in contrast to the Brahmans are strictly matrilineal and matrilocal. The household, or *taravad*, is a joint organization
housed under one roof. The eldest woman is titular head of the household, but the house, lands, and joint property are administered by the
eldest brother for the benefit of the group. All the males (brothers, sons,
and grandsons) contribute to the maintenance of the taravad and draw
their support from it. But none of their children receive any benefit from
their efforts whatsoever. Only the offspring of the women belong to the
taravad and are maintained within it. The men mate with women of
other taravad without obligating themselves to any social duties toward
their "wives" or children. Both men and women may have several mates
simultaneously, since mating involves no formal obligations. Younger
sons of the Brahman class may enter into sexual alliances with Nayar
women, but they still remain outside the taravad, as their children remain irrevocably fixed within it. Thus Nayar social organization is built
upon the susu (taravad), without even a vestige of the conjugal family.

On the other hand, it is usual for the susu to complement rather than
displace the conjugal family.

Thus in Dobu the conjugal family is the household unit, *i.e.*, its members live together. After marriage, because a man never enters his sister's
house, the susu has no household base. However, children cannot eat
food grown in their father's fields; all fishing gear, including canoes, are
used jointly by susu members only and are inherited only within the
susu. Consequently, the susu has an economic base and the conjugal family does not. Emotional security is found only in the susu, and not in the
conjugal family. Husband and wife, coming as they do from different
susus, are hostile at marriage and all their days thereafter. Each believes
the other is trying to destroy him by foul magic. All Dobus believe that
all other Dobus except those of their own susu are their magical enemies.
The susu inherits the corpse and skull of its members. It bestows personal
names and social status in relationship terms. Widows, widowers, and the
children of a dead person may never enter the village of the deceased

spouse or parent. But—susu relatives of a dead person may enter the village of the surviving spouse or children.

The differentiation and interrelationship of conjugal family and susu is also strikingly revealed by the Zuñis of New Mexico, of whom Benedict writes:

To the women of the household, the grandmother and her sisters, her daughters and their daughters, belong the house and the corn that is stored in it. No matter what may happen to marriages the women of the household remain with the house for life. They present a solid front. They care for and feed the sacred objects that belong to them. They keep their secrets together. Their husbands are outsiders, and it is their brothers, married now into houses of other clans, who are united with the household in all affairs of the moment. It is they who return for all the retreats when the sacred objects of the house are set out before the altar. It is they, not the women, who learn the word-perfect ritual of their sacred bundle and perpetuate it. A man goes always, for all important occasions, to his mother's house, which, when she dies, becomes his sister's house, and if his marriage breaks up, he returns to the same household.

This blood-relationship group, rooted in the ownership of the house, united in the care of sacred objects, is the important group in Zuñi. It has permanence and important common concerns. But it is not the economically functioning group. Each married son, each married brother, spends his labour upon the corn which will fill his wife's storeroom. Only when his mother's or sister's house lacks male labour does he care for the cornfield of his blood-relationship group. The economic group is the household that lives together, the old grandmother and her husband, her daughters and their husbands. These husbands count in the economic group, though in the ceremonial group they are outsiders.[6]

The susu exists because it offers certain advantages in which the conjugal family is weak. Yet the conjugal family enjoys a definite preference over the susu in the choice of mankind. The conjugal family is universal; the susu is not.

What is defective or objectionable in the susu? The answer will be found in the incest tabu. The basis of the susu is the fraternal bond of brother and sisterhood. Yet all societies find it necessary to tabu sex relations between brother and sister, often manifesting extreme anxiety over the consequences of incestuous relationships. The susu encourages emotional and functional ties between a pair who must never become sexually involved with each other. This is dangerous business, so much so that many societies apparently prefer to avoid it altogether. Even in

[6] Benedict, *op. cit.,* pp. 75–76.

Dobu a man may not enter his sister's house. As an additional factor, the splitting of loyalty between susu and conjugal family may produce personal and cultural conflicts that are difficult to resolve. Malinowski has shown how a primitive community can be violently upset by quarrels arising from a man's illegal attempts to favor his own son as against his sister's sons to whom he owes customary privileges.[7]

Monogamy and Polygamy. The husband-wife relationship in the conjugal family may or may not be limited to a single mated pair. *Monogamy* exists when a single pair is married. *Polygamy*, or multiple marriage, exists when more than two persons are joined in the marital relationship. It is important to realize that what is permitted in a culture and what prevails in fact may be two different things. Thus, it is usual to refer to societies whose cultures permit multiple marriages as polygamous. Yet it is unlikely that more than a few marriages in any society will actually be polygamous, since a number of factors limit multiple marriages.

First, there is the relative balance of the sex ratio. Approximately equal numbers of males and females are born. Unless some selective factor operates in favor of one sex and against the other, there will be an approximate equality in the numbers of adult males and females available for marriage. If this is the case, whenever one man has two wives, some other man in the tribe has to do without. If one man has three wives, two other men must do without. There is, of course, the possibility that the short-wived men may band together to share one wife among themselves, but such polyandrous arrangements are very rare.

If it is the current practice for a man to settle in the household of his wife, he obviously cannot live with all his wives simultaneously unless his wives are sisters. Uxorilocal (L. *uxor* wife + *locus* place) residence discourages the polygynous form of polygamy. Beyond this, the attitudes of his in-laws will discourage marriage with women from other kin groups, especially if the society is matrilineal and the wife's relationship group is in a strong position. Marriage is a kin-group alliance, and a son-in-law whose affinal allegiances are multiple is apt to be less desirable than one whose affinity is to one group alone.

Few precise statistics are available, but all reports indicate that monogamous marriages actually predominate in most societies that are permissibly polygamous.

Monogamy. Prescribed monogamy is enjoined by various tribes in several parts of the world. Its geographical distribution is quite sporadic, although there seems to be a definite monogamistic proclivity among the

[7] B. Malinowski, *Crime and Custom in Savage Society*, pp. 100–111.

tribes of the Amazonian region. Contrary to the notions of nineteenth-century anthropologists, monogamy most definitely is not the end product of an evolutionary series narrowing down from primitive promiscuity to civilized monogamy. The very primitive Andaman Islanders and the Semangs of the Malay forests limit themselves to one wife apiece, but the Semangs marry again and again in serial monogamy, Hollywood style. Inca commoners were forbidden to marry more than one wife, but a man might receive a concubine as a gift in reward for faithful service to his overlord. The occurrence of prescribed monogamy among the matrilineal, uxorilocal Iroquois in New York and the equally matrilineal, uxorilocal Hopi and Zuñi suggests that in these instances monogamy is correlated with female-dominated residence and economy. Monogamy prevails in all the Southwest Pueblos, but in the Eastern Pueblos of New Mexico, where female dominance fades out, it is impossible to tell whether this is due to ancient Pueblo custom, or whether it has been brought about by the influence of the Catholic Church. In the Zuñi and Hopi Pueblos monogamous marriages are very brittle. Among the Keresan Pueblos of the East, however, the Catholic injunction against divorce is rigidly adhered to. Clandestine relations outside of marriage occur among all these people.

Exclusive monogamy is not correlated with any stage of culture. Its absence among pastoral nomads, who are predominantly patrilineal, is nevertheless a notable fact.

Polygyny. Within polygamous marriages we have been drawing a distinction between polygyny and polyandry. *Polygamy* means multiple marriages. *Polygyny* means multiple women. *Polyandry* means multiple men. Polygyny is, therefore, that form of family in which a husband has more than one wife at one time. *Bigamy* is the more special form of polygamy in which the husband limits himself to two wives, or a woman to two husbands.

There are a number of social motives underlying polygyny as an institution. If a man has the means to support several wives, he is able to present a richer and better equipped household to the world. More women can prepare better clothes and food. If women's handicrafts are marketable or suitable for exchange, his household wealth will be enhanced. When the Blackfoot Indians found a lucrative outlet for tanned hides in the Canadian fur trade and women as tanners were an economic asset, polygyny grew to an extent unprecedented for the Plains. Bride price went up and the age of marriage for girls went down, while the age of marriage for men was set back; well-established Blackfoot entrepreneurs cornered the available women, and it took young men a longer time to acquire enough capital to purchase wives.[8]

Polygyny may also serve as a mechanism for competitive status in the sexual field when to have and to hold several wives against all comers is a dangerous task, as among the Eskimos.[9]

Strange as it may seem to us, it is repeatedly reported that in many tribes the women do not object to their husbands taking on additional wives. This is most apt to be true when additional wives are coworkers or "chore wives," as among the Comanches of the Plains. A secondary wife may be desired for the performance of special functions, as with the African Baganda, among whom a second wife is chosen from the husband's paternal grandmother's clan. This wife is charged with the responsibility of caring for her husband's hair and nail clippings.

On the other hand, instances are on record of primitive women who have shown extreme jealousy when their husbands brought home a new wife. A Cheyenne woman hanged herself because her husband took a Pawnee captive to wife, but her own grandmother remarked that, "She was foolish to hang herself over such a little thing."

Most primitives aver that polygyny works out best when a man's several wives are sisters. This is psychologically reasonable, insofar as sisters are more used to each other's ways than unrelated women; they are subject to the influence of emotional loyalty acquired in childhood as members of the same conjugal family. As representatives of the same marriage group, their nonpersonal interests in the marriage are identical, which is not the case with unrelated women. Sororal polygyny is in effect an anticipation of sororate privileges. A man does not wait for the death of his wife before he marries her younger sister. Instead, as among the Comanches, he has an expectation that if he performs his son-in-law obligations to his wife's parents, they will reward him with his wife's younger sister when she becomes of age.

Where exchange marriage prevails, the levirate will also work to produce sororal polygyny. Thus when brothers have married sisters, if a man inherits his deceased brother's wife, his two wives are automatically sisters.

Various household arrangements are made to adjust to the requirements of the multiple-wife family. The Angola practice is probably typical of Sudanese African tribes. Hambly tells of an Angola headman with

[8] O. Lewis, *The Effects of White Contact upon Blackfoot Culture, with Special Reference to the Role of the Fur Trade* (American Ethnological Society, Monograph 6, 1942), pp. 38–40.

[9] E. A. Hoebel, "Law-ways of the Primitive Eskimos" (*Journal of Criminal Law and Criminology*, Vol. 31, 1941), pp. 663–683.

eleven wives for each of whom he had a separate hut in his compound. The Ovimbundu Negroes provide each wife with a separate kitchen, which serves as the center for her brood. The husband customarily sleeps with each wife four or seven successive nights, as his personal habit may be.[10] If a Comanche had less than four wives, they usually shared the same tipi. More than four wives necessitated at least a couple of tipis for the household.

Polyandry. The actual marriage of several men to one woman is as rare as the marriage of several women to one man is common. Tibetans and the Todas of India are the most famous polyandrists.

Usually, the Toda polyandrous union is fraternal, but not always so. A few polygynous marriages occur, and quite a few monogamous ones. However, female infanticide results in a shortage of adult women, so brothers often band together as a group of husbands. Children are ordinarily betrothed in infancy and the boy gives bride-price payments two times a year all through his childhood. He also has to provide a buffalo to help pay funeral expenses of members of his betrothed's family. Just before puberty, the girl is deflorated by a man from some clan other than her own. Then she is ready for marriage. Right after puberty, she is given a dowry and taken to the home of her husband. Although she may have been betrothed to just one man, it is understood that she is also the wife of all his brothers. Even a boy yet unborn may become her husband, along with his elder brothers, when he becomes of age. All the brothers live together and share their wife without friction and, we are told, without jealousy. When the wife becomes pregnant, one of the brothers goes through a ritual of "presenting the bow." This makes him the sociological father of the ensuing child and the next couple of children to be born. There is no concern over whether he may be the biological sire or not. After he has his share of offspring to sponsor, another brother "presents the bow," thus making himself the father of the next group of children, and so on. This disregard of biological paternity in favor of ceremonially established sociological fatherhood is also manifest in a way reminiscent of Sakalava bride-price privileges mentioned previously (page 209). Occasionally, a Toda woman may leave her legitimate husbands to live with another man without official approval, or she may take a concubitant, who pays her husbands for the privilege; in either case, her subsequent children still belong to the man (her husband) who performed the bow and arrow ritual.[11]

[10] W. D. Hambly, "Source Book for African Anthropology" (*Field Museum of Natural History, Anthropological Series*, Vol. 26, Part 2, 1937), pp. 418–419.

[11] W. H. R. Rivers, *The Todas*, pp. 477–480.

Polyandry in the Darjeeling district of India is restricted to the younger brothers of the man who performs the wedding rite with the wife. If the elder brother dies and the common wife has no children, she may break the polyandrous bond by first tying a string to a finger of her No. 1 husband's corpse and binding it to one of her own fingers. Then by severing the string, she symbolically destroys the marriage tie.

Tibetan and Eskimo polyandry have been attributed to the practice of female infanticide. While it is true that both peoples practice infanticide, British census figures do not indicate a surplus of adult men in Tibet, and reliable censuses of the primitive Eskimo indicate that women exceed men in numbers in almost all Eskimo communities in spite of the common destruction of baby girls.

Although rare, polyandry is more common (at least in modified form) than was thought to be the case a decade or two ago. A form of polyandry has been reported from at least two East African tribes, leading us to expect that other unreported instances probably occur. Among the Banyankole and the Bahima, where bride price is high, a poor man may call on his younger brothers to contribute cattle to his cause.[12] All the brothers who have "kicked in" take turns in living with the bride until she becomes pregnant, when she then lives with her "husband." Whoever the sire may be, the resultant child is the social offspring of the elder brother who married the girl.

In northern Nigeria, according to Meek's observations, "A Gwari woman may have several husbands and families in different towns, living now with one, now with another, as she feels inclined. As the children belong not to the first husband but to the actual father, we have here a fairly close approximation to actual polyandry." [13]

In North America limited polyandry is now known to have existed among a number of tribes of the Great Plains [14] and the Basin area.[15] In these cases there was no shortage of women to account for the practice. Instead, in the case of the Shoshones, who considered exchange marriage between a group of brothers and sisters on an equal basis to be the most desirable form, it is easy to see that these Indians were imbued with the idea of the sexual equivalence of brothers to each other and

---

[12] J. Roscoe, *The Banyankole*, p. 123; "The Cow Tribe of Enkole in the Uganda Protectorate" (*Journal of the Royal Anthropological Institute of Great Britain and Ireland*, Vol. 37, 1907), p. 105.

[13] C. K. Meek, *The Northern Tribes of Nigeria*, Vol. 1, p. 198.

[14] A. Lesser, "Levirate and Fraternal Polyandry among the Pawnees" (*Man*, Vol. 30, No. 77, 1930), pp. 98–101.

[15] J. H. Steward, "Shoshone Polyandry" (*American Anthropologist*, Vol. 38, 1936), pp. 561–564.

sisters to each other (which is also the probable cause among the Eskimo, although there it is possible that extensive polygyny produces an artificial shortage for the weaker men).[16] Sexual rights to one sister were easily transferred to other sisters in sororal polygyny and the sororate. Likewise, the woman's rights in her husband (and his rights in her) were just as easily transferred to her husband's brothers in the levirate and fraternal polyandry. This notion of the sexual equivalence of brothers crops up in the quaint Shoshone and Comanche custom whereby an aggrieved husband courteously addresses an adulterer who has made him a cuckold as "brother." Men who have had sex relations with the same woman are "brothers" even though unrelated and even while the husband is prosecuting the adulterer for damages!

What we previously named *anticipatory levirate* (see page 199) may also be conceived of as attenuated fraternal polyandry. When a Shoshone or Comanche elder brother shares his wife with his unmarried younger brother, it is in anticipation of the younger brother's levirate privilege. Or, if emphasis is placed on the sexual equivalence of brothers, it is a polyandrous relationship—attenuated, however, since the younger brother is not married in common to the woman in the full sense of the word.

Among the Skidi Pawnee, anticipation of husband's sister's son marriage (see page 200), an extension of the avunculate, produced another variant of attenuated polyandry. According to Dorsey and Murie,

When a boy reached puberty he was taken in charge by his mother's brother's wife. From this time until his marriage, he maintained sexual relations with her, and entered a different stage immediately after having had intercourse with this woman. When her real husband was off hunting or on the warpath, the youth continued to have marital relations with her. Thus it might happen that for four or five years a woman would have an additional "husband," or possibly three or four, with a temporary state of polyandry thereby prevailing.

Inasmuch as an unmarried boy could also share his brother's wife, he could belong to two distinct types of attenuated polyandrous groups simultaneously.[17]

There is thus a borderline type of polyandry, which when combined with polygyny shades into so-called "group marriage."

[16] E. A. Hoebel, "Eskimo Infanticide and Polyandry" (*The Scientific Monthly*, Vol. 64, 1947), p. 535.

[17] G. A. Dorsey and J. R. Murie, "Notes on Skidi Pawnee Society" (*Field Museum of Natural History, Anthropological Series*, Vol. 27, 1940), pp. 96, 85.

It is a difficult, if not impossible, problem to determine why polyandry is so infrequent and polygyny not so. Does the fact that men do not often marry one woman in common mean that they are resistant to the idea? And does the fact that women do frequently marry one man in common mean that the female sex is devoid of such resistances? Or are there purely sociological factors that make polygyny functionally effective and polyandry less so?

The first possibility suggests an explanation in terms of an innate tendency toward male dominance. There is ample sociological and psychological evidence to support the idea that dominance drives are of extreme significance in human and animal behavior.[18] Innate dominance patterns as between the sexes among the subhuman primates vary by genera and species. Males among the Old World monkeys are brutal and sadistic in their terrorization of all females and weaker males, but dominance differences are weakly developed among the New World primates. Among the great apes, all of whom are Old World primates, dominance by the males is present but rarely harsh, and it is usually "strongly mitigated by friendship, affection, sympathy, and cooperation." [19]

Among human beings dominance relations are, of course, tremendously influenced, both as to degree of intensity and forms of expression, by culture. But with rare exceptions the cultures of mankind award the greater amount of dominance to the male of the species. Culture is, by and large, shaped to the advantage of males and interpreted in terms of male interests. The near universality of this condition, coupled with the significant innate dominance drives of male primates, indicates the probability of an elemental dominance drive in human males of a more intense nature than may be the case with females.

Competition for status among males also takes the form of overtly aggressive rivalry and conflict among human beings to a degree of intensity and violence rarely exhibited by females. The Musk Ox Eskimos visited by Rasmussen, who found that every adult male in the tribe had been involved in a murder, usually over some female, represent an extreme manifestation of this behavior.[20] But this is merely an exaggeration in intratribal relations of the common violence involved in the stealing or capturing of wives from alien tribes that occurs over and over in many parts of the primitive world. On the other hand, there is no evidence that any culture ever established the forceful capture of men by women

---

[18] K. Young, *Social Psychology*, pp. 360ff.
[19] E. A. Hooton, *Man's Poor Relations*, pp. 324–329.
[20] K. Rasmussen, *Across Arctic America*, p. 250.

as a social habit. Woman's weapon is "feminine wile"—a decidedly more subtle technique.

Male dominance can, therefore, be manifest over others by means of exclusive sexual possession of a woman or women desired by other males, and by limitation of the woman's sexual activity to her one husband. The husband who marries a woman in common with other men must submerge his sexual dominance within the polyandrous group. W. I. Thomas is correct in his acute observation that polyandry "represents a minimum satisfaction of the claims of men." [21] Women, who are less able in general to enforce a sexual dominance, are commonly forced to accept a polygynous relation, finding compensation in the advantages that result in such a family relationship.

The biological factor of childbearing and child nursing also contributes to polygyny rather than to polyandry. Primitive mothers are usually continent during pregnancy and nursing, which may be prolonged for years. In this situation, the husband who can manage it will find multiple wives advantageous—a need the woman does not face on this basis.

Wife Hospitality. In spite of what has just been said, it is a widespread primitive practice for men to share their wives with certain other men on specific occasions. Most commonly, a host deems that proper social form requires him to offer the hospitality of his wife to an overnight guest. An early white trader on the upper Missouri River, Jean Baptiste Trudeau, took note that, "so true is this, that husbands, fathers and brothers, are importunate with the white men who visit them, to make free with their wives, daughters, and sisters, particularly those who are most youthful and pretty." [22] Similar concepts of hospitality have been noted in all parts of the primitive world by countless explorers, travelers, and other lay observers, as well as by anthropologists. [23]

From Africa, we have Roscoe's statement on the Banyankole that "A married woman is expected to entertain any guest of her husband and invite him to her bed. This is a mark of hospitality shown by all married men to their visitors." Even if the visitor is the husband's father, the husband moves over to stay with a married neighbor while his visitor enjoys his domain. [24] Wife lending among the Eskimos is so well known as scarcely to need mention.

---

[21] W. I. Thomas, *Primitive Behavior*, p. 118.

[22] G. H. Smith, "J. B. Trudeau's Remarks on the Indians of the Upper Missouri, 1794–95" (*American Anthropologist*, Vol. 38, 1930), p. 567.

[23] *Cf.* E. Westermarck, *The History of Human Marriage*, Vol. 1, pp. 224–230, for a more detailed body of references to the custom.

[24] Roscoe, *op. cit.*, p. 123.

Many explanations of wife hospitality have been offered. Evolutionary anthropologists considered it a survival of primitive promiscuity. There is little that we can approve of in the anthropological writings of Briffault, author of the famous book on primitive sex and family relations called *The Mothers*. But it does seem that he hit the mark when he declared that, "The practice, very inaptly called 'hospitality prostitution,' is not a matter of misguided benevolence, but a necessary pledge that the guest is a friend and not an enemy." [25] Briffault cites evidence of the murder and near murder of white travelers who refused the offer of their hosts. What a delicate problem has oftentimes confronted the doughty missionary who has braved the perils of the savage world! However, Briffault is extreme in his universal implication that one who refuses to avail himself of this privilege of "tribal brotherhood" is *ipso facto* an enemy. Nevertheless, the act *is* one of real or imputed brotherhood, and it involves the reciprocity of brotherhood. It is expected that the favor will be returned whenever the host happens to visit the guest in his home. As one Comanche put it to us, "When a man lets his younger brother have his wife, he expects the younger brother to do the same for him when he marries. If the younger brother refuses, his brother won't feel right about it." There is also the unauthenticated story of an American anthropologist who enjoyed the favor of a Polynesian chieftain's wife in the Pacific, but who, much to the disgust of the chief, thought differently of the custom when the chief came to this country.

Group Concubinage. When wife lending becomes a settled arrangement among sets of men, it takes on the color of group marriage. Siberian natives and Eskimos often set up a system of partnerships (between men of different communities) within which the men regularly share their wives when any one of the partners visits in the settlements of any of the others. If the traveler is accompanied by his wife, he nevertheless exchanges mates for the duration of the visit. This gives the superficial appearance of group marriage. Yet it is hardly that, since the members of the exchanging set are not in a permanent marriage relationship to each other's wives.

This is also true of what were believed to be group marriages among certain native tribes of Australia. As Lowie has carefully pointed out for the Dieri tribe, a man marries only one woman: his mother's father's sister's daughter's daughter (a second-degree cross-cousin). The tribal elders may then designate his wife to serve as a concubine for other men,

[25] R. Briffault, "Group Marriage and Sexual Communism" in *The Making of Man*, p. 223.

who are also her second cross-cousins in the manner just noted. The husband may get other such women assigned to him as his concubines. Even single men may enjoy such a privilege. These secondary relations are concubinage and not marriage, because a "wife invariably takes precedence over the concubine when both occupy the same camp" and "the husband—the duly affianced spouse—enjoys an undisputed preemptive right over his wife." A concubitant may enjoy his rights only in the husband's absence or with his consent.[26]

In all these instances of wife lending, one important fact is present. The bestowal of the wife's favor is the prerogative of the husband. For the wife to assume the privilege on her own and without the explicit or implied consent of the husband is almost always punishable as adultery. Comanche husbands, who shared their wives with "brothers" on proper occasion, brutally mutilated and punished any wives who had extramarital relations on their own. They then invariably collected damages from the corespondent. Eskimos, for all their licentious freedom, consider adultery a killing matter, or at least cause for a song duel. Adultery, like wife stealing, is an affront to the husband's status and a challenge to his dominance position, which leads to violent reaction by the male except in societies where the culture plays down status competition among men.

Finally, sex communism, which would imply equal sexual prerogatives and marriage obligations between a group of men and women, does not exist in clear form in any known primitive society. It has been tried in one or two modern Utopian communities, but not for long.

Earlier anthropologists made much of a hypothetical stage of promiscuity preceding any restrictive family relationships. We must agree with Lowie that there is no empirical evidence of such a condition surviving in any observed system of social relationships among men. Nevertheless, inasmuch as men evolved from lower primates and inasmuch as all living primates are promiscuous, it is probable that our own primate progenitors were equally unrestrained. But there is no way of knowing when or just how emergent man came to establish marital inhibitions to promiscuity. Hypothetical speculations on this subject may be intriguing and amusing, but hardly useful. By the time anthropologists came upon the scene, notebook in hand, the conjugal family, be it monogamous, polygynous, or polyandrous, had conquered the fancy-free promiscuity of the ape man.

[26] R. H. Lowie, *Primitive Society*, pp. 52–53.

CHAPTER 16

KINSHIP BEHAVIOR

Behavior toward relatives is not the same as behavior toward non-relatives. Rich uncles win special deference. A person always owes certain obligations to his kinsmen. The status of a relative is unique as against the rest of mankind.

As a striking manifestation of this fundamental fact, that keen student of African social life, E. E. Evans-Pritchard, observes,

> If you wish to live among the Nuer, you must do so on their terms, which means that you must treat them as kinsmen and they will treat you as a kind of kinsman. Rights, privileges and obligations are determined by kinship. Either a man is a kinsman, actually or by fiction, or he is a person to whom you owe no reciprocal obligations and whom you treat as a potential enemy.[1]

Because we live in an industrialized society of great social mobility, in which we depend to a great degree upon our own efforts and those of mutual-aid associations (insurance and benevolent societies), unions, and philanthropic and governmental agencies to provide social security, rather than our relatives, it is hard for most of us to comprehend the importance of kinsmen in simpler societies. In primitive society most of these responsibilities rest with the kinship group.

The contrast is philosophically stated by an old Pomo Indian of California, who soliloquized,

> What is a man? A man is nothing. Without his family he is of less importance than that bug crossing the trail, of less importance than the sputum or exuvial. At least *they* can be used to help poison a man. A man must be with his family to amount to anything with us. If he had nobody else to help him, the first trouble he got into he would be killed by his enemies, because there would be no relatives to help him fight the poison of the other group. No woman would marry him. . . . He would be poorer than a new-born child, he would be poorer than a worm. . . . The family is important. If a man has a large family, . . . and upbringing by a family that is known to produce good children, then he is somebody and every family is willing to have him marry a woman of their group. In the White way of doing things the family is not so important. The police and soldiers take care of protecting you, the courts

---

[1] *The Nuer,* p. 182.

give you justice, the post office carries messages for you, the school teaches you. Everything is taken care of, even your children, if you die; but with us the family must do all of that.

Without the family we are nothing, and in the old days before the White people came, the family was given first consideration by anyone who was about to do anything at all. That is why we got along. . . .

With us the family was everything. Now it is nothing. We are getting like the White people and it is bad for the old people. We had no old people's home like you. The old people were important. They were wise. Your old people must be fools.[2]

The role of the kin group in government, law, and the institution of property will be discussed later on. At this point discussion shall be limited to the special relations between members of the kin groups.

Parents and Offspring. The parent-child relationship is often assumed to be determined by instinctive factors, but here as always in human affairs the cultural element obtrudes itself. Fatherhood, for instance, can mean a number of things. In its most elemental sense, it means the male biological procreator. This, surely, would seem to be a simple fact. Yet many Australian tribes dogmatically deny any knowledge of the physiology of paternity, holding persistently to the mystic notion of magical impregnation by totemic ancestral spirits. And the Banaro tribesmen of New Guinea do not permit a newly married husband to cohabit with his wife until she has borne a child sired by the best friend of her husband's father, or the father-in-law himself, for in the masquerade of a spirit ghost or goblin both cohabit with her. The infant is thought to be a goblin child.[3]

Under the discussion of bride price it was noted that a Madagascar man may claim the children of his remarried divorced wife as his own, because he paid for them, even though he did not beget them. Fatherhood may, indeed, be a matter of sociology rather than biology.

Secondarily, the father may be thought of as being the husband of one's mother. While this is commonly the case, it may or may not be so in actual practice for the reasons just indicated. In addition, the extension of the concept of father to include other men in this category by means of classificatory kinship terminology gives fatherhood a highly variable content (see Chap. 17). The consequences of polyandry should also be kept in mind.

[2] B. W. Aginsky, "An Indian's Soliloquy" (*The American Journal of Sociology*, Vol. 46, 1940), pp. 43–44.

[3] R. Thurnwald, *Banaro Society* (American Anthropological Association, Memoir 3, No. 4, 1924), pp. 251–391.

Nevertheless, if the fact of being or not being thought of as the true biological father is variable and "unrealistic," does not the role of the father have a fixed quality? Decidedly not, except perhaps that there may be a residual core of paternal affection maintained in all cultures. Malinowski, after noting how Trobriand fathers violate the formal susu requirements of their culture in order to give forbidden privileges to their sons, hazarded the belief that a paternal affective instinct is basic in human beings.[4] But it must not be overlooked that the Trobriand Islanders are virilocal (L. *vir* man + *locus* place). Relations between father and child are very intimate and tender in the early years of a child's life, so that there is every possibility for the cementing of an affective bond that is hard to suppress when the boy goes at eight to ten years of age to live with his mother's brother.

Finally, even when the father clearly plays the role of family head in the way that we understand it—as provider, protector, and preceptor for his children, especially his sons—the wide range of variation of the ways in which this role is worked out within our own cultural tradition should warn us to proceed with caution. The traditional authoritarian father of Victorian days is likely to be rare in a contemporary American society of fathers whose ideal (in the middle classes, at least) is to be "pals" to their sons, and who are indulgent, and sometimes bewildered, providers for their children—both sons and daughters.

Freud built up his Oedipus complex out of clinical experience with Europeans—primarily Central Europeans. The mixed attitudes of love and suppressed hate, of subconscious incest desires and authoritarian filial repression are a product of the special nature of European family relations. In many primitive societies the status of the father does not call for exercise of repressive authority in any degree. This is true of Malinowski's Trobrianders. Father hatred on the part of boys and suppressed mother-incest desires are found to be replaced by a sister-incest interest and maternal uncle resentment. What Freud thought was an instinct is a social product of special kin relationships.[5]

The softening of the father's role as authoritarian is by no means to be thought of solely as an aspect of matrilineal organization. Comanche kinship organization is bilateral with few matrilineal tendencies. Respect is owed the father, but the authority he exercises is mild. This is due in part to the high degree of freedom accorded boys, "who will die young in battle," but it is more than that. Petit, who has surveyed the educational and disciplinary practices of the Indians of North America, finds

---

[4] B. Malinowski, *Crime and Custom in Savage Society*, p. 107, *n.* 1.

[5] B. Malinowski, *Sex and Repression in Savage Society*.

that although the attitude prevails that punishment is for the good of a child, the idea is equally strong among the Indians that the responsibility for authoritarian repression has to come from outside the kinship group immediately concerned (the conjugal family).[6] Thus when the Comanche father avoids disciplining his son and indulges the boy's wishes, he is reflecting a general North American Indian attitude. Among the Comanches, the boy's classificatory elder sister bears the burden of exercising discipline. The result of this is that boys feel a genuine hostility toward older female relatives. It is interesting that the Comanche peace chief, who is called "father" by all the members of the tribe, never exercises the slightest disciplinary authority over his followers. This is also true of the Puebloans, whose tribal *cacique* (head chief) delegates all punishment to his executive officers, the war captains. He is also called "father" by the tribesmen. Among the southeastern Indians (Choctaw, Creek, Chickasaw) a mother does not punish her child or call on the father to do it but takes the recalcitrant to an old man, who delivers a lecture and throws cold water on the child. In many American tribes the mother's brother performs the disciplinary function, but rarely the mother or father. A Blackfoot father would ordinarily beat a mother who strikes a child. They wisely call on outsiders to carry the onus of punishment. In this way, they protect the emotional intimacy of the family in purely affective terms. The father role is protective and hortative, but not repressive.

Mead reports that the Samoan father exercises no authority as a father but only as a *matai* (the holder of a title; the titular head of a household). If a father who is not a matai attempts discipline, a child simply moves to the more congenial atmosphere of some other relative's household.[7]

Of course, there are tribes in which paternal authority, as we are accustomed to think of it, exists; this is especially apt to be true among patrilineal people, but the Roman paterfamilias is not a common primitive phenomenon. Fanciful notions about the autocratic patriarch in the prehistoric, primitive horde abound in the a priori theories of nineteenth-century anthropology and earlier psychoanalysis, but they are rooted more in fancy than in fact.

Mother-child Relations. The biological limitations imposed by nursing tend to stereotype the mother-child relation on the basis of dependency. Yet even here there is considerable variation in attitudes and behavior—especially in acceptance and rejection of children. Marquesan women,

[6] G. A. Pettit, "Primitive Education in North America" (*University of California Publications in American Archaeology and Ethnology,* Vol. 43, No. 1, 1946).

[7] M. Mead, *Coming of Age in Samoa,* Chap. 5.

whose main drive is to keep their sexual beauty, resent and reject their offspring as far as possible. Most Marquesan mothers behave as do women of our demimonde.[8] Comanche mothers, on the other hand, treat and nurse their children with great affection, and the child enjoys the security of feeling wanted. Alorese mothers, in the East Indies, neglect their children not because of vainglory, but because gardening demands so much of their time and effort. Breast feeding may be offered by other mothers who happen to be handy, or any member of the household may put some prechewed food in the child's mouth.[9] Thus, it may be seen that the nursing role of the mother is not necessarily a fixed imperative, even in a primitive society. The modern American escape by means of "formula" from the functional responsibility of motherhood has its primitive foreshadowing. In fact, the more details on mother-child relations that come in (only since psychoanalysis has roused the interest of anthropologists have we had reports of much value on this point) the more does it appear that the human mother is apt to fall short of giving ideal food and security satisfaction to the child. In human living the culture often provides other values and interests incompatible with full reproductive functioning. However, in many cultures, such as the Apache, "parents are deeply fond of their children and have them always uppermost in their minds."[10]

And as Lowie observes, a "Crow mother as a matter of course lavishes upon her children all her loving-kindness, intercedes on their behalf, and grieves over them with extravagant manifestations of sorrow."[11]

Husband-wife Relations. Among primitives relations between spouses almost always involve a certain amount of formal restraint. This probably results from the theory that marriage is an alliance of two alien groups and not, ordinarily, the consequence of romantic choice. It is unusual for husband and wife to call each other by personal name; rather, they must confine themselves to the kinship terms meaning "my husband" or "my wife." This, of course, crops up in the behavior of formalistically minded persons among us who address each other as "Mr. Applegate" or "Mrs. Smithby," or whatever the surname may be. In public the primitive man and wife rarely manifest affection, however much they may feel for each other.

Spouses are always dependent upon each other for culturally defined

---

[8] R. M. Linton, "The Marquesas" in *The Individual and His Society.*

[9] C. DuBois, *The People of Alor;* also, "The Alorese" in *The Psychological Frontiers of Society,* Chap. 5.

[10] G. Goodwin, *The Social Organization of the Western Apache,* p. 209.

[11] R. H. Lowie, *The Crow Indians,* p. 24.

services, and this leads to mutual respect relationships in most cultures. Generally, however, the male is expected to manifest a certain degree of independence from the woman, especially among warlike peoples.[12] Among matrilineal, especially matrilocal peoples, equality between husband and wife is more apt to be maintained.

Certain Melanesian people, notably the Dobu and Manus of the Admiralty Islands, emphasize hostility rather than mutual affection as the normal husband-wife relationship.[13] For Manus, Mead reports, "The blood ties of . . . parents are stronger than their relationship to each other, and there are more factors to pull them apart than there are to draw them together." [14] Contrasted to them are the Crow man and wife, who act in accordance with a deep-rooted belief that husband and wife are intimately associated in ceremonial activity.

Brother-sister (Sibling) Relations. The common rule is that brothers and sisters must practice avoidance, especially after puberty is reached. This is the consequence of extension of the incest tabu. Social intercourse entails a degree of intimacy, and primitives fear that any intimacy at all may lead down the path to forbidden sexual intimacy.

The "indecent" attitudes of white persons, who do not recognize the delicacy enjoined by avoidance, has shocked many a primitive. Let an Ifugao speak,

"Are your people like the low-landers—do they sleep in the same house with their sisters?"

"Our houses are very big." [It is the American, Barton, who is on the defensive.]

"*Nakayang!* If they are as big as a large village and if brothers and sisters sleep at opposite ends of them, it is perhaps not so bad. But the way the Fish-eaters (i.e., low-landers) do is a custom that stinks." [15]

Comanche boys resented their sisters not only because they were disciplined by older classificatory sisters, but also because the presence of a sister circumscribed their activities. "That is why boys were always glad to marry their sisters off for only a few arrows," said That's It. The boy had to sleep in a separate lodge when he reached puberty. Brother and sister avoidance does not necessarily mean hostility. Cheyenne boys avoided their sisters as an aspect of respect. This is the way they con-

---

[12] *Cf.* P. Radin (ed.), *Crashing Thunder*, Chap. 7.
[13] R. F. Fortune, *Sorcorers of Dobu*, pp. 21*ff*.
[14] M. Mead, *Growing Up in New Guinea*, p. 52.
[15] R. F. Barton, *The Half-way Sun*, p. 58.

ceived it. It was a great thing for a boy to present his sister with captured horses as a token in honor of her.

Finally, although brother-sister avoidance is the most common pattern,
there is also brother-sister interdependence as exemplified by the Manus
of the Admiralty Islands in Melanesia.[16]

It is clear that in the case of brother-sister avoidance incest fear is
the chief factor, but similar avoidances among other types of kin, to be
discussed below, indicate that numerous obscure causes and functions
may also be involved.

Avunculate and Amitate Relations. In the previous chapter, it was
seen how the susu brought the mother's brother into a position of functional prominence. The peculiar position of the maternal uncle also obtrudes in many cultures in which the susu has not been institutionalized.
It is naturally highlighted in any matrilineal clan system where succession to clan positions and functions held by men runs within the maternal clan. Since a boy in a matrilineal clan system belongs to his
mother's clan and not to his father's, inheritance from father to son is
ruled out for all clan-linked privileges. A man may pass his rights and
possessions to a brother, but generation succession is inevitable sooner or
later, and then the obvious inheritor is a sister's son. Nevertheless, avuncular relations, incipient or developed, will be found in almost all bilateral and probably in the majority of patrilineal societies too. We cannot forget that the basic conjugal family is bilateral, and whatever emphasis may be thrown on one side of the family, the other side is still
present with its interests, which cannot wholly be ignored.

To illustrate each of these situations, we may first turn attention to
the matrilineal but virilocal Haida of the Northwest Coast of North
America. At the age of ten a boy leaves his parental home and moves
into the household of his maternal uncle to have his training completed.
He serves as a page to his uncle in war and an apprentice in industry.
The uncle cares for him and subjects him to a rigorous regimen, including swimming in the winter ocean. The boy ultimately acquires titles,
supernatural power, and other property from his uncle as his due.[17]
Exactly the same practice is followed by the Trobriand Islanders, and
for the same reasons. In uxorilocal tribes with matrilineal descent, as the
Hopi and Zuñi among the Pueblos and the Iroquois in New York, the
boy continues to live at home until marriage, since that is already the
seat of the ceremonial functions he is to acquire from his maternal uncle.

[16] M. Mead (ed.), *Cooperation and Competition in Primitive Society*, pp. 213, 238.
[17] G. P. Murdock, *Our Primitive Contemporaries*, pp. 250–251.

Evidence of the strong avuncular relations that existed among the Pawnees was presented in the last chapter.

The Comanches illustrate avuncular relations in the mild form they may be expected to assume in a nonmatrilineal society. A boy always looks upon his maternal uncle as a sort of pal, who will back him up, if he gets involved in a sexual scrape. The fact that both use the same kinship term for each other (*ara*—mother's brother, sister's son) indicates the degree of status identity between the two. Avuncular indulgence is also noted in a distinct Comanche preference for the mother's father as compared to the father's father on the grandfather level.

In a host of American Indian tribes, on the other hand, the maternal uncle serves as preceptor and disciplinarian, as previously discussed.

A sociopsychological equivalent of the avunculate is the amitate: the practice of observing special relations between a child and his father's sister. In many parts of Melanesia, for example, the father's sister controls the choice of a boy's mate, and he is expected to respect her even more than his own mother. In some tribes the amitate may be found to equal the avunculate in importance, but in general the amitate is the less strongly developed of the two.

Parent-in-law Relations. A married man not infrequently has to work for his wife's parents (see page 210). He owes them something for his wife and the children she brings him. His ties and obligations to them are definite. The evidence shows that his relations to them are incipiently or grossly hostile in part; but only in part, because *in toto* they are ambivalent. The manifestations of this are in the striking rules of in-law avoidance among many primitives.

The Zulu warrior, spear in hand, is a paragon of ferocity, but when he meets his mother-in-law on the bypath, he ducks for the bushes and hides until she has passed. Among the lowly Tasmanians, a married man and his mother-in-law studiously avoid one another. Among the Arunta of Central Australia a man may not even look at his mother-in-law, to say nothing of speak to her; and for a woman to approach the men's hut of her sons-in-law results in severe social ostracism or death. In the Malay jungle almost identical restrictions are imposed, but here they also apply to father-in-law and daughter-in-law.

Avoidance rules among American Indians never bring forth the extreme penalties found in Africa and Australia. Nevertheless, social reticence is prevalent. When an Atsugewi Indian of California meets his mother-in-law on the path, the first to spy the other cries out, "Grizzly." The other one then jumps from the path to avoid that dangerous animal (the in-law). A Cheyenne never addresses his mother-in-law, nor she him. But communication is possible by subterfuge. In the hearing of her son-in-law she can tell the baby in the cradleboard what she wants her daughter's husband to know. But she will never be alone in the lodge with him, nor should they look at each other. Like an Assiniboin, she may not speak his name, nor he hers, but if his name is Knife, she may refer to him as "Something Sharp." But a Cheyenne mother-in-law is very generous to her married daughter's husband, and she has it in her power to remove the tabu if she happens to be skilled enough to belong to the honorable society of woman quillworkers. She may present him with a robe and a horse in the presence of all the female members of the society. Then and only then, may they treat each other as other people may.[18]

Primitive mother-in-law tabus almost invariably strike a responsive chord among Occidental readers. We, too, have the in-law situation. We have no explicit *rules* of mother-in-law avoidance, but there are *patterns* of avoidance in our behavior. Literature and radio humor repeat the threat of the husband to move out of house and home if mother-in-law makes good her threatened visit. There are no scientific data as to whether this is just talk or whether moving out is a common behavior pattern in this situation. Undoubtedly, there is more talk than action. Nevertheless, we do know that there is in-law trouble in our society, with which our culture provides no effective way of dealing. We do not emulate primitive people, who solve the problem by keeping in-laws apart—forbidding all social intercourse between them. Instead, we maintain the relationship and take it out in jokes. Humor can serve several functions, one of which is release of tensions. Max Eastman's analysis of humor in *The Enjoyment of Laughter* lists mother-in-law jokes as one of the primary forms of American humor. It is true that mother-in-law jokes are funny—sometimes. But they are for the most part bitter. Their humor is crude, rarely witty. Analysis of a random sample of 100 American mother-in-law jokes garnered from the press, radio, and various joke books in the past few years reveals six characteristics of these so-called jokes:

1. Ninety-four per cent are directed against the wife's mother.
2. Almost two-thirds wish the death of the mother-in-law.
3. Slightly over two-thirds emphasize the hostility of the son-in-law to his mother-in-law.
4. One-third make the mother-in-law the butt of gross ridicule.

[18] G. B. Grinnell, *The Cheyenne Indians,* Vol. 1, p. 147.

5. One-fifth give voice to resentment over the presence of the wife's mother in the household.

6. An equal number allege that the mother-in-law is a marathon talker.

Current mother-in-law jokes clearly represent a form of vicarious release from a social conflict between son-in-law and mother-in-law. This conflict is present in primitive as well as civilized society; it is a problem situation implicit in the bilateral nature of family organization. Freud attempted an elaborate psychological explanation, which the reader may find conveniently and effectively analyzed by Lowie. On only one point in his stricture of Freud must we take exception to Lowie's excellent discussion, namely, the declaration

Whenever we gain a glimpse of what the connections by marriage really feel, there is never a trace of hostility: respect is invariably the dominant note in the mutual sentiments, which are thus of a totally different character from the ones that so persistently figure in our comic weeklies.[19]

When avoidance has mastered the in-law situation respect in formal relations is easy to maintain. Respect for those of an elder generation is a common primitive characteristic. Respect is invoked in any authority situation, and in-laws always enjoy some degree of authority. But Lowie erred when he took the position that respect means the absence of hostility. Freud attempted to explain in-law avoidance as a consequence of ambivalent emotions—positive and negative, attraction and disaffection. The basic cause for in-law hostilities is, after all, psychological, conditioned by cultural factors. The parents-in-law are members of a different group of social intimacy; to them the son-in-law is an alien interloper, and from the son-in-law's point of view they are interferers in his conjugal family affairs.

In this light, because of the reasons for which they have no mother-in-law avoidance, the Seed Eater Shoshones present an interesting case. Theoretically, a boy marries his mother's brother's daughter, and his mother's brother theoretically has married his father's sister (the why's and wherefore's of this connubium are taken up in the next chapter). This being the case, his mother-in-law (wife's mother) is his father's sister—the very woman with whom he has had the most pleasant amitate relations since infancy. He feels no alienation toward her, and avoidance is not called for. But Seed Eater Shoshone cross-cousin marriage is an ideal that is rare in fact. Hence, the mother-in-law and son-in-law are not

[19] R. H. Lowie, *Primitive Society*, pp. 92–93.

usually aunt and nephew. They still feel the need for an artificial device to take them off the hostility footing of nonrelated in-laws.

The need to rely on the kin bond to overcome the implicit hostility of in-law relations is revealed in the kinship terminology of the Shoshones, who call the mother-in-law by a compound word meaning *"our mother's mother."* When a man calls his mother-in-law "our mother's mother," he is identifying himself with his children. She *is* their mother's mother, and as such she is a direct, lineal genetic ancestor, not an in-law at all. By using this terminology, a son-in-law diplomatically implies his identity with his wife's mother's group. A woman does the same when speaking of her son-in-law, whom she calls "father of my daughter's children." Here is evidence showing that the Shoshone absence of avoidance is due to factors in the kinship system, which make a genetic relative of the mother-in-law.

Another cultural factor is definitely at play in stimulating or ignoring the avoidance possibility. This is the question of residence. In the earliest attempt to apply statistical techniques to anthropology, in 1889, Tylor [20] demonstrated that in-law avoidances are correlated with the type of residence in vogue. Uxorilocal residence is positively correlated with mother-in-law avoidance; virilocal residence with father-in-law avoidance. Such association of two social conditions is what Tylor called an *adhesion*. Interpreting Tylor's results, we may observe that coresidence of in-laws of opposite sex tends to intensify the undesirable aspects of in-law interaction to the extent that formal relations are usually banned. This may account for the male orientation of our mother-in-law humor. There are no satisfactory statistics available, but direct observation indicates that when a mother in our society takes up residence with a married child, it is more often in the household of her daughter rather than of her son. Aside from the residence factor there is also the occupational factor. A son usually enters an occupational field in which his mother has no experience, and he is expected to withdraw from her sphere of dominance. Most daughters continue in the occupation that has engaged their mothers since marriage—child raising and householding. Try as she may, a mother finds it hard to suppress her directive habits over her daughter, and her participation runs naturally into her daughter's family affairs. With our individualistic orientation and generation differences in patterns of household management and child care, this well-meant participation is often resented as interference.

[20] E. B. Tylor, "On a Method of Investigating the Development of Institutions; Applied to Laws of Marriage and Descent," *Journal of the Royal Anthropological Institute of Great Britain and Ireland*, Vol. 18 (1889), pp. 245–272.

The postwar housing problem in this land has undoubtedly aggravated the problem of in-law relations for married veterans and others who have doubled up with their parents. At least one thing should be realized— the tensions are not unique to individual families. This is an old and persistent social problem.

Teknonymy. This is the practice of naming a person as the father or mother of so-and-so: Father of Swelling Rice, if Swelling Rice is the name of his first child. Prior to the birth of the child the in-laws refuse to recognize the personal name of their child's spouse. Only when he (or she) has given them a grandchild is recognition gained through a personal name. Then it is not really his own personal name but the child's name that is accorded to the parent. However, this is not the only possible cause of teknonymy. Lowie points out that with the Gold tribe of the Amur river of Siberia a woman may not address her husband by his personal name, nor may a sister her brother. But a male may use his wife's or sister's name in personal address. Thus, use of the personal name is a privilege limited to the dominant males. After a woman bears a child, she is privileged to address her lofty husband as "father of so-and-so." [21] In this case, it is manifestation of husband-wife, brother-sister restraints.

Teknonymy is regular among the Bantu Negroes. It also occurs irregularly in Melanesia, North and South America, China, India, and Siam.

Brother-in-law and Sister-in-law Relations. The sororate and levirate are ubiquitous in the primitive world. This means that a man enjoys a high expectancy of marrying his wife's sister, and a woman enjoys the same prospect with respect to her husband's brother. A man's sister-in-law and a woman's brother-in-law are potential mates. This calls for special psychological preparation. One way in which this is managed is through the custom of *privileged familiarity*. Where brothers and sisters have to avoid each other, brothers-in-law and sisters-in-law often go to opposite extremes. They may indulge in gross obscenity and horseplay. Violent practical jokes are played at each other's expense. Post Oak Jim, a Comanche, laughed uproariously as he pulled up his pants to show us the scar in the calf of his leg caused by his sister-in-law, who had thrown a knife at him, all in fun. On another occasion, she took his watch and pawned it for six dollars. It cost him seven to get it back. Post Oak Jim thought that very funny. Arapahos have similar notions. A brother- or sister-in-law may dash cold water in the face of the other, if the in-law is found sleeping late in the morning. "I always got up early so that joke

---

[21] R. H. Lowie, *Primitive Society*, pp. 107–109.

was never played on me," one Arapaho woman boasts. If not cold water, the jokester might rub kettle soot on the face of the sleeper.[22]

To joke with the wife of a younger brother is prohibited in certain cultures, while at the same time it is good form to joke with the wife of an elder brother. This distinction is correlated to some extent with the junior levirate. A man may indulge in privileged familiarity with the woman he may some day inherit as a wife, but he may not do so with the wives of his younger brothers, whom he may not marry. On this and other data, Lowie formulated the principle that "licensed familiarity *generally* obtains between potential mates." [23] It is a psychological preparation for the intimacy of a future marital union.

Reichard has recently called attention to the fact that among the Navajos the joking relationship exists between cross-cousins of either sex, but that cross-cousin marriage is strongly discountenanced.[24] In this case, Lowie's principle does not apply, but it should be noted that Lowie limited his formulation by insertion of the crucial word "generally." Further, it is obvious that the joking relationship exists in some tribes between relatives whose relationship is other than that of brother-in-law and sister-in-law. It may be between brothers-in-law, as with the Cheyennes. Members of the Tribal Council were highly revered, but when a camp crier was once making his rounds, announcing a council meeting to the tribe, Bull Head bellowed out, "Don't call them chiefs. Call them fools! There are too many fools with the chiefs." There was no blasphemy in the taunt, for everyone knew that Bull Head had a brother-in-law on the council.

Other Special Relations. It is well known that licensed familiarity is a counterpart of the avunculate relation in many tribes, too. Eggan, considering the occurrence of the joking relationship between various types of relatives, looks upon the institution as a form of social and psychological compensation that counterbalances the strong restraints imposed by the respect attitudes within primitive kinship systems.[25]

A similar conclusion has been drawn from a very careful study of joking relations in North Queensland, Australia, by D. F. Thompson, who writes, "In the joking relationship, which is regulated by the kinship system, the obligatory behavior consists of a reversal of the cus-

[22] T. Michelson, "Narrative of an Arapahoe Woman" (*American Anthropologist*, Vol. 35, 1933), p. 604.

[23] R. H. Lowie, *Primitive Society*, p. 102.

[24] G. Reichard, in *General Anthropology*, p. 448.

[25] F. Eggan, "Arapahoe and Cheyenne Kinship Systems" in *Social Organization of North American Indians*, pp. 75–81.

tomary pattern, normally of severe restraint, appropriate to the relationship." [26] Thus, the customary joking relationship may serve as a functional counterbalance to the restraints of avoidances.

There are a host of additional special relations that go along with particular relationship status in different tribes. For instance, an Apache Indian avoids all cousins of the opposite sex. On the other hand, he may joke with his brother-in-law, but not obscenely. Among the Australian tribes just referred to, the greatest joking freedom is between paternal grandfather and grandchild. Crow Indians may take terrific joking liberties with their father's clan brothers. These are all more or less unique culture patterns that would require special attention far beyond the interest of an introductory study.

[26] D. F. Thompson, "The Joking Relationship and Organized Obscenity in North Queensland" (*American Anthropologist*, Vol. 37, 1935), p. 489.

CHAPTER 17

KINSHIP SYSTEMS AND TERMINOLOGY

The patterns of kinship behavior are not biologically determined. They are all culturally conceived. Kinship relations consist of the interacting roles that are customarily ascribed to the different statuses of relationship by a people. Every culture includes a set of words, or labels, that symbolize each of its kinship statuses. These labels are called *kinship terms*, and the whole is called the *system of kinship* (or relationship) *terminology* of the culture.

The first important principle to grasp in the study of kinship systems is that *no system provides a separate and distinct term for every possible kind or position of genealogical relationship*. All systems equate, lump, or merge some relatives of different genealogical positions into one single category, which is identified by a specific term. For example, the Comanche Indians equate father, father's brother, and mother's sister's husband all under one term, *ap'*. Father's brother and mother's sister's husband (both of whom we call *uncle*) are genealogically distinct from father, but to the Comanche they are terminologically identical. Similarly, a Comanche calls his own son, his brother's son, his wife's sister's son, and his sister's daughter's husband all by the selfsame name, *tua*. All these persons are merged or equated under the same identifying term of relationship.

Kinship systems in which this practice of merging is predominant are called *classificatory systems of relationship*. Most primitive systems are of this kind.

A system in which each relationship term applies to a particular genealogical status and no other is called a *particularizing system*. We, for instance, tend to apply the terms "father" and "mother" only to our actual progenitors when referring to relatives. However, as no system is ever wholly particularizing, we also use certain classificatory terms, such as cousin, uncle, aunt, niece, nephew, grandfather, grandmother, grandson, and granddaughter.

This insistence on particularizing "father" and "mother" is sociologically significant. For you will note that in addition to particularizing "father" and "mother" we use the words "son" and "daughter" to mean only our own children and not those of our brothers or sisters. Likewise, we use "brother" and "sister" to refer exclusively to the siblings of our own conjugal family. Other relatives of our own generation level we call "cousins." Our terminology thus places strong emphasis upon the exclusiveness of our immediate conjugal family; it rigidly distinguishes more remote relatives. This reflects the great social significance of our close relatives in the small conjugal family as against the rest of our larger kinship groups. Lineal relatives are more important to us than collateral ones.

In most primitive societies, as we have noted, extended kinship groups play larger roles than is the case with us. In such societies, merging or lumping of relatives on a collateral basis is, therefore, much more likely.

Since kinship terms designate social statuses, what you must call a person ideally determines how you must behave toward him. Further, all persons who are called by the same kinship term should (and again, ideally) receive the same sort of behavior, since they enjoy theoretically identical statuses in the system of social organization.

This may be understood by examining the Comanche practice of identifying father's brother with father. A Comanche not only calls his father's brother "father" but also behaves toward him as though he were father. He also calls his mother's sister "mother," and behaves toward her as though she were a mother. On her part a woman not only calls her own offspring "son" and "daughter" but she also applies these terms to her sister's children. Do they not call her "mother"? A man also calls his brother's children "son" and "daughter." Do they not call him "father"? What is more, a man does not call his brother's wife by any term meaning sister-in-law. He simply and frankly calls her "wife." Within decorous limits he behaves toward her as though she were his wife (remember the anticipatory levirate). Since he calls her children "son" and "daughter," it is within logical reason that their mother be called "wife." Then, of course, it should follow, and does, that the woman in turn calls her husband's brother "husband."

This merging of paternal uncle with father and maternal aunt with mother does not mean that the Comanches are so simple-minded as to be unable to discern any difference between such people. For them the differences are not important. However, mother's brother is not merged with father. Nor is father's sister merged with mother. Each of these is called by a distinctive term. They, in their turn, also distinguish between the children of their brothers and sisters. A man, as we have seen, calls his brother's children "son" and "daughter," but he has a different term for his sister's children (ara). A woman, on her part, calls her sister's children "son" and "daughter" but not her brother's children (paha).

Thus, certain collateral relatives are merged with lineal ascendants or descendants; yet others of them are sharply set aside. The effect is that of a forking. The Comanche practice is therefore called *forked merging,* or more pretentiously, *bifurcate merging.*

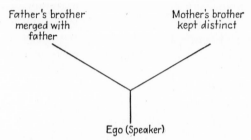

Father's brother merged with father

Mother's brother kept distinct

Ego (Speaker)

Bifurcate merging, which is a common characteristic of many primitive kinship systems, is closely correlated with unilinear descent.[1] The focusing of social interest upon one side of the relationship group leads to a fusing of certain relationship statuses within that side of the family, while setting off the other.

However, in the Comanche practice under discussion, unilineality is not a causal factor, since Comanche descent is bilateral. Comanche bifurcate merging is the functional consequence of preferential levirate and sororate marriages. It is easy to understand that when a man marries his brother's widow he becomes a stepfather to his nieces and nephews. Yet the whole psychology of stepfatherhood is one of emotional reservation. It denies complete fatherhood in filial relations. Surely it is much healthier if the substitute father can be accepted in the role of a real father. Can anyone deny that it is a greater help toward this desired relationship to call the substitute father "father"? Then think how much easier it is to do this—and to look upon him as father—if in your kinship system you have been calling him "father" since the day you could first babble *ap'.* The sting of the death or divorce of a father is surely less sharp when the child is not dependent upon just *one* father.

In anticipation of levirate marriage a man calls his brother's wife "wife." She might as well get used from the outset to future eventualities. So she responds by calling him "husband," and each calls the other's children "son" and "daughter," although their fates may never bring them together as actual husband and wife.

The consequences of the sororate are similar. With a piece of paper and a pencil it would be a good exercise to work out the equations for oneself.

[1] G. P. Murdock, "Bifurcate Merging" (*American Anthropologist,* Vol. 49, 1947), p. 60.

But although a woman may marry her husband's brother, she may not marry her own brother. The levirate may transform a *paternal* uncle into a child's father but never a *maternal* uncle. Hence, the merging of father and father's brother, but the bifurcation of father's brother and mother's brother. And although a man may marry his wife's sister under the sororate and sororal polygyny, he may not marry his own sister. So, the sororate may transform a *maternal* aunt into "mother" but may never accomplish this for the father's sister.

Among the Shoshones, from whom the Comanches stem, interfamilial exchange marriage is also a preferred marriage form. This produces additional lumpings in kinship terminology. A man calls his wife's sister's husband "brother"; a woman calls her husband's sister's husband "brother" in the same way. Likewise, a man calls his wife's brother's wife "sister"; and a woman calls her husband's sister's husband "brother," in the same way. In this system, since collateral relatives, who are distinguished from lineal, are merged, the practice is called *collateral merging*. This may all sound very confusing to the novice in anthropology, but when carefully thought through, the logical sense in it will be seen to be very nice. Note that the original logic is the primitives', not the anthropologists'.

This last illustration introduces another principle that is frequently met with in primitive systems. *Distinctions may be based on the relative ages of the speaker and the person referred to. Also, kinship terminology differs according to the sex of the speaker.*

Further consideration of the Comanche system will bring forth additional characteristics of primitive relationship systems. All cousins are lumped as siblings along with brothers and sisters. Emphasis is placed on *generation similarity*. The result is that the logically expected distinction between cross-cousins and parallel cousins is overruled and suppressed. Bifurcation of parental relatives (the distinction between father's brother and mother's brother; mother's sister and father's sister) should logically result in a separation of their children in the kinship terminology. In the absence of clans this is not a functional necessity, however, and the desire to avoid marriage with all known genetic relatives finds expression in the placement of all relatives of one's own generation in the tabued class of "brother" and "sister."

On the other hand, wherever there is a clan system, bifurcation of cross-cousins and parallel cousins consistently occurs (Fig. 65). Collateral bifurcation then supersedes generation merging on the generation level of the speaker.

Cross-cousin marriage usually produces an interesting identification of parents-in-law (who are affinal relatives, *i.e.*, by affinity) with genetic relatives. If a man marries his mother's brother's daughter, then his father-in-law is his maternal uncle. Or if he marries his father's sister's daughter, his mother-in-law is his paternal aunt. The consequences of this were discussed in Chap. 16.

Other special forms of marriage have further remarkable and, from our point of view, incongruous reflections in kinship terminology and related forms of behavior.

The Crow System. The Crow Indians possess matrilineal clans with the levirate, sororate, and secondary affinal marriage of a woman to her

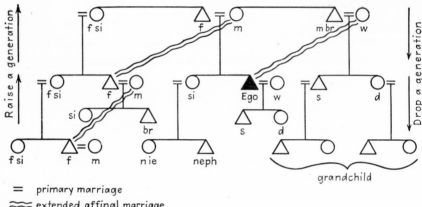

= primary marriage

~~~ extended affinal marriage

Fig. 66. Generation shifts in the Crow kinship system.

husband's sister's son. In this last form a boy marries his mother's brother's wife by means of avuncular inheritance. He calls his maternal uncle "elder brother." In the Crow system his maternal uncle is an elder clan brother, and since he may inherit this man's wife, the idea of *brother equivalence* in wife sharing exerts its influence on terminology. His uncle's wife, whom we would call "aunt," is his own potential wife, so he calls her "wife" whether she actually becomes such or not. Now see what this does to his "cousins" (as we would call them), his mother's brother's children. They are the offspring of the woman whom he calls "wife." A man's "wife's" children automatically become his "sons" and "daughters." Any offspring of these "sons" and "daughters" automatically become his "grandchildren." Thus all collateral relatives through a man's maternal uncle are dropped a generation, as illustrated in Fig. 66.

On the other hand, descendants of the father's sister are raised a generation. "Cousins" who are offspring of a man's father's sister become "father" and "father's sister." This results from the fact that the speaker's mother marries (or may marry) her husband's sister's son (the speaker's cousin), who then becomes the speaker's "father." His children are naturally elevated to become the speaker's "brother" and "sister." Generation equivalence is thrown to the winds! In the speaker's own generation, he calls his real siblings "brother" and "sister," his maternal uncle's children "son" and "daughter," and his paternal aunt's children "father" and "paternal aunt"!

In the generation of his offspring the results are even more remarkable. He calls his own offspring "son" and "daughter," the offspring of his

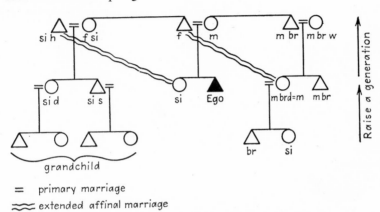

= primary marriage
≈≈ extended affinal marriage

FIG. 67. Generation shifts in the Omaha kinship system.

mother's brother's children "grandchild," and the offspring of his father's sister's children "father" and "father's sister." Lowie reports

> This odd way of putting a relative of one's own generation into the one above or below, respectively, is impressed at an early age. In my hearing a four-year-old boy, Sunrise, called a two-year-old girl, Good-Skunk, his daughter. . . . In reality she was a daughter of his mother's brother; he her father's sister's son.[2]

The Omaha System. In a tribe such as the Omaha, which has a patrilineal clan system with wife's brother's daughter marriage as the preferred type of secondary affinal mating, generation shifts of the same order as have been described for the Crow system occur. But in the Omaha system, those persons whom the Crows drop a generation are elevated, and vice versa. Figure 67 should be studied to see how these Omaha type equations are worked out.

[2] *The Crow Indians,* p. 24. After the lines above were written the ditty "I'm My Own Grandpaw" became a popular hit tune. It should help to make understanding of the Crow shifts easier.

The Hawaiian System. If tribes possessing the Crow and Omaha types of kinship systems go to extremes in ignoring generation principles, the Hawaiians go to the opposite extreme in emphasizing them. Basically, there are only five categories of kinship in the Hawaiian system:

> Grandparent
> Parent
> Sibling
> Offspring
> Grandchild

Sex distinctions are made by use of modifiers to the root word for each generation term. In the sibling generation further distinctions are drawn according to the relative ages of the parents through whom the siblings are related. Nevertheless, nearness of relationship is wholly ignored, and in terminology a remote cousin is as much a "brother" or "sister" as is a uterine sibling.

There has been much anthropological controversy over the interpretation of the significance of the Hawaiian system. Lewis Henry Morgan touched it off. He maintained that kinship terminologies are originally shaped by the social system of the society. Morgan also held that because of the stability of language, archaic terminological patterns outlive the social forms that produce them. Thus kinship terms often survive as vestiges of former usages that have undergone drastic change. Morgan, therefore, thought that he had evidence in the Hawaiian system to support his evolutionary scheme of family development in which primitive promiscuity preceded prohibition of intermarriage of brothers and sisters. Thus, when brother and sister were purportedly free to mate, there was no need to separate the maternal uncle from father, for they could be one and the same. All male relatives on the parental generation were, therefore, supposed to be lumped under a single term. There would be no need to distinguish between their children, except for sex, because all cousins could be offspring of any of these men. Hence, said Morgan, absolute generation merging resulted.[3]

A different explanation can be satisfactorily found in generation merging. This results from a psychological tendency to simplify relationships when no need to emphasize particular social obligations between kinsmen is felt.

In rejecting Morgan's interpretation of the Hawaiian kinship system, we must not err in rejecting *in toto* his principle of linguistic survivals. Historical influences do continue to operate in some instances long after

[3] L. H. Morgan, *Ancient Society*.

their functional action has been weakened to the point where they are more traditional ideals than actual behavior patterns. The Comanches shape some of their terminology to conform with interfamilial exchange marriage. Yet there does not seem to be any evidence of such marriages among the Comanches in recent times. Even the Shoshones, who are closest to the archaic social forms from which the Comanches originally developed, have produced only a few such interfamilial exchange marriages in the memory of living Indians.

Not social organization alone but a variety of interacting factors ultimately determine the form and content of each kinship system. These factors arise from social organization, language idiosyncrasies, historical contacts, and psychological tendencies.

Four decades ago Kroeber [4] identified eight principles of kinship distinctions that may be seized upon in shaping a kinship system. These eight principles of distinction are as follows:

1. Difference in generation levels (father, son; grandparent, grandchild, etc.)
2. Difference in age levels within the same generation (elder and younger brother; father's elder brother, etc.)
3. Difference between lineal and collateral relationship (father, uncle; brother, cousin, etc.)
4. Difference in sex of relatives (brother, sister; uncle, aunt, etc.)
5. Difference in sex of the speaker (males and females may have two separate systems of terms)
6. Difference of sex of the person *through* whom the relationship is established (*father's* brother, *mother's* brother; *father's* father, *mother's* father; father's *father's sister's daughter's* daughter, etc.)
7. Difference between genetic relatives and those connected by marriage (sister, mother; husband's mother; etc.)
8. Difference in status or life condition of the person *through* whom the relationship is established (as being living or dead; single or married; etc.)

Few systems make use of all eight distinctions, but many primitives use the first seven.

The Anglo-American System. The only kinship group terminologically recognized in our system is the family. The distinction between the conjugal family of orientation and the conjugal family of procreation (page 220) is one drawn by social scientists for analytical purposes only. As the sociologist Parsons observes, our term "relatives" refers to kinsmen in

[4] A. L. Kroeber, "Classificatory Systems of Relationship" (*Journal of the Royal Anthropological Institute of Great Britain and Ireland*, Vol. 39, 1909), pp. 77–84.

general and not to any organized kinship group.[5] We have no susu, clans, or moieties.

Our kinship system is merely a network of linked individual conjugal families. Throughout the whole system every linkage between any two conjugal families is in the person of only *one* individual.

Our system utilizes only four of the eight recognized principles of distinction, *viz.*, sex, generation, lineal versus collateral, and genetic versus affinal. We do not incorporate distinctions based upon the sex of the speaker, age differences within a generation, sex of the person through whom the relationship exists, or the condition of life of the person through whom the relationship exists.

Monogamy is reflected in the fact that "father," "mother," "husband" and "wife" can apply to only one person within the kinship system. When these terms are used within the Church system, they imply and evoke certain filial responses and behaviors that carry over from the kinship system, but no one makes the mistake of assuming that they imply genetic relationship! We see this also in the panhandler's claim to kinship assistance when he puts the touch with his plaintive, "Brother, can you spare a dime?" In college circles, we see it in the venerable and revered campus custodian, who is affectionately called "Dad," or the owner of a campus restaurant or pool hall, who performs the fatherly function of bailing out too exuberant students when they land in the town jail.

Affinal relatives are all distinguished by means of the "in-law" suffix. Like Shoshones, however, we often use a device of teknonymy to soften the stiffness of the "in-law" term when addressing our mother-in-law and father-in-law. This is managed by identifying ourselves with our offspring and addressing our spouses' parents as "grandmother" and "grandfather." They are lineal kin to our children, and so by this fictive device we draw them into our lineal family group.

Except for a slight linguistic emphasis given to the patrilineal line through patronymy, the consequences of which are more attitudinal than structural or behavioral, our system is symmetrically multilateral. We treat all ramifications extending out from the immediate lineal line with equal weight (or lack of it). Such distinctions in emphasis as do occur are the result of personal preferences or aversions, not the consequences of any systematic emphasis. Tendencies to exception to this characteristic exist in lineage-conscious families and the "matriarchal" family of American Negroes.[6]

[5] T. C. Parsons, "The Kinship System of the Contemporary United States" (*American Anthropologist,* Vol. 45, 1943), p. 24.

[6] *Cf.* E. F. Frazier, *The Negro Family in the United States.*

The lack of structural cohesiveness outside the inner circle of families in lineal descent in our kinship system reflects the weak role kinship groups play in our society. We emphasize the independence of separate conjugal family units.

Most of our problems of marriage and the family rise directly or indirectly from this fact. Parent-child conflict is generated because children must develop independence to be able to found their own economically independent families of procreation with separate households.

Much of the erratic behavior of adolescents, so baffling or amusing to adults, may be traced to the insecurity of the emergent boy or girl who is in transition from the bonds of his family of birth to the expectant family of procreation that he or she must soon found. Old-age insecurity is the lot of many parents whose conjugal family has been pared down until only the founding pair is left. When one of them dies the survivor is at sea with no comfortable base in which to harbor. Old people's homes, old-age security legislation, and Townsend movements are the unsatisfactory social consequences.

Few of the social relations of children are predetermined by kinship status outside the immediate conjugal family. They are thrown into open competition for social status with success and prestige for some, frustration and insecurity for others.

Marriage rests heavily on the bond of love and affection, for there are no absolutely ascribed preferential matings within the kinship group to solve the problem of mating in the Australian way, nor is there much family control of mating as in China or France.

These are only some of the upsetting consequences of our open, weak kinship system.

Advantages are those that are found in individual freedom of action in social and economic relations: freedom to choose one's friends within or without the relationship group, freedom to choose one's mate, freedom to find an occupation fairly untrammeled by kinship status, and freedom to live where one wills.

In America today the individual couple is on its own, to stand or fall as a unit according to the way in which the pair surmounts the weaknesses and hazards of our loose kinship system in a troubled society and utilizes effectively the freedoms that it offers. The divorce mills grind for those who fail, and questing college students flock to sociology courses in Marriage and the Family.

CHAPTER 18

CLANS

The clan is an extended kinship group built upon the unilateral principle. A clan system is the integrated social organization that gives to the clans of a particular society their special form, meaning, and function. Ordinarily, a clan system is either matrilineal or patrilineal. This means that children belong either to the clan of the mother or of the father. In any given culture in which there are clans one principle usually prevails to the exclusion of the others. Consequently, all the children in a conjugal family belong to the clan of the mother, if the system is matrilineal, or to the clan of the father, if the system is patrilineal. Because clans are always exogamous, a married pair must belong to separate clans. This means that while the children belong to the clan of one parent they do not belong to the clan of the other.

In a matrilineal system a woman and her brothers and sisters all belong to the same clan. Her children and her sisters' children also belong to that clan. The offspring of her brothers pass out of it. But the children of her daughters and the offspring of all her female descendants through females will remain in the clan ad infinitum. In a patrilineal society membership in a clan includes a man, his brothers and sisters, and his offspring, plus his brothers' offspring, but not the children of his sisters. In descendant generations it will include all the children of male descendants through the males only.

Clan membership is, therefore, a matter of predetermined social heredity. You do not join a clan, for it is not a voluntary association. You are born into your clan perforce. The social fiction of adoption may make possible a change of clan affiliations, however. Adoption establishes a relationship as being factually real when it actually is not. Nevertheless, on the basis of the fiction, the foster relatives and the foster child behave as though the relationship is what they pretend it to be. They assume a fictional relationship status and then enact the roles that go with those statuses. Most adoptions that occur in societies possessing clans take place within the clan, so that change of clan affiliation does not occur. Expulsion from the clan may be the dire penalty for black sheep. Otherwise, a person is born, lives, and dies in the same clan. Once a clan member, always a clan member. Only in rare societies does a woman join her husband's clan on marriage.

Clan membership is discriminating and exclusive. It arbitrarily segments the population of a tribe; artificially it separates genetic relatives one from the other. In compensation it cements the half of the genetic relatives that are included within the unilateral group into a firmer bond of kinship than is possible through bilateral extension of the family. In large or widely scattered populations the clan bond reaches out to include persons so remotely related that the actual kinship can no longer be genetically traced. Yet if people bear a common clan name, they are members of the same clan. The relationship is assumed to be real. The contemporary Chinese go to the greatest extremes of all people in this practice. The family name Wang, for example, is borne by thousands of Chinese. All Wangs form a loosely knit clan, so that no Wang may marry another Wang, and all Wangs should pull together for the glory of Wang.

A further consequence of the inclusive-exclusive character of the clan is the sharp division it makes among cousins. Cross-cousins can never belong to the same clan, although parallel cousins may. This is what makes cross-cousin marriage possible. To understand why cross-cousins cannot be members of the same clan, a simple genealogical chart helps. In Fig. 65 (page 203), we postulate a system of patrilineal descent involving only two clans. One clan is identified in black, the other in white. Of course, it should be realized that if a society includes more than two clans, it would not follow that all parallel cousins belong to the same clan, nor would it follow that all cross-cousins belong to the same clan. They would then be found dispersed among numerous clans, depending upon the clan combinations that take place among the various marriages. However, all the persons on a generation level within any one clan are theoretically, at least, parallel cousins, or "brothers" and "sisters," and none of them will be cross-cousins to each other.

In conception, therefore, all clans rest on the social fiction of genetic relationship arbitrarily based on the unilateral principle. The belief that all clan members are genetic descendants of a single common ancestor (patrilineal) or ancestress (matrilineal) follows. Because of this, clans are always exogamous. As a functioning kinship group, the clan is protected by the incest tabu. Nevertheless, it is interesting to note that when survival of the entire society is at stake, the principle of clan exogamy may be cast aside. This was done by the people of Sia Pueblo who, facing extinction in the 1870's, let down the bars to intraclan marriage. Since 1880 the population of the Pueblo has risen from 100 to more than 200 persons. In 1940 a Sia informant observed, "Now that the Pueblo is safe and growing, people don't approve of marriages within the clan any more."

Lineage and Clan. The germ of the clan is the susu and lineage, both of which are simple unilateral kin groups. Since the susu has already been discussed in detail, attention need be given only to the lineage. The lineage is an extended unilateral kinship group descended from a known founder, or common ancestor, who ordinarily lived not more than five or six generations back. He is a real person, and not a mythological or legendary figure. Some anthropologists, however, treat any recognizable subdivisions of clans as lineages. This is done by E. E. Evans-Pritchard, for instance, who describes Nuer clans as consisting of maximal, major, minor, and minimal lineages (each being a subdivision of the next higher unit).[1]

The clan founder, on the other hand, almost always existed so far in the past that often no pretense is made about who or what he or she may have been. Very often, however, the folklore of the clan includes a myth purporting to give a truthful account of how the clan came to be. Thus among the patrilineal Dahomey of West Africa, one clan was founded by the son of a horse "who, bounding from the water in a fury of passion, lay with a woman on the bank of the river." Another clan is said to have descended from the "offspring of a woman and a pig, another from that of a woman and a toad, one from that of a woman and a dog, and the royal family . . . originated from the mating of a female leopard with the King of Adja." Another clan is said to have been created when a peanut was transformed into a man by magic, who then mated with a poor woman, who lived on roots. Herskovits, who is the outstanding American authority on African peoples, says that to this day the members of the Peanut clan lack the fine smooth skin of other Dahomeans, "It is rough like the shell of a peanut." Further, the members of the Peanut clan are said to be recognizable on sight.[2] How this can be genetically possible in view of clan exogamy is a little difficult to understand.

The members of a Dahomean clan have a rather special set of attitudes toward the animal or plant creature who begat their clan founder. All clans revere their clan founder and his descendants, who are their ancestors. All Dahomean clans except one abjure the flesh of the animal species associated with the founder, and many of them bear the name of the founder. All these features give the clans a totemic tinge.

[1] *The Nuer.*

[2] M. J. and F. S. Herskovits, *An Outline of Dahomean Religious Belief* (American Anthropological Association, Memoir 41, 1933), pp. 24–27.

The usages of the Crow Indians illustrate a different kind of clan origin legend. The clan names are taken from certain alleged exploits of the founders, after the manner of Plains Indian warriors, who bestow names on children to memorialize some outstanding events in the warrior's life. It would be quite a mistake if you were to jump to the conclusion that the Crow "Greasy-inside-of-their-mouths" clan were slippery tongued, for the name is actually honorific. The clan founder was such a provident hunter that he was always surfeited with rich fat meat. His mouth was so coated with fat that when he spit in the campfire, his saliva flared up in the flames! Other Crow clan names memorialize alleged historical incidents or characteristics. The Piegan clan was originally called "They-eat-their-own-mucus," which may or not have been a praiseworthy accomplishment from the Crow point of view, but when these people once abandoned a wounded comrade in battle, they were henceforth dubbed "Piegan," meaning that they acted like the Piegan enemies, which was certainly *not* a praiseworthy epithet from the Crow point of view.[3]

In all these and similar instances, which could be drawn from a multitude of tribes, the actual origin of the clan is lost in the hoary past, but this is not the case with lineages.

Lineages may exist with or without clans. Clans may also exist with or without institutionalized lineages within them. Iroquois clans are made up of related groups of maternal lineages; the lineages are localized for the most part in long-house groupings. Very often lineage heads constitute the clan council, if there is a clan council. In most parts of Indonesia lineages are the basic functional group, for lineages or subclans form the localized village, while the clans have a more regional character.

Clan and Moiety. Reciprocity is the basis of all social relationships, for there can be no social relations without interaction. Human beings are so constituted that the isolated person is not a complete man. They are also so constituted that dependence without interdependence is not readily or for long accepted by the giver of services. He who gives would also receive. Through the building of a network of giving and receiving of services a society expands its potentialities.

The principle of reciprocity is, therefore, operative in all societies. However, some societies are content to leave it implicit in their cultures without placing much formal emphasis upon it. Others, such as the Trobrianders and many other Melanesians, go to great lengths in institutionalizing reciprocity and throwing it into the spotlight of social awareness.

[3] R. H. Lowie, *The Crow Indians*, pp. 15–16.

One of the most effective ways of institutionalizing reciprocity is to organize the society on a moiety basis. This is done by dividing the society in two equal halves, or moieties (Fr. *moitié*, half), to produce a system known as *dual division*. Moieties are exogamous with few exceptions (*viz.*, endogamous Toda moieties); each moiety supplies the other with its marriage partners. Other reciprocal services are invariably linked to the moiety alignments. Moieties thus effectively control certain types of behavior and serve to give concrete form to the reciprocity principle.

In cases where there are only two clans in a tribe, as the Water and Land groups of the Central Miwok in California, clan and moiety are automatically synonymous. Multiple clans are the more common order, however, and when clans are linked to moieties, the moiety is the larger unit and the clans are subdivisions of the moieties. Most of the Iroquois tribes have this kind of arrangement. Among the Seneca, to take a typical example, the Bear, Wolf, Turtle, and Beaver clans are aligned vis-à-vis the Deer, Snipe, Heron, and Hawk. Originally, the moieties were exogamous, but in recent centuries they have lost their control over marriage, and only the clans have retained the exogamous rule. Each moiety performs the important mourning rituals on behalf of the other; the moieties compete against each other in the old Indian game of lacrosse, which is as much a ceremonial ritual as it is a sport. On the other hand, they do not enter into the political structure, while clans and lineages do.

Many American tribes with moieties associate them with the duality of the cosmos: Sky and Earth, Water and Land, Winter and Summer, Red and White (War and Peace). This may be seen as just another way of objectifying the principle of reciprocity in the minds of the people.

Although Morgan assumed that moieties precede clans in historical development, Lowie has rightly concluded that either one may precede the other, dependent on circumstances.[4]

Phratries. Phratries (Gr. *phratria*, brother) are groups of linked clans, where there are more than two such linked groups in the tribe (if there were only two, they would be moieties). The clans in a phratry system retain their separate identities, but each clan in a phratry feels some sort of special identity to the others within its phratry. Moreover, they may have special obligations to fulfill toward each other.

The Hopi Indians have a large number of matrilineal clans, which are loosely linked into twelve exogamous phratries. The Aztecs, for their part, had four phratries embracing twenty clans among them. The Aztec

---

[4] R. H. Lowie, "Some Moot Questions of Social Organization" (*American Anthropologist*, Vol. 36, 1934), pp. 321–330; *Primitive Society*, pp. 130–137.

phratries were important political and religious divisions in the structure of the empire, and they thus played a truly significant part in the social life of the people.

Nevertheless, it may be said in general that phratry organization is a relatively rare and functionally insignificant phenomenon. It does not usually control marriage, although Crow Indians think that it is better if members of the same phratry do not intermarry. Still, they have no prohibition against such action. For the most part, the phratry sentiment seems to rest either on a tradition of common origin or common interests in ceremonial activity.

The Functions of Clans. *1. Mutual Aid and Security.* The clan provides a large mutual-aid organization on the footing of kinship. Man never stands alone. In seeking a firmer base for personal security than he can find without organization of his efforts and those of his fellow men, he casts about for some valid interests of common concern that will serve to join him in social communion with others. There can be no doubt that the most generalized interest served by the clan is that of subserving the desire for security. The family, as we noted earlier, is the incubator of personal security par excellence. The clan expands this fundamental function of the family by broadening the base in numbers of persons involved, while at the same time tightening up the structure by turning away from the diffusive effects inherent in extension along bilateral lines.

To meet the needs of security, clans always present a solid front to the rest of the world. In their personal interrelations with all persons outside the clan, every clan member must be aided, abetted, and protected at all hazards. Long before Marxist industrial workers put the words to music, the clan slogan was "solidarity forever." From the implicit maxim than clan brothers should be helpful to each other the principle of mutual aid and solidarity develops to the principle of collective protection and its counterpart, collective liability. Motivated by the urge to provide personal security, clans move to punish wrongs and injuries suffered by any member as though all members were injured by the act. "Strike my clan brother and you strike me" is the challenge the primitive clansman hurls at all comers. "The blood of the clan is my blood" is another precept of his code. The clan moves as a unit to wreak vengeance when murder has been done. The individual is strengthened in the secure knowledge that even though he may be wrong, his clan will stand behind him.

As a complement of its united protection of individual members, the clan is almost always collectively liable for the acts of its members. Thus, if a clansman commits murder, vengeance may commonly be taken on any member of the clan, for even though innocent in fact, his person is merged in that of all his fellow clansmen.

2. *Legal.* The security function of the clan inevitably leads it into the legal arena. In view of this, we may say that a second universal function of the clan is to operate as a legal instrument in the system of tribal law.[5]

3. *Control of Clan Members.* Anthropologists have recorded many instances in which a clan has cast out the black sheep who is a continuous troublemaker. After all, clan solidarity cannot be a means of unbridled license for irresponsible individuals. For the incorrigible rascal, clan disowner is tantamount to the death sentence in many societies, for then the outcast may be assaulted with impunity. There is no protection for him outside the clan.

Extrusion from the clan may come not only from having caused the clan too much trouble vis-à-vis other clans, but also from persistent refusal to carry out one's cooperative obligations within the clan. Hogbin cites a case from Ontong Java in the South Seas that shows how both impulses may be combined to form the straw that breaks the camel's back.

Two brothers were once reprimanded by their headman for something they failed to do. Instead of taking this to heart they began to abuse him. . . . Soon afterwards one of the brothers was found to have committed adultery with the wife of an important man of the tribe. The headman, not wishing any of his people to be involved in the defence, formally declared both brothers to be forever severed from their kindred, although only one of them was responsible for the trouble. The injured man was then able to take vengeance, for he was sure that none of the relatives would come to the assistance of the culprit.[6]

It is often said that a clan cannot take legal action against its own members. The old adage goes, "A clan cannot proceed against itself." However, it would be the height of foolishness to let this blind us to the fact that the clan must be able to control and shape the behavior of its members in intraclan relations.

Not all clan systems have explicit leaders or councils with directive powers. The Crow Indians, for instance, do not. But it certainly seems, in the absence of any statistical tabulations, that most clans have at least a headman with directive or even disciplinary powers, while some clan

[5] See Chap. 25 for further discussion of the clan law.
[6] H. I. Hogbin, *Law and Order in Polynesia*, p. 135.

systems provide for a council of clan elders (usually family or lineage headmen) with executive and quasi-judicial powers, as we saw in the Ontong Java case.

4. Exogamy. A fourth universal function of the clan is to regulate marriage by means of exogamy. This, if we follow Malinowski's hypothesis, is a self-protective device to ensure clan solidarity by directing the sexual drive toward persons outside the essential kinship group. We would do wrong, however, to overlook the fact that an additional security device is to be found in clan exogamy. Marriage imposes affinal obligations on the spouse's kin and clan. It tends to reduce overt aggression between the maritally allied groups; it also extends the base of support a man may count on.

5. Government. Another function that the clan may take on is that of government. The twenty Aztec clan heads, called *speakers*, made up the Aztec tribal council. This group controlled ordinary political decisions, made war and peace, and as a judicial body decided disputes between clans and members of different clans. These same clan speakers sat on the grand national council, whose jurisdiction covered the most important law cases and election of the king. Aztec clans were grouped in four phratries, each of whom had a captain-general, who served as a high-ranking military officer and in addition to his military post served on the grand national council.

Many tribes have raised one clan to the position of royalty, and the hereditary chief must come from this clan. In Melanesia this is true of the Trobriand Islanders and in Africa the Dahomeans and Ashanti provide two examples among many.

Among the American Indians the Winnebago of Wisconsin assigned political functions to seven of their twelve clans. The tribal chief was selected from the Thunderbird clan. In addition, this clan had important functions connected with the preservation of peace (its governmental functions were mainly civil). The Warrior clan, as its name implies, provided war leadership; the village and hunt policemen came from the Bear clan, while the camp crier and aide-de-camp for the chief was always selected from the Buffalo clan. The Wolf, Water-spirit, and Elk clans had less important political assignments. Not only was this true of the Winnebago, but also of the other highly organized Siouan tribes.[7]

6. Property. Among clan-organized tribes practicing hoe culture the garden lands are almost inevitably owned or administered by the

[7] P. Radin, *The Winnebago Tribe* (Bureau of American Ethnology, Annual Report 37, 1923).

clans. Aztec clans each owned its segment of the land. Assignments for use were made by the clan headman, who kept a record of all holdings. Every family head had the right to a plot of land (unless he had forfeited his clan membership for refusal to marry or carry out his clan obligations, in which case he became a common proletarian laborer). As long as a clansman was in good standing, he could use his land or rent it to a fellow clansman (but not to an outsider). He could allot it to a clan descendant by testamentary disposition, but he could not alienate it (*i.e.*, pass title to an outsider), for ownership of title was vested in the clan. He had what a lawyer would call a *possessory right of usufruct* but not ownership. This same land-use system by clans prevails throughout all of Indonesia at this very time; it is also prevalent in Africa.

Clans may own other material goods in common, such as temples, meeting houses, and sacred and ceremonial objects.

7. *Religion and Ritual.* Among the ancestor-worshiping Africans who have clan organization, the deceased clan ancestors are elevated to the status of clan deities. The clan head is usually the chief priest of the clan and the intermediary between his kinsmen and the ancestral spirits.

Among the Hopi and Zuñi, to take another example, the all-important ceremonial organization is inextricably intertwined with the clan system; each clan must perform its part of the ceremonial activities for the benefit of the whole pueblo. Winnebago clans possess sacred bundles of religious paraphernalia that are used in ceremonial activity.

Finally, clans may have totemic associations involving a feeling of identity with a plant, animal, or other natural object. This bond of emotional identity may extend from a mere feeling of kinship to actual reverence and worship. It may also lead to symbolic representation of the totemic object in clan fetishes.

To summarize the functions of the clan, we may say that the clan as an institution has two universal functions: (1) to broaden the base of the security group founded on the kinship bond by providing mutual aid and collective protection and liability in legal action and disputes; and (2) to regulate and control marriage.

Beyond this the clan is capable of taking on a variety of secondary functions, which it may assume or abjure, depending on the historical development of the culture. These functions are (1) legal, (2) governmental, (3) economic, (4) religious and ceremonial, and (5) totemic. Furthermore, clans may be localized or their members may be scattered in different communities throughout the society.

Double Descent. Until quite recently anthropologists thought that a society could embrace only one clan system, which had to be either matrilineal or patrilineal. Evidence to the contrary first came to the attention of English-reading anthropologists in R. S. Rattray's studies of the Ashanti, who were shown by this keen student of African tribes to have matrilineal clans called *abusua* and patrilineal groups called *ntoro*. The ntoro principle of inheritance is associated with the semen, and although the ntoro group is not organized, it, like the abusua, regulates marriage and sets certain incest prohibitions. It is totemic and imposes certain food tabus on its members.[8]

A subsequent report by Forde on another African tribe (the Umor) analyzes an even more precise system of dual descent.[9] The Umoran patrilineal, virilocal clan determines house and land affiliation and is called the *repun*. Of these there are twenty-two. At the same time there are four *yajima* (plural form), matrilineal, nonlocalized clans through which movable property—principally livestock and currency—is inherited and marriage exchanges (bride price and dowry) are made. "A man eats in his repun and inherits in his lejima [singular form]," is the native adage.

Herskovits has lately indicated that double descent is probably quite widespread in West Africa. Australian class systems of marriage combine matrilineal moieties, which are unnamed and intangible, with patrilineal clans.[10] Murdock has lately thrown the phenomenon into focus by showing that double descent has a widely scattered distribution in Africa, Indonesia, India, Australia, Melanesia, and Polynesia.[11]

That it took English-speaking anthropologists so long to discover double descent shows how difficult it is for even carefully trained scientists to formulate conceptions necessary to the perception of new facts when those facts are too alien to their experience and cultural background. Nevertheless, what proved to be a theoretical bombshell to English-speaking anthropologists in the 1930's need not have been, for double descent in Indonesia has long been recognized by Dutch ethnologists.[12]

Clans in Social Development. Earlier evolutionary schemes posited the priority of matrilineal clans over patrilineal ones. Morgan and Bachofen were the chief nineteenth-century protagonists of this notion. Both men based their evolutionary schemes on the idea that matrilineal clans

[8] R. S. Rattray, *Ashanti; Ashanti Law and Constitution.*

[9] C. D. Forde, "Kinship in Umor—Double Unilateral Organization in a Semi-Bantu Society" (*American Anthropologist*, Vol. 41, 1939), pp. 523–553.

[10] R. H. Lowie, *Introduction to Cultural Anthropology*, offers a simple analysis of the system as exemplified by the Murngin tribe.

[11] G. P. Murdock, "Double Descent" (*American Anthropologist*, Vol. 42, 1940), pp. 555–561.

[12] B. ter Haar, *Adat Law in Indonesia*, pp. 155–157.

were the foundation of the earliest known societies. However, as long ago as 1905 the American ethnologist J. R. Swanton in a classic study showed that the most primitive American tribes are clanless.[13] Lowie subsequently drew together other data to demonstrate in 1920 that with the exception of the Australians, the most primitive tribes of the world (the Negritos of Africa and the Pacific, the African Bushmen, and the American Shoshones) are all clanless and that there is no established pattern of priority of maternal over paternal clans.[14]

Without undertaking to discuss the mass of data available, it may be said that the majority of the higher primitive cultures have clan systems as the central features of their societal organization. However, it is absolutely impossible to correlate matrilineal or patrilineal clans with more "advanced" culture. A glance at the Pueblo Indians will quickly show why. The economic and religious organization of all Pueblos is generally similar. Yet the westernmost Pueblos (Hopi, Zuñi) have vigorous matrilineal clans. The Tewa Pueblos of the upper Rio Grande have weak patrilineal clans with descent so confused that some experts have conflicted as to whether Tewa clans are actually patrilineal or matrilineal, and the Tewa-speaking pueblos of Taos and Isleta are clanless! The Hidatsa Indians of the Plains have matrilineal clans; the Omaha have patrilineal clans. Yet both are closely comparable in culture.

Cross borrowing or diffusion is an important element, and the nature of a tribe's historical contacts may be the crucial factor in whether it acquires one sort of clan or the other, or none at all.

The Cheyennes were clanless hunters and gatherers 300 years ago. In the middle of the eighteenth century, during the course of their westward migration from the forests west of Lake Superior, they settled among the horticultural, matrilineal Arikara and Hidatsa for two generations. They acquired the techniques of gardening from their hosts. There is evidence that the Cheyennes were also beginning to incorporate the matrilineal clan organization into their culture when they acquired the horse. Early in the nineteenth century, they completely abandoned the horticultural villages for the roving life of horse-mounted buffalo hunters. This put a check to the trend toward matrilineal organization and by 1870 they were utterly clanless once more.

Historical accident threw the Cheyennes into contact with matrilineal horticulturists, and they started to imitate their more sophisticated neighbors. We can feel pretty sure that if they had gone south instead

[13] J. R. Swanton, "The Social Organization of American Tribes" (*American Anthropologist*, Vol. 7, 1905), pp. 663–673.
[14] R. H. Lowie, *Primitive Society*, pp. 147–156.

of west and settled among the horticultural, patrilineal Osages, they would have taken on a patrilineal system. As it was, a further historic event at a crucial time (the arrival of Spanish-originating horses) threw them back to a clanless state.

Nevertheless, certain generalized principles concerning the development and decline of the clan as a social form may be made.

Lowie and Titiev, among others, have emphasized the role of residence in the development of clans.[15] Lowie points out with reference to the Hupa Indians of California, certain Amazonian tribes, and the eastern Algonquian peoples of North America that the effect of virilocal residence coupled with exogamy is to retain married men in the village of their father, while girls when they marry may move off to some other village. Throughout life the men stay together as a solid unit, while the women are scattered. The inevitable social and psychological effect is to give emphasis to the male group with resultant patrilineal tendencies. Likewise, the uxorilocal Pueblos hold the group of women together, presenting a solid front to the world, so that emphasis falls on the matrilineal side. Consolidation, or institutionalization, of this tendency establishes the unilateral principle on the basis of which lineages or clans are formed. Titiev suggests that five stages of development may be demarked:

1. The unilocal group without unilateral descent (Australian hordes, Algonquian bands, the Hupa, etc.)
2. The unilocal, unilateral lineage (joint families of the Siberian Kazaks and Madagascar Tanalas)
3. The multilocal, unilateral lineage (characteristic of Java and Sumatra)
4. The multilocal, unilateral clan
5. The phratry

The first two stages are based on common residence. The last three multilocal stages are marked by a breakdown of common residence and the perpetuation of solidarity based on the theoretical unilateral principle. There is much to commend Titiev's hypothesis if one remembers that it is not intended as a fixed formula to be applied to the specific line of development of clans in each and every society. It merely formulates the sequences in the development of clans as social forms.

To establish that residence is a primary factor in determination of clan development throws us back on the question, What factors determine residence? Here again we must eschew monistic explanations, but

[15] *Ibid.*, pp. 157*ff.*; M. Titiev, "The Influence of Common Residence on the Unilateral Classification of Kindred" (*American Anthropologist*, Vol. 45, 1943), pp. 511–530.

it is possible to demonstrate that basic subsistence techniques are fundamental. It is generally believed that most tribes of collectors and gatherers consist of bands that tend to be virilocal, patrilineal, and exogamic.[16] A few are uxorilocal, but none are matrilineal (except where there is double descent in Australia). Some are bilateral. It is important to note, however, that Murdock has reported that the majority of collectors and gatherers tend to be uxorilocal, according to the data in the files of the Yale Cross Cultural Survey.[17] These facts serve as a warning not to make any determined statement concerning the residence basis of the most primitive bands. Among the lowly collectors and gatherers it is possible to observe that economic factors per se would not swing the balance toward either virilocal or uxorilocal residence. Male dominance and war tend to lend preference toward virilocality, however. The Cheyennes say that their chiefs urged young men to marry within their own bands, so that they would not deplete the war strength of the group by moving away.

Gardening is usually woman's work among primitive horticultural tribes, and garden plots are associated with women in the majority of cases.[18] Since a man has no personal use for a garden plot in those tribes where women are the gardeners, inheritance of this economic base runs from mother to daughters. The woman stays with her land, while the man, who may continue to hunt, can enjoy more mobility. In such a case, where would a married couple be expected to settle? The odds are with the wife's locale. This is why gardeners are usually uxorilocal. In uxorilocal residence, sisters and daughters form the "solid front" and matrilineal emphasis results. When lineages and clans emerge, the chances are they will be matrilineal rather than otherwise.

The domestication of animals produces just the opposite effect. Herdable animals belong to men. Jointly owned herds hold brothers together, and they bring their brides to their home band. Sons inherit from fathers, and the men form the enduring solidarity group. Emphasis is on patrilineal descent, and if lineages and clans are formed, the chances are almost 100 per cent that they will be patrilineal.[19] When the horse or ox is hitched to the plow and gardening becomes agriculture, it appears

---

[16] J. H. Steward, "The Economic and Social Basis of Primitive Bands" in *Essays in Anthropology in Honor of Alfred Lewis Kroeber,* pp. 331–350.

[17] G. P. Murdock, "Constants in Social Organization," lecture before the American Ethnological Society, New York, March, 1941.

[18] H. Bauman, "The Division of Work according to Sex in African Hoe Culture" (*Africa,* Vol. 1, 1928), pp. 289–318.

[19] W. Schmidt, "The Position of Women with Regard to Property in Primitive Society" (*American Anthropologist,* Vol. 37, 1935), p. 248.

that patrilineal tendencies gain the ascendancy over matrilineal, but in the conflict of alternatives either one may actually prevail.

The death of the clan is seeded in the growth of government based on the territorial principle of community. Even when the clan is in the ascendancy among gardeners and pastoralists, the territorial principle exerts its influence to some degree in politics and government. But the clan, like the Mesozoic dinosaur, has inherent limitations. And as the primitive Mesozoic mammal became extinct in the Cenozoic era, so the territorial principle triumphs when society reaches the stage of civilization. Clans constitute inherently divisive elements within a society. Clan loyalty always conflicts with the demands of the society as an entity. Clan feuds are internecine war endowed with fatal consequences for social serenity and stability. The suppression of clan sovereignty was one of the great tasks of growing political government, as the suppression of national sovereignty is the supreme survival need of the present day.

The clan was born to give security but ended by destroying the security it was its job to give. It was supplanted by the national state, which suppressed the clan and brought internal order. Now the national state with its inevitable wars destroys the security it was born to give. In an atomic age the national state, like the clan before it, is ultimately doomed—it, or all society.

On the higher levels of political culture the clan is always deprived of its legal, governmental, and economic functions. When shorn of its primary functions as the largest security unit for individuals, its roots are cut and its days are done. Ceremonial, ritual, and religious functions are secondary appendages to the clan. With the roots severed, these appendages drop off. The dead stump lingers on, but that, too, disintegrates in time. The clan, the proudest and most powerful social institution among the higher primitives, disappears from civilized society.

509 B.C. marks the year of its death in the Western societies that derive their political heritage from the Greeks. In that momentous year, Cleisthenes decreed that the Atticans were no longer to be represented in government by their clans but by township (*demes*) representatives of territorial divisions within the state.

C. Status and Social Role

CHAPTER 19

THE LIFE CYCLE

From a gross biological point of view life may be reduced to a simple formula: to be born, to mature, to reproduce, and to die. However, even the biologist will acknowledge that at least a few other events of significance occur along the way. Man embroiders upon the fundamental pattern.

Nevertheless, birth, maturity, reproduction, and death are the four basic and universal crises in the completed life cycle. In the earthly span of the human organism every individual who fulfills his biological destiny must pass through each of these peaks in the cycle of life. Therefore, in no human culture are these critical periods wholly ignored. They may, however, be approached and surmounted with varying degrees of intensity. Some peoples are habituated to treat one or another of the life crises in a matter-of-fact manner. Others exhibit much anxiety. In the latter situation there is considerable cultural emphasis of the crisis situation.

In general, however, since crisis periods are times of critical uncertainty—times when the fate of the individual or the group seems to hang in the balance—men are not inclined supinely to leave the outcome to mere chance or unbridled circumstance. Natural and supernatural forces may be controlled in fact and in belief. Therefore, positive techniques of rational assistance are employed, along with magic and ritual ceremonialism, to frustrate destructive and disruptive supernatural powers, or to encourage and invoke positive and helpful forces. Through ritual and ceremony, a bridge is thrown across the yawning chasms of fear and doubt wherewith to carry men over transitional states to a safe arrival and a firm footing in the new status awaiting on the other side.

Conception. The life cycle begins with conception. Yet no primitive peoples have a scientifically accurate knowledge of the nature of conception. This is not the result of prudery but of sheer ignorance. After all, even civilized man has acquired genetic sophistication only in the last few hundred years, and there is still a good deal of talk about storks in our society.

However, most primitives are able to recognize causal sequences with sufficient astuteness to be able to associate the act of sexual intercourse with conception. Some are even acute enough to be able to recognize that the male semen plays a role in the generation of life. Yet the naïve notion that the male plants a seed, which the female nurtures, is the closest primitive man can come to reality.

Explicit notions of miraculous conception abound in the primitive world. In its most common form the belief is expressed that a child is the reincarnation of an ancestral spirit, who has slipped into the womb of the mother to be regenerated. In Australia, this belief is raised to the status of a dogma so strong that the natives deny any relation between the sex act and conception other than to admit that the womb must first be opened so that ancestral spirits may enter.

Earlier anthropologists took this Australoid denial of the physiology of paternity at face value. Modern anthropology sees it as the cultural suppression of recognizable fact to sustain the shibboleths of the social system.[1] Ancestor worship and totemism are important themes in Australian culture. The continuity of the totemic group is sustained by means of the doctrine of spiritual reincarnation. To give expression to the fact of physiological paternity would be a subversive undermining of the sacred institutions of Australian social life—definitely un-Australian.

A similar functional explanation holds for the Trobriand Islanders' denial of physiological paternity. The nearby Dobu who believe that semen is voided coconut milk, which when it enters a woman causes the blood within her womb to coagulate and form a fetus, say bluntly that the Trobrianders lie. The point is verily a sore one. So many angry words have been exchanged over this moot issue in the past that nowadays when Dobus and Trobrianders meet they tacitly avoid the touchy subject. Fortune's Dobu companions scolded him for his bad taste in broaching the subject on a visit to the Trobriands.[2] Not without reason is anthropology sometimes called "the study of rude cultures by rude people."

The Dobu notion that babies are formed by the coagulation of blood is shared by many primitives, sporadically distributed about the globe. They reason from the observed fact of cessation of menstruation during gestation. By inversion they say that the clotting of the blood to form the baby stops the regular flow.

[1] Cf. M. F. Ashley-Montague, *Coming into Being among the Australian Aborigines.*
[2] R. F. Fortune, *Sorcerers of Dobu,* pp. 238–239.

Pregnancy. Life begins with conception, and conception produces pregnancy. No matter how they may conceive of conception, all primitives recognize pregnancy in empirical physiological terms. There are a number of externally observable biological alterations that occur in the mothers of all races. More notable among them are enlargement of the breasts and nipples, exudation of colostrum, cessation of menstruation, abdominal enlargement, and frequently nausea.

From the little that has been written upon this subject by anthropologists, primitives seem to focus on one or two of the symptoms as signs of coming events, although it is probable that they make note of all of them. Cessation of menstruation is the one universally recognized sign. A fair percentage of the tribes are even so alert as to calculate the expected birth at nine months after the first skipping.

Various Oceanic and African tribes make note of breast changes; the Arunta of Australia, the Pukapuka of Polynesia, and others have been put on record as noting "morning sickness." Other primitives have told field workers that a valuable sign is dimunition of appetite and a tendency to become lazy.[3]

Pregnancy is merely the foreshadowing of birth. It is, therefore, in itself a crisis condition, or a preliminary phase of the critical event of being born. Most primitive peoples seize upon the gestation period as calling for a cultural relief of their anxieties. Chief among these anxieties are (1) fear that the child will not develop ideally, (2) fear that the fetus will miscarry, (3) fear that the birth will be difficult. Pregnancy tabus and injunctions are supposed to bring freedom from these fears.

Thus Ray reports for the Sanpoil Indians of Washington that a childbearing woman and her husband may not eat trout lest the child shake like that lively fish. They may not eat rabbit, lest the child get weak legs. They may not eat "fool hen" lest the child be a moron! More than this, the mother-to-be has to rise before sunrise, stay awake through the day, swim in cold water, walk and run, and (in modern times) ride horseback to strengthen her for the ordeal to come.[4]

It may relieve some modern mothers of guilt feelings and induce some husbands to more indulgent understanding to know that queer food preferences in pregnancy are not silly whims. Quite a number of primitive peoples recognize that the pregnant woman has a craving for peculiar foods. Ford notes, however, that there do not seem to be any particular

[3] C. L. Ford, "A Comparative Study of Human Reproduction" (*Yale University Publications in Anthropology*, No. 32, 1945), p. 44.

[4] V. F. Ray, "The Sanpoil and Nespelem" (*University of Washington Publications in Anthropology*, Vol. 5, 1932), p. 124.

kinds of foods that are craved. The desire is for *variety*. What the basis of this desire may be we do not know.[5]

Childbirth. It is a strange thing that most of the anxiety over the crisis of childbirth comes before the event, not at it. Magic, ritual, and tabu dominate the prenatal period, yet when the moment of birth is reached, the obstetrical problems are in normal cases handled with matter-of-fact effectiveness free of mumbo jumbo.

For the most part, birth is strictly a woman's affair. However, a few tribes permit or require the husband to assist or to be present. Generally, however, the expectant mother retires into the house with one or two older female relatives to assist her. Midwife specialists are called upon among some people.

A widely accepted falsehood is that childbirth is easy for primitive women. It has even been anthropologically maintained that just as domestication increases birth difficulties for animals, so increasing domestication through civilization makes birth progressively more difficult for the modern mother. There is little evidence for this neat idea. On the contrary, there is much empirical evidence in the record to prove that primitive women often suffer much agony and difficulty in childbirth; the multifarious magical provisions designed to assure an easy birth are surely ample evidence of the primitive's fear of hard delivery.

Practically all primitives have special emergency medical practices to call into play when birth is unusually difficult. In easy cases, there is little use of magic at the time of birth, but in drawn-out labor medicine men and women are hastily invoked. The Cheyennes send for a medicine man who has derived power from the otter. Otters make a delightful sport of sliding down mud banks. This is the way the baby should do, and an otter medicine man can bring it about—so they say.

The Couvade. A truly quaint custom is the *couvade*. On the birth of the child the mother gets up and goes about her affairs, while the father goes to bed, apparently to recover from the effects of childbirth. During the period of his confinement, he is subjected to many tabus.

This may be variously interpreted as a petulant demand for attention on the part of the male, or it may be a symbolic assertion of the father's identification with the child. Or perhaps it is a form of magical assistance in the establishment of the child in the everyday world. But it is hardly, as some young fathers might think, a consequence of sheer exhaustion. The symbolic assertion of identification of father and child seems to be the likeliest possibility.

[5] Ford, *op. cit.*, p. 48.

As a matter of fact, not many cultures have produced the couvade. The Caribs and various of their South American neighbors are the outstanding couvadists. The Ainus of Japan and also the Chinese of Marco Polo's times should be included, as well as certain tribes of South India. In the northern mountains of the Iberian Peninsula the couvade has been practiced from the days of Strabo until very recent times.

According to Seed Eater Shoshone informants, they also practiced a real couvade in the old days.[6] When the expectant mother retired to her birth hut, the father went into a retirement hut of his own made for him by his mother. There he stayed isolated for "five days" until the umbilical cord dropped from the newborn babe.[7] He observed all the tabus that normally applied to a menstruating woman. No meat or soup could be eaten, only cereals. On the day of birth his mother came to him and he "bathed" himself with sage. If she said, "You have a boy," he took a long walk in the mountains—where the game abide—but he did not hunt. If she said, "You have a daughter," he walked down into the valleys, where the wild seeds grow. Thus he magically associated his child with its future occupation. When the five days were up, he bathed, and then when he killed his first game, he gave it away to the people.

The four widely scattered centers of the couvade (East Asia, the Pyrenees, northeastern South America, and the Plateau area of North America) indicate independent development and elaboration of the father's role in the birth crisis in these areas.

Naming and Presentation of the Child. The mere fact of birth does not necessarily complete the transition of the child from the status of fetus to that of a member of the community. Many people feel that there must be a formal presentation to the people and the spirits. Many people feel that until this act is completed mother and child must remain in isolation. The mother is contaminated by her blood and by the dangerous forces of the birth crisis. This is the putative rationalization of primitives. Practically, of course, it is a good thing for the mother to have a chance to rest.

The Hopi child and mother, although visited by relatives on the day

---

[6] E. A. Hoebel, *Shoshone Field Notes* (unpublished, 1934); also R. H. Lowie, "Notes on Shoshonean Ethnography" (*American Museum of Natural History, Anthropological Papers*, Vol. 20, Part 3, 1924), pp. 265–270.

[7] "A striking instance of numerical imposition is the frequent relationship between the sacred number of a group and the day on which the umbilical cord 'falls off': in Bali, where the mother is in a special state for the first three days after birth, the cord falls off in three days; in Itamul, where the magic number is five, it falls off in five." M. Mead, "On the Implications for Anthropology of the Gesell-Ilg Approach to Maturation" (*American Anthropologist*, Vol. 49, 1947), p. 74.

of birth, remain isolated for twenty days. On the twentieth day, mother, father, and child are bathed many times over. Relatives of every clan give the infant at least one name associated with each of their clans. Then as the sun rises the infant is carried out to be held before the Sun God, who is told all the names of the child.[8]

The Seed Eater Shoshone mother and child were isolated even longer —forty days. The birth hut was built by the woman's mother a long way from the camp. When the baby's umbilical cord dropped off after five days, the hut was moved closer to the camp. All menstrual tabus were followed exactly as by the father, but, in addition, the maternal grandmother prepared each day a bed of grass over hot coals for the mother to lie upon. (Today a hot water bottle is used.) Throughout the day the mother worked busily at weaving and other small tasks. Few friends came to visit her. After six weeks, she and the child rejoined the village.

The Omaha Indian child was touchingly introduced to the entire cosmos on the eighth day after birth in a traditional ritual always performed by a priest of a given subclan. On the eighth day the priest was sent for. When he arrived, he took his place at the door of the tipi in which the child was born. His right hand raised, palm up to the sky, he intoned this beautiful invocation in a loud, ringing voice for all the world to hear:

Ho! Ye Sun, Moon, Stars, all ye that move in the heavens,
    I bid you hear me!
Into your midst has come a new life.
    Consent ye, I implore!
Make its path smooth, that it may reach the brow of the first hill!

Ho! Ye Winds, Clouds, Rain, Mist, all ye that move in the air,
    I bid you hear me!
Into your midst has come a new life.
    Consent ye, I implore!
Make its path smooth, that it may reach the brow of the second hill!

Ho! Ye Hills, Valleys, Rivers, Lakes, Trees, Grasses, all ye of the earth,
    I bid you hear me!
Into your midst has come a new life.
    Consent ye, I implore!
Make its path smooth, that it may reach the brow of the third hill!

Ho! Ye Birds, great and small, that fly up in the air,
Ho! Ye Animals, great and small, that dwell in the forest,

---

[8] A fascinating autobiographical description of the entire birth ritual may be found in *Sun Chief*, Chap. 1.

Ho! Ye Insects that creep among the grasses and burrow in the ground,
    I bid you hear me!
Into your midst has come a new life.
    Consent ye, I implore!
Make its path smooth, that it may reach the brow of the fourth hill!

Ho! All Ye of the Heavens, all Ye of the Air, all Ye of the Earth,
    I bid you all to hear me!
Into your midst has come a new life.
    Consent ye, consent ye all, I implore!
Make its path smooth—then shall it travel beyond the four hills! [9]

Yet even this ritual did not make the child a real member of the tribe, for a baby did not complete its transition until it could walk. Then it went through a "turning of the child ritual" wherein it discarded its baby name and got new moccasins. Baby moccasins always had a hole cut in the sole, so if a messenger from the spirit world came to claim the little infant, the child could answer, "I cannot go on a journey—my moccasins are worn out!" New moccasins without holes were an assurance that the child was prepared for the journey of life and that its journey would be a long one.

In Africa, the Ashanti entertain similar notions. The child is not ceremonially named and publicly presented until eight days have passed. Then it becomes a genuine human being. Should it die before that time, its little corpse is casually thrown on the garbage heap, for it is believed to have been but the husk of a ghost child whose mother in the spirit world had pawned it off on a living mother for a short period while she went off on some jaunt or other. On returning from her undertaking, she recalled her little spirit baby.

Not all societies undertake a formal presentation, but most of them, including our own with its christenings and baptisms, seem to do so. Virtually all societies do isolate mother and child for periods of time varying from a few days to several months.

Naming, incidentally, is a universal human practice. Shakespeare to the contrary, there is much in a name. It symbolizes the individual personality and often indicates some aspects of the individual's social status. The name is usually bestowed at the end of the seclusion period. If the name is ceremonially bestowed, it is usually done by a near relative, otherwise the most common practice is for the mother to decide what her child is to be called. Names that are associated with good luck or great deeds

[9] A. C. Fletcher and F. La Flesche, *The Omaha Tribe* (Bureau of American Ethnology, Annual Report 27, 1911), pp. 115–116.

tend generally to be preferred. Thus the Menominee discard their original names, if they are chronically sick, in the hope that a new name will bring a healthier being.

Change of names or acquisition of additional ones often occurs in the course of the individual's life span in many primitive societies, as new names are assumed to indicate new statuses.

Puberty. The second crisis in the life cycle is adolescence or puberty. Puberty, like birth, is a manifestation of a basic alteration of the biological state of the individual. It is the time of maturation of the secondary sexual characteristics and the final growth to functional capacity of the sex organs. Puberty marks the twilight of youth and the dawn of adulthood.

In both boys and girls puberty is no abrupt transition, but an accelerated development extending from the eleventh to the sixteenth year. Body hair does not sprout overnight on boys; the lengthening of the vocal cords with embarrassing sound effects is not instantaneous; the relative broadening of the shoulders is a process of adolescent growth as much as is the activation of the testicles and the production of fully formed seminal fluid.

In the case of the female, the majority of puberty changes, including the emergence of body hair, broadening of the hips, increase of subcutaneous adipose tissue, especially on the hips and breasts, and the development of the sex organs, all occur over a period of months. One function alone, however, first manifests itself at a particular moment. The onset of menstruation quite definitely signals the attainment of puberty for the female.

The transition from adolescence to adulthood is fundamentally a biological phenomenon. Yet for human beings it represents also a sociological transition. Because social status is culturally defined, adolescence is for most peoples more a cultural than a biological problem.

The first fact to note is that some cultures handle adolescence most casually.[10] The second is that some ritualize it for one sex or the other, or both, with most cultures placing heaviest emphasis on adolescence rites for boys. The third factor is that puberty rites do not necessarily synchronize with biological pubescence. They fall at the point when sociologically childhood is left behind and adulthood is entered.

Negatively, this principle is admirably demonstrated in the case of

[10] For example, Samoa. "Adolescence represented no period of crisis or stress, but was instead an orderly development of slowly maturing interests and activities. The girls' minds were perplexed by no conflicts, troubled by no philosophical queries, beset by no remote ambitions." M. Mead, *Coming of Age in Samoa*, p. 157.

the Alorese in the East Indies. For boys the attainment of adulthood is a long-drawn-out process calling for extensive economic enterprising. Because of this, and since there are no men's clubs and no secret societies, there are no rites of transition, no tribal initiation. Instead, "at about sixteen the boys begin to let their hair grow long. At this time they begin to acquire male dress ornaments: sword, shields, areca basket, wide belt, bow, combs, and head plumes. This is ridiculed by the women, who hoot the men, and scoff at this manifestation of masculine vanity." [11] The boys also file their incisors halfway down and blacken their teeth.

The Polynesians, in general, present an even more decisive manifestation of the principle just enunciated. Gifford says

The absence of anything that might be called initiation rites that ushered boys into manhood is due to the fact that in Polynesia a boy left the company of women and was accepted into association with men at weaning, when the food tabu that required men to eat apart from women was laid upon him. The Polynesian boy became a man when he began to eat the food of men, not at adolescence. [12]

Thus, although the foreskin of boys was subincised by most Polynesians outside of New Zealand, the operation was performed at any time from infancy on. It was necessary only that the operation be completed before marriage.

Among the warrior tribes of the Plains and eastern North America there were no puberty rites per se. But at adolescence young men set out on vision quests to obtain the supernatural power that was so essential to a successful life. However, vision vigils were carried on by adults, too, so it cannot be said that any great emphasis was placed upon puberty by these people.

In the same manner, they treated the adolescence of girls most casually. Although all of the tribes isolated the menstruating woman, nothing much was made of the first menses, except as the Cheyenne father proudly stood in the door of his tipi shouting the good news to the whole camp and celebrated his daughter's womanhood by a giveaway of a fine horse to some poor oldster.

But the Northern Shoshones and other peoples of the Columbian Plateau made a real crisis of the event for the girl. The pubescent Shoshonean girl was isolated just for the period of her flow, but she had to be very busy, so she would not become a lazy woman. "Whatever she

---

[11] C. DuBois, "The Alorese" in *The Psychological Frontiers of Society*, p. 139.
[12] E. W. Gifford, *Tongan Society* (Bernice P. Bishop Museum, Bulletin 61, 1929), p. 187.

does then lasts for life." She could eat no meat, nor scratch herself, except with a special stick. At the end of her first isolation she was brought new clothes by her mother—women's clothes.

Northern Shoshone attitudes were but a pale attenuation of those of the Carrier Indians to the north of them. As Benedict says, "The fear and horror of a girl's puberty was at its height. Her three or four years of seclusion was called 'the burying alive.' She was herself in danger and she was a source of danger to everybody else." [13]

In such societies as those of Negro Africa and aboriginal Australia, both peoples who place much emphasis on age grading (see Chap. 20), adolescence rites become genuine "tribal initiations." This is especially true in those cases wherein men's secret societies are of great importance. Consequently, boys' initiations are also striking in many parts of eastern Melanesia.

As a mild example of the more serious forms of puberty rites, we may quote from Radcliffe-Brown's account of the Negrito Andaman Islanders. These pygmy people have no secret societies or other associations, but they do place great emphasis upon age status. To be marked and accepted as an adult each boy and girl must go through specific ceremonies. Beginning early in childhood both sexes are gradually scarred over their entire bodies with small incisions "to help them grow strong," but the culmination is reached at puberty in the following manner: For the girl on the first sign of her menses there is weeping over her by her mother and female relatives. Andaman weeping, let us hasten to say, does not express sorrow but rather marks an occasion of importance. The lass then plunges into the ocean for a two-hour bath—an act of ritual cleansing—after which she is tastefully decorated with pandanus leaves and clay.

Thus covered with leaves the girl must sit in the hut allotted to her, with her legs doubled up beneath her and her arms folded. . . . The girl sits thus for three days. Early every morning she leaves the hut to bathe in the sea. At the end of three days she resumes her life in the village. For a month following she must bathe in the sea every morning at dawn.[14]

When the friends and relatives of a boy decide that he is old enough to have the incisions made on his back, a dance is held throughout the night and the next morning.

The boy kneels down and bends forward until his elbows rest on the ground in front. One of the older men takes a pig-arrow and with the sharpened blade

[13] R. F. Benedict, *Patterns of Culture*, p. 28.
[14] A. R. Radcliffe-Brown, *The Andaman Islanders*, p. 93.

makes a series of cuts on the boy's back. Each cut is horizontal, and they are arranged in three vertical rows, each row consisting of from 20 to 30 cuts. When the cutting is finished the boy sits up, with a fire at his back, until the bleeding stops. During the operation and a few hours following it the boy must remain silent.[15]

Immediately upon completion of the puberty rites a number of food tabus are imposed upon both sexes. These are gradually removed in a series of formal ceremonies over a period of several years. Neither a boy nor a girl is considered to be a full-fledged adult until all the tabus have been removed.

If the whole ritual cycle is viewed as an entity, as should be done, then we see again that adolescence rites do not represent a fixed biological phenomenon so much as a social event roughly correlated to the biological.

In all cases, transition is the main theme—transition from the limited and undeveloped state of childhood to that of the adult endowed with the wisdom and privileges of a matured person.

Thus, death and resurrection are recurrent themes of stepped-up puberty rites. Death means the destruction of the childhood personality. Resurrection means restoration to the community in a new status with new roles. The Australian boy who retires to the hidden initiatory school in the bush, secreted from the eyes of all females and preadolescent boys, is "dead." When he returns to the camp of the band, circumcised, subincised, cicatricized, with a few teeth knocked out and with new knowledge of totemic mythology, he is a new man.

Without undertaking to be so specific about it, our college fraternities and men's secret societies use hazing to perform the same social function. Hazing the neophyte [16] is a process of degradation that destroys his ego. With his old ego destroyed, he is ready for the formal ritual initiation from which he emerges a "new man" in the ranks of the exalted.

When old-time army sergeants bully and insult rookies they are not being merely sadistic, nor are they necessarily working off personal frustrations. Although sergeants may not be aware of any principles of functional anthropology, they do know that recruits have to be made over and put through a quick transition rite. A first and unfortunately necessary act is the destruction of civilian ways and civilian thoughts. "You're in the army now." Induction means civilian death, and the "top

---

[15] *Ibid.*, p. 95.

[16] Note that the very word means "produce anew" (Gr. *neos* new + *phytos* grown).

kick" is the executioner. Completion of basic training means resurrection in a new status—General Issue.

Torture in the puberty rites of Australian and many African tribes rises to heights of sheer sadism. Yet beneath it can usually be found a functional rationalization. In Australia, circumcision and subincision, painful and dangerous surgical operations when crudely performed with stone knives, are but symbolic acts signifying the sexual and social completeness of the males in a type of society that rejects and culturally suppresses the significance of women.

The astounding sexual operations performed on girls in many parts of the African Sudan serve to exaggerate and emphasize their role as women and their status as wives.

There are a number of ancillary functions tied up with puberty ceremonialism. Cicatrization and the filing or knocking out of front teeth serve both as decorative elements and status identifications as well as tests of the neophyte's ability to endure physical pain. Strict discipline imposed during the rites works to fix the authority of the elders. The instruction in etiquette, mythology, and magic that usually accompanies puberty initiations embraces education and training in a practical sense and enhances ties of individual loyalty to the institutions of the tribal society. Yet under and through it all is the basic fact of transition—a transition that is fundamentally biological but often elaborately cultural.

Death. Death has no absolute finality for any primitive people. All of them believe in the immortality of the soul.[17] Yet all men well know that death marks the end of corporeal existence. The transition from the carnal to a wholly spiritual existence at death is an act of faith and imagination, a projection of life from a tangible and material state to an ethereal illusory condition sustained in the dogma of culture.

Because the dead are no longer constantly among the living but appear or make their influence felt only upon occasion, they are almost always relegated to another world in human cosmogony.

Funeral rites serve five basic functions: (1) Participation in mortuary ceremonies, by habitual dramatization of the faith in immortality, prepares the living for the death that awaits them. "The belief in immortality," writes Malinowski, "lived through ritually . . . makes him cherish more firmly the belief in his own future life. . . . Thus the ritual before death confirms the emotional outlook which a dying man has come to need in his supreme conflict."[18] (2) The rites serve magically

---

[17] See pp. 406–407 for the discussion of the soul concept in primitive belief.

[18] B. Malinowski, "Culture" (*Encyclopedia of the Social Sciences*, Vol. 4, 1931), p. 641.

to assure the separation of the soul from its body, to guide the deceased through the supreme transition safely and properly. (3) They serve to readjust the community after the loss of a member and to regularize the emotional disturbances that result from the upset of affective habits in connection with the deceased. Death usually evokes grief. (4) Where feasting and property giveaways are involved, mortuary rites incidentally effect a redistribution of wealth. (5) Finally, they lend high light and color, richness and depth to life through the drama of their performance.

In early prehistoric times, Neandertal man of the Mousterian epoch was the first creature to give evidence of concern over death. He deliberately buried his deceased fellow tribesmen—a boon to archaeologists and an indication that he had developed imaginative intelligence to the point where the soul concept had become possible. All later men have consistently worked into their cultures some form of disposal of the corpse accompanied by a greater or lesser development of transitional funerary rites.

Thus at each stage of the journey through life human beings have made a social issue of the biological crises. Each crisis marks a change in social status. Life is never wholly drab for any group of people. Ritual and ceremony, anticipation and anxiety, preparation and performance all color and lend zest to the act of living. Each person in turn fulfills his role and plays his part. None can escape the beginning and the end. The favored few mature and reproduce as they traverse the whole cycle and work out their potentialities within the framework permitted by the cultures of the societies within which they are destined to live and die.

CHAPTER 20

STATUS AND RANK

At no time in the history of mankind can there have been a society in which all members were identical in status. In every society that has come under anthropological scrutiny the members of those societies differentiate among themselves. Human beings do not form a colorless homogeneous mass. As Lowie aptly comments, "Primitive man is no imbecile; he is quick to perceive and to appraise those individual differences which as an inevitable biological phenomenon mark every group." [1] A suckling infant is not a gray-haired ancient; a woman is not a man; a childbearer is not a preadolescent. Nor is a master craftsman a bungling tyro. Such differences are recognized, and many lesser gradations, too. Social behavior is differentiated accordingly.

Social order is the system of interrelating and regulating individuals and groups. All individuals are alike in some respects, as they are also unlike in others. The grouping of the like into recognized social categories constitutes the status system of society.

Status. A status is the social position of an individual with reference to the other members of his society as determined by a specific attribute, cluster of attributes, or the generalized summation of all his attributes. Thus, every person has a number of statuses simultaneously. He has in the most specific and narrow sense as many statuses as there are recognized characteristics of the individual in his culture. Such characteristics are age, sex, bodily traits, and specific social experiences and affiliations. On the next level of abstraction, he has the more commonly recognized statuses that come from the possession of certain combinations of traits such as wisdom, courage, kindness, generosity, and even temper, in the case of the Plains Indian peace chief. Finally, each person may have that generalized sort of status that is referred to when the question is asked, "What is his social status?" This last sort of status identification calls for gross stereotyping of individuals. It seizes upon a small number of obvious criteria for lumping individual personalities into an undifferentiated class mass. The first sort of status identification, in contrast, calls for knowledge of numerous attributes of the individual and thus leads to a greater concern with the uniqueness of personality of the individual.

[1] R. H. Lowie, *Primitive Society*, 338.

Thus it should be kept in mind that status means "specific status" or "generalized status" with varying degrees of generalization.

The status system of every society involves also a certain amount of ranking. But, be it noted, status and rank are not synonymous. Status is a neutral term, which refers only to position. Rank refers to hierarchal status—higher or lower with reference to other statuses. The rank order of a society is its system of status gradation. A high status is one that carries prestige, *i.e.*, the attitudes associated with it are those of deference, reverence, submission, subordination on the part of those of lower status. Prestige translated into action means power—the capacity to influence or direct the behavior of others. A low status carries little prestige; the power capacities associated with it are puny.

The range embraced in a rank order will be wide or narrow dependent upon the disparities in power structures formed by the culture. In simple democratic hunting and gathering societies like the Eskimos the range is narrow. In rich class-organized societies like Dahomey the range from slave to king is great.

Role. Social psychologists have drawn an important distinction between status and role, the latter being the customary complex of behavior associated with a particular status. "When we ain't fightin'," Willie morosely acknowledges to Joe, "we should ack like sojers." [2] Every man is to some degree a poseur, for life in society is a playing of roles.

The command, "Just be your natural self," does not mean what it says. It really means, "Suppress your conscious awareness of the roles you expect to enact." A person's behavior is "natural," is free of posing, only when he has become so habituated to all his roles that he does not register awareness of them while performing them.

Newborn infants and imbeciles alone have no acquired roles as complements to their statuses. No one expects much of either of them.

Because every person has multiple statuses, he also manifests many different roles. A married professor behaves differently in the intimacy of his family (the father role) than he does in the classroom (the professor role). And if he is a volunteer fireman, he behaves quite differently when engaged in "firemanic" activities, both of an extinguishing and social nature. At different times, therefore, different roles come to the fore. Several roles may be operative simultaneously, but the intensity of their effectiveness is variable. If the professor's child visits the class, the professor activates both the role of professor and of father, but in all propriety the professional behavior should be strongest.

[2] B. Mauldin, *Up Front*, p. 83.

At times various roles may be held in abeyance or inactivated. A Pueblo Indian, while cultivating his fields, holds his dancing roles as a member of the Flint society in abeyance. The roles of a person are to be likened to a chest of clothing from which may be drawn the garb suitable to each occasion, with many quick changes called for.

Linton has recently referred to this phenomenon as *active* and *latent* status.[3] More precisely, it is the roles rather than the statuses that are activated or kept latent. Since status is an abstraction referring merely to social position and is not in itself behavior, it will be better to identify *roles* as active or latent.

Ascribed and Achieved Status. The statuses that are held by an individual are variously attained. They may be sought through striving and competitive mastery of the roles linked to the various statuses. Such statuses in the terminology suggested by Linton are called *achieved*.[4] MacIver calls them *functional determinants* of social position.[5] Other statuses devolve upon the individual by virtue of his innate biological characteristics such as sex, age, and race, or by virtue of his preexisting social affinities, such as the statuses of his parents and kinsmen and the involuntary associations into which he is born. These statuses are *ascribed* to the individual by his social system, and there is little he can do to escape them or to alter them. It is important to note that achieved statuses are attained only through the process of first mastering the roles. As Barton has observed of the Kalinga in northern Luzon, "Elevation to rank and power in the community is a gradual process of emergence in which power is attained before the rank is acknowledged by the people."[6] When the role is finally mastered the status flows from this fact. A master hunter must first master hunting.

In the case of ascribed statuses, on the other hand, the status comes first and the roles are mastered subsequently. It is even possible to inherit ascribed status without mastery of the roles. There are betimes unkingly kings, ignoble nobles.

Ascribed status distinctions based on age, sex, the premarital state, antefecundity, and kinship are the universal foundations of human social structure.

Achieved status criteria that are ubiquitous to all societies are those based on technological skill or artisanship (all peoples make tools), su-

---

[3] R. M. Linton, *The Cultural Background of Personality*, p. 78.
[4] R. M. Linton, *The Study of Man*, pp. 113–114.
[5] R. M. MacIver, *Society*, pp. 78–79.
[6] R. F. Barton, *The Kalinga* (in press).

pernaturalism (all peoples have magico-religious specialists), the marital state, fecundity, and political leadership.

Nonuniversal ascribed statuses include caste-determined occupations, inherited supernaturalism, inherited possession of wealth, inherited possession of various religious and social perquisites and paraphernalia, and inherited political position (*i.e.*, royalty).

Nonuniversal achieved statuses include those based upon hunting skills, skill in games and dances, bravery and skill in war, head-hunting, storytelling, wealth possession or distribution, bodily mutilation, and membership in various specialized associations. (This list is not exhaustive.)

The functional importance of all these different statuses rests in the fact that they limit and influence the degree and direction of cultural participation and the manner and amount of interaction for individuals and groups. No one person ever manifests all the behavior characteristic of his culture, because, for one reason, no one person ever enjoys all the statuses in his society.

The greater the number of achievable statuses in a culture, the wider is the room for full participation (potentially, at least) by all members. The more extensive and rigid the ascribed statuses, the more constrained are the individuals in their culturally prescribed roles.

Cultures that emphasize achievable status are marked by internal social mobility, social striving, and (on the whole) competitiveness and individualism. Emphasis is placed upon "fulfillment of self" and assertiveness. The social gain is ideally a greater ultimate efficiency because capable persons are not barred from effective functioning in those capacities for which they have adequate aptitudes. Conversely, caste and rigid class systems are socially wasteful because they ascribe functions to people who are not necessarily well suited to their performance, while at the same time they bar potential adepts.

On the other hand, the advantages of social systems that emphasize ascribed statuses lie in reduced strain and anxiety for the participating members of the society. Competitive insecurity is presumably reduced. Frustration born of failure to achieve a sought-after status is avoided.

When ascribed status systems begin to lose their authority, however, and persons in statuses of marked social disability begin to aspire to achievable statuses, frustration for them and anxiety for those in the threatened ascribed positions become acute and difficult, in the way that marks Negro-Caucasian relations in some parts of the American population today.

Sexual Status. Sex dichotomy is a biological fact upon which culturally determined statuses are built. But what is biological and what is cultural in sex differences is not established with certainty for all types of activity. True, certain physiological functions are sex-linked. Females produce ova, while males produce sperms; females have specialized sex organs for the nurture and incubation of fertilized ova. Males do not. Females are capable of parturition. Males are not. *Homo sapiens* is a bisexual animal in which the basic reproductive roles are biologically fixed. So long as babies are born of women, differential statuses of male and female will be recognized and culturally reflected. The real social revolution will come when perfected biogenetic techniques make possible the fertilization and incubation of the human ovum outside the womb. But that day is not at hand. Every society, therefore, assigns to the male and female different roles. But the patterns of these roles reveal a remarkable flexibility as between different cultures. Each society expects men and women to behave differently; what men do is one thing; what women do is another.

In the pueblo of San Ildefonso

. . . there is a sharp line between men's work and women's work, and in the respective attitudes of the sexes towards their work. Men's work on the whole tends to be cooperative. The ditches are dug by the male community in the spring; the fields are tended as a group enterprise. . . . Among women, on the contrary, work has tended to become competitive; women seldom carry on any of their activities as a group. . . . Theoretically, at least, women play comparatively minor roles. San Ildefonso men do work which elsewhere is frequently the task of women. Their special province is called "outside work." Traditionally they hunt, dress the skins of the animals they kill, cut and sew moccasins for themselves and for the women, weave . . . baskets, and weave and create their own dance costumes. . . . Men till the fields and the gardens, plant and reap, cut and haul firewood. Within the village itself they build the houses, care for the *kivas*, and clean the plaza before fiestas and dances. . . . Women's work is "inside." They care for the household, grind the grain, cook and tend their children. They make and fire the pottery, and if there is no man in the family who can decorate it, the women may decorate their own.[7]

Of Lesu, in Melanesia, Powdermaker writes, "It is the sexual division of labour adhered to so rigidly that first strikes the ethnological observer. Men have one kind of work and women another, and a third kind may be done by either one of them jointly." In tabular form she compiles men's and women's work as follows: [8]

[7] W. Whitman, *The Pueblo Indians of San Ildefonso*, pp. 99–100.
[8] H. Powdermaker, *Life in Lesu*, pp. 161, 163.

Masculine	Feminine	Joint
Clearing ground for new garden and building garden fence	Planting taro and yams; weeding; gathering crops and carrying them home	
Planting trees		
Getting sago		
Fishing	Catching crabs on the reef	Catching the sea worm, beta
Hunting wild pig and phalanger	Feeding domestic pigs	
Cutting firewood; making the *liga;* bringing the leaves for cooking	Drawing water	
Preparing pigs, fish, and sago to be cooked	Preparing taro and yams to be cooked	
Burying bananas in the sand		
Housebuilding and repairing	Sweeping the house and keeping it in order	
Making of masks, canoes, *malanggans,* fishing nets, spears, ornaments	Carrying heavy burdens with the exception of fish and pigs	Making baskets and mats. Taking care of children. Medicine and magic. Making "paint" for the hair

But although each society divides men's work and women's, what is distinctly men's work in one society *may* be women's work in another.

As obvious examples we may note that the weaving of Navajo blankets is women's work, while among the neighboring Hopi both spinning and weaving are confined to men. In nineteenth-century America boys were supposed to be able to swim, while girls were not; among the Yaghan of Tierra del Fuego, women are the swimmers. Among the Pueblo Indians most garden work was done by men; among the Iroquois, hunting and fighting were for men but tilling was for women only. Among the Maricopa Indians of southern Arizona pottery making was "wholly a woman's occupation and a year-round task." [9] Weaving, however, was properly men's work. Women harvested and ginned the cotton, which was grown exclusively by the men, while both sexes spun the yarn.

Sexual dichotomy, although always present, may or may not be stressed. In Australia and most of Polynesia it is. In North America it tends to be played down.

[9] L. Spier, *Yuman Tribes of the Gila River,* p. 104.

Studies by Margaret Mead have emphasized the transmutability of male and feminine roles in different cultures.[10] Of three tribes in eastern New Guinea, one (the Arapesh) is presented as equalizing the temperamental roles of men and women, another (the Mundugumor) is described as producing violent and aggressive persons of both sexes, while the third (Tschambuli) molds men in the pattern of parasitic fops whose foibles are tolerated in comfortable amusement by the energetic, realistic, hard-working women. The contrasts are striking and would conclusively demonstrate the absolute transmutability of the temperamental roles of the sexes, if the data on which Mead's interpretations rest were corroborated by independent observation. Thurnwald, Malinowski, and Fortune, however, have all rejected the factual reliability of Mead's sex temperament studies.[11] Each of them is also a Melanesian authority. Thurnwald and Fortune have worked in the specific area. Indeed, Fortune and Mead were coworkers in the field on the expedition that produced the basis for Mead's work.

In view of the serious strictures that are justifiably directed toward Mead's sex temperament studies it is not possible to accept as valid any inference from them that the temperamental roles of men and women are *wholly* culturally determined and thus interchangeable. Mead has herself lately criticized the most recent, comprehensive sociopsychological study into the origins of sexual behavior [12] on the ground that the author, a psychologist, emphasizes "sex as a value in primitive society" rather than as a developmental consequence of identifiable sex drives among animals.

As a result the primitive material interrupts a sequence which might otherwise flow smoothly from the studies of the higher apes to human societies, in which the differentiated sex drives of males and females might have been viewed as providing a dynamic framework for human interpersonal relations.[13]

[10] Especially, *Sex and Temperament in Three Primitive Societies.*

[11] R. Thurnwald, "Review of *Sex and Temperament in Three Primitive Societies*" (*American Anthropologist*, Vol. 38, 1940), pp. 663–667.

B. Malinowski, Preface, in R. Firth, *We, the Tikopia*, pp. vii–viii. "Under the deft touch of another writer the women of one tribe appear masculine, while in another males develop feminine qualities almost to the verge of parturition. . . . The reality of human life is being submitted to some queer and alarming manipulations . . . based on a few hypostasized impressions."

For Fortune's evaluations see p. 449 below.

[12] G. H. Seward, *Sex and the Social Order.*

[13] M. Mead, "Review of *Sex and the Social Order*" (*American Anthropologist*, Vol. 49, 1947), p. 309.

The sound anthropological position is that certain sex-linked behaviors are biologically based, although subject to cultural modifications
within limits. The exact nature of the biologically based differences in
behavior between the sexes and the limits of cultural modifications are
in process of investigation and not yet adequately determined. The roles
as they occur in any society, however, may be empirically observed and
ethnographically recorded.[14]

Age Status. Age statuses are recognized in all societies. Young children
may be highly valued as objects of desire, but they never have prestige
by the mere fact of their status as infants. In the exceptional instances
in which infants do enjoy high status and prestige it is always as a consequence of some special factor other than age: a princeling by birth,
or a twin by imputed supernatural qualities (among the Dahomeans).[15]

Infants have no power as infants. Youths and those of middle age
rarely enjoy favored status by virtue of their age, although prowess and
wealth may bring prestige status to them. The aged, however, almost
universally enjoy statuses of respect, reverence, and privilege because
of the attributes that are ascribed to them by virtue of their being old.[16]
It is not just being old that brings prestige. It is the accumulated wisdom
and lore of the oldsters—the association of ancient custom with ancient
people. As has been said of the Haida Indians of Queen Charlotte Island
on the Northwest Coast, "They had great respect for the aged, whose
advice in most matters has great weight." [17]

In stable societies accumulated experience builds up. Elders really do
know more than youngsters, and what they know holds good. But in a
rapidly changing culture, accumulated knowledge often becomes quickly
shopworn. What was valid in the youth of the aged is no longer so.
Wisdom based on outdated knowledge is, alas, of little credit to him
who clutches it as a source of prestige.

In the primitive world the oldsters are "elders" in politics and government, magicians and priests in supernaturalism, and owners of property in some systems of economic organization. These are sources of
power. Since such sources are more available to men than to women, old
men usually have higher status than do old women.[18] The positions of

---

[14] For example, N. M. Giffin, *The Roles of Men and Women in Eskimo Culture.*
[15] M. J. Herskovits, *Dahomey,* Vol. I, pp. 263, 270–272.
[16] L. Simmons, *The Role of the Aged in Primitive Society,* p. 79.
[17] A. P. Nibback, *The Coast Indians of Southern Alaska and Northern British
Columbia* (Board of Regents of the Smithsonian Institution, Annual Report, 1890),
p. 240.
[18] Simmons, *op. cit.,* pp. 47–49.

the aged are more secure in the settled horticultural tribes than is the case among hunting and collecting peoples, especially those who live in the Arctic and its fringes, where old people are unable to participate in primary productive activities to any extent. The support of the aged is a luxury that marginal societies find themselves unable to sustain in times of stress. Senilicide is general among the Eskimos. Old people may be blocked up in a snow hut to be abandoned to cold and starvation. Or they may be killed by more violent means when they themselves request it.[19] However, of the seventy-one societies tabulated by Simmons, only two (both Eskimo) violently remove the aged, while seven abandon or expose them to natural elements to hasten their deaths.[20] This does not mean that in these seven societies all old people are destroyed when their powers wane. It depends upon individuals and circumstances.

Almost all observers remark that old people are respected in the tribes they have visited. Only the Bushmen of South Africa and the Witotos of South America are said definitely to withhold respect from aged men. Eight of the tribes studied by Simmons deny deference to old women.

The Andaman Islands provide anthropologists with their favorite example of age as a status determinant. Kinship, which is so important in most primitive societies, is here muted. Rather,

. . . the duties that one person owes to another are determined much less by their relation to one another by consanguinity and marriage, than by their respective ages and social status. . . . There is very little of any special customs relating to conduct towards different kinds of relatives. Corresponding to this we find very few terms to denote relationships and a considerable development of terms which denote age and social status.[21]

Older persons have many food privileges denied to the young. Gradually, and with elaborate ritual, the food tabus are removed for the growing youth until at full maturity he may enjoy all the delicacies permissible to his sex. Younger persons must defer to the older in all matters.

In Australia, where as in the Andamans we find some of our most primitive peoples, seniority has reached its greatest significance—so much so that Australian social organization is dubbed *gerontocracy,* "the rule of elders." The preeminent domination of the Australian horde by old grizzled men gave birth and impetus to the nineteenth-century notion

[19] E. A. Hoebel, "Law-ways of the Primitive Eskimos" (*Journal of Criminal Law and Criminology,* Vol. 31, 1941), pp. 670–671.

[20] Simmons, *op. cit.,* Table VI.

[21] A. R. Radcliffe-Brown, *The Andaman Islanders,* p. 81.

that the primeval condition of man was that of browbeaten youth frustrated by the hoary patriarch. Australia, however, represents a special elaboration of age status in a way not universally characteristic of the lower primitives (in contrast are the African Bushmen and American Shoshones).

Wealth. Among roving collectors of food there are definite limits to the amount of goods people are able to carry around with them. It is not possible under such circumstances to accumulate wealth. Of rich men there are none. The possession of wealth is not for the lower primitives a status determinant of great significance.

The giving away of food and goods is another matter, however. Food claims are communal in nature in almost all primitive societies (see pages 340–344 below). Prestige and leadership go to hunters who have food to dispense, hides to bestow, arrows to give, and (among Plains Indians) horses to lavish upon favored friends, wayfaring visitors, and indigent neighbors. Plains Indians recognized as families of good standing those whose tipis were well-kept and decorated, whose industrious men and women kept their lodges well supplied with victuals, fine robes, and handsome clothes, but above all those who gave freely of what they possessed. Fluid wealth brought high status in its train. Hoarded wealth brought only contempt. This is what settlers on the Indian frontier could not understand when silent Indians appeared at the cabin door expecting a ready handout.

On the Northwest Coast the fluidity of wealth is guaranteed by the *potlatch*—an elaborate institution of feasting accompanied by the lavish distribution of presents by the host and his kinsmen to guests of another lineage or tribe. Its primary function is to serve as a demonstration of the family and individual statuses of the hosts. The guests are witnesses to the hosts' claims to certain statuses. Although accumulations of wealth are necessary for potlatching, it is not the wealth that gives status; it is the legitimate possession of honorific prerogatives, which are linked with specific names and titles, which are inheritable, but which may not be used until publicly assumed at a potlatch given for the purpose. To use a name not publicly notarized at a potlatch is a shameful presumption, and to address a person by a name he has inherited but has not validated is an insult to his standing.

A Tsimshian potlatch that took place around 1930 illustrates the old principle with some modern touches. It is the story of the present chief of the Gitlan tribe and a member of the Wolf clan. When Gusgai'in, chief of the Gitlan died, his nephew announced that he would take up his uncle's name at some later date. Before this could be done, he and a

Wolf clansman jammed their motorboat between the piles of a bridge, and were left hung up when the tide flowed out from beneath them. This would be enough to cause any good boatman chagrin, but when they were badgered with the remark, "We saw a wolf hanging up under the bridge," the status of all Wolves was impaired.

A potlatch was necessary to rehabilitate their position. Wherefore they undertook to give a traditional ceremony, the family Feast of the Early Snow, commemorating the exploit of the ancestral chief, Gusgai'in, whose name was now to be assumed by his descendant. This ancestor had passed beneath a glacier in his flight from enemy captors, so with poetic flavor the *pièce de résistance* of the commemorative banquet is a native sherbet made of snow mixed with olachen grease, berries, and crabapples. In keeping with the times, however, ice cream was served at this potlatch. Before each person who had taunted the hosts was placed a heaping dish of ice cream, more than he could possibly eat.

> Gorging a guest and then making fun of him was a favorite form of ridicule and provided much amusement for the guests. . . . When the feast and hilarity were over [so goes Garfield's account], the chief arose and explained the mythological background for the feast they were giving. He thanked the guests for coming and announced that, in so far as he was able, he would fill the position of his late uncle. Then La'is, the senior Wolf of the Gilutsa'u tribe, arose as the chief's spokesman and said that, as the chief had been publicly addressed as Gusgai'in, the latter was hereby acknowledging the name and assuming the position. . . . Spokesmen for each guest chief affirmed Gusgai'in's right to the name and welcomed the new chief as a brother. They also acknowledged that the bridge incident and other slurs would be forgotten. Much tribal history was narrated during the speeches and many compliments were paid the host and his lineage.

Gifts of food and handkerchiefs were then distributed among the guests. Dancing ended the potlatch.[22]

Although sensitivity as to status is shown in this account and although guests are ridiculed to the credit of their hosts, the potlatch atmosphere here described is one of congeniality and pleasure. This, from all reports, is more characteristic of the Northwest Coast potlatch than is the tense rivalry and extreme megalomania ascribed to the Northwest Coast Indians by Benedict in her well-known discussion of potlatching among the Kwakiutl Indians.[23]

[22] V. E. Garfield, "Tsimshian Clan and Society" (*University of Washington Publications in Anthropology*, Vol. 7, No. 3, 1939), pp. 205–206.

[23] R. F. Benedict, *Patterns of Culture*, pp. 173–222.

Whereas the Kwakiutls "fight with property" and have made of the potlatch a form of vicarious conflict, the more normal Northwest Coast use of the potlatch is to utilize it as a public proclamation of claims to statuses with public acknowledgment of the claims, if they are valid and deserving of public recognition.

Barnett, whose well-balanced analysis of the potlatch as an institution is based on first-hand experience combined with exhaustive comparative study, notes that "the totality of a man's potlatches, given by him or for him, is an acceptable gauge of the esteem in which he holds himself." [24] To which should be added, "within the limits imposed by his inheritance of titles and prerogatives."

Not only does the potlatch serve to affirm the status of the host, but the protocol of seating, serving of food, and distribution of gifts does likewise for the guests. Invariably the giving is in order of rank. The person with the highest rank is called upon to come up first to receive his allotted share, and so on down the line. The position of each person with respect to every other is rigidly determined by the nature of the validated titular prerogatives he holds.[25] The mere giving of a potlatch does not validate a person's claim to status. The real validation comes when he is called forth to receive his gifts when he is a *guest* at other potlatches. Only if his hosts call him forward at the moment warranted by the position he has claimed are his claims validated.

The goods distributed at the potlatch are not capital investments; lending and repayment form no part of the potlatch distribution. "Their more immediate character is that of a gift, a favor unconditionally bestowed." [26] The overdone capitalism of the Kwakiutls (with their notions of 100 per cent interest) are not representative of the usual Northwest Coast pattern.

Similar practices are prevalent in many parts of Melanesia, where "big men" get to be such through the giving of expensive feasts and the lending out of pigs or other forms of capital goods.[27] To rise through the various degrees of the all-important men's club of the Banks Islanders calls for the payment of heavy initiation fees. None but the richest of

---

[24] H. G. Barnett, "The Nature of the Potlatch" (*American Anthropologist*, Vol. 40, 1938), p. 354.

[25] P. Drucker, "Rank, Wealth, and Kinship in Northwest Coast Society" (*American Anthropologist*, Vol. 41, 1939), p. 57.

[26] Barnett, *op. cit.*, p. 353.

[27] *Cf.* C. D. Forde, *Habitat, Economy, and Society*, pp. 180*ff.* (on the Solomon Islanders); M. Mead, "The Arapesh of New Guinea" in *Cooperation and Competition among Primitive Peoples*, pp. 32–35.

men can afford to purchase the higher degrees. Indeed, as Lowie has summarized the data,

It is only the man of wealth who can reach the highest degrees and thus acquire prestige. . . . Yet the aboriginal conception is not that of avariciously hoarding wealth but rather of displaying one's greatness by exhibiting contempt for property. So a man of the loftiest status in the club may still promote his renown by providing the lavish entertainment associated with certain festivals; nay, a suggestion of niggardliness on these occasions would go far to destroy his influence.[28]

Trobriand chieftains gather great stores of yams brought in as subject tribute. But this wealth must be dissipated in public feasts eaten by the populace and chieftains alike.[29]

The stewardship of wealth is not emphasized by primitive apologists. Yet as an anthropological principle it may be said that the management of wealth rather than its possession gives social recognition among primitive peoples. Social compulsion stimulates altruism, philanthropy, and good works. In civilization it has been easier to negate this principle than is the case in the primitive world, and the contrasts in wealth and poverty that occur within civilized societies are shocking to savages.

Aptitudes. If skill's a joy to any man, it should also be true that skill in any function valued by a society brings prestige and high status to the expert. By and large, anthropological data support this supposition.

Militaristically oriented societies applaud and honor proved valor. Jivaro head-hunters count their glory in the number of shrunken heads they tally in their personal collections. The Icelandic sagas resound the fame of Gunnar of the "singing bill," mighty slayer of men. The Iroquois rewarded outstanding fighters with the opportunity to recite their deeds of valor before the admiring multitude at the victory dance, and each war leader had a war post upon which he depicted his exploits.

On the Plains, elaborate systems of coup counting were built up in a manner that inspired the merit-badge system of the Boy Scouts. A blow struck against the enemy is a *coup* in a literal sense. To ride or run into a howling mob of painted adversaries and touch an enemy stood high on the list of war merits. It was more praiseworthy than to kill him, for a dead man is not dangerous. It takes more courage to strike an enemy and run away than to lay him low. This often worked to the advantage of our own troopers in the Indian wars, who, when battle was joined,

[28] *Primitive Society*, p. 277.
[29] B. Malinowski, *Argonauts of the Western Pacific*, p. 64.

fought for keeps, not for fun. Indians who were intent on showing off made better shooting than shooters.

It was also a coup to kill an enemy, but even in this act there were degrees of merit. A kill with a knife, tomahawk, or spear rated much higher than a lethal shot with bow or gun. Scalps were desirable souvenirs of victory, but taking a scalp after the battle was over was no coup at all.

Life in a Plains Indian camp was studded with opportunities, ritual and otherwise, for brave men to recite their coups and to receive the plaudits of the people. These men became war leaders.

The pacifistic Puebloans gave special status to warriors who had killed and scalped. But it was not a glorified status. Rather, it was the status of polluted men who had to be purified through ritual initiation into the Warriors' Fraternity. In the recent war, the men of one Keresan pueblo in New Mexico were exhorted on leaving for the service not to touch any dead Germans or Japanese or to pick up any battlefield souvenirs that had belonged to the enemy, because there is no one now living who knows how to initiate them into the Warriors' Fraternity. They would remain polluted and dangerous for life, if contaminated by the enemy dead.[30]

Proficiency in supernaturalism gives special status to shamans and priests the world over—a status that bears a greater or lesser degree of prestige in almost all cases. The social position of sorcerers is esteemed or hated as the culture legitimatizes or rejects their works. There are good magicians and evil, skilful and incompetent. The test imposed by primitive man is pragmatic; he who makes magic work is always respected (whether honored or feared depends on his use of it); he who flubs his magical undertakings is scorned and debased, neither honored nor feared.

Proficiency in craftsmanship usually brings moderately high status among primitive peoples, but it tends to rank below military prowess, supernaturalism, political leadership and wealth manipulation as a prestige generator. Polynesians among all recorded primitives gave the most conscious and organized recognition to craftsmanship. The *Tuhunga*, or great adept, of the Tonga tribe in Polynesia was highly revered, whether he was a master of oratory, tribal lore, housebuilding or canoe manufacture. Only by virtue of much mana (see page 407 below) was it pos-

---

[30] Nevertheless, some of the veterans did return home thus contaminated. In the summer of 1947, therefore, the men of this pueblo were contemplating inviting the Opi (Warrior) Fraternity leaders from another Keresan-speaking pueblo to initiate the veterans.

sible for a man to excel in anything. And all Polynesians were impressed by mana.

Occupations linked to inferior castes in Africa and India bring no kudos to their practitioners, no matter how skilled the craftsman. A Masai blacksmith is doomed for life to despicable subordination, for that is the pariah status his culture ascribes to blacksmiths.

CHAPTER 21

CLUBS AND AGE GROUPS

The urge to form clubs is not an exclusive trait of civilized men. Most primitives, too, have found the means to make life more intriguing, colorful, and meaningful through club life.

When we analyze clubs from a sociological point of view, we see that structurally they are just one form of association. In the definition of associations we find it useful to follow the line laid down by Mac-Iver, who distinguishes associations from institutions in that an association is defined as a group specifically organized for the pursuit of special interests, while an institution is "the set method of procedure," the complex of behavior, characteristic of an association.[1]

We shall treat clubs as those associations that are not based on the kinship factor, that have exclusive membership within the larger society, that definitely possess a formal institutional structure and that engender a discernible feeling of congeniality among the members along with *esprit de corps*, or the "we-feeling."

Further, although it is traditional in anthropology to speak of Australian "secret societies," Plains Indian "military societies," and Pueblo Indian "curing societies," it will help eliminate confusion if we do not use "society" in the sense of club or association. It will be legitimate, however, to continue to call men's clubs "fraternities," as is traditional anthropological usage in those instances in which clubs promote the social fiction of brotherhood among their members.

Finally, associations that include all the men of a given age range are known as *age groups, age grades, age classes,* or *age sets.* They are so important in certain parts of the primitive world that they shall receive special attention in the latter part of this chapter.

Sex and Club Life. The profusion of women's auxiliaries, bridge clubs, sewing circles, women's clubs, and women's leagues that is to be seen about us today leads some myopic observers to the conclusion that women are the sociable sex. It is doubtful, even within this club-ridden society of ours, that there are more women's clubs than men's or that men spend less time and activity in club life than do women. In the primitive world, however, there is no question but that men are the devo-

[1] R. M. MacIver, *Society*, pp. 12–15.

tees of club life and women are not. The clubwoman of the modern civilized world is one of the revolutionary developments of recent times. There was nothing like her in earlier human history.

Women in primitive societies rarely participate in club life; sometimes they enter into men's organizations as auxiliaries. When they do have clubs of their own, they are weak counterparts of the vigorous organizations of the men. There are rarely all-embracing tribal associations of women, as there are of men.

Indeed, club life among primitive women is so undeveloped that Schurtz, who nearly fifty years ago gave anthropology its classic study of men's societies and age grades, advanced the theory that females are innately unsociable. They are inhibited in the formation of clubs, wrote Schurtz, because by instinct their activities and interests concentrate on reproduction, hearth, and home.[2]

This must be dismissed as androcentric prejudice. In its stead a cultural-functional explanation that is nearer the facts of human experience may be advanced. First, the demands of family nurture tend to isolate women and leave little leisure for club activities. American experience of the last few decades shows that given leisure and opportunity women take to club life. Second, primitive women, in addition to having little leisure for club activities, are in most male-dominated societies definitely discouraged from entering into the club systems set up by men. Nor do the men look with favor upon female imitations of their organizations. This is found to be true especially in tribes that link secret men's clubs with religious activities. Revelation of the secrets of ritual and hocus-pocus to women (and uninitiated boys) meant death in Australia, West Africa, and even among the matrilineal Puebloans of the Southwest. Women who might accidentally wander in upon the secret rites of Central Australian men's groups would probably still be speared upon the spot, as they would have been before the days of white police and courts. The men's secret clubs of the Banks Islands and certain other Melanesian tribes terrorize and bully the noninitiates (including all women).

When so much ado is made about the necessity of protecting the sacred secrets from women and when the sanctions imposed upon women who happen to penetrate the secrets are so fatal, is it surprising that women do not expose themselves to such risks by undertaking the formation of clubs along the lines so jealously guarded by the men?

Tribal Secret Fraternities. Secret fraternities that include all the adult men of a society are called *tribal fraternities.* The adjective "tribal"

[2] H. Schurtz, *Altersklassen und Männerbünde.*

serves to distinguish them from the more limited type of associations that are open to only a privileged few.

Tribal fraternities are a direct outgrowth of adolescence transition rites. Puberty rites, as we have seen, serve as bridges over the yawning chasms of anxiety that threaten men when they confront the crises of

Fig. 68. Structural framework of a men's clubhouse. Maipua, Gulf of Papua, New Guinea, Melanesia. (*Chicago Natural History Museum.*)

life. Those who have successfully bridged the chasms by passing through the rites of puberty do not necessarily organize into an association because of this fact. But because passage through puberty gives an exalted status of maturity and because puberty rites for boys and girls are almost always separate, all those men who have been made conscious of their newly achieved status by the rites are apt to crystallize their special status in an organized association. The puberty rite then becomes an initiatory rite. Such an initiatory rite is not only a transitional rite over a life crisis; it also opens the door into the fraternity of men.

Such rites emphasize the destruction of the preinitiation personality of the neophyte. As Webster long ago noted,

Almost universally initiation rites include a mimic representation of the death and resurrection of the novice. The new life to which he awakes after initiation is one utterly forgetful of the old; a new name, a new language, and new privileges are its natural accompaniments.[3]

A new name and a new language are not in fact always forthcoming, but seclusion from the women and children followed by "rebirth" are regular features of primitive initiatory rites.

The line to be drawn between mere puberty rites and tribal initiation ceremonies is not a sharp one. Whether we decide a ritual falls into one class or the other depends on whether it leads merely to the status of adult or whether it brings adult status *plus* membership in a specific association of adults. Sometimes there is an intermediary borderline condition on which it would be most arbitrary to make a classificatory judgment.

Thus, in the case of the Andaman Islanders' puberty rites, we contemplate solemn and elaborate but nonsecret rituals that effect status shifts for boys and girls. Full-fledged men are distinctly separated from fledgling boys, and they enjoy many perquisites of adult status. They seem to be bound together by the bonds of consciousness of their common privileges and interests. Yet they do not seem to form a men's fraternity.

On the other hand, in the case of the Central Australian tribes, the initiated married men form a domineering, tightly knit group, possessed of much secret lore and enjoying many lordly privileges, all of which indicates without doubt that here we have true tribal associations.

Aside from Central Australia and certain Melanesian groups the great center for the development of tribal fraternities is Africa, particularly West Africa from Sierra Leone into Nigeria, the Cameroons, and the jungle region of the Congo.[4] In Africa the subjugation and exclusion of women so noticeable elsewhere is much attenuated. Although the tribal associations may be exclusively for men, they often include women. And what is more notable, women frequently have powerful clubs of their own. In Sierra Leone and Liberia, although some men's associations admit females, no women's clubs admit men. In view of the greater social power and prestige of the men's organizations, when absolute exclusiveness breaks down there is more pressure from the women to penetrate the men's clubs than vice versa. Women faculty members, for example, in American universities strive for membership in the men's faculty

[3] H. Webster, *Primitive Secret Societies*, p. 38.
[4] W. D. Hambly, "Source Book for African Anthropology" (*Field Museum of Natural History, Anthropological Series*, Vol. 26, Part 2, 1937), p. 498.

clubs, but one never hears of male professors pressing for admission to the faculty clubs of the women.

For West Africa the *porro* and *bondu* fraternities and sororities of such tribes as the Mendi and Temne of Sierra Leone and Liberia are most famous. All boys upon completion of their puberty rites enter the *porro;* the girls find themselves members of the *bondu.* Among the Kpelle tribe of Liberia, Westermann found that *porro* was the central integrating and controlling feature of all tribal life—family, religious, and political.[5] The chief officer (grand master) of the *porro* outranks or rivals the king in effective political power and social prestige. Membership in the *porro* is prerequisite to marriage and to all other clubs and offices. Internally, the *porro* is loosely graded according to the general social status and ages of the members.

Nontribal Secret Fraternities. Much the most notorious of the African secret fraternities are the limited and exclusive secret orders of the Leopard, Crocodile, Snake, or other beasts, reptiles or birds. Of these the Leopards are the most feared. *Egbo, Ekkpe,* and *Ngbe* are but variant tribal names for the Leopard order. Human sacrifice and cannibalism give a terroristic aura to the Leopards. Like the Ku Klux Klan they strike in the dark against their victims, who are selected because they have evoked the ire of the membership or merely because sacrifices are needed for fertility rites. The Leopard men wear leopard-skin cloaks. With wooden dies they make false leopard imprints in the earth to leave the impression that real leopards have seized the victims. With claw-like knives they mutilate and lacerate the flesh of their victims.

In some areas the Leopard and kindred orders have been reduced to more sociable activities by the authority of European powers. But the spring of 1945 saw the police of the Singida District of Tanganyika, Kenya Colony, East Africa, arresting some sixty natives in an attempt to break up the lethal depredations of the "Lion Men" and "Lion Women." *The New York Times* on Apr. 22, 1945, reported,

> The slayings all follow a pattern. There is a scream in the night from a native hut. Fierce growls are heard. In the morning the body of the native is found some distance from his hut. It is slashed and clawed as if by a lion.
>
> Examination of thirty-five bodies of victims satisfied medical men that the killers of six were real lions. The wounds on twenty-eight were made by knives and other sharp instruments in imitation of the teeth and claws of beasts.
>
> Investigators who question the victim's neighbors find them reluctant to talk.

[5] D. Westermann, *Die Kpelle, ein Negerstamm in Liberia,* pp. 228-290.

The functions of African secret orders are by no means wholly homicidal. Their bloody activities are only incidental to deeper-lying interests. The associations are mutual-aid organizations that have taken on important social control responsibilities in addition to their magical, religious, and merely social aspects.

They counterbalance the power of the king and work to keep royal tyranny in check. Unquestionably, they serve at times as the people's solution to the trying problems that result from the need to temper anarchy with monarchy, which in turn must be stopped short of despotism. Within the framework of the tribal constitution the secret orders are often cited as assisting the king in the application of the sanctions that uphold the tribal laws.[6]

As mutual-aid protective associations the secret orders of West Africa pay especial attention to the interests of their members as against the world at large. They collect private debts from delinquent creditors on behalf of their members. They punish other transgressions against the brotherhood as well. In some sections of Sierra Leone the overextension of these practices into exploitive terrorism has caused violent public reactions, resulting in the outlawry of such clubs as the Leopard by the tribal chief.

Experience proves that secret orders are dangerous devices for use as instruments of government and social control. With the best of intentions they may serve the public weal, but since the members are not publicly accountable for their acts, there can be no safe check on the inevitable temptation to use their heady power in their own selfish interests. Exclusive secret orders are inherently corruptible and corrupting in any society, be it *Egbo* in Liberia, *tamate* in Banks Island, or Ku Klux Klan in the United States.

Secret clubs of a purely congenial, ceremonial, or magico-religious nature are generally exempt from such strictures. Thus, in Dahomey, where the power of the king appears to have become sultanistic in its strength, all secret orders were banned by royal edict. The king brooked no opposition or competition. There was, however, no objection to the banding together of men for mutual aid, so long as it was not done secretly. The Dahomean *gbe* was (and is) organized by a group of young men, not necessarily of the same age group. They socialize together, but the basic function of their organizations is to enable each member to make more impressive displays at weddings and funerals by calling upon

[6] *Cf.* Webster, *op. cit.*, pp. 115–120; R. H. Lowie, *The Origin of the State*, pp. 91–94.

the resources of all other members not in excess of a stipulated sum.[7] Women may belong to such clubs, or they may have separate clubs of their own. In effect, these secular nonsecret associations are exactly comparable to our own cooperative credit unions.

The various Pueblos of the Southwest each have their several secret fraternities whose main functions are to perform masked *kachina* dances, impersonating the gods and to perform complex rituals according to calendric cycles. The dances and rituals are performed for the benefit of all the people. Most of the ritual and accompanying liturgy is secret among the initiated members, but public dances are also performed. Thus, the village *cacique* (sacred chief) of Sia Pueblo calls upon the Flint fraternity to perform the Stick-swallowing Dance on behalf of the whole pueblo. As the dancers shove sticks down their throats the dance imitates the poking of planters' dibbles into the ground and works to ensure a good spring sowing.

The functions of such fraternities in the Pueblos are wholly religious, magical, and ceremonial. Only as the high-ranking leaders of all the secret orders form an ecclesiastical council do they enter into the governing of men.

Among the Indians of the Northwest Coast, secret ceremonial associations also play an important role in the lives of the people.[8]

Secular Associations. Purely secular organizations, given to furthering nonmystic interests and not concerned with terrorizing women and children, have no compulsive need to surround themselves with secrecy.

Such were the military and dancing clubs of the Plains Indians. These associations of warriors were fellowships for conviviality among men whose warlike flame was sustained and fanned by the stories, the rituals, the song and dance of their lodges. Their basic interests were two: warfare and congeniality. Their good times were not in roistering, but in the quieter glow that builds up in companionate smoking of a joint pipe, huddled singing about a thumping drum, parading two by two in all their finery upon their best horses, or dancing for all the tribe to see.

Although the Plains Indian men's clubs are commonly called "military societies" they were military only in the sense that the American Legion or the American Veteran's Committee are military—their members are all fighting men. Rarely did the Plains Indian men's clubs go to war as units. They did not form regular segments of an army, for Plains Indian fighting was too individualistic for that, but they idealized and

[7] M. J. Herskowitz, *Dahomey*, Vol. 1, pp. 250–253.

[8] Cf. F. Boas, *Social Organization and Secret Societies of the Kwakiutl Indians* (United States National Museum, Reports, 1895).

glorified war and labored to sustain the war ideal among their members.

Their officers were "chosen to die." In battle they planted their insignia—a crooked spear like a shepherd's crook or a trailing shoulder sash that could be pegged to the ground—in the face of the enemy. From that spot they could not retreat unless a fellow member dashed into the melee to pull up the peg or staff. Nominees for such offices were sometimes as bashful toward acceptance of the honor as are some of our own presidential aspirants. Witness what Lowie was told by the Crow Indian, Young Jackrabbit.

All declined to smoke, then they came towards me. Some one asked them, "Whom are you looking for?" They answered, "Young Jackrabbit." I was seated in the rear and tried to hide. They brought the pipe to me, but I refused to accept it. One of the pipe-carriers was my own older brother. He seized me by the hair, struck my chest, and said, "You are brave, why don't you smoke the pipe?" He wished me to die, that is why he desired me to smoke the pipe. He said, "You are of the right age to die, you are good-looking, and if you get killed your friends will cry. All your relatives will cut their hair, fast and mourn. Your bravery will be recognized; and your friends will feel gratified." I took the pipe and began to smoke. They asked me whether I wished to have a straight or a hooked-staff. I chose the hooked-staff. My comrade also smoked the pipe.[9]

Plains Indian men's clubs have been classified into ungraded and graded types. The ungraded, which occurred among the Crow, Cheyenne, Kiowa, Wind River Shoshone, and other tribes, were voluntary associations open to all men without regard to age. A man needed merely a sponsor within the club; he also gave "presents" to the club upon his entry. There was no initiation.

The number of such ungraded clubs varied in different tribes. The Crows, in 1833, had eight. Toward the end of the century this number had been reduced to only two active ones, the Foxes and the Lumpwoods (Knobby Sticks).[10] The Cheyennes had six clubs: the Fox, Elk, Shield, Bowstring, Dogs, and Northern Crazy Dogs.[11]

The graded associations occurred only among Mandan, Hidatsa, Arapaho, Gros Ventre, and Blackfoot. Each of these tribes had a system of associations that were graded in a prestige hierarchy from young to old; age qualification was prerequisite to membership in all cases. Normally, every member of a tribe, if he lived long enough, would pass

[9] R. H. Lowie, *The Crow Indians*, pp. 177–178.
[10] R. H. Lowie, "Societies of the Crow, Hidatsa, and Mandan Indians" (*American Museum of Natural History, Anthropological Papers*, Vol. 11, 1913).
[11] K. N. Llewellyn and E. A. Hoebel, *The Cheyenne Way*, p. 99.

through all grades. The higher grades naturally had progressively smaller membership, which, combined with the increasing age of the membership, gave greater prestige.

Movement from one grade to another was by collective purchase of all the rights and paraphernalia of the club just above. Among the Hidatsa, for example, all the adolescent boys banded together and, aided by their families, they made a great collection of hides, arrows, parfleches, etc. After indicating to the Kit Foxes, the lowest club, that they wanted to buy, arrangements would be made for ceremonial payment and transfer of the club to the upstarts. In addition, each neophyte chose a ceremonial father, or sponsor, who had to be a member of the neophyte's father's clan, from among the members of the Kit Foxes. To this man he offered gifts and entertainment—including his wife if he had one. The ethics of ceremonial wife lending were mixed, however. The gesture had to be made, but most ceremonial fathers were "afraid" to use the privilege.

Thus each candidate had to make individual payments to join an age society, but at the same time it was absolutely necessary that his age group act collectively to acquire the rights to the club. Such clubs were, therefore, joint incorporeal property transferable only by sale (see pages 344–345, below). Northern Plains Indian age associations are not pure age grades or age classes, *i.e.*, a series of groups each of which is automatically composed of all the persons of a given sex and approximate age. After an incumbent group of Hidatsa Kit Foxes sold their club to the next younger group, they were without any club organization until they succeeded in purchasing the Half-shaved Head club from the group above them, who then had to purchase from the Dogs, who had then to purchase from the Lumpwoods. So it went up the line, until the oldest men entered the Bull club.

The element of age grading in the Plains is a piece of fancy embroidery that was added by the more sophisticated sedentary gardening tribes of the Upper Missouri Valley to the simpler ungraded complex as seen among the nomadic tribes. From the Mandan and Hidatsa the pattern spread to the Arapaho, the Gros Ventre, and ultimately the Blackfoot. The breakdown of aboriginal Plains culture came before the complex could spread farther.[12]

[12] Lowie worked out a classic age-area distribution study directed toward historical reconstruction of the development of such clubs. See his "Plains Indian Age Societies" (*American Museum of Natural History, Anthropological Papers*, Vol. 11, 1916), pp. 877–984. This famous paper culminated the synchronized study of Plains Indian military associations instituted by the American Museum of Natural History

In the Plains there were also women's clubs. Women joined in military association festivities on many occasions. Indeed, numerous tribal systems included a few female functionaries within the men's clubs. Each Cheyenne unit had four unmarried virgins with ritual responsibilities who were called "sisters" by the members. But aside from participation in the men's clubs, women had orders of their own. Cheyenne women who had quilled thirty buffalo robes with porcupine-quill embroidery could join a club of robe quillers.[13]

Age Classes. Age classes, or *age sets* (as they are called by English anthropologists), occur in their most highly developed form in Africa. The Nandi of Kenya Colony may be taken as an illustrative example. There are a number of grades of males in this tribe. The first grade is that of the uninitiated boys. For the scion of a wealthy family initiation may occur as early as ten years of age. Or a youth may be nearly twenty before he is put up by his family for initiation. Initiations, which occur every seven or eight years, are the high light of tribal life and a rough time for the boys, who, as if circumcision were not enough, are beaten with stinging nettles and stung with hornets. Part of the initiation includes military instruction, because after initiation the boys become warriors. The initiated group receives name emblems and ornaments. War formerly was their chief concern; they could play at love and enjoy sex, but they were not to be fretted with the responsibilities of marriage and children. After four years of experience, they were ready to "receive the country" from the elder grades. The age class above them, which was retiring from active warrior status, laid aside its warrior clothing, assumed the raiment of elders and could then marry and settle down to connubial domesticity. This is not of an exclusive sort, however, since in formal custom each married man is expected to extend the hospitality of his home to any visiting classmate. Hospitality to a Nandi means wife

---

under Clark Wissler in the early decades of this century. Leslie Spier's, "The Sun Dance of the Plains Indian" (*American Museum of Natural History, Anthropological Papers*, Vol. 16, Part 7, 1921), did the same for the museum's comprehensive comparative study of the sun dance among Plains Indians. Both papers represent the height of the Boasian "school of historical reconstruction." The meticulous and painstaking methodology represented in these studies was a healthy corrective to the overeasy generalizations of nineteenth-century evolutionists. But the approach is limited by the inherent deficiencies of fact that hamper the scholar who would infer the development of institutions without historical documents. The techniques of historical reconstruction remain essential tools of modern anthropologists, but problems of historical reconstruction are not primary interests today. Emphasis has shifted to problems of dynamic interaction within societies, but such problems can never be adequately handled without historical understanding.

[13] G. B. Grinnell, *The Cheyenne Indians*, Vol. 1, pp. 159–169.

lending, a gratuity he will deny to all who are not members of his own age class.

As a class advances in age it ultimately enters the body of statesmen and tribal advisers.[14]

To the south, in the Bechuanaland Protectorate, the Swazi, a nation related to the better-known Zulus, reveal an age-class system remarkably similar to that just described. In the Swazi system, however, the whole organization is tightly controlled by the national king, who utilizes the classes of fighting age as regiments in a standing army and as work corps in time of peace. Like the Nandi warrior, a Swazi man cannot marry until his class graduates to the grade of elders.[15]

Age classes in East Africa have been made to serve well as devices of social integration and efficiency. They cause greater internal segmentation, it is true. But it is a segmentation that promotes specialization of function along effective lines. It harnesses the energies of youth to the ends of the society and gives to each age group a strong awareness of its own status. In even so widely dispersed and scattered a population as the Nuer in the Nilotic Sudan, who have only the weakest of tribal structures in spite of the fact that they number over 100,000 persons, the age-class system is one order of organization that runs through all the tribes of the nation. In a generally undeveloped social and political structure, Nuer age classes are necessarily lacking in the qualities that distinguish their counterparts in Nandi and Swazi. As Evans-Pritchard reports,

The age-sets have no corporate activities and cannot be said to have specific political functions. There are no grades of "warriors" and "elders" concerned with the administration of the country, and the sets are not regiments, for a man fights with the members of his local community, irrespective of age. In the rites of initiation there is no educative or moral training. There is no leadership in the sets.[16]

What then do they do? They fix and emphasize the status of all males toward other males as equals, juniors, and seniors. They are merely weak imitations of the functionally more significant age classes to the south of them.

In conclusion, we see that neither the structure nor the functions of primitive clubs are universal or inflexible, but that the club-forming impulse is almost irrepressible.

[14] A. C. Hollis, *The Nandi*.

[15] H. Kuper, *An African Aristocracy*, pp. 117–136.

[16] E. E. Evans-Pritchard, "The Nuer of the Southern Sudan" in *African Political Systems*, p. 289.

CHAPTER 22

SOCIAL CLASSES AND CASTES

"The history of all hitherto existing society is the history of the class struggle," trumpeted Karl Marx and Friedrich Engels just 100 years ago.[1] On this generalization rests the ideology of class struggle that motivates militant Communism today.

The authors of this declaration recognized that in its pronounced form it is patently false, after they had become familiar with August von Haxthausen's studies in the rural sociology and land economics of Russia,[2] the historical culture studies of old Germanic communities by George Ludwig von Maurer,[3] and the anthropology of Lewis Henry Morgan (especially his *Ancient Society*). These works emphasized the communal and classless nature of tribal society. Hence, in 1884 Engels undertook to explain that by history he and Marx had meant no more than "all written history."[4] Primitive communism was then said to antedate class divisions, and the class struggle was said to have begun with ancient civilization.

The fundamentals of the Marxian proposition in Engels's phraseology are

. . . that in every historical epoch, the prevailing mode of economic production and exchange, and the social organization necessarily following from it, form the basis upon which is built up, and from which alone can be explained, the political and intellectual history of that epoch; that consequently the whole history of mankind (since the dissolution of primitive tribal society, holding land in common ownership) has been a history of class struggles, contests between exploiting and exploited, ruling and oppressed classes; that the history of these class struggles forms a series of evolution in which, now-a-days, a stage has been reached where the exploited and oppressed class—the proletariat—cannot attain its emancipation from the sway of the exploiting and ruling class—the bourgeoisie—without, at the same time, and once and for all, emancipating society at large from all exploitation, oppression, class-distinctions and class struggles.[5]

[1] *The Communist Manifesto*, p. 12.
[2] *Studien über die inneren Zustände, das Volksleben und inbesondere die ländlichen Einrichtungen Russlands.*
[3] *Geschichte der Dorfverfassung in Deutschland.*
[4] F. Engels, *The Origin of the Family, Private Property and the State in the Light of the Researches of Lewis Henry Morgan*, p. 6.
[5] *The Communist Manifesto*, pp. 7-8.

It is this class-conscious conception of culture history and economic determinism that today lends such critical significance to the phenomena of social class. It is not within our province to assay the historical validity of the entire Marxian thesis. But it is proper to investigate the nature of primitive society with respect to the problems of class and caste.

The Nature of Classes. "The concept of class," in the view of Mombert, "is concerned with the social differentiation of groups." [6] But if a clean-cut definition is asked for, the problem of what *kind* of groups is one that poses a knotty question. In its broadest sense a class would cover any category of people within a population who possess some diagnostic trait in common. All people whose feet take 10B shoes would constitute this sort of class. This is not what is meant by a social class, however.

The working criteria of social class are both objective and subjective. Economic determinists emphasize the objective criteria of relationship to the instruments of production; *i.e.*, ownership or nonownership of land and capital. This is the Marxian choice. Max Weber includes economic criteria in his analysis of class, but he adds also the nature of the external standard of living (which is only indirectly related to the possession of economic means), plus cultural and recreational opportunities. American sociologists, reflecting the more fluid and blurred nature of classes in our society, emphasize the subjective nature of class. There are no social classes but thinking makes them so. MacIver declares,

We shall mean by a social class any portion of a community which is marked off from the rest . . . primarily by a sense of social distance. Such a subjective character involves as a rule objective differences, income levels, occupational distinctions and so forth, within the society. But these differences, apart from a recognized order of superiority and inferiority, would not establish cohesive groups. It is the sense of status, sustained by economic, political, or ecclesiastical power and by distinctive modes of life and cultural expressions corresponding to them, which draws class apart from class, gives cohesion to each, and stratifies a whole society.[7]

A social class is, therefore, a group within a society, whose members hold a number of distinctive statuses in common and who, through the operation of the roles associated with these statuses, develop an awareness of their like interests as against the unlike traits and interests of other groups. A social class can exist only with reference to other social classes. A one-class society is necessarily a classless society. Furthermore, if there is no consciousness of class, there can be no dynamics of class

---

[6] P. Mombert, "Class" (*Encyclopedia of the Social Sciences*, Vol. 3, 1930), p. 531.
[7] R. M. MacIver, *Society*, pp. 78–79.

action; then the classes will have no functional significance. People must act in terms of class if the class concept is to be functionally significant.

Finally, there are a number of things that a social class is not. It is not organized. Classes are not in themselves associations. But there may be, of course, associations representing the interests of specific classes, as the CIO does for certain segments of the industrial workers in this country, or as the NAM does for a portion of the industrial owners and manufacturers. Yet even in Russia only a small part of the proletariat is organized within the Communist Party and its affiliate associations. Social classes ignore sex and age criteria. All classes embrace both young and old, males and females.

Classes in Primitive Society. There is clearly a direct and positive correlation between the degree of complexity of culture and the presence of social classes. Rude simple cultures do not provide the basis for differentiation of function and role sufficient to produce class identifications. Eskimos, Andaman Islanders, Australians, Semangs, Veddas, Great Basin Shoshones, Fuegians, and African Bushmen are conspicuously free of social classes. There is no possibility of the accumulation of capital goods; all persons have equal access to all natural resources; and none have notable political power over others. Victory in battle does not lead to conquest; slaves are not taken, nor do the victors saddle themselves on the necks of the defeated. A worker in a food-gathering economy produces no surplus beyond what it takes to feed himself. On this level of production there is nothing to be gained from enslavement.

The probability is that the majority of hunting societies are also classless. Certainly this is true of North and South America, except for those tribes who kept captive slaves.

Plains Indians. Among the Plains Indians a nascent sense of class was noticeable. Grinnell wrote,

Family rank, which existed among the Cheyennes as among other Indians, depended on the estimation in which the family was held by the best people. A good family was one that produced brave men and good sensible women, and that possessed more or less property. A brave and successful man has raised his family from low to very high rank; or a generation of inefficient men might cause a family to retrograde.[8]

But there was no real social gap between good and not-so-good families. The poor, instead of being driven into servitude to the upper crust by means of debt, wage dependence, or clientage, seem rather to have sponged upon the chief, the successful hunter and the taker of war booty.

[8] G. B. Grinnell, *The Cheyenne Indians*, Vol. 1, p. 129.

Recent researches have shown the Kiowa Indians to have had a fairly strong sense of class ranking.[9] Four classes were recognized by name: *onde, ondegupa, kɔɔn,* and *dapom.* The *onde,* who constituted about a tenth of the population, were those whose family heads were handsome on a horse, wealthy and generous, proud in bearing and courteous in demeanor, but above all, possessed of an outstanding war record. The *ondegupa* were the able artisans, hunters, herders and medicine men, who had wealth and were generous, noble in character and behavior, but lacking in sufficient war credits. They made up a third of the tribe. The *kɔɔn* were the common stuff, undistinguished in war or other accomplishments. They lived with their more illustrious kinsmen as poor relatives. Half the tribe was lower class. The *dapom* were simply *déclassé.* Shiftless and lazy, they filched and stole within the camp. Practically disowned by their own relatives, they were virtual outcasts. They sucked upon the generosity of the good people; theft was not looked upon or treated as a legal infraction. The *dapom* was not punished or extruded from the group. He was merely scorned and suffered to be borne.

Northwest Coast. Class was more marked on the Northwest Coast of North America, where in every tribe a sharp division existed between freemen and slaves—unfortunates captured from other tribes. In the early nineteenth century slaves numbered 10 to 30 per cent of the total populations of various Northwest Coast tribes. They were in effect a depressed caste whose function was by hunting and fishing to produce food for their masters and to do the menial work around the village, as well as to paddle the seagoing canoes. Whatever their rank in their own tribe, all slaves were reduced to the level of productive capital in the tribe of their masters. Just as any valuable good, a canoe or copper, could be destroyed at a potlatch, slaves too could be killed to show their masters' unconcern for wealth.

Most authorities have described the body of freemen in Northwest Coast society as consisting of two classes: nobles and commoners. Nobles were those men and their wives who had attained the rank of chieftain through the inheritance of chiefly titles, which they had validated by potlatching. Since most tribes held to primogeniture, the nobility consisted of first-born, while subsequent children or nephews (in matrilineal societies) became commoners. Among the Tsimshian, according to Jenness, distinctions were drawn even finer. Intermarriage among the first-born children of the highest ranking families of the nobility was

[9] J. Richardson, *Law and Status among the Kiowa Indians* (American Ethnological Society, Monograph 1, 1940); B. Mishkin, *Rank and Warfare among the Plains Indians* (American Ethnological Society, Monograph 3, 1940).

reputedly obligatory, so that there was even an endogamous "royalty" within the nobility.[10]

Drucker, who has studied Northwest Coast culture at first hand, takes issue with the orthodox view of Northwest Coast social classes. He flatly maintains that there was no class of nobility set off from a class of commoners, much less a three- or four-fold class system. What actually occurred as he sees it was "that each society consisted not of two or more social classes, but of a complete series of statuses graded relatively, one for each individual of the group." [11] He argues that between high and low there were differences in degree but not in kind.

This particular conflict of interpretations is not resolvable; it merely points up the ambiguity of the concept of class in certain settings. It precisely parallels the situation in which most Americans argue that we have no social classes, at the same time that Warner and his coworkers are assiduously dividing us into Upper upper, Lower upper, Upper middle, Lower middle, Upper lower, and Lower lower (than which there are no lower) classes.[12]

Aztec. Among the peoples of high culture in Central America and the Andean region of South America class differentiation was strongly fixed.

The Aztecs in their meteoric rise and fall developed from an apparently classless unsegmented society with a rude material culture, prior to 1300 A.D., to a highly organized, sophisticated protocivilization in the fourteenth century. At the time of the arrival of the Spaniards in 1518 they were rapidly evolving a feudal aristocracy at the expense of the earlier clan socialism. The society then consisted of royalty, nobility, common freemen, propertyless proletariat, and slaves.

The core and largest part of the Aztec population was the body of free commoners, members of one or another of twenty localized clans (*calpulli*). Every married man enjoyed the right to cultivate a plot of clan garden land and to have a flat-roofed, dingy, one-room hut of adobe or clay-plastered wattle. He might become a craftsman specializing in one of the many productive arts and trades. He had security and continuous employment and an obligation to perform military service. But he was hedged in by a code of sumptuary laws that reserved to the rich and to distinguished warriors and officials the rights of wearing fine cotton, jewelry, and particular hairdos. Presumption above one's rank was sum-

[10] D. Jenness, *The Indians of Canada* (National Museum of Canada, Bulletin 68, Anthropological Series, No. 15, 2d ed., 1934), p. 337.

[11] P. Drucker, "Rank, Wealth, and Kinship in Northwest Coast Society" (*American Anthropologist*, Vol. 41, 1939), p. 57.

[12] W. L. Warner and P. S. Lund, *The Social Life of a Modern Community.*

marily and severely punished. The upper classes in Mexico were not harassed by a dizzily whirling style cycle, in which the pace setters must have a new fashion every two or three years in order to keep ahead of the imitative masses.

Class distinctions cut across kinship groups, for the class of honorary lords was recruited from all clans. They formed a nonhereditary order of merit with various grades conferred by the government as a lifetime reward for outstanding military accomplishment, service in civil office, service to the state as a traveling merchant-spy, or exceptional religiosity. They wore the beautiful and elaborate costumery depicted in Aztec art. They lived in the mansions of Tenochtitlan. They received homage and led a rich life apart from their common fellow clansmen. In theory, the huge parcels of conquered lands that they received as rewards for their services could not be inherited as family estates. All such rewards were to be redistributed to a new worthy after the death of the holder. This was always done, but, by a process not difficult to understand, a system of preference was crystallizing whereby sons of nobles were appointed to their fathers' positions of nobility. Inheritance of rank and landed estates were thus leading rapidly to the freezing of a hereditary aristocracy.

Above the nobles in luxuriant splendor stood the royal lineage from among whose members the *tlacatecutli*, or king, was elected by the great council of lords.

Far below the royalty and nobles was the hapless proletariat. Aliens whose goods and lands had been expropriated by the state, and Aztecs who had lost their clan privileges for failure to fulfill clan obligations eked out a meager and sweaty existence as burden-bearing coolies on the streets of the city and roads of the country. Or they grubbed for their livelihood upon the estates of the lords. Taxes and feudal services left little to them.

Slavery was the lot of impecunious Aztecs who could not meet their bills. In like manner crooks who could not make restitution for their thefts became the slaves of the freemen they had victimized. Children were sold into slavery by impoverished parents, and even adults among the proletariat might voluntarily sell themselves into servitude. Many slaves were alien boys and girls taken as tribute from conquered neighbors.

The society of the Aztec Indians was on the road to the same type of pyramidal, exploitive society that is so familiar to us in the flourishing days of the archaic Mediterranean civilizations. The Aztecs, however, had not hardened the inequalities of their society. Children of slaves were born free (into the proletariat); slaves could not be killed or abused by their masters; they could even acquire property in their own right (although it is not likely this opportunity meant much to many slaves); they could not be sold to another master except by self-consent, and if married by master or mistress they became freemen.[13]

Natchez. To the north, where now stands the charming city of Natchez, Mississippi, lived a gardening tribe that gave its own peculiar twist to the Central American concepts of religion and social classes. This was the Natchez tribe, an outstanding member of the great southeastern Muskogean language family.

The Natchez people were devoted worshippers of the sun, and their towns were dominated by small pyramids at either end of a plaza. Upon each mound was a temple or the dwelling of a priest-chief. Each morning the Sun of Suns, exalted ruler, brother of the celestial sun, greeted his illustrious ancestor before the Sun Temple. In another temple was tended the perpetual sacred fire of the village.

The people, as was usual in the Southeast Woodlands, were divided into moieties. What was unusual about Natchez moieties was their unequal social positions. Reciprocity in dual organization had become neglected in favor of aristocratic exaltation. The result was a monstrosity in social organization. Interest in aristocracy as a principle had produced a three-fold subdivision of the aristocratic moiety into Suns, Nobles, and Honored People. For the common moiety there were no such grandiloquent names. They were all Stinkers. The meager material culture of the Natchez allowed for no such economic ostentation as the Aztec royalty and nobility drew to themselves, but the social superiority of the Natchez Suns and Nobles colored the behavior of all life in the tribe.

A startling Natchez rule was that the aristocrats had to marry *outside* the aristocracy; there was no alternative for them but to marry Stinkers. Such a rule is compatible with the principle of moiety exogamy but not in the least with the principle of aristocratic exclusiveness. Indeed, a recent criticism of the traditional scheme of Natchez social organization has centered upon the objection that the scheme is impossible as a reality, since in a few generations' time almost everyone would be aristocrats. A truly comic-opera situation would result, and the system would be self-liquidating.[14] This is because in all intermoiety marriages, except that of Honored Person with Stinker, the children were born aristocrats. The

---

[13] G. C. Vaillant, *Aztecs of Mexico.*

[14] C. W. M. Hart, "A Reconsideration of the Natchez Social Structure" (*American Anthropologist*, Vol. 45, 1943), pp. 374–386.

population of Stinkers would not be self-replacing and would soon be exhausted.

If we look at the descent system in more detail, we find that when aristocratic women married, their children belonged to the same moiety and class as the mother. When aristocratic men married, their children were debased one grade; thus, the children of a Sun male married to a Stinker female became members of the Noble class. When the boys of this group married Stinker women, their children in turn became members of the Honored class. When Honored men married Stinker women their offspring dropped out of the aristocracy to become common Stinkers (Fig. 69).

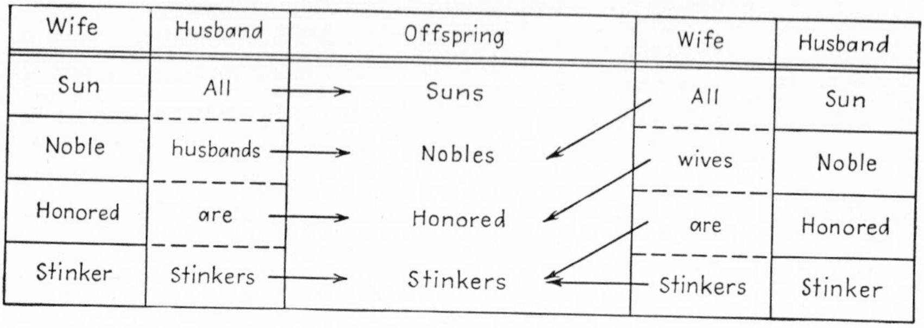

Wife	Husband	Offspring		Wife	Husband
Sun	All	→ Suns		All	Sun
Noble	husbands	→ Nobles		wives	Noble
Honored	are	→ Honored		are	Honored
Stinker	Stinkers	→ Stinkers		Stinkers	Stinker

Fig. 69. Marriage and descent in the Natchez class system.

The rule of exogamy did not apply to Stinkers. If not espoused to an aristocrat, a Stinker could marry a Stinker, and their children assumed that status. There was nothing lower than a Stinker.

Hart's contention that the Natchez social system was inherently self-destructive rests on the assumption of a stable population. Contrary to this, Quimby has effectively brought together historical and archaeological data to demonstrate that the Natchez actually replenished the Stinker moiety by absorption of shattered remnants of neighboring tribes decimated by enemies. Adopted foreigners were always Stinkers.[15] Quimby's excavations in Natchez sites indicate that the Natchez archaeological culture came into its own around 1600 A.D.[16] The French smashed the Natchez nation in three wars between 1716 and 1731, annihilating hundreds. Nearly 500 Natchez captives went as slaves into Santo Domingo, while surviving remnants were sheltered by the Chickasaw and the English colony of South Carolina. It is thus likely that the unique

[15] G. I. Quimby, "Natchez Social Structure as an Instrument of Assimilation" (*American Anthropologist*, Vol. 48, 1946), pp. 134–136.

[16] G. I. Quimby, "The Natchezan Culture Type" (*American Antiquity*, Vol. 7, 1942), pp. 255–275.

Natchez class system was a social mutation sustainable for a short period by absorption of outside populations but inherently incapable of long enduring. Its social survival value was negative. That it was not an ancient system is indicated by the fact that it did not occur among any other tribes of the Southeast, who were essentially similar in other fundamentals of culture.

Indonesia. When we turn our attention to the Pacific area we find that the rice-culture societies of Indonesia (outside the areas of strong Hindu influence) are almost all democratically organized communities of persons who hold their land in usufruct from the communally owned territory. Communities are congeries of kinsmen among whom no class distinctions are drawn. But the Indonesian village tends to form a closed society. Indonesians from other parts may obtain permission to live and work land in a strange community, but they may not enter into the political democracy; they remain residents without franchise, tolerated members of the village but not citizens. Aliens thus form a class apart, and it takes many generations for a family finally to enter the inner circle of First Families. In most parts of the Indies, until recent years, slaves taken in war formed another class.

Wherever Hindu princedoms were established in Indonesia (900–1300 A.D.), great gaps of social distance between Hinduized masters and the lower castes and classes were formed. In Javanese-Balinese court etiquette several different forms of language, to be used according to the relative social positions of the persons engaged in conversation, give a strong flavor to notions of superiority and inferiority.[17] Multifarious rules of behavior keep relations of higher and lower class people rigidly formal.

Polynesia. In Polynesia, native usage tends to run to class distinctions hedged in by much preferential etiquette. All Polynesians recognize a divine nobility, a gentry, a body of commoners, and slaves. Direct descent from a god gives a claim to nobility and innate mana to the class of sacerdotal chiefs. In democratic Samoa, the social and political power of the nobles is limited and subject to personal modification. In Hawaii, Tonga, and Tahiti, on the other hand, the sacredness of royalty before the days of white dominion was such that all the king touched became tabu to lesser men. Commoners were humbled before the royalty in the few contacts they had with it. Relations approached the feudal in nature. In Tonga, commoners paid in kind for the privilege of using their local chief's land. He in turn passed on some of this wealth to the higher chiefs. The basic reciprocity between chief and people, described with respect

[17] E. M. Loeb, "Javanese Word Formation, High and Low" (*Journal of the American Oriental Society*, Vol. 64, 1944), pp. 113–126.

to food as property in a previous chapter, had become phrased as a "right" of royalty rather than as a service to the society.

In Samoa, deemphasis of divinity was accompanied by emphasis upon craft skill, so that occupational guilds tended to enjoy the functional role played by royal classes elsewhere in the area.

Melanesia. In the western and interior parts of Melanesia inhabited by the more primitive Papuans, social classes as such are practically non-existent. In the eastern islands, where the Melanesian-speaking people predominate, differentiation into social classes is characteristic, even though there are classless tribes such as the Dobu. The actual governing of men throughout Melanesia is usually in the hands of a council of village elders, but there is commonly a class of wealthy chiefs who enjoy much social prestige by reason of their economic, ceremonial, and religious if not political powers.

Melanesian chiefs are almost always an immigrant group that has bamboozled the local populace into believing that because they have superior magical powers and control valuable ritual that will benefit the community (and that can be used to threaten the indigenous natives if they do not behave), it is only right that the chiefly class shall enjoy exalted sanctity and privileged superiority. The chiefly class is also universally regarded by the people and themselves as a class of feast givers and ceremonialists who reflect glory upon their people.

Fiji, on the Melanesian-Polynesian border line, is typical enough. About ten generations ago a group of warriors moved into the island of Lau. They may have muscled in with forceful measures, but present tradition has it that the local population accepted them as "civilizers" who brought light (*rarama*) to those who were living in darkness (*mbutombuto*).

The primordial clan system of the original people was reworked into a graded hierarchy in which every clan stood in a definite relationship to every other clan. Clans descended from the immigrants formed the chiefly class (*yavasu turanga*), and clans descended from the original indigenous population formed a peasantry, or "land class" (*yavusa vanua*). Through intermarriage the sibs of the newcomers also have acquired some land, but in this instance there has been no expropriation of the lands belonging to the lower class. Sibs of the land people still own most of the land. They also show more interest in gardening, while they are excelled by the chiefly class in sailing, fish spearing, and craftsmanship.[18]

[18] L. Thompson, "The Culture History of the Lau Islands, Fiji" (*American Anthropologist*, Vol. 40, 1938), pp. 185–189.

Africa. In Africa the range of social differentiation is from homogeneous democracy, as exemplified by the Nuer, to heterogeneous conquest states with formal caste systems. In illustration of the latter we shall take the Kingdom of Ankole in Uganda as an example of East African stratified societies.

The basic caste division in Ankole is between pastoralists calling themselves *Bahima* and gardeners known as *Bairu*. The Bahima are Hamitic or Hamiticized Negro cattle people, who came down the grassland corridor between Lake Victoria on the east and the mountain and lake chain on the west. Their original home was probably southern Abyssinia. Racially and culturally they were and are distinct from the Bantu horticulturalists, who had preceded them in occupation of the country. As they moved southward, the Bahima proved themselves as fighters to be superior to the Bantu-speaking Bairu and capable of effective enlargement of their social groups for politico-military ends. They conquered the Bairu and proceeded successfully to subjugate them, without apparent difficulty, although the Bairu outnumbered them ten to one.

Unbreachable disabilities were imposed upon the Bairu:

1. All Bairu are forbidden to own fecund cattle. It is true that they are sometimes given barren cows or bull calves for services rendered a Muhima,[19] but any Muhima can arbitrarily expropriate any productive cows found in the possession of a Mwiru.

2. While all Bahima males were liable to be called for military service, the Bairu were barred from bearing arms. They were kept militarily ineffective, and the chances of successful revolution were kept at a low level.

3. There can be no intermarriage between Bahima and Bairu. Aside from the customary prohibition of intermarriage, the injunction against Bairu cattle holding is an effective bar. No marriage is valid without bride price in cattle, and the Bairu can receive no reproductive cows, nor do they have any to give.

4. Bahima men (especially chiefs) can take Bairu girls as concubines, but Bairu men do not have an equivalent privilege with Bahima girls.

5. No Bairu may hold high political office. At best, they may serve as district tax collectors under a Muhima.

6. All Bairu have to work for and pay tribute to the Bahima chieftains, who in turn distribute the garden products and derivatives to their fellows. The Bahima have had no desire to kill the goose that lays the

---

[19] In Bantu speech the prefix "Mu" refers to a particular person, "Ba" the tribe collectively, "Bu" the tribal territory, and "Lu" the language. Thus we have Bahima, Muhima, Buhima, and Luhima; also Bairu and Mwiru.

golden eggs. Therefore the individual Muhima is barred from abuse of the Bairu, who is privileged to plead before a Bahima chief for compensation when ill-treated or exploited by an unauthorized Wahima.

7. When a Mwiru killed a Mwiru, that was a matter for retaliatory revenge among themselves. But if a Muhima killed a Mwiru, the law denied the right of direct action to the Bairu kin group. The most they could hope for was to be able to plead with the Bahima king that he obtain compensation on their behalf, and they were lucky if they got anything at all. But if a lowly Mwiru dared to kill a Muhima, the Bahima dispatched him forthwith.

Domination and exploitation in the Banyankole state is direct, unabashed, and efficient. It is an example par excellence of the oft-repeated story of the parasitic mastery of a sedentary people by nomadic herdsmen.

However, the class structure is not the simple dichotomous arrangement we have thus far described. The Banyankole kingdom does not exist in a vacuum, and there are other Bahima kingdoms and tribelets in the area. Although racially self-conscious, the predatory Muhima has not been adverse to raiding alien Bahima. To put a stop to this, the kingdom of Ankole undertook the subjugation of various Bahima neighbors, who were then incorporated into the Banyankole tribal society as a separate tribute-paying class, known as *Abatoro*. These can intermarry with their conquerors and they suffer no serious legal disabilities.

Yet a fourth class is the *Abambari*. Prohibition of intermarriage never prevents miscegenation. Out of the Bahima-Bairu concubine relations come half-caste offspring. Legally the *Abambari* are classed as Bairu, in the same way as most American laws class mulattoes as Negroes. But the personal interest of a Muhima father often mitigates the strict working of this rule. Those who have no legitimate heirs often raise the son of a concubine to the status of heir. Thus the exclusive separatism of the ruling caste has been self-defeated and, ironically enough, to the greatest degree among the chiefly families and lineages. For it is just in this group that today a definitely larger percentage of dark Bantu Negroid physical types is found than occurs among the ordinary Bahima herdsmen in the more remote rural districts.

Lastly, there were the *Abahuku*, or slaves. Because of the convenience and effectiveness of the system of exploiting the Bairu and the limited economic possibilities in slavery when Bairu tools and gardening methods are used, slavery has never been extensive. The slaves were Bairu taken in raids upon neighboring kingdoms. Ankole Bairu were never enslaved.

Slaves were used as menials in the households of the very rich. They neither gardened nor tended the herds. They were chattels of their individual masters, and their ears were cut off to keep them from passing as Bairu if they succeeded in running away.[20]

Caste. Caste is the result of intensification of the class principle. It is the freezing of social classes by means of endogamy and hereditarily ascribed status. It is thus a device by which a dominant group attempts to perpetuate and guarantee unto itself and its descendants a special and favored position in life. In theory, no person can escape his caste, whatever his potentialities and capabilities may be. Kroeber has pointed out that the caste "resembles the clan in being a sub-grouping within the larger political or cultural whole, and in being marriage regulating." [21] However, it differs from the clan in that while clans are exogamous, castes are endogamous. Clans are usually (but not always) of more or less equal social rank whereas castes are implicitly higher or lower in social status. The very existence of castes is a denial of any concept of social equality. The American dilemma rests in the contradiction between our devotion to the Christian ideal of brotherhood and to the democratic ideal of political equality and fraternity among all men and the occurrence of racial castes, which have resulted from our earlier conquests of Negroes and Indians.[22]

Slavery in Primitive Society. Slaves have entered several times into our discussion of class systems. Slavery is one of the most important of human social institutions and at the same time one that has not been adequately studied by anthropologists. It is by no means a universal institution, but it is very widespread and one that goes deep into human relations.

Our democratic morality has condemned slavery in such terms that we recoil from it with emotional horror. It is now hard for us to conceive of involuntary servitude as an implicit aspect of any society. Yet slavery has been an important part of civilization far longer than the period in which civilizations have extirpated it from the social body.

Slavery is not in itself an absolute concept. In operation it ranges from the complete degradation of a whole class of people by means of dogmatic denial of their humanity (slaves as chattels) to the inclusion of

[20] K. Oberg, "The Kingdom of Ankole in Uganda" in *African Political Systems,* pp. 121–162.

[21] A. L. Kroeber, "Caste" (*Encyclopedia of the Social Sciences,* Vol. 3, 1930), p. 254.

[22] Thirty of our forty-eight states have criminal laws prohibiting interracial marriages.

slaves as adopted members of the masters' family and kinship group. Slavery, we are safe in saying, is a condition rarely welcomed by the slaves. There are few social advantages in being a slave and usually a good many disadvantages. The lot of the slave depends to a large degree on whether the tribe customarily utilizes its slaves as household servants or field workers. If the former, the relation of slave to master is unavoidably intimate, and slaves reap the benefit. If slaves are used as field workers, the master's chief interest becomes one of sheer economic exploitation, and, especially where there are great numbers of slaves, relationships become impersonal and harsh.

Slaves are derived both from within and without a society. Internal slavery occurs only in the more advanced primitive societies with quasi-capitalistic practices of borrowing and lending. A borrower may pledge himself or a son or daughter as security on a loan. Default means servitude. Or, as in the case of the West African Ashanti, a man could pawn his brother's son to raise a sum. The boy then worked for the creditor until the loan was repaid; the labor he performed constituted the interest on the loan.

Debt slavery does not produce huge masses of slaves, nor are their positions ordinarily harsh. A second internal source of slaves is the condemnation of criminals to servitude. This, too, is found only in the more highly advanced cultures, since a strongly centralized law system is a necessity.

The great source of slavery is war and the exploitation of war captives. Warfare may or may not be waged to take captives. The lower primitives, for two reasons, rarely enslave war captives: (1) The community is primarily on a kinship basis and there is no room for nonkinsmen in the group; consequently, captives are quickly adopted into the family, with the result that the exploitive advantages of slavery are dissipated. (2) On the level of food gatherers and lower hunters the population usually presses close upon its food resources; extra mouths to feed are a disadvantage, and since slaves do not produce an appreciable surplus over what they consume, they are not desired. It is not that simpler peoples are more humane than more advanced peoples. Hunters are just as active in killing captive enemies as people on any other economic level of development.

Although slavery occurs with greater frequency among higher hunters than lower, it is among advanced agriculturalists and pastoralists that it first came into its own.

In the studies of Hobhouse, Wheeler, and Ginsberg, the relation be-

tween the occurrence of slavery as an institution and the level of subsistence culture is indicated in the following chart.[23]

This rising curve continues right on into civilization, ancient, medieval,
and modern. Although the nineteenth century saw extensive abolition
of slavery, the mid-part of the twentieth has seen its recrudescence in
hideous forms, first in the forced labor camps of Russia and then in the

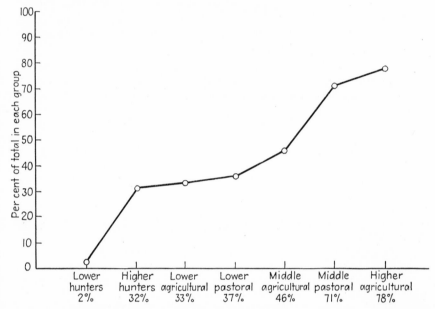

FIG. 70. Percentage occurrence of slavery according to subsistence categories.

nightmarish brutality of slave labor exploitation of subjugated peoples
by Nazi Germany.

That slavery is shunned by peoples on the same level of economic
development as others who incorporate it into their society warns us
that the high correlation between the development of technology and
slavery is not absolutely positive. In Africa slavery has long been a characteristic part of native life throughout most parts of the continent.
Thus, such pastoralists as the Bahima quite readily impose it on the Bairu.
But the pastoralists of Siberia, Central Asia, and India do not know the
institution, nor do the pastoralists of extreme South Africa.

In North America, as we have observed, the hunters and fishers of
the Northwest Coast kept numerous slaves. Yet the gardening Indians of

[23] L. H. Hobhouse, G. C. Wheeler, and M. Ginsberg, *The Material Culture and
Social Institutions of the Simpler Peoples,* p. 236.

the Southwest, although culturally more advanced, held no true slaves although they did keep a few captive children.

Even more striking is the absence of slavery among the Indians of the Southeast Woodlands, notably the Creeks. In gardening and social organization they were quite sophisticated, yet they had no class of slaves. Their institutional configuration was not conducive to the enslavement of enemies. Wars were fought to give men prestige (just as in the Plains); as in the case of the Pueblo Indians, economic goods did not provide the basis for prestige rating. Finally, kinship sentiments equalized most property usages.

In conclusion, our review of the anthropological data indicates that primitive society is neither classless nor class-ridden. Both forms of social organization occur. It is, nevertheless, perfectly clear that the most ancient societies were devoid of social classes, as they were also devoid of clans. Segmentation into classes is in part a function of increasing complexity of culture and differentiation of function and privilege. Subjugation and conquest commonly lead to enslavement or caste-organized states among peoples on the barbaric and archaic civilizational levels of cultural development. But this is not the sole form or origin of state structure, as Marxist students of social politics have maintained.[24] States evolve also from the internal needs of historically homogeneous groups.

[24] Cf. F. Oppenheimer, The State, p. 15. "A social institution, forced by a victorious group of men on a defeated group, with the sole purpose of regulating the dominion of the victorious group over the vanquished, and securing itself against revolt from within and attack from abroad."

D. Property

CHAPTER 23

REAL AND MOVABLE PROPERTY

The Nature of Property. Property is a universal feature of human culture. The land upon which the social group is located, from which it draws its sustenance, the beasts that rove upon it wild, the animals that graze upon it tame, the trees and the crops, the houses that men erect, the clothes they wear, the songs they sing, the dances they execute, the charms they incant, these and many more are subjects of property. Whatever men rely upon for the maintenance of life or hold dear because of the sociopsychological compensations to be derived therefrom, they tend to bring within the scope of property. So it is that property is as ubiquitous as man, a part of the basic fabric of all society.

Property may be held variously—individually (personal property), by groups (joint property), or by the society at large (communal property). It may be fixed and immovable (real estate), or it may be movable. It may be material and concrete, or it may be an idea or a way of acting (incorporeal). It may be transferable by gift, barter, sale, inheritance, or confiscation, or it may be inalienable. It may or it may not be protected by law. Most people by habit think of property only as a thing or things, whereas the thing itself is in fact the least important element in the reality of property. The genuine nature of property is found in its qualities as a social institution. Property in its full sense is a web of social relations with respect to the utilization of some object (material or nonmaterial) in which a person or group is tacitly or explicitly recognized to hold quasi-exclusive and limiting connections to that object.

As an illustration, a stone conveniently shaped for use as an axhead lies unnoticed and unused for untold time on the surface of the ground. It is not property. A wandering tribesman finds it, takes it to his cave, and uses it as a hand ax. This in itself is mere possession. If the social practices of the possessor's tribe are such that any other person could appropriate this tool at will, it would still be a mere matter of possession. But if the custom is such that his fellow tribesmen, at least, recognize that he has a special *right* to possess that piece of rock and all others have

329

a *duty* to desist from using or taking it, then it is an object of property. The stone has not changed, but the social pattern with respect to it has. It is the special and peculiar set of social relations that have transformed the rock into an object of property. Thus, we have two irreducible aspects of property: (1) the object and (2) the web of social relations that establishes a limiting and defined relationship between persons and the object.

This limiting relationship is often referred to by lawyers and economists as an *exclusive right of use*. It is exclusive insofar as it excludes non-owners from legitimate use without the express or tacit approval of the owner. However, the right is rarely, if ever, so absolutely exclusive that the owner may utilize the object in any way his whim may dictate. His right of use is always limited to some extent by the demands of society. After all, society, not the individual, is the creator of property. This is not to say that society created the *object*. The point of emphasis is that an object does not become property until the members of the society at large agree to bestow the property attribute upon the object by regulating their behavior in a self-limiting manner. This is done because social experience has led to the conclusion that social benefits are derived from granting "exclusive" rights to individuals and groups with respect to certain classes of objects that they have created or acquired. By the same token, men always limit the extent of that exclusiveness in accordance with their conception of the needs of social good. Property— a social creation—is consequently always subject to social limitations, even in the most individualistic societies. Thus it is that as social concepts change from time to time, the specific content of property concepts undergo alterations. The form and content of property notions are not the expression of immutable instinct nor of any imagined laws of nature. Property in mid-twentieth-century United States is not what it was in the mid-nineteenth century, nor what it will be at the dawn of the twenty-first.

As an example of the way in which property is constituted, we may briefly analyze canoe ownership among the Yuroks of California—a highly individualistic people. A Yurok boat owner nominally possesses his canoe as private property. It is his. He has a series of demand rights against all other persons not to molest or damage his boat. He has the privilege right to use it upon the public waters. He does not have to sell or give it away. These are all marks of exclusive rights. Yet he is also subject to a series of well-recognized duties that limit his exclusive prerogatives. For one thing, he is under a duty to ferry any sojourner over the river when called upon to do so. Failure to perform this duty gives the traveler a demand right for legal damages equal to one dentalium shell. On the other hand, if the owner suffers injury because of the service he has to render, then the traveler is subject to damages. Thus, when one canoeman's house burned down while he was in midstream, his passenger had to pay for the house.

This is what Cook meant when he said "ownership denotes—not only an indefinite number of rights in the strict sense or claims available against an indefinite number of persons, each of whom is under a corresponding duty, but also a large and indefinite number of privileges, powers and immunities." [1]

Finally, we should take note in our introductory comments of the relation of property to law. In the modern world it is a fact that a vast proportion of the law of the state is devoted to the definition of the relationships between owners of property. Much of the activity of our courts and police is devoted to maintaining and enforcing these relationships. Government feeds and grows on the complexity of property in a heterogeneous industrial civilization.

But to state, as does one of our best sociologists, that property rights "exist only because government recognizes and protects them" [2] is an expression of an amazingly myopic point of view. Property rights are tacitly and explicitly recognized and upheld by all forms of social sanction, legal and nonlegal alike. And in the case of primitive society the recognition and support of property institutions is in fact more frequently nonlegal than legal. Even when legal in nature, primitive property law falls predominantly within the area of private law, which operates independently of the formal governmental machinery.

Land Tenure among Food Gatherers and Hunters. Land is a *sine qua non* of human existence. It is therefore the most important single object of property. All societies are territorially based,[3] and most sustenance is drawn from the soil, either directly or indirectly.

[1] W. W. Cook, "Ownership and Possession" (*Encyclopedia of the Social Sciences*, Vol. 11, 1933), p. 521.

[2] R. M. MacIver, "Government and Property" (*Journal of Political and Legal Sociology*, Vol. 4, 1946), p. 5. See *contra*, A. I. Hallowell, "The Nature and Function of Property as a Social Institution" (*Journal of Legal and Political Sociology*, Vol. 1, 1943), pp. 115–138, especially pp. 130ff. Above all, every student should read the article by W. H. Hamilton and I. Till, "Property" (*Encyclopedia of the Social Sciences*, Vol. 12, 1934), pp. 528–538.

[3] One notable, possibly the only, exception to this is found in the case of the *Orang Laut*, the Malayan sea gypsies of the Java and Flores Seas. These tribes are autonomous units, living a roving existence entirely in boats.

Various observers have reported a tendency, presumably instinctive, for local groups among certain animals to fight to keep outside intruders from their territory. This is especially true of the primates, for whom Hooton has recently summarized all the available data relative to this subject.

Territoriality, or the residence of a primate group within well-defined territorial limits, has been established for howler monkeys, red spider monkeys, various baboons, gibbons, and, in all probability, orang-utans. The list is restricted by the number of field studies made. It is quite possible that nearly all primate genera share this habit of remaining within a certain area which they regard as their own and from which they attempt to expel trespassers, especially those belonging to their own species. If, as is stated, different species of lemurs in Madagascar are separated by fairly easily traversable natural boundaries, such as narrow rivers, it would appear that this primate tendency to maintain territoriality must be closely bound up with the differentiation of races and varieties, and even of species, by selection and inbreeding. Further, it would seem necessary to postulate some such innate or acquired habit of relative immobility within a narrow environmental range to account for the early differentiation of the very distinct physical varieties or races of man.

Thus it would appear that the feeling of ownership of real estate or of a certain habitat area is a very ancient primate inheritance.[4]

Various writers have at times naively assumed this sort of behavior to represent property in land among animals. At best it represents no more than a possessive tendency. Territorial control on the animal level cannot involve the "socially recognized and socially sanctioned rights in valuable objects that characterize property in human societies."[5]

However, most human societies claim property rights in land as communities. The Australians, African Bushmen, the Veddas of Ceylon, and the Tasmanians recognize clearly discernible natural boundaries as marking off local group territories. Each resents uninvited or surreptitious incursions—usually reacting with recourse to war or to regulated expiatory combat (see pages 390–393). Recognition of the possessory communal right as a true communal property right is seen in the Australian practice whereby one band sends an emissary to another to ask permission to collect certain foods on the lands of the second community. It is up to the tribal elders to grant or reject the request.

In addition to the obvious economic reasons for tribal exclusiveness in the use of their land, Australian tribes have a vital mystic relation to

[4] E. A. Hooton, *Man's Poor Relations*, pp. 331–332.
[5] Hallowell, *op. cit.*, pp. 135–138. For a fuller discussion, see E. Beaglehole *Property*, Part 1.

the land. The land is tied up with their dead ancestors, and as they cannot migrate from the land because that would break an immutable tie to the ancestors, neither do they wish to have upsetting strangers poking around their sacred territory.

However, not all food gatherers and lower hunters hold land as communal property. We may cite the Shoshones of the Great Basin in the western part of the United States. Steward, our chief authority on this area, categorically states, "The Shoshoni lacked any form of ownership of land or resources on it (except eagle nests). No group habitually and exclusively utilized any clearly defined territory for hunting, fishing or seed gathering." [6] Wyeth, who was among the Shoshones 110 years ago, noted the same: "None of the roving tribes claim ownership of the soil." [7] Evidence taken among the Northern Shoshone in 1934 corroborates these reports.

Steward has given an admirable explanation of the situation in terms of ecological factors. The uncertainty and variability of the pine nut and wild seed crops are so great that territories exploited by different groups varied greatly from year to year. When there were good crops in any locality, they ripened so fast and fell to the ground so quickly that the people who ordinarily lived in the area could not possibly gather them all. When a good harvest was promised, they therefore spread the news abroad, so that people whose crops had failed could come to share their bounty with them. "Under such conditions," notes Steward, "ownership of vegetable food resources would have been a disadvantage to everyone." [8]

Among the Eskimos land is not property in any sense. Nor is local group sovereignty applied to territory. Anyone, whatever his local group, may hunt where he pleases; the idea of restricting the pursuit of food is repugnant to all Eskimos (except for some groups in western Alaska, who were influenced by the very property-minded Indians of the Northwest Coast). [9]

Eskimo interest is in game per se. Land is ignored and not conceptualized as property, in spite of the fact that each local group is identified by the territory in which it lives.

[6] J. H. Steward, *Basin Plateau Aboriginal Socio-political Groups* (Bureau of American Ethnology, Bulletin 120, 1938), p. 254.

[7] *Ibid.*, p. 255.

[8] *Ibid.*

[9] But even here Lantis reports that when Eskimos from the mainland came to hunt on Nunivak Island, it never occurred to the Nunivakers to object to, or apparently even resent, the intrusion, although the supply of game was limited. (Oral communication.)

Such exceptions as these indicate that territorial exclusiveness is by no means universal. However, it is perfectly correct to say that the vast majority of food-gathering and hunting tribes do hold their land in common. Any member of the tribe may hunt where he will, as Neighbors once wrote of the Comanches, "No dispute ever arises between the tribes (bands) with regard to their hunting grounds, the whole being held in common." [10]

On the other hand, a few hunting peoples have developed practices of joint, and even individual, ownership of hunting and fishing areas. Notable among these are the Algonquian tribes of Canada and certain Indians of California and the Northwest Coast. There is a considerable body of analytical material on Algonquian land tenure, beginning with Speck's classic paper, "The Family Hunting Band as the Basis of Algonkian Social Organization," [11] and summarized and weighed by Cooper in 1939, who writes,

> The [Algonquian] band territory is divided up into sections or segments . . . each section being claimed by a particular "family." It appears . . . that the title to the land rests more in the individual than in the family as such, . . . the right to the hunting ground is a permanent and abiding one.[12]

Beavers and muskrats, which are the chief game, are sedentary. Unlike the roving beasts, they stay close to their home sites. Hence, it is possible for individual owners to conserve and protect the supply of such game on their individual tracts. To set traps on another man's property without invitation leads to violent sanctions—bloodshed or sorcery. A hunter who follows the trail of a large fur bearer, such as the fox or bear, into the land of another man may kill the beast, although he usually takes pains to notify the landowner, with whom he usually divides the spoils. Berry picking, fishing, root gathering, and birch-bark collecting are prohibited by some Algonquians but not by others. Among the Têtes de Boule, studied in the field by Cooper, there is a superfluity of berries, and fish are plentiful. "There is no scarcity, and no need for individual claims on such resources."

The Tungus of Siberia have very similar notions, although hunting areas are owned by families rather than by individuals. A man should not hunt or trap in the territory of another family, although he may follow in wounded game for the kill.

[10] R. S. Neighbors, in *History of the Indian Tribes of the United States,* Vol. 2, p. 131.

[11] *American Anthropologist,* Vol. 17, 1915, pp. 289–305.

[12] J. M. Cooper, "Is the Algonquian Family Hunting Ground System Pre-Columbian?" (*American Anthropologist,* Vol. 41, 1939), pp. 66–90.

The Kwakiutls of British Columbia partitioned coastal areas of water as private property for fishing purposes. All intruders were driven off.

In a similar vein, the California Yuroks exhibited a partial private proprietary right to ocean areas. Kroeber tells of a Yurok family that "owned" a portion of the sea off the beach extending about four miles in either direction from their house site. Other people could fish there, but they had to surrender the flippers of all sea lions taken within the area.[13]

In summary: food gatherers, hunters, and fishers usually hold large land and water areas communistically as common property, excluding from exploitation of their "sovereign possession" all aliens except such friends as those to whom they may extend privileges. Exceptions are found in the Shoshones and Eskimos, who at the one extreme have *no* exclusive concepts with respect to land, and the Algonquians and West Coast Indians, who permit individual or family holdings of hunting and fishing grounds.

Land Tenure among Pastoralists. Among pastoral herders there is a notorious "carelessness as to land." The Comanches, for instance, who were horse herders and hunters of game, had no concept of land. "Land was a matter of unconcern for them, being held neither individually, jointly nor communally." [14] Buffalo herds could be found anywhere and pasturage for their horses was unlimited.

Even among people whose grazing resources are limited the tendency is to treat the pasturage as public domain. Notable exceptions have, nevertheless, been reported for the Tungus reindeer herders of Siberia and the Kazaks (or Kirghiz, as the Russians call them to avoid confusion with the Cossacks) of Central Asia east of the Caspian Sea.

Although the Chukchi and Samoyed, neighbors of the Tungus, do not subdivide their pastures within the tribe, the Tungus treat the pastures as the common property of a group of cooperating and intermarrying clans, from which they exclude other groups and their herds by force, if necessary. In some instances a territory is divided among clans as such. In recent times individual families have utilized customary grazing grounds somewhat exclusively and irrespective of clan ties.[15]

[13] A. L. Kroeber, lecture, *Seminar in Psychological Approaches to Culture* (University of California, spring, 1941). An interesting legal case arising from failure to surrender the flippers is analyzed in E. A. Hoebel, "Fundamental Legal Concepts as Applied in the Study of Primitive Law" (*Yale Law Journal*, Vol. 51, 1942), p. 958.

[14] E. A. Hoebel, *The Political Organization and Law-ways of the Comanche Indians* (American Anthropological Association, Memoir 54, Contributions from the Laboratory of Anthropology, 4, 1940), p. 118.

[15] C. D. Forde, *Habitat, Economy, and Society*, p. 361.

Kazak practices are even more distinctive. These excellent horsemen subsist on large flocks of sheep and a few goats and camels. As is so often the case in primitive economy, they vary their life and social organization according to the seasons. It is their custom to summer in the lowlands, where they graze their herds at will in the tribal territory. In April, each household sneaks out of the winter village in an attempt to get to good pasturage before the others. In midsummer, drought so parches the land that constant movement from one grass spot to another is necessary. The families and clans do not lay claims to any piece of the country at this season, for the richness of the herbiage varies greatly from year to year. Winter camps are fixed settlements conveniently located near a well-protected pasturage amid the trees in a deep river valley. Each lineage or family group has its winter grazing sites established with natural boundaries or rock piles and stakes.

Land Tenure among Food Growers. Gardening and agriculture set quite different situations from those we have thus far discussed. Since full-fledged gardeners and farmers are more or less intimately bound to the soil, it is hardly surprising that they show greater interest in it.

For the most part, primitive gardeners work their lands either individually, by lineages, or by clans, and occasionally by clubs, but the ultimate title to the land commonly rests in the community. This makes it necessary to draw a clear distinction between proprietary title and usufruct. The last is merely a right-of-use granted by the property owner to someone else. Usufruct may be for a lifetime; it may even extend through a family for generations, but the ultimate control rests in the owner. Sometimes the distinction between usufruct and ownership is very real; at other times it is more ideological than active.

In a number of monarchistic West African tribes a sort of feudal system prevails. All land "belongs" to the paramount chief. He assigns it to various chiefs, who in turn allocate it to clans, whose headmen assign individual plots to each gardener. In return, the land-working populace owes fealty to the chiefs and above all to the king. They must do public work, pay taxes, and perform military service. As long as they are loyal and faithful in their duties, as long as they are not involved in serious crime, they may not be ousted from their lands. The privilege of use passes down through the family. However, a man may not transfer or sell his plot outside the family without approval of his clan elders. Often the family will pawn or sell a member into slavery in order to avoid alienation of its hold on the land. Since the services that are called for from landholders are general public duties, they are actually only services to the king in theory. The king's ownership of all land is, therefore, largely ideological. The kingship serves as the symbol of community unity, and landed property is phrased in terms to fit the ideal.

In Indonesia, where the rules of land ownership among the primitive rice growers have been carefully studied by numerous Dutch scholars, we find the relationship between communal ownership and individual holding clearly delineated. In the autonomous villages of the independent tribes all land belongs to the village, which is made up of a core of related clansmen. The solidarity of the group is strong and mystically symbolized in the possession of a common temple and sacred relics. The deceased village ancestors are buried in the soil, which contributes to the sacred feeling of intimacy of the group to its land. The land, all of which belongs to the community, is technically called by the Dutch the *area of disposal* (het Beschikkingsgebied). Any member of the community may reclaim and cultivate from the unused communal land as much ground as he can handle, provided he first informs and obtains the consent of the headman and makes a ritual sacrifice. Then he alone is entitled to cultivate that land as long as he works it and keeps it clear. He has continuing right of usufruct. Among some Indonesians, however, if he neglects to prepare the field at the start of any season, he may be confronted by someone else who wants to take it up. Then he must set to work or let the field go. Generally, however, if he abandons a field, he retains a right of exclusive usufruct until the jungle has reclaimed it. Then it reverts wholly to the community area of disposition. If he has built dikes, it may be that his hold remains unimpeded until all traces of the dikes have disappeared.

He may borrow goods or money on such lands as he holds by pledging the land as security. But he may never "sell" the land, nor can a creditor ever obtain a complete foreclosure. There is no possibility of alienation. Land belongs forever to the community.

Outsiders may acquire use of land from the community area of disposal by arranging for payments to the local headman. The contract is in theory for one year only and must be renewed annually. The importance of inalienability to survival of native life was recognized by the Dutch in the last century when they forbade the selling of land to nonnatives and limited the duration of leaseholds by Europeans and other aliens.

Among the natives of a village the right of usufruct is inheritable within the family line, but if a line dies out the land reverts directly to the area of disposal for redistribution by the headman. An interesting aspect of the close social bond between the community and its land is seen in the event of a secret murder of an outsider on community land. If the murderer cannot be found, the community that owns the land must indemnify the victim's kinsmen! After all, he died on their common property, so it is presumed that he was killed by someone in that group.[16]

In the Philippines, the Ifugaos reveal a pattern basically similar to that which has just been generalized for Indonesia at large. The Ifugaos are extreme individualists, however, and have no organized villages. Terraced rice fields belong to families, with usufruct inherited by both males and females as a part of their marriage portions. *Camote* fields are hewn from the public domain in the mountainside forests by man and wife together and are owned by them jointly as long as they are cultivated. Soil depletion in *camote* fields is so rapid, however, that such fields are abandoned after several years. Still, the title remains with the clearers of the fields until the second growth of underbrush has reached the thickness that prevailed before clearing.

Abandoned rice fields may be taken up without permission by a person other than the owner for a period equal to the exact number of years they have lain unused. After that the title of the original owner becomes active once again. This certainly seems to be a sensible safeguard against withdrawal of needed land from production by overlanded gentry.[17] How different from the depression condition in California where squatting "Okies" were ejected from large idle holdings and their pitiful gardens destroyed!

The sound regulation that lands recently acquired from the public domain must be worked to retain title is a general and basic rule among primitive gardeners the world over. It effectively guards against one of man's besetting social evils—land hoarding by a wealthy few and the closing of the doors of opportunity to the land-hungry.

How fundamental the African and Indonesian land-use principles are in the primitive gardening complex can be seen from Titiev's comment on the Hopi Pueblo of Oraibi in Arizona:

The Village chief is the theoretical owner of all his town's lands; these lands are divided among the clans residing in his pueblo; and each individual farms a specified portion of his clan's holdings. In addition, there is a large piece of unassigned land, part of which may be used by any villager with his chief's consent. Under such a system land is never bartered or sold, and only rarely exchanged. Ownership is restricted to the privilege of use, but this right

[16] B. ter Haar, *Adat Law in Indonesia*, p. 88.
[17] R. F. Barton, "Ifugao Law" (*University of California Publications in American Ethnology and Archaeology*, Vol. 15, 1919), pp. 40–44.

is so carefully recognized that if a man decides to allow some of his fields to lie fallow, no other farmer may use them without the specific permission of the owner.[18]

Grazing land for sheep, goats, cattle, and horses is communally shared.

In summary: primitive gardeners assign the right of usufruct to individuals or families. In some instances, title is vested in the clan, but usually ultimate ownership is vested in the community. In parts of Africa this communism is transformed into a type of feudal monarchy, where the king symbolizes community entity. Unused land is public domain from which enterprising individuals may carve their plots, with or without official approval, depending on tribal practice.

On the whole, primitive peoples overwhelmingly treat their land resources as a communal asset. In this sense, they are preponderantly communistic. Pastoralists are, for the most part, land communists, because the necessity to rove makes individual ownership impractical. In the case of the hunters and gatherers, there is also little impulse to private ownership of land, since so far as the hunters are concerned most animals are free-ranging and it is more advantageous to rove at will when on the chase. When the habits of prized animals make it feasible, such primitives as the Algonquians and Northwest Coast Indians are quite ready to abandon land communism for vested rights. The primeval savage is not by nature a communist. But he is unwittingly Marxist enough to respond to ecological and economic determinism when it is advantageous to do so and when noneconomic values do not block it.

Theories of social evolution that assume "primitive communism" as the first mile on man's rough road thus have some foundation, so far as use of the basic land resources go.

People among us who take the institutions of private property for granted are prone to point to the widespread communism of primitive man as proof of the "advanced" quality of private-property institutions. Communism, they hold, is representative of a primitive state, and the spread of modern communism is a reversion to a condition of savagery.

With equal lack of balance many Communists see the land communism of the primitives as proof that communism is the "natural" and, therefore, the proper and manifest condition for human decency and social purity.

The anthropologist notes that the real-estate practices of primitives are not properly to be conceived as a justification for any particular eco-

[18] M. Titiev, "Old Oraibi" (*Papers of the Peabody Museum of American Archaeology and Ethnology, Harvard University,* Vol. 22, No. 1, 1944), p. 181.

nomic forms in modern civilization. They demonstrate merely that men can adjust their social institutions to the special needs of their subsistence technologies and natural resources and often will do so. Yet men are not always realistic about it, since emotional values may be quite as powerful as rational utilitarianism.

Game Food. Food is undoubtedly one of the most basic property interests of omnivorous man. Land may seem important, but that is largely because it is the chief original source of the food supply. We have already seen that some foodstuffs are in some societies free goods, as is the air we breathe. But elsewhere and oftentimes access to food is limited; the ethics of food use fluctuate. The sense of mutual aid and a realization of the inescapable interdependence of man to man struggle eternally with the self-assertive urges of bare-bones survival (when resources give but slim pickings) and selfish gratification of desires. Selfishness corrupts altruistic ideals; mutual aid tempers the harshest self-interest.

Property rights in food are the formal crystallization of each society's struggle to regulate the distribution and use of this basic essential.

Wild plants and animals on communal lands are communal property. But the slaying of game and the collection of plant stuffs alter the economic condition of these goods, subjecting them to altered property statuses. So it is that while the general principle of collective ownership of free-running game and unharvested plants holds good, we find that in most instances the expenditure of work in reducing the game and plants into consumable food stocks converts them into private property. All peoples recognize private ownership of food. Yet inasmuch as private ownership never entails absolute exclusiveness and since among hunters and gatherers the food is derived directly from communally owned resources, the communal claim upon privately owned foodstuffs is insistent.

Among the Comanches anyone coming upon a hunter who had just made a kill could claim the choicest quarter of the animal merely by placing his hand upon it. If four different people happened on the unfortunate hunter, they took everything except the hide. This, custom decreed, he could retain by hanging onto the tail of the beast. Far to the north Boas recorded as typical for the Baffin Land Eskimos, "Who first strikes a walrus receives the tusks and one of the forequarters; the next man, the neck and head; the following, the belly; and each of the next two, one of the hindquarters." [19]

[19] F. Boas, *The Eskimo of Baffinland and Hudson Bay* (American Museum of Natural History, Bulletin No. 15, 1907), p. 116.

Again, in the practice of the Comanches, any hunter returning to the camp with game was obliged to come in openly and to share his spoils with all who came to his lodge for a share in it. "If a man won't give it away, they camp on him until he does." To frustrate this social lien on the products of their individual efforts some families camped alone during hard times.

After the communal antelope hunts of the Plains Indians, the meat was equally divided among all participating families, for the whole project was a gigantic cooperative undertaking. In communal bison hunts, after the acquisition of horses, all Plains tribes allowed each man whose marked arrow had killed a bison to keep the meat. But even so, the old and infirm who could not hunt and the wives of luckless hunters received their shares from those who had, and it was the usual thing to teach a boy to give away all of his first kill of any large game animal.

Sharing of food, even though privately owned, is the basic virtue of almost all American Indian tribes and of most of the primitive hunters of the world. To be generous with food, that is the ideal. But as Lowie has pointed out, etiquette which demands that all comers be fed from a man's private larder is something quite different from actual communal ownership of a common hoard by all the members of the group.[20] The psychological and social response to private beneficence results in a different order of social prestige ranking than is produced by common ownership.

Outright pooling of food occurs less commonly among the hunting and collecting peoples than it does among the gardeners. In the South Pacific it is associated with prestige competition between local groups and tribes. Great quantities of produce are offered to the chief to be used in feasting rival tribes. The chief's storehouses among the Maori, for example, were the people's storehouses, for the people identified his needs as their needs. They were regularly fed from the great storehouses, but above all their great concern was that the chief should be able to entertain visitors munificently. Should he fail in this, their outraged pride made them ashamed before the world. Eating was to the Maori the supreme pleasure, and only by the joint efforts of all could it reach the great heights they so cherished.

Communal pooling of certain foods is also characteristic of our Pueblo Indians. Annual rabbit hunts are held every fall. All men must participate as a religious duty. The dried rabbits are offered to the head priest-chief of the pueblo, who stores them in his house to be used in ceremo-

[20] R. H. Lowie, *Primitive Society*, p. 207.

nial meals and to be doled out by him to the poor and hungry families of his pueblo in time of need.

At the opposite extreme, certain Algonquian hunters of North America such as the Ojibwa demonstrate the ideological lengths to which rugged individualism in food procured from wild game can go. Says Landes,

> The game and fish that a man catches in the winter are his private property. When he returns with them to his lodge . . . he decides what to do with them. . . . When he gives game to his wife, . . . he has lost all claim to it. It is never said that he gives game to his wife for her use in making food and clothing for the family; but they phrase it that a man gives game to his wife and therefore the game belongs to her to do with as she pleases. . . . The wife now employs "her" property in the manufacture of food and clothing. She gives the finished product to her husband, immature children, and herself. When these gifts have been given, they become the property of the recipient.[21]

The Ojibwa are committed to individualism as an ideal. The fact that they operate an objectively cooperative economy does not daunt them in the least. For their purposes, they are what they think they are, although an anthropologist can tell them otherwise.

Among many hunting tribes, animals that have a fixed abode such as a hibernating bear, a bee, or the eagle are often seized upon as objects of private ownership, even where all other claims to animals are communal. The Nama Hottentot places a few broken twigs before a wild beehive, and a Sia Indian publicly announces the location of bee trees that he has discovered—not to invite others to find the way to the delicacy, but to warn them off. Eagle nests are privately owned among all the Pueblo Indians, so that eagles born in the nest belong to the owner of it. A Pueblo hunter who finds a bear's den marks it, and the bear is his to take in the spring.

Similarly, wild fruit trees in Indonesia and among many peoples of the South Pacific may be blazed or otherwise marked by an individual so that he alone may harvest the tree's yield. In the Melanesian area the tree is guarded by a magic charm that brings foul diseases to any violator of the property right of the owner. Ownership of such trees is usually divorced from the land upon which the tree stands. In some places it is even possible to own a tree that stands on another man's land.

Livestock. The word *chattel*, which means any object of personal ownership, is derived from the Old French *chatel*. The modern Anglo-

[21] R. Landes, "The Ojibwa of Canada," in *Cooperation and Competition among Primitive Peoples*, pp. 90–91.

American word *cattle* has the same origin. *Chatel* has its ultimate etymology in the Latin *caput*, or head. *Chatel* in ancient France referred to property of greatest value, head property. Cattle were so much the chief form of property among our pastoral ancestors that our specialized word for personal property grew from the same root.

This small fragment of word history formulates the universal principle of stock ownership among all primitive peoples. Cattle are chattels. Livestock is privately owned. The one great known exception was that remarkable progenitor of totalitarian socialism, the Inca Empire. Private citizens in Incaland could own up to ten llamas, but the vast majority of the beasts were state property. The wool collected from the state herds was stored in government warehouses, to be distributed annually in equal allotments to each family head.[22]

Grazing land among migratory primitive pastoralists does not economically lend itself to subdivision. Hence, as has been noted, it is usually communally held and used. But livestock comes in individual units to which individuals may readily attach themselves. Undoubtedly, there is a deep emotional impulse underlying this tendency. Domestication begins in a symbiotic relationship between man and animal that is fundamentally personal. It is most clearly seen in the affectionate relation between man and his dog, the first of the domesticated beasts. It runs through all herders in greater or lesser degree. Nuer men, when they have nothing more pressing to do, spend hours in sensuous contemplation of their cattle.[23]

"Some men," said Post Oak Jim of the Comanche herders of seventy-five years ago, "loved their horses more than their wives." Favorite horses among most Plains Indians were treated almost as members of the family. Among the Solomon Islanders and many other Melanesians, pigs are the chief objects of value. Most men in the Solomons cannot bring themselves to slaughter their own beloved pigs, so they manage to get meat for their great pork banquets in an exchange of pigs for pigs, or pigs for shell money for pigs.

In the history of mankind the domestication of animals has undoubtedly been a great stimulus to the development of private-property institutions.

Garden Produce. Ownership of foodstuffs produced by gardening tends generally to be vested in individuals or family households, but the lines are not drawn with universal consistency. Since most garden plots

[22] J. H. Rowe, "Inca Culture at the Time of the Spanish Conquest," in *Handbook of South American Indians*, Vol. 2, pp. 219, 267.
[23] E. E. Evans-Pritchard, *The Nuer*.

are worked under private usufruct or outright ownership and most of the expended effort is individual effort, harvests are commonly individually owned. Polynesian practices in contravention of this usage have already been noted, however. In the Keres-speaking Pueblos, just as rabbit hunts are communal duties, so is the planting and cultivating of the cacique's garden. The harvest is stored in the cacique's house for communal use.

Susu practices in Melanesia require that a man raise his crops on his sister's behalf. Since his sister's household is not his own household, he must in effect transfer the yams from his garden to the storehouses of his sister's husband. His storehouses in turn are filled in part by his wife's brother. What a man produces does not necessarily remain his own property.

Artifacts. Weapons and implements for individual use are ordinarily owned either by their creator or by their user. According to the *principle of individual effort*, proprietary ownership of movables is usually vested in the person who has wrought the object through the expenditure of individual effort. Primitive women ordinarily own the pottery they have modeled. A man owns the spear or ax he has shaped himself. There is to some extent a psychological identity between the artisan and his creation, as though it were an "extension of his personality." Most of mankind has recognized this identity and respected it by establishing protective devices in the form of personal-property institutions. Recognition of this aspect of property does not entail forgetfulness that social limitations on the rights of the individual owner are always present.

The personal attribute attached to property is an incorporeal element that is almost a property feature in itself.

Incorporeal Property. It no longer surprises us that nonmaterial things of value are objects of property in primitive society. It never would have surprised us at all if it had not been that our grandfather's generation and its predecessors were so smugly comfortable in their self-assurance that savages were of childlike mentality and that Europeans alone were capable of mental abstraction. Even to this day many legal historians cling pathetically to this absurd bolster to our egos in spite of conclusive evidence put forth by anthropologists.[24]

Thus, consider the case of a Plains Indian visionary who has fasted and sought supernatural power. A bear has appeared to him in a dream;

---

[24] Cf. R. H. Lowie, "Incorporeal Property in Primitive Society" (*Yale Law Journal*, Vol. 38, 1928), p. 551; also *Primitive Society*, pp. 235–243; also E. A. Hoebel, "Fundamental Legal Concepts as Applied in the Study of Primitive Law" (*Yale Law Journal*, Vol. 51, 1942), pp. 963–965.

it spoke to him and taught him four new songs. It also instructed him in the preparation of a rawhide shield to be painted with a bear symbol and other devices. The bear in the vision also instructed his tutelary that a shield made in accordance with the instructions would provide immunity in battle if the four songs were sung before an engagement began. The visionary has made a shield as instructed; he has sung the songs; his comrades have heard the words; and he has deliberately exposed himself to the missiles of the enemy, coming through unscathed. The value of the shield and the songs has been publicly demonstrated. The shield, as Lowie has made clear, is a material object that is clearly personal property. But the shield as such, in the culture of the Plains Indians, is of little value. What is of value in conjunction with the shield are the songs and the mystic power that the two engender together. The incorporeal property is the thing of worth. The complex of shield, song, and power may be transferred as a gift to son, nephew, brother, or friend (in at least one Comanche case which the author has recorded, the transfer had to be followed by a vision on the part of the recipient before the mystic power would become operative, however, and this may frequently be the case among other tribes). Or this same complex may be sold in a commercial transaction that has the qualities of contractual sale. In either case, the recipient may use the complex if he has properly acquired the rights through regularized transfer, but not otherwise. The consequence of unauthorized use of the shield and songs is that the usurper will most certainly be killed by enemy missiles, because of the punitive action of the supernatural power. But there is no reason to believe that the true owner may not recover the shield if it is stolen, and with it his enjoyment of the songs.

Certainly we have here a sufficiently large aggregate of rights denoted by ownership so that we may properly speak of them as incorporeal property. Thus, we find again and again that magic rites and charms, songs, dances, and names are the property of persons and groups of persons. Myths and legends may belong to lineages, as among the Indians of the Northwest Coast. These are objects of property in exactly the same sense as are our copyrights, patents, and "good will." After all, if a people is capable of creating intangible patterns for behavior, such as magic and songs, it is not a great step into the abstruse to attach protective social rules to these abstractions when and if they become objects of value.

CHAPTER 24

GIFTS, TRADE, AND INHERITANCE

Gift giving is a human activity of fundamental and universal social significance. It functions as a concrete symbolic representation of mutual interdependence among the members of a society, enhancing social solidarity and effecting a redistribution of economic goods. Psychologically it is an effective means of satisfying the ego of the giver; sociologically it serves as a means of prestige attainment.

Normally a gift is an outright transfer that alienates the donor's proprietary title. Anglo-American law requires that the donor must part not only with the possession but also with the dominion. It holds that a perfect gift is irrevocable. Among primitive peoples, however, there are circumstances in which the gift may be conditional. Thus in Africa bride price (which may from one point of view be looked upon as a highly formalized marriage gift) is conditional upon the production of offspring. Sterility may require the return of the marriage gift to the husband's family. The distinction between gift and purchase is often hard to define.

A pure gift should be a gratuity offered as a free enrichment of the recipient without desire for reciprocity. Only anonymous giving meets this ideal qualification, however. Motives for gift giving are many, and in all instances the donor receives some sort of return, be it no more than the self-gratification of his ego known to himself alone.

The fundamental key to gift giving is the reciprocity underlying all social relations. Each social action on behalf of others evokes, or is taken in expectation of, a reciprocal action. The passing of a gift is a beneficence that brings a return in expectancy. "Do unto others as you would have others do unto you" has positive as well as negative connotations.

Gift Exchanges in Primitive Societies. On the lowest level of culture the Andaman Islanders nicely exemplify primitive behavior in gift exchange. Movables are all privately owned by these people, yet no one may long possess a particular article.

When two friends meet who have not seen each other for some time, one of the first things they do is to exchange presents with one another. Even in the ordinary everyday life of the village there is a constant giving and receiving of presents. A younger man or woman may give some article to an older one without expecting or receiving any return, but between equals a person

346

who gives a present always expects that he will receive something of equal value in exchange. At the meetings that take place between neighboring local groups the exchange of presents is of great importance.

Almost every object that the Andamanese possess is thus constantly changing hands.[1]

Among our Plains Indians generosity was one of the highest virtues; accumulation of property was socially limited. Gifts of horses were constantly being made. Whenever a guest admired an object, his host forthwith made a gift of it. Sooner or later, a return gift was expected, but it did not have to be of equivalent worth. Chiefs above all other people were obligated to give, for this is one way of attracting and holding followers (as our own politicians well know). Cheyenne Indians today are reluctant to become chiefs in the old way now that they have become "Americanized." They do not want to have to give away their property. Political leaders among all people are in fact subject to the demands of compulsive giving. Marquesas Island chieftains, according to Linton, used the sexual favors of their wives as a form of gift to attract and hold their henchmen.[2]

Among many primitives, gift giving that builds into gift exchange marks every important crisis period in the individual life cycle or any other change of personal status. Birth, puberty, marriage, and death, entrance into a club or assumption of an office are called to public attention by the bestowal of gifts. The famous potlatches of the Northwest Coast with all their lavish expenditure of gifts center around such occasions. Contractual arrangements such as marriage call for immediate two-way exchanges, often extending over months.

Gift exchange of economic significance may border on trade. Yet it may be merely symbolic in nature when the rule of equivalence is strong. The person who takes a utilitarian view of our ceremonial gift exchanges on the occasion of the Christmas festival naturally thinks the whole business is silly. But he, poor soul, misses the point. Quite true, we all end up with a number of things we neither need nor want. Quite true, it would be more rational to offer gift certificates or even money to one's friends or family so they could then buy what they want and need. But how flat are such gifts! Their donors confuse the sociology of gift giving with economics. They forget that the gifts are symbolic of a social bond between giver and receiver. They represent a state of social relations and a set of emotions, not business.

[1] A. R. Brown, *The Andaman Islanders*, pp. 42–43.
[2] R. M. Linton, in *The Individual and His Society*, pp. 152ff.

Trade. The essential difference between trade and gift exchange is in their relative functions. In trade the emphasis is on economic redistribution. In gift exchange the emphasis is on social relationships. Trade rests on and fosters social interaction, but its main concern is with the distribution of goods. Gift exchange distributes goods, but its main concern is with personal relations.

Within small tribes there is little trade. Gift exchange suffices for the most part. The level of culture is also a factor of some influence. Simple cultures with little specialization of labor do not call forth much intratribal trade. It is primarily the high cultures with large populations that are capable of considerable specialization of effort among their members. Services and products are then available for exchange and trade.

However, virtually all societies, large and small, engage in intertribal or international trade. Every culture has its unique goods or possesses natural resources from which to supply materials not available elsewhere.

Salt-water shells find their way hundreds of miles inland in New Guinea and North America. In the Bronze Age, copper from Cyprus followed trade routes over all Europe. Beeswax flint from Grand-Pressigny, France, found wide use over all western Europe in Neolithic times. Melanesian inlanders trade vegetables for fish with the coastal dwellers.

Specialization based on custom rather than limitation of resources induces a good deal of trade. In New Mexico, Sia women make excellent pottery. The pueblo of Jemez, less than ten miles distant, makes none, although the same clays are available to both. Jemez exchanged corn for pots in the old days. Hopis trade maize with the nearby Havasupai for buckskins and paint, and maize for wood and wool with the surrounding Navajo. But within the Hopi tribe only the women of the pueblos on Second Mesa make coiled baskets, while those who live on Third Mesa make them of wicker; painted pottery is produced only on First Mesa.

The Crow Indians of the Plains were capable of growing tobacco. Indeed, they had a ceremonial organization, the Tobacco Society, whose interest centered around the growing of tobacco as a sacred ritual. Nevertheless, the nicotine plant was not grown for use, and common tobacco had to be obtained by trade with other tribes.[3]

In western Melanesia the Southern Massim own large seagoing canoes, which they could manufacture themselves but do not. Instead, they obtain them in trade from the tribes of the Northern Massim district.

Within the small group of Trobriand Islands local specialization is very marked. Two towns alone produce the red shell disks so valued in the *kula* exchange (see below). The people of the island of Kayleula

[3] R. H. Lowie, *The Crow Indians*, pp. 274ff.

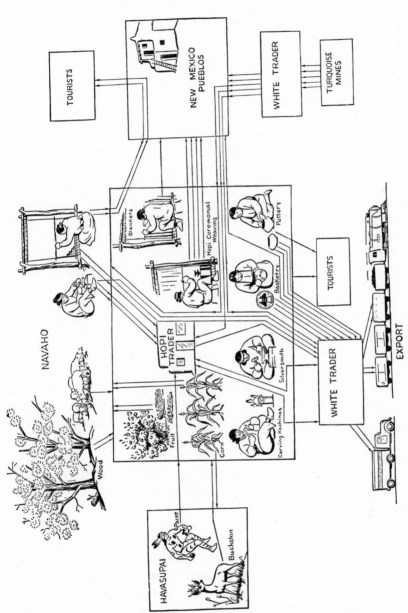

Fig. 71. Trade relations of the Hopi Indians. *(From L. Thompson and A. Joseph, The Hopi Way, p. 23.)*

make canoes and trade with the inhabitants of the western D'Entrecasteaux Islands for betel nuts, sago, pottery, and turtle shell.

To the east of the Trobriands the natives of Woodlark Island produce homogeneous greenstone for tools and the best carved ebony of the area; both of these products are valued objects of trade.[4]

Dumb Barter. It shocks many people to discover that businessmen carry on trade with enemy nations. A high command will deliberately spare certain enemy plants, because by means of trade through neutrals it is possible to secure products of those plants. Enemies not infrequently find it advantageous to let economic interests override their antagonisms.

This is the basis of the dumb barter, or silent trade, among certain primitives. The pygmy Semang of Malaya, for example, exchange forest products for goods offered by their enemies, the Sakai. Neither group sees the other party during the transaction. The Semang place their goods in a customary place and retire. When the Sakai find the offering, they appropriate the stuff and replace it with whatever they wish to exchange. Later the little Semangs come back to pick up the goods before retiring to their jungle fastness. In like manner, the Mountain Vedda of Ceylon trade game for iron arrowheads with the Singhalese smiths. They lay their game in front of the smiths' huts at night, to return the next night to gather the returns.

Heroditus describes how Carthaginian merchants carried on dumb barter with the natives of the northwest coast of Africa. The Carthaginians placed their goods on shore and retired to their ships, sending up a smoke signal. The natives came and replaced the goods with gold. Then they withdrew, while the Carthaginians came ashore. If satisfied, the Carthaginians reembarked and sailed away. If not, they returned to their ships and awaited more gold. They got what they deemed necessary, for the natives knew that if the mariners were shortchanged they would not return again.[5] Dumb barter still occurs in parts of Africa.

Markets. Open trade is naturally much more convenient, and primitive peoples often develop elaborate machinery for this purpose. In Nigeria huge market towns of great antiquity are in existence. Native artisans bring their brasswork, pottery, mats, baskets, leatherwork, and foodstuffs many miles to these trading centers. The Kede tribe of northern Nigeria acts as river transporters of trade goods, for the Kede are the consummate canoemen of the Niger. They carry kola nuts and palm oil

---

[4] B. Malinowski, *Argonauts of the Western Pacific*, Chap. 1.

[5] W. D. Hambly, "Source Book for African Anthropology" (*Field Museum of Natural History, Anthropological Series,* Vol. 26, Part 2), p. 650.

north from Nigeria, bringing back gowns, mats, fish, rice, horses, and potash from the Hausa and Nuse tribes.[6]

In Africa the market place is often under the magical protection of some great native chief, whose supernatural authority evokes the "peace of the market" so that enemy tribes may trade in safety.

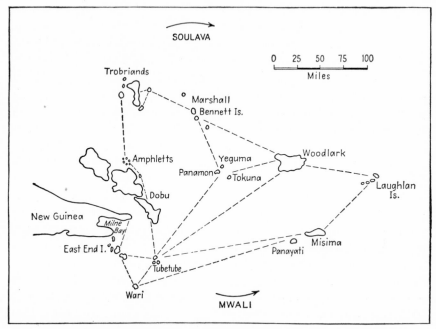

Fɪɢ. 72. The kula ring. Lines show overseas trade routes. Arrows indicate directions followed by necklaces (*soulava*) and arm bands (*mwali*). (*After Malinowski.*)

The Kula. Without doubt the most elaborate and exciting system of trade yet noted for the primitive world is the *kula* of northwestern Melanesia. Malinowski's thorough description of the kula will stand as a classic of anthropological economics for many years to come. The kula enterprise is a vast complex of trade, magic, ceremonial exchange, overseas travel, and pleasure seeking that involves the enterprisers of tribes many miles apart. The framework on which the whole organization rests is the exchange of white shell arm bands, called *mwali* (Trobriand), and long necklaces of red shell, called *soulava*. Exchange is intertribal and interisland. *Soulava* are always traded in a clockwise direction. *Mwali* go counterclockwise (Fig. 72). There is no exception to this rule.

[6] S. F. Nadel, "The Kede," in *African Political Systems*, p. 169.

Each of these articles [wrote Malinowski] meets on its way articles of the other class, and is constantly being exchanged for them. Every movement of the Kula articles, every detail of the transactions is fixed and regulated by a set of traditional rules and conventions, and some acts of the Kula are accompanied by an elaborate magical ritual and public ceremonies.

On every island and in every village, a more or less limited number of men take part in the Kula—that is to say, receive the goods, hold them for a short time, and then pass them on. . . . Thus no man ever keeps any of the articles for any length of time in his possession. One transaction does not finish the Kula relationship, the rule being "once in the Kula, always in the Kula," and a partnership between two men is a permanent and lifelong affair. . . .

The ceremonial exchange of the two articles is the main, the fundamental aspect of the Kula. But associated with it, and done under its cover, we find a great number of secondary activities and features. Thus side by side with the ritual exchange of arm-shells and necklaces, the natives carry on ordinary trade, bartering from one island to another a great number of utilities, often improcurable in the district to which they are imported, and indispensable there.[7]

Not all trade among primitives is by means of direct barter. Various media of exchange are known in several parts of the world. Shells serve most commonly as a species of money: cowrie shells in the Pacific area and in Africa; dentalium shells among the Indians of California. Wampum beads were used in exchange among our eastern Indians, and the early Dutch in New York treated them as good cash. Importation of poor counterfeits caused the city council of New Amsterdam in 1650 to pass an ordinance pegging the exchange value of good beads at six white and three black per *stiver*. Poor wampum was pegged at eight and four. Polished stone axheads and bronze celts were extensively used in late prehistoric times in Europe. Livestock—pigs in the Solomon Islands, cattle in East Africa—are used in such a way that they may properly be called media of exchange.

Iron hoes serve as a medium of exchange in parts of Africa, but the strangest of all primitive moneys are the huge limestone wheels of the Island of Yap in Micronesia.

Value. People engage in trade and commerce to obtain the things they value but do not have. Value is defined as "the believed capacity of any object to satisfy a human desire." [8] As such it is to be sharply distinguished from utility, because its reality is psychological and not in the object itself.

[7] Malinowski, *op. cit.*, pp. 82–83.
[8] H. P. Fairchild (ed.), *Dictionary of Sociology*, pp. 332–333.

Economists have been taught a hard lesson by anthropologists, *viz.*, values are by no means always rationally determined. Economic man, that creature of Adam Smith and classical economics, the wraithlike ghost of *laissez faire*, has been driven from the scene by anthropological facts.

Malinowski's analysis of the kula makes perfectly clear that the value of the shell necklaces and arm bands is largely nonutilitarian. Yet men work, plot and plan, and endanger their lives on overseas journeys to keep up the exchange. Utilitarian trade is carried on too, it is true, but only secondarily. The kula is for fun and prestige.

Plains Indians went on horse raids even after they had more horses than they could handle. The more horses the more glory and prestige to the brave—and the more fun!

East African cattle raisers milk their cows, but in the eyes of its owner and his neighbors the main value of the cow is its beauty.

Land is of basic importance to the gardeners of Indonesia, but the objects of supreme value are village and family heirlooms, gongs, jars, skulls, and queerly shaped stones, all of magical import. Such things are so valuable as to be without economic worth; they cannot be bought or exchanged.

Value is usually vested in those objects that satisfy basic drives. Value also arises from wants (acquired drives) that are not basic and not necessary to biological existence. This is especially true where value is attached to those things that bring social recognition and prestige. To mention the Trobrianders once more, they stint on eating that they may have food surpluses left to rot in their storehouses at the end of the year. To be able to raise more than you can possibly use—that is the goal of the "good man."

What is it that drives our businessmen on after they have all the wealth they can possibly personally consume?

Value is always enhanced by scarcity, but the scarcity need not be genuine. It may be artificially created and maintained in social attitudes. Yuroks have plenty to eat, but they teach their children that they must always rise hungry from a meal, that their resources must be hoarded, and that while eating they must not pay attention to food but concentrate their thoughts on wealth and more wealth.

In societies that have institutionalized emphasis on gift exchange, the main value of goods is not in themselves or in their possession but in the fact that one can give them away. Samoa is typical of most Pacific tribes. "Property is valued for its mobility, for its power of validating ceremonial and increasing prestige; there is no hoarding and no benefit given one generation by any accumulation of capital goods by the preceding generation." [9] In the Admiralty Islands among the people of Manus "recognition within the community goes to a man in terms of the amount of wealth which has passed through his hands." [10]

Inheritance. Inheritance, in the quaint wordage of G. D. H. Cole, "is the entry of living persons into the possession of dead persons' property." [11] That is one way of putting it. We prefer to say that inheritance *is the transference of a deceased person's rights in property to certain of his survivors.* Inheritance is thus linked to the institution of private property and exists only in connection with it. Communal property is non-inheritable for the reason that, although the group is constantly replenished by the addition of newly born members, the group is a continuum and there is no hiatus in succession.

In the simplest societies inheritance is poorly developed. Nomadic hunters and collectors have few goods. Most of these are the personal working equipment of a man or woman. Because of the universality of belief in an afterlife many primitives naively assume that the deceased want and need their goods. The result is, as Radcliffe-Brown has noted,

With us one of the most important aspects of succession is the transmission of property by inheritance. Yet in some of the simplest societies this is a matter of almost no significance at all. In an Australian tribe, for example, a man possesses a few weapons, tools, utensils, and personal ornaments, things of little value or permanence. On his death some of them may be destroyed, others may be distributed among his relatives or friends. But their disposal is of so little importance, unless in relation to ritual, that it is often difficult to find any rules of customary procedure.[12]

The same may be said of the African Bushmen, the Andaman Islanders, the Semangs, the Eskimos, and the Shoshones.

In the instance of the Comanches,

. . . in the disposal of a deceased's property there is but one rule which stood out with constancy: upon the death of a person all effects of his (or her) personal usage were destroyed. This included clothing, weapons, saddles, tools, paraphernalia, and horses customarily ridden by the deceased. . . . Further, even the tipi in which the dead person, man or woman, lived was totally destroyed; also for a child, but not for a baby. Articles of intimate

[9] M. Mead, *Cooperation and Competition among Primitive Peoples*, p. 294.
[10] *Ibid.*, p. 214.
[11] G. D. H. Cole, "Inheritance" (*Encyclopedia of the Social Sciences*, Vol. 8, 1932), p. 35.
[12] A. R. Radcliffe-Brown, "Patrilineal and Matrilineal Succession" (*Iowa Law Review*, Vol. 20, 1935), p. 286.

personal usage were buried with the corpse. Other less important articles were burned. Possessions with medicine powers were either destroyed by throwing them into the river, or by placing them in an unfrequented tree where they could rot.[13]

All Plains Indians had similar rules. Surpluses were variously handled. The Comanches passed the residual estate to the widow, who in turn was obliged to pass some of it on to her husband's friends and relatives, and especially to nonrelatives, who hung around as enthusiastic mourners; they mourned and mourned until they were given sufficient gifts to stop them. Inheritance by nonrelatives was, in point of fact, characteristic in the Plains area. A family that went the whole way in mourning made itself destitute, until in due time friends and relatives reoutfitted them with gifts.

On the lower levels of culture it is difficult to generalize inheritance rules with accuracy. Often there is no single rule of inheritance controlling all situations, or any single line of practice under any of the legal rules. Our canny Cheyenne informant, Calf Woman, cautioned, "Some families did differently than others."

In general, it may be said that husband and wife do not inherit from each other in the primitive world. This is an easily understood consequence of the nature of marriage as an alliance of two kin groups.[14] What is left by either spouse is more than likely to revert to the family or lineage from which he came. Men's goods are inherited by men, and women's by women. Two factors that are present on the primitive level are responsible for these conditions. The first is the absence or undeveloped state of a free market and money economy. Goods cannot be divorced from use with any appreciable degree of ease. They are not readily convertible into fluid capital. Therefore, they must be possessed by a competent user; the sexual division of labor bars inheritance of sex-linked property across sex lines. Secondly, in all primitive societies a person is more closely tied to his or her kinship group than to the marriage partner. The claims of surviving kinsmen outweigh the claims of the surviving spouse.[15]

[13] E. A. Hoebel, *The Political Organization and Law-ways of the Comanche Indians* (American Anthropological Association, Memoir 54: Contributions from the Laboratory of Anthropology, 4, 1940), pp. 120–121.

[14] *Cf.* R. F. Barton, "Ifugao Law" (*University of California Publications in American Archaeology and Ethnology*, Vol. 15, 1919), p. 26, for the Ifugao exemplification of this rule.

[15] *Cf.* R. F. Benedict, "Marital Property Rights in Bilateral Society" (*American Anthropologist*, Vol. 38, 1936), pp. 368–373.

In the event that a death is followed by a sororal or levirate marriage, the movable property of the deceased spouse stays right in the household of the surviving spouse, and the landed property remains in the relation to the survivor that it exhibited before the death of the spouse. But this is only because of the coincidence of identity of status between the deceased spouse and the one who replaces her (or him) in the household. The inheritance runs from deceased wife to her sister who replaces her, not from deceased wife to husband to his second wife.

Inheritance of usufruct in land follows fairly clear lines. Among matrilineal gardeners, where women till the soil, inheritance runs from mother to daughters. If the picture is complicated with matrilineal organization coupled with virilocal residence and male gardening (as in Trobriand), then inheritance runs from mother's brother to sister's son. In parts of Melanesia, although land is inherited matrilineally, fruit trees privately owned by males are inherited patrilineally.

Whether matrilineal or patrilineal organization prevails also strongly influences the lines of inheritance of movable and incorporeal property.

Patrilineal societies favor filial inheritance. Matrilineal societies favor inheritance from maternal uncle to sister's son. It is quite possible for a tribe to subject some forms of property to the avunculate and other forms to paternal succession. It is not necessary that the inheritance system be absolutely consistent with one principle or the other.

The sexual equivalence of brothers in marriage arrangements is reflected in the equivalence of brothers in relation to property. Thus *collateral inheritance*, or inheritance by brothers or sisters from brother or sister in preference to the children, indicates that the members of a fraternity have a solidarity that supersedes that of the conjugal family. Plains Indians applied this rule to the inheritance of horses especially. The generation tie outweighs the filial or avuncular. This may well be reinforced in political inheritance of chiefship, where it is advantageous to avoid letting the mantle of leadership fall on a callow youth.

Incorporeal properties, especially magic formulas and medicine powers, must be partially transferred before death, if they involve secret knowledge. A man may transfer his charms or songs to son or nephew as a gift or without anticipation of his departure from life. In such an event we have a gift *inter vivos*, not properly a matter of inheritance. Or, it may be that the necessary knowledge is taught without transfer to the beneficiary of the right of use until after the death of the donor. Then we have a true case of gift *causa mortis*, gift made in the prospect of death and properly an aspect of inheritance.

Testamentary disposition, or verbal wills, are general among primitives, contrary notions of orthodox legal historians notwithstanding. But such devices are troublemakers, for so far as can be determined with the limited evidence at hand, few primitives have developed clear rules for the execution of wills or have officials charged with disinterested responsibility in their execution.

Primogeniture. In societies of growing populations given to gardening or agriculture on limited land resources, there is always the problem of dispersal of the family holdings through inheritance by too many heirs. Primogeniture is the solution hit upon by some peoples. All property devolves upon the eldest son, who then has the duty to support the other members of the family in exchange for their labor. "A family must have a strong center," say the Ifugaos. Primogeniture more often applies to inheritance of chiefship and office, however, than to landed property. The *mana* of the Polynesian chief passes to the first-born son in an unending line. So strong is the primogeniture rule among the Maoris of New Zealand that on occasion a first-born woman takes a man's name and the status of a first-born son.

Primogeniture can be a force in an expansionistic movement. Power and glory are available to second-born sons who found new lineages by leading a group of colonists to unsettled territory.

The evidence is clear for the Maori, and we may infer that primogeniture was a force in Polynesia that worked to drive younger sons out on overseas expeditions of exploration and colonization.[16]

How much of the brunt of empire building was born by the younger sons of Britain who were shut out at home by the laws of primogeniture? In the classical laissez-faire economics of nineteenth-century England primogeniture was hailed as a double-acting social device: it avoided inefficient division of the family inheritance and it forced the younger members to fend for themselves, thus enriching society by their efforts. Those primitives who practice primogeniture recognize the first of these benefits, but it is unlikely that the second ever entered their conscious thoughts. Primogeniture is not much favored in the western world today. Feudalism is gone, and enterprise capitalism is not favorable to primogeniture.

There are a few tribes that turn the tables completely about. By means of *ultimogeniture*, or the mimorat, the youngest son inherits the greater portion of the family estate. Among certain peoples of India,

---

[16] B. W. Aginsky and P. H. Buck, "Interacting Forces in the Maori Family" (*American Anthropologist*, Vol. 42, 1940), pp. 195*ff*.

Asia, and Africa, the elder brothers are set up with herds or households in part by family resources used in bride purchase. What is left over at the father's death tends in cases of ultimogeniture to go to the youngest of them all on the ground that he is the least likely to be well set up in life.

In concluding a discussion of primo- and ultimogeniture a note of caution should be sounded. The vast majority of societies adhere to neither of the set rules.

E. Social Control

CHAPTER 25

LAW AND THE SOCIAL ORDER

"If your subject is law, the roads are plain to anthropology," for "it is perfectly proper to regard and study the law simply as a great anthropological document. The study pursued for such ends becomes science in the strictest sense." Such is the judgment of one of the greatest jurists of the age.[1]

The analytical study of law is a social science called *jurisprudence*. The practice of law is a trade or a profession according to the level on which it is practiced. Just as advanced medicine rests on medical science, so must the practice of law rest on juridical science. Anthropological jurisprudence is a branch of juridical science that treats of law as an instrument of society created by man for the use of man. Law has its existence solely in and through society. "The life of the law has not been logic; it has been experience."[2]

What Is Law? To seek a definition of law is to set forth upon a quest for the Holy Grail. Anyone who has made the search will readily sympathize with the lament of Max Radin, "Those of us who have learned humility have given over the attempt to define law."[3] However, if there is a science of law, there must be a determinable body of phenomena for it to study. We must have some idea of what constitutes law.

Law is obviously a complex of human behavior. The problem is, What kinds of behavior? What sets off legal behavior from that which is nonlegal or other than legal?

Anthropologists must turn to the students of law for assistance in answering these questions. At the very outset the anthropologist must rid himself of the strange notion that a field worker going out to study a primitive culture must have no preconceptions about the nature of social

---

[1] O. W. Holmes, Jr., "Law in Science and Science in Law" (*Harvard Law Review*, Vol. 12, 1899), p. 443.

[2] O. W. Holmes, Jr., *The Common Law*, p. 1.

[3] M. Radin, "A Restatement of Hohfeld" (*Harvard Law Review*, Vol. 51, 1938), p. 1141.

institutions for fear that he may warp the behavior of the primitives into a mold cast in the image of our civilization. He has seen how the early Spanish recorders made a Catalonian monarchy of the Aztec empire when in fact it was something quite different. He knows how easy it is to phrase primitive property concepts in terms of our values when the property institutions of the primitives may have an entirely different quality. He fears that if he has *any* preconceptions about legal institutions, he may find himself seeing and phrasing primitive law in terms of our modern experience and not in terms of the primitives'. As a canon of method the kernel of this caution is eminently sound. A social science has always to struggle to keep the biases and cultural compulsives [4] of its formulators under strict control. But the flowering of this germ into a rejection of all preconceptions is a rank weed of noxious quality. Without preconceptions, *i.e.,* hypotheses, properly shaped and properly used, a scientist has no tools with which to work. He cannot see, for he cannot organize, interpret, or test what he does see. Specifically, if he has no idea as to what constitutes law, he will be unable to see law. He should not forget that the very reason anthropologists are able to draw attention to much in primitive society that misses the eye of the ordinary layman is just because anthropologists have already learned a good deal of what to expect and look for before they ever visit a primitive society in the field.

If, then, it is imperative that we have a suitable conception of what may constitute law or be significant in relation to law, we may properly put the question, What is it that makes law law?

It is not legislation, despite contrary notions of typical code-trained European lawyers. Most primitive law is not legislated, and modern sociological jurisprudence and legal realism from Holmes down have made it perfectly clear that much of modern law is not legislated either.[5] English jurisprudence has long since given assent to this point of view, as witness the remarks by Salmond:

> But all law, however made, is recognized and administered by the Courts, and no rules are recognized by the Courts which are not rules of law. It is therefore to the Courts and not to the Legislature that we must go in order to ascertain the true nature of Law.[6]

The now classic formulation of this concept of the nature of law is Cardozo's statement that law is "a principle or rule of conduct so estab-

---

[4] V. F. Calverton, "Modern Anthropology and the Theory of Cultural Compulsives" in *The Making of Man*, pp. 1–41.

[5] O. W. Holmes, Jr., "The Path of the Law" (*Harvard Law Review*, Vol. 10, 1897), p. 457.

[6] J. W. Salmond, *Jurisprudence*, p. 49.

lished as to justify a prediction with reasonable certainty that it will be enforced by the courts if its authority is challenged." [7]

This behavioristic concept of law gives the anthropologist a handle he can grasp, but it is still not enough. For if we think of courts in our traditional manner, *i.e.*, a formal sitting of professional judges, with bailiffs, clerks, and advocates, we must conclude: no courts, no law. This is what bothered Max Radin, who well understands the anthropologist's problem, and perhaps led him to assert,

> But there is an infallible test for recognizing whether an imagined course of conduct is lawful or unlawful. This infallible test, in our system, is to submit the question to the judgment of a court. In other systems exactly the same test will be used, but it is often difficult to recognize the court. None the less, although difficult, it can be done in almost every system at any time.[8]

Max Radin is right. But what sort of courts does he have in mind? Some courts are difficult to identify. Anthropologically, they may be regularly constituted tribal courts such as the tribal council of an American Indian pueblo sitting in judicial capacity, or a court of the West African Ashanti, constituted of the chief, his council of elders, and his henchmen.

That type of primitive court is not hard to recognize. Any member of the American Bar Association would readily see it for what it is. But a more obscure type of court may be found in the Cheyenne Indian military fraternity. Consider the case of Wolf Lies Down, whose horse was "borrowed" by a friend in the absence of the owner. When the friend did not return from the warpath with the horse, Wolf Lies Down put the matter before his fraternity, the Elk Soldiers. "Now I want to know what to do," he said, "I want you to tell me the right thing." The fraternity chiefs sent a messenger to bring the friend in from the camp of a remote band. The friend gave an adequate and acceptable explanation of his conduct and offered handsome restitution to the complainant in addition to making him his blood brother. Then said the chiefs, "Now we have settled this thing." But they went on, half as a legislature, "Now we shall make a new rule. There shall be no more borrowing of horses without asking. If any man takes another's goods without asking, we will go over and get them back for him. More than that, if the taker tries to keep them, we will give him a whipping." Can anyone deny that the Elk Soldiers were in effect sitting as a court for the entire tribe? The test is first, one of responsibility. That they knew. It is second, one of effective

---

[7] B. N. Cardozo, *The Growth of the Law*, p. 52.
[8] Max Radin, *op. cit.*, p. 1145.

authority. That they achieved. It is third, one of method. Unhampered by a system of formal precedent that required them to judge according to the past, they *recognized* that the rule according to which they were settling this case was *new*, and so announced it.[9]

Among the Yurok Indians of California, as typical of a less specifically organized people, the court was less definite, but it was nevertheless there. An aggrieved Yurok who felt he had a legitimate claim engaged the services of two nonrelatives from a community other than his own. The defendant did likewise. These persons were called *crossers*, because they crossed back and forth between the litigants. The litigants did not face each other in the dispute. After hearing all that each side offered in evidence and argument the crossers rendered a judgment on the facts. If the judgment was for the plaintiff, they rendered a decision for damages according to a well-established scale that was known to all. For their footwork and efforts each received a piece of shell currency called a *moccasin*. Here again we have a court.[10]

On an even more primitive level, if an aggrieved party or his kinsmen must institute and carry through the prosecution without the intervention of a third party, there will still be a court, if the proceedings follow the lines of recognized and established order. There will be then at least the compulsion of recognized legal procedure, although the ultimate court may be the bar of public opinion. When vigorous public opinion recognizes and accepts the procedure of the plaintiff as correct and the settlement or punishment meted out as sound, and the wrongdoer in consequence accedes to the settlement because he feels he must yield, then the plaintiff and his supporting public opinion constitute a rudimentary sort of court, and the procedure is inescapably legal.

Consider the Eskimo dealing with recidivist homicide. Killing on a single occasion merely leads to feud, inasmuch as the avenger enjoys no recognized privilege of imposing the death penalty on the murderer or his kinsman with immunity against a counterkilling. A feud, of course, is an absence of law, since blood revenge is more a sociological law than a legal one. But to kill someone on a second occasion makes the culprit a public enemy in the Eskimo view. It then becomes incumbent upon some public-spirited man of initiative to interview all the adult males of the community to determine whether they agree that he should be executed. If unanimous consent is given, he then undertakes to execute the

[9] For a full account of this case, see K. N. Llewellyn and E. A. Hoebel, *The Cheyenne Way*, p. 127.

[10] *Cf.* A. L. Kroeber, "Yurok Law" (*22d International Congress of Americanists*, 1922), pp. 511*ff.*

criminal, and no revenge may be taken on him by the murderer's relatives. Cases show that no revenge is taken.[11] A community court has spoken. Such are the kinds of courts Max Radin has in mind.

Although courts in this sense exist in most primitive societies, insistence on the concept of courts is not really necessary for the determination of law. The really fundamental *sine qua non* of law in any society is the legitimate use of physical coercion. The law has teeth, and teeth that can bite, although they need not be bared, for as Holmes put it, "The foundation of jurisdiction is physical power, although in civilized times it is not necessary to maintain that power throughout proceedings properly begun." [12] We would merely add to that declaration that it was not necessary to limit the latency of power to civilized times; primitive men often found that it was not necessary to display the power behind the law when the defendant acceded to proceedings carried through properly. Jhering has emphasized the factor of force in law. "Law without force is an empty name." Again, more poetically we find, "A legal rule without coercion is a fire that does not burn, a light that does not shine." [13] In this we agree.

But force in law has a special meaning. Force means coercion, which in its absolute form is physical compulsion. There are, of course, as many forms of coercion as there are forms of power, and only certain methods and forms are legal. Coercion by gangsters is not legal. Even physical coercion by a parent is not legal, if it is extreme in form. The essentials of legal coercion are general acceptance of the application of physical power, in threat or in fact, by a privileged party, for a legitimate cause, in a legitimate way, and at a legitimate time. This distinguishes the sanction of law from other social rules.

The privilege of applying force constitutes the official element in law. He who is generally or specifically recognized as rightly exerting the element of physical coercion is a fragment of social authority. It is not necessary that he be an official with legal office or a constable's badge. In any primitive society the so-called "private prosecutor" of a private injury is implicitly a public official *pro tempore, pro eo solo delicto*. He is not and cannot be acting solely on his own, his family's, or his clan's behalf and yet enjoy the approval or tacit support of the disinterested remainder of his society. If the rest of the tribal population support him

---

[11] For a type case, see F. Boas, *The Central Eskimo* (Bureau of American Ethnology, Annual Report 6, 1888), p. 668.

[12] O. W. Holmes, Jr., *McDonald v. Maybee* (*Supreme Court Reporter*, Vol. 37, 1917), p. 343.

[13] R. von Jhering, *Law as Means to an End*, p. 190.

in opinion, even though not in overt action, it can only mean that the society feels that the behavior of the defendant was wrong in its broadest implications, *i.e.*, contrary to the standards of the society as a whole. Thus it is in itself an injury to the society, although the group feeling may not be strong enough to generate overt and specific action by the group as a group and on its own initiative. However, the private prosecutor remains the representative of the general social interest as well as that which is specifically his own. This fundamental fact is ordinarily ignored in discussions of primitive law, and it is in this sense that we may say that the difference between criminal law and private law is a difference in degree rather than in kind, though there can be no doubt that some matters touch the general interest in fact and feeling much more vigorously than others in primitive law, *e.g.*, sacrilege, homicidal tendencies, and, frequently, treason.

Regularity is what law in the legal sense has in common with law in the scientific sense. Regularity, it must be warned, does not mean absolute certainty. There can be no true certainty where human beings enter. Yet there is much regularity, for all society is based on it. In law, the doctrine of precedent is not the unique possession of the Anglo-American common-law jurist. Primitive law also builds on precedents, for new decisions rest on old rules of law or norms of custom, and new decisions tend to supply the foundation for future action.

Hence we may say that *force, official authority*, and *regularity* are the elements that modern jurisprudence teaches us we must seek when we wish to differentiate law from mere custom or morals in whatever society we may consider.

Thus we may form a working definition of law that fits primitive as well as civilized law in the following terms: *a law is a social norm the infraction of which is sanctioned in threat or in fact, by the application of physical force by a party possessing the socially recognized privilege of so acting.*

It is necessary to qualify the element of application of physical force with the phrase "in threat or in fact," since substitutes for physical force are often used in the form of confiscation of property by means of damages or fines. But always there is the final resort of physical punishment, if the offender balks at confiscation or resists whatever other substitutes the law enforcers apply.

Recognition of the privilege of applying the sanctions prevents revenge reactions by the offender or his kin. Where this does not exist there is no legal law. Thus the so-called "law of blood revenge" unrestrained by social limitations is no law at all but is merely a social norm.

When the killing of a murderer by his victim's kinsmen leads to a counterkilling, and on and on, we have the reign of feud, not of law. Feud is internecine warfare. It is a form of anarchy, not order. Such is the present law of nations, which measured against the background of the world society is amazingly similar to private law on the primitive level.

Primitive law is predominantly private law. The concept of community of interests is not easily recognized by men on the more primitive levels of life. For them kinship is more real than society. The family and the clan are often preferred as the security group, as has been seen in an earlier chapter. Thus, offenses are more often seen and treated as injuries primarily to individuals and the kin group rather than as crimes against the society as an entity.

Eskimo Law. The Eskimos serve well as an example of law on the lowest levels of cultural development. The small Eskimo local group rarely numbers more than 100 heads. Its organization is based on the bilateral family, beyond which there is nothing. There is no lineage, no clan, no clubs of either men or women, and no government. Each group has its headman, he who is "tacitly, half-unconsciously recognized as first among equals"; he who is variously called *ihumatak* "he who thinks (for others)," *anaiyuhok* "the one to whom all listen," or *pimain* "he who knows everything best." The headman leads, but he does not govern. He lends direction to his people's activity, but he does not direct. No Eskimo will give an order to another; therefore the headman exercises no legal or judicial authority.

Many acts that we consider heinous are accepted as necessary by the Eskimos. Thus certain forms of homicide are socially justified and legally privileged. Infanticide, invalidicide, suicide, and senilicide fall in this category. They are all responses to the basic principle that only those may survive who are able, or potentially able, to contribute to the subsistence economy of the community. Life is precarious in the Arctic.

There can be few legal offenses against property among the Eskimos, since there is no property in land, and free borrowing of goods makes stealing pointless.

Eskimo law grows out of the aggressive status struggle that bedevils the men. The society is wholly democratic, but prestige rivalry among the men is strong. Status is attainable by superior hunting skill and by stealing the wives of other men. The better the reputation of a man, the more likely he is to have his wife stolen. The reason behind wife stealing is not primarily sexual. An Eskimo can enjoy sex without running the risks involved in home breaking. The motive lies in an attempt to out-rank the man whose wife he takes, if he can get away with it.

Wife stealing is not a crime, but most litigation arises from it. The challenge results either in murder or wager of song, wrestling, or buffet-ing. Rasmussen found that all the adult males in a Musk Ox Eskimo group had been involved in murder, either as principals or as accessories; "the motive was invariably some quarrel about a woman." [14] The fact that Eskimo husbands will lend their wives does not mean that they are free of sex jealousy. If a man lends his wife, he enjoys the prestige of a giver of gifts. But if another man assumes sexual rights without permis-sion, that is adultery and an assault on the husband's ego that cannot go unchallenged. Murder must be revenged, sooner or later. And since it is usual Eskimo custom for the killer to marry his victim's widow and to adopt his children, a man may raise the boy who will slay him when he comes of age.

The alternative to killing an aggressor (and thus becoming involved in feud) is to challenge him to a juridical song contest. In the manner of Provençal troubadors of the thirteenth century, the two litigants scur-rilously abuse each other with songs composed for the occasion.

> Now I shall split off words—little sharp words
> Like the splinters which I hack off with my ax.
> A song from ancient times—a breath of the ancestors
> A song of longing—for my wife.
> An impudent, black-skinned oaf has stolen her,
> Has tried to belittle her.
> A miserable wretch who loves human flesh.
> A cannibal from famine days.

Like amateur night at the local theater, he who receives the most ap-plause wins. Thus is the case settled without reference to the right or wrong of the case. But what is more important, the dispute is laid to rest.

Recidivist homicide, excessive sorcery (which is *de facto* recidivist homicide), and chronic lying are crimes punishable by death under the procedure described earlier in this chapter. Such is the nature of rudi-mentary law in the Eskimo anarchy.[15]

Comanche Law. Comanche Indian law ways represent a somewhat higher development on the same general plane as Eskimo law.

The Comanches had chiefs, both civil and military. The band was

[14] K. Rasmussen, *Across Arctic America*, p. 250.

[15] E. A. Hoebel, "Law-ways of the Primitive Eskimos" (*Journal of Criminal Law and Criminology*, Vol. 31, 1941), pp. 663–683.

larger than the Eskimo local group, and the Comanches had considerable property, especially in horses.

They shared with the Eskimos a fierce drive toward male dominance and competitive rivalry among males for status by means of wife stealing. To this they also added the road of military glory. The Comanches recognized nine common legal offenses against the individual, *viz.*, adultery, wife absconding, violation of levirate privileges, homicide, killing a favorite horse, sorcery, causing another person to commit suicide (a form of homicide), failure to fulfill a contract, and theft.

Homicide called for the killing of the offender by the aggrieved kin of the dead man. This was a true legal penalty inasmuch as custom prevented the kin of the man so executed from retaliating.

Adultery and wife absconding were handled variously, but in every case the aggrieved person was forced by public opinion to act. He could, and often did, proceed directly against the erring wife, killing her, cutting off her nose, or otherwise mutilating her hapless body. This was a husband's legal privilege. Or, if he preferred, he could collect damages from the male offender. This would be done by a direct demand. Whether he got what he first went after or not depended on how courageous the defendant was. If the aggrieved husband, on his part, was not strong enough or fearless enough, he could call in his friends or kinsmen to prosecute for him. But then "the lawyers got the a' of it." Or, lacking kin and friends, he could call upon any brave warrior to prosecute for him. Great braves were willing, for prestige reasons, to do this without any material recompense whatever.

The Comanches recognized no clear-cut types of criminal offenses. There are a couple of cases, half-legendary, of obnoxious sorcerers who were lynched, which indicates that excessive sorcery was a crime. Unlike most Plains tribes, the Comanches did not consider violation of the rules of the communal buffalo hunt to be a clearly defined crime.[16]

Ifugao Law. The Ifugaos represent yet another interesting example of law on the primitive level of organization. These mountain-dwelling head-hunters of Luzon possess no government worthy of being called such. Over 100,000 tribesmen live scattered throughout the deep valleys that crease their rugged homeland. Although there are clusters of houses in the more favorable spots, they have not even formed true villages, nor do they have a clan organization. But the bilateral group of kinsmen is tightly knit. In the course of centuries, the Ifugaos have carved the steep

---

[16] E. A. Hoebel, *The Political Organization and Law-ways of the Comanche Indians* (American Anthropological Association, Memoir 54; Contributions from the Laboratory of Anthropology, 4, 1940).

walls of their mountains into stupendous rice terraces fed by intricate irrigation systems. Their paddies are privately owned and protected by a complex body of substantive law. Ifugaos are capitalists who have many legal rules controlling credit and debt. In addition, they are litigious in the extreme, for each man is sensitive about his "face" and quick to take offense. Their list of possible legal wrongs is long indeed.

How do they handle a legal case? A man with a grievance or a claim tries first to exact a satisfactory settlement from the opposite party. Failing this, he must go to a *monkalun*, a man of the highest social class, who has a reputation as a man of affairs and a number of enemy heads to his credit. The *monkalun* hears his story. Next he accosts the defendant with the charges. The defendant in turn pleads his cause. Meanwhile, both plaintiff and defendant are marshaling their fighting relatives—just in case. The *monkalun* shuttles back and forth between the two parties, wheedling, arguing, threatening, cajoling—attempting to induce them to give ground so that they may meet on terms acceptable to each. Customary law makes the penalties and obligations of both parties quite explicit for every conceivable offense. But first there must be agreement on the exact nature and degree of the offense. Claim must be balanced against counterclaim. Each side weighs the fighting strength and inclination of the other. But at long last, if the patience of the *monkalun* and the litigants endures, a settlement is reached and damages are paid (if it is an assault case) or the debt is satisfied (if it is an economic dispute). But if no settlement satisfactory to each disputant is reached, the *monkalun* finally withdraws from the case. Then the plaintiff or his kinsmen undertake to kill the defendant—or any convenient kinsman of his. Feud is forthcoming. The creaking legal machinery has broken down.

The *monkalun* represents the public interest by his intervention. Yet he is only incipiently a public officer. He makes no decision and enforces no judgment, but he provides the means through his good offices of bringing disputants to a resolution of their conflict. All Ifugao legal offenses are wrongs to be prosecuted by the aggrieved individual. There are no recognized crimes against society at large.[17]

Cheyenne Law. The Cheyenne Indians represent a more mature and sophisticated development of law on the middle level of primitive society. The state was well organized. It had a large tribal council of civil chiefs with a ten-year tenure of office. There were no clans, but military societies flourished.

Adultery was still a private wrong, but most rare. Wife absconding

---

[17] R. F. Barton, "Ifugao Law" (*University of California Publications in American Archaeology and Ethnology*, Vol. 15, 1919).

was not culturally countenanced and gave little cause for trouble. Prestige drives in Cheyenne life had been effectively socialized or turned against the outside world. A man made his aggressive record against enemies, not against fellow tribesmen.

Homicide was a sin and a crime. As a sin it corrupted the viscera of the killer, which "rotted within him," so that he gave off a putrid odor. His stench was obnoxious to the buffaloes, who shunned the Cheyennes, so that starvation threatened. What is more, murder still pollutes the four sacred Medicine Arrows that are the tribal fetish. Blood gets on the feathers. And while blood is on the Arrows, bad luck dogs the tribe. To purify the Arrows and clear the air, two things must be done. In the old days, the great tribal council sat in judgment. The murderer was exiled. Then an impressive ceremony of purifying the arrows was performed before the whole tribe—with the exception of murderers and their families.

Such a system makes blood revenge, feud, and capital punishment impossible. The Cheyennes in their own way had found the means to suppress internal disruption without recourse to autocracy.

Violation of the rules of the annual communal buffalo hunt was summarily punished by the military society in charge of the occasion. The culprit's weapons were destroyed and his horse beaten. But if he showed contrition, the very men who punished him bestowed free gifts upon him to set him once more on the road to right living. The Cheyennes understood that the purpose of punishment is to correct and reform.[18]

Ashanti Law. Finally, the Ashanti of West Africa may be cited as a primitive people well on the road toward civilized law.

The Ashanti are a powerful nation with a constitutional monarchy. Clan feuding has been checked and all private law brought within the potential jurisdiction of the royal criminal courts. Any private dispute ordinarily settled between the household heads of the two disputants can be thrown into royal hands by the simple device of one of the quarreling persons swearing an oath on the Great Forbidden Name of a god that the other is guilty of an offense against him. In rebuttal his adversary swears on the same forbidden name that he did not commit the wrong. One or the other is guilty of a false oath—perjury. This act is a capital crime for which the liar must lose his head.

Whoever hears the swearing must arrest the two, for every citizen is the king's agent in such an event. He leads them to a log kept for the purpose and chains them to it, after which he trots off to the king's bailiff with the news. A day for the trial is set. When hauled before the

18 Llewellyn and Hoebel, *op. cit.,* Chaps. 4–7.

king and his council of elders, each litigant tells his story. The stories are repeated verbatim by the king's speaker, and each affirms the accuracy of the repetition. So is the issue joined. Now one or the other of the prisoners before the bar names a witness. He is brought forth to swear a deadly conditional curse that what he shall say is the truth of the matter. In this the Ashanti place implicit faith, for the whole trial hinges on what is now said. On the testimony of the single witness, one party is freed and the other condemned to be beheaded—unless the king in deference to the needs of his treasury allows the luckless one "to buy his head," *i.e.*, pay a fine.

Aside from this crude but remarkable device for extending the king's peace, there is also a great body of criminal regulations, every one of which is punishable by death. These range from homicide—"only the king may wield the knife"—to carrying a chicken on top of a load. Even suicide is a capital offense. It constitutes a usurpation of the king's exclusive right to kill. The corpse of the suicide is hauled into court, tried, and decapitated. As a more practical gesture, his properties are also confiscated on behalf of the king.

Ashanti criminal law overreached the mark in much the same way as the law of eighteenth-century England with its 200 capital crimes. It is significant as an example of the way that monarchy becomes the means of expressing the social interest in the maintenance of order by replacement of private law by criminal. This is a genuine social advance over the chaos of societies that allow feuding.[19]

The Growth of Law. Modern jurisprudence has much to tell the anthropologist about leads for the study of the formation of law through the processes of litigation. Sociological jurisprudence points up the fact that breach and disputes in conflicts of claims are the most constant source of the law. "Breach," says Seagle, "is the mother of law as necessity is the mother of invention." [20] On the authority of Holmes we have it that "a law embodies beliefs that have triumphed in the battle of ideas and then translated themselves into action," and in the same vein Pound has written, "The law is an attempt to reconcile, to harmonize, to compromise . . . overlapping or conflicting interests." [21] Law exists in order to channel behavior so that conflicts of interest do not come to overt clash. It comes into existence to clear up the muddle when interests do clash. New decisions are ideally so shaped as to determine which inter-

[19] R. S. Rattray, *Ashanti Law and Constitution.*
[20] W. Seagle, *The Quest for Law*, p. 35.
[21] R. Pound, "A Theory of Legal Interests" (*American Sociological Society, Publications,* Vol. 16, 1920), p. 44.

ests best accord with the accepted standards of what is good for the society. Of course, it is unfortunately true that tyrants, usurpers, and pettifoggers can and do pervert the ends of law to their own designs without regard to social interests or prevailing standards of what is right.

As a canon of realistic law it may be said, and this is particularly important for anthropologists, that unless a dispute arises to test the principles of law in the crucible of litigation, there can be no certainty as to the precise rule of law for a particular situation, no matter what is said as to what will or should be done. A law that is never broken may be nothing more than an omnipotent custom, for one will never know more than this until it is tested in a legal action.

The role of the claimant is the most important single factor in the development of law in primitive societies. Numerous writers have commented upon the relative absence of legislative enactment by primitive government. Lowie, who is distinguished among American anthropologists for his unique contributions to the study of legal phenomena, has offered a general statement that is fairly typical of the prevailing opinion: ". . . it should be noted that the legislative function in most primitive communities seems strangely curtailed when compared with that exercised in the more complex civilizations." [22] Salmond parallels this with the statement that "the function of the State in its earlier conception is to *enforce* the law, not to *make* it." [23] Lowie continues, "All the exigencies of normal social intercourse are covered by customary law, and the business of such governmental machinery as exists is rather to exact obedience to traditional usage than to create new precedents." [24]

Now this would be true for wholly static societies, but, as Lowie would be among the first to acknowledge, no society is wholly static. New exigencies always arise. One thing permanent about human society is its impermanence. Especially when strange cultures come into contact do new materials, new ways of behaving, and new ideas enter into the cultural picture.

These new elements are not usually adopted simultaneously by all members of the society. The inevitable consequence is that when some members get new goods and new ideas, they have new interests for which the old lines of the culture have made no provision. Their use of their new acquisitions almost certainly comes into conflict with the old standards held by others. New custom and new law must then be generated.

[22] R. H. Lowie, *Primitive Society*, p. 358.
[23] Salmond, *op. cit.*, p. 49.
[24] Lowie, *op. cit.*, p. 358.

However or by whomsoever the judgment may be rendered in any dispute, it is the claimant and the defendant who lay the grounds of the claim and counterclaim or denial. If one or the other does it skillfully, soundly, and wisely, the basis of decision is likely to be found in his statement of his claim. No matter how selfish the motivation of a disputant may be, unless he be a fool indeed, he poses his claim against the background of "right" social principles, general rightness, and the well-being of the entire social group. How else can he gain enduring social acceptance of his position? Naturally, also, the more skillfully he argues his case in terms of the consonance of his claim with the well-established principles of social order, the greater the probability that he will shape the law as he wishes it to be determined.[25]

Evidence. Any lawsuit or criminal trial involves at least two questions. Is the alleged offense an illegal act? If so, is the defendant guilty of the offense? The first is a question of law. The second is a question of fact. If the first can be brought to a negative answer, then there is no need to seek an answer to the second. The case must be dropped.

Assuming there is a legal rule covering the alleged act, how are the facts then determined?

On the lower levels of legal development the question of evidence is not of great importance. In a small community not much behavior is secret. As a Shoshone once commented to the author, "They just wait around. Sooner or later the facts will come out." In Comanche trials the question of guilt or innocence was rarely raised. The usual point of argument was only the extent of damages.

Judges or prosecutors with skill in cross-examination or detectives with mastery of the techniques of scientific investigation are not of the primitive world. Extortion of confessions by third-degree methods occur in a few tribes, as in the case of the Comanche husband who could choke his wife or hold her over a fire until she named her lover. But more commonly the primitive man when he cannot get at the facts by direct means has recourse to the supernatural.

Divination is the most common device. An Eskimo seer ties a thong around the head of a reclining person, or a bundled coat, or even the diviner's own foot. When the proper spirit has entered the object, the

[25] Many examples of this process may be found in Llewellyn and Hoebel, *op. cit.*, or in J. Richardson, *Law and Status among the Kiowa Indians* (American Ethnological Society, Monograph 1, 1940). Because Cheyenne and Kiowa societies were undergoing rapid change during the period covered by these studies, the process of judicial lawmaking was more intensified than is the case in more stable cultures.

questions may be put. As it is hard or easy to lift, the answer is "yes" or "no."

Among many North American Indians, the still surface of water that has been put into the abdominal cavity of an animal reveals the image of the culprit. "Just as easy as reading a newspaper," says Post Oak Jim, the Comanche. Trobriand Islanders dig up the newly buried corpse of a dead person to see what signs it may reveal. Maggots mean the lamented one was killed by the chief's sorcerer for having been too successful with women. If the lips are pursed, the same conclusion is indicated. Blotches of color on the skin mean he painted his house too ostentatiously for one of his social station, and so was done in by a jealous chief.

Conditional curse enters into trial procedure among almost all peoples. It is the assertion that always includes or implies the clause, "if what I say is not true, *then* may the supernatural destroy me." "You [Sun] saw me. May the one who lies die before winter." [26]

Even our own courts do not rely wholly upon our laws against perjury, since every witness must first swear a conditional curse—"So help me God." ("May God smite me, if I lie!") Or is it, since the laws of criminal perjury are more recent than the conditional curse, that the courts do not have full faith in the efficacy of the curse?

Oath is merely a formal declaration that the testimony given is true. It may or may not imply the sanction of a supernatural power against falsehood. Often it is accompanied by a ritual act, as touching the pipe to the lips among Indians, or touching an arrow laid across the horns of a buffalo skull.

Ordeal is peculiarly rare in the New World, which was to the good fortune of the Indians, to say the least. But most of the hideous forms known to medieval Europe were practiced with variations throughout Asia, Indonesia, and Africa. The ordeal by hot iron with which Ibsen opens his historical play *The Pretenders* had its counterpart in Ifugao. Various Philippine tribes used the old technique of tying up the two litigants and throwing them in a river. He who rose to the surface first was guilty. Ordeal by poison is popular in Africa. In Ashanti the defendant to a trial may drink a poison brew. If he vomits, he is innocent. If he does not vomit, he dies. And that is proof enough for any man.

Trends in the Growth of Law. Law is a consequence of social differentiation and increasing complexity in society. Simple societies have little need of law, and on the earliest levels of human existence there were probably no legal institutions. In such rude groups as the Shoshones,

26 R. H. Lowie, *The Crow Indians*, p. 217.

Eskimos, Andaman Islanders, and African Bushmen there is little of what we would call law. Almost all relations in the tribe are face-to-face and intimate. The demands imposed by culture are relatively few; child training is direct and comprehensive. Ridicule is keenly felt, for there is no escape in anonymity. Tabu and the fear of supernatural sanctions cover a large area of behavior. Special interests are few, for there is little accumulated wealth. Conflict arises mostly in interpersonal relations. Hence, homicide and adultery are the most common legal focuses. Sorcery as a form of homicide always looms large as an illegal possibility, but among the simpler peoples sorcery, which uses supernatural techniques, is usually met with supernatural countermeasures rather than with legal action.

Among the higher hunters, the pastoralists, and the ruder gardening peoples, the size of the group and the increased complexity of the culture make possible greater divergence of interests between the members of the tribe. Conflict of interests grows and the need for legal devices for settlement and control of the internal clash of interests begins to be felt. Private law emerges and spreads. It exerts a restraining influence but, like the clan, it has inherent limitations that prevent it from completely satisfying the need it must meet. As no man is competent to judge his own cause, procedure under private law leads too often not to a just settlement but to internecine fighting. A society that is to advance beyond the limited horizons of barbarism must master the feudistic tendencies of kin-group organization.

Experience in the development of other branches of culture is also accompanied with experience in the manipulation of the social-control phases of culture. Instruments and devices of government are created. To a greater and greater extent private law is replaced by public law. The state and its agencies corrode away the family and its legal powers. "Through all its course," the development of society, wrote Maine, "has been distinguished by the gradual dissolution of family dependency and the growth of individual obligation in its place." [27]

The individual takes his place in a legal system sustained and operated almost wholly under public control. The kinship element is not dead in modern civilization but it is much reduced in relative importance, and government and public law have filled much of the space formerly occupied by it.

The next development is clearly the final emergence of an area of law framed and administered by a world commonwealth. Ultimately, it

[27] H. S. Maine, *Ancient Law*, p. 163.

shall be this or regression. Today primitive law prevails between nations. By and large, what passes as International Law consists of no more than normative rules for the conduct of affairs between nations as they have been enunciated and agreed upon from time to time by means of treaties, pacts, and covenants. In addition, a body of prevailing custom in international intercourse, recognized by tacit consensus or verbalized in arbitration, World Court awards and United Nations decisions, provides the other main source of its substance. But this body of social norms for international intercourse is as yet no more than the by-laws of the sub-groups we call nations. International law now consists of substantive rules without imperative legal sanctions.

The United Nations today, like the League of Nations of yesterday, because the power of universal coercive, absolute force is withheld from it, cannot make law of the international norms upon which it determines. Whatever the idealist may desire or the nationalist fear, force and the threat of force remain the ultimate power in the implementation of law between nations, as it does in law within the nation or tribe. But until the use of force or the threat of force as now exercised by nation against nation are brought under the socialized control of a world community, by and for world society, they remain not the sanctions of world law but the instruments of social anarchy and the constant threat to the survival of present civilizations.

The metamorphosis from primitive law to modern on the plane of international intercourse awaits the emergence of the consciousness of world community by all men. If the fulfilment comes in our times, it shall be our happy destiny to participate in the greatest event in the legal history of mankind. If not—

CHAPTER 26

GOVERNMENT

The only kind of society that could be said to be without political organization would be one consisting of a single bilateral extended family within which there were no organized subdivisions. Sex and age differences would be present, to be sure, and there would be one or two religious specialists. But the society would be organized as a single large family operating under familial controls. All problems would be settled as family problems, and there would be no other divisive groupings within the community. Family and community would be one.

This kind of society is approximated among some of the simpler primitive peoples, as the Shoshones, but it exists nowhere among men today, nor has it been observed to have existed since written records have been kept.[1]

Political organization comes into being wherever societies are segmented on the basis of kinship, economics, religion, sex, fraternities, or community. Where there are subgroups that are discrete entities within the social entirety, there is political organization—a system of regulation of relations between groups or members of different groups within the society at large.

The State. It follows that where there is political organization, there is a state. If political organization is universal, so then is the state. One is the group, the other an institutionalized complex of behavior.

Whether state and society are one has long vexed political philosophers. The social scientist sees no problem here. The state is but an aspect of society, the group organization of society when seen from the angle of the political control of its members and its formal relations to other societies. Thus, as Linton observes, the tribe is a social entity marked by a sentiment of community due to common culture, while the state is a political entity marked by common governmental organization.[2]

Although we often speak of the state in terms of government, the

[1] "Among all known people—the autonomous, land-owning socio-political group is greater than the bilateral family." J. H. Steward, "The Economic and Social Basis of Primitive Bands" in *Essays in Anthropology in Honor of Alfred Louis Kroeber*, p. 333.

[2] R. M. Linton, *The Study of Man*, p. 240.

state is more than mere government. It is the organized association of men (the group) for whom a specialized suborganization functions to transmute state policy into social action. Thus I, a citizen, am a member of the state, but I am not a part of its government in a strict and formal sense. Government is to be thought of as the practicing executive instrument of the state. Says MacIver, "When we speak of the state we mean the organization of which government is the administrative organ." [3]

In simple democratic societies of the order of the early New England town, the personnel of the state and government are nearly identical. This is true of the simplest primitive societies. But in complex societies with highly developed political structures serviced by special functionaries it is quite otherwise.

A variety of grossly defined labels are applied to different forms of states in terms of the preponderant power sources in the matter of control of the governmental machinery:

1. *Oligarchy* is that state whose government is controlled by a small group within the larger society.
2. *Monarchy* vests power (in theory at least) in one man, the king.
3. *Gerontocracy* puts governmental power in the hands of the old men as a class.
4. *Democracy* retains control in the hands of a large part of the people.
5. *Theocracy* leans to supernaturalistic domination of the government by priests or other religious specialists endowed with sanctity.

Such labels must be used with caution, for they are apt to be quite misleading in that they induce us to oversimplify the pluralistic nature of the state in which a multitude of divergent interests meet and merge or clash. African monarchies have all the external appearance of absolute autocracies. But if an observer centers attention on the powers of the royal elders, he will emphasize their oligarchic nature. Yet the "voice of the people" is also so insistently heard by the rulers as to give a strong democratic tinge to the functioning of the monarchy.

There are also classifications of states based on the size and composition of the politically organized unit. These may be ranged in an ascending scale in which each higher unit presupposes the existence of those below it (see diagram on page 378).

The Local Group. The local group is the seedbed of all statism. In face-to-face relations in the daily round of life it is the first group beyond the family to which personal loyalty is attached. In the *esprit de corps* of the local group lies the germ of patriotism. It is the simplest

[3] R. M. MacIver, *The Web of Government*, p. 31.

unit of territorial organization known to man, and it is presumably the only territorial unit of society known to early humanity as it emerged from apehood to manhood. As we see it among the lower contemporary tribes—the Shoshones, Eskimos, Andaman Islanders and all other Negritos, the Bushman, and Australians—the local group is autonomous and politically sufficient unto itself. It is bilaterally organized and, due to male dominance and hunting ecology, is usually patrilocal. It is autonomous, or nearly so, maintains communal property claims to its recognized territory, and is nomadic *within* its defined land area. It is small and com-

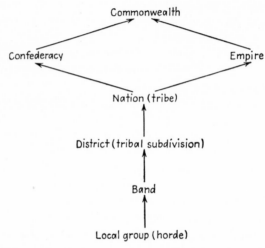

pact (20 to 100 persons) and usually holds 100 or more square miles of land.[4] Because all members of the local group are usually close relatives, the Bushmen, Negritos, and Australians prescribe local group exogamy. Eskimos and Shoshones do not force exogamy on a locality basis, but anyone within three degrees of relationship is tabued as a mate. Local groups may share a common culture with other local groups within a tribe and be part of a larger society. Yet they may be so discrete that it is scarcely proper to speak of them as constituting a tribe. This is certainly true of the Shoshones.

New local groups come into being through fission. Small groups break off from parent groups and find a new territory to occupy. This may come about through increase of the population beyond the maximum sustainable with the food resources available in the traditional band territory. Or it may result from internal dissension. Or an ambitious political aspirant may draw off a group of followers when he cannot gain

---

[4] Cf. Steward, *op. cit.*

leadership ascendancy in his home group. These processes occur over and over, and it is likely that the peopling of the earth in prehistoric times was done more in this wise than in the wholesale migration of already established local groups.

The Band. When a new group splits off from the parent group it does not sever all ties with it. Its members carry the same old attitudes and habits of life. There lingers a certain amount of loyalty for the old group, although the new one has first claim on the affections of its members. Intermarriage is maintained, as well as other forms of social intercourse. Resources of the environment permitting, the local groups get together occasionally for ceremonial purposes and visiting. Sometimes they join forces for war and defense.

The impulse for the getting together of local groups springs basically from the desire to see new faces and old acquaintances, to enjoy the social pleasures that are possible in a large gathering, to break with games, dance, and ceremony the routine of everyday grubbing. Dance and ceremony in turn function not only to satisfy the psychic need for sociability but to reinforce the appetite for it by building up the feeling of unity between local groups. In the end they and the pressures of war solidify the local groups into bands: social units with political organization embracing a number but not all of the local groups within the tribe.

Shoshones live through the summer months in scattered local groups. Bands constitute the winter villages, which endure through the spring fertility ceremonies. Australian local groups gather for tribal initiation and fertility rites whenever the need corresponds with the accumulation of food surpluses.

Kirghiz herders gather in band villages during the winter months and spread out in local groups to find summer pasturage. Cheyenne Indians scattered in small local group camps to weather out the winter, gathered in great tribal conclaves for the early summer ceremonies, then broke up into band groupings for the remainder of the summer, finally to split into local groups again as fall arrived. Seasonal variations in food supply thus usually control the time and duration of band consolidation among the more precariously existing hunters and gatherers.

The Nation. A consolidation of local groups and bands into a permanent political organization, which embraces the whole tribe, produces the nation. The Cheyenne Indians with tribal council and tribal chiefs represent this stage.[5] A tribe may or may not be organized as a nation. The Cheyennes were but the Comanches were not.

[5] Cf. K. N. Llewellyn and E. A. Hoebel, *The Cheyenne Way*, Chaps. 7 and 8.

Confederacy. The union of two or more nations for purposes of war and peace produces a confederacy. Each, however, keeps a larger measure of its own identity and autonomy. Confederacy involves more than mere alliance, which is at best a temporary makeshift (as our recent wartime love match with Russia too potently demonstrates). It calls for a relatively permanent and moderately subtle wedding of interests and organizations among the several nations involved. Yet confederacy as a political device can never achieve enduring stability, since by its nature the component states reserve to themselves the right to place their particularistic interests above those of the united body. The thirteen American colonies quickly realized the fallibility of confederacy. After the years of confederation they had the wisdom to move on to federation in the greatest single act of political creation in all history. The inherent weaknesses of confederacy were the fatal defects of the erstwhile League of Nations, and they likewise constitute the crippling features that have doomed the present United Nations to impotence.

For all its shortcomings, confederacy is a social scheme that is not easily attained. Each nation is jealous of its own uniqueness. Voluntary sacrifice of self-determination comes hard. Outside of North America confederacy among primitive nations was rare indeed. Even on our continent few tribes attained it. But the Iroquois and the Southeastern Indians of the United States showed how it could be done even by illiterate savages, and confederacies were not unknown in Central and South America.

Empire. Consolidation of nations or tribes into large units of political organization through conquest by a dominant nation produces empire. In its most elemental form it is enough if even a single conquered tribe is brought under the continued controlling power of the conquerors. In its more usual and elaborate form empire involves a cluster of subjugated tribes drawn into the state system of the conquerors. Most empires are of this order, for once a victorious nation masters the technique of holding its victims in permanent subjugation and has tasted the fruits of its yield, it strives to extend its sway in an ever-increasing scope.

Empire is found only on the higher levels of primitive culture. The conquerors must have a well-knit political organization to give coordination to their military adventures, and above all they must have enough political centralization to be able to set up and maintain an administrative system over the conquered peoples. Further, the cultures of one or both of the tribes must have attained at least the gardening stage of economy so that the labor of the subject peoples can be utilized to produce food or handicraft surpluses for appropriation by the master nation. Tribute is the goal of empire.

Empire in the long run tends to be self-dissolving. It rests on force and may always be destroyed by force. Revolt is an ever-present possibility. Other power states eye rival empires as juicy plums. If only they can displace the ruling group within the empire structure, the fruits of the exploitative organization are theirs for the harvesting. Aside from destruction from without, however, social processes work continuously within the empire to transform it. The end result is either a stabilized conquest state with caste organization or a commonwealth. Primitive peoples ordinarily arrive at the first solution. Modern empires tend toward the second.

In Africa, given sufficient time, as also in ancient India, the empire fuses into a higher type of tribal organization in which the conquerors become a ruling caste and the various subjugated tribes lower castes or social classes.

Caste and conquest states are exploitative states. The Marxist definition of the state as a system of politico-economic domination by one class for the exploitation of another aptly applies to them. But the Marxist desire to make of this a universal definition of the state leads to false conclusions from false premises. The state on lower levels of primitive society is not of this order. Nor are the states on the higher levels of social organization necessarily so. The Leninist dictum that in a classless society the state will wither away and die may be true of the state defined solely in terms of class exploitation. But when we see the state as a social organization whose function is to determine general social policy for the social whole, an organization equipped with privileged power to enforce social policy, it will be recognized as an inevitable and continuing feature of the social life of men.

Governmental Functions. The basic function of law is, as has been seen, to resolve conflicts of interest between individuals and groups within a society. In its internal activities this is also one of the important functions of the state. For this reason, the state assumes more and more control over the legal system of a society as its culture becomes more complex and the possibilities for interest conflicts between members increase in number. Every person and subgroup naturally strives to influence the state to make its decisions in terms favorable to the ideas and interests of that person or group. They do this through legislative action and pleading cases at law. Every legal disputant argues his claim in terms of its being in harmony with the established usage of the tribe and what is right custom. The state decision goes to one party or the other, and as Holmes once remarked, "There never has been a judicial decision that did not hurt somebody."

Within the limitations imposed by social restraint, it is obviously desirable to acquire as much control over the judicial and state machinery as is possible. Decisions will then be made according to principles harmonious to your own interests and concepts of right rather than the other fellow's. A large part of political struggle in any segmented society is of this order. The political goal is to get in the driver's seat with your hands on the control levers of the governmental machinery. Politics *is* in a broad sense the process of determining who gets what, when, and how.

Thus the state, which is a cultural creation to meet general social needs through government, is always in danger of having the government captured by special interest groups who undertake to usurp the power of the state to their own limited ends and interests. Because the instrument of the state is socially endowed with physical force, the state in larger societies is easily susceptible to tyranny. There is less danger of this in small primitive societies where interests are quite homogeneous and the range of material culture is limited.

It is an eternal paradox of society and a basic sociological principle that increasing complexity of culture requires delegation of authority and specialized functions to professional or semiprofessional personnel, while on the other hand the specialized functionaries are always driven by self-interest to think and act as though the job exists for them, not they for the job. In government the struggle endures through the ages. The problem is how to give the governors sufficient power to do what needs to be done, while at the same time limiting their urge to abuse the power that must be put at their disposal. Government is a dynamic process in which no solution can be permanent. The price of liberty *is* eternal vigilance.

"The final justification of all government rests on the need for maintaining the superiority of the general interest without sapping the social initiative of the community." [6]

The Headman. The earliest and most primitive type of governmental leader is not the chieftain but the headman. Notions about patriarchal tyrants among lower primitives have little reality.[7] Of course, there is no

---

[6] F. M. Marx, "Administrative Ethics and the Rule of Law" (mss.).

[7] Promulgated a half-century ago by J. J. Atkinson in *Primal Law*, made popular by H. G. Wells's *The Outline of History*, utilized by S. Freud as the foundation for his unfortunate essay into anthropology, *Totem and Tabu*, and still clung to by psychoanalysts such as Theodore Reik in his *Ritual: Psychoanalytic Studies.*

way of knowing for certain just how Stone Age man disported himself, but at least we can observe the general characteristics of the primitive hunters that have survived into the modern age.

"The headman of a Chiricahua [Apache] local group can be thought of as a natural-born leader, one who earns the confidence and support of his neighbors. His influence is considerable, but it is of an informal nature." [8]

The leader is expected to speak on all important occasions. Among the Yavapai of Arizona, the headman was moderate in speech, stopped quarrels, and knew the best camp sites. People followed him because his personality won their confidence. Of the Comanche headmen, That's It sagely observed, "I hardly know how to tell about them; they never had much to do except to hold the band together." [9] That's It put his finger on it. The headman in the primitive world rarely has explicit authority; his functions are so subtle that they defy easy description. Yet he is the focal point of the local group.

As Harrasser notes among the Central Australians, the "chief is at most *prima inter pares* with few exceptions among the Dieri and in West Victoria." [10] Similar evidence comes from the Shoshones and the Eskimos. The Shoshone headman is called *tegwɔni*, which in its fullest sense means "good talk thrown out to the people." In western Alaska the headmen are those who "by their extended acquaintance with the traditions, customs and rites connected with the festivals, as well as being possessed of an unusual degree of common sense, are deferred to and act as chief advisers of the community." [11]

The simplest primitive societies are always democracies; rarely does dictatorial political leadership crop up among savages.

Chieftains. Complexity of social life sharpens the need for leadership and the delegation of responsibility. Societies that are developed enough to have a tribal state always possess chiefs. A chief is differentiated from the headman merely by degree of authority and social distinction. His position may or may not be inherited. His functions and powers are variable among different peoples.

[8] M. E. Opler, *An Apache Life-way*, pp. 233–234.

[9] E. A. Hoebel, *The Political Organization and Law-ways of the Comanche Indians* (American Anthropological Association, Memoir 54: Contributions from the Laboratory of Anthropology, 4, 1940), p. 18.

[10] A. Harrasser, *Die Rechtsverletzung bei den australischen Eingeborenen* (Beilageheft zur vergleichende Rechtswissenschaft, Vol. 50, 1936).

[11] E. W. Nelson, *The Eskimos about Bering Strait* (Bureau of American Ethnology, Annual Report 18, 1899), p. 304.

In North America it was unusual for a chief to have strong power. Great care was taken in many tribes to separate the offices of peace chiefs and war chiefs. Peace chiefs were the civil governors. Usually they were band or clan headmen elevated to the status of membership in the tribal council. They supervised internal tribal relations and had judicial powers over a few classes of crime. Most legal offenses, however, remained in the area of private wrongs to be settled by the parties concerned. Sometimes, as in the case of the Cheyennes, Omahas, and Iroquois, the civil chiefs were explicitly chosen for limited tenure. War chiefs were the heads of military fraternities, or a war chief could be any man who had an outstanding war record. Naturally, such war chiefs could make their opinion felt in the tribe, but they had very limited constitutional powers in the operation of the camp in peacetime. The most militaristic American Indians were astute enough to realize that military dictatorship is the greatest of all threats to the democratic way of life.

The main social functions of chiefs, it may seem strange to contemplate, need not be political. Yet there is really nothing strange about this, if we consider the King of England. His political functions have atrophied, but his symbolic and ceremonial functions evoke a stir of emotion in British hearts the world over.

In the primitive world the Trobriand chief enjoys high status and many privileges. Tribute must be paid him, but he utilizes it mostly to put on ceremonial feasts on behalf of his people. His functions are more to serve as a mainspring of ceremonial activity than as political officer.

This is true in greater or less degree for all of Oceania (even in tribes where chiefs stem from conquerors), for as Forde observes,

The origin and development of chieftainship in Melanesia is by no means clear, but everywhere the chiefs claim the same essential rights and powers. They are nearly always real or alleged immigrants who make similar claims to sanctity, superiority and to the control of valuable ritual.

The chiefs of the Sa'a people on the island of Ulawa, Solomon Islands, are aliens who established and maintained their position by arrogance and determination, who are regarded not as political directors but as feast givers and the controllers of certain ceremonies. "By the splendor of their feasts they enhance the prestige of their district and win the approval of the commoners who make gifts of food for yet more feasts." [12]

Exactly the same could be said of the Indians of the Northwest Coast of North America with their potlatching chiefs (see pages 296–299).

[12] C. D. Forde, *Habitat, Economy, and Society*, pp. 182, 183.

Hereditary Monarchies. Kingship results from the development of the hereditary tendency into a hereditary principle. Its main function is to introduce stability into the administration of government. Strong clans make for intratribal strife. The law of blood revenge must be superseded by a stronger law of the whole society. This can conveniently be the king's law and the king's peace. But the power of paramount chieftains is in itself a luscious prize for power-hungry men. With bloody intrigue and with turmoil in their struggles to project themselves into chieftainship they can rend the peace of the tribe. Clearly defined hereditary succession puts a check on such social abscesses. Yet the oftentimes fatal defect of the hereditary principle is that the heir to succession may have no aptitude for the job. The king may be a feeble weakling, or worse still, a dangerous egomaniac. In the one event, the state may fail to function effectively in times of crisis. In the other, tyranny supplants social justice, and men suffer under corruption.

Kingship is so common among advanced primitive societies that we must conclude that the need for centralized control outweighs the urge for democratic freedom at this level of social development. The resurgence of democracy comes later. But where democracy fails, the need for centralization produces dictatorship or fitful moves for the restoration of monarchy.

The hereditary principle is no thought-out device. It develops quite naturally and without conscious awareness. We can see this among those American Indian tribes who explicitly deny hereditary succession to chieftainship. In spite of the fact that any good man may become a chief, records show again and again that a chief is succeeded by one of his sons or maternal nephews. Chiefship runs in family or susu lines. This arises from the fact that the training and high example set by the senior relative give chiefly qualities to their boys.

People become habituated to expectancy of leadership from such lines. The boys assume that people will respond to their superior leadership—and they do. Eventually, the tendency may become a prescription.

In Polynesia and Africa primogeniture often fixes succession upon the eldest son. Yet most tribes maintain functional flexibility by leaving succession open to selection from among the chiefs' heirs by the royal council or the matriarch (in Africa, the Queen Mother; in Iroquois, the oldest woman in the lineage). This is a sound device except as it leads to palace feuds between the parties of the heirs who rely on the *coup d'état* to circumvent council deliberations. Civil war and temporary anarchy are the usual concomitants of the death of a monarch in many a Bantu kingdom. Indeed, as a precaution against this sort of thing the death of the king is often kept secret until his successor is chosen and everything is ready for the coronation.

Sacerdotal Chiefs and Kings. The skeins of religion and politics are composed of separate threads. They are woven into the tapestry that makes the web of society, sometimes carefully separated, each forming its own design, sometimes intertwined, joining church and state in one pattern. The warrior's sword and the magician's wand are different artifacts. A man may wield one or the other, but if he is skilled enough and if his culture permits, he may seize the sword in his right hand and the wand in his left. Then, indeed, he becomes a power to cope with. The essential doctrine of separation of church and state in American democratic tradition is a needful defensive reaction to that awful power.

Shamans and priests are specialists in controlling the action of the supernatural; headmen, chiefs, and kings are specialists in controlling the actions of men. But the actions of men must be controlled in their relations to the supernatural; the priest always has temporal influence. The politician uses religious means for political purposes when he is able to control religious power; the priest in turn is apt to use political means to attain religious ends when he has the techniques to do so. When either one has specialized his own peculiar techniques to a high degree and religious and political instruments are clearly developed, it sometimes occurs in the primitive world, as it so often does in the modern world, that rivalry and hostility between church and state is sharp. Among primitive men, however, a working agreement between the two often exists—as the Trobriand chief employs his hereditary sorcerer to destroy upstarts,[13] and the Yokuts-Mono chiefs in California connive with medicine men to mulct the guileless public.[14] On the other hand, use of supernatural power for self-advantage through black magic is almost universally treated as a deadly crime if carried too far.

In general, supernaturalism is so ubiquitous in the primitive world that it colors all government to a greater or lesser degree. Political officers almost invariably possess some magic power or religious sanctity. War making, legislation, and judicial procedure inevitably involve religious ritual.

In highly organized gardening societies of sedentary peoples dependent on fixed crops, the chief is usually the high priest of the rain, fertility, and garden cults. As he is the supervisor of politico-legal relations, so is he also responsible for the economic well-being and religious

[13] B. Malinowski, *Crime and Custom in Savage Society*, pp. 85–86, 92–93.

[14] A. H. Gayton, "Yokuts-Mono Chiefs and Shamans" (*University of California Publications in American Archaeology and Ethnology*, Vol. 24, 1930), pp. 361–420.

security of his folk. If his society is that of ancestor worshipers, as is usually the case in Africa and Oceania, he is also the ancestral viceroy on earth—his people's highest link to the ancestral spirits. He is himself a direct descendant of the gods and has godhood in him. In Africa, again and again, he symbolizes the tribal soul: a soul that must be hale and vigorous, else the tribe wanes and dies. Hence, the fate of the king who becomes feeble or ill is the poison cup or strangulation by his chief councilors.[15] It is no unalloyed privilege to be a ruler. Eminence entails responsibility.

The extreme sacredness of the god-king limits his activities. In Tonga (Polynesia) the *tuithonga* may not walk abroad, for where he places his foot, that earth becomes tabu.

The Talking Chief. "A White House spokesman announced to-day. . . ." The device of presidents is a possession of primitive chiefs and kings the world over. The Ashanti king or the paramount chief of a district rarely speaks in public. To do so is bad etiquette and policy on his part. He has his *okeyame* to serve as his mouthpiece. Most African kings have a court mouthpiece. In Polynesia each chief has his Talking Chief, who recites his lord's genealogy before every meeting of the native "parliament." He speaks his chief's mind in debate. Kwakiutl and other Northwest Coast chieftains have their speakers at potlatches to extol the ancestry and virtues of their masters. Every Plains Indian peace chief had his crier, who announced decisions to the camp at large. His "loudspeaker," the Cheyenne interpreter, High Forehead, always called him.

The reason for these spokesmen is subtle but sound. When chieftains rise above the level of headmen their power increases. He who wields powers of decision and enforcement must not be too familiar to the multitude. Some good men can maintain influence and fraternity simultaneously, but they are rare. It is a safer and surer technique to let a minion undertake the vulgar task of shouting to the masses.

The Council. The one universal instrument of government is the council. No tribe or nation does without it. No man can govern alone, nor is he permitted to. Monarchy, if taken literally, is a misnomer. Every king or chief operates within the network of his advisers and cronies. Some are helplessly enmeshed in it.

In small primitive bands and tribes the council is a democratic gathering of adult males. In gerontocratic Australia participation is limited to

---

[15] *Cf.* J. G. Frazer, *The Golden Bough*, Chap. 24, "The Killing of the Divine King."

the elders. Elsewhere, it is mostly open to all the males. Among American Indians decision of the council had to be unanimous, and one stubborn holdout could block action. Still there were neat devices for attaining unanimity.[16] Tribal councils commonly consisted of all the band headmen or clan headmen, as the case might be. Among the Aztecs, for a special example, every family sent its headman to a clan council. Each clan council had a clan headman, a war chief, and a speaker. The speakers of the twenty clans formed the tribal council, which worked with the king and his executive officer, the Snake Woman, who was a man.

Among the great African monarchies the king bears the superficial appearance of absolute autocracy. Yet he can rarely act without council approval, and this is not forthcoming until the royal elders have sounded out tribal public opinion. Kings who abused their power could be deposed or destroyed in the old days.

Monarchy, like every other social relation, rests on reciprocity. If the exalted ruler receives great social privilege, he must give service to his people in return. Some kings and dictators forget it, but it is difficult for them successfully to ignore for long the sociopolitical principle voiced in the proverb of Bali: "the ruler owes his might to the people."

Nonpolitical Organizations in Government. It is simple-minded to think of government only in terms of the organs explicitly designed for governmental purposes. All government is pluralistic and various extra-state organizations play their part in determining and executing social policy.

The author for some years belonged to a small-town volunteer fire company. It is a closed fraternity, which elects its members by secret vote. It has all the trappings of a lodge: sworn secrecy, uniforms with gold buttons, rituals, dances, and ceremonial feasting. It also puts out fires. This "firemanic" fraternity is a private club that is at the same time an official agency of government. The costs of its equipment and meeting rooms are met by public taxation. It is regulated by public law and is controlled by publicly elected fire commissioners. It remains a club, and yet it is an organ of government, just as the Plains Indian military fraternities,[17] which have already been discussed in their social aspects in Chap. 21. Fraternity, feasting, dancing, and social enjoyment were the primary functions of these men's clubs. But they also took on police, judicial, and, ultimately, legislative powers when the need arose. The

---

[16] *Cf.* Llewellyn and Hoebel, *op. cit.,* pp. 91–93.

[17] R. H. Lowie, *Primitive Society,* p. 415; *The Origin of the State,* pp. 94–107; "Property Rights and Coercive Powers of the Plains Indian Military Societies" (*Journal of Legal and Political Sociology,* Vol. 1, 1943), pp. 59–71.

tribal councils constitutionally possessed all judicial and legislative powers covering criminal activity. However, the council chiefs were peace chiefs not given to coercive action. When coercive restraint or punishment was needed, they were not suited to the task. They were "fathers" to all the tribe, and Indian fathers do not punish their children. What was more natural than that the extragovernmental societies of warriors should take over policing the hunt, the rice harvest, the great tribal ceremonials of the sun dance? This they did with vigor and dispatch. In later years, as the Plains tribes began to crumble before the onslaught of the white men, the Cheyenne military societies assumed more and more governmental power as crisis piled on crisis. But to no avail; they were overwhelmed.

In Africa, as we have already seen, various secret societies among certain West Sudanese tribes imposed peace, collected debts on behalf of their members, and, in the case of the Egbo society, punished wrongs.

In Melanesia the numerous men's secret societies also directly and indirectly determine policy and operate as law-enforcing agencies.

Plains Indian military societies were not secret, and as a result their role in government was essentially democratic. It is quite otherwise with the exclusive secret orders of Africa and Melanesia. They are more akin to the Ku Klux Klan, Christian Front, and Columbians, who spring up in our midst to usurp the functions of the state and to corrupt democracy. That these extralegal bodies can sporadically attain a measure of success is testimony to the Hydra-headed nature of government in society.

CHAPTER 27

WAR—THE DEADLY ISSUE

Unfortunately for mankind, war is one of the great social institutions. Techniques of destroying fellow men, their homes and goods have concerned men from the beginning of human history. Indeed, a large part of the history of material culture and social organization has been the history of the development of lethal weapons and their application to human beings.

War may usefully be studied in three aspects: (1) the techniques of warfare, (2) the motivations underlying war, and (3) the consequences of war. Each of these shall be treated in turn.

By war is meant organized assault by one social group upon another with the intent to further the interests of the one group at the expense of the other through the willful destruction of life and goods. War is often, but not always, an extension of politics. Politics is also the mitigation of war—a substitution of ballots for bullets. It is not sheer whimsy to say that a politician "campaigns" for office, "attacks" his opponent, and "fights" a good fight—or a dirty one.

All kinds of fighting have something in common with war, as do all forms of social struggle. Nevertheless, individual brawls are not war. Nor are sporting bouts, even though people may be killed and goods destroyed. Feud, on the other hand, is a kind of war—internecine war—as is civil war within a society.

Regulated Combat. A number of primitive peoples engage in warfare by means of regulated or expiatory combat. This is common among the Australian aborigines, for whom the *makarata* of the Murngin tribe, as described by Warner, is a nice example:

When a clan has had a member hurt or killed, and when sufficient time has elapsed for their emotions to calm, the men send a message to their enemies saying they are ready for a *makarata*. The other side usually agrees to enter into this peace-making ceremony although there is always suspicion of treachery. The injured group always sends the invitation, and the other must wait for them to decide when they wish to have it. Very frequently *makarata* are held after some of the totemic ceremonies have taken place, since it is at that time most of the clans will be present. When the warriors of the injured clan or clans arrive on the dueling ground they are covered with white clay. They dance in, singing a song which is descriptive of the water of their totemic well. The other side has also painted itself. The two sides stand a little more than spear throwing distance apart, and each is so situated that it has a mangrove jungle back of it for protection in case the *makarata* becomes a real fight, and it is necessary to take cover. The clan which considers itself injured performs the dance connected with its chief totem. It is of the *garma* variety, or nonsacred form. The Waruweri clan, for instance, would dance the *garawark* (mythological fish) totemic dance, or the Djirin clan would perform its shark dance. The challenging group dances over to the people who have inflicted an injury upon it and stops, and without further ceremony walks back to its own side. After the men have reformed their ranks, their opponents dance toward them, using the latter's totemic dance for this military ritual. They return to their own side and reform their line to make ready for the actual duel.

The men who are supposed to have "pushed" the killers then start running in a zigzag manner in the middle of the field, while they face their opponents. They are accompanied by two close relatives who are also near kin of the other side. The function of the latter runners is to prevent spears from being thrown with too deadly an intent from the aggrieved clan for fear of hitting their friends who are running with the foe and to help knock down spears which might hit the actual runners. When the "pushers" run they are made a target for spears whose stone heads have been removed. Every member of the clan or clans which feels itself injured throws at least once at the men who are running before them. When an individual's turn to throw arrives, he advances from the group and moves toward the runners. He continues throwing spears if he feels very strongly about the matter until he has chased the runners into the jungle. This is repeated by the more indignant members of the offended clan three or four times. Finally, when their emotions have subsided to a considerable extent, one of the older men of the group says that they have had enough and the spear throwing stops. While the spearmen are still active the injured clan curses the members of the other group; the offending group cannot reply, for this is supposed to add additional insult. They must run and say nothing.

After the "pushers" have been chased and thrown at, the actual killers run. The spear head is not removed from the shaft; the throwers continue hurling their spears at them, at first as a group and finally as individuals, until they have exhausted their emotions. While all this is taking place the old men of both sides walk back and forth from one group to the other, telling the throwers to be careful and not kill or hurt anyone. The offending clan's old men ask the younger men to be quiet and not become angry, and when they hear insults thrown at them not to reply or throw spears since they are in the wrong. When the old men of the injured clan feel that they have sated their anger as a group they call out to the young men to stop, and each man then throws singly at the killers. He may throw as long as he pleases.

When this has been completed the whole group dances up to the other, and one of the latter jabs a spear through the thigh of the killer. If this happens it means that no further attempt will be made to avenge the killing of one of their members. The killers can feel free to go into the country of their enemies and not be injured. If only a slight wound is made they know that they are not forgiven and that this is only a temporary truce. Sometimes no wound is made at all. This acts as a direct statement of the intention of the offended clan to wreak vengeance on the other side.

After the wound has been made the two sides dance together as one group to prove their feeling of solidarity and to express ritually that they are not openly warring groups, but one people. They do the usual water dance.[1]

Among early American Indians quite similar practices occurred in California and in the Northern Plains. In prearranged fights among the Maidu of California both sides lined up out of arrow range, women and children behind the chiefs of both sides standing together on a knoll to watch the fun. When all was ready, the young men of the "defendants" advanced within range, unarmed. A volley of arrows was released against them. But because the men had been trained as artful dodgers since boyhood, no one would be hit. While they retired to get their weapons, the children of the attackers ran out to pick up the arrows for reuse. Next their fighters advanced to be shot at. So it went for hours, until at last some tired leaper was struck. At this, his side, defeated, broke and ran. The victors chased them with yells of triumph. Those who were caught were pummeled. Then it was over. Everyone returned to the battlefield. The women brought forth food, and both sides together enjoyed a peace feast—or was it a picnic? The victors paid compensation to the losers for having wounded their man.

Somewhat more serious but hardly more dangerous were the early fights on the northern Plains. When a group of Cree joined with the Blackfoot to make war on the Shoshones, about 1725, they spent a few days in speeches, feasting, and dancing before marching off to meet the foe. The Shoshones were ready for them. According to the account of Sankamappee, the Cree chief,

Both parties made a great show of themselves. After some singing and dancing, they sat down on the ground and placed their large shields before them, which covered them. We did the same. . . . Theirs were all placed touching each other. . . . Our headed arrows did not go through their shields, but stuck in them; on both sides several were wounded, but none lay on the ground;

[1] W. L. Warner, "Murngin Warfare" (*Oceania*, Vol. 1, 1931), pp. 445–447.

and night put an end to the battle without a scalp being taken on either side, and in those days such was the result, unless one party was more numerous than the other.[2]

And this was a battle in which some 800 men took part.

Such formal combats as we have just been discussing are not real warfare. They come closer to William James's "moral equivalents of war." They release aggressions harmlessly; they provide exercise, sport, and amusement without destruction; and only mildly is there any imposition of desires by the one party on the other.

At the opposite pole are the more common primitive assaults by ambush and assassination. Ruthless, cowardly guerrilla fighting is known among all the lowest Negritos. Among the more advanced Indians of the Northwest Coast, battles were rarely open and aboveboard. Attackers preferred to slip into a village in the early dawn to murder warriors in their beds and steal away their wives and children. Head-hunters of South America and the more primitive Indonesians prefer to waylay the unwary. Punan fighters of Borneo prefer to stick an enemy with a poisoned dart propelled from a blowgun in the hands of an assassin hidden beside the trail. For them, like the tribesmen of modern Iran, "war consists in pillage; they assassinate, but they do not come to blows." [3]

The Criteria of War. Such behavior is rudimentary warfare, but it hardly deserves to be called war. War is a complex institution that involves definite purpose and organized sustained assault. True war has four necessary conditions:

1. A group motive rather than merely individual ones
2. Leadership (command and direction)
3. Tactical operations (movement designed to bring the warriors to advantageous fighting positions)
4. Ability to sustain a series of assaults until the aim of the war is attained. On the highest levels of warfare, the ability to plan and carry through campaigns [4]

Weapons. The tactical operations of primitive warfare are many and varied. They are limited by the weapons the culture makes possible, although the same weapon can be handled in various ways. All weapons fall in three categories: projectile, shock, or a combination of the two.

---

[2] J. B. Tyrell (ed.), *David Thompson's Narrative of His Explorations in Western America, 1784–1812*, p. 329.

[3] J. de Morgan, *Feudalism in Persia*, p. 592.

[4] H. H. Turney-High, *The Practice of Primitive War* (The University of Montana Publications in the Social Sciences, No. 2, 1942), pp. 21–22.

All tactics revolve around the applications of the principles of projectile and shock. A war can be fought without projectiles, but few wars can achieve their ends without shock contact.

Any weapon that is hurled at an enemy from a distance is a projectile. The most ancient of all such missiles is the simple rock heaved in the direction of an adversary. In this case, the arm of man serves as a compound projecting lever of fairly limited power.

The South American *bolo* is one development of the simple stone projectile. It consists of a number of stones each sewn into a leather pouch fastened to a thong. The loose ends of all the thongs are tied together. The whole is hurled through space after swinging it overhead like a lariat. As it whirls through the air, centrifugal force keeps the stones spread out, so that it covers a wide striking area. Although it is effective in bringing down fast-moving animals and birds, the bolo has not had wide adoption as a primitive weapon. One obvious reason is that it can be used only in open areas and by widely spaced warriors.

Throwing sticks, such as the Australian boomerang, constitute another type of primitive projectile, but one of limited usefulness in war. Complicated multiedged iron throwing weapons such as those used by the Azande of Africa are more deadly, to be sure, but like the boomerang they are a poor kind of projectile. They are heavy to carry and wasteful to use.

Pointed shafts of wood, hurling spears, were the true heavy artillery of early primitive man. When Stone Age man learned to tip spears with barbed points of stone, bone, or reindeer horn, he set a pattern that spread to all continents of the prehistoric world and persisted through the civilizations of the classical world into medieval times.

However, the most efficient projectile of primitive man, serving as his light artillery, was the arrow sped from an elastic bow. Invented in the Neolithic, it was tipped with chipped-stone points in a variety of shapes. When bronze and iron were later invented, these materials supplanted stone. Among the Melanesians of the South Pacific, however, elaborately carved arrow points of wood are still made for war purposes. Many primitives of South America and the Pacific area add poisons to their arrow tips to increase their deadliness.

The bow and arrow is a development originating in the more primitive dart throwers (*atlatl*) found in common use among Central Americans and Eskimos. An arrow or dart is hurled with a bone or wooden lever, which serves as an extension of the human arm. Aesthetically carved dart throwers were made by Cro-Magnon man 20,000 years ago.

Catapults were not known to any primitives, for these clumsy engines of siege war were developed by the ancients of the Mediterranean. They served as mechanical and more powerful equivalents of the brawny, rock-heaving arm of the cave man.

Civilization's greatest projectile improvement has been, of course, the application of the expansive power of combustible materials to drive a missile through space. Primitive man anticipated it with the blowgun, the favorite weapon of the jungle tribes of South America, Southeastern United States, and Indonesia. The infantry rifle and the giant 16-inch naval rifles of our floating behemoths are nothing more than high-powered blowguns, exploding powder instead of breath.

German buzz bombs and modern rockets are further refinements of the projectile principle. An air-force bomber is the same. The plane merely sustains the projectile until over the enemy target when the bombardier releases his missile to gravity for delivery.

The function of all projectiles, called *fire weapons* in contemporary military usage, is to strike at, disable, destroy, and disorganize the enemy from a distance. They are a convenient way of getting at him with minimum risk.

In the hands of those primitive people who prefer assassination to genuine war, the projectile is a tool to be launched from a safe ambush. In the hands of braver men who understand the basic principles of warfare, primitive or civilized, projectiles function merely as a preliminary "softening up" of the enemy preparatory to decisive contact with the shock weapons.

Shock weapons are "the crushers and piercers which are held in the hand of the assailant." [5] They are the lethal tools of man-to-man contact. An armed body may be dispersed by projectile assault, but it is rarely destroyed by such. Smashing, close-in fighting by aggressive warriors is necessary to close the issue.

It is for this reason that in modern preatomic war the infantry was still the "Queen of Battles." Tarawa, Eniwetok, Iwo Jima, Okinawa—battleship, rocket launcher, and bomber pounded away for days, but it took shock troops to beat down the enemy yard by yard, hole by hole, from shore to shore.

Strategic bombing across the Channel did its part in destroying German supply and communication, but armored and infantry divisions had to force their way from Normandy to the heart land of the Axis to end

[5] *Ibid.*, p. 7.

the war in Europe. Projectile and shock together are the basic offensive techniques of all war.

It may be that atomic fission has changed the age-old principles of warfare, as it shall certainly change many centuries-old principles of social politics. It may be that atomic bombs, extensively used, will relegate shock weapons to the status of Boy Scout knives. Atomic bombs are basically projectiles, but their demonstrated shock power is so paralyzing that they may utterly destroy the enemy's will to fight, as apparently happened with the Japanese. Whether this will be so or not, when both antagonists are equipped with such weapons, remains to be seen, when and if men are so supremely human in their perversities as to put the matter to the test.

The basic shock weapon of primitive man is the war club or skull crusher. Popular fancy always pictures Stone Age man as a hairy ruffian with a big stick. Although no Paleolithic war clubs have survived for archaeological discovery, Cro-Magnon man did picture them on cave walls. Rugged wooden clubs are truly the most popular shock weapons of recent primitives. Tomahawks of hafted stone are functional brothers to them. Battle axes of the Bronze and Iron ages are descendants of the cruder clubs of the Stone Age, and the direct antecedents of the fancy battle-axes and maces with which medieval knights bludgeoned each other for the glorification of chivalry. The stock of an infantryman's automatic rifle has the same function when he swings it butt-end-to in close fighting.

The other great shock weapon is the knife in all its myriad forms. Stone knives with puncturing points go back to Paleolithic times. The dagger and sword are merely elongated knives. Of these the dagger and short sword have always been the more effective weapons. The sword has had its vogue, for the heft of so much metal in the hand gives a comforting assurance to its wielder. But the more self-confident and aggressive warrior who does not shrink from in-fighting prefers the greater efficiency of a dagger. Thus it is that to this day the combat knife is essential military equipment, while the sword has become nothing but the peacetime vanity of officers on parade.

The pike and spear have long contended with the sword and club for favor as shock weapons. Among some peoples, as North American Indians, the club and spear virtually supplanted the knife for shock purposes. The lance, like the sword, has the psychological appeal of apparently greater safety for its user, who can put a few more feet between himself and a redoubtable enemy. Yet there is a real advantage in the spear, for its very weight lends greater thrusting power. On the other hand, it is fatiguing for fast-moving troops to carry.

The bayonet, be it noted, serves either as a short sword, or, affixed to a rifle as it is supposed to be, this projectile tool converts into a good old-fashioned primitive pike. Spears ought best be used as pikes, not as javelins. When it comes to contact, a spear in the hand is worth twenty that have been thrown at the enemy.

Defensive Devices. Warfare is not all offensive action, even though the best defense may be offense. The truth of this military adage depends upon circumstances. However, fighters who shun such protection as may be reasonably devised are less likely to survive. Each inventive development of an offensive implement has trailed its shadow in a defensive counterpart. Military inventiveness has been a continuing race between new and better methods for killing men and effective means for nullifying their lethal effects. Wooden, wicker, and leather shields were the answers to the arrow, sword, and pike. Shields are world-wide in their distribution, although a few primitives fight without them. Modern fighters mount their shields on caterpillar tracks and call them tanks.

Body armor of slats of wood or leather was used by American Indians and Oceanic peoples, while those of Asia often employed heavily quilted suits. Only the African Negro consistently abjured the protection of any kind of armor.

When carried too far, recourse to body armor involves the sacrifice of mobility to bodily protection; or, perhaps, with the knights of the late Middle Ages the transformation of the noble warrior into a canned mannikin was due to an overelaboration of armor as a status symbol distinguishing the knight from the churl.

Helmets were at first an answer to the war club and sword. Their late revival is a response to shrapnel and the high lethality of head wounds among men who fight from trenches or foxholes.

Among primitive peoples, fixed defenses serve primarily as a hindrance to surprise attack and as a protection for the women and children. They slow down the assault of unannounced invaders long enough to enable the defense to organize itself. If the defense is purely defensive and obstinate, breastworks, palisades, and moats may enable the defenders to hold at little cost to themselves while at the same time inflicting severe damage to the attackers. They may force the attackers to withdraw in discouragement without bringing the issue to a successful conclusion. Thus defensive works may lead to a negative victory for the defenders. But fixed defenses are deathtraps for those who are content to hide behind them when the attackers are strong and persistent, for mobility and the initiative are then in the hands of the attackers.

The simplest primitive peoples pay scant attention to fixed defenses, on the whole, for this is precluded by their nomadic lives. Especially is this true of desert and steppe hunters and collectors as well as pastoral nomads.

Quite reasonably, settled gardeners and fishers often fortify their villages. Most Melanesians and Indonesians do not, but Polynesians, especially the Maori of New Zealand, palisaded their towns, as did the Eastern Woodland Indians of North America. Extensive earthwork embankments still survive from prehistoric times, as at Fort Ancient in Ohio. Even Plains Indians staked their tipis side to side when they expected a serious enemy attack.

Of all primitive men, the Pueblo Indians reached a defensive peak when they raised their doorless, windowless stone houses upon inaccessible mesas. Pueblos became the village citadels of pacifistic gardeners.

Motivations of Warfare. The ways in which people undertake the waging of war depends not only upon the tools they possess but also upon their social organization and motivations. The chief reasons for war among primitive peoples are not economic. Real or fancied grudges, the desire for revenge, extroverted antipathy, come first. Reciprocity, both positive and negative, is the basis of all social relations, and tit is returned for tat. In 1933 an old Comanche gave voice to this in the expressed desire to scalp a young anthropologist "because he looks like a German," and no one had brought old Mumseka a German scalp for the life of his grandson who had fallen in France in 1918.

"Those are the fellows we used to like to kill," said the Cheyenne, High Forehead, of the three Crow Indian guests who sat across from us in a peyote ceremony on the Tongue River in 1936.

Warner took a count of Murngin battles in Australia over a twenty-year period. Fifty out of seventy assaults sprang from a desire for revenge for a previous killing. Ten were launched because of woman stealing.[6]

Religious and magical notions probably rank next after revenge drives. All head-hunting is tied up with supernaturalism and the belief that dead men's power can be taken with their heads. Polynesian wars were frequently undertaken to obtain sacrificial victims. Ashantis and other West Africans kept prisoners for sacrifice. The bloody religion of the Aztecs called for thousands of war prisoners for human sacrifice

---

[6] Warner, *op. cit.*, p. 457.

to the gods—a fact that proved their undoing when they came to grips with stout Cortez. The Aztecs fought to take prisoners; the Spaniards fought to kill. They baptized only survivors.

The essential difference between the religious warmaking motivations of civilized and primitive men is that while the latter wage war to obtain victims for sacrifice they never have sought to force their beliefs on others by means of war.

The seeking of status and excitement are other important motivations for war. Pueblo Indians allow no special honor to warriors, but Plains Indians made the measurement of a man his war record. Few are the tribes that do not honor the warrior. Again and again, we find that a boy is not eligible for marriage until he has participated in his first raid or brought back his first head. When a Cheyenne lad, who had not been to war, attempted to woo a maiden by seizing her within his blanket, she could turn him to precipitous flight with an archly put "And how many times have you blocked the way of an enemy?" The coup-counting system of the Plains Indians required of men that they go on the war-path many times to establish and maintain their social prestige.

Outright conquest was undertaken by Inca, Aztec, and many African kings as a means of enhancing personal glory and power. Among peoples who esteem the military life, expeditions are sometimes launched for the sheer fun of it. Young Plains warriors were actually disappointed when older chieftains called off prospective fights through peace parleys. War can be loved by those who play it as a game and are willing to pay the croupier, Death.

In the period of disillusionment following the First World War it became the fashion to maintain that all wars spring from sordid economic greed. Self-enrichment is a mighty driving power. War can serve well as a means of depriving other peoples of access to natural resources. Or it may be used positively as an instrument of subjugation for the purposes of callous exploitation. Whether it is so used or not depends upon various factors culturally determined.

It is safe to say that among the lower primitives of recent times wars were not fought for economic reasons. Australians, for example, cannot conceive of dispossessing another horde of its land, because of an intimate tie between the living and their ancestral spirits, who haunt the rocks and springs of their territory. Eskimos fight for grudges but not to acquire territory. Linton reports that in certain areas of Madagascar the concept of expropriating the land of defeated enemies simply does not exist.

Food gatherers and lower hunters just do not possess enough property to make booty raids worth while, and victors in fights among the lower nomads do not have the means to carry surplus goods with them. Hence there is no advantage in appropriating such goods as the vanquished may possess.

It is quite otherwise when peoples have reached a settled gardening stage of cultural development. Workers are capable of producing more food and goods than they must consume to live. It pays conquerors to become masters and exploiters. Thus, as we have seen in Chap. 22, slavery and caste systems develop in the form of conquest states, and war is a useful if unjust instrument of enrichment and cultural development. The capture of women for chore wives and children for slaves is an important feature of war on the higher primitive and lower civilizational levels of culture.

War has become the deadly issue of the twentieth century. It now threatens the very existence of the societies that have brought it to its high peak of destructive perfection. After all, no culture can long nourish a trait that is actively and efficiently self-destructive. But we are attempting just this. Like the dinosaur, who overdeveloped his bulk into extinction, we are overdeveloping war. Unlike the dinosaur, who did not know what he was doing, we do. Our poignant tragedy is that we can see where we are heading and yet seem unable to alter our course. Like the reputed behavior of the lemmings, who supposedly travel relentlessly over hill and dale when the migration instinct moves them, blindly plunging into the sea when they reach the shore and swimming on and on in an unswerving direction until at last they sink beneath the waves, we seem intent on pushing forward into the sea of blood and fire that threatens ultimately to engulf us.

War and Instinct. Is man's propensity to war an instinct? Obviously warfare as such is not, for war is an elaborate cultural complex. But that it rests on certain innate tendencies of mankind is a possibility that must be seriously considered.

Antipathy toward other persons or groups is a universal characteristic of all human beings in greater or lesser degree. On the other hand, so is sympathy. The first is an emotional state of displeasure stimulated by the existence of persons whose behavior is unlike your own. It leads to rejection or withdrawal in social relations. Antagonism is an overt manifestation of antipathy producing active opposition to, or interference with, the object of antipathy. Sympathy, the sharing of emotions and interests, draws people together in common behavior. Sympathy builds social groups; antipathy sunders them.

Antipathy as an emotional state may or may not lead to pugnacity, which is an overt state of actual or threatened physical assault on the object of opposition. It is true that in most societies pugnacity is manifest by some individuals at some times. But it is also true that the forms of pugnacity are culturally shaped, the stimuli that evoke pugnacity are culturally controlled, and in a few cultures pugnacity is reduced to a minimum or entirely suppressed. A culture can build on the primeval urge to make people more or less antipathetic and pugnacious. Compare, for example, the pacifistic Shoshones and the violent Comanches (see pages 292–293 above). In 1600 they were culturally and racially one.

War and Natural Selection. Natural selection operates among all organisms. In the competition for food and space each individual and each organic group must find adequate room and sustenance or die prematurely. In the world of lower animals the struggle is relentless, even though mitigated by mutual aid and symbiosis. Organisms best adapted to resist the onslaughts of other organisms and to exploit particular aspects of the physical environment have greater survival potentialities than others. The weeding-out process of natural selection operates between groups and on individuals within a group. The rocks are strewn with fossils of forms that have gone the way of the dodo.

Man is not exempt. He too is faced with the inexorable facts of a finite world of limited resources and space. He must struggle as any other animal for access to these two essentials for living. The thousands who shall die of starvation this very year in Asia and Europe do not have to read a book to learn this bitter truth.

Man cannot escape natural selection, but he does not have to be its abject slave. He can and does modify the operation of the process.

Man has been engaged in killing his fellow men and animals through all the ages of his existence on earth. He does it either by direct assault or by denial of access to available food and space. We exterminate beasts, fish, and insects on a large scale. We wipe out whole areas of plant life to serve our needs and desires. For a million years the Neandertal strain dominated the prehistoric Old World, but *Homo sapiens*, aided perhaps by pestilence, completely wiped out Neandertal man some 50,000 years ago. Anthropological records are replete with the total destruction of one tribe or local group by another. In our own times, the Tasmanians have disappeared under the onslaught of ruthless European settlers, and while the Indians as a whole are now surviving, numerous tribes disappeared from the face of the earth in the nineteenth century. War and pestilence were the primary agents of their extinction.

Does this mean that the destroying groups of man were superior to their victims? In terms of sheer survival, yes. Innately? Not necessarily, for culture is an extension of man's survival equipment. Human groups equipped with cultures that bring about larger and more effective group organization, so that they can force the displacement, subjugation, or exploitation of other groups, are in the position of being superior. Many Indians, consciously aware of this after defeat, deliberately turned to the white man's way, "because it is stronger than ours."

All primitive cultures are doomed in the next hundred years. They cannot survive against civilization. Selection is operative, and primitive man is disappearing even as we study him.

This is not to say that all primitive *peoples* are doomed. Many such groups can and will survive by modified adaptation to the ways of civilization and incorporation into the larger society of the civilized world.

Among the societies of civilized man does war operate with positive selection? To some extent, yes, and in some circumstances, no. Rome put a complete and total end to Carthage. The means were war. Many were the lesser societies that lost their discrete existence through the power of Rome. Anglo-Saxon Britain as it existed in the tenth century was brought to an end by the Normans, although neither it nor its culture was wholly destroyed, and the Normans with their culture were fused into the new civilization of later Britain.

In opposition to the proposition that war works for the selective survival of peoples and cultures, it may be argued that superior fighters are often defeated by accident and circumstance. There is general agreement that in military organization and ability the Germans were superior to any of the nations who fought them in both World Wars. Yet they were brought to their low estate because the *total* military organization that confronted them was superior to theirs. Their culture has been deficient and in survival value inferior, for it has led them twice into the maelstrom of disaster. War is a part of the total culture, and it cannot be considered separately.

It is only when equally matched forces lock in war and uncontrollable accident gives smashing victory to one side and brings about the destruction of the other that selection in terms of survival superiority can be denied. This probably has happened many times.

This discussion is no argument for war as a necessary instrument of social selection. It merely attempts to give honest recognition to the fact that war does operate as a selective agent among societies and their cultures; it seeks to drive home that only those who win in wars of annihilation survive, while those who win in limited wars may dominate—at least temporarily.

If war has consequences in social selection, the case is less clear with respect to biological selection. In combat today we destroy the cream of our manhood. The selection works negatively. Selective service and preliminary training screen out the physically and mentally weaker men. They never make the combat team. Those who fail under fire are sent home. Only the strongest remain, gradually to be destroyed, until after prolonged fighting the whole personnel of combat units have been filled by replacements. Among the wounded there may be some positive selection. In critical cases, other things being equal, the physically strong may survive to reproduce another day, while the weaker go under, but this is hard to measure.

Among the civilian population exposed to the ravages of war the results are uncertain. Here the mentally and physically weak and the strong are alike exposed to mass bombing and fire raids. Among those killed outright there is little selection. Among the wounded results may parallel those of the soldiers. Starvation and pestilence, those silent servants of war, do select the constitutionally weak for extinction.

No balance sheet worthy of scientific consideration can be drawn. We do not know if war has beneficial biological results in the long run. Probably not. After all, there is no evidence that man today is physically superior to Neolithic man. Warfare over 15,000 years does not seem to have made any difference. True, modern men have double the life expectancy of Neolithic men, but that is clearly the result of medical advance, not war.

If ever war made contributions to the moral and social advance of mankind in measure outweighing its moral and social destructiveness, that day is past. War has assuredly become a luxury that modern civilization can ill afford.

The hard lesson of psychology and anthropology is that all men have their aggressions, which can be mastered only by superior authority.[7] Each society has its system of social control to accomplish this end among its members. World society is still in the infant stage, wherein the necessary control system does not yet exist. The deadly issue of the times is, Do we have the will and intelligence to master the mass antipathies and aggressions of nations and societies by enabling sympathy to triumph through creation of an authoritative world social order? By "we" is meant not just America—or America and those who stand with

[7] R. West, *Conscience and Society.*

her—but all the major societies of mankind. Will the western democracies and the eastern communistic countries succeed in making of the United Nations a true world authority? Or will they keep it hamstrung with the limitations of jealous national sovereignty? By the first means alone can war be brought under permanent control. By continuance along the old route catastrophic disorder becomes an increasing certainty.

F. Religion

CHAPTER 28

ANIMISM, MAGIC, AND THE SUPERNATURAL

Of all the manifestations of man's social life none is so elusive of definition as religion. It presents so many aspects, intertwines with so many phases of culture, and is so variable that it is difficult to delineate religion in terms both broad enough to encompass the whole and discriminating enough to isolate it for study.

As is often the case, it is best to clear the ground by a negative statement of what religion is not. Religion does not depend on belief in God. Many religions are polytheistic. Nor yet does religion depend upon a belief in deities, single or multiple. Many religions have not developed the concept of such exalted spiritual beings as may properly be called gods. Religion does not depend upon bodies of worshipers organized in church or cult. Many religions are almost completely individualistic. Nor, for the same reason, does religion necessarily involve a priesthood. Religion does not depend upon the existence of a formulated body of dogma; and, obviously, among primitive peoples it cannot involve sacred books.

Religion is rooted in the mind of man. On the subhuman level there is no religion. Men alone possess it. Men alone developed it, for animals have neither the awareness nor the reflective intelligence to formulate the conceptual abstractions that underlie religion.

Religious belief and behavior are a universal aspect of culture. No society of men has possessed a culture devoid of religion. Indeed, in the primitive world religion dominates most culturally determined activity. Only in the sophisticated, civilized world are men capable of eliminating religious belief and action from their behavior. And even among the non-religious, residues of religious and magical thinking remain.

Religion rests upon belief in the supernatural, which embraces *animism* and *mana*.

Animism. Animism, as defined by the great nineteenth-century anthropologist Tylor, is the belief in spiritual beings. This constitutes his famous minimum definition of religion.[1] What then are spiritual beings? We all know them by name. Souls, ghosts, goblins, genii, trolls, sprites, elves, pixies, leprechauns, fairies, witches, demons, devils, and gods. Their essential quality is their disembodiment, although they are real enough to those who believe in them.

As spirits they are not subject to the laws of nature. They are uninhibited by the limitations of physical matter, by the weaknesses of human flesh. They transcend matter, time, and space. They are supernatural. It is this that makes them wonderful, mysterious.

Tylor saw the origin of animism in the phenomena of dreams, of life and death. Dreams are a form of hallucination, an illusory experience. But that men dream is empirical fact. In dreams we transcend reality. We soar to great heights of attainment and pleasure; we experience horrible happenings; we relive the past and anticipate the future; we visit places once visited and those where our feet have never yet been; we commune with the dead and departed, or the living who are far distant. Neither time, nor space, nor any limitations of the body hinder us—in our dreams.

Yet in sleep or in coma the body does not leave its resting place. We wake where we lay down to rest—barring the unfortunate somnambulist. The body has not performed the miracles dreamed, but it is hard, even for the sophisticate, not to take dream experiences as real. To the primitive and, indeed, to most civilized men, the dream experience *is* reality.

Primitive man reflected and concluded that there are two parts to man: the bodily self of mortal flesh and the spiritual alter ego, the soul. The soul concept is the root of animism. It is a universal concept.

The soul is in itself quite intangible. In the language of many peoples it is synonymous with "shadow" or "shade." Intangible though it be, it is oftentimes perceptible in the image of the body it normally inhabits.

The soul is the vital force. Its presence animates the body. Its departure stills it. It is in the stillness of sleep that the soul goes wandering. Absence in dreams brings the restless body of man to the quiescence of sleep. Man's restlessness is of the spirit, not the body.

The long sleep that is death comes when the sojourning soul does not return. The body that is the vessel for the soul has no further function once its soul has abandoned it. Disintegration follows. Illness is due to intrusive corruption of the soul, or to soul loss.

This is the logic of the soul concept—in part.

Man lives not alone. The beasts of wood and field, the fowl of the air, the fish of the waters are also endowed with vitality. So too are the

[1] E. B. Tylor, *Primitive Culture,* Vol. 1, p. 424.

plants. By means of analogical reasoning, primitive man attributes souls to them as the cause of their vitality. Yet it is not completely by false analogy, for animals appear in dreams, even as man. Thus, in most primitive belief, not only man but all living beings possess souls.

Souls after death become ghosts or free spirits wholly disembodied. They live on in the world of man, within his very community or in a special realm which the spirits of living men may on occasion visit, or from which souls may come to visit the living.

Whether or not the concept of free spirits could arise only from the soul concept, as Tylor thought, or whether early man was imaginatively capable of creating the spirit concept out of mere nothingness, we shall never know. It is enough that pure spirits inhabit the believing minds of people in all societies and that these imaginary beings are thought to be above the laws of nature. They and souls are living elements in all religions.

Mana. Mana is a force, but not a vitalistic force. It exists as a supernatural attribute of persons and things. Mana is sheer power. Above all, it is exceptional power. Mana is therefore manifest in the unusual, when the unusual is not the work of spirits.

Extraordinary aptitudes of men are explained in terms of mana. The master craftsman in Polynesia excels in his skill because he possesses mana. The learned pundit excels in lore and knowledge because he possesses mana. The mighty warrior excels in the killing of men because he possesses mana. The outstanding healer, the expert canoeman, and any others who stand above their fellow men, do so because of personal possession or control of mana. Mana, though it is an impersonal force, can be manifest in and through persons.

Mana can also be manifest in things. The queerly shaped, or unusually marked, stone may be believed to possess miracle-working power. This is its mana. The canoe that can outdistance all others, the song that heals, the war club that smashes more than a normal quota of skulls, the talisman that in itself brings good luck—all these have power, power that is mana.

The power that is extraordinary is not a mundane force. It does not follow the regular laws of ordinary technologies or skills. Like the power of spirits, it transcends the natural. Mana is supernatural.

Animism and mana are the raw materials of supernaturalism. But they do not persist in a social vacuum. They act on man and man interacts with them.

Supernaturalism thus has two aspects: the subjective and the objective. The subjective consists of the belief in spirit beings and mana. The objective consists of the ways of interacting with the supernatural: concilation, appeasement, sacrifice, petition, adoration, worship, prayer, ritual and ceremony, magic. The relative importance of faith, which is inner, and deeds, which are external, is a problem in balance that has always plagued the religious idealist.

We may now essay an anthropological definition of supernaturalism as *the complex of man's interrelations with imagined powers that he believes transcend the mechanical laws of nature.*

It is necessary only to add that what constitutes the supernatural is dependent upon each culture and the thought systems of the individuals within each society. As mechanistic thinking and natural science spread, the area of the supernatural shrinks. In the primitive world there are few secular skeptics. Modern thought has certainly narrowed the scope of the supernatural, but it is still too early to predict its ultimate disappearance from the lives of men.

Magic and Religion. Supernaturalism is fundamental to both religion and magic, for these are merely two special categories subsumed under the more general one of supernaturalism. That which distinguishes religion from magic is neither the goodness of one nor the evil of the other, but the state of mind of the believer and his consequent modes of behavior. This is the valid distinction that was originally pointed out by Frazer.[2] In the religious state of mind man acknowledges the superiority of the supernatural powers upon whose action his well-being depends. His attitudes are preponderantly those of submission and reverence. The objective behavior put forth is manifestly that of beseechment, petition, and appeasement in prayer, offerings, and sacrifice.

> Father have pity on me,
> Father have pity on me,
> I am crying for thirst,
> I am crying for thirst,
> All is gone—I have nothing to eat,
> All is gone—I have nothing to eat.

Such is the tenor of an Arapaho ghost dance song, "sung to a plaintive tune, sometimes with tears rolling down the cheeks of the dancers."[3] It epitomizes the religious attitude, as does the Lord's Prayer with its

---

[2] *Cf.* J. G. Frazer, *The Golden Bough*, Chap. 4. Frazer argued a theoretical priority of magic over religion in prehistoric origins. This is a futile and irrelevant problem for which there are no empirical data upon which to base a conclusion.

[3] J. Mooney, *The Ghost Dance Religion and the Sioux Outbreak of 1890* (Bureau of American Ethnology, Annual Report 14, 1896), p. 977.

"Hallowed be thy name" (reverence); "Give us this day our daily bread" (petition); "Thine is the Kingdom, the Power and the Glory, forever" (subordination and awe).

"O, spirits, here humble in heart I stand beseeching you" is the opening plaint of the Winnebago on a vision quest.

The magician, on the other hand, believes that he *controls* supernatural power under certain conditions. He has power over power. He feels confirmed in his belief that if he possesses a tested formula and if he executes the formula perfectly, barring outside interference he will get the results which that formula is specified to give. The supernatural power has no volition or choice of its own. It must respond. Even as the student in the laboratory knows that if he follows the manual instructions correctly, he will obtain a predictable result, so the magician works in a similar confidence.

Magic often does produce the expected results. It appears to meet the pragmatic test. At least, it must do so in its initial applications, or the formula is usually rejected as false or worthless. When magic works, it does so for two reasons: (1) coincidence—if sufficient time is allowed, the desired event may well come to pass; (2) psychological suggestion—when magic is directed against persons who suspect or fear that they are its objects, hysteria or compulsion grips them; they sicken and often die. Psychologists call this *somatic compliance* and *thanatomania* (the depression of the will to live to the point of extinction). The records of travelers and anthropologists abound with cases from the primitive world. Clinical records reveal many authentic cases among civilized men. Doctors well know the importance of the psychological state of the patient in crucial illness or injury.

Magic also serves its ends by giving the magician and his clients a needed psychological boost. As Malinowski reiterated, magic begins where mechanical technology ends. A Melanesian knows that magic cannot dig the soil in which he must plant his yams, so he does his own digging. He knows that he must hoe to keep down weeds, so he hoes. But he also knows that no matter how great his skill, pests, foraging animals, and climate are beyond his technological ability to control. Yet these and unknown factors affect his crop for better or worse. He desperately needs a good crop. It is the object of his most ardent wish, so he endeavors to control the unknown element by magic or religion. The confidence they give him quite definitely helps him to outdo himself in achievement of his wished-for goal.

The warrior who believes he has magical invulnerability can surmount fear to leap to heroism far more easily than the man who confronts danger without its support. Magic takes over when technology falls short; astrology boomed in Wall Street after the 1929 crash as financiers deserted the statistical charts of economists for the heavenly charts of star fakers.

Not only does magic actually aid the magician to attain his end in reality, it also fosters the illusion of attainment. When the dogma of magic is strong the practitioner often thinks the magic result has come to pass when nothing of the sort has occurred at all. Magic has much in common with daydreaming as a form of autistic thinking.

Magic is thus in some of its aspects pseudo science, as Frazer held. When the magician proceeds on the mechanistic assumption that the magical formula is a cause that must produce a given effect, his thinking parallels that of the scientist. But his method is not scientific method, and his method is false science at best. It would, perhaps, be more accurate to call magic a social technique based upon autistic thinking—imaginative fantasy as a means of wish fulfillment.

Finally, it should be noted that magic often appears to work because the primitive magician may be as skilled a prestidigitator as the Mohammedan fakir. He simply bamboozles the credulous.

It is thus possible analytically to distinguish magic from religion, and the distinction is much more than a mere play on words. The difference between the two methods of approach to the supernatural has tremendous social consequences. Religious emphasis in supernaturalism leads to subordination of men to gods and to the power of cult functionaries—the priesthoods. Religion is much more readily centralized and organized than is magic, which is inherently more individualistic in nature. Although organized religions always use a certain amount of magic in their rituals, the church is implicitly antagonistic to magic, since the magical attitude is incompatible with the religious attitude of submission. The conflict endures through the ages. As recently as February 6, 1944, the Reverend Harry Emerson Fosdick, as reported in *The New York Times,* decried contemporary resort to magic and expressed regret "that millions turn to cheap superstitions as substitutes for faith."

Primitive man, however, does not greatly concern himself with the ideological distinction between magic and religion. Rather, he blends them as best he may to attain his ends.

The Plains Indian on his vision quest makes himself pitiable in the eyes of the spirits. If they favor him, they give power along with sundry paraphernalia and the ritual wherewith to invoke power. The Indian reveres his tutelary spirit from whom he has received his magic. Pueblo Indians, for example, are most deferential in their relations to the gods who bless them with rain and fertile crops. At the same time their dances, which are pleasing to the gods, are full of magical enactment. Their prayers are petitions, true, but they are highly colored with magical word imagery and accompanied with magic acts. Piled-up yucca seeds bring the clouds, sprinkled water produces the rain, and rolling stones bring on thunder.

There is a bit of the magician in every priest, and every magician is partly priest.

Magic is built for the most part on two aspects of the principle of association. First, there is the assumption that like is linked to like. Second, there is the belief that things once in contact are thereafter associated with each other. The first produces imitative, or homeopathic, magic—that magic in which the magician puts the hex on an effigy of the person or object on which he would work his desire. The second produces contagious magic—that magic in which a hank of hair, a bit of clothing, or even excrement is filched from the victim, and upon which the magician works his spell. If these things are also put into an effigy, thereby combining both principles, the magic is of course doubly potent.

Tabu. Tabu is an inevitable element in supernaturalism. Supernatural power is in itself amoral. It may work for good or evil without discrimination, a quality that makes it implicitly dangerous. It is like fire or a heavy charge of electricity. When under control and directed toward desirable ends, it is beneficent. When out of control, it may well be disastrous. Man cannot get along without fire, yet he must fight a constant battle against it. Modern civilization cannot function without harnessed electricity, yet it must be handled with insulated tools and gloves.

Spirits and mana are deemed absolutely essential forces in the human conception of man's universe. They must be used for human ends, but if improperly used, they can backfire most dangerously.

Supernatural power, be it remembered, is above the realm of the ordinary. It does not operate according to understood natural laws. Because of this, it may not be approached or dealt with casually. It too must be handled with rubber gloves. Figuratively, tabu is a great *Caution! Handle With Care!* sign. Tabu does not mean *verboten*, in the German sense. Rather, it carries the overtones of the French *défense de toucher*.

In content, tabu consists of a series of negative rules, each of which states a form of behavior that will cause a supernatural power to backfire or get out of control. In reality, very few tabued acts are physically or socially dangerous. The function of tabu is predominantly psychological, originating in man's fear of dealing with forces he does not wholly understand. It also engenders respect and cautious care for the supernatural. Inasmuch as supernatural power always involves tabu, no man can ever take his possession of power wholly for granted.

Typical of the irrelevance of most tabus was the injunction that went with the war bonnet of the famous Cheyenne chieftain, Roman Nose. His bonnet had the power to give invulnerability in battle. With it Roman Nose rose unscathed to fame on the western plains. One of the rules of the bonnet was that its wearer must not eat any food taken from a dish with an iron utensil. If he did, a bullet or iron-tipped arrow could pierce him, just as the sharp metal pierced the meat. The protective power of the hat would be nullified, until restored through a long and elaborate ceremony of purification and atonement.

Just before the famous Beecher's Island fight with General Forsyth's men on the Republican River of western Nebraska, in 1868, Roman Nose ate as a guest in the camp of the Sioux Indians. When it was pointed out to him that the wife of his host was using a fork in her cooking, he said, "That breaks my medicine." The battle began before Roman Nose could make atonement so, like Achilles, he sulked in his tent. But under pressure, like Achilles, he donned his war gear, saying, "My food was lifted with an iron tool. I know that I shall be killed today." Roman Nose was killed by a bullet before he had a chance to strike a single blow in the battle.[4]

Violation of a tabu not only nullifies the positive power of medicine, it brings certain disaster as a consequence.

In Polynesia, whence comes the word *tabu*, high-ranking nobles possess mana because of their direct descent from the gods. So potent is their charge of mana that their very persons are surrounded with tabus, as is everything they touch. Sin, in Polynesia as elsewhere, is the violation of a tabu—an act punishable by supernatural sanction.

Prayer and magic are the two basic techniques of dealing with the supernatural. The first is a means of seeking spiritual rapport on a basis of subordination to animistic beings. The second is a technique of external compulsion over supernatural powers, animistic and mana.

Between these poles every possible form of interpersonal behavior may find its religious counterpart. As Benedict observes, "There is probably no customary behavior towards one's fellows that is not to be found somewhere as a religious technique."[5]

Gods may be flattered and bribed by sacrificial offerings. The Ifugao, Galangi, who had had his left hand burned to a stump in an ordeal with

---

[4] A thrilling account of the whole fight is given in G. B. Grinnell, *The Fighting Cheyennes*, pp. 267–282.

[5] R. F. Benedict, "Religion" in *General Anthropology*, p. 641.

red-hot iron, although he was innocent, complacently explained, "The Gods of Justice would rather do justice than injustice, but they can be bought just as other gods can be bought. The rich man sacrificed many fat hogs and chickens to them." [6] In this spirit the Plains Indian chopped off his own fingers to make himself pitiable to power-giving spirits, and so, too, apparently did Cro-Magnon man. Finger mutilation was almost universal among South African Bushmen of the nineteenth century "to insure safe passage to the next world or a long career of feasting after death." [7]

The world over, offerings of food and goods are made to the gods and spirits. Human sacrifice became the most extreme form of offering with its highest centers of development in Africa, Central America (especially Aztec), and Polynesia.

Although reverence and appeasement are the characteristic tones of men's relations to their gods, cavalier treatment is sometimes found. Bantu Negroes dupe their ancestral spirits by putting on disguises when they wish to violate a tabu. Some Bantus, when angered by the failure of their gods to bring them prosperity, make offerings accompanied by irreverent imprecations.

Similar scoldings are not uncommon in Polynesia. In the bitterness of extreme disappointment many a man has blasphemed his gods.

[6] R. F. Barton, *The Half Way Sun*, p. 89.
[7] G. G. MacCurdy, *Human Origins*, Vol. 2, p. 172.

CHAPTER 29

SHAMANS, PRIESTS, AND CULTS

Shamans. There is little doubt but that the accolade for the world's oldest profession goes to the religious specialist. Long before there were chieftains, kings, judges, lawyers, artists, teachers, or prostitutes, there were shamans and, possibly, priests.

We have seen societies in which there were no clearly defined political leaders or any other nonreligious functionaries. But no anthropologist has yet penetrated to a tribe so primitive that it does not have shamans.

A shaman is the possessor of supernatural power derived directly from the original supernatural source. He has personal and favored access to gods and spirits above and beyond that of ordinary men. The shaman is quite definitely a chosen one.

Throughout large areas of the primitive world every man is potentially a shaman. In true democratic belief supernatural power is there for all to seek. For example, every Plains Indian boy made his vision quest as a matter of course. Only the most unfortunate were never favored by at least one power-giving vision experience. Women, too, could share in this store of power, although a woman's chances of getting power were somewhat less than a man's. Thus, practically every one in the tribe was an incipient shaman.

In North America shamans excelled in thaumaturgy, and because they excelled, they tended to specialize. As specialists they exercised more than a normal share of influence in the affairs of men. Supernatural power always engenders temporal power, for the specialist can aid his fellow men to attain their hearts' desires or he can threaten them with dire consequences according to his own desires.

The center of the most intensive development of shamanism in the primitive world is aboriginal Siberia. The very word *shaman* comes from a native Siberian tongue. Synonyms also meaning shaman are medicine man (usually applied to American Indians), witch doctor (usually applied to Negroid shamans of Africa and Melanesia), and *angakok*, in Eskimo.

The Siberian shaman is more definitely set off from his fellow men than is his North American counterpart. For one thing, his personality is more clearly marked. For another, his "call" and training are more definite. Bogoras, the famous Siberianist, wrote of the Chukchee,

> For men, the preparatory stage of shamanistic inspiration is in most cases very painful, and extends over a long time. The call comes in an abrupt and obscure manner, leaving the young novice in much uncertainty regarding it. He feels "bashful" and frightened. . . . The young novice, the "newly inspired," loses all interest in the ordinary affairs of life. He ceases to work, takes little food and without relishing it, ceases to talk to people, does not even answer their questions. The greater part of his time he spends in sleep.[1]

Bogorus observed that they were as a rule excitable and hysterical. He even opined that not a few of them were "half crazy." Psychiatry was not the vogue in Bogorus's day or he would have attached the label *schizophrenic* to the personality of the Siberian shaman.

Suggestibility and a greater or lesser degree of emotional instability are essential traits of the shaman who obtains power by mystic experience. He or she must be capable of hallucinations. The person who cannot respond with visions and hallucinations to the pervading cultural suggestion that these form the road to power is out of luck if he would be a shaman. Crashing Thunder, the Winnebago Indian, was one of these. Even when he faked a vision and luck seemed to confirm his power, he knew in his inner self that his power was false. An extrovert whose aggressive personality demanded social prestige and the opportunity to amount to something, he was frustrated by his intellectual hardheadedness. Not finding the social means (supernatural power) to greatness open to him, he took the antisocial road—drunkenness, rowdyism, debauchery, murder, and fraud. Then when peyote at last reached the Winnebagos, the vision-stimulating drug brought visions and power to the tortured man. With power came reorientation of his personality. The bum became a pillar of society, a moral leader, and a decent citizen—much to the relief of his fellow tribesmen.[2]

The evidence is clear that to be a spirit-endowed shaman the odds favor those who belong to the "lunatic fringe."

The shaman as inheritor of magical power is a different matter. True, the magician is the dupe of his own beliefs, but it is possible for him to work with cold calculation. Highly developed magic often involves sheer fraud—skill in prestidigitation and the creation of optical illusions. Siberian and Eskimo shamans are skilled ventriloquists, using

---

[1] W. Bogoras, "The Chukchee I: Religion" (*Jessup North Pacific Expedition,* Vol. 7), p. 420.

[2] P. Radin (ed.), *Crashing Thunder.* This book should not be missed by any student of anthropology.

their tambourines so to deflect their voices that the listeners, "after a few minutes . . . begin to lose the power to locate the source of the sound. . . . The song and drum seem to shift from corner to corner, or even to move about without having any definite place at all." [3]

Algonquian Indian shamans hold impressive séances in which the tent rocks and pitches violently upon the arrival of the shaman's "spirit." The tent is cleverly constructed to be manipulated mechanically with ropes and thongs.[4]

However, the deceit practiced by shamans may not always be such crass charlatanism as it at first appears. Eskimo shamans often disclaim their own skill, as did one of the best of them to Peter Freuchen. "This is nothing for a man like you to look at. I am only a big liar, and even if these idiots are stupid enough to believe me, I never expected you to stand for it. I am a foolish old man, and what happens here has nothing to do with the truth." [5] But the effect of his performance on the people in the iglu was ecstasy. People are not adverse to being fooled, if it gives pleasure. Beyond that, of course, credulous ones are duped without their being the wiser.

It is difficult to draw an accurate balance between the exploitative and social-service activities of the primitive shamans. It is a false gesture to dismiss them solely as a class of exploiters. Yet it is true that they often turn their position and power to self-advantage. Eskimo shamans can impose almost any tabus they wish on individuals. They can sexually exploit women, married and unmarried, to gratify themselves in the name of spirits. Shamans can use their power particularly to consolidate the position of the elders as against the younger generation. But for this they must pay a price in self-denial of many things, for their work is dangerous in its own terms, and the burden of shamanism is often hard.

Priests. Priesthood is a manifestation of developed religion. It occurs in the more ordered primitive societies whose cultures are rich and complex. On the whole, it calls for an economic base of sufficient richness to support fairly large populations, plus some food and wealth surpluses. It is necessary to be able to organize and sustain permanent cults. Priesthood presupposes organized groups with standardized ceremonial ritual. The priest may have mana, but his power is less his own than the power resident in the office he holds. Unlike the shaman, he does not acquire his sacredness personally. He is vested in his succession to the *office* of priest. He becomes part of a religious corporation.

[3] Bogoras, *op. cit.*, p. 430.

[4] F. Densmore, "An Explanation of a Trick Performed by Indian Jugglers" (*American Anthropologist*, Vol. 34, 1932), pp. 310–314.

[5] P. Freuchen, *Arctic Adventure*, p. 133.

Priesthood emerges along two basic lines: (1) the family heads in ancestor-worshiping religions who serve as priestly intermediaries between the kinship group and the deceased ancestors; and (2) the priests who serve cult groups whose interests are directed toward special spirits or deities.

Priestesses are much less common than female shamans, probably for the reason that the organization of associations tends to be correlated almost exclusively with the male sex in primitive societies (see Chap. 21).

Ancestor Worship and the Cults of the Dead. Ancestor worship is by no means a universal form of religious expression, although belief in the spiritual immortality of the dead is. All cultures call for cognizance of ghosts, and all provide some means of dealing with them. However, the intensity of ghost awareness and concern over the activity and feelings of ghosts is variable. In North America, the Pueblo Indians pay little attention to ghosts, the Plains Indians fear them but their ghosts are not too prevalent, while the Navajos and Eskimos are bedeviled by ghost anxiety. They possess definite ghost cults, a body of practices and ritual observances associated with the propitiation or avoidance of ghosts.

Most Plains Indians and the Navajos abandon any house in which a person has died. The ghost haunts the house and disturbs the inhabitants. Navajos, therefore, take a seriously ill patient who is about to die outdoors in order to save the house. The Arizona desert is dotted with hogans abandoned because a death has occurred within. One of my Shoshone friends compromised this problem by dismantling a log house, moving it a few hundred feet, and then reassembling it, after mixing up the logs to fool the ghost of his brother, who is now unable to recognize the new house. Ghost fear has long been a hindrance to Indian Service efforts to provide modern housing on some reservations. In the northern Plains a workable expedient acceptable to the Indians in some places has been to fumigate the house as an effective antidote to ghosts!

Eskimos believe that ghosts are harmful and relentlessly malicious as long as they remain in the memory of the living. On death the corpse is not removed from the iglu by way of the door; this would make it too easy for the lingering ghost to reenter. Rather, a hole is chopped in the back, later to be refilled after removal of the body. This baffles the ghost. Then, lest the ghost does find the entrance, knives are set in the snow floor of the doorway for three nights after burial. Such booby traps discourage ghosts. Among Eskimos, as with many other people, the name of the dead is tabued, lest it summon the reappearance of the ghost. Later, the name is given to a newborn child, reincarnating the name soul of the deceased ancestor.

Comanches also tabu names of the dead, but when they wanted to mention a defunct friend named Pork, they called him Bacon. Ghosts are literal-minded, but people can get the idea.

Eskimos, like many other people, bury the dead with grave offerings—the personal equipment and gifts of friends and relatives to serve the ghost in the other world. These are "killed." They are broken to release the animate soul of the object. For it is the spiritual counterpart of the goods that obviously is used in the spirit world.

Plains Indians also sacrificed a warrior's favorite horse on his grave, as did medieval Europeans at times. This is no longer Occidental practice, but the officer's horse led behind the casket-bearing caisson with reversed saddle and upturned stirrups still follows the hero to his grave, only to be spared the final sacrifice.

Grave sacrifices were stepped up to extravagant heights for the royalty of Africa and India. Into the nineteenth century Hindu wives were immolated on the funeral pyres of their princely husbands. In Dahomey in West Africa whole corps of wives and retainers were slain to provide an adequate retinue for the deceased king. Shoshone and Comanche tradition has it that in ancient times wives were killed to accompany their husbands' spirits, but in more recent days the wives followed the general Plains Indian practice of self-mutilation and abnegation.

Ghost cults usually, but not always, emphasize the malevolence of ghosts. Manus in Melanesia is an exception. The ghost of the last deceased household head is the preceptor and protector of his family. He punishes their moral derelictions, but above all he is busy thwarting the malignant efforts of other ghosts. All ghosts are malicious toward people not of their own kin group. The social and economic rivalry that is characteristic of everyday Manus life continues in the afterworld through the jealousy and rivalry of the ghosts. Each family ghost enjoys a brief span of immortal existence, while his skull adorns the doorway of his family hut. But the death of an adult male in the household is indication that the family ghost has not been on the job. He has been negligent enough to permit a rival ghost to kill his descendant. He is no good. Therefore his skull is thrown out and replaced by that of his successor, who then rules as the Honored Ghost of the household until he, too, fails in his duty.[6]

Ancestor worship is both an elaboration and an abstraction of the ghost cult. As an elaboration it is best seen among the Bantu tribes of Africa. Every lineage and clan has its distinct ancestral deities, who are

---

[6] R. F. Fortune, *Manus Religion* (Proceedings of the American Philosophical Society, 1935); M. Mead, "The Manus of the Admiralty Islands," in *Cooperation and Competition among Primitive Peoples*, pp. 210–239.

gods to their descendants and ignored by the members of other kinship groups. The gods of royal clans, because the heads of such clans must be honored by all the kingdom, are not only worshiped by the royal clan itself but by all the subjects of the king. In ancestor-worshiping cults of this order the eldest ranking member of the kin group is not only its headman but also its priest. He stands nearest to the ancestral gods. He is the intercessor on behalf of his kinsmen. On the gods' behalf he is the intermediary who is responsible for controlling the acts of his family or clan members. As in modern Japan, he has to keep the ancestral gods informed of the state of affairs within his domain. The Mikado has merely to make a ceremonial report at the ancestral shrine, but in Dahomey in West Africa it was customary to execute a couple of victims to carry the royal message to the ancestors whenever the king had anything of moment to report.

Periodic elaborate feasts and sacrifices on behalf of the ancestral gods are characteristic of the western Sudan. In Dahomey, such ceremonies are held by each clan every year, with litanies, dancing, offerings of food and libations of liquors and sacrifice of animals. In the annual ceremonies of the royal clan human victims used to be offered.

Vodun,[7] among West Indies Negroes, is nothing more than a syncretism of Dahomean ancestral rites and Catholicism.[8] The clan founders of Dahomey are known as *tovudun*, from whom the *vodun* cult is named. Vodun rites are fundamentally family rituals with offerings and sacrifices accompanied by chants and dances, in which various gods are impersonated and called upon to visit the ceremony. Dancers representative of specific gods are possessed in turn as each god is called with his drum *salute* (greeting). The trance behavior of the votaries and the ecstasy of the worshipers lend the eerie wildness to the performance that has given vodun its exotic reputation.

Ancestor worship as an abstraction of ghost worship occurs where gods are thought once to have been human beings but the more recently deceased are not believed to be potent deities. This may be said to be true of Polynesian and Pueblo Indian religions. Maori chieftains are lineal descendants of gods through primogeniture. Honor is due these gods, but there is no cult of the dead. The masked gods, *kachinas*, of the

---

[7] *Vodun* is the phonetically correct name for the cult complex popularly called voodoo.

[8] Cf. M. J. Herskovits, "African Gods and Catholic Saints in New World Negro Belief" (*American Anthropologist*, Vol. 39, 1937), pp. 635–643; G. E. Simpson, "The Vodun Service in Northern Haiti" (*American Anthropologist*, Vol. 42, 1940), pp. 236–254.

Pueblos are vaguely thought of as ancestral beings, but dead ancestors are not worshiped as such.

Social conservatism is a characteristic feature of ancestor-worshiping religions. The ancestors as moral preceptors do not favor change from the social practices they knew as men. Since they punish moral lapses with death and illness and their standards are the old ones, the religious sanctions toward conformity are powerful.

Nature Worship. Cults deifying various features of nature abound in the primitive world. Among agricultural and gardening peoples, sun, rain, and fertility deities are outstanding. Solstitial rites marked the annual crisis of the sun in the religion of the megalith builders of Neolithic Europe. Mysterious Stonehenge and Avebury in England, and the cromlechs of Carnac in Brittany are aligned to the rising sun at the time of the spring solstice, as is the sun stone in the famous Sun Temple of Mesa Verde National Park, built by prehistoric Pueblo Indians 700 years ago. In ancient Rome, the solstice rites of the Mithraic cult gave way to the Christian Christmas celebration of the birth of Christ as the new light of the world. Each pueblo in the Southwest today has its priestly sun watcher, who controls the ceremonial cycle with the movements of the sun. Pious people greet the sun with prayer each day.

All the religions in the great Central American culture complex made much of the sun. The Pyramid of the Sun near Mexico City is one of the truly great monuments of our southern neighbors. The Natchez of Mississippi and the Incas of Peru built theocratic states around the principle of sun divinity. The Natchez high chief was also high priest, called the Sun, or brother of the Sun. The Inca of Peru was the personification of the divine sun. And until the disaster of 1945 induced the Emperor of Japan to deny it by imperial edict, he was supposed to be a divinity directly descended from the mythical sun goddess Amaterasu.

The sun figured greatly in Plains Indian religion. All tipis opened east, and tribal camp circles likewise. By the nineteenth century the midsummer sun dance had come to be one of the most spectacular of Plains ceremonials.[9]

Although the sun looms large in the mythologies of the peoples of the Pacific area, it does not assume importance as an actual deity. This

[9] *Cf.* G. A. Dorsey, "The Cheyenne, II, The Sun Dance" (*Field Columbian Museum, Publication 103, Anthropological Series*, Vol. 9, No. 2, 1905) for a good description of a typical sun dance with many illustrations. Volume 16 of the *Anthropological Papers of the American Museum of Natural History* contains descriptions of other tribal sun dances.

is true also of Africa and most of North America. Ancient Europe, the countries of the Mediterranean basin, and India were the great seats of sun worship.

In Africa and Polynesia, although the sun is not glorified, nature worship is not neglected. The entire universe is departmentalized among gods of the skies, earth, waters, trees, and thunder, with myriads of subdivisions among the specialized deities. On the less-than-god levels all primitive religions include multitudes of nature spirits associated with particular spots, trees, volcanoes, mountains, rivers, lakes, and rocks. Barton, in his recently published work on *The Religion of the Ifugaos* [10] lists 1,240 deities for this single Philippine tribe and estimates that the total number known to the best informed priests is probably more than 1,500. Many of these are nature gods.

To primitive man the whole world lives. Souls animate things, and whatsoever embodies the soul is a spirit being to be treated with religion or magic—or both.

Fetishism. When a material object is believed to possess mana or to be possessed by a spirit being, and when it is venerated or cherished because of this, it is a fetish. Because of its imputed value, it receives special attention and care, and it is this attribute that leads to our popular phrase "to make a fetish of something." The word is derived from the Latin *facticius*, an amulet, by way of the Portuguese *feitiço*, after the use of the word by the Portuguese adventurers, who first met with it in their voyages along the west coast of Africa.

Fetishes are symbolic repositories of supernatural power, and they serve the psychological function of objectifying the belief. They are a rallying point for faith, a visual stimulant to faith.

Fetishes may be simple or precious stones, implements, trees, mountains, or often art objects endowed with power. It is commonly recognized that art receives much stimulus from the attempt to express religious belief in concrete form. However, mere art as such is not *ipso facto* fetishistic. As Lowie comments,

The representation of a human figure is not an effective fetish until it has been through the hands of the medicine-man and received its power from him. What confers upon the object its supernatural potency is solely the mysterious spell sung over it or the substance, wonder-working in its own right like the *ngula* paint, thrust into a ventral cavity. Hence, only a moderate percentage of the human or animal figurines are in reality fetishes. . . . Any object can become a "fetish" if only it has been ritualistically consecrated.[11]

[10] American Anthropological Association, Memoir 65, 1946.
[11] R. H. Lowie, *Primitive Religion*, p. 269.

The High God Concept. The time has passed when informed civilized men could think the primitive mind incapable of conceiving of a Supreme Being or High God. Tylor's greatest error was to infer that the High God concept could be only the end product of a long intellectual evolution, beginning with the soul concept and leading through ghost and ancestor worship to polytheistic nature worship on to monotheism.[12]

Andrew Lang,[13] before the turn of this century, proved that Australian, Polynesian, African, and American Indian notions of the High God were not derived from Christian teachings. The indefatigable Austrian anthropologist Wilhelm Schmidt has confirmed it with his stupendous four-volume work, *Der Ursprung der Gottesidee*.[14]

The essential beliefs of primitive men concerning the High God are that he is the original creator of the world; that the world as he made it was good; that he is not a spirit being (in the usual sense); that he is non-anthropomorphic, nonnatural, lives in the sky remote from earthly affairs, has retired from active participation in daily events (is otiose), and is on the whole unapproachable and disinterested. Because of this, there is little ritual and cult ceremonial directed in his favor. Temples are not raised to him, no sacrifices given (except offerings of first fruits), and prayers are offered only infrequently and by few people.

In cosmological lore his acts of creation are generally only vaguely conceived. Myth tells how he created departmental, executive sub-deities charged with the responsibility for filling in the details of creation and running the universe. These are the gods men must appease and pray to. They are the ones who deliver or withhold the goods.

Evil in life is due to their perversity or maliciousness. A common counterpart of the High God is a Trickster or Transformer, like Coyote among the western American Indians, who spoils or modifies the good work of the creator to burden man with death, sin, and travail. The Trickster is the equivalent of the serpent in the garden of Eden.

Lang felt that the formulation of the High God concept was a consequence of contemplative religious thought. The corruption of this idealism and the creation of the less pure deities he conceived as due to a "myth-making mood" and "the Old Adam" in man—the unsocial desire to obtain advantage over fellow men. In this the Supreme Being is too ethical to lend a hand; hence, ghosts, spirits, and corruptible gods were formulated in playful and erratic fantasy, which is irrational and

[12] E. B. Tylor, *Primitive Culture*.

[13] A. Lang, *The Making of Religion*.

[14] See W. Schmidt, *The Origin and Growth of Religion*, pp. 167–217, a condensed version of Schmidt's thesis.

debases the gods. Thus, to Lang early primitive man when he was in his higher mood was capable of rational philosophic thought. Yet man also expressed his baser mood of selfish desire to elaborate the pantheisms of the savage world.

Civilized religious reformers have struggled long to suppress the supremacy of the second religious mood, striving to reestablish the Supreme Deity in absolute and undefiled dominance.

The Mohammedan, Hebrew, and Christian concepts of God are of this order. But the God concept is still corrupted by petty claims for personal and tribal (national) favor by people known as civilized.

Subsequent to Lang, Radin has modified Lang's notions in a way worth noting.[15] He forgoes the notion of an original purity of the High God later corrupted. Instead, he posits two contrasting types of human mentality, the idealist and realist. The idealists are men of intellectual and reflective temperament, men whom anthropological experience has shown are present in small numbers among all peoples. They philosophize on the conundrum of life and the universe. Their thought seeks a direct, unified, orderly cause in explanation of the universe. The product of their thought is the Supreme Being. As idealists they are little concerned with crass material desires. Their god is free from the petty demands of men.

The bulk of men, alas, are materialists. Their bellies, their health, wealth, and social power mean much to them. They develop religion in terms of gods and spirits, who control the means to satisfy these needs. When prayer, appeasement, and magic suffice to win the desired results, all goes well. But hunger, illness, failure, and death stalk the earth, for which the lesser gods and the forces of evil are responsible. Toward them man's emotions are ambivalent. The gods and spirits are both loved and feared. The emotional overtones of religion are mixed indeed. But taken in the main, the anthropologist cannot on the facts concur in the idealistic belief that religion in all its history represents solely man's striving for the highest values of life.

Nor is it possible to derive religion from any single mainspring of motivation. Belief in souls, fear of ghosts, fear of fear, worship of ancestors, traffic with hosts of spirits, nature worship, and philosophical reflection all play their parts. Emphasis shifts from culture to culture, but religion is a growth with many roots and many fruits.

[15] P. Radin, *Monotheism in Primitive Religion;* see also *Primitive Man as Philosopher.*

Part Five: Society and Culture

CHAPTER 30

SOCIETY AND CULTURE

Throughout all previous sections of this book we have been describing various aspects of culture and human behavior. The concept of culture is the analytical key fashioned by the anthropologist to solve the mysteries that have enveloped the relations of man toward man. All our discourse thus far has assumed the concept of culture as its foundation. In this last interpretative section of the book it will be well at the outset to make the nature of the concept explicit.

Culture is a uniquely human phenomenon. Among all the creatures of the animal kingdom man stands alone in his capacity to create and sustain culture.

The human capacity for culture rests in man's complex and plastic nervous system. It takes brains to produce culture, and for all his stupidities man alone has crossed the critical threshold in the evolutionary development of a central nervous system equal to the task of creating culture. For culture is created in the mind of man. Every item of culture is a product of invention—a way of behaving is introduced that was not preset in the genetic organization of the human animal. It is transmitted to other members of the group and becomes a more or less standardized form of behavior.

Learned Behavior. By definition cultural behavior is learned behavior. It is essential to the concept of culture that instincts, innate reflexes, and any other biologically predetermined forms of behavior be ruled out. Culture is, therefore, in a sense artificial behavior. But it is as much a part of the natural universe as are the stars in the heavens.

That cultural behavior is learned behavior may be demonstrated by answering the question, What would happen if a collection of babies were cut off from all adult care, training, and supervision? The answer is, of course, they would die. Therefore, we must modify our question and put it in this form, What would happen if a collection of babies could be fed and protected without supervision, training, or any form of contact with adults? Would they manifest any of the special traits of behavior that were characteristic of their parents?

Our answer cannot be based upon direct empirical observation; legend, mythology, and the testimony of honorable men notwithstanding, neither wolves nor jailers nor scientific experimenters have ever set up such a situation under conditions of control or observation that meet the elementary canons of scientific acceptability.[1] But enough is known of infant physiology, learning, and psychology to justify an answer in unequivocal terms. Assuming the survival of the infants, they would eat, drink, defecate, urinate, and gurgle and cry. These would be direct responses to basic biological drives. But what they would eat, when they would eat, and how they would eat would not be according to the tastes and palates of any group of men we now know. It is quite unlikely that they would cook their food. Presumably they would sooner or later get up on their hind legs, and even before adolescence they would experiment in mating without benefit of incest tabus or any preferred approaches of courtship. They would communicate emotional states through gesture and sounds. But they would be devoid of language, utensils, fire, arts, religion, government, and all the other features of life that distinguish man among the animals. Left solely to their own instinctive devices the children of men would remain undeveloped brutes, which is something less than brats.

In spite of their shortcomings, however, these hapless children would enjoy a social life. They would constitute not only an animal aggregation but also an animal society.

Many animals in addition to man experience social life and even possess social organization. Ant society has long been recognized for its well-delineated division of labor among drones, workers, fighters, males, females, and queen. The organization of the colony with its living quarters and storage rooms for eggs presents the picture of a well-ordered society. The ants interact among each other in an integrated sustained set of relationships. These relationships are preset in the genetic organization of the ants. So far as is known, little if any of their behavior is behavior learned from adult ants. If eggs are hatched without any adult ants present, they produce a host of new ants who when they attain maturity reenact every single aspect of all of the forms of social life that have characterized their species for untold generations.

On the other hand, we would be blessing ourselves with undue credit if we denied all culture-creating capacity to all subhuman creatures.

---

[1] For a cruelly sarcastic debunking of the wolf-child stories, B. Evans, *The Natural History of Nonsense*, is good reading.

Monkeys and apes are quite capable of solving problems posed for them by experimenters. Köhler's early experiments are now endowed with classic prestige.[2] Who is not now familiar with his demonstrations of the ingenuity and intelligence of chimpanzees in joining sticks, piling boxes, untwisting ropes, and picking locks in order to reach a banana? Yerkes and others of Köhler's epigoni have worked out even more complicated tests of the chimp's discriminatory powers and retentive memory.[3] The apes show considerable intelligence and inventiveness. What is more, they are quite definitely capable of learning from each other through direct imitation. Apes ape each other.

When one of a group of experimental apes accidentally jabbed the end of a pole into the ground and found to his immense delight he could hoist himself skyward, all the other members of the colony were soon searching for sticks; pole vaulting was the rage. Another discovered that by scattering bread outside the bars of his cage he could lure unwary yard chickens in close, while he lurked with a stick in his hand with which to jab them. Annoying the chickens then became the current sport of the group. The alarmed squawks of the hens provided rich simian diversion. These and other tricks were discovered by the apes without help from psychologists. When they spread among the group, they had for the time being all the qualities of customs. But, alas, when interest wore off and enthusiasm waned, as it always did after a few days or weeks, each practice was forgotten never to be done again. Their destiny was that of fads; they could not endure to become customs. The permanency of culture was lacking. Apes can spread a pattern of learned behavior through direct imitation, but they cannot talk about it, nor can an older ape tell a younger ape how things were done when he was young. Apes fall short of real culture, because although they can make rudimentary inventions and although their brains are essentially similar to man's, they do not have brains enough to work out and retain complex interrelations between things, and above all they are absolutely incapable of symbolizing things and relationships in speech.

Culture exists in and through communication. Man still remains the sole producer of genuine culture.

The Group. A culture is always carried and made manifest by a group. No individual ever knows or exhibits all the traits of his culture. A culture is the integrated system of learned behavior traits characteristic of the members of a society. The culture and the society are not one. A society of animals, like a society of men, is more than just an animal

[2] W. Köhler, *The Mentality of Apes.*
[3] Effectively summarized by E. A. Hooton in *Man's Poor Relations,* pp. 42–56.

aggregation. It is bound together by an awareness of belonging together—by the social sentiment of the consciousness of kind. It is integrated by instinctive patterns of herd or flock behavior. A human society has just these qualities *plus* cultural control and direction of the behavior of its members. We may then rephrase this by saying that a human society is a permanently organized population acting in accordance with its culture. Reduced to simple formula: S (society) $= P$ (population) $+ C$ (culture).

The Superorganic. We have already said that culture is a part of the natural world—a phenomenon of nature. Culturology, the science of culture, as a specialized branch of anthropology, is a natural science in the same degree as is anthropology. In the natural world, however, culture represents a distinct level of phenomena, the superorganic. And here there is controversy. Not all anthropologists see eye to eye on the superorganic. As a legacy of behaviorism in psychology, a goodly number of anthropologists hold fast to the proposition that since all culture can exist only through the behavior of men, culture is wholly a psychological phenomenon existent in the human nervous system and subject only to psychological laws.[4]

Kroeber, Wissler, Lowie, and White, among others of contemporary anthropologists, hold that culture is a *sui generis* controlled and governed by its own laws and to be understood in its own terms.

This means that if we are going to understand the techniques of housing and the social aspects of housing, there is little or nothing in the psychology or biology of the individual that will tell us anything of use in arriving at an analysis of the origin, development, and function of different housing forms. True, we start with the proposition that there is a basic need for shelter. We also suggested (in Chap. 9) that conservatism in housing development may be linked to security desires and habits set early in life. But psychology does not determine whether a Southwest Indian builds a stone and mortar pueblo or a wood and mud hogan. That is a consequence of his culture. Further, we found that Navajo Indians cannot build pueblo-type houses, because such houses are incompatible with their culture. The elements of Navajo culture have to be understood in terms of Navajo culture. This determines Navajo psychology, not vice versa.

What is true of housing and Navajos is true of all other aspects of culture and all other peoples. Thus the systems of kinship terminology that we discussed in Chap. 17, except as they are limited by the physio-

[4] *Cf.* L. A. White, "The Expansion of the Scope of Science" (*Journal of the Washington Academy of Sciences,* Vol. 37, 1947), pp. 181–210, especially pp. 201*ff.*, for a detailed presentation and critique of some anti-superorganic points of view.

logical principles of sound, are shaped not by psychology but by the forms of marriage and familial relations set by the culture and by influences emanating from culture-historical contacts. A Shoshone calls his father's brother "father," not because of any psychological traits of Shoshone organism but because his father's brother may marry his mother. This is a cultural fact.

The level of phenomena at which culture occurs has been labeled *superorganic*. The nature of the superorganic is best seen in schematic relation to the lower levels of natural phenomena. The prototype of the

THE LEVELS OF NATURAL PHENOMENA AND THEIR RESPECTIVE SCIENCES

Level of phenomena	Type of phenomena	Hierarchy of sciences
IV. Superorganic.......	Culture	Anthropology, culturology, sociology, political science, economics, history
III. Psychic organic....	Sentient animals	Psychology, neurology, social psychology
II. Vital organic.......	Protozoa, metazoa, plants, and nonsentient animals	Organic chemistry, zoology, biology, botany, physical anthropology, anatomy, physiology
I. Inorganic..........	Earth and cosmic matter	Chemistry, physics, geology, astronomy

idea represented in the table was first formulated by the founder of modern sociology, Auguste Comte, more than 100 years ago. Herbert Spencer gave it its later elaboration, and Kroeber brought the concept into anthropology three decades ago.[5]

The lowest level of natural phenomena was the first to take evolutionary form. It consists of inorganic matter—earth materials and cosmic stuff.

With the birth of life something new was added. The inorganic became organic, and in the emergence of vitality a new level of phenomena was reached. No one mistakes the fact that between living organisms and inorganic matter there is *a difference in kind* even though all organisms are composed of inorganic elements. Note this well: the vital organic rests upon the organic level from which it emerged, but the presence of vitality raises it to an entirely different plane. An understanding of the

[5] A. Comte, *Positive Philosophy;* H. Spencer, *The Principles of Sociology,* Vol. 1, pp. 2–16; A. L. Kroeber, "The Superorganic" (*American Anthropologist,* Vol. 19, 1917), pp. 163–213.

principles of chemistry is helpful in the working out of the laws of life, but the scientist who works with the principles of chemistry alone will not get far in the field of biology and the other vital sciences. Organic phenomena have their own body of principles that are not unfolded by the rules and techniques of the basic sciences. Nor does the baffling mystery of the nature of life keep us from recognizing the difference between organic and inorganic phenomena.

Quite late in organic evolution the more advanced life forms became sentient. They developed nervous systems. For the third time in emergent evolution a new order was established. Animals developed the notochord and psyche. Sentient animals are different in kind from nonsentient plants, viruses, metazoa, and protozoa. They represent a different level of phenomena, and no one fails to see the difference between the two levels, although all psychic manifestations are rooted in the vital organism and the nature of the nervous impulse still remains unexplained.

Thus we come to cultural phenomena, the latest and most advanced product of the evolutionary process. As happened twice before, something new was added to what had previously existed. The psychic capacity of man crossed the culture-producing threshold, and he produced a yet higher level of phenomena—that which while it rests on the organic and the psychic is more than either—the more-than-organic, the superorganic, culture.

Boas branded the concept of the superorganic as "mystical" and, therefore, unacceptable.[6] It is most certainly true that it is extremely difficult to see culture as a phenomenon different in kind from the mere psychic—for cultures cannot be seen. But who has seen an atom or a vitamin? Yet from their attributes we know they exist.

An interesting and incidental bypath of the sequence of levels of phenomena is the historical sequence of the development of the sciences. Astronomy, physics, chemistry, and geology—the sciences that deal primarily with the lowest order of phenomena, the inorganic, are the oldest and most highly developed of the sciences. Zoology, biology, physiology, and those sciences predominantly concerned with the vital organic were next in birth and approach to maturity. Psychology and the social sciences were last upon the scene. Among these infant sciences anthropology and culturology were the very last to emerge as full-fledged disciplines. Mastery or near mastery of the lower levels of phenomena seems to have been a necessary prerequisite to scientific awareness of the existence of the higher levels.

---

[6] F. Boas, *Anthropology and Modern Life*, p. 245.

Given 200 years of development of methodology in psychology, sociology, and anthropology, there is some hope that these sciences will approximate the sure-handed skill that has at last been mastered by the other sciences.

Components of Culture. A culture trait or a culture element is a simple functional unit of culture. On the material side it may be a knife or a canoe. It may be a word or a gesture or an idea. It may be an aspect of kinship relations or an action in government. We did not say a culture trait is the simplest functional unit of culture, because each of them is actually a cluster of smaller culture traits. A simple stone knife, for instance, involves the traits of selection of a particular kind of stone, holding it in a particular way to flake it with blows struck in a definite direction with specific force, etc. Irreducible culture traits there are, but anthropologists rarely attempt to phrase their descriptions or pursue their analyses on the lowest levels of irreducible elements. The traits or elements that they treat as though they were the smallest fractions are almost always of a higher order. They are, we might say, trait clusters.

Culture complexes are nothing but larger clusters of traits organized about some nuclear point of reference: the hunting of buffalo, the pursuit of war, the organization of sex. A culture complex is very much akin to a social institution as it was defined on page 302.

.The culture whole or *the* culture of a society is an abstraction of a high order. When we speak of a culture we speak of it as though it were a neatly taped-off entity. Each society, we say, has its own unique culture and is therefore unlike any other society in all its details. This is quite true. But it is equally true, and not usually kept in mind, that no culture in all its details is exactly the same from one moment to the next. Cultures are processes of behavior constantly changing and modifying. Yet in anthropology we investigate a society on a field trip of greater or lesser duration, after which we write up a monograph describing its culture. In so doing, we fix for the moment those main lines of characteristic behavior that we have perceived and noted as though they were all taking place at any given moment. It is as though we stopped a fast action with a high-speed shutter to obtain an instantaneous picture of a continuous action. We get the main contours of the action frozen for an instant in what Linton calls the *culture construct*.[7] It is a statement that lumps together descriptions of modal behavior, in which each mode typifies or represents what is actually a variable range of behavior produced in the members of a society by a given stimulus.

[7] R. M. Linton, *The Cultural Background of Personality*, pp. 43*ff.*

Thus the culture of a people, as described by anthropologists, consists of a set of social norms, a phrasing of the mass habits of a people. In statistical terms a mass habit is nothing but a norm of behavior, that which is "normal." The norm may be that behavior which occurs with greatest frequency (the mode), or that which is average (the mean), or that which falls at the mid-point in the whole range of variation (the medium). When an anthropologist describes a custom, he is usually stating what appears to him to be the modal form of behavior. Only in extremely rare cases does he make an actual statistical count of all behavior over a given period of time to determine an arithmetically accurate distribution. Such precision may be ideally desirable but under the given situation either impossible or impractical. Modern canons of anthropology at least call for observation of the behavior described whenever possible. Yet sometimes it is not possible to observe what is recorded, since the behavior may have died out, or may be secret, or the field worker may not be around at the particular time the event comes off. Therefore, to find out whether a given habit is modal or not we often take a people's word for it. They say this is what they always do, or usually do, or would do, if they did it.

Unfortunately, such pseudo modes do not even provide us with a reasonable facsimile of a genuine culture construct. What they do give us is a formulation of the *ideal culture*. It is the idealization of normal behavior as phrased by the native informants and recorded by the field worker as though it were the culture construct. It is never the real culture. We say this categorically, because all people idealize their norms of conduct to some degree. There are always gaps between what a people think they do, say they do, and actually do. Every society has what Judge Jerome Frank calls "pretend rules"—rules mouthed but not acted upon.[8]

This seeming hypocrisy is an inevitable concomitant of social life; it is inherent in the nature of culture. Culture is a complex web covering all aspects of life, and every culture is derived from many sources. It is an accretion of the ages and the result of multifarious influences. No culture can ever be wholly consistent in its underlying values. Where gaps exist between ideal and real norms, the ideal is often rooted in one set of values, while real behavior is set on another. In addition to this unwholesome influence, there is yet another that mounts from the duality of the person in society: the inevitable clash of interests of the person acting in terms of his immediate self-interests and the person acting as

[8] J. Frank, "Lawlessness" (*Encyclopedia of the Social Sciences*, Vol. 9, 1933), p. 277.

a responsible member of the group. Ideal norms are generally selected and phrased in terms of group well-being. The individual has learned that he had better subscribe to them publicly, even though he is going to act differently outside of the public view.

An outstanding example of this is found in Malinowski's account of the Trobriand Islanders with respect to clan incest.

If you were to inquire into the matter among the Trobrianders [wrote Malinowski, who did precisely that], you would find that . . . the natives show horror at the idea of violating the rules of exogamy and that they believe that sores, disease and even death might follow clan incest. [But] from the point of view of the native libertine, *suvasova* (the breach of exogamy) is indeed a specially interesting and spicy form of erotic experience. Most of my informants would not only admit but actually do boast of having committed this offense or that of adultery (*kaylasi*); and I have many concrete, well-attested cases on record.[9]

The natives manage to get away with it, provided they keep it from becoming a publicly recognized scandal, because they have a system of magic which ensures immunity from the threatened diseases if a person has the proper charms.

One department of the culture provides the means for making a mockery of the other. Preservation of the clan is a group interest loudly acclaimed. Intercourse with a clan cousin is an individually motivated sport that is a genuine custom.

A similar conflict of norms existed among the Comanches, who married their young girls to older men. Ideally, they loved and respected one another—especially the girl her husband. Actually, a considerable number of romance-seeking wives ran off with dashing young warriors. This was against the law—for the law is on the side of husbands. The Comanche husband could, and as a matter of fact had to, sue for damages. He could, and often did, kill his wife, if not cut off her nose. This was his privilege by law. But the interesting part of it all is that a deserting wife and her absconder always ran off with a war party. It was the custom. So they were aided and abetted in flaunting the marital norms by fellow Comanches. It was a group custom to break the law.[10]

We need not discuss here the gaps that exist between our ideals of

[9] B. Malinowski, *Crime and Custom in Savage Society*, pp. 79, 84.

[10] A number of cases are presented and discussed in E. A. Hoebel, *The Political Organization and Law-ways of the Comanche Indians* (American Anthropological Association, Memoir 54: Contributions from the Laboratory of Anthropology, 4, 1940), pp. 49–66.

democracy and our practices that negate them, even though they are a tender spot in our social body.[11]

It is because of such ever-present gaps between the thought and the deed, between the ideal and the action, that the modern realistic social-science behaviorist will no longer take a people's say-so as valid evidence of the real behavior norm.

An important feature of culture traits that is frequently forgotten by sociologists in their discussions of folkways and mores is a manifestation of social differentiation and leeway. In the chapters on status and role, kinship, and clubs, the internal segmentation of societies was discussed in some detail. Each social status has its distinctive role or concatenation of behavior patterns. Many norms of behavior apply only to certain members of a given status in the society. A culture is not shared evenly throughout. Some people are privileged to carry more of it than others. Some culture traits are characteristic of some subgroups within the society but not of others.

Linton has on this basis formulated a useful breakdown of norms in terms of their relative applicability to a social population. These he has named universals, alternatives, and specialties.[12] Those norms which apply to all members of the society and from which there is no permissible deviation are called *universals*. An example would be the prohibition of incest in most societies. All persons must refrain from sexual relations with brother, sister, parent, child. Universals are relatively rare within any given culture.

Much more numerous are the norms that are known as *alternatives*, the patterns that exist where several different norms apply to the same situation. A permissible range of choice and leeway is available. Neckties may be called for, but the choice may be between black, white, or colored four-in-hands or bows. Meat should be cooked, but the individual may choose between baking, boiling, roasting, or broiling, rare, medium, or well done, seasoned or unseasoned.

The traits that are restricted to a particular group, as the common tabus of medicine men or the cut of the hair of the boys in an Omaha clan, are *specialties*.

The specialties of one group may be known to the other members of the society and yet not be used by them, because they are not patterns for their behavior. Many American adult men know the Boy Scout salute, having once been Scouts, but they do not use it as a form of greeting after they have left Scouting behind. In a complex society, however,

---

[11] Cf. G. Myrdal, *An American Dilemma*.
[12] R. M. Linton, *The Study of Man*, pp. 272–275.

most specialties remain unknown to most of the people. This may be because the specialties require unique aptitudes or a rigorous course of training undertaken only by a few. Or, it may be that the specialties are the secret and hidden knowledge of a few, kept within their closed circle for the benefits that may be derived from secretiveness. The result is that no individual can ever acquire or manifest in himself all the elements of his society's culture. It means also that no anthropologist, even the most assiduous, can ever make note of, to say nothing of record, all the aspects of any culture, even the simplest known to man.

This then, provides the answer to the question often asked, "How can one speak of American culture when there are such divergences in the cultures of New Yorkers and the Kentucky Highlanders? Between the Italians of Lower Manhattan and the Scandinavians of Minnesota? Between the Yankees of Vermont and the *paisanos* of Monterey?" The universals shared by all Americans are the common binding and integrating elements of American culture and society. The specialties of the different regional groups and socio-economic classes are merely differentiating elements.

The cohesive strength of a society is in part a product of the relative proportion of universals to specialties. In any analysis of a society and its culture it is absolutely essential, in the interests of clarity and accuracy, to keep the subgroup you are talking about always before yourself and your listeners. A social scientist must never generalize from the norms of a subgroup to make statements about the society as a whole, unless he has observed that the norms of the subgroup are also characteristic of the whole. Americans who live west of the Hudson River and north of Long Island Sound can appreciate the meaning of this injunction, if they will reflect on their feelings about European authors who write about America after a visit to New York City.

When we speak of culture as the integrated system of learned behavior characteristic of the members of a society, we cover both *overt* and *covert* behavior under the term. Overt behavior, of course, is that which is manifest in motor activity. Covert behavior consists of attitudes, emotional orientations, presets of the organism that may profoundly influence overt behavior without becoming themselves overtly expressed. All subconscious behavior falls within this realm. Covert culture is hidden culture, for which anthropology and psychology are only now beginning to shape reliable tools of study.

Finally, we should take note that what is traditionally called *material culture* is not really culture at all. It is nothing more than the concrete products of overt cultural behavior.

Archaeology, which deals in a scientific manner with the recovery and study of the objects of material culture buried in the earth, is always limited in the results it can produce. It is doomed always to be the lesser part of anthropology. The use and meaning of any object depends almost wholly upon nonmaterial behavior patterns, and the objects derive their true significance from such patterns. A pointed stick may be a dibble, a weapon, a scepter, a stake, or a phallic symbol. What it is can be determined only through contact with the living culture.

Thus when the archaeologist uncovers a prehistoric culture, it is not really the culture that he unearths but merely the surviving products of that culture, tangible remnants of the intangible reality. The actual culture became extinct when the society that carried it passed out of existence. No culture can exist divorced from living beings, for culture and society are inseparable, as are mind and body on a lower level.

CHAPTER 31

CULTURE AREAS AND CULTURE SYSTEMS

Classification is nothing more than a grouping of phenomena in accordance with certain of their qualities. There are as many possible and valid classifications of a group of things as it possesses qualities or traits. Any classification is valid, providing the basis or criterion for classification is a true attribute of the thing being classified and providing the criterion is held constant throughout that particular classification. When the requirements of validity of criterion and consistency of application have been met, one classification is as *true* as another.

Classifications have greater or lesser significance and usefulness, however, depending upon the interests of the investigator and the problems he is attempting to solve.

Take a barrel of mixed apples. What possibilities for classification are there in it? Color, size, shape, flavor, juiciness, number of seeds, and toughness of skin are obvious attributes. You may properly and scientifically classify your apples by using any one of these attributes as a criterion for grouping. But if you are going to select the best apples for cider making, then the only classification of significance will be one based upon flavor and juice content. Color and shape are irrelevant. On the other hand, if you want to select apples to be sold in *bon voyage* baskets, color and size will be the criteria of greatest significance.

Cultures may be classified according to any attributes shared among a number of cultures. This can be done for single elements of culture such as stepdaughter marriage, domestication of dogs, or the use of salt.[1] Culture complexes may be classified and compared in terms of shamanism, peyote cult, guardian spirits, bow and arrow, etc.[2] Or cultures may be classified and compared with respect to basic institutions, such as food economy, religion, or law.

[1] A. L. Kroeber, "Stepdaughter Marriage" (*American Anthropologist*, Vol. 42, 1940), pp. 562–570; "Culture Element Distributions: XV, Salt, Dogs, Tobacco" (*Anthropological Records*, Vol. 6, No. 1, 1941), pp. 1–20.

[2] W. Z. Park, *Shamanism in Western North America;* W. LaBarre, *The Peyote Cult* (Yale University Publications in Anthropology, No. 19, 1938); R. F. Benedict, *The Concept of the Guardian Spirit in North America* (American Anthropological Association, Memoir 29, 1923).

It is also possible to classify and compare cultures on the basis of more abstract attributes, such as degree of integration, internal homogeneity, or the social processes of cooperation and competition.[3] Finally, classification may be attempted in terms of general categories of configuration, as Benedict has done with her famous categories of Dionysian and Apollonian, or, as Dr. Morris Opler suggests, in terms of *theme*, which he defines as "a postulate or position, declared or implied, and usually controlling behavior or stimulating activity, which is tacitly approved or openly promoted in a society." [4]

Culture Areas. The culture area concept is a classificatory device based upon cultural similarities and geographic distribution. A culture area may be defined as a segment of geographic space within which the cultures reveal a degree of similarity sufficient to set them off from cultures lying outside the area.

The similarities within the area are brought about by diffusion, or borrowing, of traits from one tribe to another *and* the selective processes arising from the basic physiographic characteristics of the area and the nature of the food resources it offers for human exploitation.

Boas was the first to conceive of culture areas as an anthropological tool in the arrangement of museum displays. Wissler first used it extensively in ethnological analysis, but his original map of culture areas for this continent is unfortunately oversimplified. His classifications are so broad that they convey an impression of homogeneity in culture over wide areas in a way that is hardly justified. This is especially true of the Southwest area. Pueblo culture cannot be lumped with that of the Navajos and the Apaches. Nor should any of these be lumped with the cultures of the Yuman tribes of the Gila and Lower Colorado rivers. There is also a great gap between the cultures of the sedentary gardening tribes of the river valleys of the Plains (the Mandan, Hidatsa, Arikara, Pawnee, Ponca, Oto, etc.) and the roving, hunting tribes of the grasslands.

Further, Wissler's areas are based primarily upon subsistence techniques and material culture. His classification tends to ignore the fact that the distributions of many traits of nonmaterial culture do not conform to area patterns based on food and implements. This fact was pointed up in a critical comment by Boas some time ago, as follows:

[3] See the "Interpretative Statement" in M. Mead (ed.), *Cooperation and Competition among Primitive Peoples*, pp. 458–516.

[4] M. E. Opler, "Themes as Dynamic Forces in Culture" (*The American Journal of Sociology*, Vol. 51, 1945), pp. 198–206.

Like every other classificatory device built upon a selection of typical traits, the concept of culture areas contains a strong subjective element and varies according to the stress laid upon one or the other of the traits of culture. To those who see the principal trait of culture in economic conditions and inventions and to those who lay particular stress on psychological attitudes, folkloristic material or social organization, the culture areas will not be the same.[5]

To overcome this criticism, Kroeber took meticulous care, in his study of culture areas, to lump together only those tribes which showed congruity in a really large number of traits.[6] This led him to identify eighty-four culture areas for North America, grouped within ten larger areas loosely similar to those originally set forth by Wissler. Such an analysis better serves the purposes of advanced detailed study of American Indian culture. But even Kroeber's method cannot meet the fact that cultures change drastically through time. Culture area maps are good only for delimited periods.

We may sketch the main features of each of the primary culture areas of North America as follows:

I. Arctic.
  1. Main tribes: Eskimos.
  2. Environment: Arctic maritime and coastal, with migration to interior tundras in summer.
  3. Food source: Sea mammals and fish in winter; caribou and fresh-water fish in summer.
  4. Housing: Iglus of snow or dugouts in winter; skin tents in summer.
  5. Social organization: Bilateral family; no clans. Autonomous tribelets with weak chiefship; no organized council or government.
  6. Religion: Shamanism, séances, individual guardian spirits, manifold tabus, and public confession of sins; masks used in impersonation of deities.
  7. Material culture: Skin boats, harpoons, bow, dog sled, snow knife, stone kettles, tailored skin clothing.
  8. Art: Carved and incised ivory figurines.

II. Northwest Coast.
  1. Main tribes: Tlingit, Haida, Tsimshian in north; Kwakiutl, Bella Coola in central part; Salish, Nootka, Chinook in south.

[5] F. Boas, "Anthropology" (*Encyclopedia of the Social Sciences*, Vol. 2, 1930), p. 105.
[6] A. L. Kroeber, "Cultural and Natural Areas of Native North America" (*University of California Publications in American Archaeology and Ethnology*, Vol. 39, 1939).

2. Environment: Deeply indented coast heavily forested with fir. Mild, moist climate.
3. Food source: Salmon and other sea foods, berries and some hunting of wild animals. Fish smoked and dried.
4. Housing: Large rectangular plank houses with gabled roofs.
5. Social organization: Strong emphasis on ranking—nobility, commoners, and slaves. Totemic heraldry with carved wooden crests representing family mythologies. Societies with complex initiation rituals. Moieties and clans. Chiefs with exalted rank but weak governmental structure. War for revenge. Potlatch.
6. Religion: Family guardian spirits. Ritual dramatization of mythology. Elaborate masking.
7. Material culture: Highly developed wood-carving technique. Wooden bowls and boxes. Large dugout canoes. Basketry. No pottery. Polished stone tools. Bow and war club. Loose skin mantles and basketry hats. Skin and slat armor with wooden helmets. No shields.
8. Art: Highly stylized and unique painting and carving.
   These traits prevail in the northern group of the area. In the south influences from California and the Plateau have effected some modifications.

III. California.
   1. Main tribes: Yurok, Karok, Hupa, Shasta, Pomo, Miwok, Maidu, Wintun, Mono, Yokut, Serrano.
   2. Environment: Considerable range of climate from moist to dry. Equable temperature.
   3. Food source: Primarily acorns. Limited hunting and fishing except in north. Shellfish extensively on coast.
   4. Housing: Simple brush structures in considerable variety in south. Plank houses in north.
   5. Social organization: Hereditary chieftains, but weak governmental organization; lineages, and moieties. Emphasis on rank and status in north; absent in south. Men's house. Puberty ceremonies.
   6. Religion: Shamanism. Weak ritualism. High God concept.
   7. Material culture: Scanty skin clothing, superb basketry. No pottery. Little woodwork. Sinew-backed bow. Canoes in north; absent in central part.
   8. Art: Carving in the north. Basketry in central and southern parts.

IV. Mackenzie-Yukon.
   1. Main tribes: Kohotana, Kutchin, Yellowknife, Dogrib, Slave, Carrier, Chipewyan, Sarsi, Caribou-eater.
   2. Environment: Subarctic swamp and forest.
   3. Food source: Caribou, small forest animals, fresh-water fish, berries.
   4. Housing: Predominantly double lean-tos of brush, tipis in east, plank and log houses in west.

5. Social organization: Weak clans and totemism in west, with social classes. Bilateral family predominant in east. Weak political organization. Puberty institutionalized.
6. Religion: Shamanism and personal guardian spirits. Little ceremonialism.
7. Material culture: Snowshoe, bark canoe, toboggan. Skin clothing. Net bags and fish nets. Bark vessels. No pottery. Baskets. Spears and fish hooks. Strike-a-light instead of fire drill.
8. Art: Weak and undeveloped.

V. Basin-Plateau.

A. Basin.
1. Main tribes: Shoshone, Ute, Goshiute, Paiute, Paviotso.
2. Environment: Desert interspersed with mountains.
3. Food source: Pine nuts, seeds, roots and vermin.
4. Housing: Conical brush shelters and windscreens. Puebloid houses and pit dwellings in late prehistoric times.
5. Social organization: Bilateral bands. Band headmen. No tribal government; no clans; no fraternities.
6. Religion: Simple shamanism and guardian spirit complex.
7. Material culture: Coiled basketry, little pottery, rabbit skin robes.
8. Art: Virtually lacking.

B. Columbia Plateau.
1. Main tribes: Thompson, Shushwap, Flathead, Nez Percé, Northern Shoshone.
2. Environment: High plateau. Semi-arid in the south, forested in the north.
3. Food source: Salmon, game, berries and roots.
4. Housing: Pit dwelling predominant.
5. Social organization: Emphasis on puberty rites; band and tribal organization weak. Attenuated ranking after the manner of the Northwest Coast.
6. Religion: Similar to Basin.
7. Material culture: Excellent basketry but no pottery. Skin clothing and rabbit skin robes. Simple bark fiber weaving. Fishhooks, spears, weirs and nets.
8. Art: Weak and undeveloped.

VI. Plains.

A. Village tribes.
1. Main tribes: Mandan, Hidatsa, Arikara, Ponca, Iowa, Omaha, Pawnee.
2. Environment: Open grasslands, limited rainfall, well-watered river bottom lands.
3. Food source: Maize with subsidiary game.

4. Housing: Large polygonal log houses covered with earth and sod. Tipis on expeditions.

5. Social organization: Clans, phratries, and moieties. Strong tribal councils. Military and dance societies.

6. Religion: Individual guardian spirits. Vision quest. Well-developed ceremonials.

7. Material culture: Skin clothing, ceremonial feathered headdress. Bow, lance, war club, hide shield. Rawhide boxes. Pottery poor or lacking, no baskets, or weaving. Travois. Domesticated the dog and horse.

8. Art: Stylized but realistic painting on hides. Porcupine-quill and bead-work embroidery on hides in geometric designs.

B. Nomadic tribes.

1. Main tribes: Blackfoot, Gros Ventre, Assiniboin, Crow, Cheyenne, Dakota, Arapaho, Kiowa, Comanche.

2. Environment: Open, semiarid plains.

3. Food source: Bison, antelope, roots, and berries.

4. Housing: Skin tipis.

5. Social organization: Clans in north and east, absent in west and south. Democratic political organization with tribal councils (except Co-manches) and differentiation of peace and war chiefs. Male status based on coup counting and generosity. Military and religious associations. Camp circle.

6. Religion: Sun dance and other group rituals. Guardian spirit complex with vision quest. Medicine bundles. Medicine men (shamans).

7. Material culture: Essentially similar to that of nomadic tribes (above).

8. Art: Essentially similar to that of nomadic tribes (above).

VII. Southwest.

A. Pueblo.

1. Main tribes: Eastern: Taos, Santa Clara, San Ildefonso; Central: Cochiti, Santo Domingo, San Felipe, Santa Ana, Jemez, Sia, Isleta, Laguna, Acoma; Western: Zuñi, Hopi.

2. Environment: High desert plateau interspersed with wooded mountains.

3. Food source: Maize, beans, squash. (Sheep, goats, and cattle in modern times.)

4. Housing: Stone or adobe, multistoried, compound community apartment houses.

5. Social organization: Dual division with paternal clans in east, dual division with weak clans in central, strong maternal clans in west. Strong complex theocratic government. Strong ceremonial and religious associations.

6. Religion: Sun cult, ancestor cults, kachinas, ritual prayers. Complex, pervasive, dramatic ceremonialism. Witch complex. Ritual curing. Sand painting. Kivas.
7. Material culture: Excellent pottery and weaving; basketry less developed. Cloth clothing. Metate. Bow, throwing stick.
8. Art: Decorative pottery and blankets. Wall paintings. Sand paintings. In modern times silver and turquoise jewelry.

B. Nomadic tribes.
  1. Main tribes: Navajo and Apache (Jicarilla, Mescalero, Western, etc.).
  2. Environment: Same as Pueblo.
  3. Food source: Maize and small animals, plus sheep in modern times (Navajo). Hunting (Apache).
  4. Housing: Wood and earth hogans (Navajo); skin tipis and brush arbor (Eastern Apache); brush lodges (Western Apache).
  5. Social organization: No tribal government. Headmen with limited political power. Maternal clans. Band organization.
  6. Religion: Ritual priests or singers. Complex curing rituals or chants (Navajo).
  7. Material culture: In most respects quite meager. Excellent weaving. Weak pottery and basketry (Navajo). Apache similar to Plains in many respects, but good in basketry.
  8. Art: Elaborate sand paintings. Geometric designs on woven blankets. Silver work (Navajo). Plains type beadwork (Apache).

C. Colorado-Gila.
  1. Main tribes: Mohave, Yuma, Pima, Papago, Maricopa, Yavapai, Walapai.
  2. Environment: Low-elevation desert.
  3. Food source: Maize and beans, small game, seeds, and berries.
  4. Housing: Adobe or flat-roofed brush lodges.
  5. Social organization: Weak governmental organization. Bands. Headmen.
  6. Religion: Individualistic. Little ceremonial development.
  7. Material culture: Irrigation. Good to excellent basketry. Weaving. Poor pottery.
  8. Art: Poorly developed.

VIII. Northeast Woodlands.
  1. Main tribes: Cree, Ojibway, Montagnais (in Canada), Iroquois, Mohican, Delaware, Erie, Potawatomi, Winnebago, Sauk, Fox, Menominee.
  2. Environment: Deciduous forests with cold winters.
  3. Food sources: Maize, squash, beans (except in extreme north). Extensive hunting and trapping of forest animals. Fish; wild rice in Great Lakes region.

4. Housing: Birch bark over pole frames. Stockaded villages in east.
5. Social organization: Clans with totemism. Strong government, except in north. Iroquois league.
6. Religion: Individual guardian spirit complex. Algonquian midewiwin.
7. Material culture: Bow and ball-headed war club. Bark and dugout canoes. Skin clothing, snowshoes. Bark mats and vessels. Pottery and wampum.
8. Art: Floral-design beadwork. Iroquois wooden masks.

IX. Southeast Woodlands.

1. Main tribes: Shawnee, Cherokee, Creek, Choctaw, Natchez, Seminole.
2. Environment: Forest with warm winters.
3. Food sources: Maize, cane, pumpkin, melon. Extensive hunting and trapping of forest animals.
4. Housing: Rectangular or round houses with thatched roofs, set in palisaded villages.
5. Social organization: Moieties and clans. Strong governments and tribal confederacies. Social classes.
6. Religion: Sun and fire ceremonies. Temples set on mounds. Priesthood. Strong shamanism. Complex agricultural rituals.
7. Material culture: Skin clothing, some of woven bark. Special forms of mats and basketry. Notable use of cane for knives and darts. Blowgun. Well-developed pottery and stone implements. Dugout canoes.
8. Art: Shows Central American influence.

Provisional outlines of culture areas have been set up for other parts of the world in addition to North America north of the Rio Grande. The assiduous reader may seek out the descriptive analyses of the areas in the sources given below.[7]

Configurations of Culture. A culture is built up of elements and traits, but the significance of a culture is less in its inventory of traits than in the manner of its integration of traits. For this reason we have phrased our definition of culture in terms of "the integrated system of learned behavior."

Benedict, who introduced the configurational idea into modern anthropological thought, has written of culture that "The whole, as modern science is insisting in many fields, is not merely the sum of all its parts,

[7] Africa: M. J. Herskovits, "A Preliminary Consideration of Culture Areas of Africa" (*American Anthropologist*, Vol. 26, 1924), pp. 50–63; "The Culture Area of Africa" (*Africa*, Vol. 3, 1930), pp. 59–77; see also his *Backgrounds of African Art* (Denver, 1945); Madagascar: R. M. Linton, "Culture Areas in Madagascar" (*American Anthropologist*, Vol. 30, 1928), pp. 363–390; Asia: E. Bacon, "A Preliminary Attempt to Determine the Culture Areas of Asia" (*Southwestern Journal of Anthropology*, Vol. 2, 1946), pp. 117–132; Indonesia: R. Kennedy, *Islands and Peoples of the Indies* (Smithsonian Institution War Background Studies, No. 14, 1943), pp. 11–30.

but the result of a unique arrangement and interrelation of the parts that has brought about a new entity." [8]

This is a sound principle for the understanding of the nature of cultures and the uniqueness of divergent societies, for it is theoretically possible for two societies to possess identical inventories of culture elements and yet so to arrange the relationships of the elements to each other as to produce two quite unlike systems of integration. By simple analogy, a mason may take two identical piles of bricks and equal quantities of mortar. Yet with these materials he may build a fireplace, a cesspool, or a garden wall, depending on the way he integrates the bricks.

The configuration of a culture may be defined as its delineated contours as formed by the structural interrelation of all its elements. It presumes internal integration in accordance with some basic and dominant principles or value systems underlying the whole scheme.

Pueblo Culture. In Benedict's discussion of the configuration of culture, the Pueblo Indians of the American Southwest have been shown to possess a culture that stresses restraint and orderliness in behavior, avoidance of emotional excess and display in personal experience and ritual, rigorous suppression of individual initiative and innovation, with quiet cooperation in group endeavor.[9] Pueblo culture presents a philosophy of a carefully ordered universe in which man is but one harmonious part of a delicate balance that involves all nature. As long as each man plays his ordained roles in the traditional manner, all people will prosper, for the relation between man and the universe is reciprocal. The rain gods will make water-giving clouds; the gods of plants and fertility will mature the colored corn; the dancing gods will visit the village. All functions necessary to the good life and survival of the pueblo will be fulfilled. But if any person fails to perform his roles in the traditional and proper way, it will upset the delicate universal balance and bring down disaster upon the people.

Pueblo culture is a rich culture in a physically poor environment. Ceremonialism and ritual drama in elaborate religious complexes are supported upon a skillfully managed horticultural base precariously sustained in a romantically beautiful but realistically harsh desert.

The nature of Pueblo house structure—the compact, masonry built, collective dwellings into which the members of each tribe are jammed—was discussed in Chap. 9, as well as the physically imposed need for cooperative responsibility, the impossibility for much individual leeway. The cosmic and social philosophy of the Pueblos emphasizes what Bene-

[8] *Patterns of Culture*, p. 47.
[9] *Ibid.*, Chap. 4.

dict has called the *Apollonian ideal*—the middle-of-the-road way of life that avoids all extremes of sensate behavior and, in the Pueblos, distrusts and suppresses individualism as a disruptive unbalancing force.

Economic wealth is of little cultural interest to Pueblo Indians. Food is important but they are not obsessed with its worth. Rather, religion has displaced economics as a center of social interest.

Alorese Culture. To draw the lines of another configuration, we may briefly turn to the culture of the people of Alor in Indonesia.[10]

Like the Pueblo Indians the Alorese are gardeners, but for them the environment is that of the tropical forest. For women the main cultural activity is gardening; for men it is an endless round of wealth exchanges, the making and collecting of loans. Money, which in Alor consists of pigs, Javanese bronze vessels (*moko*), and gongs, is lent out at interest with tight bonds of obligation that bind the debtor to his creditor. Marriage and death, among other occasions, call for extravagant consumption of pork along with tremendous exchanges of *moko* and gongs. The heavy burdens of these occasions force the principals deep into debt; except as it stimulates the growing of pigs by the men, all this exchange activity contributes little to utilitarian needs or actual economic production.

Capitalism in Alor is reduced to a vehicle for egotistical dominance over one's fellow men. In the family the internal tensions and hostilities of the Alorese household have already been cited as an example of a family type that fails to gratify the security needs of the infant child (see pages 465–466). Alorese culture is integrated about the basic insecurity of the individual. Dominance through credit control is a futile attempt at compensatory adjustment.

In like manner, Alorese war rested not upon any military interest. War was only a means of getting even, a sort of irritable gesture expressed not in any art of warfare but in a series of long-drawn-out feuds marked by cowardly assaults carried out by trickery and stealth with women the victims as well as men.

In the Pueblos and Alor we have two cultures with reasonably distinct clear-cut configurations producing two quite divergent types of societies. These examples indicate in a brief manner the way in which variant cultures shape variant societies.

At this point it becomes advisable to turn a somewhat more critical eye to this enticing device of cultural analysis and classification. Along

---

[10] C. Du Bois, *The People of Alor*. A condensed summary can be found in A. Kardiner, *The Psychological Frontiers of Society*, Chap. 5.

with its alluring attractions the configuration method harbors some less obvious but definitely dangerous pitfalls.

Culture is no simple matter. It may not be, as Lowie paraphrases Gilbert and Sullivan, a "thing of shreds and patches." [11] Nevertheless, it is a complex web drawn from many sources. Its integration is, as has been noted, never perfect, nor are its values wholly consistent.

The configurationalist is tempted to make it consistent. To make the configuration of a culture stand out clearly, the analyst is apt to draw the lines of the configuration in bold forceful strokes. The representation slights or even ignores those incongruent features of the culture that unbalance or disturb the patterns of the composition envisaged in the mind of the author. The consequent portrayal may well lend subjective insight into human motivations; it may strike an enthusiastic emotional response with the effectiveness of high art. In art this is legitimate. Indeed, it may be the very function of art. But is it a legitimate aim for anthropology as science? A bit of art in the work of the scientist is needful for high science, but when the impulse of the artist overcomes the realistic objectivity of the scientist in the work of anthropology, *caveat emptor!*

The purpose of anthropology is to make possible a fuller understanding of the nature of man and his ways of life. How it does this is a matter of method. The method of anthropology is and must be the method of science: observation and description, classification of the data observed, analysis, interpretation, and—if the data allow it—generalization. In the nineteenth century, anthropology made great headway in the collecting and recording of data. It opened up new worlds of factual information concerning man. At the same time it moved overeagerly to generalization. Great and impressive schemes of evolutionary systems were formed by intellectual giants like Tylor and Morgan. Early in the twentieth century a critical reaction set in, primarily under the rigorous leadership of Boas. Emphasis was shifted to facts and the testing of theory against hard fact. Anthropology, especially in America, became rigorously empirical. The zenith of this trend was manifest in Lowie's *Primitive Society* (1920), of which Justice Oliver Wendell Holmes wrote to his British confrere, Sir Frederick Pollock,

I shall first devote myself to reading Primitive Society by Robert H. Lowie, which seems to be an advance on all previous books in the same sense as Tourtoulon's *Principes philosophique de l'histoire du droit*, distrusting and even discrediting the too sweeping and easy generalizations of our earlier day.[12]

[11] *Primitive Society*, p. 441.
[12] *Holmes-Pollock Letters*, letter of Nov. 22, 1920, Vol. 2, p. 59.

This and the many monographic reports on field investigation by Boas and his followers (not forgetting Boas's important book, *The Mind of Primitive Man*) put anthropology on firm ground. Careful field studies by a number of English and German anthropologists and non-Boas-trained Americans contributed to the same end.[13] Anthropology rose to a status of high respect among the social sciences; it acquired a well-earned reputation for scientific reliability. It also earned from those who prefer a social philosophy to a social science the scornful epithets "creeping empiricism" and "anthropology for anthropology's sake." The brilliant and impatient legal scholar Seagle recently scolded that the works of "the critical school of anthropology . . . are thus often meaningless conglomerations of data."[14]

Such carping is hardly justified, for no collection of data is meaningless so long as the data represent actual facts. The meaning in the data has to be extracted by the analyst and subjected to interpretation. But first there must be data—good data and sound. The meaning of data depends upon their relations to other phenomena. That is why any system of classification is useful or useless, depending upon the nature of the problems chosen for solution.

The tenet of Boas and those who held to his method and orientation was that interpretation must wait on the facts. The first job in any science is to get the facts—lots of them. Interpretation based on partial data is at best highly provisional, at worst false and misleading.

How many facts the anthropologist must have before he leaves off field work for analysis and interpretation is hard to say. Certain it is that he will never get all the facts. And certain it is that if he does not stop to organize and communicate his data to fellow workers, his efforts will produce no contribution to science and knowledge.

When it comes to interpretation he must use all the pertinent facts—not just those that buttress a thesis or an ideology. He must never lay himself open to the charge the elder Huxley is said to have hurled at the sociologist Herbert Spencer: "For him the supreme tragedy is a hypothesis destroyed by a fact."

Where then does this lead us in our evaluation of configurational anthropology?

Enthusiasm for startling and contrasting configurations in order to show the effect of culture on behavior and personality produces results

[13] For examples, see the works of Spencer and Gillen on the tribes of central Australia; Seligman, Malinowski, and Thurnwald on Melanesia; Rattray and others on Africa; and Gusinde on Tierra del Fuego.

[14] W. Seagle, *The Quest for Law*, p. 427.

of particular appeal to the intelligent nonanthropologist. As the Melanesianist Thurnwald wrote of Mead's *Sex and Temperament in Three Primitive Societies*, "It will win friends for anthropology," [15] but Thurnwald was sharply critical of the factual basis of the book.

Fortune, who participated in the investigations of one of the three tribes described by Mead, has observed,

> It is not an easy task to view Arapesh social culture in its entire sweep, . . . [While] the theory of Arapesh social culture having the one, uniform tendency, so called maternal, remains a hypothetical creation, it is not proper to assume that the Arapesh must be conceived either in terms of that hypothesis, or in terms of alternative hypothesis. It is better to make no hypotheses.[16]

To doubt the validity of a hypothesis is justifiable. To reject hypothesis making *in toto* is not. Without hypotheses no science can advance. Hypotheses are legitimate scientific tools, and no scientist should be criticized for making what turns out to be an erroneous hypothesis. What scientists are obligated to criticize is any tendency to force a hypothesis beyond its limits. The squeezing and distortion of facts to fit a hypothesis on a supposed configuration is the offense against scientific method that causes concern (see also note 11, page 293, above).

Pueblo and Plains configurations were sketched in terms similar to those set forth by Benedict in her formulation of the Apollonian configuration for Pueblo culture and the Dionysian configuration for Plains culture. The Peace Chief pattern in Plains culture, which is surely Apollonian in character, is, however, ignored in Benedict's treatment of the two cultures. Morris Opler feels it is also overlooked in Benedict's appraisal of the Chiricahua Apache, on whom Opler has published a rich and meticulous monograph. Opler has challenged Benedict's characterization of Chiricahua Apache culture [17] because "it virtually ignores the cooperative and peaceful aspects of Chiricahua life in order that these Apaches may be interpreted as Dionysiacs." [18]

The presentation of Pueblo configuration in *Patterns of Culture* seems to have reversed the selective process in order to emphasize an Apollonian configuration. The individualistic and terroristic aspects of

[15] R. Thurnwald, "Review of *Sex and Temperament in Three Primitive Societies*" (*American Anthropologist*, Vol. 38, 1940), p. 667.

[16] R. F. Fortune, "Arapesh Warfare" (*American Anthropologist*, Vol. 41, 1939), p. 37.

[17] R. F. Benedict, "Review of *An Apache Life-Way*" (*American Anthropologist*. Vol. 44, 1942), pp. 692–693.

[18] M. E. Opler, "On the Method of Writing Anthropological Monographs" (*American Anthropologist*, Vol. 45, 1943), p. 329.

Pueblo life are virtually ignored to highlight the cooperative restraint of Pueblo living. The idealized composition is beautiful. In the modern world of discord, strife, and insecurity it is soothing to contemplate. But what are the facts?

In the first place, Pueblo culture is not so homogeneous with respect to social organization that a configuration for "The Pueblos of New Mexico" [19] can be drawn from a description of the single Pueblo of Zuñi.

The Western Pueblos (Hopi and Zuñi) are uxorilocal, matrilineal, and have strong clans. But it is wrong to leave the impression that this is a universal Pueblo characteristic. Among the several Keres-speaking Pueblos of Central New Mexico (Cochiti, Santo Domingo, San Felipe, Santa Ana, Sia, Acoma) clans, although matrilineal, are weak. Moieties, which are lacking in the west, are strong. Fraternal associations also play a correspondingly greater role. Among the Eastern Pueblos north of Santa Fe (Santa Clara, San Ildefonso, Taos, etc.), clans are patrilineal and relatively unimportant. Patrilineal moieties dominate social life. Houses are owned by the men, and residence is consequently virilocal.[20]

"Torture," according to Benedict's configuration, "was . . . consistently rejected." [21] "The Pueblo practice of beating with stripes is likewise without intent to torture." [22] But at Zuñi, at the climax of initiation "the boys are terrified." [23]

Against the purely symbolic nature of whipping just cited, the empirical observer Voth reported long ago that in the Hopi initiations at the pueblo of Oraibi "on several occasions some of the boys, probably as a result of fear and pain, involuntarily micturated and in one or two cases even defecated." [24] Naughty Pueblo children are terrorized by cannibal kachinas, called in by their parents to give them a good fright.[25]

[19] Title of Chap. 4, *Patterns of Culture*.

[20] Cf. F. M. Hawley, "Pueblo Social Organization as a Lead to Pueblo History" (*American Anthropologist*, Vol. 39, 1937), pp. 504–522, for a useful summary of the contrasts in organization of the different pueblos. For a superb and meticulous detailing of the whole range of Pueblo variability see E. C. Parsons, *Pueblo Indian Religion*, Vol. 1, Chap. 1.

[21] Benedict, *op. cit.*, p. 90.

[22] *Ibid.*, p. 91.

[23] *Ibid.*, p. 69.

[24] H. R. Voth, "The Oraibi Powamu Ceremony" (*Field Columbian Museum, Anthropological Papers*, Vol. 3, 1901), p. 104.

[25] E. S. Goldfrank, "Socialization, Personality, and the Structure of Pueblo Society" (*American Anthropologist*, Vol. 47, 1945), pp. 524ff. Also, "Linguistic Note to Zuñi Ethnology" (*Word*, Vol. 2, 1946), pp. 191–196.

The hanging up of offenders by the wrists has been a feared and fearsome trait in the Eastern Pueblos for more than 300 years. It is not surprising that Pueblo Indians do not inflict self-torture, when we realize that in many pueblos they live in deep dread of tribally imposed torture. Plains Indians, on the other hand, do inflict self-torture to obtain the patronage of a supernatural spirit. But tribal law there rarely inflicted torturous punishment on individuals as in the pueblos.

Sorcery is fear projection. Belief in witchcraft terrorizes Pueblo Indians. The Pueblos are sorcery-ridden. Among the Keresans, people are afraid to cross the plaza at night for fear they will meet witches or be taken for one. Father Dumarest, who worked and lived for years among the Central Pueblos, asks,

Why are the Pueblo Indians so pacifistic? Why do they not try to defend themselves even in quarrels? Because from their youth their elders have taught them that nobody can know the hearts of men. There are witches everywhere, and woe to him who has trouble with them. . . . They can be overcome with great difficulty, if at all.[26]

Parsons, whose knowledge and reliability as a Pueblo scholar is unexcelled, made note that,

Indeed much of Pueblo mannerliness is motivated by fear of witches. At Zuñi if you ask for an article, it is straightway given to you—you might be a witch. . . . "The reason we always ask visitors to eat is because a witch might enter and be angry if not asked." [27]

The ultimate Pueblo penalty for witchcraft is death, and as Benedict indicates, any deviant person is apt to be hailed into a witchcraft trial.

Finally, Benedict makes much of the rejection of alcohol by the Pueblo Indians, because

. . . in their strict Apollonian *ethos*, the Pueblos distrust and reject those experiences which take the individual in any way out of bounds and forfeit his sobriety. This repugnance is so strong that it has even been sufficient to keep American alcohol from becoming an administrative problem.[28]

Field work among the Central Pueblos in 1945 to 1947 revealed the Pueblo governments almost helpless in the face of uncontrollable drunkenness and violence. Drunkenness is not confined to the young men, although greatest within this group. It is undoubtedly aggravated by

[26] N. Dumarest, *Notes on Cochiti, New Mexico* (American Anthropological Association, Memoirs, Vol. 6, No. 3, 1919), p. 162.

[27] E. C. Parsons, editor's note, in Dumarest, *op. cit.*, p. 162, *n.* 2.

[28] Benedict, *op. cit.*, p. 89.

personal disorientation due to conflicts resulting from Americanization as against the old repressive Pueblo way of life. But rather than being a nonexistent administrative problem it heads the list.

So also, with suicide, which "is too violent an act, even in its most casual forms, for the Pueblos to contemplate. They have no idea of what it could be." [29] But in the summer of 1946 a war captain of Zuñi shot and killed himself after reiterating all day "that someone was talking to him, or that someone wanted him." The United Pueblos Agency records show two other Pueblo Indian suicides between 1940 and 1946.

Such facts lead the Chinese anthropologist Li An-che, who has done field work in Zuñi, sagely to conclude that the configurational pictures of culture "painted with all the processes of elimination and selection" may be very misleading.[30]

The configurational analysis of culture, pioneered by Benedict and Mead, is stimulating the development of a deeper understanding of human behavior. Benedict's recent analysis of Japanese culture and national character shows the benefits of more careful use of a more fully developed technique.[31] The strictures advanced in this chapter constitute not a rejection of the method but a warning to nonanthropological specialists that cultures are not as streamlined as they may sometimes be depicted.

[29] *Ibid.,* p. 117.

[30] Li An-che, "Zuñi: Some Observations and Queries" (*American Anthropologist,* Vol. 39, 1937), p. 63.

[31] R. F. Benedict, *The Chrysanthemum and the Sword.*

CHAPTER 32

PERSONALITY AND CULTURE

As a culture is the integrated system of behavior traits characteristic of the members of a society, so a personality is the integrated system of traits characteristic of an individual. This is essentially the conception of personality offered by Kimball Young, who in more detail proposes that personality is the "totality of habits, attitudes, ideas, and characteristics of an individual which grow out of his role and status in the various groups of which he is a member." [1]

Determinants of Personality. Early in the development of the social psychology of personality, Young framed an analytical scheme of personality determinants embracing three main categories: (1) the physical characteristics of the individual, (2) the culture under which the individual lives, and (3) the unique social experience of the individual.[2]

Morphological factors directly influencing personality are stature, weight, and physical appearance. The personality of a dwarf cannot be that of a giant. Always we keep in mind, however, that the social meaning of a physical characteristic is culturally determined. We expect big men to be dominant in ascendant-submissive relations.

In further illustration of this point we may contrast the situation that exists among ourselves and the Trobrianders with respect to identification of physiognomy among kinsmen. Every newborn babe hereabouts is carefully evaluated by relatives and friends to see whether it looks like its mother or father, or this uncle or that aunt, or this grandfather or that grandmother. We have an obsession to find points of resemblance to kinsmen. Maternal kinsmen project maternal identities upon the infant. Paternal kinsmen project their counterparts. If the physical traits are quite definitely identifiable with those of one line or the other, the stimulus value is quite marked and the role behavior is definitely influenced one way or the other.

In the Trobriands, on the other hand, the dogma of the culture is that children do not and cannot resemble their mother or her kin. To hint as much is offensively bad taste. Yet resemblance to the father is always

---

[1] K. Young, *An Introductory Sociology*, p. 598.

[2] K. Young, lectures in *The Individual and Social Adjustment* at the University of Wisconsin, 1927.

assumed and affirmed. Physical aspects of the father's personality, but not of the mother's, are thus transferred to the children. (Of course, a great many of the mother's traits are transferred to her children in association and learning.)

A queerer quirk in Trobriand culture is the suppression of perception of physical similarity between brothers. When Malinowski suggested apropos of some Trobrianders' remarks on how much a group of brothers looked like their father that it followed from this that the brothers must then look like each other, the natives made it plain enough how crude they thought his manners were to make such a gauche remark.[3]

Studies in the correlation of constitutional typologies with personality types among Occidentals date from Lombroso's famous investigations into the physical anthropology of criminals. Unfortunately, neither Lombroso's materials nor those of his contemporary counterpart Hooton meet the tests of rigorous statistical and scientific methodology.[4] Their correlations between type of physique and type of criminal propensity cannot be considered as validated.

In the field of psychopathology, Kretschmer's correlations between physical type and psychosis have been much discussed but little tested. Currently, Sheldon is seriously pushing an elaborate series of studies with the goal of testing correlations between constitutional typologies and temperament.[5] The materials in this area of cooperative study between physical anthropology and psychology have been recently summarized in a competent monograph by Lessa,[6] to which the student who wishes to inform himself on just how far the studies in this area of investigation have gone is recommended. Problems in the effects of variable endocrine activity upon temperament and personality also are an aspect of physical constitution in relation to personality. The state of health or general organic well-being of the individual is but a broader facet of the same problem.

The cultural determinant sets the patterns and limits for permissible behavior within a given society. It shall be discussed specifically later.

The third factor noted by Young is the unique personal experience of the individual's life history. Not all phases of the society's culture are

---

[3] B. Malinowski, *The Father in Primitive Psychology*, pp. 87–92.

[4] Cf. R. Merton and M. F. Ashley-Montague, "Crime and the Anthropologist" (*American Anthropologist*, Vol. 42, 1940), pp. 384–408.

[5] W. H. Sheldon and S. S. Stevens, *The Varieties of Temperament;* also W. H. Sheldon, S. S. Stevens and W. B. Tucker, *The Varieties of Human Physique.*

[6] W. A. Lessa, *An Appraisal of Constitutional Typologies* (American Anthropological Association, Memoir 62, 1945).

open to all persons. Differences in status mean differences in social opportunity and experience. These mean differences in status roles and personalities. Even more important, however, is the fact that persons of identical status never have the same experiences. The mother prefers one child over the other. One child burns his finger, another does not. One woman has an auto accident, another does not. One infant falls in the river, another does not. No two persons ever have the same social experience, not even identical twins. From psychoanalysis we have learned how important the fortuity of history can be in shaping the direction of personality development.[7]

Culture tends to standardize personalities by channeling the experience of all individuals along the same broad stream. But life is made up of so many instances, so many situations, such rich variety of experience that absolute standardization is never realized and never will be.

Personality, therefore, in Young's analysis is seen as the behavioral synthesis of the individual's physical (including neural and glandular) constitution, the patterns of his culture, his contact with those patterns, and his moment-to-moment experiences with people and things.

The Kluckhohn-Mowrer classification of personality factors. More recently Kluckhohn and Mowrer have elaborated Young's type of analytical scheme into a logically exhaustive set of categories.[8] The Kluckhohn-Mowrer scheme recognizes the biological, cultural, and social determinants of personality, and adds a fourth—the physical environment. Whether one lives in a desert or a tropical rain forest makes a difference.

These determinants, we may note, reflect the diverse levels of natural phenomena discussed in Chap. 30. The criterion for this classification of personality determinants is, therefore, *level of natural order.*

The really new development in the Kluckhohn-Mowrer scheme, however, is the addition of four cross categories of determinants based upon the criterion of *degree of universality among human beings.* The four determinants based upon this principle are (1) the *universal,*[9] those determinants which are relatively constant for all mankind, whatever the environment, whatever the culture, whatever the race; (2) the *communal,* those determinants which are relatively constant and unique for all the members of a given society as against the members of other societies; (3) the *role,* those determinants which are linked to different statuses

[7] See J. Dollard, *Criteria for the Life History,* for a handbook discussion of this significant aspect of personality analysis.

[8] C. Kluckhohn and O. H. Mowrer, "Culture and Personality" (*American Anthropologist,* Vol. 46, 1944), pp. 1–29.

[9] Not to be confused with universals in cultural norms, p. 434.

within a society; and (4) the *idiosyncratic,* those determinants which are uniquely individual, either in constitution or life history.

Combining the eight determinants gives us the fifteen components of personality [10] as presented in the table on page 457.

The advantage of the elaborated Kluckhohn-Mowrer scheme over the simpler one of Young is that whereas the Young formula enables us to see the stuff that goes into individual personalities clearly, the Kluckhohn-Mowrer formula in addition provides the means for sifting out "group personalities." Thus the universal determinants, which apply to all mankind, produce what there is of human nature the world over. The communal traits lead to national or societal personality types. The role determinants shape the distinctive personalities of persons belonging to various age, sex, occupational, class, and caste groupings within societies. The idiosyncratic determinants account for the world's freaks, queers, crackpots, and geniuses at the far extremities; they guarantee the uniqueness of every individual so long as men shall endure.

Psychosis and Culture. Psychoanalysis, from the days of Freud until quite recently, was to a great extent a therapeutic technique concerned with clinical correction of individual behavior aberrations. It assumed certain psychobiological universals such as the Oedipus complex and recognized certain communal-cultural mores that either permitted gratification or caused frustration of the biological-universals, but it directed its analytical attention almost wholly to probing out the idiosyncratic experiences that were presumed to have produced the patients' psychological abnormalities.

The primary service of anthropology to psychoanalysis has been to force an awareness of cultural conditioning of psychological states and the degree of relativity of such states. Malinowski, for instance, tested the Oedipus complex idea upon his Trobriand Islanders and found that in that matrilineal society the Oedipus complex of mother lust and father hatred does not exist.[11] Anthropology has borne in upon psychiatry that certain psychoses such as running amok and the cannibalistic *windigo* madness of the Ojibway are culturally predetermined.[12]

Some recently gathered unpublished material recorded by Dyk on Navajo incest cases, or what purport to be incest cases, focuses a sharp

[10] Because cultural phenomena are possible only where two or more persons establish and maintain a mode of behavior, there can be no idiosyncratic culture component. This reduces the sixteen potential components to fifteen.

[11] B. Malinowski, *Sex and Repression in Savage Society.*

[12] *Cf.* J. M. Cooper, "Mental Disease Situations in Certain Cultures," and A. I. Hallowell, "Culture and Mental Disorders" (*The Journal of Abnormal and Social Psychology,* Vol. 29, 1934).

The Components of Personality

Modified from Kluckhohn and Mowrer, *op. cit.*, Fig. 1, p. 4.

Determinants based on level of natural order	Determinants based on degree of universality among human beings			
	Universal	Communal	Role	Idiosyncratic
Cultural	Incest tabu, kinship systems, property, magic, religion, housing, time reckoning, etc.	Special forms of kinship, property, magical and religious beliefs, etc.	Special roles culturally differentiated for status groups within each society	
Social	Group life, child care	Size, distribution, density of population, etc.	Play groups, congeniality groups, cliques, etc.	Fortuitous experiences in social relations
Biological	Birth, death, hunger, thirst, metabolic action, skeletal-muscular structure, basic drives, etc.	"Racial" variations of universal traits, health conditions of society at large, etc.	Age and sex differences, racially based class and caste	Individual peculiarities of stature, physiognomy, glandular functions, etc.
Physical environmental	Atmospheric pressure, gravity, earth, sun, moon, stars, clouds, water, wind, precipitation, etc.	Local climate, topography, wild plant and animal life, other natural resources, etc.	Differential access to material goods by different status groups	Unique relations to flood, storm, lightning and other physical phenomena

light on the cultural determination of psychoses.[13] In each case the incester went psychotic and became the victim of a self-destruction-by-fire obsession. At night when others in the hogan relaxed their watchfulness in sleep these poor psychotics burned off their hands or feet or lay on their bellies in the quiet embers of the hearth. In each case the psychotic claimed to have committed incest. Navajos believe that incest is punished by the fire madness. Psychiatrists are thoroughly familiar with the fact, however, that neurotics and psychotics may be convinced of their guilt in acts they have never committed. It is clear that the Navajo psychosis with the fire-self-destruction symptom is a culturally determined abnormality; it is also quite possible that the incest guilt follows the mental aberration rather than causes it.

To a greater and greater extent psychiatry is coming to look for the social roots of psychoses. Even medical practitioners are expanding their awareness of the etiology of seemingly organic diseases in sociopsychological maladjustment. "From concern with the individual as a biological unit psychiatry has progressed to a consideration of him as a social science. . . . Psychiatry has become a social science as well as a medical science."[14]

Anthropology has proved that within limits "abnormals are those who are not supported by the institutions of their civilization."[15] This means that he who is abnormal in one society may be the approved ideal in another. Crashing Thunder, the Winnebago realist (see page 104), was a misfit in his tribal society, whose culture required visionary experience for success, but he had the personality equipment to make him a successful, hardheaded, two-fisted, go-getting businessman. Siberian shamans definitely have unstable neurotic personalities. In their society they are leaders and men of influence. In our society they would be crackpot members of the lunatic fringe, whom many judges would consider fit candidates for a mental hospital.[16]

Homosexuality. In our society the habitually homosexual male is looked upon with emotionally intense hostility. His rejection by the normal elements of our world is complete and devastating—for him. His conflicts

[13] W. Dyk, *Navajo Field Notes* (unpublished).

[14] W. C. Menninger, "Psychiatry Today" (*The Atlantic Monthly*, Vol. 181, 1948), p. 65. The best and most recent of books with this orientation is N. Cameron, *The Psychology of Behavior Disorders.*

[15] R. F. Benedict, *Patterns of Culture*, p. 258.

[16] One of the archaic lags in our culture is the still prevalent handling of mental ailment as a crime. Mental hospitals, as our asylums are euphemistically called, are subconsciously recognized as prisons. Therefore patients must be committed like criminals and be legally protected from unwarranted incarceration.

of guilt, remorse, and frustration are usually enough to turn him into a psychopath no matter how healthy his early personality may have been. Homosexuality usually accompanies a rejection of the normal social roles fixed for the two sexes.

In Plains Indian culture the way out of the dilemma for the boy who found himself unable to meet the demands of the aggressive warrior role was that of the institutionalized *berdache* or transvestite. At the time of the vision quest he would be ordered by some tutelary spirit to take up a woman's role, to wear women's clothes, and to perform women's tasks. Because the order was a supernatural one, there was no blame affixed to the transvestite. Indeed, although the half-men half-women were looked upon with awe by children, they were respected and sought out by young men who hoped to procure love medicine from them with which to lure the affection of a desired girl. Thus, Plains Indian berdaches, while relatively rare, were not abnormal personalities, because they were supported by their culture.[17]

Personality Conflicts. Still another lead to the understanding of mental disorganization that derives from the cultural approach is an awareness of personal conflict resulting from the varying demands of the society's culture.

Mead has phrased this very nicely in terms addressed to the problem of adolescent conflict but pertinent to the whole distressing miasma of uncertainty and the continuing demands for decision that our culture imposes upon all but the most circumscribed persons.

Our young people are faced by a series of different groups which believe different things and advocate different practices, and to each of which some trusted friend or relative may belong. So a girl's father may be a Presbyterian, an imperialist, a vegetarian, a teetotaler, with a strong literary preference for Edmund Burke, a believer in the open shop and a high tariff, who believes that woman's place is in the home, that young girls should wear corsets, not roll their stockings, not smoke, nor go riding with young men in the evening. But her mother's father may be a Low Episcopalian, a believer in high living, a strong advocate of States' Rights and the Monroe Doctrine, who reads Rabelais, likes to go to musical shows and horse races. Her aunt is an agnostic, an ardent advocate of woman's rights, an internationalist who rests all her hopes on Esperanto, is devoted to Bernard Shaw, and spends her spare time in campaigns of anti-vivisection. Her elder brother, whom she admires exceedingly, has just spent two years at Oxford. He is an Anglo-Catholic, an enthusiast concerning all things mediaeval, writes mystical poetry, reads Chesterton,

[17] Cheyenne informants estimated that there were usually about five among the 3,000 members of the tribe.

and means to devote his life to seeking for the lost secret of mediaeval stained glass. Her mother's younger brother is an engineer, a strict materialist, who never recovered from reading Haeckel in his youth; he scorns art, believes that science will save the world, scoffs at everything that was said and thought before the nineteenth century, and ruins his health by experiments in the scientific elimination of sleep. Her mother is of a quietistic frame of mind, very much interested in Indian philosophy, a pacifist, a strict non-participator in life, who in spite of her daughter's devotion to her will not make any move to enlist her enthusiasms. And this may be within the girl's own household. Add to it the groups represented, defended, advocated by her friends, her teachers, and the books which she reads by accident, and the list of possible enthusiasms, of suggested allegiances, incompatible with one another, becomes appalling.[18]

Fanatics are people who acquire fixations on one scheme of life, religion, or politics because they cannot thread their way through the maze of conflicting alternative demands that modern life imposes. They escape a breakdown by settling into a less complete form of insanity.

If the multiplicity of conflicting cultural demands drives to near madness people who are trained wholly within a single cultural tradition, how much more disrupting of the personality is the situation when people are subject to the demands of two or more unlike cultures. This is the case with immigrants to this country.

Thus we see that not only do culturally induced conflicts produce psychoses but the configurations of the cultures influence the kind of insanity that results.

Acculturation and Personality. This, then, is the sort of thing that occurs on the level of civilized people caught between two cultures. Generically similar but not necessarily identical phenomena often occur when a primitive culture is in the process of being destroyed by a civilized one. Aside from the ravages of disease on the biological level, the too rapid destruction of a people's culture means disruption of individual personality for most of the members of the primitive group. A small minority manage quickly to simulate the conquering culture. These persons are usually those who were (1) misfits in their own society, on the biological or social level unable to adjust to their cultural standards; or (2) assigned by ascribed status to roles of limited prestige and power, who therefore hope to better their position under the new dispensation; and (3) well-integrated leaders who see the inevitable end of their culture and are able consciously and intelligently to make the shift without crack-up, although with heavy hearts. The annals of American history

[18] M. Mead, *Coming of Age in Samoa,* pp. 202–203.

are studded with the moving declarations of great Indian chieftains announcing their determination to follow the white man's road.

Again and again in the history of recent culture contact the majority of the overwhelmed tribes have lapsed into alcoholism tempered with lassitude. "Lazy, drunken, good-for-nothing Indian" became a tragic byword in America. But not because Indians are inherently such. Rather it was because when the Indian way of life was gone there was nothing for most Indians to live for. Interest and motivation were dead. The spice of life lost its savor. Dull drifting on government dole or escape in chronic drunkenness was the result.

Personality conflict of a different order is generated by cultural disparities when a primitive culture engulfed by a civilized culture still remains strong. Consider the possibilities in the situation that must have confronted some of the young Pueblo Indian men in the last war. A common Southwest Indian notion is pollution through killing an enemy. In most of the pueblos those who have killed and taken a scalp must join the Warriors' or Scalp Society. Initiation is a form of absolution.

In 1941 membership in the Warriors' Society of one of the Keresan pueblos [19] was reduced to one surviving old man who did not know the details or have the power to initiate new members. The society was functionally defunct but the power of its beliefs was not. Thus the rejoinder of a member of the pueblo to the author's speculation that some of the boys who had been drafted would bring back German and Japanese scalps and revitalize the Warriors' Society was

No. When our boys go off to the army we give them very strong instructions. They must not pick up any souvenirs on the battlefield or touch anything that belonged to the enemy. They must not touch any dead enemy bodies. If they do they are contaminated and there will be no way to clear them of it. They will stay that way for life.

Consider the mental anguish of the Pueblo G.I. who might be ordered to do burial-squad duty or battlefield salvage work. The possibilities for psychoneurosis due to no deficiency of the individual are much heightened in such a situation.

As a sequel it may be added that in the summer of 1947 the pueblo was considering inviting in the officers of the Warriors' Society of a cognate pueblo to initiate several veterans who had been polluted in spite of injunction.

[19] See note 30, p. 330.

To this point our discussion has turned about problems of culture and its relation to psychopathology—problems of what might be called *clinical anthropology*. Let us now turn our attention to another aspect of the interrelation of culture and personality, that of the *ideal personality type* and the *basic personality structure*.

The Configuration of Culture and the Ideal Personality Type. The central thesis of Benedict's approach to this problem is that the ideological contours of a tribal culture are impressed upon individuals in an ideal personality type. Each society has a more or less clear idea of what constitutes the good man, the kind of a man a person ought to be. The precepts, maxims, rewards, and punishments doled out by the *publicum* are directed toward molding all men in the image of the ideal. He who approximates the ideal is an object of social cynosure. The character of this ideal personality is equated with an abstracted tribal character structure. Or, when the method developed for analysis of primitive peoples is transferred to civilized societies, the collective ideal personality type becomes the "national character." [20]

Like culture, the ideal personality type is a construct. It suffers from the same dangers of oversimplification that we discussed in connection with the configuration concept in the last chapter. But like the configuration idea it is fundamentally useful. French national character is different from the British, and the British in turn from the German. Plains Indian personalities are typically strikingly unlike those of Pueblo Indians, and in turn those of Central Australians. The Benedict-Mead approach has pointed up and driven home the theory that the personalities of the majority in any society are largely reflections of the ideal personality type presented by each society's culture.

The collective actions of a nation are to a certain degree the reactions of the ideal personality type to given stimulus situations. Accurate analyses of national character aid in understanding national conduct. The problem from the point of view of social science is to see that such characterizations are validated by adequate empirical data and critical checking.[21]

The Basic Personality Structure. Although the concept of basic personality structure developed by Kardiner originated in the concept of the

[20] See M. Mead, *And Keep Your Powder Dry*, and G. Gorer, *The American People*, on American character; R. F. Benedict, *The Chrysanthemum and the Sword*, on Japanese character.

[21] *Cf.* O. H. Klineberg, "A Science of National Character" (*Journal of Social Psychology*, S.P.S.S.I. Bulletin 19, 1944), pp. 147–162; and E. Beaglehole, "Character Structure" (*Psychiatry*, Vol. 7, 1944), pp. 144–162.

ideal personality type, it is a development on the latter and is not identical with it.[22]

Whereas the use of the concept of ideal personality type demonstrates the close interrelation between culture and personality, it presents a characterization that is essentially descriptive and nongenetic. It describes what type personalities are without attempting to probe deeply into questions of how they got that way.

Kardiner, who is a psychoanalyst by training and in practice, has focused interest on the psychodynamics of personality and culture. The unique aspect of his approach is in the way he undertakes to determine the effect of social institutions upon personality and personality upon institutions.

Some fifteen years ago William Morgan wrote in the *American Anthropologist:*

Investigations of human adults show that their behavior consists of patterns derived from processes of conditioning in early childhood. Furthermore, some of these patterns are of such a nature that they may be called character traits. The most important factors conditioning an infant's behavior have been found to be the father and the mother. Thus there is interaction between the innate impulses of the child and the conscious and unconscious energies of the parents. In this way, the child is deprived of a series of satisfactions but the impulses remain and may, in later life, manifest themselves in ways which are by no means obvious. The human organism's responses to a life-long conditioning process can be arranged in categories and in open equilibrium equations. These responses can be demonstrated not only in conscious acts and attitudes, but also in dreams, and the rites and institutions of group life. The most comprehensive set of concepts dealing with these responses and innate impulses has been named psycho-analysis. These concepts need not concern those who are primarily interested in the essential work of recording what can be seen and heard, but they do concern those who are interested in the meanings and derivations of individual and group behavior, myths, tales, and institutions.[23]

Out of the interaction of this generalized psychoanalytic proposition and the anthropological materials on cultural determinism have emerged the following constructs: (1) Certain culturally established techniques

[22] A. Kardiner, *The Individual and His Society; The Psychological Frontiers of Society.* A concise summary of the historical development of the concept may be found in Kardiner's article, "The Concept of Basic Personality Structure as an Operational Tool in the Social Sciences" in *The Science of Man in the World Crisis,* pp. 107–122.

[23] "Review of G. Roheim, *Psycho-analysis of Primitive Cultural Types*" (*American Anthropologist,* Vol. 34, 1932), p. 705.

of child treatment shape basic attitudes toward parents; these attitudes exist throughout the life of the individual. (2) The "group of nuclear constellations" of attitudes and behavior formed by the culturally standardized patterns of child treatment in any society, and persisting among the adults, is the *basic personality structure* characteristic of that society. (3) The complexes of child treatment are called *primary institutions*. (4) By means of the mechanisms of projection the nuclear constellations derived from primary institutions are subsequently reflected in the development of other institutions such as religion, government, mythology, etc. Institutions derived as a result of projective systems are called *secondary institutions*.

The Kardinerian system is a limited system that attempts two things: (1) the identification of the basic personality structure and the process of its formation as a reaction to child-care customs; and (2) the carryover effect of the basic personality patterns into certain of the larger institutional structures of the society.[24] In other words, he is striving to show how one phase of culture shapes personality and how the resultant personality in turn shapes other phases of the culture. He really is probing the interrelation between culture and personality, not just the influence of culture on personality.

The method in its present stage of development is avowedly self-limited. It does not attempt to discover how the primary institutions, the child-care complexes, came into being. "The primary institution is treated as the taking-off point for the individual, not for the culture." [25] Furthermore, it assumes that various elemental aspects of culture, such as certain technologies (*e.g.*, basket making), may have no direct bearing on the basic personality structure. And yet further, it acknowledges that in many cultures there are institutions that lie outside and independent of the projective system.

On the positive side, a precept of psychodynamics which is essential to the whole scheme and which we have not yet mentioned is that the individual is not wholly the passive receptor of his cultural system. Culture is transmitted through learning, but the individual works emotionally upon what he experiences.

---

[24] Note that Kardiner's secondary institutions are institutions in the ordinary sociological sense (see p. 301, above). However, his primary institutions are what anthropologists usually call *trait complexes*. In a strict sense they are not institutions at all. This leads Kardiner in his later work to amend the concept of primary institution to read: "primary institution or related practices, whether institutionalized or not." (*The Psychological Frontiers of Society*, p. 25.)

[25] *Ibid.*, p. 25.

The point is that learning processes do not account for the integrative character of the human mind in so far as the emotional relationships of the individual to his environment are concerned. . . . In addition to direct learning processes, the individual builds up a highly complicated series of integrative systems which are not a result of direct learning.[26]

The integration of the personality, like the integration of a culture, is more than the sum of its parts.

It is quite impossible to convey the meaning of the operational application of the basic personality structure with anything like reasonable adequacy here. Yet a skeletal sketch will portray the idea better than none at all. We select Alor for the purpose, since it is the only one of the primitive cultures on which Kardiner has published results of psychodynamic analysis that is really based upon adequate data. All the other analyses of primitive cultures (Marquesan, Tanala, Comanche) must be recognized as experimental probing; the conclusions drawn from such probing must be treated as wholly provisional and indicative of potential results rather than final fact.

The Alorese Basic Personality Structure. In discussing the family (Chap. 15) the Alorese family was cited as one type that failed to meet the basic security needs of its offspring. This point now needs more detailing. The Alorese child is neglected. It is wanted, not rejected, but neglected. The mother works, and works hard, in her scattered fields. After the fourteenth day she has little time for her child. The father is away from home much of the time. The hunger pangs of the infant are irregularly and inconsistently met. The mother does not take the child to the fields with her. Someone else around the house must tend it—grandma, an older child, the father, if he is home. Several women may nurse it now and then; it is given gruel and premasticated bananas almost from the outset. Its hunger cravings are physiologically met, but no consistent image of any person upon whom it can depend for relief of hunger tensions is developed. Premasticated food may be given by anyone who wants to stop the infant's incessant bawling. But rejection and spitting out of such food indicates that it does not relieve the emotional tensions of the child. Hunger is more than an empty stomach.

Although the child is not left alone and is usually lugged around half-sitting in a shawl, it is not fondled or caressed by its parents to relieve its tensions. But the mother or elder brother or sister, or whoever else is paying any attention to the infant, masturbates it to calm it down. This

[26] A. Kardiner, "Concept of Basic Personality Structure as an Operational Tool in the Social Sciences" in *The Science of Man in the World Crisis*, pp. 109–110.

is merely a distraction and does not help to build the child's ego, for it is no more than an absent-minded gesture.

In the primary institutions of Alor child feeding there is no possibility of production of a parental image as a reliever of tensions. The intermittent appearance of the mother makes of her a tantalizing object who gives but inadequately the satisfactions so desperately needed.

Early childhood illnesses are indifferently treated and irritated by rough handling and irritating medication.

Learning to walk is accomplished in spite of lack of assistance and encouragement. Again there is no one to enter into a relationship eliciting trust and dependence in response for giving security and abetment.

Defecation and urination are not brought under any particular coercive control. At this point Alorese child neglect is a slight psychological benefit to the growing child. No anal eroticism is produced.

Comes weaning, and the rejection of the child by its mother and mother substitutes, while not abrupt, is damaging. The breast-seeking child is pushed away or slapped. Then jealousy and rage are deliberately evoked by taking another child to the breast. Food is promised but not given. The adults think this is very funny.

These are the main lines of the primary institutions.

What is the basic personality structure? Some of its features emerged in the last chapter.

As children the Alorese are shy and reserved—they do not expect favorable response—but they fly readily into tantrums and become vituperative. Because they cannot obtain their desires or rewards in a direct way they steal and forage as a regular thing. Aggression becomes canalized and predatory. The child, in turn, may reject his family by running away from home to live with some remoter relative.

This is the most extreme gesture of defiance and independence that the child is permitted and offers both a safety valve for pent-up aggressions and an opportunity to sustain the hope that the child may find in one of its other relatives the long-sought-for kind parent.[27]

None of the childhood patterns build toward emotional solidarity within the family.

The essentials of the adult male roles and character have already been sketched in our discussions of puberty (page 282) and in our outline of the configuration of Alor culture (page 446).

The ego development and social conscience (superego in Freudian ter-

[27] A. Kardiner, *The Psychological Frontiers of Society*, p. 156.

minology) are very weak. There is little self-confidence or sense of responsibility to others or to society. Relations to women are a projection of the almost complete defeat of the child in its relations to its mother. Husband to wife relations are bitter and nonintimate. Woman is the economic provider and the male is dependent upon her. Yet he cannot really dominate her. Compensation is found in the elaborate tomfoolery of loans and exchanges, the functions of which are essentially to gratify psychological rather than the production-consumption needs of the economy.

Warfare and religious institutions in Alor bear quite clearly the impress of the projective system. War, we saw, was disorganized, fitful, and vengeful. Religion falls within the category of ancestor worship as is characteristic of the cultures of this part of the world. But the ancestors are neither exalted nor revered. Their powers for good are not exaggerated and there is no desire to assuage them by suffering or renunciation in their names. Because there is no interest in, possibility of, or benefit to be derived from getting back in their good graces, there is no restitution by penance. One expects no more from the ancestral gods than one expects from parents.

Ancestors, however, want to be fed. Failure to feed the gods makes them angry (failure to feed the child was the supreme frustration). Angry gods punish their descendants. With great reluctance and only under the duress of misfortune the Alorese make sacrificial food offerings to the ancestral spirits.

Religious art is careless and slipshod. Gods are projected "fathers" and "mothers." With no idealization of parents in the culture there is no idealization of the gods. Representative carvings of ancestral deities are carelessly made, perfunctorily used, and quickly discarded. The dead are projections of the powerful and insistent creditors who bedevil adult life. In short:

> The basic personality in Alor is anxious, suspicious, mistrustful, lacking in confidence, with no interest in the outer world. There is no capacity to idealize the parental image or deity. The personality is devoid of enterprise, is filled with repressed hatred and free floating aggression over which constant vigilance must be exercised. The personality is devoid of high aspirations and has no basis for the internalization of discipline. Individuals so constituted must spend most of their energy protecting themselves against each other's hostility. Cooperation must be at a low level and a tenuous social cohesion can be achieved only by dominance-submission attitudes, not by affection and mutual trust.[28]

[28] *Ibid.*, p. 170.

Alor is a society with an old culture. It has survived for quite some time. This means that it has made the necessary minimal adjustments to the physical and biological imperatives. Yet that it is a precarious adjustment there can be no doubt; "the continuance of the society must hang on a very thin thread." It has had the protection of island isolation sealed off from too much external competition.

As an object lesson in the interaction of culture upon personality and personality upon culture it is superb.

CHAPTER 33

INVENTION AND DIFFUSION

Culture grows by accretion of inventions. But what is an invention? Does it differ in any way from discovery? These questions are not merely queries of theoretical importance for analytical purposes. They are of tremendous practical significance in the operation of modern patent law where an invention is patentable, while a discovery is not.

In the view of a United States District Court of Appeals, a valuable patent on the process of irradiation of foodstuffs by exposure to ultraviolet light was invalid because it merely utilized a physical-chemical process that has existed since life began. A distinction is drawn between the invention of a lamp for producing ultraviolet light and the discovery of the fact that exposure to ultraviolet rays increases the vitamin content of the exposed organic materials. The one is patentable (subject to certain legal limitations); the other is not.[1]

Invention. A discovery is the process of becoming aware of something which has been existing but which has not been previously perceived. Vitamins and sunspots were discovered, not invented.

An invention is an alteration in or a synthesis of preexistent materials, conditions, or practices so as to produce a new form of material or action. We have to deal with new patterns of action that are translated into concrete form (material inventions), and we have to deal with inventions that remain in the realm of action patterns solely. These latter are sometimes called *social inventions*, or by philosophers, *moral inventions*.

To illustrate the distinction between discovery and invention more fully, let it be noted that the first ninety-two elements, from hydrogen to uranium, were discovered by means of scientific perception. But the two new transuranium elements (neptunium and plutonium), which first came into being in 1940 as a result of the experiments in atomic fission leading to the invention of the atom bomb, are truly invented elements. They did not previously exist in nature; they were produced as a result of human ingenuity in the development of techniques for separating neutrons from their elemental nucleus and causing them to enter another ele-

---

[1] *Vitamin Technologists v. Wisconsin Alumni Research Foundation* (*Federal Reports,* 2d series, Vol. 146, 1945), pp. 941ff.

mental nucleus without producing fission. Wholly new sets of nuclear combinations of protons, neutrons, and electrons produced the two new elements.

Contrary to casual belief, invention does not have to be intentional or sought after. Because in our culture invention is highly valued and richly rewarded, we have hordes of aspiring minds struggling to find new relations as solutions to set problems. In the process of volitional invention the inventor recognizes a need or thinks he sees an insufficiency in some form or function. He sets a problem for solution on the basis of this recognized need and proceeds from this point to attempt a rational solution in the form of a practicable invention. *Popular Science* magazine, for example, capitalizes upon and stimulates this process by running a monthly column of suggested needs for inventions submitted by its readers. Volitional invention, however, is characteristic only of highly sophisticated societies with a cultural bent toward dynamic change. Even among advanced civilized nations relatively few include within their populations many active willful inventors.

In the primitive world volitional inventiveness is truly a rare occurrence. Conscious tinkering with the social structure or with gadgetary improvement is not the order of the day. Most primitive inventions are nonvolitional. They result from what Greenman has called *accidental juxtaposition.*[2]

The operation of the principle of juxtaposition on the crudest level may be illustrated by taking recourse once again to the activities of Köhler's famous apes. The fact that Sultan was able to join two sticks together and so obtain the banana outside his reach was mentioned in Chap. 30. The fact that other apes were able to imitate his invention was cited as evidence of incipient cultural capacity among chimpanzees. The details of the inventive process were not mentioned, but it shall be done now, for it is important to the point under discussion.

Sultan was presented with a problem, how to get that banana. He was also presented with two hollow bamboo sticks, neither long enough in itself to reach the banana. Both, however, were so fashioned that one could be snugly fitted within the other to make a stick long enough to meet the need. An invention was called for, and the means were at hand. Sultan strained his simian brain for a solution, but the best he could work out was to push one stick toward the banana with the other. This failed to capture the banana. At length, like many another disgusted in-

[2] E. F. Greenman, "Material Culture and the Organism" (*American Anthropologist*, Vol. 47, 1945), pp. 212*ff.*

ventor, he gave up. His efforts at volitional invention were a flat failure. He dropped the sticks and turned his attention to less frustrating activities.

As he roamed around his cage looking for amusement, his attention was once more directed to the sticks. He picked them up and began to play with them in a casual manner and entirely without interest in the elusive banana. Suddenly he found himself holding the two sticks end to end. He pushed the one into the other. Lo, he had it! At this critical point his intelligence was equal to the occasion. He could recognize a useful relationship when he saw it. Immediately he went to the bars, used his tool, and swallowed the banana.[3]

We actually know very little of the precise steps by which most primitive inventions came into being, since those steps were in most instances taken before civilized observers came upon the scene to make their notations. Long archaeological sequences such as have been established for European prehistory and in the Southwest reveal the external form of the gradual steps by which many artifacts have been developed over generations of time. A less empirical method, of which earlier anthropologists were quite fond, was to reconstruct the inventive steps by mesological inference. This is a most intriguing pastime, but too often the result is more of a "Just so" story rather than an objectively substantiated analysis worthy of scientific attention.

The Cheyenne Indian account of the invention of the tipi is of this order. Grinnell recorded that,

The first lodge of modern shape is said to have been suggested by a man who was handling a large poplar leaf, and quite by accident bent it into the shape of a cone—that is to say, of a lodge, such as are used today. As he looked at the leaf it flashed into his mind that a shelter like it would be better than those they then had. He showed it to the people and they made lodges in the shape of this leaf, and have used them ever since.[4]

Although it is extremely unlikely that any Cheyenne Indian invented the conical lodge in this manner,[5] the story illustrates quite perfectly the operation of the principle of juxtaposition. Sultan's invention was the result of the close juxtaposition of two objects (the sticks); the supposed invention of the Cheyenne tipi was the result of the juxtaposition of two mental images, the cone formed by the leaf and the potential house.

[3] W. Köhler, *The Mentality of Apes*, pp. 130–133.

[4] G. B. Grinnell, *The Cheyenne Indians*, Vol. 1, p. 50.

[5] The Cheyennes did not acquire the conical skin tipi until well into the nineteenth century. Other Plains and Woodlands tribes had it before them, so it is quite certain that the Cheyennes borrowed the idea.

The two accomplishments together exemplify Greenman's final definition of juxtaposition:

The creation of a new implement as the sequel to the establishment of a close spatial relationship between two or more objects, or of a close temporal relationship between the mental images of two or more objects, by natural or artificial means without foreknowledge of the result.[6]

In the technical field, therefore, the creation of a new type of artifact as a result of juxtaposition is a mental reaction to a stimulus in the environment. For the most part, "the progressive evolution of technical forms had to wait upon such accidental juxtapositions." [7]

Of course, accidental juxtaposition can lead to inventive errors as well as to beneficial creativeness. The heavy freight of shibboleths, nonsense tabus, and false dogma carried through the ages by mankind results from erroneous association of images in juxtaposition.

Furthermore, mere juxtaposition does not in itself automatically generate an invention. The use, meaning, and function [8] of particular artifact or social forms may be such as to block acceptance of new forms, uses, meanings, and functions that are proposed in conjunction with new inventive ideas. Resistance to new inventions is proverbial, and inventors are by no means always heroes.

Anthropological data and historical fact combine to establish that invention is rarely mutational. Complex tools and institutions develop gradually as the result of contributions by many men over a considerable period of time. Our discussion of the development of domesticated plants in the New World (see pages 108–109, above) constituted a brief summary of the multifarious sources of this complex social invention. The gradual nature of the developmental process was implicitly indicated in that discussion. As a contrasting example of what primitive invention is not, the following flight of uninhibited imagination is noteworthy:

What vision some ancient fellow must have had to start this process [the domestication of corn]! Can you imagine some primitive hunter of long ago as he sat in the mouth of his cave after an unsuccessful hunt? This man's empty stomach had stimulated his mind and he began to reason, which is the

[6] Greenman, op. cit., p. 215.

[7] Ibid., p. 218.

[8] Cf. H. G. Barnett, "Culture Processes" (American Anthropologist, Vol. 42, 1940), pp. 21–48. Form: how it looks to an objective observer; meaning: what a people think and feel about it; function: what it really does for them. See also R. M. Linton, The Study of Man, pp. 402–404, for a detailed discussion of these analytical concepts. Linton also distinguishes use: an ax is used to chop wood; it functions to satisfy the need for wood.

process that distinguished this man from the animal he hunted. A bird was eating grass seeds before him. If only those seeds were as large in relation to the man as they were to the bird! Could they be made larger? Possibly by picking out the very largest seeds and those which tasted best, and planting them next year, he might have a larger plant with larger seeds. The process was started.[9]

Invention proceeds not only by small steps, but until very recent times it was also quite rare. Remember, it took a good 900,000 years and more for our European antecedents to pass through the inventive sequence of the Old Stone Age.

The vast majority of human societies can claim relatively few inventions to their credit. There is abundant evidence to prove that most trait accretions are through borrowing. This leads to a consideration of diffusion.

Diffusion of Culture Traits. When we find a particular trait or trait complex spread over a wide area and practiced by a number of different tribes we are confronted with several theoretical possibilities. Either each tribe invented the same trait independently, or one tribe invented it, after which it spread to the others through borrowing, or several tribes separately invented it, after which it subsequently spread over the area.

We can safely say that the first possibility never occurs. Historical observation establishes that all peoples are always borrowing from others. We know, for instance, that Indians did not invent domestication of the horse, nor the art of riding, nor halters, bits, reins, saddles, or any of the other accouterments of riding. They were all adopted from the Spaniards, first by the tribes of the Southwest frontier, who passed them on to the north and east.[10] An interesting fact to note is that the Western saddle, horn-pommeled and deep-backed, was copied from the Spanish-type saddle, as was also the Indian's. But the Eastern riding saddle is copied from the English type that made its appearance first on the Atlantic Coast. The McClelland army saddle is a fusion of the two types.

Even such simple matters as hide dressing are acquired by borrowing. According to Grinnell,

When the Cheyennes first found the buffalo, they had no knowledge as to how to dress hides. Later, the Sioux on the east side of the Missouri showed

---

[9] F. C. Hibben, "Corn" (*The Atlantic*, Vol. 175, 1945), p. 121.

[10] C. Wissler, "The Influence of the Horse in the Development of Plains Culture" (*American Anthropologist*, Vol. 16, 1914), pp. 1–25; F. Haines, "Where Did the Plains Indians Get Their Horses?" (*American Anthropologist*, Vol. 40, 1938), pp. 112–117; also, "The Northward Spread of Horses among the Plains Indians" (*American Anthropologist*, Vol. 40, 1938), pp. 429–437.

them how to cut hides in two, dress them, and sew them together again. These they used as robes. After they reached the Black Hills the Kiowas and Comanches taught the Cheyennes how to dress buffalo-hides in one piece and also showed them the use of a mixture for softening the hide.[11]

Much more complex cultural structures also spread through borrowing. It is a canon of anthropological analysis that when a complex consisting of a number of internal traits appears in two or more contiguous cultures the probability of diffusion is high, especially if the nature of the traits is such that nothing in their component characteristics forces the formation of the particular complex in question.

Tylor was the first to formulate and apply this principle in a study of the diffusion of the ancient East Indian game of pachisi into prehistoric America where it appeared among the Aztecs as *pattoli* and in various other forms among other Indians.[12] Tylor undertook to prove historicogenetic connection between the Asiatic and American forms of these games by "analysing such phenomena into constituent elements showing so little connection with one another that they may reasonably be treated as independent. The more numerous such elements, the more improbable the recurrence of the combination." [13]

The technique may be applied to any aspect of culture, but it is particularly apt in the case of folklore. The ideas and objects treated in a folk myth are adjusted to the framework of each people's culture, but the distorting pressures are not as great as are commonly exerted in the field of material culture. Ideas range freer of the material environment than do artifacts.[14] Hence, there is a greater stability the world over in myth complexes than there is in tool or house complexes.

For a fascinating study of comparative distributions of Old World myth complexes, Frazer's *Folklore in the Old Testament* is challenging reading. For our demonstration of the application of the principle of diffusion analysis by means of internal congruity of traits, the "Tale of the Wandering Animals" will be used.

This story is familiar to all readers of Grimm's *Fairy Tales* as the

[11] Grinnell, *op. cit.*, Vol. 1, p. 51.

[12] E. B. Tylor, "On the Game of Pattoli in Ancient America and Its Probable Asiatic Origin" (*Journal of the Royal Anthropological Institute*, Vol. 8, 1879), pp. 116–129.

[13] E. B. Tylor, "American Lot Games as Evidence of Asiatic Intercourse before the Time of Columbus" (*Internationales Archiv für Ethnographie*, Vol. 9, supplement, 1896), p. 66.

[14] F. Boas, *Tsimshian Mythology* (Bureau of American Ethnology, Annual Report 31, 1916), pp. 393–558. This is the classic study of the reflection of a people's material culture and social organization in their mythology.

"Musicians of Bremen." The old donkey, the worn-out hound, the abused cat, the rooster destined for the pot, and other rejected decrepit animals all joined forces to go to the fair port of Bremen to become *Stadtmusikantern*. Night closed in on them as they found themselves deep in the woods. They frightened the robbers out of their hut and made themselves at home, each in his favorite spot—the cat on the hearth, the rooster in the rafters, the dog on the doorstep, the donkey on the dung-heap. The robbers sent back a spy in the darkness. But when he lighted the fire, the cat flew in his face; the dog chewed his leg as he fled through the door; the donkey planted a kick; and the rooster crowed his doom. The weak and despised animals frightened away the robbers (symbolic of mankind) and lived prosperously ever after in their nice snug little cot in the woods.

In Southeast Asia and Japan is told an ancient story, which in its simplest outline runs as follows:

An egg, a scorpion, a needle, a piece of feces, and a rice mortar (or any hard, heavy object) come together upon a journey. They enter the house of an old woman during her absence, and in order to do her harm, they dispose themselves in different places. The egg lies on the hearth, the scorpion in the water basin, the needle on the floor, the feces in the doorway, and the mortar over the door. When the old woman comes home in the evening, she goes to the hearth to light the fire, but the egg springs up and smears her face. When she goes to the basin to wash, she is stung by the scorpion. Seized by terror, she rushes from the house, but the needle sticks her in her foot, she slips on the feces and is upset, while the mortar falls on her head, killing her.[15]

Here are the Musicians of Bremen all over again. Aarne justifiably concluded that "The concurrences between the tales are so significant that in my opinion we must conclude that the stories stand in an interdependent relationship in their origin."[16] The story is traced through India by this scholar, into south Russia, up through central Europe and into Germany, where it arrived in the late Middle Ages.

Now let us shift our attention to the Northwest Coast of North America. A favored story of the Northwest Coast Indians has now a familiar ring. It is Raven's War on the South Wind.[17] Raven is the mythological culture hero of this area and the south wind often brings too much rain from the ocean.

[15] A. Aarne, *Die Tiere auf der Wanderschaft* (Folklore Fellows Communications, No. 11, 1913), p. 100.

[16] *Ibid.*, p. 162.

[17] Eleven versions are recorded by Boas in his *Tsimshian Mythology*, pp. 79–81, 658–660.

The South Wind, so the story runs, was blowing so incessantly that all the creatures had to stay in their huts. They could not hunt, and they were hungry. The smoke blew back down their smoke vents and made their eyes sore. At last Raven called a council of war to propose an attack on the Master of the South Wind. A special canoe was procured, and the war party made the journey to the home of the South Wind. They had trouble landing, because the gale caused by the flatulence of the Master of the South Wind was so strong that they were nearly overcome.

But once ashore, Halibut and Flounder or Skate (all flat, slippery fish) arranged themselves according to Raven's orders just outside the South Wind's doorstep. Red Cod or the Wren went in and started a smudge (in another version, Mouse went in and bit the South Wind's nose). As the Master of the South Wind staggered from the house, he slipped on the fish, slithered down the beach where the waiting animals tried to beat his brains out with clubs—which are as hard as a rice mortar or a donkey's hoof. The South Wind made a successful deal for his life— four days of good weather to alternate with four days of bad.[18]

Here, then, is a basic plot in which pusillanimous animals overcome masterful human beings in their very houses by combining their own little natural aptitudes to undo mankind. No matter that men were the authors of the tale. It is the story of the little men triumphing over the big men who order their lives. Its appeal as a vicarious release of suppressed resentments is clear. The ludicrousness of the event provides a Mack Sennett sort of gusty humor. The story is too good to keep. It has a broad appeal because it meets a common need. From Asia it spreads westward into Europe, northeastward into the northwest corner of North America. This, however, is not the end of its history. In post-Columbian times variants of the Musicians of Bremen form of the tale were brought to the eastern Indians by early trappers, and in the Plains and Woodlands they were adapted into a charming story known as Big Turtle's War Party.

Thus, by word of mouth, crossing language barrier after language barrier, the Tale of the Wandering Animals has girdled the globe; penetrating North America from the west and from the east, it met itself along the rocky spine of the western mountain area (Fig. 73).

The spread of tobacco may be followed from the New World to Europe and Africa, from Europe to the South Seas and Asia, and to

[18] An analysis in full detail is given in E. A. Hoebel, "The Asiatic Origin of a Myth of the Northwest Coast" (*Journal of American Folklore*, Vol. 54, 1941), pp. 1–12.

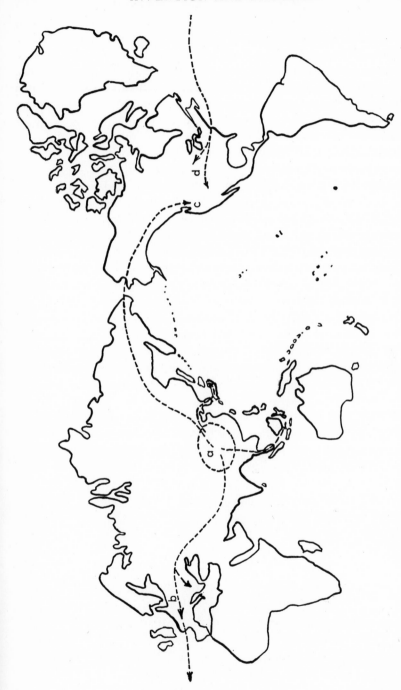

FIG. 73. Diffusion of the Asiatic Wandering Animals Tale: *a*, original Asiatic center of origin; *b*, The Musicians of Bremen version; *c*, Raven's War on the South Wind; *d*, Big Turtle's War Party.

Siberia whence it went into Alaska even before it reached the Eskimos from the south. Although Indians 1,000 miles away had native tobacco, it had to travel some 15,000 miles around the world before the Eskimos could enjoy a smoke. In this case, the essential factor was the difference between limited primitive transportation of an item that can be grown only in favored locales and the extensive communication established by European civilization with the Commercial Revolution.

Trait after trait may be followed through the course of its diffusion either by reliance upon historical data or by inferential reconstruction through distributional analysis.

Dynamics of Diffusion. Diffusion is no simple straight-line process in which some originating people put an idea on wheels, figuratively speaking, and give it a shove to send it on its way around the world.

Every spreading trait or complex as it moves from one society to another must face the test of its acceptability in the culture of the receiving people; and if it is accepted, it invariably is reworked either in form, use, meaning, or function. No people take an alien trait without altering it to some degree.

The fate of the Plains Indian sun dance may be used to illustrate this. The sun dance is a fairly complex ritual shared by a score of tribes in the western part of the Plains area. The ceremony is most elaborated and developed among the Arapaho and Cheyenne. From these tribes, according to Spier's classic analysis, the complex spread out among the other nomadic tribes.[19] In its core the sun dance shows remarkable stability wherever it occurs. The fundamental form of the dance is universalistic within the area of its distribution. Nevertheless, considerable variation in content occurs from tribe to tribe. As Spier observed, strong systematic selection was exercised.

Selection often works in subtle ways that we cannot determine *ex post facto.* In more obvious points, however, the determinants may be quite clear. Thus, a feature of the Arapaho sun dance is the use of medicine bundles and special roles played by the military fraternity of the man who sponsors the dance. Among the Wind River and Idaho Shoshones neither of these occur in connection with the dance. The reason is simply that in the crude Basin culture of the Shoshones there is no social structure of military societies and no priesthood of bundle owners. The Shoshones stripped the complex ritual down to the structure of their meager social framework. It is quite reasonable that in the eyes of an

[19] L. Spier, "The Sun Dance of the Plains Indians" (*American Museum of Natural History, Anthropological Papers,* Vol. 16, Part 7, 1921).

Assiniboin Indian the Shoshone version should be "a travesty, nothing more."

Not only is form modified in diffusion, but also meaning. To the Cheyennes the sun dance has been the fulfillment of a conditional contract with the sun. A man in dire straits in battle or a desperately ill person pledges himself to give a sun dance if he survives his crisis. It is also a means of acquiring supernatural power. Masochistic torture on the part of some dancers is seen as a sacrifice to supernatural powers who are moved to pity by man's devotion.

To the Shoshones the sun dance is primarily a curing ceremony and one designed to bring general well-being to the entire tribe. It is almost wholly a purificatory rite with emphasis (in the minds of the Shoshones) upon cleansing of the body and spirit, the shedding and "blowing away" of badness. Self-torture is wholly absent.[20] For the closely related Utes the meaning of the dance is quite similar, although there is possibly more emphasis upon dreaming.[21]

In the case of the Comanches it is doubtful that the sun dance had acquired any meaning, since the one and only sun dance they held was a prelude to disaster never to be repeated.[22]

The function of the sun dance varied as it was worked into one tribal culture after another. Among the buffalo hunters of the middle of the century its chief function was that of tribal integration. The scattered bands that had been eking out the winter in separation were brought together in the early summer for a grand socializing prior to the communal buffalo hunt. For individuals the dance functioned to relieve anxiety. It was an escape from danger. It also expressed subconscious submissiveness to the dominant supernatural—self-imposed hunger and thirsting, bloody immolation of the self in gratification of the spirit forces. It functioned to make more probable the acquisition of power through visions by means of heightened social suggestion. As the dances are performed on the reservations today they function mostly as reinforcers of tribal integrity in the face of the disintegrating acids of white civilizational contact.[23]

[20] E. A. Hoebel, "The Sun Dance of the H3kandika Shoshone" (*American Anthropologist*, Vol. 39, 1935), p. 580.

[21] M. K. Opler, "The Integration of the Sun Dance in Ute Religion" (*American Anthropologist*, Vol. 43, 1941), pp. 550–572.

[22] Cf. E. A. Hoebel, "The Comanche Sun Dance and Messianic Outbreak of 1873" (*American Anthropologist*, Vol. 43, 1941), pp. 301–303.

[23] J. W. Bennett, "The Development of Ethnological Theories as Illustrated by Studies of the Plains Indian Sun Dance" (*American Anthropologist*, Vol. 46, 1944), pp. 162–181.

The Comanche sun dance in its one performance functioned as a messianic vehicle, a tribal unifier, and a stimulator of courage to undertake the annihilation of the whites.

Diffusion may be of a whole complex of the order just discussed. In this situation the block of traits *en gros*, but not *in toto*, is taken over by the receiving culture. Changes take place in form, meaning, and function.

Diffusion and resistances to diffusion also occur with respect to more minuscule elements of culture. Minor items of material culture may remain wholly constant in form but be given entirely altered use, meaning, and function in the accepting culture. The external appearance of the result is often ludicrous in the eyes of the donors. An explorer may give a used film spool to a native, who receives it with delight, puts it through the slit in his ear-lobe and proudly struts his beauty. The form of the spool is unaltered, but its use becomes that of an ear labret, its meaning aesthetic, and its function that of prestige enhancement and ego gratification. The spool is culturally acceptable because it readily fits into the context of the native culture in a positive way.

On the other hand, traits may be rejected because their form is associated with negatively colored uses, meanings, and functions.

In a Northern Cheyenne peyote meeting the author once became interested in a decorative staff used in the ritual. It seemed to be carved with figures of bison quite similar to those of the Franco-Cantabrian cave art. The thought was intriguing. Upon closer examination, however, the carved scenes proved to be those of toreadors and charging bulls. There was also the Mexican eagle sitting on his cactus. But the snake in his claws had been scraped out with a knife. Black Wolf, the peyote leader, explained that the staff came from Mexico, and he pointed out that the eagle is good medicine. The toreador confronting the bull has connotations of the vision-seeking Indian confronted by a bison. However, "those people down there worship snakes, but we don't. So we took the snakes out. We can't have any snakes in our ceremony." The Cheyennes in point of fact are more than neutral with respect to snakes. In their mythology the Horned Snake (= Plumed Serpent) is a creature much to be feared and avoided.

Barnett has detailed a number of such rejections for several northern California tribes. When the bobbing of women's hair came into vogue a few years ago, it met heavy resistance because that hair form was believed to cause death. Corsets and hairpins were rejected at first because they resemble the warrior's rod armor and the bone pins that he used in his hair.[24]

The likelihood of misinterpretation of the Christian rite of communion by the Tsimshian Indians induced one wise and not too doctrinaire Episcopalian missionary to omit the ritual from his services. Cannibalism among the Northwest Coast Indians, although quite different in meaning for the Indians, was too close to the communion in form and function to risk presentation of the Christian rite. Not only in this but in other points as well did Duncan, the missionary in question, deliberately and as a matter of policy eliminate "many of the potential danger spots in Christian metaphysics for a native whose only basis for interpreting new belief was in terms of the old." [25]

This fundamental anthropological fact (that in cultural transference a trait or complex will be evaluated and rejected, or accepted and modified, in terms of the meaning it has for the receiving people) is one of the most difficult principles for professional civilizers (be they teachers, officials, or missionaries) to perceive and to apply. The mischief worked in consequence of this ignorance is mountainous.

Transfer of form with alteration of meaning and function is the most common type of intercultural exchange.

Occasionally, the obverse situation occurs; an alien people present a trait strange and new in form but familiar in meaning and function. The usual tendency is then for the receiving people to accept the idea but to alter the formal expression of it. This is the sort of thing that occurs when a Chinese weaver portrays Jesus in a portrait rug as a veritable Chinese shepherd tending a goat. In like manner, when an ardent missionary preached the concept of the Holy Ghost and direct revelation to the Tsimshians at Metlakatlan, British Columbia, to whom spirit possession was a violent part of their indigenous religion, they responded by putting on ecstatic dances four or five days long in which they captured the power of God in the manner of inculcating spirit power in cult initiates in the old Dionysian way.

A very special type of diffusion situation has recently been discussed by Kroeber under the heading of *stimulus diffusion*.[26] This is the sort of diffusion that occurs when the general idea of a culture trait or complex is transferred from one people to another without a transmission of the

---

[24] Barnett, *op. cit.*, pp. 31–32.

[25] H. G. Barnett, "Applied Anthropology in 1860" (*Applied Anthropology*, Vol. 1, 1942), p. 24.

[26] A. L. Kroeber, "Stimulus Diffusion" (*American Anthropologist*, Vol. 42, 1940), pp. 1–20.

actual detailed content. The content of the pattern is more or less wholly invented by the borrowers of the idea. Sequoya, the Cherokee inventor of the syllabary used by the Cherokees for writing their tongue, got the idea of writing from contact with whites, but he did not learn to write the English language. He took some alphabetic symbols directly from English, modified some, and invented others. His English symbols, however, bear no relation to the English phonetic system. He made them stand for Cherokee syllables. He took the idea but not the form of writing.

Stimulus diffusion as a process stands midway between independent invention and genuine diffusion. Awareness of a need or an inventive possibility is stimulated by the presentation of a trait or a complex from an alien source. The stimulated people, who lack the trait, attempt independently to invent an equivalent of it. If the Russians succeed in inventing an atomic bomb on their own, it will be a case in point (assuming no diffusion along espionage channels).

Acculturation. The diffusion processes that have been under discussion are all aspects of a specialized process called *acculturation* in modern anthropological literature. It is the process of culture change that occurs when a culture undergoes drastic alterations in the direction of conformity to another culture from which it borrows numerous traits or principles. The acculturating society, although drastically modified, retains its discrete identity. It becomes adjusted to, but not assimilated in, the dominant society. Most of our Indian tribes have made adjustments through acculturation. A few have become assimilated, and others have suffered annihilation, as a result of social and cultural contact with whites. The early contacts, incidently, were such as lead to diffusion. Trappers, traders, and missionaries brought new traits to the Indians and borrowed in return buckskin clothes, canoes, snowshoes, tobacco, corn, maple sirup, etc. Diffusion was stimulated, but there was not yet acculturation. Only when settlers arrived to disorganize the ecological and economic basis of Indian life, and soldiers and administrators disorganized the political structure, did the setting for acculturation take shape. The white colonizers continued to borrow a few ideas and traits from the Indians, but there has been no acculturation in that direction. On the other side the Indians were posed by manifest destiny with the dictum: "Acculturate— or else." [27]

Independent Invention. Very little attention has been given to parallelism, or independent invention, in this discussion for the reason that

---

[27] See R. M. Linton (ed.), *Acculturation in Seven American Indian Tribes;* M. J. Herskovits, *Acculturation;* O. LaFarge, *The Changing Indian.*

relatively few of the total mass of cultural traits possessed and shared by the peoples of the world have been invented more than once. This is not to take an extreme diffusionistic stand and deny the occurrence of independent invention. Although manifold, the possibilities in human culture are limited. Man is physiologically quite homogeneous the world over. His psychological mechanisms seem to be almost universally standardized. The problems that he faces tend to have much in common. Within the confines of limited possibilities the same solutions to similar problems sometimes recur without any historical contact between the societies involved.

Yet it is clear that cultures grow more through cross-fertilization and diffusion than in isolation through independent invention. There is no surer way to destroy the growth vigor of a culture than to attempt to keep it "pure." Isolated cultures invariably stagnate. The world's highest flowering of cultures has almost without exception occurred at crossroads of culture contact.[28] The peripheral cultures of the Australians, Tasmanians, Fuegians, and African Bushmen are all testimonials to the sterilizing effects of isolation.

Too much culture contact may be a dangerous thing, however, as in the case of the too universalistic scholar who learned less and less about more and more, until he became intellectually unbuttoned. A culture may lose its integration, its people become disorganized, and its society destroyed or seriously impaired by a too sudden exposure to the culture of a more powerful society.

As yet we know very little concerning the dynamics of the ebb and flow of particular cultures, why they are so vigorous and dynamic at given periods in their history, why at other times they fall into desuetude. The formalistic schemes of a Spengler or a Toynbee are of no great help, for they have not the means to reach the internal dynamics of the process. Anthropology has much work cut out for it in this area.

[28] The Maya of Yucatan appear superficially to have been more or less isolated, but very few competent Americanists agree with the contention that "the Maya developed their unique civilization practically without influences from the outside." S. G. Morley, *The Ancient Maya*, p. 14.

CHAPTER 34

EVOLUTION

The formulation and establishment of the principle of evolution is universally recognized as one of the great intellectual events of the nineteenth century. Contrary to common belief, its recognition and application in the field of sociology and anthropology was not a mere copying of Darwinism. The facts of social science had been pointing to the realization of evolution in culture ever since the seventeenth century.[1] Herbert Spencer had clearly fixed and formulated his version of the principle of evolution some years before Darwin formulated his masterwork. Comte, before the mid-point of the nineteenth century, had foreshadowed the thought of cultural evolution in considerable detail. Indeed, all scientific knowledge of the period was leading toward evolutionism. Spencer was influenced not only by his predecessors in social philosophy but also by the work of the embryologist von Baer and the great Lyell in geology. From Malthus's *Essay on Population*[2] Spencer derived the principle of the survival of the fittest. Darwin, too, was stimulated from the same source, for, as he acknowledged,

In October 1838 . . . I happened to read for amusement "Malthus on Population," and being very well prepared to appreciate the struggle for existence which goes on, . . . it at once struck me that under these circumstances favorable variations would tend to be preserved, and unfavorable ones to be destroyed. The result would be the formation of a new species.[3]

An excellent example, incidently, of juxtaposition in invention. Darwin felt the need of some principle to explain the biological facts he had long since sensed; quite by accident he read Malthus whose ideas combined with Darwin's to form the greatest thought invention of the era. Malthus, in turn, found in an essay by Benjamin Franklin the critical stimulus for his formulation of the reproductive capacities and consequent competition for survival of living things.[4]

[1] See the writings of Bousset (1681), Turgot (1750), Condorcet (1793), and Hume (1742).

[2] T. R. Malthus, *An Essay on the Principle of Population.*

[3] F. Darwin (ed.), *The Life and Letters of Charles Darwin*, Vol. 1, p. 83.

[4] B. Franklin, "Observations concerning the Increase of Mankind" in *The Interests of Great Britain Considered.*

On the record it is clear that cultural evolution in the late nineteenth century was no mere vapid imitation or simulation of the idea of biological evolution. All science was moving together toward the idea, because the principle is inherent in the facts. This is emphasized, because a common error in more recent times has been to condemn the application of the principle of evolution to culture as a misplaced transference of the biological principle induced by the great appeal and prestige of the principle in natural science.

In the later development of cultural evolution Tylor, Morgan, Bachofen, McLennan, Lang, Frazer, Westermarck, Brinton, and Haddon stand out as leaders.[5]

The Boasian Reaction. With the turn of the century a strong reaction led by Boas in America set in against much of the work of these men.

The main line of the Boasian attack was in terms of the numerous errors in fact that were exposed by careful empirical field study. To a considerable degree the nineteenth-century cultural evolutionists were more social philosophers than empirical scientists. They grasped the large idea of evolution and then moved in to formulate detailed schemes of the development of various aspects of culture without waiting for sufficient factual data to come in. Indeed, except in the case of Morgan, they hardly bothered themselves to raise a finger to add to factual knowledge by means of field studies. Truly, they earned the epithet "armchair anthropologists." Too much of their work rested on a priori premises and uncritical handling of the tales of travelers and accounts of officials and missionaries, who were themselves in most cases without scientific training; they mistook masses of library references for critical scholarship.

With Boas anthropology planted its feet firmly upon empiricism. Primitive cultures were fast disappearing. The job to do was to get in the field and make objective studies before the sands of time ran out. As factual knowledge scientifically obtained began to come in and be collated, the known errors in the current evolutionary schemes began to pile up.

As the recognized errors increased, so did the Boasian scorn of evolutionism as then practiced. To pull the pillars from under the structures so grandiosely built by Morgan *et al.* became a primary interest. The cold

[5] E. B. Tylor, *Researches into the Early History of Mankind; Primitive Culture; Anthropology.* L. H. Morgan, *Ancient Society.* J. K. Bachofen, *Das Mutterrecht.* J. F. McLennan, *Primitive Marriage; The Patriarchal Theory.* A. Lang, *Myth, Ritual, and Religion; The Making of Religion; Social Origins.* J. G. Frazer, *The Golden Bough; Totemism and Exogamy.* E. Westermarck, *The History of Human Marriage.* D. G. Brinton, *Religions of Primitive People.* A. C. Haddon, *Evolution in Art.*

enthusiasm for the truth that Boas insisted upon became inverted in some extreme instances to a near-fanatic scorn of all theory.[6]

Scientific caution so hypertrophied to scientific negativism, that Kluckhohn ten years ago reported the mental state of American anthropologists to be such that "to suggest something is 'theoretical' is to suggest that it is slightly indecent." [7]

Along another line of history, cultural evolutionism has suffered the fate of becoming caught up in the mesh of revolutionary dogma. Marx and Engels embraced Morgan and turned his particular schema of evolutionary development into a scathing, often bitter, treatise on the origin of bourgeois sex and family morals in their relations to the institution of private property.[8] They took many of the specific errors of Morgan and compounded them. They undertook to turn evolutionism into an ideological weapon to assure the downfall of capitalism and the inevitable triumph of the proletarian communist state. Evolution was to make Manifest Destiny of *The Communist Manifesto.*

On two counts this happenstance further discredited evolutionism with the early Boasian group. It doubled the methodological and factual errors of Bachofen and Morgan. And, in the opinion of Radin, the agglutinated revolutionary interpretation of cultural evolution was intellectually and emotionally antipathetic to the "anti-evolutionists." [9]

Thus on scientific grounds certainly, and on socio-economic-political grounds possibly, the principle of evolution suffered almost a total eclipse in the anthropology of this country, as also in England and Germany.

Only among avowed socialists and communists has old-time evolutionism prevailed. And Morgan, capitalist lawyer and railroad manager, sits enshrined as a minor communist saint with his *Ancient Society* as one of the sacred books.

Evolution Today. The problem of anthropological science today is to divorce the principle of evolution from Morganism and Marxism and to redevelop it in scientific terms. Unfortunately, the revived discussion of

---

[6] "I must confess that I am in a state of mind where I would no longer give a dime for a new theory, but I am always enthusiastic about new facts." B. Laufer in the *American Anthropologist,* Vol. 32, 1930, p. 162.

[7] C. Kluckhohn, "The Place of Theory in Anthropological Science" (*The Philosophy of Science,* Vol. 6, 1939), p. 333.

[8] F. Engels, *The Origin of the Family, Private Property, and the State in the Light of the Researches of Lewis Henry Morgan.* Those who have been shocked by the sexual morals of ardent young communists will better understand the ideological basis of their activity after reading the first two chapters of this book.

[9] P. Radin, "The Mind of Primitive Man" (*New Republic,* Vol. 98, 1939), p. 303.

evolution that is enlivening the anthropological journals of today is not directed toward this end. Instead it has currently been resolved into a series of occasionally ill-tempered and acrimonious debates about the intellectual orientation of Morgan, Tylor, Boas, Lowie, White, and others. Little or no reexamination of the data of anthropology in evolutionary terms is being published.[9a] Constructive work in evolutionary analysis has been in abeyance for forty years. Since a large part of the original evolutionary formulations have been proved wrong in content and since the efforts of anthropologists for two generations have been applied not to the working out of valid formulations of evolutionary principles, but only to the proper decimation of invalid evolutionary formulations, there are few constructive data that can be offered in the present state of anthropological science.

However, some clarifications can be made and tentative formulations proffered.

Biological evolution "means primarily the passage from simplicity to complexity, from homogeneity to heterogeneity, which, from empirical observation of living creatures and their remains, may be deduced to have occurred and to be still occurring in the world of life." [10]

In like wise, cultural evolution may be taken to mean the passage from simplicity to complexity, from homogeneity to heterogeneity, which, from empirical observation of living societies and their material remains may be deduced to have occurred and to be still occurring in the world of social life among men.

To study the evolution of culture is to study the processes of differentiation of culture. To study the evolution of culture is to determine the courses along which human societies have arrived at more distinct patterns of behavior to fulfill more distinct functions. As MacIver has said in writing of *The Reality of Social Evolution*, "the main interest of the evolutionary method is not the modification of specific form into specific form but the emergence of a variety of more specific forms from the less specific." [11]

The process of social change and cultural modification in a particular society is best considered as *cultural change*, not *cultural evolution*. Evolution cannot be studied with reference only to a single form. Evolution

[9a] While this book was in press J. H. Steward published an important article generalizing evolutionary sequences for five prehistoric centers of civilization. See his "Cultural Causality and Law: A Trial Formulation of the Development of Early Civilization" (*American Anthropologist*, Vol. 51, 1949), pp. 1–27.

[10] J. Needham, "Evolution" (*Encyclopedia of the Social Sciences*, Vol. 5, 1931), p. 649.

[11] R. M. MacIver, *Society*, p. 424.

deals with differentiation, and differentiation can only be referred to several forms.

Failure to hold fast to this principle has engendered confusion among both the earlier cultural evolutionists and their critics. Morgan, as Lowie has shown, did reconstruct unknown aspects of ancient societies in terms of his general evolutionary formula.[12] Morgan's analysis of American Indian house types was wholly vitiated because he had a predilection for an a priori scheme of evolution of clan and family; he specifically attributed earlier matrilineal clans to the patrilineal Ojibwa, for example, because according to his scheme it had to be that way (see page 116, above).

Tylor, too, as Lowie has indicated, was guilty of the same error, though less crassly than Morgan.[13] At times, therefore, the early evolutionists did treat cultural evolution and the processes of social change (culture history) in a given society as one and the same thing. This is the fatal error.

One thing evolution as a working tool does not do, and cannot do, is to formulate a line of specific detailed development through which all species or societies must pass. A whale and a dog are both mammals and each is the product of evolutionary divergence, but the detailed phylogenetic histories of the two species are quite unlike, and the one cannot be transferred to the other. In sociocultural terms, the history of any particular society does not recapitulate the evolution of culture. It cannot, for evolution covers the differentiation of cultures as wholes and of institutions and customs within them. No one culture ever embraces all the patterns of all cultures, either past or present. From this it follows that the *history* of a given society is not to be reconstructed from general patterns of evolution.

When the early evolutionists attempted to do just that and when they implied, as they often did, that all societies must by the force of natural evolutionary law pass successively through the same forms of culture and social organization,[14] they exposed a weakness to which their critics were not slow to take exception.

[12] R. H. Lowie, "Lewis H. Morgan in Historical Perspective," in *Essays in Anthropology in Honor of Alfred Louis Kroeber,* pp. 171–172. The article (pp. 169–181) is a balanced and well-considered appraisal of Morgan's strength and weaknesses.

[13] R. H. Lowie, "Evolution in Cultural Anthropology" (*American Anthropologist,* Vol. 48, 1946), pp. 229–230.

[14] This is what is known as *lineal evolution* or *parallelism, i.e.,* that the culture history of each society will parallel that of all others. It is not the same as independent invention, although numerous writers have used the terms synonymously.

It has not been difficult to demonstrate that diffusion and the accidents of historical contact between peoples with different levels and forms of culture play hob with any serial scheme of cultural development *for particular cultures.* Cultures grow, as was shown in the last chapter, mostly through acquisition of diffused traits. Whether a particular people is exposed to one or another form of a trait is often the result of sheer accident. The Cheyennes were clanless hunters and gatherers in their early habitat in the woods of the western Great Lakes region. When they moved west to settle among the Arikara in the Missouri River Valley, they learned gardening from their sedentary neighbors, and there is evidence that they acquired the rudiments of a maternal clan system. Had their migration led them southward to settle among the gardening Omahas, who have paternal clans, it is quite probable that they would have copied gardening and acquired the rudiments of a paternal clan organization.

Numerous comparable cases have led evolutionary critics to conclude that the consequences of diffusion disprove the principle of evolution. A false antagonism has been posed in the common phrasing of the problem, "Diffusionism vs. Parallelism," wherein parallelism is identified with evolutionism.[15]

The established importance of diffusion vitiates parallelism but not evolutionism. Diffusion is one of the processes whereby the products of evolution are distributed. Were it not for diffusion, evolution would be much slowed down and would truly creep along at a snail's pace. This is also true of biological evolution, of course, where traits are diffused through reproductive contacts.

The understanding of evolution requires us, therefore, to be able to abstract and separate the idea of a cultural form from its history in particular societies. We follow the degrees and varieties in development of the institution or artifact as such rather than its historical vicissitudes in a given culture. Above all, it must be remembered that evolution deals with differentiation through time. Evolutionary anthropology must be both science and history without becoming schizophrenic.

Consider the evolution of the ax. The development and differentiation of the chipped flint hand ax in the Paleolithic Age leads from crude homogeneous pre-Chellean types without hafting up to the moderately variegated Chellean forms. Chellean forms could not come into being

[15] *Cf.* L. A. White, " 'Diffusion vs. Evolution' " (*American Anthropologist,* Vol. 47, 1945), pp. 339–355. White's attitudes are so defensive with respect to Morgan and Tylor and at the same time so aggressively combative toward their critics that he fails to see that his heroes are responsible for the emergence of the false issue.

until the pre-Chellean types had preceded them. Differentiation between Chellean types and natural flint nodules was too great to be taken in one single step. In the Neolithic Age the introduction of two new technologies, abrasion and hafting, led to greater differentiation and complication in ax forms. The development of metallurgy continued the process in the Bronze and Iron ages as numerous specialized types of axes were worked out. The process continues into the present with new differentiations developing as the need arises into varieties of woodsmen's steel axes, firemen's axes, and butchers' cleavers. A full study of the evolution of the ax would cover the emergence of every single type of ax that has ever been invented; it would also cover the development and differentiation of different meanings attributed to axes (*e.g.*, the ax as a sacred symbol) and the social functions of axes. Developed and differentiated meanings and functions would be found to rest upon prior meanings and functions, for the more complicated patterns cannot come into being until the simpler ones have been in existence.

The fact that the Stirling Expedition brought steel axes to a certain group of Negritos in the mountains of Dutch New Guinea, who previously had had only stone axes, would be unimportant so far as the evolution of the ax is concerned. To be sure it is a significant fact in the history of those pygmies that the Stirling Expedition came bearing steel axes in the first quarter of the twentieth century. But that they leaped from the Stone Age to the Iron Age in a day does not invalidate any general formulation of the evolution of the ax *qua* ax.

If the reader will recall our discussions of food getting, housing, and handicrafts, he will see how the evolution of these forms and activities is implicit in the treatment of the materials.

The determination of the evolution of material artifacts is naturally much easier to accomplish than that of social forms, because with respect to form they lend themselves to direct archaeological evidence, even if not with respect to use, meaning, and function.

Yet, through the treatment of kinship (from susu to lineage to clan), of political organization (from local group to band to tribe to nation to empire or confederacy to commonwealth), of political leadership (from headman to chief to king, emperor, or president), of religious organization (from undifferentiated animism and mana to differentiated cults and churches), of specialization of religious personnel (from shamanism to priesthood), and of law (from limited private law to differentiated private law to increasing displacement of private law [torts] by public law [crime]), many expressions of evolutionary development in social organization have been implicit in this book.

They aid in giving meaning to the materials of anthropology. Especially with respect to the development and relation of subsistence techniques (food gathering, hunting, gardening, pastoralism, and agriculture) has the evolutionary principle been of great use in organizing and interpreting the data of anthropology. The concept of evolution vitalizes the data of culture by fitting them into the larger framework of cultural dynamics.

It is purblindness to hold that

. . . the order of events in which they all [anthropologist, psychologist, and historian] deal in common is best studied without the complications of any attempted evolutionary arrangement. . . . The historian is not helped in the reconstruction of Plantagenet England by any scheme of cultures arranged according to an ascending scale of evolution.[16]

Quite true, the historian will derive no facts of Plantagenet history from any knowledge of political evolution, but he most certainly will be able to deal more intelligently and understandably with his facts of Plantagenet, or any other, history, if he can bring a set of *sound* evolutionary concepts to bear upon them. Likewise, the anthropologist.

It behooves the anthropologist to be scientifically eclectic in his approach to man and culture. The phenomena are complex. The concept of evolution is a tool of thought with which to handle one aspect of the data of anthropology. The concepts of basic personality structure and ideal personality types are yet others. The concepts and principles of functionalism, of linguistic analysis, of statistical treatment are still others among many more.

Indeed, as Lowie warned long ago, *there is no royal road to the comprehension of cultural phenomena.*[17] Nor is there any single road, though some may seem like broad avenues and others wandering bypaths.

Finally, as we draw to the close of this study, let us observe that the pace of evolution does not follow a steady curve. Cultural evolution manifests the characteristics that biologists have in their field come to call *emergent.* "Whether the process of evolution has taken place continuously or discontinuously is a problem which probably will never be solved," writes Needham, "for continuity and discontinuity are two alternating modes of scientific expression neither of which is permanently victorious."[18] Biological evolution takes a spurt and then settles down

[16] R. F. Benedict, "The Science of Custom" in *The Making of Man,* pp. 809–810
[17] R. H. Lowie, *Primitive Society,* p. 107.
[18] Needham, *op. cit.,* p. 649.

to slow development and differentiation until a new unbalance induces a new spurt. This is evolution by mutation combined with gradual modifications.

White has recently emphasized that one important consequence of cultural evolution is the progressive increase of the amount of energy put under control for utilization by men.[19] The potential daily average energy output of a healthy man is estimated as equal to approximately 3,000 pounds lifted one foot in one minute, or roughly one-tenth of a horsepower. Counting infants, the sick and feeble adults, the amount of energy per capita available in the earliest societies was approximately one-twentieth of a horsepower per person. For a very primitive local group this would amount to an energy utilization of no more than two to three horsepower of energy a day for the entire society. Not much could be accomplished with that productively. As long as man was restricted to such a level, the development of culture was destined to be limited. This condition prevailed throughout the Old Stone Age and was characteristic of all societies before the development of hoe culture and the domestication of animals.

The great revolution of the Neolithic Age was wrought by the domestication of plants and animals. Domestication of plants increased man's control over solar energy, which is stored in plants. Domestication of animals made him an exploiter of animal energy. More efficient tools reduced energy waste and new tools made possible new applications of energy. All culture expanded rapidly; the mode of life changed from that of hunters to gardeners and pastoralists. Old institutions and customs went down and new ways had to be worked out. The savages became barbarians.

The ages of Bronze and Iron are but extensions of the Neolithic. Metal was substituted for stone. Increased efficiency in tools leading to stepped-up productiveness in handicraft industries and gardening (which the plow transformed to agriculture) gradually expanded the cultures of the Old World.

The next cultural revolution awaited the harnessing of steam, the invention of the internal-combustion engine, and the artificial production of electricity. With the industrial revolution, feudalism gave way to modern capitalism. The reorganization of society and culture shook the modern world through and through. The repercussions are still with us.

[19] L. A. White, "Energy and the Evolution of Culture" (*American Anthropologist*, Vol. 45, 1943), pp. 335–356.

Ten years ago, according to Millikan's estimates,[20] we in the United States expended about 13½ horsepower-hours of electrical and internal-combustion-engine energy per day per person. This has been made possible by the technological evolution of our culture, which in turn has been made possible in large part by the increases in energy released and brought under control.

Whether this is progress or not is another matter, but it is a most important aspect of cultural revolution. It writes large upon the wall a great lesson for today.

In 1945 the most stupendous energy conquest of all time was accomplished. Einstein's theory of the equivalence of mass and energy ($E = mc^2$) indicates that 1 kilogram (2.2 pounds) of matter, if it could be converted entirely into energy, would release 25 billion kilowatt-hours of energy, or approximately 33 billion horsepower. Splitting the uranium atom as was first done in 1945 converted one-tenth of 1 per cent of the uranium mass into energy. Today 33 million horsepower of energy may be released from 1 kilogram of uranium.[21] And this is but the beginning.

What do the laws of evolution teach us as to the meaning of this new outburst of energy? Not what the future forms of society will be. But as the Neolithic technologies induced a thoroughgoing revision of previously existing societies and drove the expansion of culture ahead in a great spurt, as the technological innovations of the industrial revolution forced similar alterations in the ways of men, so the atomic age will be one in which old modes will become quickly outworn. We are destined to see such cultural changes in the new era that has burst upon us as will make all prior evolutionary development seem static by comparison.

Certain cultural forms have persisted through all human vicissitudes. Our studies have shown what they are. They may continue into the future. Other cultural forms, like the sovereign national state, are clearly incompatible with present prospects. Rational men will turn all their knowledge of society and culture, all their skills of social science analysis, to making the needed cultural changes as quickly and as effectively as possible.

The near future is bound to be unsettled and painful. With atomic wars it may become a nightmare. On the other side of the probable dark age of transition, however, is the possibility of a great era.

Man, too, may take an emergent spurt. Physically and neurologically

[20] R. A. Millikan, "Science and the World Tomorrow" (*Scientific Monthly*, Vol. 37, 1939), p. 211.
[21] H. D. Smyth, *Atomic Energy for Military Purposes*, pp. 2, 224.

there has been little evolutionary development in the human stock for 50,000 years and more. Radiation does strange things to the germ plasm. A notable increase in gross mutations is reported from Hiroshima and Nagasaki. Mutation produces monstrosities, but it may also produce traits that break through the ceiling of present known aptitudes and capacities of men. It may well be that a new order of men is in the offing.

GLOSSARY

abusua. The matrilineal clan in Ashanti society.

acculturation. The process of interaction between two societies by which the culture of the society in the subordinate position is drastically modified to conform to the culture of the dominant society.

Acheulean. A culture of the Lower Paleolithic Age in western Europe.

adobe. An unfired, sun-dried clay brick.

affinal. Related by marriage.

age class, age grade, age set. An organized association that includes all the members of a tribe who are of a given age and sex.

agoraphobia. An obsessive state of discomfort stimulated by large open spaces.

alignment. A series of standing stones (menhirs) arranged in rows.

alter ego. The soul, spirit, ghost, or other self of a person.

alternative. A behavior pattern in which two or more permissible response norms occur for a given stimulus situation.

amitate. The complex of special behavior patterns governing relations between a child and its father's sister.

amok (to run amok). A form of psychotic behavior prevalent among Malayan peoples. It is characterized by inattention followed by a violent outbreak, often directed toward homicidal assault.

Anasazi. The prehistoric and contemporary culture of the Pueblo Indians of the Southwest.

androcentric. Centered about the male.

androcratic. Ruled by males.

angakok. An Eskimo shaman.

animatism. The attribution of life to inanimate objects.

animism. The belief in the existence of spiritual beings. (Tylor's minimum definition of religion.)

anthropogeography. The study of the effect of geographical factors upon man and society.

anthropoid. Having the characteristics of the highest family (that of man and the tailless apes) within the primate order.

anthropometry. The division of physical anthropology concerned with the measurement of man's bodily characteristics.

anthropomorphism. The attribution of human form to any object.

anthropophagy. Cannibalism.

Apollonian. A configuration of culture that emphasizes restraint, moderation, and "middle-of-the-road" behavior in human conduct.

artifact. Any material object that has been "worked" or has been used as a tool.

association. A social group specifically organized for the pursuit of special interests.

atlatl. The Aztec name for a dart or spear thrower.

Audi blade. An Aurignacian flint artifact developed from the Levallois flake of the Mousterian epoch.

Aurignacian. The first culture of the Upper Old Stone Age in Europe.

Aurignacian man. *Homo sapiens aurignaciensis*, a variety of modern man associated with the Aurignacian culture.

Australopithecus africanus. A genus of fossil ape with humanoid characteristics found at Taungs, South Africa.

autistic thinking. Wishful daydreaming.

avoidance. The inhibition of social interaction, especially between affinal relatives.

avunculate. The complex of special relations between a mother's brother and his sister's child.

Azilian. A culture that is transitional between the Upper Paleolithic and Neolithic ages in western Europe; usually associated with the Tardenoisean.

band. A territorially based social group that is less inclusive than the tribe.

Bandkeramik. Neolithic pottery decorated with incised parallel lines about the neck.

barbarism. A classification of cultures possessing gardening, agriculture, or domesticated herds but devoid of written language.

barrow. The English term for a burial mound.

barter, dumb. Exchange of goods between hostile people without face-to-face contact and without the use of middlemen.

Basket Maker. A prehistoric culture (or the people who produced it) widely spread throughout the southwestern parts of the United States and antecedent to the Pueblo cultures.

bast. The fibrous inner bark of certain trees.

berdache. A person who assumes the social roles ascribed to the opposite sex.

bifurcation. Separation into two branches or sections.

blastula. A mass of cells, usually in the shape of a hollow sphere, resulting from the cleavage of an egg.

bolo. A weapon made of several stones, each encased in a leather pouch at the ends of a string. The free ends of the strings are joined together.

Bondu. The women's tribal secret society among the tribes of Sierra Leone and Liberia in West Africa.

brachiation. Use of the hands; in a special sense, movement through the trees by swinging from the branches.

brachycephalic. Roundheaded; cephalic index 80 to 84.9.

brother equivalence. The classifying of brothers within a single kinship status.

bull-roarer. A flat board that, when whirled at the end of a string, makes a low whirring noise.

cacique. The Spanish word for "chief"; often used for the sacerdotal head of a Pueblo Indian tribe or any Central or South American tribe.

calvarium. The skullcap, or upper portion of the cranium.

caste. An endogamous social group, usually linked with a specific occupation.

Caucasian race. The so-called "white" race.

celt. A polished stone axhead.

cephalic index. A metric expression of the ratio between head breadth and head length. $\text{C.I.} = \dfrac{\text{HB}}{\text{HL}} \times 100$

chalcedony. A white, waxy "flint."

Chalcolithic Age. The Copper Age.

Châtelperron point. A long, sharp-pointed Aurignacian blade developed from the Audi blade.

Chellean. A culture of the Lower Paleolithic Age in Europe.

chert. An impure form of flint.

chief, peace. A chief whose functions are largely concerned with the direction of civil affairs.

chief, talking. In many societies the chief does not publicly address the people. A "speaker" or talking chief does this for him.

cicatrization. A pattern of scar tissue produced by making incisions in the skin.

cire perdue. *See* lost wax method.

cist. An individual, slab-lined grave.

civilization. A classification of cultures possessing gardening, agriculture, or domesticated herds and a written language.

Clactonian. A first interglacial culture found in East Anglia.

clan. A unilateral kinship group that maintains the fiction of common genetic descent from a remote ancestor, usually legendary or mythological.

coccyx. The hidden tail in man formed of the last several vertebrae at the end of the spinal column.

concubinage, group. A group of men, as an African age class, sharing concubines in common.

concubitant. A male who has the status of marriageability to a person without necessarily being married to that person.

conditional curse. A ritual declaration that if the facts are not as stated, or if certain conditions come to pass, ill fortune may strike the person cursed.

convergence. A process of cultural dynamics in which two or more cultures contain similar institutions or behavior patterns independently arrived at, *i.e.*, without historical connection.

cosmic time. All time prior to the formation of the earth.

coup. An attested deed of valor among the Plains Indians.

coup counting. The social practice of publicly reciting coups.

coup de poing. A flint hand ax characteristic of the Chellean, Acheulean, and Mousterian cultures.

couvade. The practice whereby a husband retires to bed upon the birth of his offspring and acts as though he had just gone through childbirth.

cranial capacity. The interior volume of the cranium measured in cubic centimeters.

cranium. That portion of the skull which encloses the brain.

Cro-Magnon man. A variety of *Homo sapiens* dominant in western Europe during the last half of the fourth glaciation.

cromlech. A circular arrangement of standing stones.

cross-cousins. Cousins whose related parents are siblings of unlike sex. Offspring of a person's mother's brother or father's sister.

cultural orthogenesis. The relative overdevelopment of one aspect of a culture.

culture. The sum total of learned behavior traits characteristic of the members of a society.

culture area. A geographical territory within which the cultures tend to be similar in some significant aspects.

culture complex. An integrated system of culture traits organized about some nuclear interest.

culture configuration. The characteristic arrangement of traits that gives to a culture its distinctive contours.

culture construct. A selective and descriptive formulation of the modal or normal behavior characteristic of the members of a society.

culture, ideal. A verbalized formulation of normative patterns for behavior as stated by the members of a given society.

culture pattern. A normative form of behavior laid down by the consensus of the members of a society.

culture trait or element. A reputedly irreducible unit of learned behavior pattern or material product thereof.

Cyprolithic. The Copper Age.

deadfall. A type of trap so constructed that a weighted lever, rock, or ceiling drops on the victim when released by a trigger.

deme. A territorial political unit in Attica after the reorganization by Cleisthenes in 509 B.C.

dibble. A pointed digging stick.

diffusion. A process in cultural dynamics wherein culture elements or complexes spread from one society to another.

Dionysian. A categorical label attached to cultures that emphasize sensate experience.

dolichocephalic. Long- or narrow-headed. Cephalic index less than 75.

dolmen. A structure formed of three or more slabs of rock set on edge and covered with a flat slab. Hence called *table rock*.

double descent. The existence of a maternal and a paternal clan system side by side within the same culture.

Dryopithecus. A genus of Miocene fossil ape from which man and the great anthropoids evolved.

dysteleology. *See* vestigial remains.

earth lodge. A house built wholly or partially of sod or made of a framework covered with dirt.

ecology. The study of the relationships between organisms and their physical environments.

Egbo. A secret fraternity identified with the leopard in certain African tribes.

egomaniac. A person whose self-centeredness reaches psychotic proportions.

Ekpe. *See* Egbo.

embryology. The study of the embryo, the organisms in its earliest stages of development.

endocranial. The inner surface of the cranium or brain case.

endogamy. The rule that requires a person to marry within a given social group of which he is a member.

Eoanthropus dawsoni. Dawson's Dawn man, otherwise known as *Piltdown man*. A fossil genus of man found in first interglacial deposits in East Anglia.

Eocene. The first period of the Cenozoic era.

eolith. Dawn Stone Age artifacts. Stone implements so crudely made that their shape is more fortuitously than purposefully determined.

Eolithic Age. The Dawn Stone Age. The first age in the evolution of human culture, characterized by eoliths.

epicanthic fold. An overlap of the upper eyelid.

Epipaleolithic. The stage of prehistoric cultural evolution between the Paleolithic and Neolithic ages. Also called the Mesolithic or transitional age.

Ertebolle. A local manifestation of Early Neolithic culture in Denmark.

ethnography. The division of anthropology devoted to the descriptive recording of cultures.

ethnology. The division of anthropology devoted to the analysis and systematic interpretation of cultural data.

evolution, biological or organic. The passage from simplicity to complexity, from homogeneity to heterogeneity, which, from empirical observation of living creatures and their remains, may be deduced to have occurred and to be still occurring in the world of life.

evolution, cultural. The passage from simplicity to complexity, from homogeneity to heterogeneity, which, from empirical observation of living societies and the material remains and records of those now defunct, may be deduced to have occurred and to be still occurring in the world of social life among men.

evolution, divergent. The process of evolutionary development that results in several lines of progressive modification from an original common form.

evolution, unilinear. The theory that predicates the evolution of social forms in a universal and ordered sequence.

exogamy. The rule that requires a person to marry outside a specific social group of which he is a member.

extrovert. A person whose interests and concerns are predominantly in external objects and actions.

family. A bilateral kinship group.

family, conjugal. A social group consisting of spouses and their offspring.

family, consanguine. *See* susu.

family, extended. A social group consisting of near relatives in addition to the mated pair and their offspring.

fatherhood, sociological. The institution whereby the adult male who is the husband of a child's mother stands in the functional relationship of fatherhood to the child, regardless of his biological relationship.

felting. A cloth-making technique in which the fibers are matted together, not spun and woven.

femur. The thighbone.

fetish. An object that is revered because it is believed to house a supernatural power.

fibula. (1) The long bone that, with the tibia (shinbone), makes up the lower part of the leg. (2) A Bronze or Iron Age safety pin.

foramen magnum. The "great window." The hole in the base of the skull through which the spinal cord leaves the cranium.

fossil. An organic object that has been transformed into stone by a natural process of replacement.

fraternity. (1) An association of men. A men's society. (2) The children of a woman. *See* sibling.

Galley Hill man. A neoanthropic fossil of mid-glacial age found at Galley Hill, England.

gastrula. A stage in embryonic development in which the embryo consists of an outer layer of cells, enclosing a cavity and having an opening at one end.

generation equivalence. The classifying of relatives of different genetic relation, but within the same generation level, within a single kinship status.

genotype. An organic specimen in which both the genes that determine a specific trait are dominant or recessive. The somatic characteristic therefore directly reflects the gene combination.

gens. A patrilineal clan.

geologic time. All time since the first formation of the earth.

gerontocracy. A society dominated by the old men.

Gigantopithecus blackii. A genus of giant fossil ape from South China.

God, High. The supreme deity in a polytheistic system.

gravette. A small, sharp-pointed Aurignacian flint blade used for engraving and carving.

G-string. A string or band of material worn between the legs and fastened around the waist.

hallcist. *See* passage grave.

headman. A leader of a band, clan, or tribe who is not endowed with specific and determinative authority; less than a chief.

Heidelberg Man. A Neandertaloid fossil man found in first interglacial deposits at Mauer, near Heidelberg, Germany.

hieroglyph. A highly conventionalized symbol developed from pictorial representation and used as an element in certain archaic writing systems.

hogan. The Navajo dwelling.

Hohokam. A prehistoric culture localized in the desert areas of central Arizona.

Homo sapiens. The sole existing species of man. Modern man.

ideograph. A conventionalized pictograph that symbolizes an idea rather than a thing.

idiosyncrasy. A form of behavior uniquely characteristic of an individual.

incest. Sexual contact between persons who are both members of the same socially defined kinship group.

infanticide. The killing of infants.

institution, social. A complex of behavior patterns organized about some dominant nuclear interest.

introvert. A person whose interests are predominantly concerned with himself.

invalidicide. The killing of invalids.

invention, independent. *See* parallelism.

joking relationship. An institutionalized pattern of privileged familiarity or joking between persons of specific social statuses.

Kanam man. *Homo kanamensis.* A purported species of modern man represented by a fossilized symphysis found in Kenya Colony, East Africa.

kachina. The gods in certain Pueblo cultures, who are represented in ceremonials by masked dancers.

kaylasi. Adultery among the Trobriand Islanders.

kinship, classificatory. The lumping, merging, or equating of relatives of differing genetic relationship into one and the same kinship status.

kinship system. The customary complex of statuses and roles governing the behavior of relatives.

kinship terminology. The set of names applied to the various statuses in a kinship system.

kitchen midden. A refuse heap.

kiva. A semisubterranean ceremonial chamber, usually round, in the Southwest Pueblos.

Krapina man. A local type of Neandertaloid fossil man found at Krapina in Croatia in second interglacial deposits.

kula ring. The system of intertribal ceremonial exchange of shell arm bands and necklaces in southwestern Melanesia.

Kulturkreis. A conception of large culture complexes that, in the theory of the culture historical school (*Kulturkreislehre*) of ethnology, diffuse en bloc over large areas of the globe.

labret. A plug worn through an incision in the lip, ear, or nose.

laurel-leaf point. A flint blade shaped like a laurel leaf and characteristic of the Solutrean culture.

law. A social norm sanctioned by the application of physical coercion, in threat or in fact, by a person or group possessing the recognized privilege of so doing.

lejima. The nonlocalized maternal clan in Umor society.

lemur. A primitive type of primate that first emerged in the Eocene period.

leprechaun. A sprite or fairy in Irish folk belief, usually in the form of a little old man.

Levalloisian. A Lower Paleolithic culture characterized by a flint flake tool with a prepared striking platform.

levirate. Brother-in-law marriage. The marriage of a woman to her deceased husband's brother.

levirate, anticipatory. The practice in which a husband extends limited sexual privileges with his wife to his younger brother.

liga. A pile of heated stones used for baking taro in New Ireland.

linea aspera. The longitudinal ridge on the posterior surface of the femur.

lineage. A unilateral kinship group that traces descent from a known common ancestor, who lived not more than five or six generations back.

lobola. Bride price among the Bantu-speaking tribes of South Africa.

lost wax method. A process of casting metal objects in molds shaped about a wax form, which is then melted out.

Magdalenian. The final culture of the Upper Paleolithic Age in Europe.

magic. The control of supernatural forces by means of compulsive formulas.

magic, contagious. A form of sympathetic magic. It operates on the principle that things once in contact with each other can exert a continuing influence upon each other.

magic, imitative. A form of sympathetic magic. It operates on the principle that like influences like.

magic, sympathetic. Magic that operates on the principle of homeopathic association; *i.e.*, that one object can exert an influence upon others that have an identity with it.

Maglemosian. A local manifestation of the Mesolithic Age in the Great Swamp of the Baltic Coast.

makarata. A formal regulated combat among the Murngin of Australia.

malagan. A complex of memorial festivals in New Ireland, Melanesia.

mana. Supernatural power that does not occur in the form of a spirit being.

manioc. A tropical plant of the genus *Manihot*, whose roots yield a nutritious starch. Also called *cassava*.

mano. *See* muller.

marriage. The social institution that regulates the special relations of a mated pair to each other, their offspring, their kinsmen, and society at large.

marriage, affinal. Marriage to a spouse's relative. In-law marriage.

marriage, cross-cousin, asymmetrical. A preferred marriage form that is restricted to one type of cross-cousin only. Marriage of a man to his mother's brother's daughter is permitted, while marriage to his father's sister's daughter is prohibited, or vice versa.

marriage, cross-cousin, symmetrical. Marriage in which either type of cross-cousin is permissible or preferred as a spouse.

marriage, extended affinal. Marriage to an affinal relative of a higher or lower generation. Marriage based upon an extension of the levirate or sororate principles.

mastaba. An Egyptian subterranean burial chamber that is prototypic of the pyramids.

matai. The titular head of a Samoan household.

matriarchate. A society distinguished by uxorilocal residence and matrilineal descent.

matrilineal. The reckoning of descent through the mother.

matrilocal. *See* uxorilocal.

mean, arithmetical. The average. That point in the range of variability of a phenomenon at which exactly equal quantities fall on either side.

median. The mid-point. That point in the range of variability of a phenomenon which falls exactly at the middle of the two extremes.

megalith. A large stone used as a marker, altar, or monument.

megalithic complex. A cultural system centering about large stone monuments.

Meganthropus paleojavanicus. A giant fossil man from Java.

Melanesia. Black islands. The island area of the Southwest Pacific.

menhir. An elongated, standing stone raised as a monument or altar.

merging (in kinship systems). *See* kinship, classificatory.

mesocephalic. Medium-headed. Cephalic index 75 to 79.9.

Mesolithic. The Middle Stone Age. Also called *Epipaleolithic*.

mesological. Semi- or quasi-logical. Applied to the method of reasoning used by the nineteenth-century lineal evolutionists, who by inference reasoned that beginning with assumed starting points the successive stages of each form of social institution or material invention could be described.

metate. A flat or grooved grinding stone that functions as a mortar.

Microlith. A minute stone artifact made from fine flint flakes.

Micronesia. Small islands. The island area of the West Central Pacific.

milpa. The Maya Indian method of gardening, involving the slash and burn technique of clearing garden plots in the forest.

Miocene. The middle, or third, period of the Cenozoic era.

Mithraic cult. The religious system devoted to the worship of Mithras, the Persian god of light, upholder of the truth and the foe of evil.

mode. The high point. That point in the range of variability of a phenomenon which occurs with the greatest frequency.

Mogollon-Mimbres. A prehistoric culture localized in the mountainous area of southeastern Arizona and southwestern New Mexico.

moiety. Half. The social unit based upon kinship that occurs when the tribe is divided into two recognized units.

monogamy. Marriage of one man to one woman.

monolith. A structure consisting of a single stone.

monotheism. The worship of one god.

morphology. The study of the form and structure of an organism or social manifestation.

Mousterian. The culture associated with Neandertal man during the third interglacial and fourth glacial epochs in Europe.

muller. A grinding stone held in the hand and rubbed over a metate.

mutation. An abrupt modification of the genetic composition of an organism.

nasal index. The relation between the breadth and height of the nasal orifice. $N.I. = \dfrac{N.B.}{N.H.} \times 100$

nasion. The intersection of the internasal suture with the frontal bone of the skull.

Neandertal man. An extinct fossil race of man dominant in the Old World from the third interglacial epoch to the climax of the fourth glacial.

Neoanthropic man. A "modern" or *sapiens* type of man.

Negroid. Characteristic of Negroes.

Negrito. The "little Negro" or Pygmy race.

Neolithic. The New Stone Age.

neurosis. A mild form of behavior disorder.

Ngbe. *See* Egbo.

Nilotic. People who live on the River Nile.

nobility. A class or caste with hereditary status of high prestige and ceremonial or political power.

normative. The quality of inducing conformity to a norm.

notochord. A rod of cells that forms the beginning of the backbone in vertebrate animals.

ntoro. The patrilineal clan in Ashanti society.

oath. A formal declaration that the facts are as stated. (Not to be confused with conditional curse.)

occiput. The bone that forms the rear and lower segment of the cranium.

Oedipus complex. A psychological state of a male characterized by sexual desire for the mother and antagonism toward the father.

okeyame. The talking chief in Ashanti society.

oligarchy. A state whose government is controlled by a small group within the larger society.

ontogeny. The natural history of an individual, beginning with the fertilized egg.

ordeal. A ritual method of verification of testimony in which the litigants are subjected to a physical test designed to injure the falsifier seriously or to kill him.

Paleolithic. The Old Stone Age.

paleosimia. A genus of Miocene fossil ape that is ancestral to the orangutan.

Paleozoic. The third era of geological time.

papyrus. The Egyptian paper made from the pith of *Cyperus papyrus*, an Egyptian sedge.

parallel cousin. The offspring of a person's mother's sister or father's brother.

parallelism. The development of similar cultural forms through identical steps without historical interaction or contact.

parapithecus. A genus of fossil primate found in Oligocene deposits and believed to be ancestral to man, the apes, and monkeys.

parfleche. An oblong rawhide box made by Plains Indians.

passage grave. A long narrow burial chamber.

pastoralism. A culture marked by a subsistence technique centered about the herding and husbandry of domesticated animals.

paterfamilias. The authoritarian father in the Roman family.

patriarchate. A society dominated by the father as head of the kinship group, characterized by patrilineal descent and virilocal residence.

patrilineal. The reckoning of descent through the father. Children belong to the kinship group of their father.

patrilocal. *See* virilocal.

patronymy. The custom of giving children the name of their father's kinship group.

pattoli. The Aztec form of pachisi, a game played with dice.

percussion flaking. The technique of shaping flint artifacts by removing flakes with blows of a hammerstone.

personality. The sum total of behavior traits, overt and covert, characteristic of a person.

personality, basic structure. The constellation of behavior traits and attitudes established in the members of a given society by their childhood reactions to the methods of child training characteristic of their culture.

personality, ideal type. The construct of the personality configuration most highly emphasized in a culture.

personality, modal. The personality configuration most commonly manifest by the members of a society or group.

petroglyph. A symbol incised in rock.

peyote. A variety of cactus (*Lophopora williamsii*) ingested by Indians (notably Plains Indians) as a means of stimulating visions as a form of religious experience.

phenotype. An organic specimen in which one of the paired genes determining a trait is dominant and the other recessive. The presence of the recessive trait is not directly revealed in the somatic manifestation of the trait.

phratry. A social unit consisting of two or more linked clans between which exists a special bond of unity as against clans joined in other phratries within the society.

phylogeny. The natural history of a species or variety.

physical anthropology. The study of the bodily characteristics of mankind.

pictograph. A simple picture, or series of pictures, intended to describe a situation or record some event.

pile dwelling. A house raised from the ground or built over water on piling.

pit dwelling. An earth lodge built over an excavated pit.

Pithecanthropus erectus. Upright ape man. An early Pleistocene type of man, whose fossil remains were discovered at Trinil, Java (Java man).

Pithecanthropus robustus. A large-sized variety of the genus pithecanthropus, also found in Java.

planetesimal. Fragmentary solar materials from which the planets are hypothetically believed to have been formed.

Pleistocene. The fifth period of the Cenozoic era. The glacial age during which man rose to dominance among life forms.

plesianthropus. A genus of fossil ape recently discovered in South Africa.

Pliocene. The fourth period of the Cenozoic era. A warm period during which early human types became differentiated from apes.

pliopithecus. A genus of Pliocene fossil ape that is directly ancestral to the gibbon.

polyandry. The marriage of a woman to two or more men simultaneously.

polyandry, attenuated. The marriage relationship in which a married brother extends limited sexual privileges in his wife to his unmarried younger brothers. Also called *anticipatory levirate*.

polyandry, fraternal. A polyandrous marriage in which the husbands are brothers.

polygamy. Any multiple marriage.

polygenesis. The evolutionary hypothesis which assumes that the several genera of prehistoric man have evolved from different species of Pliocene apes.

polygyny. The marriage of a man to two or more women simultaneously.

Polynesia. Many islands. The area of the Central Pacific that falls within a triangle formed with Hawaii, Easter Island, and New Zealand as the apices.

polytheism. Many gods. A system of religion recognizing multiple gods.

Porro. The men's secret fraternity in Sierra Leone and Liberia, West Africa.

potlatch. The Northwest Coast Indian institution of ceremonial feasting accompanied by lavish distribution of gifts.

preferential marriage. A form of marriage that is enjoined or preferred between two persons of specifically defined statuses.

pressure flaking. The technique of shaping flint artifacts by removing fine flakes by means of steady pressure applied with a hard stick or bone.

priest. A religious functionary whose supernatural authority is bestowed upon him by a cult or organized church, in contrast to the shaman, who derives his power directly from supernatural sources.

primate. An order within the mammalian class.

primitive. A culture, or an aspect of a culture, or an individual whose culture is not characterized by the inclusion of a written language; therefore, nonliterate or preliterate.

primogeniture. Inheritance by the first-born son or child.

privileged familiarity. A culturally permissive relation of free joking between individuals of certain statuses.

prognathous. Having a projecting jaw.

promiscuity. The absence of any social restraints limiting or regulating sexual behavior.

property. The special and socially sanctioned relation of a person or group to the utilization of some object.

property, communal. Property that is owned by the entire community.

property, incorporeal. Property that involves a nonmaterial object.

property, joint. Property that is owned by a group smaller than the entire community.

propliopithecus. A genus of fossil ape found in Oligocene deposits of Egypt. It is a prototype of the gibbon.

Proterozoic. The second era of geological time.

psychosis. An extreme form of behavior disorder marked by relatively fixed patterns of maladaptive attitudes and responses.

pueblo. A village constructed of clay bricks (adobe) or stones. Characteristic of the Indians of southwestern United States and northern Mexico.

Pygmy. *See* Negrito.

pyrite. A mineral, such as flint, used for striking fire.

quern. A grinding stone.

race. A biologically inbred group possessing a distinctive combination of physical traits that tends to breed true from generation to generation.

racism. A doctrine that assumes the inherent superiority of one or another race over others.

relatives, affinal. Persons related through marriage.

relatives, genetic. Biologically related persons.

repun. The virilocal, patrilineal clan in Umor society.

Rhodesian man. A fossil human type with remarkably heavy supraorbital ridges found at Broken Hill in Rhodesia, South Africa.

rite de passage. *See* transition rites.

rite, fertility. A ritual complex designed to promote genetic reproduction.

role. The customary complex of behavior associated with a particular status.

rostrocarinate. A Pliocene artifact found in East Anglia. So called because it is "beak-keeled" in shape.

sacerdotal. Of a priestly nature.

sacrum. The wedge-shaped bone formed by the joining of the vertebrae that form the posterior segment of the pelvis.

sanction. Any social reaction operating to induce conformity to a normative standard of behavior.

sanction, legal. A coercive penalty involving the use of physical force in threat or in fact, attached to the violation of a social norm, when the application of the sanction is considered legitimate according to the prevailing standards of the culture.

sarong. A loose girdle-like skirt originally made of bark cloth and worn by Polynesian women.

savagery. A state of cultural development marked by the absence of gardening or agriculture and written language.

scarification. The process of mutilation of the body through the artificial raising of scar tissue.

schizophrenia. A behavior disorder marked by a replacement of the learned behavior systems with desocialized behavior dominated by private fantasy.

Schnurkeramik. Neolithic pottery decorated with imprints of cord.

senilicide. The killing of the aged.

shaman. A religious specialist who has received his power directly from supernatural sources. Synonymous with medicine man, witch doctor, angakok (Eskimo).

sib. A unilateral kinship group. Synonymous with clan.

sibling. Brother or sister; a member of a sib or clan.

silent trade. *See* barter, dumb.

simian. Apelike.

Sinanthropus pekinensis. Peking man. An Early Pleistocene fossil race found at Chow Kow Tien, China, related to Java, Heidelberg, and Neandertal men.

Skhūl man. A highly variable type of fossil man found in Palestine. It reveals both neandertaloid and *Homo sapiens* characteristics.

slavery. The institution whereby persons are subjected to involuntary servitude, are denied the right of freedom of movement or action, and must place their productive efforts at the disposal of the master.

social distance. A term covering the relative "spatial positions" of two statuses. Generally used to emphasize limitations on social intercourse.

society. An aggregation of human beings (a population) living as a distinct entity and possessing a distinct culture.

society, military. An association of warriors.

society, secret. A fraternity or association whose membership and activities are shrouded in secrecy. A tribal secret society embraces all adult males in its membership.

Solo man. *Homo soloensis.* A fossil species of a Neandertaloid type found on the Solo River in Java.

Solutrean. The middle culture of the Upper Paleolithic Age in western Europe.

sorcery. The use of supernatural power as an aggressive instrument to further the interests of the sorcerer. *Magic* is a more neutral term.

sororal polygyny. The simultaneous marriage of two or more sisters to one husband.

sororate. The practice whereby a younger sister marries the widowed husband of her deceased elder sister.

soulava. The red shell necklaces exchanged in the Melanesian kula.

state. The association within a society that undertakes to direct and organize social policy on behalf of and in the name of the entire society.

status. The social position of an individual with reference to the other members of his society.

Steinheim man. A type of fossil man (*Homo sapiens*) found in mid-glacial deposits at Steinheim, Germany.

stimulus diffusion. The process of cultural dynamics in which one people receive the idea of a cultural invention from another but give a new and unique form to the idea.

Stone Age. *See* Eolithic; Paleolithic; Neolithic.

stratigraphy. Analysis of geological deposits in terms of discernible layers. Derivative time sequences are inferred from the relative positions of the strata or layers.

subincision. A surgical operation in which the urethra of the male sex organ is slit open. A mutilation performed as a part of the male puberty rites in certain Australian tribes.

suitor service. A substitute for, or equivalent of, bride price, in which the potential groom works for his intended bride's kin.

superorganic. The phenomena, known as *cultural*, that occur on a level over and above the organic; *i.e.*, they are not preset in the organic structure.

supraorbital ridge. A bony ridge above the orbits, or eye sockets.

survival. A culture element or complex the genetic function of which has altered with the passage of time so that the usage has become a mere formal convention.

susu. The kinship group formed of a woman, her children, and her brother.

suvasova. Breach of exogamy among the Trobriand Islanders.

Swanscombe man. A *Homo sapiens* type of man found in mid-glacial deposits at Swanscombe, England.

symphysis. The chin region of the lower jaw.

syncretism. The act of fusing or joining two distinct systems of belief, especially religions.

tabu. An act that is enjoined or forbidden and punishable by supernatural sanctions.

tapa. Polynesian bark cloth.

taravad. The joint household consisting of the members of a susu among the Nayar caste of the Cochin state of the Malabar Coast of India.

Tardenoisian. A local manifestation of the Mesolithic Age in northern France. Usually linked with the Azilian to form the Azilian-Tardenoisian culture.

taro. A plant grown extensively in the Pacific area, where its root provides a staple food.

Taungs ape child. See *Australopithecus africanus.*

teknonymy. The practice of naming a parent after his child.

teleolith. A purposefully shaped stone artifact.

thanatomania. The depression of the "will to exist" to the point of death. Somatic compliance to the "death wish."

thaumaturgy. The performance of miracles. Magic.

theocracy. A social order controlled by religious officers.

till, glacial. An unstratified deposit of earth and rock deposited by a glacier.

tipi. A conical tent.

tort. An offense against an individual subject to legal sanctions applied by the wronged person or his kinsmen.

totem. An object, often an animal or a plant, held in special regard by the members of a social group, who feel that there is a peculiar bond of emotional identity between themselves and the totem.

totemism. The institutional complex centering about a totem.

tovudun. The ancestral gods in Dahomean religion from whom is derived the American word *voodoo.*

transition rites. Ritual complexes associated with important changes in personal status, such as birth, adolescence, marriage, death.

transvestite. An individual who effects a transfer of sex roles, such as occurs when a male takes on the status and roles of a female or vice versa.

travertine. A porous limestone. Also called *tufa*.

travois. A carrying device of two poles hitched to a draft animal like the tongues of a buggy. The free ends of the travois drag along the ground.

tribe. A social group speaking a distinctive language or dialect and possessing a distinctive culture that marks it off from other tribes. It is not necessarily organized politically.

Trickster. A character in mythology who alters the order of things by tricking man or animals into choices or circumstances that they do not expect or desire.

Trinil man. See *Pithecanthropus erectus*.

troll. A giant or dwarf in old Scandinavian belief.

tumulus. A mound of earth covering a dolmen or burial chamber.

ultimogeniture. Inheritance by the youngest son or daughter.

unilateral. Reckoning descent through one parent only.

unilocal. The practice whereby a married couple regularly settles with, or close to, the parents of one of the spouses. *See* uxorilocal, virilocal.

universal. A behavior pattern characteristic of all the members of a society.

usufruct. The right to use of an object of property without possessing title of ownership.

uxorilocal. The practice whereby a married couple settles in the domicile of the wife's family. Also called *matrilocal residence*.

vestigial remains. Organs whose physiological functions have been lost (so far as can be determined).

virilocal. The practice whereby a married couple settles in the domicile of the husband's family. Also called *patrilocal residence*.

vodun. A system of religious belief and practice developed by Caribbean Negroes and combining elements of Catholicism and African, particularly Dahomean, religions. Magic is only a minor element in the entire complex. Called *voodoo* in the American vernacular.

wampum. Elongated beads drilled out of clamshells, used by Indians of the Northeast Woodlands.

warp. The parallel-lying foundation threads of a fabric.

weft. The threads woven at right angles through the parallel-lying foundation threads, or warp. Also called the *woof*, or *filler*.

wergild. The money payment made by the kin of a murderer to the kin of a murdered man.

Weimar man. A local Neandertaloid type of fossil man found near Weimar, Germany.

wickiup. A beehive-shaped grass hut.

wife lending. The custom whereby a husband extends to a household guest the sexual favors of his wife as a symbolic gesture of brotherhood.

wigwam. A domed bark hut of the Algonquian Indians of the Northeast Woodlands.

willow-leaf point. A long, slender flint blade characteristic of the Solutrean culture.

windigo. A type of culturally induced insanity among the Ojibway and other Algonquian Indians.

woof. See *weft*.

wrong, private. An offense against an individual that is customarily punished by legal action instituted by the injured person or his kinsmen. Private wrongs make up the body of private law.

wrong, public. An offense against the social entity punished by the legal action of the group at large or by its official representatives.

wurley. A lean-to shelter built by Australian aborigines.

yucca. A plant belonging to the lily family and possessing long fibrous leaves. The sap of its roots produces suds in water.

BIBLIOGRAPHY

AARNE, A.: *Die Tiere auf der Wanderschaft* (Folklore Fellows Communications, No. 11, 1913).

AGINSKY, B. W.: "An Indian's Soliloquy" (*The American Journal of Sociology*, Vol. 46, 1940), pp. 43–44.

—— and P. H. BUCK: "Interacting Forces in the Maori Family" (*American Anthropologist*, Vol. 42, 1940), pp. 195–210.

AMSDEN, C.: "The Loom and Its Prototypes" (*American Anthropologist*, Vol. 34, 1932), pp. 216–315.

ASHLEY-MONTAGUE, M. F.: *Coming into Being among the Australian Aborigines* (New York, 1938).

——: *Man's Most Dangerous Myth: The Fallacy of Race* (2d ed., New York, 1945).

——: "On the Origin of the Domestication of the Dog" (*Science*, Vol. 96, 1942), pp. 111–112.

ATKINSON, J. J.: *Primal Law* (London, 1903).

BACHOFEN, J. K.: *Das Mutterrecht: eine Untersuchung über die Gynaikokratie der alten Welt nach iherer religiosen und rechtlichen Natur* (Stuttgart, 1861).

BACON, E.: "A Preliminary Attempt to Determine the Culture Areas of Asia" (*Southwestern Journal of Anthropology*, Vol. 2, 1946), pp. 117–132.

BAITSELL, G. A. (ed.): *The Evolution of Earth and Man* (New Haven, 1929).

BALFOUR, H.: *The Evolution of Decorative Art* (London, 1893).

BARNETT, H. G.: "Applied Anthropology in 1860" (*Applied Anthropology*, Vol. 1, 1942), pp. 19–32.

——: "Culture Processes" (*American Anthropologist*, Vol. 42, 1940), pp. 21–48.

——: "The Nature of the Potlatch" (*American Anthropologist*, Vol. 40, 1938), pp. 349–358.

BARRETT, S. A.: "Pomo Indian Basketry" (*University of California Publications in American Archaeology and Ethnology*, Vol. 7, 1908).

BARTON, R. F.: "Ifugao Economics" (*University of California Publications in American Archaeology and Ethnology*, Vol. 15, No. 5, 1922).

——: "Ifugao Law" (*University of California Publications in American Archaeology and Ethnology*, Vol. 15, 1919).

——: *Philippine Pagans: The Autobiographies of Three Ifugaos* (London, 1938).

——: *The Half-way Sun: Life among the Headhunters of the Philippines* (New York, 1930).

——: *The Religion of the Ifugaos* (American Anthropological Association, Memoir 65, 1946).

BAUMAN, H.: "The Division of Work according to Sex in African Hoe Culture" (*Africa*, Vol. 1, 1928), pp. 289–318.

BEAGLEHOLE, E.: "Character Structure: Its Role in the Analysis of Interpersonal Relations" (*Psychiatry*, Vol. 7, 1944), pp. 144–162.

——: *Property: A Study in Social Psychology* (London, 1931).

BELO, J.: "A Study of a Balinese Family" (*American Anthropologist*, Vol. 38, 1936), pp. 12–31.

BENEDICT, R. F.: "Marital Property Rights in Bilateral Society" (*American Anthropologist*, Vol. 38, 1936), pp. 368–373.

——: *Patterns of Culture* (New York, 1937).

——: *Race: Science and Politics* (New York, 1940).

——: "Religion" in *General Anthropology* (New York, 1938).

——: "Review of *An Apache Life-way*, by M. E. Opler" (*American Anthropologist*, Vol. 44, 1942), pp. 692–693.

——: *The Chrysanthemum and the Sword: Patterns of Japanese Culture* (Boston, 1946).

——: *The Concept of the Guardian Spirit in North America* (American Anthropological Association, Memoir 29, 1923).

——: "The Science of Custom: The Bearing of Anthropology on Contemporary Thought" in *The Making of Man* (New York, 1931), pp. 805–817.

—— and G. WELTFISH: *The Races of Mankind* (New York, 1943).

BENNETT, J. W.: "The Development of Ethnological Theories as Illustrated by Studies of the Plains Indian Sun Dance" (*American Anthropologist*, Vol. 46, 1944), pp. 162–181.

BENNETT, W. C., and R. M. ZINGG: *The Tarahumara: An Indian Tribe of Northern Mexico* (Chicago, 1935).

BOAS, F.: "Anthropology" (*Encyclopedia of the Social Sciences*, Vol. 2, 1930), pp. 73–110.

——: *Anthropology and Modern Life* (rev. ed., New York, 1932).

——: *Decorative Designs of Alaskan Needlecases* (United States National Museum, Reports, Vol. 39, 1908), pp. 221–344.

——: *Primitive Art* (Oslo, 1929).

——: *Social Organization and Secret Societies of the Kwakiutl Indians* (United States National Museum, Reports, 1895).

——: *The Central Eskimo* (Bureau of American Ethnology, Annual Report 6, 1888), pp. 399–669.

——: *The Eskimo of Baffinland and Hudson Bay* (American Museum of Natural History, Bulletin No. 15, 1907).

——: *Tsimshian Mythology* (Bureau of American Ethnology, Annual Report 31, 1916), pp. 393–558.

—— and others: *General Anthropology* (New York, 1938).

BOGORAS, W.: "The Chukchee I: Religion" (*Jessup North Pacific Expedition*, Vol. 7, 1904–1909).

BRAIDWOOD, R. J.: "The Interrelations of Core and Flake Tool Traditions in Europe," in *Human Origins, Selected Readings*, Series 2 (2d ed., University of Chicago, 1946), pp. 145–152.

BRIFFAULT, R.: "Group Marriage and Sexual Communism" in *The Making of Man* (New York, 1931).

——: *The Mothers: The Matriarchal Theory of Social Origins* (3 vols., New York, 1927).

BRINTON, D. G.: *Religions of Primitive People* (New York, 1897).

BROWN, A. R.: *The Andaman Islanders: A Study in Social Anthropology* (Cambridge, 1922).

BUCK, P. H.: *Vikings of the Sunrise* (New York, 1938).

BUNZEL, R.: "The Pueblo Potter" (*Columbia University Contributions to Anthropology*, Vol. 8, 1929).

BURGESS, E. W.: Introduction in E. F. Frazier, *The Negro Family in the United States* (Chicago, 1939).

CALVERTON, V. F. (ed.): *The Making of Man: An Outline of Anthropology* (New York, 1931).

CARDOZO, B. N.: *The Growth of the Law* (New Haven, 1924).

CARTER, G. F.: "Origins of American Indian Agriculture" (*American Anthropologist*, Vol. 48, 1946), pp. 1–21.

CHAMBERLIN, T. C.: *The Origin of the Earth* (Chicago, 1916).

CHAPPLE, E., and C. COON: *Principles of Anthropology* (New York, 1942).

CHILDE, V. G.: *The Dawn of European Civilization* (New York, 1925).

CLELAND, H. F.: *Our Prehistoric Ancestors* (New York, 1928).

COLE, G. D. H.: "Inheritance" (*Encyclopedia of the Social Sciences*, Vol. 8, 1932), pp. 35–43.

COMTE, A.: *Positive Philosophy* (trans. from the French by H. Martineau, London, 1893).

COOK, W. W.: "Ownership and Possession" (*Encyclopedia of the Social Sciences*, Vol. 11, 1933), pp. 521–525.

COOPER, J. M.: "Is the Algonquian Family Hunting Ground System Pre-Columbian?" (*American Anthropologist*, Vol. 41, 1939), pp. 66–90.

———: "Mental Disease Situations in Certain Cultures" (*Journal of Abnormal and Social Psychology*, Vol. 29, 1934), pp. 10–17.

———: "The Yahgan" in *Handbook of South American Indians* (5 vols., Washington, 1947–), Vol. 1, pp. 81–107.

———: "The Patagonian and Pampean Hunters" in *Handbook of South American Indians* (5 vols., Washington, 1947–), Vol. 1, pp. 127–168.

CUPPY, W.: *How to Tell Your Friends from the Apes* (New York, 1931).

CURTIS, E. S.: *The Kwakiutl* (New York, 1919).

DARWIN, F. (ed.): *The Life and Letters of Charles Darwin* (3 vols., London, 1887).

DAVIDSON, D. S.: "Knotless Netting in America and Oceania" (*American Anthropologist*, Vol. 37, 1935), pp. 117–134.

DENSMORE, F.: "An Explanation of a Trick Performed by Indian Jugglers" (*American Anthropologist*, Vol. 34, 1932), pp. 310–314.

DOLLARD, J.: *Criteria for the Life History, with Analyses of Six Notable Documents* (New Haven, 1935).

DOMENECH, E.: *Seven Years' Residence in the Great Deserts of North America* (2 vols., London, 1860).

DORSEY, G. A.: "The Cheyenne: II, The Sun Dance" (*Field Columbian Museum, Publication* 103, *Anthropological Series*, Vol. 9, No. 2, 1905).

——— and J. R. MURIE: "Notes on Skidi Pawnee Society" (*Field Museum of Natural History, Anthropological Series*, Vol. 27, 1940).

DRUCKER, P.: "Rank, Wealth, and Kinship in Northwest Coast Society" (*American Anthropologist*, Vol. 41, 1939), pp. 55–65.

DuBois, C.: "The Alorese" in A. Kardiner (ed.), *The Psychological Frontiers of Society* (New York, 1945), pp. 101–145.

———: *The People of Alor* (Minneapolis, 1944).

DUMAREST, N.: *Notes on Cochiti, New Mexico* (American Anthropological Association, Memoirs, Vol. 6, No. 3, 1919).

EGGAN, F. (ed.): *Social Organization of North American Indians* (Chicago, 1937).

EMBREE, J. F.: *The Japanese Nation: A Social Survey* (New York, 1945).

ENGELS, F.: *The Origin of the Family, Private Property, and the State in the Light of the Researches of Lewis Henry Morgan* (London, 1884).

EVANS-PRITCHARD, E. E.: *The Nuer: A Description of the Modes of Livelihood and Political Institutions of a Nilotic People* (Oxford, 1940).

——: "The Nuer of the Southern Sudan" in *African Political Systems* (Oxford, 1941).

FAIRCHILD, H. P. (ed.): *Dictionary of Sociology* (New York, 1944).

FLETCHER, A. C., and F. LaFLESCHE: *The Omaha Tribe* (Bureau of American Ethnology, Annual Report 27, 1911).

FORD, C. L.: *A Comparative Study of Human Reproduction* (Yale University Publications in Anthropology, No. 32, 1945).

FORDE, C. D.: *Habitat, Economy, and Society: A Geographical Introduction to Ethnology* (2d ed., New York, 1937).

——: "Kinship in Umor—Double Unilateral Organization in a Semi-Bantu Society" (*American Anthropologist*, Vol. 41, 1939), pp. 523–553.

FORTUNE, R. F.: "Arapesh Warfare" (*American Anthropologist*, Vol. 41, 1939), pp. 22–41.

——: *Manus Religion* (Proceedings of the American Philosophical Society, 1935).

——: *Sorcerers of Dobu: The Social Anthropology of the Dobu Islanders of the Western Pacific* (New York, 1932).

FRANK, J.: "Lawlessness" (*Encyclopedia of the Social Sciences*, Vol. 9, 1933), pp. 277–279.

FRANKLIN, B.: *The Interests of Great Britain Considered* (Boston, 1760).

FRAZER, J. G.: *The Golden Bough: A Study in Magic and Religion* (1 vol., abridged ed., New York, 1941).

——: *Totemism and Exogamy* (4 vols., London, 1910).

FRAZIER, E. F.: *The Negro Family in the United States* (Chicago, 1939).

FREUCHEN, P.: *Arctic Adventure: My Life in the Frozen North* (New York, 1935).

FREUD, S.: *Totem and Tabu* (reprinted in *The Basic Writings of Sigmund Freud*, New York, 1938).

GARFIELD, V. E.: "Tsimshian Clan and Society" (*University of Washington Publications in Anthropology*, Vol. 7, No. 3, 1939).

GARRETT, H. E.: "Negro-White Differences in Mental Ability in the United States" (*The Scientific Monthly*, Vol. 65, 1947), pp. 329–333.

GARTH, T. E.: *Race Psychology: A Study of Racial Mental Differences* (New York, 1931).

GAUCH, H.: *New Foundations for Research into Social Race Problems* (Berlin, 1933).

GAYTON, A. H.: "Yokuts-Mono Chiefs and Shamans" (*University of California Publications in American Archaeology and Ethnology*, Vol. 24, 1930).

GIFFORD, E. W.: *Tongan Society* (Bernice P. Bishop Museum, Bulletin 61, 1929).

GILLIN, J. L., and J. P. GILLIN: *An Introduction to Sociology* (New York, 1942).

GILLIN, J. P.: "The Barama River Caribs of British Guiana" (*Papers of the Peabody Museum of American Archaeology and Ethnology, Harvard University*, Vol. 14, 1936).

GOLDENWEISER, A.: *Anthropology* (New York, 1937).

GOLDFRANK, E. S.: "Socialization, Personality, and the Structure of Pueblo Society (with Particular Reference to Hopi and Zuñi)" (*American Anthropologist*, Vol. 47, 1945), pp. 516–539.

——: "Linguistic Note to Zuñi Ethnology" (*Word*, Vol. 2, 1946), pp. 191–196.

GOODWIN, G.: *The Social Organization of the Western Apache* (Chicago, 1942).

GORER, G.: *The American People: A Study in National Character* (New York, 1947).

GREENMAN, E. F.: "Material Culture and the Organism" (*American Anthropologist*, Vol. 47, 1945), pp. 211–231.

GRIFFIN, N. M.: *The Roles of Men and Women in Eskimo Culture* (Chicago, 1930).

GRINNELL, G. B.: *The Cheyenne Indians: Their History and Ways of Life* (2 vols., New Haven, 1928).

———: *The Fighting Cheyennes* (New York, 1915).

GUNTHER, J.: *Inside U.S.A.* (New York, 1947).

HAAR, B. TER: *Adat Law in Indonesia* (trans. from the Dutch and edited with an introduction by E. A. Hoebel and A. A. Schiller, New York, 1948).

HADDON, A. C.: *Evolution in Art* (London, 1895).

HAINES, F.: "The Northward Spread of Horses Among the Plains Indians" (*American Anthropologist*, Vol. 40, 1938), pp. 429–437.

———: "Where Did the Plains Indians Get Their Horses?" (*American Anthropologist*, Vol. 40, 1938), pp. 112–117.

HALLOWELL, A. I.: "Culture and Mental Disorders" (*Journal of Abnormal and Social Psychology*, Vol. 29, 1934), pp. 1–9.

———: "The Nature and Function of Property as a Social Institution" (*Journal of Political and Legal Sociology*, Vol. 1, 1943), pp. 115–138.

HAMBLY, W. D.: "Source Book for African Anthropology" (*Field Museum of Natural History, Anthropological Series*, Vol. 26, Part 2, 1937).

HAMILTON, W. H., and I. TILL: "Property" (*Encyclopedia of the Social Sciences*, Vol. 12, 1934), pp. 528–538.

HARRASSER, A.: *Die Rechtsverletzung bei den australischer Eingeborenen* (Beilegeheft zur vergleichende Rechtswissenschaft, Vol. 50, 1936).

HART, C. W. M.: "A Reconsideration of Natchez Social Structure" (*American Anthropologist*, Vol. 45, 1943), pp. 374–386.

HAWLEY, F. M.: "Pueblo Social Organization as a Lead to Pueblo History" (*American Anthropologist*, Vol. 39, 1937), pp. 504–522.

HAXTHAUSEN, A. VON: *Studien über die inneren Zustände das Volksleben und inbesondere die ländlichen Einrichtungen Russlands* (3 vols., Hanover and Berlin, 1847–1852).

HERSKOVITS, M. J.: *Acculturation: The Study of Culture Contacts* (New York, 1938).

———: "African Gods and Catholic Saints in New World Negro Belief" (*American Anthropologist*, Vol. 39, 1937), pp. 635–643.

———: *Backgrounds of African Art* (Denver, 1945).

———: "The Culture Area of Africa" (*Africa*, Vol. 3, 1930), pp. 59–77.

———: "A Note on 'Woman Marriage' in Dahomey" (*Africa*, Vol. 10, 1937), pp. 335–341.

———: "A Preliminary Consideration of Culture Areas of Africa" (*American Anthropologist*, Vol. 26, 1924), pp. 50–63.

———: *Dahomey: An Ancient West African Kingdom* (2 vols., New York, 1938).

——— and F. S. HERSKOVITS: *An Outline of Dahomean Religious Belief* (American Anthropological Association, Memoir 41, 1933).

HIBBEN, F. C.: "Corn" (*The Atlantic*, Vol. 175, 1945), p. 121.

HOBHOUSE, L. H., G. C. WHEELER, and M. GINSBERG: *The Material Culture and Social Institutions of the Simpler Peoples* (London, 1930).

HOEBEL, E. A.: "Anent Blood Relationship" (*Science*, Vol. 103, 1946), pp. 600–602.

———: "Comanche and H3kandika Shoshone Relationship Systems" (*American Anthropologist*, Vol. 41, 1939), pp. 440–457.

HOEBEL, E. A.: "Eskimo Infanticide and Polyandry" (*The Scientific Monthly*, Vol. 64, 1947), p. 535.

——: "Fundamental Legal Concepts as Applied in the Study of Primitive Law" (*Yale Law Journal*, Vol. 51, 1942), pp. 951–963.

——: "Law and Anthropology" (*Virginia Law Review*, Vol. 32, 1946), pp. 836–854.

——: "Law-ways of the Primitive Eskimos" (*Journal of Criminal Law and Criminology*, Vol. 31, 1941), pp. 663–683.

——: "The Asiatic Origin of a Myth of the Northwest Coast" (*Journal of American Folklore*, Vol. 54, 1941), pp. 1–12.

——: "The Comanche Sun Dance and Messianic Outbreak of 1873" (*American Anthropologist*, Vol. 43, 1941), pp. 301–303.

——: *The Political Organization and Law-ways of the Comanche Indians* (American Anthropological Association, Memoir 54: Contributions from the Laboratory of Anthropology, 4, 1940).

——: "The Sun Dance of the H3kandika Shoshone" (*American Anthropologist*, Vol. 39, 1935), pp. 507–581.

HOGBIN, H. I.: *Law and Order in Polynesia: A Study of Primitive Legal Institutions* (New York, 1934).

HOLLIS, A. C.: *The Nandi* (Clarendon, 1909).

HOLMES, O. W., JR.: "Law in Science and Science in Law" (*Harvard Law Review*, Vol. 12, 1899), pp. 443–463.

——: *McDonald v. Maybee* (*Supreme Court Reporter*, Vol. 37, 1917), p. 343.

——: *The Common Law* (Boston, 1881).

——: "The Path of the Law" (*Harvard Law Review*, Vol. 10, 1897).

HOLMES-POLLOCK LETTERS: *The Correspondence of Mr. Justice Holmes and Sir Frederick Pollock 1874–1932* (2 vols., Cambridge, 1942).

HOLMES, W. H.: *Ancient Art of the Province of Chiriqui* (Bureau of American Ethnology, Annual Report 6, 1888).

HOOTON, E. A.: *Man's Poor Relations* (New York, 1942).

——: "The Wages of Biological Sin" (*The Atlantic*, Vol. 164, 1939), pp. 435–445.

——: *Up from the Ape* (New York, 1932).

HOWELLS, W. W.: "Fossil Man and the Origin of Races" (*American Anthropologist*, Vol. 44, 1942), pp. 182–193.

HOWITT, A. W.: *The Native Tribes of South-east Australia* (New York, 1904).

HRDLIČKA, A.: "The Neandertal Phase of Man" (*Smithsonian Institution, Annual Report*, 1928), pp. 593–623.

JAMES, P.: *An Outline of Geography* (Boston, 1935).

JENNESS, D.: *The Indians of Canada* (National Museum of Canada, Bulletin 68, Anthropological Series, No. 15, 2d ed., 1934).

JHERING, R. VON: *Law as Means to an End* (trans. from the German, New York, 1924).

JUNOD, A. H.: *The Life of a South African Tribe* (2 vols., London, 1913).

KARDINER, A.: *The Individual and His Society* (New York, 1939).

——: *The Psychological Frontiers of Society* (New York, 1945).

KEITH, A.: "A Resurvey of the Anatomical Features of the Piltdown Skull with Some Observations on the Recently Discovered Swanscombe Skull" (*Journal of Anatomy*, Vol. 63, 1938–1939), pp. 155–185, 234–254.

——: *New Discoveries Relating to the Antiquity of Man* (New York, no date).

——: *The Antiquity of Man* (2 vols., Philadelphia, 1925).

KENNEDY, R.: "Bark Cloth in Indonesia" (*Journal of the Polynesian Society*, No. 172, 1934).

———: *Islands and Peoples of the Indies* (Smithsonian Institution War Background Studies, No. 14, 1943).

KLINEBERG, O. H.: "A Science of National Character" (*Journal of Social Psychology*, S.P.S.S.I. Bulletin 19, 1944), pp. 147–162.

———: "Mental Tests" (*Encyclopedia of the Social Sciences*, Vol. 10, 1933), pp. 323–328.

———: *Race Differences* (New York, 1935).

KLUCKHOHN, C.: "The Place of Theory in Anthropological Science" (*The Philosophy of Science*, Vol. 6, 1939).

——— and O. H. MOWRER: " 'Culture and Personality:' A Conceptual Scheme" (*American Anthropologist*, Vol. 46, 1944), pp. 1–29.

KÖHLER, W.: *The Mentality of Apes* (New York, 1925).

KROEBER, A. L.: "Caste" (*Encyclopedia of the Social Sciences*, Vol. 3, 1930), pp. 254–256.

———: "Classificatory Systems of Relationship" (*Journal of the Royal Anthropological Institute of Great Britain and Ireland*, Vol. 39, 1909), pp. 77–84.

———: "Cultural and Natural Areas of Native North America" (*University of California Publications in American Archaeology and Ethnology*, Vol. 39, 1939).

———: "Culture Element Distributions: XV, Salt, Dogs, Tobacco" (*Anthropological Records*, Vol. 6, No. 1, 1941), pp. 1–20.

———: "Decorative Symbolism of the Arapaho" (*American Anthropologist*, Vol. 3, 1901), pp. 308*ff*.

———: "Stepdaughter Marriage" (*American Anthropologist*, Vol. 42, 1940), pp. 562–570.

———: "Stimulus Diffusion" (*American Anthropologist*, Vol. 42, 1940), pp. 1–20.

———: "The Superorganic" (*American Anthropologist*, Vol. 19, 1917), pp. 163–213.

———: "Yurok Law" (*22d International Congress of Americanists*, 1922), pp. 511*ff*.

KUPER, H.: *An African Aristocracy: Rank among the Swazi* (Oxford, 1947).

LABARRE, W.: "Potato Taxonomy among the Aymara Indians of Bolivia" (*Acta Americana*, Vol. 5, 1947), pp. 83–102.

———: *The Peyote Cult* (Yale University Publications in Anthropology, No. 19, 1938).

LAFARGE, O.: *The Changing Indian* (Norman, 1942).

LANDES, R.: "The Ojibway of Canada" in M. Mead (ed.), *Cooperation and Competition among Primitive Peoples*, New York, 1937, pp. 87–126.

LANG, A.: *Myth, Ritual, and Religion* (London, 1887).

———: *Social Origins* (London, 1903).

———: *The Making of Religion* (London, 1898).

LANTIS, M.: "The Alaskan Whale Cult and Its Affinities" (*American Anthropologist*, Vol. 40, 1938), pp. 438–464.

LEAKEY, L. S. B.: *Adam's Ancestors: An Up-to-date Outline of What Is Known about the Origin of Man* (New York, 1935).

———: *The Stone Age Races of Kenya* (London, 1935).

LESSA, W. A.: *An Appraisal of Constitutional Typologies* (American Anthropological Association, Memoir 62, 1945).

LESSER, A.: "Levirate and Fraternal Polyandry among the Pawnees" (*Man*, Vol. 30, No. 77, 1930), pp. 98–101.

Lewin, J.: *Studies in African Native Law* (Cape Town and Philadelphia, 1947).

Lewis, M., and W. Clark: *History of the Expedition of Captains Lewis and Clark 1804-5-6* (Hosmer ed., 2 vols., Chicago, 1902).

Lewis, O.: *The Effects of White Contact upon Blackfoot Culture, with Special Reference to the Fur Trade* (American Ethnological Society, Monograph 6, 1942).

Li An-che, "Zuñi: Some Observations and Queries" (*American Anthropologist*, Vol. 39, 1937), pp. 62-75.

Linton, R. M. (ed.): *Acculturation in Seven American Indian Tribes* (New York, 1940).

———: "Culture Areas in Madagascar" (*American Anthropologist*, Vol. 30, 1928), pp. 363-390.

———: *The Cultural Background of Personality* (New York, 1945).

———: *The Marquesas*, in A. Kardiner, *The Individual and His Society* (New York, 1937).

——— (ed.) *The Science of Man in the World Crisis* (New York, 1945).

———: *The Study of Man* (New York, 1936).

———: "The Tanala," in A. Kardiner, *The Individual and His Society* (New York, 1937).

———: "The Tanala, A Hill Tribe of Madagascar" (*Field Museum of Natural History, Anthropological Series*, Vol. 22, 1933).

——— and P. S. Wingert: *Arts of the South Seas* (New York, 1946).

Llewellyn, K. N., and E. A. Hoebel: *The Cheyenne Way: Conflict and Case Law in Primitive Jurisprudence* (Norman, 1941).

Loeb, E. M.: "Javanese Word Formation, High and Low" (*Journal of the American Oriental Society*, Vol. 64, 1944), pp. 113-126.

——— and J. O. M. Broek: "Social Organization and the Long House in Southeast Asia" (*American Anthropologist*, Vol. 49, 1947), pp. 414-425.

——— and G. Toffelmier: "Kin Marriage and Exogamy" (*The Journal of General Psychology*, Vol. 20, 1939), pp. 181-228.

Lowie, R. H.: *An Introduction to Cultural Anthropology* (rev. ed., New York, 1940).

———: "Evolution in Cultural Anthropology: A Reply to Leslie White" (*American Anthropologist*, Vol. 48, 1946), pp. 229-230.

———: "Incorporeal Property in Primitive Society" (*Yale Law Journal*, Vol. 38, 1928), pp. 551-563.

———: "Kinship" (*Encyclopedia of the Social Sciences*, Vol. 3, 1931), pp. 568-572.

———: "Lewis H. Morgan in Historical Perspective" in *Essays in Anthropology in Honor of Alfred Louis Kroeber* (Berkeley, 1936), pp. 169-181.

———: "Notes on Shoshonean Ethnography" (*American Museum of Natural History, Anthropological Papers*, Vol. 20, Part 3, 1924).

———: "Plains Indian Age Societies: Historical Summary" (*American Museum of Natural History, Anthropological Papers*, Vol. 11, 1916), pp. 877-984.

———: *Primitive Religion* (New York, 1924).

———: *Primitive Society* (New York, 1920).

———: "Property Rights and Coercive Powers of the Plains Indian Military Societies" (*Journal of Legal and Political Sociology*, Vol. 1, 1943), pp. 59-71.

———: "Societies of the Crow, Hidatsa, and Mandan Indians" (*American Museum of Natural History, Anthropological Papers*, Vol. 11, 1913).

Lowie, R. H.: "Some Moot Questions of Social Organization" (*American Anthropologist*, Vol. 36, 1934), pp. 321–330.

——: *The Crow Indians* (New York, 1935).

——: "The Northern Shoshone" (*American Museum of Natural History, Anthropological Papers*, Vol. 11, Part 2, 1909).

——: *The Origin of the State* (New York, 1927).

MacCurdy, G. G.: *Human Origins* (2 vols., New York, 1926).

MacIver, R. M.: "Government and Property" (*Journal of Political and Legal Sociology*, Vol. 4, 1946), pp. 5–18.

——: *Society: Its Structure and Changes* (New York, 1931).

——: *The Web of Government* (New York, 1947).

Maine, H. S.: *Ancient Law: Its Connection with the Early History of Society, and Its Relation to Modern Ideas* (3d American ed., New York, 1879).

Malinowski, B.: *Argonauts of the Western Pacific: An Account of Native Enterprise and Adventure in the Archipelagos of Melanesian New Guinea* (London, 1922).

——: *Coral Gardens and Their Magic* (2 vols., New York, 1938).

——: *Crime and Custom in Savage Society* (New York, 1926).

——: "Culture" (*Encyclopedia of the Social Sciences*, Vol. 4, 1931), pp. 621–646.

——: Preface in R. Firth, *We, The Tikopia* (London, 1936).

——: *Sex and Repression in Savage Society* (New York, 1927).

——: *The Father in Primitive Psychology* (New York, 1927).

Malthus, T. R.: *An Essay on the Principle of Population: or, A View of Its Past and Present Effects on Human Happiness; with An Inquiry into Our Prospects Respecting the Future Removal or Mitigation of the Evils Which It Occasions* (London, 1798).

Manglesdorf, P. C., and R. G. Reeves: "The Origin of Maize: Present Status of the Problem" (*American Anthropologist*, Vol. 47, 1945), pp. 235–243.

Marx, F. M.: "Administrative Ethics and the Rule of Law" (mss.).

Marx, K., and F. Engels: *The Communist Manifesto* (authorized English translation by S. Moore; edited and annotated by F. Engels, London, 1888; American reprint, Chicago, 1946).

Mason, O. T.: *Aboriginal American Basketry* (United States National Museum, Annual Report, 1904), pp. 171–548.

Mauldin, B.: *Up Front* (New York, 1945).

Maurer, G. L. von: *Geschichte der Dorfverfassung in Deutschland* (2 vols., Erlangen, 1865–1866).

McLennan, J. F.: *Primitive Marriage* (Edinburgh, 1865).

——: *The Patriarchal Theory* (London, 1885).

Mead, M.: *And Keep Your Powder Dry* (New York, 1942).

——: *Coming of Age in Samoa: A Psychological Study of Primitive Youth for Western Civilization* (New York, 1928).

—— (ed.): *Cooperation and Competition among Primitive Peoples* (New York, 1937).

——: *Growing Up in New Guinea: A Comparative Study of Primitive Education* (New York, 1930).

——: "On the Implications for Anthropology of the Gesell-Ilg Approach to Maturation" (*American Anthropologist*, Vol. 49, 1947), pp. 69–77.

MEAD, M.: "Review of *Sex and the Social Order*, by G. H. Seward" (*American Anthropologist*, Vol. 49, 1947), pp. 309–311.

——: *Sex and Temperament in Three Primitive Societies* (New York, 1935).

MEEK, C. K.: *The Northern Tribes of Nigeria* (2 vols., Oxford, 1925).

MENNINGER, W. C.: "Psychiatry Today" (*The Atlantic*, Vol. 181, 1948), pp. 65*ff*.

MERTON, R., and M. F. ASHLEY-MONTAGUE: "Crime and the Anthropologist" (*American Anthropologist*, Vol. 42, 1940), pp. 384–408.

MÉTRAUX, A.: "The Botocudo," in *Handbook of South American Indians* (5 vols., Washington, 1947–), Vol. 1, pp. 531–540.

MICHELSON, T.: "Narrative of an Arapaho Woman" (*American Anthropologist*, Vol. 35, 1933), pp. 604*ff*.

MILL, J. S.: *Principles of Political Economy* (2 vols., New York, 1899).

MILLIKAN, R. A.: "Science and the World Tomorrow" (*Scientific Monthly*, Vol. 49, 1939), pp. 212–240.

MIROV, N. T.: "Notes on the Domestication of the Reindeer" (*American Anthropologist*, Vol. 47, 1945), pp. 393–408.

MISHKIN, B.: *Rank and Warfare among the Plains Indians* (American Ethnological Society, Monograph 3, 1940).

MOMBERT, P.: "Class" (*Encyclopedia of the Social Sciences*, Vol. 3, 1930), pp. 531–536.

MOONEY, J.: *The Ghost Dance Religion and the Sioux Outbreak of 1890* (Bureau of American Ethnology, Annual Report 14, 1896).

MORGAN, J. DE: *Feudalism in Persia; Its Origin, Development and Present Condition* (Washington, 1914).

MORGAN, L. H.: *Ancient Society, or Researches in the Lines of Human Progress from Savagery, through Barbarism to Civilization* (New York, 1877).

——: "Houses and House Life of the American Aborigines" (*Contributions to American Ethnology*, Vol. 4, 1881).

MORGAN, W.: "Review of *Psycho-analysis of Primitive Cultural Types*, by G. Roheim" (*American Anthropologist*, Vol. 34, 1932), p. 705.

MORLEY, S. G.: *The Ancient Maya* (Stanford University, 1946).

MURDOCK, G. P.: "Bifurcate Merging: A Test of Five Theories" (*American Anthropologist*, Vol. 49, 1947), pp. 56–68.

——: "Constants in Social Organization," lecture before the American Ethnological Society, New York, March, 1941.

——: "Double Descent" (*American Anthropologist*, Vol. 42, 1940), pp. 555–561.

——: *Our Primitive Contemporaries* (New York, 1934).

——: "The Science of Culture" (*American Anthropologist*, Vol. 34, 1932), pp. 200–215.

NADEL, S. F.: "The Kede; A Riverian State in Northern Nigeria" in *African Political Systems* (Oxford, 1940), pp. 166–195.

NEEDHAM, J.: "Evolution" (*Encyclopedia of the Social Sciences*, Vol. 5, 1931), pp. 649–656.

NELSON, E. W.: *The Eskimos about Bering Straits* (Bureau of American Ethnology, Annual Report 18, 1899).

NELSON, N. C.: "Prehistoric Archaeology," in F. Boas (ed.), *General Anthropology* (Boston, 1938).

NEWMAN, H. H.: "The Nature and Origin of Life" in *The Nature of the World and Man* (rev. ed., Chicago, 1933), pp. 166–176.

NIBLACK, A. P.: *The Coast Indians of Southern Alaska and Northern British Columbia* (Board of Regents of the Smithsonian Institution, Annual Report, 1890).

NISSEN, H. W.: *A Field Study of the Chimpanzee* (Comparative Psychology Monographs, Vol. 8, No. 1, Serial No. 36, 1931).

OBERG, K.: "The Kingdom of Ankole in Uganda" in *African Political Systems* (Oxford, 1940), pp. 121–162.

OPLER, M. E.: *An Apache Life-way: The Economic, Social, and Religious Institutions of the Chiricahua* (Chicago, 1942).

———: "On the Method of Writing Anthropological Monographs" (*American Anthropologist*, Vol. 45, 1943), pp. 329–332.

———: "Themes as Dynamic Forces in Culture" (*The American Journal of Sociology*, Vol. 51, 1945), pp. 198–206.

OPLER, M. K.: "The Integration of the Sun Dance in Ute Religion" (*American Anthropologist*, Vol. 43, 1941), pp. 550–572.

OPPENHEIMER, F.: *The State* (trans. from the German by Gitterman, New York, 1922).

PARK, W. Z.: "Paviotso Polyandry" (*American Anthropologist*, Vol. 39, 1937), pp. 366–368.

———: *Shamanism in Western North America: A Study in Cultural Relationships* (Evanston and Chicago, 1938).

PARSONS, E. C.: *American Indian Life* (New York, 1923).

———: *Pueblo Indian Religion* (2 vols., Chicago, 1937).

PETTIT, G. A.: "Primitive Education in North America" (*University of California Publications in American Archaeology and Ethnology*, Vol. 43, No. 1, 1946).

PORTEUS, S. D.: *The Psychology of a Primitive People: A Study of the Australian Aborigine* (New York, 1931).

POUND, R.: "A Theory of Legal Interests" (*American Sociological Society, Publications*, Vol. 16, 1920).

POWDERMAKER, H.: *Life in Lesu: The Study of a Melanesian Society in New Ireland* (London, 1933).

PROVINSE, J. H.: "Cooperative Ricefield Cultivation among the Siang Dyaks of Central Borneo" (*American Anthropologist*, Vol. 37, 1939), pp. 77–102.

QUIMBY, G. I.: "Natchez Social Structure as an Instrument of Assimilation" (*American Anthropologist*, Vol. 48, 1946), pp. 134–136.

———: "The Natchezan Culture Type" (*American Antiquity*, Vol. 7, 1942), pp. 255–275.

RADCLIFFE-BROWN, A. R.: *The Andaman Islanders* (Cambridge, 1922).

———: "Patrilineal and Matrilineal Succession" (*Iowa Law Review*, Vol. 20, 1935), pp. 286–298.

RADIN, M.: "A Restatement of Hohfeld" (*Harvard Law Review*, Vol. 51, 1938), pp. 1141*ff.*

RADIN, P. (ed.): *Crashing Thunder: The Autobiography of an American Indian* (New York, 1926).

———: *Monotheism in Primitive Religion* (New York, 1927).

———: *Primitive Man as Philosopher* (New York, 1927).

———: "The Mind of Primitive Man" (*New Republic*, Vol. 98, 1939), p. 303.

———: *The Winnebago Tribe* (Bureau of American Ethnology, Annual Report 37, 1923).

RASMUSSEN, K.: *Across Arctic America* (New York, 1927).

RATTRAY, R. S.: *Ashanti* (Oxford, 1923).

——: *Ashanti Law and Constitution* (Oxford, 1927).

RATZEL, F.: *Anthropogeographie* (2 vols., Stuttgart, 1882).

RAY, V. F.: "The Sanpoil and Nespelem: Salishan Peoples of Northeastern Washington" (*University of Washington Publications in Anthropology*, Vol. 5, 1932).

REDFIELD, R.: *The Folk Culture of Yucatan* (Chicago, 1942).

REICHARD, G.: "Social Life," in F. Boas (ed.), *General Anthropology* (New York, 1938).

REIK, T.: *Ritual: A Psychoanalytic Study* (New York, 1947).

RICHARDSON, J.: *Law and Status among the Kiowa Indians* (American Ethnological Society, Monograph 1, 1940).

RIVERS, W. H. R.: *The Todas* (London, 1906).

ROSCOE, J.: "The Bahima" (*Journal of the Royal Anthropological Institute*, Vol. 37, 1907), pp. 93–118.

——: *The Banyankole* (London, 1923).

——: "The Cow Tribe of Enkole in the Uganda Protectorate" (*Journal of the Royal Anthropological Institute of Great Britain and Ireland*, Vol. 37, 1907).

——: *The Northern Bantu, An Account of Some Central African Tribes of the Uganda Protectorate* (2 vols., Cambridge, 1915).

ROSS, E. A.: *Social Psychology* (New York, 1915).

ROWE, J. H.: "Inca Culture at the Time of the Spanish Conquest" in *Handbook of South American Indians* (5 vols., Washington, 1947–), Vol. 2, pp. 183–330.

SALMOND, J. W.: *Jurisprudence* (7th ed., New York, 1924).

SAUER, C.: "American Agricultural Origins: A Consideration of Nature and Culture" in *Essays in Anthropology in Honor of Alfred Louis Kroeber* (Berkeley, 1936), pp. 279–298.

SCHMIDT, W.: *The Origin and Growth of Religion* (trans. from the German by H. J. Rose, New York, 1935).

——: "The Position of Women with Regard to Property in Primitive Society" (*American Anthropologist*, Vol. 37, 1935), pp. 244–256.

SCHOOLCRAFT, R. H. (ed.): *History of the Indian Tribes of the United States* (Philadelphia, 1860).

SCHUCHERT, C.: "The Earth's Changing Surface and Climate during Geologic Time" in G. A. Baitsell (ed.), *The Evolution of Earth and Man* (New Haven, 1929), pp. 47–82.

SCHURTZ, H.: *Altersklassen und Männerbunde* (Berlin, 1902).

SEAGLE, W.: *The Quest for Law* (New York, 1941).

SEWARD, G. H.: *Sex and the Social Order* (New York, 1946).

SHELDON, W. H., and S. S. STEVENS: *The Varieties of Temperament, A Psychology of Constitutional Differences* (New York, 1942).

—— and W. B. TUCKER: *The Varieties of Human Physique* (New York, 1940).

SIMMONS, L. (ed.): *Sun Chief: The Autobiography of a Hopi Indian* (New Haven, 1942).

——: *The Role of the Aged in Primitive Society* (New Haven, 1945).

SIMPSON, G. E.: "The Vodun Service in Northern Haiti" (*American Anthropologist*, Vol. 42, 1940), pp. 236–254.

SMITH, G. H.: "J. B. Trudeau's Remarks on the Indians of the Upper Missouri, 1794–95" (*American Anthropologist*, Vol. 38, 1936), pp. 565–568.

SMYTH, H. D.: *Atomic Energy for Military Purposes: The Official Report on the Development of the Atomic Bomb under the Auspices of the United States Government, 1940–1945* (Princeton, 1946).

SPECK, F. H.: "The Family Hunting Band as the Basis of Algonkian Social Organization" (*American Anthropologist,* Vol. 17, 1915), pp. 289–305.

SPENCER, H.: *The Principles of Sociology* (3 vols., London, 1887–1896).

SPIER, L.: "Plains Indian Parfleche Designs" (*University of Washington Publications in Anthropology,* Vol. 4, No. 3, 1931).

———: "The Sun Dance of the Plains Indian" (*American Museum of Natural History, Anthropological Papers,* Vol. 16, Part 7, 1921).

———: *Yuman Tribes of the Gila River* (Chicago, 1933).

——— and E. SAPIR: "Wishram Ethnography" (*University of Washington Publications in Anthropology,* Vol. 3, No. 3, 1930).

STEGGERDA, M. G.: "Physical Measurements on Negro, Navajo, and White Girls of College Age" (*American Journal of Physical Anthropology,* Vol. 26, 1940), pp. 417–431.

STEWARD, J. H.: *Basin-Plateau Aboriginal Socio-political Groups* (Bureau of American Ethnology, Bulletin 120, 1938).

———: "Cultural Causality and Law: A Trial Formulation of the Development of Early Civilization" (*American Anthropologist,* Vol. 51, 1949), pp. 1–27.

———: "Ecological Aspects of Southwestern Society" (*Anthropos,* Vol. 32, 1937), pp. 82–104.

———: "Shoshone Polyandry" (*American Anthropologist,* Vol. 38, 1936), pp. 561–564.

———: "The Economic and Social Basis of Primitive Bands" in *Essays in Anthropology in Honor of Alfred Louis Kroeber* (Berkeley, 1936), pp. 331–350.

STIRLING, M. W.: *Historical and Ethnographical Materials on the Jivaro Indians* (Bureau of American Ethnology, Bulletin 117, 1938).

STOW, G. W.: *The Native Races of South Africa, A History of the Intrusion of the Hottentots and Bantu into the Hunting Grounds of the Bushman* (London, 1905).

SUMNER, W. G.: *Folkways: A Study of the Sociological Importance of Usages, Manners, Customs, Mores and Morals* (Boston, 1913).

SWANTON, J. R.: "The Social Organization of American Tribes" (*American Anthropologist,* Vol. 7, 1905), pp. 663–673.

THOMAS, W. I.: *Primitive Behavior* (New York, 1937).

THOMPSON, D. F.: "The Joking Relationship and Organized Obscenity in North Queensland" (*American Anthropologist,* Vol. 37, 1935), pp. 460–490.

THOMPSON, J. E. S.: "A Survey of the Northern Maya Area" (*American Antiquity,* Vol. 2, 1945), pp. 2–24.

———: *The Civilization of the Mayas* (Field Museum of Natural History, Anthropology Leaflet 25, 4th ed., 1942).

THOMPSON, L.: "The Culture History of the Lau Islands, Fiji" (*American Anthropologist,* Vol. 40, 1938), pp. 181–197.

——— and A. JOSEPH: *The Hopi Way* (Lawrence, 1944).

THURNWALD, R.: *Banaro Society* (American Anthropological Association, Memoir 3, No. 4, 1924).

———: "Review of *Sex and Temperament in Three Primitive Societies,* by M. Mead" (*American Anthropologist,* Vol. 38, 1940), pp. 663–667.

TILNEY, F.: *The Brain from Ape to Man* (2 vols., New York, 1928).

TITIEV, M.: "Old Oraibi: A Study of the Hopi Indians of the Third Mesa" (*Peabody Museum of American Archaeology and Ethnology, Harvard University*, Vol. 22, No. 1, 1944).

————: "The Influence of Common Residence on the Unilateral Classification of Kindred" (*American Anthropologist*, Vol. 45, 1943), pp. 511–530.

TURNEY-HIGH, H. H.: *The Practice of Primitive War: A Study in Comparative Sociology* (The University of Montana Publications in the Social Sciences, No. 2, 1942).

TYLOR, E. B.: "American Lot Games as Evidence of Asiatic Intercourse before the Time of Columbus" (*Internationales Archiv für Ethnographie*, Vol. 9, supplement, 1896), pp. 55–67.

————: *Anthropology: An Introduction into the Study of Man and Civilization* (London, 1881).

————: "On the Game of Pattoli in Ancient America and Its Probable Asiatic Origin" (*Journal of the Royal Anthropological Institute of Great Britain and Ireland*, Vol. 8, 1879), pp. 116–129.

————: "On a Method of Investigating the Development of Institutions; Applied to the Laws of Marriage and Descent" (*Journal of the Royal Anthropological Institute of Great Britain and Ireland*, Vol. 18, 1889), pp. 245–272.

————: *Primitive Culture: Researches into the Development of Mythology, Philosophy, Religion, Language, Art and Custom* (2 vols., New York, 1874).

————: *Researches into the Early History of Mankind* (2 vols., London, 1871).

TYRELL, J. B. (ed.): *David Thompson's Narrative of His Explorations in Western America, 1784–1812* (Toronto, 1916).

VAILLANT, G. C.: *Aztecs of Mexico: Origin, Rise and Fall of the Aztec Nation* (New York, 1948).

VAVILOV, N.: *Studies on the Origin of Cultivated Plants* (Bulletin of Applied Botany and Plant Breeding, Leningrad, 1926), pp. 109*ff.*

VOTH, H. R.: "The Oraibi Powamu Ceremony" (*Field Columbian Museum, Anthropological Papers*, Vol. 3, No. 2, 1901).

WAITZ, F. T.: *Anthropologie der Naturvölker* (6 vols., Leipzig, 1859–1871).

WALLIS, W. D.: *An Introduction to Cultural Anthropology* (New York, 1926).

WARNER, W. L.: "Murngin Warfare" (*Oceania*, Vol. 1, 1940).

———— and P. S. LUND: *The Social Life of a Modern Community* (New Haven, 1941).

WASHBURN, S. L.: "Thinking about Race" (*Science Education*, Vol. 28, 1944), pp. 65–76.

WEBSTER, H.: *Primitive Secret Societies: A Study in Early Politics and Religion* (New York, 1908).

WEIDENREICH, F.: "Giant Early Man from Java and South China" (*American Museum of Natural History, Anthropological Papers*, Vol. 40, 1945), pp. 1–34.

————: "Man or Ape?" (*Natural History*, Vol. 46, 1940), pp. 35*ff.*

————: "Some Problems Dealing with Ancient Man" (*American Anthropologist*, Vol. 42, 1940), pp. 375–383.

WELLS, H. G.: *The Outline of History* (New York, 1920).

WELTFISH, G.: "Prehistoric North American Basketry Techniques and Modern Distributions" (*American Anthropologist*, Vol. 32, 1930), pp. 454–495.

WEST, R.: *Conscience and Society: A Study of the Psychological Prerequisites of Law and Order* (New York, 1945).

WESTERMANN, D.: *Die Kpelle, ein Negerstamm in Liberia* (Göttingen, 1921).

WESTERMARCK, E.: *The History of Human Marriage* (3 vols., London, 1925).

WHITE, L. A.: "A Problem in Kinship Terminology" (*American Anthropologist,* Vol. 41, 1939), pp. 569–570.

———: " 'Diffusion vs. Evolution:' An Anti-evolutionist Fallacy" (*American Anthropologist,* Vol. 47, 1945), pp. 339–355.

———: "Energy and the Evolution of Culture" (*American Anthropologist,* Vol. 45, 1943), pp. 354–355.

———: "The Expansion of the Scope of Science" (*Journal of the Washington Academy of Sciences,* Vol. 37, 1947), pp. 181–210.

WHITMAN, W.: *The Pueblo Indians of San Ildefonso* (New York, 1947).

WILSON, G. R.: "The Hidatsa Earthlodge" (*American Museum of Natural History, Anthropological Papers,* Vol. 33, 1934).

WISSLER, C.: *The American Indian* (3d ed., New York, 1938).

———: "The Influence of the Horse in the Development of Plains Culture" (*American Anthropologist,* Vol. 16, 1914), pp. 1–25.

WOODRUFF, L. L.: "The Origin of Life" in G. A. Baitsell (ed.), *The Evolution of the Earth and Man* (New Haven, 1929).

WOODWARD, S.: "Fourth Note on the Piltdown Skull" (*Quarterly Journal of the Geological Society,* Vol. 73, 1917), pp. 1–10.

WUNDT, W.: *Völkerpsychologie* (10 vols., Leipzig, 1910–1920).

YERKES, R. M.: *Psychological Examining in the U.S. Army* (National Academy of Sciences, Memoirs, Vol. 15, 1921).

YOUNG, K.: *An Introductory Sociology* (rev. ed., New York, 1939).

———: *Social Psychology* (New York, 1941).

INDEX